The Birth of the Orchestra

The Birth of the Orchestra

HISTORY OF AN INSTITUTION, 1650–1815

John Spitzer

AND

Neal Zaslaw

OXFORD

UNIVERSITY PRESS

OXFORD

UNIVERSITY PRESS

Great Clarendon Street, Oxford OX2 6DP

Oxford University Press is a department of the University of Oxford.
It furthers the University's objective of excellence in research, scholarship,
and education by publishing worldwide in

Oxford New York

Auckland Bangkok Buenos Aires Cape Town Chennai
Dar es Salaam Delhi Hong Kong Istanbul Karachi Kolkata
Kuala Lumpur Madrid Melbourne Mexico City Mumbai Nairobi
São Paulo Shanghai Taipei Tokyo Toronto

Oxford is a registered trade mark of Oxford University Press
in the UK and in certain other countries

Published in the United States
by Oxford University Press Inc., New York

© John Spitzer and Neal Zaslaw 2004

The moral rights of the authors have been asserted
Database right Oxford University Press (maker)

First published 2004

First published as an Oxford University Press paperback, 2005

British Library Cataloguing in Publication Data
Data available

Library of Congress Cataloging in Publication Data
Data available
ISBN-13 978-0-19-518955-1 (pbk.)
ISBN 0-19-816434-3; 0-19-518955-8 (pbk.)

3 5 7 9 10 8 6 4 2

Preface

Two heads may be better than one, but they are certainly no faster. We outlined this book together fifteen years ago, and we've been chipping away at it ever since. Neal Zaslaw wrote the first drafts of Chapters 3 and 6; the remaining chapters were drafted by John Spitzer. The two of us edited, rewrote, and reedited the entire book together. Our two heads bear collective responsibility for any insights and all errors that readers may find.

As we finished the book we realized, not entirely to our surprise, that we had written a narrative history—not a chronological account by any means, but a narrative in the sense that we tell a story that has a beginning, a middle, and an end. Once upon a time there were no orchestras. In the second half of the seventeenth century, at the courts of kings, princes, and cardinals, instrumentalists began to organize into ensembles that combined strings, winds, and continuo instruments and that put several players on each of the string parts. Over the course of the eighteenth century these ensembles developed distinctive repertories, distinctive performance practices, distinct personnel, and their own administrative structures, until by the 1790s and early 1800s the orchestra had become recognizable as the institution that, with changes, still exists in concert halls and opera houses in many parts of the world.

Narrative histories seem to have gone somewhat out of fashion these days. "Grand narratives," says Lyotard, "have lost their credibility"—by which he seems to mean that people since the middle of the twentieth century have become increasingly skeptical of Christian, Marxist, and/or scientific accounts of history as the story of human progress. Postmodern literary critics and historians have extended Lyotard's dictum to encompass all narratives great or small, proclaiming somewhat gleefully that narrative in general is dead.

We reject this notion. To say that historical narratives are impossible is to say that we can no longer tell a story about what happened in the past, or that we must tell as many stories as there are readers. And this means in turn that the past no longer has any meaning for the present, or that it has an infinite number of meanings, which amounts to the same thing.

We propose to tell a single, if multilayered, story of the orchestra—who created orchestras, what the details of this process were, and when, where, and why orchestras came into being. Our story by itself is at most a middle-sized narrative, but it is linked to a grander narrative: the creation of modern institutions. Armies, navies, banks, bureaucracies, factories, corporations, secondary schools, scientific societies, and more all came into being during the seventeenth and eighteenth centuries, in developments that were, if not part of the same process as the birth of the orchestra, at least parallel. If readers choose to make our story a chapter in this grand narrative of modern institutions, we have no objection.

Besides those whose assistance is acknowledged in our footnotes, we give our warm thanks to the following people who helped us at various stages of the project: Katherine Flegal, Ellen Zaslaw, Kyra Voss, Douglas Laing, Kelly Pask, Jennifer Strauss, Michele Cabrini, Kate van Orden, Brooks Kuykendall, Marc Mellits, Bonnie Blackburn, and Jane Dieckmann. We also thank the National Endowment for the Humanities, the American Council of Learned Societies, Peabody Conservatory, and Cornell University for grant and research support.

J.S.
N.Z.

Baltimore, MD
Ithaca, NY
December 2002

List of Credits

Acknowledgment is made to the following for photographs and permission to reproduce illustrations:

Archivio di Stato, Bologna: Pls. IV, XVI

Bayerische Staatsgemäldesammlungen, Alte Pinakothek, Munich: Pl. V

Biblioteca Nazionale Vittorio Emanuele III, Naples: Fig. 5.3

Bibliothèque de Lille, Médiathèque Municipale Jean Lévy: Pl. VIII

Bibliothèque Nationale de France, Paris: Pl. VII

Civica Raccolta delle Stampe Achille Bertarelli, Milan: Fig. 5.4

Carl A. Kroch Library, Cornell University Library, Ithaca, NY: Fig. 7.3

Courtauld Institute of Art, London: Fig. 2.1

The Folger Shakespeare Library, Washington, DC: Fig. 2.3

The Johns Hopkins University, Garrett Library: Fig 8.1

Kungliga biblioteket, Stockholm: Fig. 4.1

Library of Congress, Washington, DC: Fig. 5.1

Lord Hastings: Pl. X

Metropolitan Museum of Art, New York: Fig. 6.1

Dr. Jürgen Meyer: Fig. 10.7

Museo Correr, Venice: Fig. 2.4

Museo di Roma: Pl. XII

Museo Nacional del Prado, Madrid: Pl. XIV

Museum of Fine Arts, Boston: Pl. VI

National Archives of Hungary: Fig. 12.1

Nationalmuseum, Stockholm: Pl. II

The New York Public Library: Figs. 2.2, 7.5

Réunion des Musées Nationaux/Art Resource, New York: Pl. XIII

Rijksmuseum, Amsterdam: Fig 10.6

Sächsische Landesbibliothek, Dresden: Fig. 10.1

Staatliche Kunstsammlungen, Dresden: Fig 7.2

Staatsarchiv, Hamburg: Fig. 7.6

Stadtarchiv Leipzig: Fig 10.5.

Contents

List of Plates

(Plates appear between pp. 300 and 301.)

List of Figures

List of Tables

List of Documents

List of Music Examples*

★ All music examples are notated at sounding pitch.

Abbreviations

Chapter One

Introduction

THE LYRE OF ORPHEUS

The story of Orpheus has provided the subject for operas, ballets, tone poems, and other musical works, beginning with Poliziano's *Orfeo*, produced in Mantua in 1480, and continuing to the present. Plucking a lyre in time to his words, says Ovid in his classic formulation of the myth, Orpheus makes the pale shades weep; the thirst of Tantalus is momentarily appeased, Sisyphus sits down on his stone to listen, and the Furies' cheeks are moist with tears.[1] Poliziano's Orpheus accompanied himself on a lute or perhaps a bowed lira di braccio.[2] In later musical versions the lyre of Orpheus was represented by a variety of different musical instruments. For Peri's *Euridice* (Florence, 1600) four performers hid backstage to accompany Orpheus on the harpsichord, chitarrone, viol, and lute.[3] Monteverdi's Orfeo in 1607 pleaded his case to the accompaniment of a succession of instruments: a pair of violins, a pair of cornetts, two harps, a string trio, and finally a four-part bowed-string ensemble. Orpheus in Luigi Rossi's *Orfeo*, at the French court in 1647, pretended to pluck a lyre, but what the audience heard was an ensemble of twelve violins hidden backstage.[4] *Le Ballet des*

[1] Ovid, *Metamorphoses*, 10. 45–52. For a survey of musical settings of the Orpheus story see Frederick W. Sternfeld, "Orpheus, Ovid and Opera," *PRMA* 113 (1988), 172–202; id., "Orpheus," in *GroveO*, ii. 776–77; Alexander Becker, Britta Schilling-Wang, and Kara Kusan-Windweh, "Orpheus als Opernthema," in *MGG*², Sachteil 7, cols. 1103–8; Reinhard Kapp, "Chronologisches Verzeichnis (in progress) der auf Orpheus bezogenen oder zu beziehenden Opern, Kantaten, Instrumentalmusiken, literarischen Texte, Theaterstücke und Filme," in Sigrun Anselm and Caroline Neubaur (eds.), *Talismane: Klaus Heinrich zum 70. Geburtstag* (Basel, 1998), 425–57.

[2] Nino Pirrotta, "Orpheus, Singer of *Strambotti*," in id. and Elena Povoledo, *Music and Theatre from Poliziano to Monteverdi*, trans. Karen Eales (Cambridge, 1982), 29.

[3] Jacopo Peri, *Le musiche sopra l'Euridice* (Florence, 1600), "A lettori."

[4] The manuscript of Rossi's *Orfeo* (I-Rvat, QV 58, 234 ff.) has only a basso continuo accompaniment at this spot in the score. However, a contemporary scenario of the opera (I-Rvat, Barb. lat. 4059) gives details about

muses, performed at the court of Louis XIV in 1666, included the Orpheus story as the seventh of thirteen danced entrées. In the original performance the part of Orpheus was played by the King's favorite composer, Jean-Baptiste Lully, who did not sing but instead played a solo on his violin, alternating with a large string band, which presumably represented his lyre.

In Antonio Sartorio's *Orfeo* (Venice, 1673) Orpheus entered "with a lyre in his hand," but he sang the aria that moves the wild beasts to the accompaniment of four-part strings. *Le Carnaval de Venise* by André Campra (Paris, 1699) presented the story of Orpheus as a play within a play in the third act. Orpheus descended into the underworld accompanied by a "sweet symphony" of two flutes plus continuo; he then addressed Pluto to the accompaniment of two violins. In J. J. Fux's *Orfeo ed Euridice* (Vienna, 1715) Orpheus' lyre became an ensemble of pizzicato violins and cellos. Gluck in both the Italian and French versions of his *Orpheus and Euridice* (Vienna, 1762; Paris, 1774) gave Orpheus an entire orchestra of his own—an offstage ensemble of four-part strings and harp—while the Furies, who bar his path to the underworld, were accompanied by a second orchestra of strings, woodwinds, and trombones.[5] Karl Ditters von Dittersdorf wrote a program symphony on the subject of Orpheus and Euridice, which was performed in Vienna in 1786. Here both the singer and his lyre were represented by instruments: Orpheus by a solo violin, the lyre by the rest of the orchestra.[6] Haydn too composed an Orpheus opera, *L'anima del filosofo* (1791), written for the King's Theatre in London, and rehearsed but never performed. Haydn's Orpheus tamed the wild beasts in Act I to the accompaniment of pizzicato strings and harp.

The great differences between the ensembles that represented the lyre of Orpheus in this series of operas composed between 1600 and 1791 can be seen by comparing some of their scores. Peri's *Euridice* has no individual parts for instruments, only a basso continuo (Ex. 1.1). The four players backstage, whom Peri names in his introduction to the score, probably improvised their parts from the bass line. Perhaps harpsichord, chitarrone, viol, and lute all played together as Orfeo pleaded with Pluto; perhaps only one or two of them played. Scoring was a matter of performance practice. The only other instruments in the entire opera are a pair of recorders, which play onstage to accompany a shepherd's song. In Lully's *Ballet des muses* (Ex. 1.2) the scoring is more explicit. Lully writes out five parts for a band of violin-family instruments, plus a solo violin part for himself. The string band, which always plays as a unit, alternates with the solo violin, which is accompanied by basso continuo as though it were a singer. With several players on the lower parts, there is less room for improvisation. Little crosses above the notes in the score show the players where to place their ornaments.[7]

what was actually played at the Paris performance; see Frederick Hammond, "Orpheus in a New Key: The Barberini and the Rossi–Buti *l'Orfeo*," *Studi musicali*, 25 (1996), 103–25 at 124.

   [5] Gluck designates the two ensembles "Orchestra I" and "Orchestra II" in the score.
   [6] Carl Krebs, *Dittersdorfiana* (Berlin, 1900), 178.
   [7] Later in this entrée the score notates the ornamented *double* that Lully added to the melody when he repeated a passage.

Ex. 1.1. J. Peri, *Euridice*, 1600, "Quai pianti" ("Such tears and such lamentation your dear Orpheus pours from his heart. Weep at my tears, O shades of Hell")

Ex. 1.2. J. B. Lully, *Le Ballet des muses*, 1666, "Symphonie d'Orphée"

Ex. 1.2. J. B. Lully, *Le Ballet des muses*, 1666, "Symphonie d'Orphée" (*Cont.*)

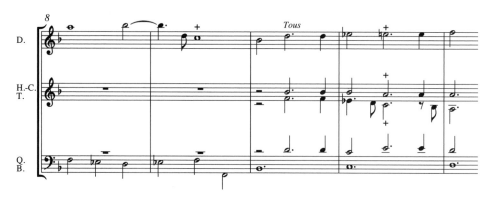

Proserpina's aria from Fux's *Orfeo ed Euridice* presents a different kind of alternation (Ex. 1.3). The full four-part string band begins the piece with a ritornello, but when the voice enters, the ensemble is reduced to a concertino with single players on the parts. This enables the instruments to play along with the singer without drowning her out. The roles of the instruments in the texture have become more flexible: for the first eight measures the viola plays an inner part; when the voice enters, the viola takes

Ex. 1.3. J. J. Fux, *Orfeo ed Euridice*, 1715, "Credi a me" ("Believe me, never is a heart desperate that boasts of constancy in love")

Ex. 1.3. (*Cont.*)

over the bass line. In the the overture to Haydn's *Anima del filosofo*, the orchestra does not accompany a singer at all (Ex. 1.4). Haydn's orchestra consists of four-part strings plus wind pairs, and he uses them in a kaleidoscope of instrumental combinations: the

Ex. 1.4. J. Haydn, *L'anima del filosofo*, 1791, Sinfonia

Ex. 1.4. (*Cont.*)

full orchestra in measure 70, a wind choir in measure 76, a melody played by the first violins colored by a solo oboe (m. 80) and answered by a solo flute (m. 81). Scoring, which was left up to the performers in the first example, has become an opportunity for the composer to display his skill.

These four short examples highlight some of the changes that instrumental ensembles underwent during the seventeenth and eighteenth centuries. Over the years ensembles came to include more instruments and more different kinds of instruments. Peri's ensemble was dominated by plucked strings, Lully's and Fux's by bowed strings, Haydn's by mixed strings and winds together. Composers became more specific about which instruments they wanted in their ensembles. They also wrote out more of what they wanted the instruments to play, so there was less opportunity for improvisation. Scorings and instrumental combinations became more complex. From an improvised bass line played by four backstage instruments in 1600, the lyre of Orpheus had evolved by 1791 into a large ensemble of winds and strings playing an orchestral score.

The size and makeup of the ensembles that played at the first performances of all 11 of the Orpheus settings mentioned above can be determined, at least approximately, from pay records, reports, and other archival materials. Table 1.1 shows not just the instruments that represented Orpheus' lyre but those that played at any point in the work.[8] The changes from earlier to later Orpheus ensembles run parallel to the developments seen in the scores. Earlier ensembles emphasize keyboards and plucked strings, while later ensembles are based on bowed strings and tend to contain more winds. Unfamiliar instruments in the early ensembles—lira grande, cornett, basse de violon—are replaced by instruments that are the direct ancestors of those still in use today, like violins, violas, clarinets, and bassoons. The balance of instruments within the ensembles also changes. Violins increase as a proportion of strings; violas decrease; there are more winds. Finally, Table 1.1 suggests that instrumental ensembles grew considerably larger during the two centuries between 1600 and 1791.

At the beginning of the published score to his *Orfeo* Monteverdi printed a list of "Personaggi" and "Stromenti" required to perform the work (Fig. 1.1). Charles Burney, the historian and chronicler of music, looked at Monteverdi's list and opined that "the orchestra . . . for the performance of this drama was greatly superior to that of [Peri's] Euridice."[9] John Hawkins, Burney's contemporary and rival, looking at the same list, concluded that each singer was accompanied by a different group of instruments and that therefore "no accompaniment of a whole orchestra was required."[10]

Were the instruments that accompanied Monteverdi's *Orfeo* an orchestra or not? If an orchestra is simply a large number of instruments assembled together for a performance, the 33 instruments in Fig. 1.1 seem more than enough to be an orchestra. But then the marching band at an American football game would have to be considered an orchestra too, and so would a Balinese gamelan or a hundred Suzuki violinists playing "Twinkle, Twinkle Little Star" in unison. On the other hand, if an orchestra has something to do with what kinds of instruments play, the balances between different kinds of instruments, and how the players of these instruments interact with one another, then perhaps Monteverdi's *Orfeo* ensemble was not an orchestra after all, because the instruments in it functioned in ways quite different than they did in later

---

[8] In several instances (Campra, 1699; Fux, 1715; Gluck, 1774) Table 1.1 shows not just the instrumentalists known to have played in the Orpheus opera but rather the payroll of the entire orchestra.

[9] Charles Burney, *A General History of Music* (1776, 1786–89), ed. Frank Mercer (New York, 1935), 519.

[10] John Hawkins, *General History of the Science and Practice of Music* (1776) (London, 1875), 525. Hawkins, reading the list somewhat naively from left to right, imagined that Orfeo was accompanied throughout by two contrabass viols, Euridice by 10 viole da brazzo, the nymphs by a double harp, and so on. Had he looked more carefully through the score, he would have seen that Orpheus is accompanied by other instruments besides two contrabass viols, and Euridice is never accompanied by 10 viole da brazzo.

TABLE 1.1. *Orpheus orchestras, 1600–1791*

Composer: opera (place, date)	Keyboard and plucked strings	Bowed strings	Woodwinds	Brass and drums	Source
Peri: *Euridice* (Florence, 1600)	gravicembalo chitarrone liuto grosso	lira grande	2 flutes		Peri, *Le musiche*
Monteverdi: *Orfeo* (Mantua, 1607)	2 gravicembali 2 organi di legno 1 regal [2] arpe doppia 2 chitaroni	10 viole da brazzo 2 violini piccoli 2 contrabassi 3 bassi da gamba	[2] flautini	4 tromboni 2 cornetti 1 clarino 3 trombe [1 vulgano]	Kelly, "'Orfeo'"; Zaslaw, "Three Notes"
Rossi: *L'Orfeo* (Paris, 1647)	2 lutes 2 chitarri 4 harpsichords 4 theorbos	20 violins and violas 4 violoni	"piffari" cornamuse	cornetti 4 trumpets drums	Hammond, "Orpheus," 114
Lully: *Ballet des muses* (Saint-Germain-en-Laye, 1666)		1 violin soloist 5 dessus de violon 3 haute-contres de violon 3 tailles de violon 3 quintes de violon 5 basses de violon			Lemaître, "Sources," 200; *État* (1692), 227
Sartorio: *L'Orfeo* (Venice, 1673)	3 harpsichords 2 theorbos	2 violins 2 violas 1 violone			Orchestra for Cavalli's *Ciro*, 1665; Arnold, "L'Incoronazione," 177

	Continuo	Strings	Winds	Brass and percussion	Source
Campra: *Le Carnaval de Venise* (Paris, 1699)					Paris Opéra in 1704; La Gorce, "L'Orchestre," 25–26
petit choeur:	1 harpsichord 2 theorbos	2 violins 2 viole da gamba 2 basses de violon			
grand choeur:	1 harpsichord 2 theorbos	12 violins 8 violas 10 basses de violon	4 flutes and oboes 4 bassoons		
Fux: *Orfeo ed Euridice* (Vienna, 1715)	[2 harpsichords] 1 lute 1 theorbo	22 violins and violas 6 cellos 3 basses 1 viola da gamba	6 oboes 3 bassoons 1 chalumeau 1 flute	1 cornetto 3 trombones trumpets drums	Imperial Kapelle in 1715; Selfridge-Field, "Viennese," 124
Gluck: *Orfeo ed Euridice* (Vienna, 1762)	[2 harpsichords] 1 harp	20 violins 3 violas 4 cellos 4 double basses	2 oboes 2 flutes 2 bassoons 1 chalumeau 2 English horns	2 cornetti 2 trombones 2 horns 2 trumpets timpani	B. A. Brown, *Gluck*, 370–72
Gluck: *Orphée et Euridice* (Paris, 1774)	[1 harpsichord] 1 harp	22 violins 5 violas 9 cellos 6 double basses	2 flutes 4 oboes [2] clarinets 8 bassoons	2 horns [3 trombones] [2] trumpets 2 drums	*Almanach* (1775)
Dittersdorf: Orpheus and Euridice Symphony (Vienna, 1786)	[1 harpsichord]	12 violins 4 violas 3 cellos 3 double basses	2 flutes 2 oboes 2 clarinets 2 bassoons	2 horns 2 trumpets 1 timpani	Burgtheater orchestra in 1788; Edge, "Mozart's," 74
Haydn: *L'anima del filosofo* (London, [1791])	[1 harpsichord] 1 harp	12–16 violins 4 violas 5 cellos 4 basses	2 flutes 2 oboes 2 English horns 2 clarinets 2 bassoons	2 horns 2 trombones 2 trumpets timpani	Salomon's orchestra in 1793; McVeigh, "Professional," 121

Fɪɢ. 1.1. Claudio Monteverdi, *L'Orfeo*: list of characters and instruments

orchestras. The majority of the opera was accompanied by the keyboards and plucked strings, improvising their music from the basso continuo part; bowed strings and winds were used only for dances and special effects. Some of the instruments played behind the scenes, some at the side of the room; others appeared onstage.[11] The 10 viole da brazzo (violin-family instruments in several sizes) played one on a part most of the time, rather than as a section. And Monteverdi does not designate the instruments in

[11] See Thomas Forrest Kelly, " 'Orfeo da Camera': Estimating Performing Forces in Early Opera," *Historical Performance*, 1 (1988), 3–9; also Neal Zaslaw, "Three Notes on the Early History of the Orchestra," *Historical Performance*, 1 (1988), 63–69.

Fig. 1.1 with a corporate noun like "cappella," "sinfonia," or "orchestra"; rather he calls them "stromenti," that is, instruments or instrumentalists.

Was Rossi's *Orfeo* ensemble of 1647 an orchestra? According to the manuscript scenario, 20 viole, four violoni, four harpsichords, and eight theorbos, lutes, and guitars "all played together before the curtain was raised."[12] The same large ensemble played during the prologue and at the ends of the acts. The 20 viole and four violoni must have been a standing ensemble, because they played the next day for a dance in the same theater.[13] Presumably they were the Vingt-quatre Violons du Roy, string players who held official appointments at court and who are mentioned in French court records as early as 1618. In the opening *sinfonia* and at the ends of the acts, however, where the scenario describes large ensembles, the score has only a figured bass. Either the violins improvised their parts, or their music was filled in by a composer other than Rossi, perhaps one of the violinists. In ritornellos and dance numbers, on the other hand, Rossi writes out four lines with different clefs, presumably for a four-part violin band, though the parts are not labeled. The score contains no parts for wind instruments.

The King's Vingt-quatre Violons may also have accompanied Lully's *Ballet des muses*, but more likely Lully used the Petits Violons, an ensemble that he himself led.[14] The Petits Violons, according to a report in 1664, had 19 or 20 members, all of whom played bowed stringed instruments. Table 1.1 assumes that their balances were more or less the same as the balances of the Vingt-quatre Violons during the same period, with the top and bottom parts slightly more heavily staffed than the inner parts. At the end of the scene a nymph, who, according to the libretto, happened to be sitting on a nearby rock, recites a flattering verse in Lully's praise:

> This Orpheus has delicate and refined tastes.
> The ornament of our times, he can inspire
> Men, animals, trees, and even rocky wastes,
> With the melodious sound of his charming lyre.[15]

Other entrées of the *Ballet des muses* used other instruments besides the string band. Songs were accompanied by lutes and perhaps keyboards. A battle scene in the fifth entrée was accompanied by two recorders and a drum; a Spanish dance was accompanied by two guitars and a harp.[16] These instruments did not play together with one

[12] Hammond, "Orpheus," 118.

[13] Hammond, "Orpheus," 125.

[14] See James Anthony, "More Faces than Proteus: Lully's *Ballet des muses*," *EM* 15 (1987), 336–44. On Lully's relations with the Vingt-quatre Violons, see Ch. 3.

[15] Victor Fournel, *Les Contemporains de Molière* (Paris, 1866), 602, freely translated. The original reads: "Cet Orphée a le goust très-délicat et fin; / C'est l'ornement du siècle, et n'est rien qu'il n'attire, / Soit hommes, animaux, bois et rochers enfin, / Du son mélodieux de sa charmante lyre." Here and elsewhere we translate verse as verse—if not rhymed, then at least metrical. We give the original in a footnote, so readers may translate more literally for themselves.

[16] Ibid. 595, 597.

another or with the strings, however, but as separate ensembles. The players appeared onstage, in costume, and in character.

In Sartorio's *Orfeo* (Venice, 1673) the majority of arias are accompanied by continuo instruments only. However, when Orpheus appears "lyre in hand" at the beginning of the third act to lament the death of Eurydice, he is accompanied by an onstage ensemble of four-part strings [*viole*].[17] Perhaps these were different performers from the five bowed-string players who worked in the pit of the Teatro San Salvatore. Whether there was one ensemble or two, the musicians probably played one on a part, since the surviving performance rosters from Venetian opera orchestras of the seventeenth century suggest that there were very few violins and violas.[18]

In Campra's *Carnaval de Venise*, the Orpheus episode is sung in Italian and set to Italian-style music. The instrumental ensemble, however, is divided according to French practice into two groups—a *petit choeur*, which accompanies recitatives and solo singing, and a *grand choeur*, which plays overtures and interludes and accompanies dances and choral numbers. Orpheus, when he pleads with Pluto to release Euridice, is accompanied by the two violins and the continuo of the *petit choeur*. When he rejoices in his next aria at Euridice's return, the entire *grand choeur* plays along in five parts.

Fux had all fifty instrumentalists from the Imperial *Hofkapelle* at his disposal for *Orfeo ed Euridice* in 1715, but he may not have used all of them, since he labeled the work a "chamber opera" (*componimento da camera*); it was performed at the Emperor's summer palace at Laxenburg, outside Vienna. The score shows a four-part string ensemble playing not just in the overtures and dances, but in most of the arias as well. However in lyrical arias like Ex. 1.3 Fux reduced his forces to just a concertino when the singer enters, a procedure similar to Campra's use of the *petit choeur*. Fux made use of the great variety of wind instruments in the Imperial Kapelle, mainly as obbligato soloists in individual arias. He treated the instruments, winds and strings, as a unified ensemble: no instruments were placed onstage or backstage.

Burney and Hawkins would surely have agreed that the ensembles for Gluck's *Orpheus*, in both its Vienna and its Paris incarnations, were orchestras. The Vienna production used the orchestra of the Burgtheater, a standing ensemble that played for spoken and sung dramas, augmented with supernumeraries from the *Hofkapelle* and the Kärntnertor theater orchestra.[19] The Paris production, *Orphée et Euridice* (1774), was accompanied by the orchestra of the Paris Opéra, one of the largest orchestras in Europe at the time. Gluck took advantage of the opportunity to rewrite and to add wind parts to the Vienna score.

---

[17] The instruction to place the strings onstage does not appear in the score of the 1673 Venice premiere but in a score from a later Viennese performance (Antonio Sartorio, *L'Orfeo*, ed. Ellen Rosand (Milan, 1983), p. xxxiv). Rosand believes it probably applied to the original performance as well. See also Susanne Kübler, "Die musikalische Ohnmacht des *Orfeo* von Antonio Sartorio," in Antonio Baldassarre, Susanne Kübler, and Patrick Müller (eds.), *Musik denken: Ernst Lichtenhan zur Emeritierung* (Berne, 2000), 35–46.

[18] See below, Table 2.1.

[19] Bruce Alan Brown, *Gluck and the French Theatre in Vienna* (Oxford, 1991), 369.

Dittersdorf's "Orpheus" symphony was the tenth of twelve symphonies based on stories from Ovid's *Metamorphoses*. The score is lost, but a published description gives a detailed acount.[20] In the first movement the wind instruments, playing in unison, portray Orpheus' grief over the death of Euridice. In the second movement a long violin solo with orchestral accompaniment represents Orpheus singing to Pluto and Proserpina in the underworld.[21] The third movement depicts the reunion of Orpheus with Euridice, and the fourth, a march, represents their trek back to the world of the living. The journey is interrupted by an orchestral grand pause, as Orpheus glances back at his bride, then a vivace in which Euridice is snatched back to the Underworld. In his autobiography Dittersdorf mentions that he performed his Orpheus symphony in a Viennese theater along with five more of his Ovid symphonies, and that he hired "an orchestra of forty persons" for the occasion.[22] Dittersdorf does not say which theater he used, but the orchestras in the two principal Viennese theaters were similar in size and composition. Table 1.1 uses the orchestra of the Burgtheater in 1788 as a proxy for Dittersdorf's Orpheus orchestra.

Haydn wrote his setting of Orpheus, *L'anima del filosofo*, for the reopening of the King's Theatre in London in 1791. He coached the singers and held at least one general rehearsal before the production was canceled and replaced by a ballet.[23] This was his first meeting with the orchestra organized and led by John Peter Salomon that played his London Symphonies later that year. It included a full complement of strings, plus woodwind and brass instruments in pairs. In addition, Mme Anne-Marie Krumpholtz, the only woman in Table 1.1, was engaged to play the Act I imitation of Orpheus' lyre on her harp.[24] Haydn, who had not yet learned English, began the rehearsal by borrowing a violin and demonstrating how to play the first three notes of the overture, a gesture that, according to his biographer Dies, endeared him greatly to the orchestra musicians.[25]

In the end it is impossible to decide whether the ensemble for Monteverdi's *Orfeo*, or Rossi's, or Fux's, or even Gluck's, was or was not an orchestra. That depends on what Hawkins or Burney or modern critics and readers mean by "orchestra." Nonetheless, the beginning and end points of the process are clear. The lyre of

---

[20] The description, by J. T. Hermes, is reprinted in Krebs, *Dittersdorfiana*, 177–79.

[21] Hermes reports that he asked Dittersdorf why he hadn't given Orpheus' song to a wind instrument, a more naturalistic representation of the human voice. Dittersdorf replied: "because these days the only real virtuosos are violinists" (ibid. 178).

[22] Karl Ditters von Dittersdorf, *Lebensbeschreibung—Seinem Sohne in die Feder diktiert* (1800), ed. Norbert Miller (Munich, 1967), 230.

[23] The King's Theatre in the Haymarket, which had burned in 1789, was scheduled to reopen with the performance of Haydn's new opera. At the last moment, however, the theatre was denied a license for dramatic performances and was allowed to present only concerts and ballets. See Joseph Haydn, *L'anima del filosofo*, ed. Helmut Wirth (Joseph Haydn: Werke, XXV/13), pp. vii–viii; H. C. Robbins Landon, *Haydn: Chronicle and Works* (Bloomington, Ind., 1976–80), iii. 71.

[24] Simon McVeigh, "The Professional Concert and Rival Subscription Series in London, 1783–1793," *RMA Research Chronicle*, 22 (1989), 1–135 at 13; Landon, *Haydn: Chronicle and Works*, iii. 331.

[25] Albert Christoph Dies, *Biographische Nachrichten von Joseph Haydn* (1810), ed. Horst Seeger (Kassel, 1964), 84–85.

Orpheus in 1600, Peri's four-man, backstage ensemble for *Euridice*, was not an orchestra in any sense of the word. The lyre of Orpheus in 1791, the ensemble that rehearsed Haydn's *L'anima del filosofo*, resembled orchestras of the nineteenth and twentieth centuries in most essential respects. It seems, then, that the orchestra must have come into being during the two centuries that separated the two productions. At the beginning of the seventeenth century the orchestra did not exist: no instrumental ensemble was called by that name; no ensemble looked or behaved like an orchestra; no ensemble of that time was the direct ancestor of a modern orchestra. By the end of the eighteenth century there were orchestras in most of the major cities and courts of Europe. People called them "orchestras"; they played a repertory of music written specifically and idiomatically for orchestras; a few of them, like the orchestra of the Paris Opéra and the orchestra of the Gewandhaus concerts in Leipzig, were the direct ancestors of orchestras that still exist. Thus, the orchestra must have been "born" at some time between 1600 and 1791.

Just *when* the orchestra was born is hard to say, because instrumental ensembles took on so many different forms in the seventeenth and eighteenth centuries that it is often impossible to decide what was an orchestra and what was not. Instead of searching for "the first orchestra," it is more productive to view the birth of the orchestra as a process stretching over the course of two centuries and culminating around 1800 in a social institution that was distinctive and durable, and has remained a central feature of Western art music from that time to the present.

Our book tells the story of the birth of the orchestra during the seventeenth and eighteenth centuries. Other authors have told the story before—indeed they have told various stories, according to which aspects they chose to emphasize. In the literature on the history of the orchestra at least five approaches can be identified:

1. *Etymology*: the history of instrumental ensembles that people call "orchestra";
2. *Taxonomy*: the classification of orchestra-like instrumental ensembles;
3. *Organology*: the history of the instruments that have played in orchestras;
4. *Orchestration*: the history of how composers have written for instruments as an orchestra;
5. *Social history*: the history of relations among orchestra musicians, composers, patrons, and audiences.

This introductory chapter will tell the story of the birth of the orchestra five times over, once from each of these perspectives.

THE ETYMOLOGY OF "ORCHESTRA"

The origins of the word "orchestra" and the changes in its meanings over time can be traced in dictionaries and encyclopedias as well as in letters, documents, and other writings about music. Martin Staehelin, in the *Handwörterbuch der musikalischen*

Terminologie, provides an overview of the history and etymology of the word "orchestra" and its cognates in major European languages.[26] This Greek word was revived by Renaissance humanists to designate the area in the theater between the stage and the audience. In sixteenth-century theaters the instrumental ensemble did not usually occupy this space but was placed in a balcony, onstage, or behind the scenes, as in Peri's *Euridice*. In the first half of the seventeenth century theaters did begin to put the instrumental ensemble between the stage and the audience, and "orchestra" began to refer to the place where the instrumentalists played.

Edward Phillips, in his *New World of English Words* (1658), considers "orchester" to be a genuine English word, meaning "that part of the Scene in a Theater, where the Chorus useth to dance; it is also sometimes taken for the place where the Musicians sit."[27] Across the Channel, Richelet in his *Dictionnaire* of 1679 accepts the word as French:

ORCHESTRA [*orchestre*]. Among the Romans this was the place where the senators sat, and among the Greeks it was the place where ballets were danced. But among us nowadays ORCHESTRA designates the place where the instrumental ensemble [*simphonie*] is enclosed as well as any other performers on musical instruments who play between the acts of spoken plays and for ballets.[28]

In Italy the word "orchestra" referred as early as 1629 to a place set aside for musicians, as evidenced in Buttigli's description of an outdoor festival in Parma:

a platform extended out from the foundation. It was about a yard above the ground and about ten yards wide, and it formed a half-ellipse, raised up on little pedestals and surrounded by a balustrade. This provided a place for the musicians where they could sing and play at the appropriate times, and where they could see everything that was happening on the stage without being seen themselves. And this place is what Vitruvius calls the Orchestra.[29]

Buttigli seems to throw in the word "orchestra" as a sort of an afterthought, and he invokes Vitruvius' classical treatise on architecture, as though he does not expect the term to be familiar to his readers. It seems, however, that "orchestra" must have been familiar to Italians of the day, because it had already appeared in Florio's Italian–English dictionary of 1598, where it is glossed as "a theatre or scaffolde where musitions and singers sit."[30]

---

[26] Martin Staehelin, "Orchester," in *Handwörterbuch der musikalischen Terminologie*, ed. H. H. Eggebrecht (Wiesbaden, 1972–). Graham Strahle's *Early Music Dictionary* adds several interesting usages of the word in English and Italian before 1700 (Graham Strahle, *An Early Music Dictionary: Musical Terms from British Sources, 1500–1740* (Cambridge, 1995), 258–59). See also Helmut Rösing, "Zum Begriff 'Orchester' in europäischer und aussereuropäischer Musik," *Acta musicologica*, 47 (1975), 134–43.

[27] Quoted in Strahle, *Early Music Dictionary*, 258.

[28] Pierre Richelet, *Dictionnaire françois* (Geneva, 1679), 95.

[29] M. Buttigli, *Descrizione dell'apparato fatto per honorare la prima e solenne entrata in Parma della Serenissima Principessa Margherita di Toscana . . . 1629*, quoted in Irving Lavin, "On the Unity of the Arts and the Early Baroque Opera House," in Barbara Wisch and Susan Munshower (eds.), *Art and Pageantry in the Renaissance and Baroque* (State College, Pa., 1990), 518–79 at 554.

[30] John Florio, *A Worlde of Wordes, or most copious and exact Dictionarie in Italian and English* (London, 1598), quoted in Strahle, *Early Music Dictionary*, 258. Already in an earlier dictionary, the Latin

Florio's explanation suggests that the "orchestra" did not have to be in front of the stage but could be a sort of stage itself, and that singers, as well as instrumentalists, could be placed in an orchestra. The description of a performance of an oratorio in Rome in 1689 explains that a riser (*scalinata*) was erected for one group of instrumentalists, a gallery (*tribuna*) for another, and an "orchestra" for the singers, the harpsichords, and the other instruments necessary for the accompaniment.[31] This meaning of "orchestra" as a gallery or a bandstand was also well established in French, so much so that the word could be put to use in imaginative and imaginary contexts. In Aulnoy's story "The White Cat" (1698) a prince attends a banquet at a mysterious castle and is entertained by cats,

who took their places in a small orchestra [*orquestre*] erected for the occasion. One held a part-book with the cleverest little notes in the world; another beat time with a roll of paper; others had little guitars. On the downbeat they all began to miaow on different pitches and pluck the strings of the guitars with their claws . . .[32]

Soon the meaning of "orchestra" extended itself by metonymy to the instrumentalists (human not feline) who made music in places called orchestras. Enea de' Vecchi, a Roman writing in 1679, remarks that Queen Christina of Sweden sent her own carriage to fetch the young Alessandro Scarlatti "so that he could play in the orchestra."[33] Here "orchestra" could mean a place, but it could also also mean the group of people that Scarlatti joined in that place. By the first part of the eighteenth century, "orchestra" had come to refer unequivocally to the instrumentalists and to their collective identity as an ensemble. The new usage seems to have established itself first in Italian and French. A violinist-composer at the church of Santa Maria Maggiore in Bergamo complains in a memo dated September 1702 about the expense of buying paper and copying out his music for "tutti li virtuosi della Sacra Orchestra." Here the word has taken on its new sense, of an instrumental ensemble considered as a single unit, distinguishing between the individual instrumentalists ("virtuosi") and the group of which they are members.

In 1702 the French writer François Raguenet, comparing musical life in Rome with life in Paris, uses the word *orchestre* in a similar way:

Il faut tout Paris pour former un bel Orchestre, on n'y en trouveroit pas deux comme celui de l'Opéra; à Rome où il n'y a pas la dixième partie du monde qui est à Paris, on trouveroit de

---

"orchestra" is explained in English as "a theatre or scaffold whereon musitians, singers, and such like shew their cunning." Thomas Thomas, *Dictionarium linguae Latinae et Anglicanae* (London 1587), quoted in Strahle, *Early Music Dictionary*, 258.

[31] "Dispozizzioni dei musici" for *Santa Beatrice d'Este* by Giovanni Battista Lulier. Transcribed in Adriano Cavicchi, "Prassi esecutiva (IV Tavola Rotonda)," in *Studi corelliani: 1° Congresso Internazionale di Studi Corelliani, Fusignano, 1968*, ed. Adriano Cavicchi, Oscar Mischiati, and Pierluigi Petrobelli (Florence, 1972), 111–25 at 116–17.

[32] Marie-Catherine Aulnoy, *Les Contes des fées par Madame d**** (1698) (London [*i.e.* Paris], 1782), 67–68.

[33] Letter of 15 Feb. 1679 from Enea de' Vecchi to Marucelli. Quoted in Frank D'Accone, *The History of a Baroque Opera: Alessandro Scarlatti's* Gli Equivoci nel Sembiante (New York, 1985), 158.

quoi fournir sept & huit Orchestres composez de Clavessins, de Violons, & de Thüorbes, tous également bien remplis.[34]

Raguenet's essay was translated into English a few years later, but when the translator got to the word "orchestre," he did not use the English cognate, which for him still meant a place in the theater. Instead he translated it as "band":

You must rummage all Paris to fit out a good Band, 'tis impossible to find two such as that in the Opera: At Rome, which is not a tenth Part so populous as Paris, there are Hands enow to compose seven or eight Bands, consisting of Harpsichords, Violins and theorbo's, equally good and perfect.[35]

In each European language "orchestra" had to carve a niche for itself in an already well-populated semantic field.[36] A passage from Johann Mattheson's *Das neu-eröffnete Orchester* maps the topography of this field in the Germany of 1713:

I have chosen to use the word *Orchestre* or *Orquestre* as a not yet very common and thus galant expression, instead of *Concert, Capelle, Chor,* or similar terms . . . The word Orquestre may be applied not only to the instrumental ensemble at the opera [*Opern Symphonie*] but equally and without exception to whatever place the leadership and direction of the music is found, whether it be sacred or secular music.[37]

Mattheson considers the word orchestra to be a neologism, hence fashionable and *galant*. His list of synonyms—*Concert, Capelle, Chor, Opern Symphonie*—shows that he is aware of how many neighbors the word orchestra has in German vocabulary. He implies, however, that orchestra is a better word for what he is talking about, because it is potentially more widely applicable. It can be used to denote an instrumental ensemble in and of itself, whatever its location or purpose.

Dictionaries were slow to acknowledge the new usage of orchestra as designating people rather than places. The first edition of the *Dictionnaire de l'Académie françoise* (1694) gives only the meanings from antiquity. The second, third, and fourth editions (1718, 1740, 1762) acknowledge "orchestra" as "the place where the instrumentalists [*la symphonie*] are located," but not as the instrumental ensemble itself. Not until the edition of 1798 does the Academy admit that "The word is also applied to the collection of all the musicians: e.g. a well-staffed orchestra."[38] German dictionaries by Walther (1732) and Zedler (1740) also limit their definitions to the place in the theater where the musicians sit. Adelung's *Grammatisch-kritisches Wörterbuch* (1777) finally extends the definition to include "all the musicians assembled to play a

---

[34] François Raguenet, *Parallele des Italiens et des François en ce qui regarde la Musique et les Opéra* (Paris, 1702), 109–10.

[35] François Raguenet, *A Comparison between the French and Italian Musick and Opera's* (London, 1709).

[36] See John Spitzer, "Metaphors of the Orchestra: The Orchestra as a Metaphor," *MQ* 80 (1996), 234–64.

[37] Johann Mattheson, *Das neu-eröffnete Orchester* (Hamburg, 1713), 34.

[38] Académie françoise, *Dictionnaire de l'Académie françoise, revu, corrigé et augmenté par Académie elle-même* (Paris, 1798).

piece."[39] Although "orchestra" was used in Italian as early as 1600 to designate a place and from around 1700 to refer to a group of people, the word does not appear at all in Italian dictionaries until the nineteenth century. Perhaps it was considered to be Greek rather than a genuine Italian word. Antonini's French–Italian dictionary of 1760 has an entry for the French "orchestre" but none for the Italian "orchestra."[40]

Jean-Jacques Rousseau, however, recognized the new meaning of "orchestra" clearly in an article he wrote in the 1750s for Diderot and d'Alembert's *Encyclopédie*:

At present this word . . . means sometimes the place where those sit who play on the instruments, as the orchestra of the opera-house; and sometimes the place where the whole band in general are fixed, as the orchestra of the spiritual concert at the Château des Tuilleries; and again the collection of all the symphonists. It is in this last sense, that we say of the execution of music, that the orchestra was good or bad, to express that the instruments were well or ill played.[41]

Rousseau's definition of "orchestra" as "the collection of all the symphonists" reflected contemporary parlance not only in French but also in English, German, and Italian. By the mid-eighteenth century the word orchestra and its cognates had come to designate an instrumental ensemble and the musicians who belonged to that ensemble—not just any instrumental ensemble, but the sort of ensemble that played for an opera or a concert, the sort of ensemble that people listened to attentively enough to care whether the instruments were well or poorly played.

The history and usage of the word "orchestra" in four major European languages narrows the search for the birth of the orchestra to the period between 1650 and 1750. At the beginning of the period "orchestra" was an archaic, unfamiliar word that referred to a place in the theater where instrumentalists occasionally sat. By the end of the period the word had become familiar in all European languages, referring not only to the place but also to the instrumentalists themselves and to their identity as an ensemble. This suggests that the orchestra itself arose during this same period: in the first half of the seventeenth century there was no word for orchestra because there were no orchestras; by the last half of the eighteenth century the word had acquired general currency because by then the orchestra had emerged as an acknowledged, distinctive social institution. The observation that the word "orchestra" took on its modern meanings earliest in Italian and French suggests further that the orchestra developed first in France or Italy, and that both the word and the institution were imported slightly later into Germany and England.

---

[39] Quoted from Johann Christoph Adelung, *Versuch eines vollständigen grammatisch-critischen Wörterbuches der hochdeutschen Mundart* (Leipzig, 1777), col. 916.

[40] Annibale Antonini, *Dictionnaire italien, latin, et françois*, new edn. (Lyon, 1760). Antonini glosses the French "orchestre" as "orquestro" in Italian, a word not encountered elsewhere.

[41] Jean-Jacques Rousseau, *A Complete Dictionary of Music*, trans. William Waring (London, 1779), 301–2. Rousseau reprinted his *Encyclopédie* article in his *Dictionnaire de musique* of 1768. The earlier version is dated there by a parenthetical comment: "ceci s'écrivoit en 1754" (Jean-Jacques Rousseau, *Dictionnaire de musique* (Paris, 1768), 353–54).

THE EVOLUTIONARY TAXONOMY OF THE ORCHESTRA

One way to recognize the birth of the orchestra by whatever name would be to specify the traits that distinguish orchestras from other sorts of instrumental ensembles.
This approach resembles the methods of paleontologists and taxonomists, who, on
the basis of living creatures and the fossil record, classify plants and animals into
species and genera, attempting to establish when and where a given organism first
appeared.

The taxonomic approach is one that we ourselves have espoused in a series of articles, beginning with Neal Zaslaw's "When is an Orchestra not an Orchestra?"
(1988).[42] The article looks at the "Baroque orchestras" of the late seventeenth and
early eighteenth centuries and proposes seven characteristics that define these ensembles as "orchestras" in contrast to earlier ensembles:[43]

1. An orchestra is based on bowed stringed instruments of the violin family.
2. In an orchestra several instruments of the same type play each of the string parts.
   The violins are doubled more heavily than the other strings.
3. The instrumentation of orchestras is considerably standardized within a given
   time and place. As a consequence, repertories emerge of specifically orchestral
   music.
4. Orchestras include one or more bowed bass instruments sounding in the 16-
   foot (double bass) register.
5. Orchestras have a keyboard continuo, usually either a harpsichord or an organ.
   They may also include plucked string continuo instruments like lutes and
   theorbos.
6. Orchestras perform as unified ensembles under centralized control and discipline.
7. Orchestras have distinct organizational identities and administrative structures.

This list of traits serves pretty well to define the orchestra as it existed in the first half
of the eighteenth century and to distinguish this "Baroque orchestra" from earlier,
less orchestral ensembles. The list makes it possible, for example, to settle the argument between Burney and Hawkins by showing that the accompaniment for
Monteverdi's *Orfeo* was not an orchestra, because it was not based on violin-family
instruments, because the stringed instruments were distributed evenly rather than

---

[42] Neal Zaslaw, "When is an Orchestra not an Orchestra?," *EM* 16 (1988), 483–95. Other articles that take
a similar approach include John Spitzer, "The Birth of the Orchestra in Rome: An Iconographic Study," *EM*
19 (1991), 9–28; Neal Zaslaw, "The Origins of the Classical Orchestra," *Basler Jahrbuch für historische
Musikpraxis*, 17 (1993), 9–40; John Spitzer and Neal Zaslaw, "Orchestra," in *NG II*, xviii. 530–84.

[43] Actually there are two lists in Zaslaw's article, the first (pp. 484–86) with eight traits, the second (p. 487)
with only seven traits. The disappearing trait involves the presence of wind instruments in the ensemble. Wind
scorings remained in flux during the 18th c., so here we use the shorter list.

unevenly on the parts, because the instrumentation was unique to that one opera, and so on. The ensemble that played for Rossi's Paris *Orfeo* of 1647 embodied more of the listed traits—it contained a large number of violin-family instruments, it played as a unified ensemble, etc.—but others were lacking, for example the organizational identity and the 16-foot bass. Thus Rossi's ensemble can be said to be more orchestral than Monteverdi's, but not yet an orchestra.

It is possible to determine, at least approximately, when and where most of the traits on the list above first appeared.

1. *Violin-based ensembles.* Administrative documents and extant music show that violin bands were operating in Paris by the second half of the sixteenth century, at the English court at the beginning of the seventeenth century, and in Italian churches by the second half of the seventeenth century.

2. *Part doubling.* Contracts that Parisian violinists drew up in the 1580s and 1590s to regulate their association into ensembles sometimes specify which persons should play what parts. Two, three, and even four players are assigned to the treble and bass parts, one or two players to the middle parts.[44] In 1636 Marin Mersenne, the French philosopher and music theorist, stated that in a violin band of twenty-four members there should be six violins on the upper part, four violas on each of three middle parts, and six basses on the bottom part.[45]

3. *Standardized instrumentation and repertory.* The earliest string bands played music in four, five, or six parts. The five-part scoring specified by Mersenne became standard in France in the first quarter of the seventeenth century, and a repertory of five-part music for string band has been preserved from that time. In the last quarter of the seventeenth century suites of Lully's overtures and dances—in both five-part originals and four-part arrangements—circulated so widely as to constitute a sort of international orchestral repertory.

4. *16-foot bass.* In the seventeenth century the bass part in string bands and other instrumental ensembles was played by 8-foot instruments. The double bass, which had previously been used to reinforce the bass part in church music, began to turn up in large instrumental ensembles around the beginning of the eighteenth century.

5. *Keyboard continuo.* Sixteenth- and seventeenth-century string bands did not include keyboards or plucked-string continuo instruments. With the advent of opera at the beginning of the seventeenth century bowed strings were combined with keyboards and lutes in the theater. At first their functions did not overlap: the continuo instruments accompanied singers; the string band accompanied dancers. Gradually, over the course of the seventeenth century, the string ensemble took a larger role alongside the continuo in vocal accompaniment, not only in the theater but in church and other contexts as well.

---

[44] François Lesure, "Les Orchestres populaires à Paris vers la fin du XVIᵉ siècle," *Revue de musicologie*, 36 (1954), 39–54 at 51–52.

[45] Marin Mersenne, *Harmonie universelle* (Paris, 1636), iii. 185.

6. *Unity and discipline.* Orchestras achieve unity by means of performance practices like centralized leadership, uniform bowing, and control of improvised ornamentation. Early orchestra leaders like Lully (Paris, 1660s–1680s), Corelli (Rome, 1680s–1700s), and Buxtehude (Lübeck, 1680s–1690s) established new, higher standards of orchestral discipline.

7. *Administrative structures.* In the seventeenth and eighteenth centuries most orchestras were subsumed within larger organizations, such as courts, theaters, or churches. During the eighteenth century a few orchestras, like the Concert Spirituel in Paris, the Professional Concert in London, and the Grosse Konzert in Leipzig, emerged with their own administrative apparatus.

According to this taxonomic analysis, the birth of the orchestra took place gradually, in a process that began at the end of the sixteenth century and continued until the late eighteenth century, when all seven traits on the list above could be found in many large instrumental ensembles. Most of the traits—including violin-based ensembles, part doubling, standard repertory, and centralized leadership—appeared earliest in France, which would thus get credit for being the birthplace of the orchestra.

Why, though, should the "Baroque orchestra" of the mid-eighteenth century be the standard for what is or is not orchestral? If, for instance, one were to take Haydn's ensemble for *L'anima del filosofo* in 1791 as the model, then the list of traits would look somewhat different. Violin-family instruments, unequal doubling, standardized instrumentation, and several others would remain, but some important new traits would have to be added:[46]

8. *Wind instruments.* By the end of the eighteenth century wind instruments had become an integral part of the orchestra. These included flutes, oboes, clarinets, bassoons, horns, and trumpets, all of them usually present in pairs.

9. *Leadership.* Late eighteenth-century orchestras were led by the first violinist, who set tempos, led rehearsals, and maintained discipline. Around the beginning of the nineteenth century, violin leaders began to be replaced by conductors, who did not play an instrument but beat time with their bows or with batons.[47]

10. *Specialization.* By the end of the eighteenth century most orchestra musicians had become specialists on their instruments. Instrumental specialization represented a change from earlier periods, when most players were double-handed and could play several different instruments in the ensemble as needed.

11. *Placement.* Orchestras became central to events in which they participated. The orchestra was assigned a place of its own: on a bandstand, on a stage, or in an enclosure directly in front of the stage.

[46] For an expanded list with 12 traits, see Zaslaw, "Origins."

[47] Some French orchestras, including that of the Opéra in Paris, were directed already in the 18th c. by a timebeater, who by the 1770s exercised many of the functions of a baton conductor. See David Charlton, "'A maître d'orchestre . . . conducts': New and Old Evidence on French Practice," *EM* 21 (1993), 341–53.

12. *Nomenclature.* By Haydn's time the orchestra was universally called by the name "orchestra." Other names persisted, like *Kapelle, symphonie, suonatori,* and band, but by the end of the eighteenth century, the name "orchestra" had come to designate a unique sort of instrumental ensemble.

At the same time, based on orchestras of the 1790s, at least one trait would have to be crossed off the original list: the keyboard continuo. Although a piano was still used for *secco* recitative in opera, keyboards had disappeared from orchestras in most other circumstances. Haydn sat at a piano during the Salomon concerts in London, but it was Salomon who led the orchestra with his violin. At the rehearsal of *L'anima del filosofo* Haydn used a violin, not the piano, to make his point about the first three notes of the overture.

The taxonomical definition of the orchestra depends, then, on which orchestra is selected as a model. If the list of traits were based on orchestras of the 1890s, the definition would change yet again—but perhaps not as much this time, because the more firmly the orchestra established itself as an institution, the more it conserved its old traits and resisted change. Unless one wants to break the orchestra down into subspecies ("Baroque orchestra," "Classical orchestra," "Romantic orchestra," etc.), a taxonomic approach cannot draw a line between what is and what is not an orchestra.

THE HISTORY OF ORCHESTRAL INSTRUMENTS

Another way to tell the story of the orchestra is as a history of musical instruments. One version of this history is the story of "firsts and lasts," identifying the earliest appearance of each instrument that plays in the modern orchestra, as well as the last vestiges of obsolete instruments. Scholars like Adam Carse, Charles Sanford Terry, and Jérôme de La Gorce try to ascertain what instruments were in use in orchestras of a given period and place, and what the characteristics of these instruments were.[48] A second approach is to tell the story as a history of orchestral size and balances: how many of what kinds of instruments various orchestras contained and how these balances changed over time. This approach generates the formidable tables of orchestras and instruments that appear at the end of the "orchestra" articles in the *The New Grove Dictionary, Die Musik in Geschichte und Gegenwart,* and elsewhere.

The story of instrumental firsts and lasts can be sketched here only in broad terms. Already at the beginning of the seventeenth century violin-family instruments

---

[48] Adam Carse, *The Orchestra in the XVIIIth Century* (Cambridge, 1940); id., *The Orchestra from Beethoven to Berlioz* (Cambridge, 1948); Charles Sanford Terry, *Bach's Orchestra* (London, 1932); Jérôme de La Gorce, "Some Notes on Lully's Orchestra," in John Hajdu Heyer (ed.), *Jean-Baptiste Lully and the Music of the French Baroque: Essays in Honor of James R. Anthony* (Cambridge, 1989), 99–112; id., "L'Orchestre de l'Opéra et son évolution de Campra à Rameau," *Revue de musicologie,* 76 (1990), 23–43.

formed the core of the instrumental ensembles that would eventually become orchestras. Seventeenth-century violins and violas had much the same shape as modern instruments and were usually tuned like their modern counterparts. However, all their strings were made of gut, they had no chin or shoulder rests, and their bows were convex rather than concave.[49] Seventeenth-century violas were built in a variety of sizes, from instruments only slightly larger than a violin to instruments 15–20 percent larger than modern violas. When scores and personnel lists from the seventeenth century refer to viole—like the 12 viole in Rossi's *Orfeo* that imitated Orpheus' lyre backstage—they usually mean violin-family instruments rather than viols. Viols and other bowed stringed instruments—violino piccolo, viola d'amore, viola da caccia—turn up occasionally in eighteenth-century orchestral scores, but usually as soloists rather than as members of an orchestral string section.

The identity of bass stringed instruments in the second half of the seventeenth century is a confusing, contentious topic. The sources transmit a profusion of names—violone, basse de violon, basso di viola, violone grosso, contrabasso—but it is hard to tell what instruments these names refer to or how the instruments were tuned. In the seventeenth century violone, the commonest name, seems to have referred most often to a violin-family instrument with a long neck that sounded in the 8-foot register.[50] The violoncello, smaller than the violone but sounding in the same register, was introduced around 1675 in Italy.[51] By 1700 cellos could be found in orchestras throughout Europe, often alongside the older violone. Around the same time 16-foot string basses, which had been available since the early seventeenth century, came into widespread orchestral use, under the names contrabasso, contre basse, and (confusingly) violone.[52] By the 1730s the situation had clarified itself considerably: 8-foot cellos and 16-foot double basses usually played the bass line together; a separate cello part was occasionally added as a tenor obbligato.

During the first half of the seventeenth century ensembles often included large numbers of plucked stringed instruments—like the two lutes, two guitars, and four theorbos that played in Rossi's *Orfeo*. From this initial high point plucked strings declined more or less steadily. By the end of the seventeenth century the only plucked strings to be found in large instrumental ensembles were archlutes and theorbos, which realized the bass line in vocal accompaniments and occasionally had an obbligato part, like the theorbo that imitates Orpheus' lyre in Fux's *Orfeo*. The last theorbist retired from the

[49] David D. Boyden, *The History of Violin Playing from its Origins to 1761* (London, 1965). There were structural differences as well between 17th- and 18th-c. violins and modern instruments.

[50] Stephen Bonta, "Terminology for the Bass Violin in Seventeenth-Century Italy," *JAMIS* 4 (1978), 5–42. Planyavsky argues, probably incorrectly, that the violone was usually a viol-family instrument and often sounded in the 16-foot register (Alfred Planyavsky, *The Baroque Double Bass Violone*, trans. James Berket (Lanham, Md., 1998), 10 ff.). In the 17th c. violone more often referred to a bass violin.

[51] See Stephen Bonta, "From Violone to Violoncello: A Question of Strings," *JAMIS* 3 (1977), 64–99.

[52] Mary Cyr, "*Basses* and *Basse continue* in the Orchestra of the Paris Opéra 1700–1764," *EM* 10 (1982), 155–70.

Paris Opéra in the 1720s, from the Turin *Cappella* in the 1730s, and from the Kapellen at Mannheim, Dresden, and Vienna in the 1750s.[53] Harpists, such as Haydn's Mme Krumpholz, did not become regular members of orchestras until the nineteenth century.

Keyboard instruments, sometimes several at a time, participated in orchestra-like ensembles already in the early seventeenth century, though at first they seldom played at the same time as the bowed strings. In his list of instruments for *Orfeo* Monteverdi calls for two harpsichords, two wooden pipe organs, and one reed organ (regal), and at several points in the score he directs multiple harpsichords and/or organs to play simultaneously. He also instructs the keyboards to play along with the bowed strings in several passages. Likewise, in Rossi's *Orfeo* four harpsichords played with the string band in the overture. Orchestras for Italian opera continued to use two harpsichords during much of the eighteenth century. Other kinds of eighteenth-century orchestras, however, generally used only a single keyboard, and orchestras for dancing had none. Symphonies, both in the theater and in concert, were often performed without keyboard.[54] By the 1770s pianos (what today are called "fortepianos") had begun to replace harpsichords, first in German orchestras, then elsewhere. However, with the rise of the symphonic repertory and the growing fashion for accompanied recitative in opera, keyboards of all types were used less and less. By the 1780s some opera orchestras were beginning to do without a keyboard altogether.

Wind instruments present the greatest problems for the story of orchestral firsts and lasts. Many different types of wind instruments were used in instrumental ensembles between 1600 and 1800, and many different forms of the same instruments. In their Orpheus settings Peri, Monteverdi, and Rossi borrowed cornetts, trombones, and trumpets from churches and civic bands. For pastoral scenes they added flutes (usually recorders rather than transverse flutes), shawms, and bagpipes. The winds usually formed separate ensembles, which played by themselves, often onstage and in costume, as in the *Ballet des muses*. They rarely played at the same time as the strings or the continuo instruments. The redesign of wind instruments undertaken by French musicians and craftsmen in the second half of the seventeenth century made it easier for them to play along with an ensemble of violin-family instruments, and wind players began to sit in the "orchestra" with the strings, where they often doubled the string parts and sometimes played an obbligato line. French-style oboes and bassoons

---

[53] La Gorce, "L'Orchestre de l'Opéra"; Marie-Thérèse Bouquet, *Musique et musiciens à Turin de 1648 à 1775* (Turin, 1968); Eugene K. Wolf, "On the Composition of the Mannheim Orchestra ca. 1740–1778," *Basler Jahrbuch für historische Musikpraxis*, 17 (1993), 113–38; Christoph-Hellmut Mahling, "Orchester und Orchestermusiker in Deutschland von 1700 bis 1850" (Diss., Universität Saarbrücken, 1971); Eleanor Selfridge-Field, "The Viennese Court Orchestra in the Time of Caldara," in Brian W. Pritchard (ed.), *Antonio Caldara: Essays on his Life and Times* (Aldershot, 1987), 115–51.

[54] James Webster, "On the Absence of Keyboard Continuo in Haydn's Symphonies," *EM* 18 (1990), 599–608.

were introduced to England by the 1670s; they appeared in Germany by the 1680s, in Italy by the 1690s.[55]

Trumpets had been used in theater music since the sixteenth century, usually to play introductory fanfares, like the toccata at the beginning of Monteverdi's *Orfeo*, or for battle scenes, like the four trumpets that "sound a warlike alarm" in Rossi's *Orfeo*. In the second half of the seventeenth century trumpets were integrated more often with other instruments, as obbligato soloists in opera arias and also in church music, where they added splendor to concertos and masses.[56] Trumpet players, however, along with the drummers who accompanied them, were seldom members of the same music establishment as other instrumentalists but instead belonged either to a corps of court or cavalry trumpeters or to a city or military band. Not until the second half of the eighteenth century did orchestras begin to include a pair of trumpets and a kettle drummer as regular members.

Two important new wind instruments were introduced into orchestras in the eighteenth century: the horn and the clarinet. The horn, which had been used onstage for fanfares and hunting calls in a few seventeenth-century operas, was first combined with the string ensemble by German composers such as Keiser (*Octavia*, 1705) and Buxtehude (*Templum honoris*, 1705).[57] The invention *c*.1700 of interchangeable crooks, which could be assembled to make up various lengths and fit between the mouthpiece and the body of the horn, greatly increased the usefulness of the horn as an orchestral instrument. From Bohemia and Germany horns and hornists spread to England (by 1711), Italy (by 1715), and belatedly to France (by 1748).

The chalumeau, a single-reed instrument shaped like a recorder, appeared at the beginning of the eighteenth century. Fux used a chalumeau in 1715 to lend a pastoral flavor to one of Orpheus' arias in *Orfeo ed Euridice* (1715), and, although the instrument had become scarce by mid-century, Gluck managed to find a chalumeau player for his Viennese *Orfeo* in 1762.[58] The clarinet, a chalumeau re-engineered to play in the upper register, functioned chiefly as a novelty instrument during the first half of the eighteenth century. By the 1730s a few German court orchestras had acquired pairs of clarinets, initially played by oboists or string players, later by specialists.[59] Regular clarinetists were not hired at the Paris Opéra until 1771, just in time for Gluck's *Orphée et Euridice* (1774), where they played in the ballets and the choruses.

[55] Bruce Haynes, *The Eloquent Oboe: A History of the Hautboy, 1640–1760* (Oxford, 2001), 132–52. In Turin, where the court maintained close connections with France, oboes were in use already in the 1670s.

[56] For a survey of early trumpet repertory, see Edward H. Tarr, "The Trumpet before 1800," in Trevor Herbert and John Wallace (eds.), *The Cambridge Companion to Brass Instruments* (Cambridge, 1997), 84–102.

[57] See Horace Fitzpatrick, *The Horn and Horn-Playing and the Austro-Bohemian Tradition from 1680 to 1830* (London, 1970), 50 ff.; Renato Meucci, "Horn," in *NG II*, xi. 709–25.

[58] For more examples of orchestral repertory for chalumeau, including several pieces by Vivaldi, see Colin Lawson, "Single Reeds before 1750," in id. (ed.), *The Cambridge Companion to the Clarinet* (Cambridge, 1996), 1–15.

[59] See Albert Rice, *The Baroque Clarinet* (Oxford, 1992), 151 ff.

As new wind instruments were added, old ones disappeared. By 1700 cornett and trombone players had become rare on personnel lists, and composers seldom called for them in theater or concert music. As late as 1762, however, Gluck could evoke the underworld with cornetts and trombones in his Viennese *Orfeo*: players were available because the instruments were still used in Viennese churches.[60] Evidently there were no cornettists left in Paris in 1774 for *Orphée et Euridice*, so Gluck replaced cornetts in the score with clarinets. He was able to keep the trombones, however, which, although not on the roster of the Opéra in 1774, must have been available. The recorder too slipped out of use during the first half of the eighteenth century. Lully called specifically for transverse flute only in one work (*Le Triomphe de l'Amour*, 1681); but by the 1690s French composers were writing for it often. By the 1730s flute specialists were beginning to appear on orchestra rosters throughout Europe, and composers were writing parts idiomatic for transverse flute rather than for recorder.[61] By the last quarter of the eighteenth century orchestral wind sections had become considerably standardized. Almost anywhere in Europe a composer could expect to find pairs of flutes, oboes, clarinets, bassoons, horns, and trumpets.

This familiar story of orchestral firsts and lasts has some drawbacks. For one, naming an instrument does not tell very much about it. Did the "first" double bass have three strings, four, or more? Was Lully's "hautbois" an oboe, a shawm, or neither? Also, the story of firsts and lasts tends to take on a teleological cast: it concentrates on those instruments that became part of the modern orchestra and ignores those that disappeared. The theorbo, the tenor violin, and the serpent were all common and potentially important orchestral instruments, but the story ignores them because they have not been retained in the modern orchestra. Finally, the story of firsts and lasts only identifies the instrumental building blocks of the orchestra; it does not say anything about how many of these instruments there were, what the proportions of the instruments to one another may have been, or how they were employed.

ORCHESTRAL SIZE AND BALANCES

A great deal of information survives about numbers of players and numbers of instruments in orchestras, particularly in the eighteenth century. This information comes from a variety of sources, including scores, musical almanacs, personnel records, pay lists, instrument inventories, and pictures. It is typically summarized in tables of

---

[60] Otto Biba, "Die Wiener Kirchenmusik um 1783," *Beiträge zur Musikgeschichte des 18. Jahrhunderts. Jahrbuch für österreichische Kulturgeschichte*, 1/2 (1971), 7–79; Markus Spielmann, "Der Zink im Instrumentarium des süddeutsch-österreichischen Raumes 1650 bis 1750," in *Johann Joseph Fux und die barocke Bläsertradition—Kongressbericht Graz, 1985*, ed. Bernhard Habla (Tutzing, 1987), 121–55.

[61] See Adrienne Simpson, "The Orchestral Recorder," in John Mansfield Thomson (ed.), *The Cambridge Companion to the Recorder* (Cambridge, 1995), 91–106 at 101–3. Handel frequently scored for recorders up to 1738, almost never thereafter.

orchestral sizes and balances, of which Table 1.1 is a modest example. Adam Carse, in *The Orchestra in the XVIIIth Century*, assembled a table of 91 reports of how many of what sorts of instruments played in 60 different European orchestras between 1697 and 1791. Ottmar Schreiber topped this in *Orchester und Orchesterpraxis in Deutschland* (1938) with a table of 159 reports on 79 different orchestras in Germany alone between 1780 and 1850—to which he appended another 85 reports of one-time-only festival orchestras, most of them very large.[62] Such tables of orchestral forces, with violins, oboes, and trumpets marshalled in tidy columns, have become a sort of topos in the musicological literature, each table more ambitious than the last.[63] The current record holder is probably C.-H. Mahling's table in the 1994 edition of *Die Musik in Geschichte und Gegenwart*, where 236 reports on sizes and balances are given for 134 different European orchestras, the earliest dating from 1610, the latest from 1877.[64]

Historians sometimes use these tables to trace the development of orchestras in the seventeenth and eighteenth centuries, while performers occasionally use them as guides to performance practice. Both these uses are problematic. The tables are based for the most part on rosters and pay lists from court Kapellen and theaters—that is, on the records of music establishments, not of performing ensembles. Such records often make orchestras look larger than they really were.[65] Retired musicians kept their places on the payroll long after they had ceased to play; other musicians whose names appeared on the roster were actually on tour or on leave. In addition, the full number of musicians present and active did not necessarily play for a given performance: instrumentalists could be excused when a piece did not call for their instrument or when the event needed only a small orchestra. Theater orchestras were often reduced to about half their usual size when they performed opera buffa. According to this line of reasoning, the number of musicians on a payroll or a roster should be considered not as an actual orchestra but rather as a maximum—a pool of available performers from which to assemble smaller orchestras.

Such cautionary observations are well founded, but they are also influenced by the modern predilection for performing seventeenth- and eighteenth-century music with small orchestras in order to make it sound different from nineteenth-century music. An actual eighteenth-century orchestra might just as well have been larger than the number of names on a roster would indicate. It might include trumpeters playing violin or viola, or unpaid apprentices (*Accessisten*), or dilettantes who played

---

[62] Ottmar Schreiber, *Orchester und Orchesterpraxis in Deutschland zwischen 1780 und 1850* (Berlin, 1938), 10 ff.

[63] More examples of orchestral size and balance tables may be found in Carse, *The Orchestra from Beethoven to Berlioz*; Neal Zaslaw, "Toward the Revival of the Classical Orchestra," *PRMA* 103 (1976–7), 158–87; Mahling, "Orchester und Orchestermusiker"; Jack Westrup and Neal Zaslaw, "Orchestra," in *NG*, xiii. 679–91; and John Spitzer and Neal Zaslaw, "Orchestra," in *GroveO*, iii. 719–35.

[64] Christoph-Hellmut Mahling and Helmut Rösing, "Orchester," in *MGG*², Sachteil 7, cols. 812–54.

[65] Dexter Edge, "Manuscript Parts as Evidence of Orchestral Size in the Eighteenth-Century Viennese Concerto," in Neal Zaslaw (ed.), *Mozart's Piano Concertos: Text, Context, Interpretation* (Ann Arbor, 1996), 427–60; Wolf, "On the Composition."

along in concerts.[66] Theater orchestras hired supernumeraries when they wanted extra string players or when a score called for special instruments. Thus rosters and paylists sometimes overstate, sometimes understate the size of the orchestras that performed seventeenth- and eighteenth-century music. The relation between tables based on such documents and actual orchestras remains tenuous.

Tables of orchestral numbers and balances can be useful to trace changes over time and also to compare contemporary orchestras with one another. However, producers and consumers of such tables need to observe at least two principles:

1. Tables should be based on primary sources, not on other tables. The sources on which they are based should be evaluated critically and the numbers adjusted to address the issues raised above.

2. Tables should compare apples with apples—that is, they should follow a single orchestra over time or compare orchestras of the same period with one another, or orchestras that played in similar venues or played similar repertories. Tables that compare all kinds of ensembles playing all manner of music in all sorts of venues are impossible to interpret.

THE HISTORY OF ORCHESTRATION

The story of the orchestra as a history of instruments is often combined with the story of how the instruments functioned musically, that is the history of orchestration. Adam Carse recounts the two stories simultaneously, illustrating them with musical examples in his *History of Orchestration* (1925). For Paul Bekker in *The Story of the Orchestra* (1936) and Henry Raynor in *The Orchestra* (1978) the history of the orchestra is once again the history of instruments and the ways they are used in the works of famous composers. Essays by several authors in the anthology *The Orchestra: Origins and Transformations* (1986) update the story.[67] All these accounts propose more or less the same periodization of the history of orchestration before 1800. It is a tripartite scheme based on the traditional style periods of music history:

1. *Renaissance ensembles.* The first period lasted from the sixteenth into the seventeenth century. Renaissance writing for instrumental ensembles tended to be generic rather than idiomatic: instruments often doubled or substituted for voices; scores either said nothing at all about instrumentation or gave options for different combinations of instruments. The number of parts varied greatly: church music might have parts for ten or more different instruments; theater music often had just a bass line (cf. Ex. 1.1).

---

[66] Wolf, "On the Composition," 116; Neal Zaslaw, *Mozart's Symphonies: Context, Performance Practice, Reception* (Oxford, 1989), 3–4.

[67] Joan Peyser (ed.), *The Orchestra: Origins and Transformations* (New York, 1986). Essays in this collection that discuss the history of orchestration include those by Robert Weaver, George Stauffer, and Larry Todd.

When composers did take the trouble to specify which instrument should play which part, the instruments were often chosen not so much for how they sounded as for what they represented.[68] Monteverdi adhered to this notion in *Orfeo*: the recorders signify shepherds and rural life; trombones and cornetts are associated with the underworld, bowed and plucked strings with the gods and the heavens. When Orpheus ascends from the underworld at the beginning of Act IV, Monteverdi's instruction reads: "Let the cornetts, trombones, and reed organ cease playing, and let the violins, organs, harpsichords, contrabass, harps, chitarroni, and ceteroni come onstage to play the ritornello."

2. *The Baroque orchestra.* Baroque orchestration, beginning in the mid-seventeenth century and lasting until about 1740, combined idiomatic writing for bowed strings and winds with a generic basso continuo. The string ensemble was divided into a fixed number of parts or groups, arrangements that became standardized by region over long periods. Northern Italian ensembles used a five-part scoring during much of the seventeenth century. In Sartorio's *Orfeo* most of the ritornellos are scored for two violins, two violas, and a bass. A slighty different five-part scoring (1 violin, 3 violas, 1 bass) was typical in French orchestras, as in Lully's *Ballet des muses* (Ex. 1.2) and Campra's *Carnaval de Venise*. German and southern Italian orchestras tended to score for four-part strings (2 violins, viola, bass), the scoring that Fux uses in his *Orfeo* (Ex. 1.3). Within these basic schemes, however, there was great flexibility. The bass usually played throughout, but there could be anywhere from one to four violin parts and one to three viola parts, according to how dense or how thin a texture the composer desired.

Innovations in instrument design made it possible to add bowed bass instruments and bassoons to the continuo part, previously played by plucked strings and keyboards. Usually, however, composers did not specify the instrumentation of the basso continuo; its makeup was a matter of performance practice, which varied from genre to genre and from one location to another. Technological innovations also enabled oboes and flutes to play at the same pitch level as the strings and hence to double the string parts, a scoring that composers sometimes wrote out, but just as often left to performance practice.[69] The same improvements encouraged composers to use winds more as obbligato soloists. In Fux's *Orfeo ed Euridice*, for example, flute and chalumeau accompany the aria that Orpheus sings on the banks of the River Lethe, and duetting bassoons accompany Pluto's entrance aria. A wind obbligato, once initiated, usually continued throughout the movement.

3. *The Classical orchestra.* The "Classical" orchestra usually refers to the orchestra and orchestration techniques of Haydn and Mozart, but the term can be extended to music and composers from the 1740s through the beginning of the nineteenth century—that is from Jommelli and Stamitz to Spontini and Beethoven. The four-part

[68] See Robert Weaver, "Sixteenth-Century Instrumentation," *MQ* 47 (1961), 363–78.
[69] Haynes, *The Eloquent Oboe*, 57, 93 ff.

string layout became standard, although the violas were occasionally divided and the cello was sometimes given its own part distinct from the double bass. Treatment of the bass line became increasingly flexible, with violas, bassoons, sometimes even second violins called upon to provide the orchestral bass line (cf. Ex. 1.4).

Taking advantage of new instruments like flutes, clarinets, and horns, composers for the Classical orchestra used winds more often and more flexibly than did earlier composers. Winds could still be obbligato soloists for entire movements, like the flute and oboe in "Che puro ciel" from Act II of Gluck's *Orfeo*. However, they could also be used for shorter solos, emerging for a few bars of melody, then relinquishing their solo role, often to be supplanted by a different wind instrument. Winds in the Classical orchestra could also be used for their tone quality, sometimes doubling a string part to add a touch of color, sometimes as a little band to contrast with the strings, as in the overture to Haydn's *L'anima del filosofo* (Ex. 1.4).

In this conventional account the history of orchestration is seen as being driven mainly by the technology of musical instruments. As old instruments were redesigned and new instruments introduced, composers found new and different ways to use instruments. The same story can be told as a history of the combination and recombination of groups of instruments and performers. This version of the story retains the same three periods of orchestration but characterizes them differently: as separate ensembles, nested ensembles, and sections.

1. *Separate ensembles.* Most fifteenth- and sixteenth-century instrumental music was conceived for "consorts," that is groups of instruments, often of the same type but sounding in different registers, one on a part. By the seventeenth century several instruments could play the same part (particularly the bass part), but the principle of separation of ensembles by instrument type still obtained. The two most characteristic ensembles in the first half of the seventeenth century were continuo ensembles of keyboards and plucked strings, which accompanied singers, and string bands, which played for dancing. These two ensembles were administratively and socially separate, with different personnel and different functions. Continuo ensembles and string bands were sometimes combined in operas and other dramatic productions, but they usually alternated rather than playing the same music together. In Monteverdi's *Orfeo*, for example, singing is accompanied by keyboards and lutes, while ritornellos and dances are played by the five-part string ensemble.[70] Winds constituted a third ensemble, again with its own identity and organization, and again treated as a separate entity by composers. For example, the underworld scenes of Monteverdi's *Orfeo* and also of Rossi's are introduced by ritornellos played by trombones and cornetts.

---

[70] In Orfeo's aria "Possente spirito" and again in his plea to Pluto in Act IV, the instruments accompany the singer directly, but only pairs of soloists, not an ensemble. Only at the end of "Possente spirito" do stringed instruments play at the same time as Orfeo sings, marking a shift from vocal virtuosity to heartfelt expression of emotion.

The separation of ensembles began to break down in the late seventeenth century. Composers began to combine the three ensembles in their orchestrations, adding wind parts to string music and strings to vocal accompaniments. For example, occasional figures above the bass line in Sartorio's *L'Orfeo* suggest that theorbos and/or the harpsichord may have played along with the string band in dances. In Campra's *Carnaval de Venise* pairs of flutes are included in the *petit choeur* and accompany several of the arias.

2. *Nested ensembles.* As previously distinct groups of instruments merged in the late seventeenth century, the somewhat amorphous new ensemble was given shape by treating it as a smaller ensemble nested within a larger one. The old vocal accompaniment ensemble became the continuo group, clustered around the harpsichord or organ. In fully scored music the continuo group played along with the string band, setting tempos, helping to maintain good ensemble, and filling in harmonies.

Another sort of ensemble within an ensemble was "concerto grosso" orchestration, in which the smaller group, usually two violins and a cello, were designated as "concertino," the larger group as "concerto grosso" or simply as "tutti." Fux, in *Orfeo ed Euridice*, uses this device frequently, alternating concertino and ripieno to avoid covering the singer (Ex. 1.3). In another passage he uses the contrast of the small ensemble with the large one to imitate an echo. The differentiation of smaller vs. larger groups had another advantage: a composer could assign more difficult passages to the more expert players, reserving the full orchestra for simpler passages where volume and power were needed.

3. *Sections.* As orchestras became more integrated during the second half of the eighteenth century, ensembles within ensembles were replaced by "sections," that is, groups of identical instruments considered as parts of a greater whole. Because each section was internally homogeneous, composers could treat instruments more idiomatically. Composers began to conceive of the orchestra as a vast reservoir of possible sounds, from which they could pick and choose the sounds they wanted. A composer could give the same musical "idea" a number of different orchestral realizations; or he could reorchestrate an existing piece, as Gluck did with several numbers in *Orfeo ed Euridice* when he reworked the opera for Paris.

Neither history of orchestration—the story of instrument technology or the story of instrument groups—presents an entirely satisfactory account of the birth of the orchestra. For one thing, successful techniques of orchestration are tenacious. Symbolic instrumentation did not disappear with the advent of "Baroque" orchestration: Monteverdi, Gluck, and Haydn all use trombones to suggest the underworld; indeed so does Stravinsky in his ballet *Orphée* (1947). Gluck's two orchestras—one for Orpheus, one for the denizens of the underworld—recall the separate ensembles of the Renaissance. Another problem with histories of orchestration is that they almost always turn into a parade of well-known works by famous composers, culminating in the "Classical" orchestral music of Haydn, Mozart, and Beethoven. Innovations by less well-known composers are ignored or seen as forerunners of the works of the masters. Finally, the history of the orchestra is not just a story of things—instruments and scores—but a story about people: performers, composers, patrons, and listeners. The story of the birth of the orchestra needs to tell their stories too: who these people were, what sort of lives they led, and how they interacted to make orchestras function.

THE SOCIAL HISTORY OF THE ORCHESTRA

Social histories of the orchestra address the lives and careers of orchestra musicians, the politics and mechanisms of patronage, the role of the orchestra in social activities, and the social meanings of the orchestra. No one has undertaken a comprehensive social history for the period before 1800, but valuable contributions can be found in Adam Carse's *The Orchestra in the Eighteenth Century* (1940), Ottmar Schreiber's *Orchester und Orchesterpraxis in Deutschland* (1938), and *The Orchestra in England: A Social History* by Reginald Nettel (1946).[71] All these authors tell more or less the same story: the orchestra began in the seventeenth century in a courtly milieu with royal and aristocratic patronage; then it shifted during the eighteenth century to the concert hall and patronage by the middle class.

The earliest standing ensemble of violin-family instruments with several players on each part seems to have been the Vingt-quatre Violons du Roy at the French court in the first half of the seventeenth century. The original and primary function of the Vingt-quatre Violons was to play for dancing, but they soon began to play for the King's suppers, for dramatic entertainments, and at public festivities. The members of the Vingt-quatre Violons held appointments at the French court, just like other court functionaries. As individuals the 24 players participated in the musical life of Paris— indeed, they used the prestige of their position to get the best jobs—but as a single ensemble they played primarily at court. The prototype orchestra, then, was a monopolistic professional group, operating in an exclusive social milieu. The Vingt-quatre Violons had a external function as well: to display the grandeur of the French king and the magnificence of his court to the rest of the world.

The Vingt-quatre Violons were imitated during the seventeenth century by other large European courts, for example London and Vienna, and also by smaller courts, like Stuttgart, Stockholm, and Turin. Everywhere the social function and organiza-

---

[71] See also Christoph-Hellmut Mahling, "The Origin and Social Status of the Court Orchestral Musician in the 18th and Early 19th Century in Germany," trans. Herbert Kaufman and Barbara Reisner, in Walter Salmen (ed.), *The Social Status of the Professional Musician from the Middle Ages to the 19th Century* (Stuyvesant, NY, 1983), 219–64, and Michael Broyles, "Ensemble Music Moves out of the Private House: Haydn to Beethoven," in Peyser (ed.), *The Orchestra: Origins and Transformations*, 97–122.

tional model were the same: the incipient orchestra was administered as part of the household of the ruler; musicians were employees of the court; the ensemble performed mainly at court functions; the orchestra displayed the magnificence of the prince and his court to the rest of the world. Music-loving princes competed with one another to maintain the biggest, best-dressed, and best-sounding orchestras.

During the eighteenth century, as orchestras were formed in imitation of one another in courts and cities all over Europe, they came increasingly to resemble one another: in the way they were organized, in the kinds of instruments they contained, in the music they played, and in their performance practices. The movement of players from one orchestra to another and the movement of repertory between orchestras reinforced these similarities. By the second half of the eighteenth century the culture of the orchestra had become international. There were standing orchestras in all the major courts and theaters of Europe, with the same or similar instruments, the same performance practices, and some of the same repertory.

At the same time musical culture in the European capitals began to outgrow the confines of the court milieu. The influx of people and of wealth into London, Paris, and Vienna during the course of the eighteenth century created a level of cultural demand that kings and courts could no longer meet. In music, as in art, literature, and dress, the courts remained leaders in taste and style, but they could not maintain their position as the principal purveyors of orchestras and orchestral music to the aristocracy and the populace. The orchestras of the English, French, and Austrian courts became peripheral to the musical life of London, Paris, and Vienna. In these capitals, as in cities like Venice, Hamburg, Brussels, and Leipzig where there was no court, theaters constituted the backbone of an orchestra musician's livelihood. Each theater had a standing orchestra, which played several nights a week during much of the year, for spoken theater as well as for opera and oratorio. Members of this theater orchestra could be engaged, as individuals or as an ensemble, to provide orchestras in other venues: in aristocratic homes, in pleasure gardens, at concerts, or for dances. Under this system the patronage for orchestras was considerably broader than under the court system.

The second half of the eighteenth century also saw the emergence of the public concert as a newly characteristic venue for orchestras. Public concerts by orchestras in the early eighteenth century were put on gratis by princes, often outdoors, to celebrate their regime while displaying their wealth and magnanimity to the aristocracy and the people. The first indoor public concert series with a standing orchestra and a regular schedule of performances was the Concert Spirituel in Paris, established in 1725 to provide entertainment to the public and employment to the singers and instrumentalists of the Opéra during Lent and other days when the theaters were closed. Concert series featuring standing orchestras soon emerged in other European cities, for example the Grosse Konzert in Leipzig, which began in 1743, and the Bach–Abel concerts in London, beginning in 1765. Concert series were financed almost entirely by ticket sales, usually by subscription.

Concert series and public theaters offered a way for people other than kings, princes, and the upper aristocracy to gain access to orchestras on a regular basis. Conversely, concerts and theaters provided a way for orchestras to exist outside the court milieu. The shift in patronage brought a shift in the meaning of the orchestra. As orchestras became identified with cities rather than with courts, they became emblems, not of the power and taste of a prince, but of civic prosperity and of the musical and cultural level of the educated public. Most social histories of the orchestra regard the expansion of the orchestra and the development of concert life as manifestations of the rise of the bourgeoisie and its seizure of cultural hegemony from the aristocracy in the eighteenth and early nineteenth centuries.

This oft-told tale of the social history of the orchestra as the transformation of a courtly luxury into a middle-class institution fails to account for the early success of orchestras in cities that were not ruled by a prince or a king and where, consequently, there were no courts. Already by the last third of the seventeenth century large, proto-orchestral ensembles were thriving in Rome, Hamburg, Lübeck, and Venice. In the absence of a single patron, instrumentalists were organized as a city-wide network of overlapping ensembles, on the payroll of the municipality, churches, theaters, and aristocratic households. In these cities, and later in others like Amsterdam, Leipzig, and Bologna, the orchestra was adopted enthusiastically by merchant oligarchs, professionals, and a general public of culturally sophisticated people.

At the same time, social histories of the orchestra tend to downplay the continuing importance of royal and courtly patronage in the nineteenth century. Several German courts maintained Kapellen for much of the nineteenth century. Aristocratic patronage remained central both to theaters and to concert series. During most of its history the orchestra has functioned, indeed it has thrived, in several different social situations and milieux simultaneously. In the eighteenth century the same violinist might play one year in a German court Kapelle, the next year in an Italian theater orchestra, the next in a London pleasure garden. And the same symphony could be performed with success in each of these milieux too. By the early nineteenth century theaters, courts, churches, festivals, concerts, spas, circuses, and dance halls all maintained orchestras or assembled them for special occasions. And the orchestras that played in these different settings resembled one another in most essential respects. Social historians need to consider the orchestra not simply as a manifestation of social forces and social classes but as a social institution in its own right.

An "institution" in this sense is a social structure that is legitimized by beliefs and sanctions.[72] Many (though not all) institutions are embodied in organizations, often in sets of organizations with similar purposes. These organizations resemble one another in structure, they are maintained by the same beliefs, and they exchange

---

[72] Schmuel N. Eisenstadt, "Social Institutions," in *International Encyclopedia of the Social Sciences*, ed. David L. Sills (New York, 1968), 409–29 at 409–10.

goods, services, and personnel with one another. The more "institutionalized" such organizations are, the more they resemble one another.[73]

The concept of institutionalization fits the orchestra and its history very well. Orchestras are groups of people working toward common purposes; they constitute parallel organizations with similar structures and are maintained by similar beliefs and expectations on the part of composers, performers, patrons, and audiences. The homogeneity of modern orchestras is striking: symphony orchestras tend to be the same size; they include the same instruments; they play the same repertory; they play in similar venues; they even dress like one another.

The "birth of the orchestra" can be defined as the emergence of the orchestra as an institution. To put the same thing another way: the birth of the orchestra was the process by which instrumental ensembles were institutionalized as orchestras. When Jacopo Peri composed his *Euridice* and presided over its performance in 1600, instrumental ensembles were temporary, ad hoc organizations that resembled each other only incidentally and rarely exchanged repertory or personnel. By the time Haydn composed (but did not perform) *L'anima del filosofo* in 1791, the orchestra was recognizable and recognized as an institution throughout Europe. Orchestras at the end of the eighteenth century constituted a set of parallel organizations within an internationally integrated field. European orchestras were by no means homogeneous, but the process of homogenization was well advanced. They were made up of similar numbers of similar instruments; they exchanged personnel across regional and national boundaries; they exchanged repertory even more extensively. By the end of the eighteenth century a consciousness had emerged of the orchestra as an institution. A set of beliefs had emerged about how orchestras should be organized, how they could be financed, how they ought to play, how orchestra musicians ought to act, and about the role of orchestras in culture and society.

PLAN OF THE BOOK

We aim to tell the story of the birth of the orchestra as an institution, from the first proto-orchestra ensembles in the sixteenth century until the beginning of the nineteenth century, when the orchestra becomes recognizable as the direct ancestor of modern orchestras. The first part of the book is organized chronologically and geographically. We begin with large instrumental ensembles of the sixteenth and early seventeenth centuries (Ch. 2); then we examine the two ensembles that provided organizational models and repertory for later orchestras: Lully's orchestra in France (Ch. 3) and Corelli's orchestra in Rome (Ch. 4). Chapters 5 through 8 proceed

---

[73] Paul J. DiMaggio and Walter W. Powell, "The Iron Cage Revisited: Institutional Isomorphism and Collective Rationality in Organizational Fields," *American Sociological Review*, 48 (1983), 147–60 at 148.

geographically, examining individual orchestras and the orchestra as an institution, as it developed in Italy, France, Germany, and England during the seventeenth and eighteenth centuries. Chapter 9 looks at the "classical orchestra" as it had emerged by the second half of the eighteenth century—a large number of similar organizations spread throughout the courts and cities of Europe. The second part of the book proceeds analytically and systematically, looking at the social arrangements, structures, and beliefs that made it possible for instrumental ensembles to become orchestras: at the placement and acoustics of orchestras in the spaces where they played (Ch. 10), at orchestral performance practices (Ch. 11), at the daily lives of orchestra musicians in various regions of Europe (Ch. 12), and at new ways of composing for instrumental ensembles as orchestras (Ch. 13). The final chapter (Ch. 14) attempts to say what the newly born orchestra meant to people in the seventeenth and eighteenth centuries.

Chapter Two

Pre-orchestral Ensembles

The five accounts of the birth of the orchestra summarized in Chapter 1 agree more or less on chronology: the orchestra began to emerge in the second half of the seventeenth century, and the process of its birth stretched over the next hundred years. This does not mean that there were no large instrumental ensembles before 1650. Reports from the sixteenth and early seventeenth centuries document many instances in which large numbers of instrumentalists were assembled in the same place at the same time and played together, or at least played in coordination with one another. These "pre-orchestral" ensembles were made up of different instruments than orchestras of later times; they were organized according to different principles, and they played different roles in the events in which they participated.

ENSEMBLES FOR INTERMEDII

The Florentine intermedii of the sixteenth century provide several examples of pre-orchestral ensembles. The intermedii of 1589, staged to celebrate the wedding of Ferdinando de' Medici and Christine of Lorraine, are particularly well documented. Before, after, and between the acts of *La Pellegrina*, a play by Girolamo Bargagli, six entr'actes (*intermedii*) were presented, featuring songs, instrumental music, spectacular sets, costumes, and theatrical effects. A report by Cristofano Malvezzi, who composed much of the music, names at least 30 instruments that played during the course of these intermedii, including seven lutes, two harps, five viols, a violin, a cornett, four trombones, reed and pipe organs, and more.[1]

[1] The figures are based on Malvezzi's instructions in his *Intermedii et concerti fatti per la commedia . . .*, as reported in D. P. Walker, *Musique des intermèdes de "La Pellegrina"* (Paris, 1963), pp. xxxvii–lviii. See also Howard Mayer Brown, *Sixteenth-Century Instrumentation: The Music for the Florentine Intermedii* (n.p., 1973), 107–32.

The instruments and instrumentalists at the 1589 intermedii were organized according to three principles:

1. *Shifting ensembles.* Except for the instrumental *sinfonia* at the beginning of the first intermedio and the final chorus at the end of the last, the full ensemble of 30 instruments never played together. Instead, it was broken down into a succession of sub-ensembles, which followed one another onto the stage. In the second intermedio, for example, the *sinfonia* was played by two harps, two lutes, two lire, a basso di viola, a violin, a viola bastarda, and a chitarrone—10 instruments in all.[2] The first song was accompanied by two lire and a harp, the second by bass lute, chitarrone, and basso di viola, the third by an unspecified combination of lutes and viols. The fourth and final song was accompanied by the same 10 instruments as the *sinfonia*. The next intermedio was accompanied by groups of two to 12 instruments—including lutes, viols, harp, trombone, cornett, and violin—assembling and reassembling for a succession of numbers. The intermedii were, thus, played not by a single ensemble but by a kaleidoscope of shifting ensembles, whose size, sound, and appearance changed according to the number of parts in each piece and the requirements of the drama.

2. *Equal distribution on parts.* In the majority of songs and instrumental *sinfonie* the number of instruments was a multiple of the number of parts in the polyphonic texture. When in the first intermedio eight singers representing the Sirens sang *Noi che cantando* by Malvezzi, they were accompanied by eight instruments—two lire, two harps, two bassi di viola, chitarrone, and bass lute—divided, like the singers, into two four-part choirs. In the third intermedio a song in 12 parts by Luca Marenzio was accompanied by an ensemble of 12 instruments: four lutes, a harp, two lire, two bassi di viola, a bass trombone, a cornett, and a violin. Presumably the instruments played one on a part along with or in alternation with the voices. The same principle applied to instrumental *sinfonie* without voices. For example, the sinfonia *à 6* by Malvezzi that opened the fifth intermedio was played by two lutes, basso di viola, chitarrone, violin, and reed organ—six instruments for six parts. In other cases the instruments were distributed two or even three on a part, as in the *sinfonia* in the fourth intermedio, where six parts were played by 12 instruments, or in the sixth intermedio, where 18 instruments accompanied a six-part madrigal, *O qual risplende nube.*

This arithmetic did not apply in every case. Plucked stringed instruments and keyboards sometimes seem to have taken several parts or perhaps played as a continuo, as in *Chi dal delfino* in the second intermedio, where six vocal parts were accompanied by only three instruments—a large lute, a chitarrone, and a basso di viola—or *O valoroso dio* from the third intermedio, where four vocal parts were accompanied by two

---

[2] Walker, *Musique des intermèdes*, pp. xli–xliii; Brown, *Sixteenth-Century Instrumentation*, 113–17. The lira da braccio, a bowed instrument with a violin-like body and five strings, was used to accompany sung poetry. The viola bastarda, called in English the lyra viol, was a relative of the viola da gamba.

instruments (harp and lira). For the most part, however, instruments were evenly distributed along with the voices from top to bottom of the polyphonic texture.[3]

3. *Symbolic instrumentation.* The choice of instruments for the various sub-ensembles of the Florentine intermedii was influenced by a tradition of programmatic stereotypes.[4] Instrumentalists appeared on the stage and in character; the instruments they played and the sounds of those instruments served a symbolic function. For example, in the fourth intermedio of *La Pellegrina* the spirits in the heavens who prophesy an Age of Gold are accompanied by what Weaver calls an "Olympian" ensemble of harp, lutes, lire, psaltery, flute, and violin, the same instruments that appear in contemporary paintings of heavenly choirs. When the scene is transformed to the gates of Hell, the heavenly spirits are replaced by a chorus of devils, and the accompaniment changes to an "infernal" ensemble of trombones and viole da gamba, low instruments that by convention denoted the underworld. The "Olympian" ensemble makes another appearance in the sixth and final intermedio, where gods and goddesses seated on clouds sing Malvezzi's *Dal vago e bel sereno* accompanied by chitarroni, lire, lutes, violin, and basso di viola.

Besides "Olympian" and "infernal" ensembles, Weaver identifies other stereotypical configurations of instruments in the Florentine intermedii. To accompany nymphs, shepherds, and other rustic characters, instruments like recorders, crumhorns, bagpipes, and rebecs formed "pastoral" ensembles. Warlike characters and battle scenes were accompanied by "martial" ensembles of trumpets and drums. Maritime subjects called for ensembles of flutes, lutes, and bowed strings.[5]

Another set of intermedii, staged in 1608 to celebrate the wedding of Cosimo de' Medici to Archduchess Maria Magdalena of Austria, extended the intermedio tradition into the seventeenth century.[6] Engraved illustrations depict large instrumental ensembles in three of the six intermedii.[7] All are "Olympian" ensembles, perched on clouds and composed of lutes, bass viols, violins in various sizes, flutes, cornetts, and organs. A roster of instrumentalists for the sixth intermedio, "The Temple of Peace

---

[3] Brown, *Sixteenth-Century Instrumentation*, 114, 119. For most songs and *sinfonie* Malvezzi's account states the number of parts and the names of the instruments that played, but it does not say which instruments played which parts. The distribution of instruments on parts is a matter of conjecture. Brown proposes distributions of instruments on parts in the 1589 intermedio ensembles quite different from those given here. He thinks that the keyboards and plucked strings functioned as "foundation" instruments: they played several parts or realized the bass line rather than taking one part in the texture (p. 78). We believe that, although lutenists and organists may have added harmonic filler to that part as they played, the principle was one of equal distribution on parts, not foundation vs. ornamenting instruments.

[4] Weaver, "Sixteenth-Century Instrumentation."

[5] Ibid. 369–70, 372–73. On the instrumentation of other Florentine intermedii in 1539, 1565, 1568, and 1586, see Brown, *Sixteenth-Century Instrumentation.*

[6] See Tim Carter, "A Florentine Wedding of 1608," *Acta musicologica*, 55 (1983), 89–107. The wedding in 1600 of Maria de' Medici to Henri IV of France had been celebrated with innovative melodramas: Peri's *Euridice* and Caccini's *Il rapimento di Cefalo*. The wedding of 1608 rejected these experiments and returned to the intermedio tradition.

[7] Arthur R. Blumenthal, *Theater Art of the Medici* (Hanover, NH, 1980), 41–57.

Fɪɢ. 2.1. *Tempio della pace* from the sixth intermedio for the *Judgment of Paris*, Florence, 1608

in the Heavens," lists a total of 42 instruments, over half of them plucked strings (lutes, chitarroni, citterns), plus seven cornetts and trombones, and a sprinkling of bowed strings, flutes, and keyboards.[8] The list pairs several of the instruments with singers, suggesting that the principle of equal distribution still obtains. However another kind of organization, new to the intermedii, is also evident. Singers and instrumentalists are divided into two choirs, each comprising voices and instruments in several registers, from soprano to bass. Figure 2.1 shows this sixth intermedio as portrayed in an engraving. Instrumentalists can be seen on the cloud in the center, on the left-hand side of the stage, and at the right of the stage.[9] A sketch by the author and stage designer, Michelangelo Buonarotti the Younger (son of the famous

[8] See Carter, "Florentine Wedding," 105–7.

[9] According to a printed key, the instrumentalists on the cloud in the center represent the 12 Blessings. See Blumenthal, *Theater Art*, 55–56.

painter), makes it clear that the singers and instruments on the left of the stage represent the first choir, while the singers and instruments on the right are the second choir.[10]

Besides the music for the intermedii, large instrumental ensembles appeared in other contexts during the festivities of 1608. An evening's entertainment at the Pitti Palace culminated in a ball accompanied by a band of 12 French violinists, which the Medici court had brought to Florence especially for the festivities. An equestrian ballet in the Piazza Santa Croce was also accompanied by a violin band, with the parts heavily doubled so that it would be loud enough to be heard in the noisy, outdoor surroundings.[11] Perhaps the French violinists were reinforced with local fiddlers.[12] Finally, at a banquet in the Palazzo Vecchio a large number of singers and instrumentalists were placed on risers in a balcony high above the hall to serenade the royal couple and the rest of the diners.

TABLE MUSIC

The instrumental ensemble at the Medici wedding banquet in 1608 continued a tradition of table music that was well established already in the sixteenth century. An account of a state banquet at Ferrara in 1529 and the music that accompanied it is transmitted in a cookbook written by Cristoforo da Messisbugo, a steward at the Este court. A 17-course seafood banquet given by Ippolito II d'Este, Archbishop of Milan, in honor of his brother, Ercole II, was accompanied by vocal and instrumental music organized according to principles similar to the ensembles for the Florentine intermedii. There were 16 instrumentalists in all, but they did not play together until the final number. Instead, a succession of sub-ensembles accompanied one course after another, the diversity of their timbres paralleling the diverse flavors and aromas of the dishes on the table. A first course of sea bream, boiled sturgeon in garlic sauce, and pike's entrails fried with oranges, cinnamon, and sugar was accompanied by an ensemble of three trombones and three cornetts. For a course of cream-filled French pastries, artichokes, olives, fermented apples (*pome guaste*), and oyster pies, the instruments were three flutes, three bagpipes (cornamuse), and one violone. For the seventeenth and last course—candied orange and lemon rinds, ices, nougat with mounds of cinnamon, pine nuts, pistachios, and melon

---

[10] Buonarotti's sketch is reproduced in Victor Coelho, "Public Works and Private Contexts: Lorenzo Allegri and the Florentine Intermedi of 1608," in *Luths et luthistes en Occident—Actes du colloque organisé par la Cité de la Musique, 13–15 mai 1998* (Paris, 1999), 121–32 at 131. We want to thank Victor Coehlo for sharing this sketch with us and for helping us decipher it.

[11] Camillo Rinuccini, *Descrizione delle feste fatte nelle reali nozze de' serenissimi principi di Toscana d. Cosimo de' Medici e Maria Maddalena Arciduchessa d'Austria* (Florence, 1608), 32, 62; Carter, "Florentine Wedding," 101. Rinuccini writes "violoni" rather than "violini," suggesting, perhaps, that he is thinking of the French word.

[12] Edmund A. Bowles, *Musical Ensembles in Festival Books, 1500–1800: An Iconographical and Documentary Survey* (Ann Arbor, 1989), 161.

seeds—the musicians gathered for a grand finale: six singers, accompanied by six viols, lira, three flutes, kit fiddle (sordina), trombone, lute, cittern, and two keyboard instruments, one large and one small. "This music was so well played," Messisbugo reports, "that everyone judged it to be even better than what had come before."[13]

A similar succession of ensembles accompanied a banquet at the wedding of Wilhelm V, Duke of Bavaria, and Renée of Lorraine in Munich in 1568.[14] There were only eight courses at the Munich banquet, but, with 20 or more dishes in each course, there was plenty of food, and some of the same dishes turn up on the Munich menu as in Ferrara. During the first course a seven-part motet by Orlando Lasso, the *Kapellmeister*, was sung, accompanied by cornetts and two trombones. For the second course a six-voice madrigal by Alessandro Striggio was performed by the choir with six trombones. Between the third and fourth courses six viole di braccio accompanied a six-voice motet by Cipriano da Rore, and so on until dessert—piles of sweets shaped like castles and mountains—for which 12 instrumentalists were organized into three choirs: one choir of four viole da gamba, one of four flutes, and a third comprising a dolzaina, a cornamusa, a shawm, and a cornett. The final course—fresh fruit—featured a grand finale in 24 parts, accompanied by eight viole da gamba, eight violins, and eight winds. A picture of the Munich banquet (Fig. 2.2) shows the musicians in the foreground. In the center of the ensemble an organist plays a portative organ. To the right of the organ stand 10 singers, three of them boys. To the left is an instrumental ensemble with four violins of various sizes, two basses, and a lute. On the chest in front of the organ lie three trombones—left over, perhaps, from the Striggio madrigal—and three flutes, waiting, perhaps, for the dessert course. These banquet ensembles at Ferrara and at Munich lacked the symbolic connotations of the intermedii, but they followed the same principles of shifting ensembles and equal distribution on the parts.

ENSEMBLES FOR COURT OPERAS AND MASQUES

Monteverdi's *Orfeo*, staged in Mantua in 1607, shared many features with the Florentine intermedii. The 30-plus instrumentalists who accompanied *Orfeo*, like the players in the intermedii, seldom played together as a single ensemble. Instead they

[13] Cristoforo da Messisbugo, *Banchetti, composizione di vivande e apparecchio generale* (1549), ed. Fernando Bandini (Venice, 1960), 37–38, 42. See also Howard Mayer Brown, "A Cook's Tour of Ferrara in 1529," *Rivista italiana di musicologia*, 10 (1975), 216–41; Susan F. Weiss, "Medieval and Renaissance Wedding Banquets and Other Feasts," in Martha Carlin and Joel Rosenthal (eds.), *Food and Eating in Medieval Europe* (London, 1999), 159–74. According to Weaver's typology the ensemble of trombones and cornetts that accompanied the first course would have been an "infernal" ensemble and the next ensemble a "pastoral" one. It is hard to see why pike's entrails should have been infernal or artichokes and oyster pies pastoral.

[14] Reported by Massimo Troiano, *Discorsi delli trionfi, giostre, apparati, et delle cose piu notabile . . .* (Munich, 1568), 86 ff., and id., *Dialoghi di Massimo Troiano* (Venice, 1569). Like Messisbugo, Troiano gives the full banquet menu.

FIG. 2.2. Wedding banquet for Wilhelm V of Bavaria and Renée of Lorraine, Munich, 1568 (detail)

were divided into smaller ensembles, usually with one instrument for each part in the score. For example, the 10 violins ("Dieci viole da brazzo") listed at the beginning of the score (see above, Fig. 1.1) were divided during most of the opera into two ensembles: five visible to the audience, the other five hidden backstage.[15] Since most of Monteverdi's string scorings are in five parts, this means that each violin ensemble played one on a part. The numbers of trumpets, cornetts, and trombones also match the number of parts for them in the score. A stage direction at the end of the fourth act tells violins, organs, harpsichords, contrabass, harp, chitarroni, and cittern to enter and play a ritornello while the scene changes. This probably refers to more offstage instrumentalists, who came onstage at this point and remained for the grand finale in the fifth act, with the strings now two on a part. In addition Monteverdi followed the intermedio principle of symbolic instrumentation. The shepherds in Act II are accompanied by a pastoral ensemble, first two little French violins, then two recorders. The underworld scenes in Acts III and IV are scored for cornetts, trombones, and bass viols. Thus, *Orfeo* embodied all three intermedio principles: shifting ensembles, equal distribution on parts, and symbolic instrumentation.

[15] Claudio Monteverdi, *L'Orfeo—Favola in musica*, ed. Wolfgang Osthoff (Kassel, 1998), 32; Kelly, " 'Orfeo da Camera,' " 7.

An important exception in the Orfeo ensemble to the principle of equal distribution on parts was the bass line, which in many scenes was realized by several continuo instruments at the same time. For the offstage ensemble in Act II the score specifies that the bass line should be played by four instruments: harpsichord, bass viol, and two chitarroni. For the ritornello at the end of the fourth act Monteverdi indicates that organs, harpsichords, contrabass viol, harp, chitarroni, and citterns should all play. If all these instruments realize the bass, then the texture, instead of being a balance of equal parts, becomes one to four upper parts supported by a diffuse continuo. *Orfeo* also differed from the intermedii in its use of obbligato instruments to accompany singing, like the pairs of violins, cornetts, and harps that represent Orpheus' lyre when he pleads with Charon for passage to the underworld.

Finally, Monteverdi broke away from the principle of shifting ensembles by using the same string ensemble throughout for *sinfonie*, ritornelli, and dance music. In the prologue "La Musica," an allegorical figure, greets the noble guests and tells them that they will see represented the extraordinary powers of music to alter emotions and influence human behavior, as exemplified by Orpheus and his lyre. La Musica sings three verses, preceded, punctuated, and followed by a ritornello, which is played by a five-part string band. The ritornello is heard again between the second and third acts and also between the fourth and fifth, as a kind of leitmotif, reminding the audience of the powers attributed to music by the ancient writers. The same ensemble of five-part strings also accompanies dances. Thus the string band forms a structural and textural counterpoint to the sung drama, which is accompanied by the continuo plus occasional obbligato instruments. In the underworld scenes five-part strings are replaced by a wind ensemble, but for the balance of the opera the string band serves as a core ensemble and instrumental point of reference.

Monteverdi's *Arianna* (1608), staged to celebrate the wedding of Francesco Gonzaga, Duke of Mantua, to Margherita of Savoy, seems to have been an even more magnificent production than *Orfeo*, performed before an audience of thousands in a theater specially built for the occasion. Unfortunately the score has not survived, and all that is known about the instrumental ensemble is that it was located offstage throughout, that before the prologue it performed "a sweet concerto of diverse instruments," that "a fine dance tune" ended the last act, and that Ariadne's famous "Lament" was accompanied by violin-family instruments ("viole et violini").[16] *Orfeo* and *Arianna* stand at the beginning of a tradition of "festival operas," staged, like the intermedii, by royal or ducal courts to celebrate dynastic marriages or other special occasions.[17] Because of the importance of

---

[16] Angelo Solerti, *Gli albori del melodramma* (Milan, 1904–5), i. 99; ii. 145, 185. This information comes from a letter by the Modenese ambassador. Perhaps "viole e violini" in his account should read "viole e violoni," i.e. violins and bass violins.

[17] On the distinction between "festival operas" and other sorts of 17th-c. operas, see Edward H. Tarr and Thomas Walker, " 'Bellici carmi, festivo fragor': Die Verwendung der Trompete in der italienischen Oper des 17. Jahrhunderts," *Hamburger Jahrbuch für Musikwissenschaft*, 3 (1978), 143–203 at 148, and Ellen Rosand, *Opera in 17th-Century Venice* (Berkeley, 1991), 10.

the events that they commemorated and the deep pockets of their patrons, festival operas were usually lavish productions with large, diverse instrumental ensembles.

For the visit of a Polish prince to Florence in 1625 the Medici court staged *La liberazione di Ruggiero*, a "balletto" with music by the singer and composer Francesca Caccini. The prologue and the first three scenes were enacted on a specially built stage in the courtyard of a Medici villa. The instrumental ensemble for this outdoor performance seems to have resembled the shifting, one-on-a-part, symbolic ensembles of the intermedi, with flutes for pastoral episodes, violins doubling the voices for a scene in an enchanted forest, and trombones for an underworld episode.[18] For the end of the entertainment the audience moved to the front of the palace to watch an equestrian ballet (*balletto a cavallo*) in which magnificently dressed riders put 24 caparisoned horses through intricate maneuvres to the accompaniment of a band of violins.[19]

Outside of Italy too, festival operas preserved features of Renaissance intermedii. Luigi Rossi's *Orfeo* (Paris, 1647) was sponsored by Cardinal Mazarin during Carnival as a showcase for Italian culture.[20] It retained the instrumental symbolism of the intermedio ensembles. A simulated assault on a walled city in the prologue was staged to the sounds of a "martial" ensemble of trumpets and drums. The underworld scenes featured the traditional "infernal" ensemble of trombones, cornetts, and reed instruments. Most of the rest of the opera, however, was accompanied either by a continuo group of harpsichords, theorbos, lutes, and guitars or by the King's Vingt-quatre Violons.[21] There must have been several string players on each of the four parts in Rossi's score, but there is no way to tell whether they were equally or unequally distributed. Like Monteverdi's operas, Rossi's *Orfeo* departed from the Renaissance principles of shifting, symbolic ensembles and moved toward a standardized ensemble in which plucked strings and keyboards accompanied singers, while bowed strings, now with several to a part, played instrumental interludes and dances.

Likewise, at German courts events of state were celebrated with festival operas, drawing on the intermedio tradition. The wedding of the daughter of the Duke of Hesse-Darmstadt was celebrated in 1673 with an operatic entertainment entitled *Representation of the Triumph of True Love*, which featured martial music played by the court trumpeters, pastoral music by shawms, flutes, and bagpipes, and a string band playing behind the scenes.[22] The libretto for *The Judgment of Paris*, staged in Stuttgart

---

[18] Francesca Caccini, *La liberazione di Ruggiero dall'isola d'Alcina* (Northampton, Mass., 1945), 54, 73–74. It is possible that the "viole" parts were played by viole da gamba rather than by violins.

[19] Angelo Solerti, *Musica, ballo e drammatica alla Corte Medicea dal 1600 al 1637* (Florence, 1905), 183.

[20] Neal Zaslaw, "The First Opera in Paris: A Study in the Politics of Art," in John Hajdu Heyer (ed.), *Jean-Baptiste Lully and the Music of the French Baroque: Essays in Honor of James Anthony* (Cambridge, 1989), 7–23.

[21] See Ch. 1, and esp. Table 1.1.

[22] Hermann Kaiser, *Barocktheater in Darmstadt* (Darmstadt, 1951), 56–62.

in 1686, mentions accompaniments by a trio of oboes, a trio of flutes, as well as a "Symphonia" of trumpets and violins.[23]

Probably the most ambitious festival opera of the seventeenth century was *Il pomo d'oro*, commissioned for the wedding in Vienna of Emperor Leopold I to Margherita Theresia of Spain in 1666 but not performed until July 1668. This grandly pretentious spectacle contained 66 scenes, required 23 separate sets, and lasted for eight hours. Most of the music was by the Venetian composer Pietro Antonio Cesti, but Heinrich Schmelzer, the violinist and Austrian court composer, wrote the instrumental "sonatas" at the beginning of each act, and Emperor Leopold himself composed two arias.[24] An engraving by Matthäus Küssel (Fig. 2.3) depicts the instrumentalists, but they are not displayed as part of the scenery as in Fig. 2.1. Rather they are placed in an enclosure in front of the stage. A harpsichord and a lutenist face one another in the center; to their left are two shadowy trombone players, to their right a man playing what seems to be a bass viol; other musicians are hidden behind the statues and columns on the left. Traces of the instrumental symbolism of the intermedio tradition persist in *Il pomo d'oro*. The underworld scenes—the court of Pluto and Proserpine in Act I and Charon at the river Styx in Act II—are accompanied by an "infernal" ensemble of two cornetts and three trombones, plus bassoon and regal. Cesti introduces an aria by a shepherd with a "pastoral" ritornello for two flutes. For the aria itself, however, he uses a trio of viole da gamba. A battle scene in Act IV featuring two elephants carrying soldiers to assault a city is accompanied by a martial ensemble of two trumpets. These, however, were the only remnants of the principles of intermedio instrumentation. The greater portion of *Il pomo d'oro* is accompanied either by keyboard and plucked string continuo or by a five-part ensemble of bowed strings.

Large instrumental ensembles were also assembled for the masques staged at the Stuart Court in England during the first four decades of the seventeenth century. Lord Hay commissioned a masque at Whitehall in 1607 to celebrate his marriage. Music and words were by Thomas Campion; the stage designer was Inigo Jones; the guest of honor was King James I. In all, Lord Hay's masque employed 42 singers and instrumentalists. As in the Florentine intermedii, the instrumentalists were organized into distinct ensembles, which played in turn. There was a "consort of ten"—five lutes, two violins, bass trombone ("double Sackbott"), bandora, and harpsichord; a "consort of twelve"—nine violin-family instruments of various sizes, plus three lutes; and finally, a consort of six cornetts. Each ensemble had its own raised platform—the consort of 10 on one side of the "dancing place," the consort of 12 on the other side, the cornetts between them. According to Campion's careful description, the consort of 10, dominated by plucked strings, provided the principal accompaniment for

---

[23] Samantha Kim Owens, "The Württemberg Hofkapelle, c.1680–1721" (Ph.D. diss., Victoria University of Wellington, 1995), 17.

[24] Carl B. Schmidt, "Pomo d'oro, Il," in *GroveO*, 1051–54; id., "Antonio Cesti's *Il pomo d'oro*: A Reexamination of a Famous Hapsburg Court Spectacle," *JAMS* 29 (1976), 381–412 at 391, 407–8.

Fig. 2.3. *Il Pomo d'Oro*, Vienna 1668 (detail)

songs, while the consort of 12, a violin-based ensemble, played for the dances. The cornett ensemble played processional music between numbers, and at one point it doubled the six singers in a "sollemne motet of six parts." The cornettists also played "Hoboyes" (shawms) for the King's entry at the beginning of the masque. In the grand choruses, Campion explained, the three ensembles did not play together but worked in close alternation: "This Chorus was in the manner of an Eccho, seconded by the Cornets, then by the consort of ten, then by the consort of twelve."[25] The instrumental ensemble for Lord Hay's masque thus followed the first two principles of the intermedio: shifting ensembles and equal distribution on parts. The three consorts seem not to have had any symbolic implications, however. Instead, they were distinguished by function according to the same tradition that obtained in festival operas: plucked strings accompanied singing; bowed strings accompanied dancing; winds played processional music. The close alternation of ensembles and the echo effects seem to have been novelties.

[25] Thomas Campion, *Lord Hay's Masque* (Menston, 1973), facs. of 1607 edn., unpaginated; Stephen Orgel and Roy C. Strong, *The Theatre of the Stuart Court* (Berkeley, 1973), 115–21.

The largest and most spectacular of all the Stuart masques was *The Triumph of Peace*, staged for Charles I at Whitehall in 1634. The libretto, several printed descriptions, and the manuscript notes of Sir Bulstrode Whitlocke, the organizer of the event, combine to paint a vivid picture of the instrumental forces assembled for this spectacle.[26] Whitlocke recruited approximately 70 instrumentalists, reflecting a cross-section of London's musical life. There were nine lutenists and viol players from the King's Lutes and Voices, 14 string players from the King's Violins, 12 flute, cornett, shawm, and trombone players from the King's Winds, 12 string and wind players from the Blackfriars and the Cockpit theaters, two waits from the City band, 11 trumpeters from various noble households, and 14 freelance musicians, including several lutenists and a "harper." This aggregation of instrumentalists was organized into a series of shifting and overlapping ensembles. In the parade of the masquers from Chancery Lane to Whitehall six different ensembles walked beside six parade floats. Setting off the elegant portions of the masque, a burlesque ensemble of fire tongs and keys accompanied a "Beggar's antimasque," and an ensemble of whistles "in excellent consort" accompanied an "Antimasque of birds." For the songs and dances of the masque proper two sub-ensembles were selected. Songs were accompanied by "The Symphony," an ensemble of 12 lutes and viols. Dances were accompanied by the King's Violins, playing 14 violin-family instruments of various sizes in a five-part consort. The singers, Symphony, Violins, and King's Winds combined for a grand finale.[27]

Masques and other danced entertainments were also given at the Spanish court in the early seventeenth century, accompanied by instrumental ensembles similar to those of English masques. *El premio de la hermosura* by Lope de Vega, staged outdoors at the estate of the Duke of Lerma in 1614, made use of a wind band and a violin band, installed along with singers in a gallery to one side of the stage. In addition, plucked-string players accompanied singers onstage. The instruments for a court theatrical in 1622 included violins, viols, lutes, guitars, theorbos, shawms, cornetts, trombones, flutes, trumpets, and drums, divided into four choirs placed in galleries on either side of the stage.[28] As in English masques, the wind instruments played for entrances and processions, while the violins mainly accompanied dances, and the plucked strings accompanied singers.

In 1653 *Las fortunas de Andrómeda y Perseo*, more of a festival opera than a masque, with a libretto by Calderón and music by Juan Hidalgo, was performed at the Buen Retiro palace to celebrate the recovery of Queen Mariana from an illness. A plucked-string continuo accompanied recitative and songs, but other instruments formed

[26] See Murray Lefkowitz, "The Longleat Papers of Bulstrode Whitelocke: New Light on Shirley's *Triumph of Peace*," *JAMS* 18 (1965), 42–58; id., *Trois Masques à la cour de Charles Ier d'Angleterre* (Paris, 1970); Orgel and Strong, *Theatre*, 537–66; Andrew J. Sabol, "New Documents on Shirley's Masque 'The Triumph of Peace,'" *M & L* 47 (1966), 10–28.

[27] Lefkowitz, "The Longleat Papers," 46–49, 55; id., *Trois Masques*, 33–35, 48; Sabol, "New Documents," 17.

[28] Louise Stein, *Songs of Mortals, Dialogues of the Gods* (Oxford, 1993), 76, 90–91.

symbolic ensembles, like the muted trumpets and drums that accompanied Andromeda's lament and the pastoral ensemble of reed pipes (zampoñas) in the last act. Curiously, a battle scene in the first act was accompanied not by trumpets and drums but by violins. An engraving of the final scene resembles the "open heavens" tableaux of the Florentine intermedii, with an "Olympian" ensemble of lutes, violins, harps, and bass viols perched on clouds above the the stage.[29]

All these entertainments, at the Hapsburg, Stuart, Medici, and other courts, brought large numbers of instrumentalists together in performance. However, rather than constituting standing ensembles with fixed instrumentation, they were organized as combinations of overlapping, shifting groups, assembled and arranged for one festive event, then dispersed afterward. In the later festival operas, however, like Rossi's *Orfeo* (1647) and Cesti's *Pomo d'oro* (1666), ensembles became standardized by function: plucked strings and keyboards to accompany singers, bowed strings for ritornelli and dances.

ENSEMBLES IN THE THEATER

Music was an important attraction at the semi-permanent public theaters that established themselves in several large European cities during the seventeenth century. Instrumental ensembles played during performances of spoken dramas; they also accompanied the increasingly popular sung dramas, especially Italian operas. The instrumental ensemble was usually placed to the side of the stage or in front of it and did not participate in the action. Rather than being assembled ad hoc for a special event, a theater ensemble was often engaged for the duration of a season. And rather than appearing in a succession of shifting ensembles, the same players accompanied from beginning to end.

Ensembles in the theater were seldom as large as those for courtly entertainments like intermedio or masque. In Venice, the birthplace and principal center of public opera in the seventeenth century, the ensembles for opera were quite small. A French visitor commented in 1680: "The Symphony is mean[,] inspiring rather Melancholy than Gaiety: It is composed of Lutes, Theorbos and Harpsichords, yet they keep time to the voices with the greatest exactness imaginable."[30] Extant pictures of Venetian theaters in the seventeenth century do not depict orchestral ensembles at all. An engraving of San Giovanni Grisostomo theater at the beginning of the eighteenth century shows a small ensemble in front of the stage (Fig. 2.4). There are 12 instrumentalists: seven playing

---

[29] Ibid. 144–67, 342. The Spanish court in Naples staged similar masques and danced entertainments. A "festa a ballo" in 1620 featured 40 instruments, arranged into violin bands, rustic ensembles, martial ensembles, and an ensemble of winds that accompanied a ballet of "savages and monkeys." See *A Neapolitan Festa a Ballo and Selected Instrumental Ensemble Pieces*, ed. Roland Jackson (Madison, 1978).

[30] Saint Didier, *The City and Republic of Venice, in three parts, Originally written in French by Monsieur de S. Desdier* (London, 1699), 62.

Fig. 2.4. Teatro San Giovanni Grisostomo in 1709

violins or violas, three playing what might be basses, one lute, and what could be a harpsichord. An ensemble of this size would have played four- or five-part music with one to three players on a part.

The only written records that document the size and composition of instrumental ensembles in the seventeenth-century Venetian theaters seem to be the account books for two Cavalli operas—*Antioco*, at the San Cassiano theater in 1659 and a revival of *Ciro* at the Teatro di SS. Giovanni e Paolo in 1665.[31] For the 1659 production three players are identified as violinists, one as a violist, and two as theorbo players; two

[31] Denis Arnold, "'L'Incoronazione di Poppea' and its Orchestral Requirements," *Musical Times*, 104 (1963), 176–78 at 176–77. The character of this source, the Faustini account books, is discussed in Lorenzo Bianconi and Thomas Walker, "Production, Consumption, and Political Function of Seventeenth-Century Italian Opera," *Early Music History*, 4 (1984), 209–96 at 221 ff.

additional players are not identified by instrument. Assuming that the ensemble included a bowed bass instrument and a harpsichord, and that the composer played an additional harpsichord, this makes an ensemble of nine, distributed as shown in Table 2.1.[32] The score to *Antioco* has not survived, but most of the operas Cavalli wrote for San Cassiano have strings in five parts, which would imply that the strings played one on a part in *Antioco*. For *Ciro* in 1665 the ensemble consisted of three keyboards, two violins, violetta, viola da brazzo, violone, and two theorbos (Table 2.1). The *sinfonie* and ritornelli in *Ciro* are scored in five parts, so here again the strings must have played one on a part. Of the instrumentalists hired for *Ciro* four were members of the *capella* at St Mark's.[33] The third keyboardist was a woman, "Sig[ra] Prudenza," unusual in the theater at that time and for more than two centuries thereafter.

The small size of the ensemble for seventeenth-century Venetian opera was dictated to some extent by economic constraints. Singers were already demanding and receiving such high fees that not much remained to hire instrumentalists. The size of the ensemble may also have been influenced by aesthetic considerations.[34] Unlike the intermedii, masques, and festival operas, which were court rituals, public opera was theater first and foremost. The function of the instruments was to accompany the singers and to provide framing *sinfonie* and ritornelli. The ensemble did not represent anything; it did not convey meanings to the audience; and it did not need to be any larger than what was necessary to get the singers through the show with the "greatest exactness imaginable."

Instrumental ensembles for opera in other cities were no larger than those in Venice. Because of papal restrictions on theater of any sort, Roman opera productions during much of the seventeenth century took place not in public but in private theaters built in the palaces of wealthy families like the Orsini, the Barberini, and the Pamphili. However, their instrumental resources resembled those of Venetian public opera, rather than of festival opera. In 1636 at the Barberini palace a performance of *I santi Didimo e Teodora* employed 15 instrumentalists: two keyboards, four plucked strings, seven bowed strings, plus cornett and flute (Table 2.1).[35] For *San Bonifatio* in 1638, also sponsored by the Barberini family, there were only seven players: two violins, two violoni, organ, harpsichord, and theorbo. Since the score has two violin parts, the violins must have played one on a part.[36] For *Chi soffre speri* in 1639 there were 10 players, with a relatively large continuo group but violins again one on a part (Table 2.1).[37]

[32] See Jane Glover, *Cavalli* (New York, 1978), 107.

[33] Eleanor Selfridge-Field, *Venetian Instrumental Music* (Oxford, 1975), 39.

[34] See Robert Weaver, "The Orchestra in Early Italian Opera," *JAMS* 17 (1967), 83–89.

[35] These and following figures are taken from Frederick Hammond, "Girolamo Frescobaldi and a Decade of Music in Casa Barberini: 1634–1643," *Analecta musicologica*, 19 (1979), 94–124. See also Frederick Hammond, *Music and Spectacle in Baroque Rome* (New Haven, 1994), 199–243.

[36] For scorings, see Margaret Murata, *Operas for the Papal Court, 1631–1668* (Ann Arbor, 1981), 258, 289.

[37] Instrumental ensembles for Roman oratorios were often much larger than ensembles for opera during this period. See Ch. 5.

TABLE 2.1. *Instrumental ensembles in seventeenth-century Italian opera*

Place, date, title	Keyboard and plucked strings	Bowed strings	Winds	Source
Rome, 1636 *SS. Didimo e Teodora*	1 organ 1 harpsichord 2 lutes 1 theorbo 1 guitar	3 violins 3 violoni 1 lira	1 cornett 1 flute	Hammond, "Girolamo Frescobaldi," 112
Rome, 1638 *S. Bonifatio*	1 organ 1 [harpsichord] 1 theorbo	2 violins 2 violoni		Ibid. 117; Hammond, *Music and Spectacle*, 234
Rome, 1639 *Chi soffre speri*	2 harpsichords 2 lutes 1 harp 1 cittern	2 violins 2 violoni		Hammond, "Girolamo Frescobaldi," 120
Venice, 1659 *Antioco*	[2 harpsichords] 2 theorbos	3 volins 1 viola [1 violone]		Arnold, "L'Incoronazione," 177

Venice, 1665 *Ciro*	3 harpsichords 2 theorbos	2 violins 1 viola 1 viola da brazzo 1 violone		ibid.
Florence, 1679 *Con la forza d'amor*	1 harpsichord 1 lute	2 violins 2 violas 2 bass viols		Holmes, *Opera*, 27
Reggio Emilia, 1683 *Il talamo*	2 harpsichords 1 theorbo	5 violins 3 violas 1 cello 1 double bass	2 trumpets	Cavicchi, "Musica," 111
Rome, 1684 *La vita è un sogno*	1 harpsichord	2 violins 1 viola 1 cello		Marx, "'Giustificazioni,'" 147

Elsewhere in Italy ensembles for opera followed a similar pattern. A performance of *Con la forza d'amor si vince amore* at Florence in 1679 was accompanied by a harpsichord, a lute, and six bowed strings. Late in the century opera ensembles seem to have become slightly larger. Seven performances of *Il talamo* by P. A. Ziani in 1683 at the Teatro Reggio in Reggio Emilia employed 15 instrumentalists: 10 bowed strings, theorbo, two harpsichords, and two trumpets borrowed from the nearby Duke of Modena (Table 2.1).[38]

Instrumental ensembles played important roles in the theater outside of Italy during the seventeenth century—in spoken theater as well as in opera. As in the Italian opera, ensembles in French, English, and German theaters tended to be smaller than ensembles for courtly entertainments like festival operas and masques. Instrumentalists appeared onstage as characters in the drama, often cast as fiddlers or pipers, accompanying singers or playing for dancers.[39] However, many theaters also maintained a standing ensemble placed in front of the stage or in a gallery above the stage, which performed before, after, and between the acts as well as accompanying singing and dancing.

In Paris there were instrumental ensembles already in the late sixteenth century in the theater at the Hôtel de Bourgogne, and in the seventeenth century at the Théâtre du Marais and the Palais-Royal. For a series of plays at the Hôtel de Bourgogne in the early 1640s "there were 10 or 12 string players [*violons*] in the rear boxes who played before, after, and between the acts."[40] Apparently this was not a standing ensemble. Rather the violins were provided by the playwright himself for the duration of the show. By the 1660s, however, all of the main Parisian theaters had standing instrumental ensembles.[41] Samuel Chappuzeau reported in 1674 on the role of the instrumental ensemble in Parisian theaters:

There are usually six violins, selected from the best players. In former times they were placed either backstage, in the wings, or in a pit [*retranchement*] between the stage and the parterre. Lately, however, they have been placed in one of the rear loges, from whence they sound louder than from any other location. It is best for them to memorize the last couple of lines in each act, so that they can begin the symphony immediately, without waiting for people to shout "Jouez," something that happens all too often.[42]

Chappuzeau's "six violins" presumably included violin-family instruments in several sizes, but he does not mention lutes and other plucked strings that were so important in the opera theaters of Italy.

---

[38] Bianconi and Walker, "Production, Consumption, and Political Function," 232.

[39] See Harold Love, "The Fiddlers on the Restoration Stage," *EM* 6 (1978), 391–99; Curtis Price, "Restoration Stage Fiddlers and their Music," *EM* 7 (1979), 315–22; David Lasocki, "The Recorder in the Elizabethan, Jacobean and Caroline Theater," *American Recorder*, 25 (1984), 3–10.

[40] Gédéon Tallemant des Réaux, *Les Historiettes de Tallemant des Réaux* (Paris, 1938), vi. 162.

[41] John S. Powell, *Music and Theatre in France, 1600–1680* (Oxford, 2000), 35.

[42] Samuel Chappuzeau, *Le Théâtre françois* (1674), ed. Georges Monval (Paris, 1875), 146–47.

In the theaters of Elizabethan England instrumentalists usually appeared in character and onstage, like the musicians who play the strain with the "dying fall" at the beginning of *Twelfth Night* or the "Hoboyes Playing lowd Musick" for the banquet in Act I of *Timon of Athens*.[43] The practice of employing a regular group of instrumentalists who had their own place in the theater and entertained the audience between the acts seems to have been an innovation of the choirboy companies around 1600.[44] Soon the adult companies too added instrumental ensembles: a roster for the King's Men at Blackfriars in 1624 lists six musicians, of whom one may have played violin, another the lute, another the bass.[45] *The Siege of Rhodes* (1656), an opera in English with music by several composers, was accompanied again by an ensemble of six instruments: three violins or violas, bass viol, theorbo, and harpsichord.[46] After the Restoration the Twenty-four Violins of the King's Musick were made available to the public theaters, and instrumental ensembles grew larger. It seems, however, that the 24 were divided between the King's and Duke of York's companies, so that the actual ensembles in the theaters numbered only 12 instruments.[47]

Documentation of instrumental ensembles in public theaters in Germany is scanty. The Hamburg theater in the Gänsemarkt, built in 1678, presented public opera on the Venetian model, accompanied by a standing ensemble. The instruments were probably located in front of the stage, although directions in scores occasionally mention onstage ensembles.[48] An undated sketch of the ensemble shows first and second violins, keyboard, cello, bass, and trumpets, but it provides no information about how many of each of these instruments there may have been in the theater.[49]

Instrumental ensembles in the seventeenth-century theater, for Italian opera, for German opera, for spoken and sung theater in France and England, tended to be relatively small—from six to 15 players at most. The ensembles for Italian opera contained nearly as many continuo instruments—keyboards and plucked strings—as bowed strings. Theater ensembles in France and England tended to use more violin-family instruments, probably because they did not have the responsibility of accompanying voices. Of European public theaters in the seventeenth century, only the Opéra in Paris, from the 1670s on, employed a large, standing instrumental ensemble.

[43] *Twelfth Night* I. i. 4–6; *Timon of Athens* I. ii.

[44] Peter Holman, "Music for the State I: Before the Civil War," in *Music in Britain—The Seventeenth Century*, ed. Ian Spink (Oxford, 1992), 282–305 at 294.

[45] David Lasocki, "Professional Recorder Playing in England, 1500–1740," *EM* 10 (1982), 23–29 at 27.

[46] Peter Holman, "Thomas Baltzar (?1631–1663), the 'Incomparable *Lubicer* of the Violin,'" *Chelys*, 13 (1984), 3–38 at 5.

[47] Peter Holman, introduction to Matthew Locke, *The Rare Theatrical*, ed. Holman (London, 1989), p. xvii.

[48] Andrew McCredie, "Instrumentarium and Instrumentation in the North German Baroque Opera" (Ph.D. diss., Universität Hamburg, 1964), 37, 39, 42 ff.

[49] Reproduced in Wilhelm Kleefeld, "Das Orchester der Hamburger Oper 1678–1738," *Sammelbände der IMG*, 1 (1899–1900), 219–89 at 234. Kleefeld says this sketch was copied by Friedrich Zelle "in a foreign library."

POLYCHORAL ENSEMBLES FOR SACRED MUSIC

For the music on Christmas Day, 1602, at St. Mark's in Venice the regular choir of 22 singers was adequate for the occasion, but the church's instrumental ensemble, consisting of seven performers on cornett and trombone, was not. Thirteen additional instrumentalists were engaged at the rate of 2 scudi apiece. They were:

Zuane di Prioli, player of the little organ on the platform;
S[ignore] Ventura, player of the Violone;
S. Nicolo da Mosto, bassoonist;
S. Alvise Grani, trombonist;
S. Gasparo Sanson, trombonist;
Nicolo Moreto, trombonist;
S. Vivain, cornettist;
S. Battista Caliger, trumpeter;
S. Francesco Bonforte, the violinist;
S. Vicenzo, cornettist;
S. Silvio, trombonist;
S. Zuane de Salo, trombonist;
S. Francesco da Treviso, violinist.[50]

Just what music this large, diverse ensemble may have played in 1602 is not known. It might well have included motets by Andrea or Giovanni Gabrieli or by Giovanni Bassano, who played cornett at this very event. A Christmas motet by Giovanni Gabrieli, "Quem vidistis pastores" from the *Symphoniae sacrae* of 1615, is written in 14 parts—some with texts, some without—plus a "basso per l'organo."[51] Several of the textless parts are labeled with the names of the instruments that played them. In addition to accompaning singers in concerted pieces, the ensemble at St. Mark's probably performed music for instruments alone of the type represented by Gabrieli's *Canzoni e sonate* of 1615.

Gabrieli accommodated the large numbers of instrumentalists at festive occasions at St. Mark's by writing a large number of parts. The motets in the *Symphoniae sacrae* of 1615 have 15 to 20 parts, some for voices, some for instruments, some perhaps intended for voice and instrument together on the same part. The instrumental

---

[50] Denis Arnold, "Con ogni sorti d'istromenti: Some Practical Suggestions," *Brass Quarterly*, 2 (1958), 99–109 at 104. Eleanor Selfridge-Field, in her discussion of the same performance, counts one more cornettist (Eleanor Selfridge-Field, "Bassano and the Orchestra of St. Mark's," *EM* 4 (1976), 153–58 at 155). On the size of the St. Mark's choir in 1602, see James Harold Moore, *Vespers at St. Mark's: Music of Alessandro Grandi, Giovanni Rovetta and Francesco Cavalli* (Ann Arbor, 1981), 76–77, 247.

[51] Giovanni Gabrieli, *Mottetta (Symphoniae sacrae, 1615)*, ed. Denis Arnold (Opera Omnia, 5; Rome, 1969), 1 ff.

Canzoni e sonate have anywhere from five to 22 parts. Comparing the size of regular and festival ensembles at St. Mark's with the scorings of pieces by Gabrieli and other Venetian composers, it seems likely that the instrumentalists at St. Mark's usually played one on a part.[52] Only the bass lines are likely to have been doubled—by organ plus violone, bassoon, or trombone.

Large numbers of instruments playing large numbers of parts were organized by means of the practice of *cori spezzati* (dispersed choirs). Instrumentalists, along with singers, were divided into separate "choirs," each one a quasi-independent musical unit with four to seven parts. Some choirs were made up of singers only, some of instruments only, some were mixed, either with separate parts for singers and instruments or with instruments doubling vocal lines. Thus, in Gabrieli's *Quem vidistis* the 14 parts are divided into two choirs, with three voices and four instruments in each choir. The score has a single bass part for the organ, but at St. Mark's each choir usually had its own organ, and extra parts were copied for the organists.[53] Given that St. Mark's had two organists on the payroll in 1602, the addition of Zuane di Prioli on a third organ implies that the Christmas music of 1602 was probably scored for three choirs. The first two choirs were most likely placed in the organ lofts on either side of the chancel. The choir for which Zuane played organ was located on a temporarily erected platform, probably on the floor of the chancel.[54]

Multiple choirs and spatial separation led to problems in coordination. The solution seems to have been to put the *maestro di cappella* with one of the choirs in a central location and to designate one person in each of the other choirs to serve as timebeater, relaying the beat to his fellows. The author of a memorandum in 1607 noted: "it is necessary that there be some accomplished person to stand next to the organ and display the beat as it is laid down by the maestro at the keyboard. . . . Giovanni Bassano, the leader of the instrumentalists, is stationed at the organ played by Gabrieli to do this service; on the other side it is Brother Agostin . . . a singer in the choir . . ."[55]

Other Italian churches during the seventeenth century used the same system of multiple choirs to organize large numbers of singers and instrumentalists. Records preserved for the yearly Feast of the Assumption at the church of Santa Maria Maggiore in Bergamo show the evolution of the system over time. Judging from the number of organs, the music for the event was always polychoral. S. Maria Maggiore,

[52] Arnold is of the opposite opinion, suggesting that "there must have been a considerable amount of doubling," but he does not provide any evidence for this view. See Arnold, "Con ogni sorti d'istromenti," 104; also Moore, *Vespers at St. Mark's*, 99.

[53] For a list of organists at San Marco, see Selfridge-Field, *Venetian Instrumental Music*, 294 ff.

[54] Denis Arnold, *Giovanni Gabrieli* (London, 1974), 166. See also David Bryant, "La musica nelle istituzioni religiose e profane di Venezia," in *Storia della cultura veneta*, ed. Girolamo Arnaldi and Manlio Pastore Stocchi, iv/1 (Vicenza, 1983), 433–47 at 438.

[55] Quoted in David Bryant, "Liturgy, Ceremonial and Sacred Music in Venice at the Time of the Counter-Reformation" (Ph.D. diss., University of London, King's College, 1981), 114.

like St Mark's, had two organs, one in each choir loft, but in most years, a third and sometimes a fourth organ were rented and additional organists engaged. Extra musicians, both singers and instrumentalists, were engaged from Milan, Brescia, and as far away as Padua.[56] Although polychoral organization persisted at S. Maria Maggiore throughout the seventeenth century, between 1600 and 1650 the makeup of the instrumental ensemble changed markedly from an ensemble dominated by brass instruments to a violin-based ensemble. In 1602 the only string players on the regular payroll were two violinists—as against seven brass players, some of whom could double on strings as needed. For the Feast of the Assumption that year a tenor viola and a violone were added, but also another cornett and two trombones.[57] By 1637 there were no trombonists or cornettists on the regular payroll. Now the ensemble was dominated by bowed and plucked strings; brass players were hired only for the Feast of the Assumption.[58] Given the continued use of multiple organs, however, violins, violas, and basses probably did not function as a unified ensemble but as members of separate choirs.

The polychoral principle spread from Italy northward, particularly to German-speaking lands. At the Munich wedding in 1568, several of the pieces for the banquet were organized polychorally, for example, Lasso's grand finale in which 24 instruments were evenly distributed among three choirs. Yet more ambitious polychoral music was performed at the same festivities: a 24-part, three-choir mass by Annibale Padovano, and a 40-part, four-choir motet by Alessandro Striggio.[59] There were not enough instruments in the Munich Kapelle to staff a 40-voice piece; some of the parts were sung but not played.

A *multiplicatio ad absurdum* of the principle of organizing large ensembles by adding individual parts and increasing the number of choirs was the so-called *Missa Salisburgensis*, written in 1682, most likely by Heinrich Biber for the millenium of the founding of the Archbishopric of Salzburg.[60] Fifty-three separate parts—16 for voices, 37 for instruments—were organized into eight choirs, some with voices only, some with only instruments, some mixed. Two of the choirs were composed exclusively of trumpets and timpani. The score shows the following distribution:

---

[56] Maurizio Padoan, *La musica in S. Maria Maggiore a Bergamo nel periodo di Giovanni Cavaccio (1598–1626)* (Como, 1983); id., "La musica liturgica tra funzionalità statutoria e prassi," in A. Colzani, A. Luppi, and Maurizio Padoan (eds.), *La musica sacra in Lombardia nella prima metà del Seicento* (Como, 1987), 369–94.

[57] Padoan, *La musica in S. Maria Maggiore a Bergamo*, 76, 109.   [58] Padoan, "La musica liturgica," 390.

[59] Troiano, *Dialoghi di Massimo Troiano*, 147; id., *Discorsi delli trionfi*, 182; Anthony F. Carver, *Cori Spezzati* (Cambridge, 1988), 70 ff.

[60] The *Missa Salisburgensis* was long attributed to Orazio Benevoli and dated 1628, but both the date and the attribution have been shown to be impossible. See Ernst Hintermaier, "The Missa Salisburgensis," *Musical Times*, 116 (1975), 965–66; id., "'Missa Salisburgensis': Neue Erkenntnisse über Entstehung, Autor und Zweckbestimmung," *Musicologica Austriaca*, 1 (1977), 154–96; Eric Thomas Chafe, *The Church Music of Heinrich Biber* (Ann Arbor, 1987), 63.

Choir 1: 8 voices, Organ
Choir 2: 2 violins, 4 viole
Choir 3: 2 oboes, 4 flutes, 2 clarini [high trumpets]
Choir 4: 2 cornetts, 3 trombones
Choir 5: 8 voices
Choir 6: 2 violins, 4 viole
Choir 7 (gallery 1): 4 trumpets, timpani
Choir 8 (gallery 2): 4 trumpets, timpani

Plate I, an engraving by Melchior Küssel of the Salzburg Cathedral in 1682 with the festivities in progress, corresponds to the general features of Biber's score, although it probably does not represent a performance of the *Missa Salisburgensis*.[61] Only six choirs are visible. Two trumpet choirs can be seen in galleries, foreground right and left, but the timpani are hidden. Two more choirs in galleries are seen further back, directly across the transept from the trumpets. The right-hand choir seems to be composed of singers plus three bowed-string players and an organ; the choir in the left gallery includes two trombones and a cornett, as well as singers.[62] The final two choirs are on the floor, just behind the altar rail. On the left are eight singers, six seated and two standing. On the right are an organist (with a boy who pumps the bellows), two violoni, a cornett, a trombone, and at least eight singers. In the left-hand gallery at the corner of the transept the rearmost figure beats time with a rolled-up scroll of paper; the rearmost figure in the right-hand gallery seems to be doing the same. At the Salzburg cathedral, like St. Mark's, polychoral music seems to have been coordinated by relaying the beat from the maestro, who probably stood with one of the choirs on the floor, to the choirs in the galleries.

While polychoral practices continued to thrive in southern Germany during the first half of the seventeenth century, the organization of instrumental ensembles in northern Italian churches was moving in a different direction—toward the consolidation of ensembles into more manageable units. Rather than multiplying parts, *maestri di cappella* began to multiply instruments on fewer parts. Lodovico Viadana, in the introduction to his *Salmi a 4 chori* (Venice, 1612), explains how this several-on-a-part practice could be reconciled with polychoral organization and also with the use of instruments. Viadana calls the first of his four choirs the *coro favorito*. It consists of five vocal soloists plus organ and, if desired, a chitarrone doubling the bass line. The second choir, the *cappella*, must contain at least 16 singers—that is, four singers to a part—and it will be even better if it has 20 to 30 voices and instruments. The third and fourth choirs can also have several voices on each part, as well as violins, cornetts, trombones, double basses, and bassoons. If all Viadana's instructions were followed to

[61] Chafe, *Church Music*, 40–47.
[62] Singers are recognizable because they hold music. This iconographical convention persisted throughout the 17th and 18th cc.

the letter, it would take something like 50 voices and 30 instruments to perform the *Salmi a 4 chori*. However, he goes on, "these psalms can also be sung by two choirs alone, namely the first and second choirs." He calls the moments where everyone sings and plays together "ripieno" (full), as opposed to passages where the *coro favorito* sings alone. Because only two choirs are essential, a single timebeater can lead the entire ensemble:

The Maestro di Cappella should stand with the first choir à 5, watching the organist's basso continuo so that he can see how the music is going and indicate when one person sings alone, when 2, when 3, when 4, and when 5. And when the *ripieni* come in, he should turn to face all the choirs, and raise both his hands as a sign for everyone to sing together.[63]

Thus Viadana transforms polychoral techniques into a solo vs. ripieno practice. The essence of the music is presented by a choir of soloists plus a thorough bass, while the second, third, and fourth choirs, including all the instruments, have become a ripieno that adds occasional volume and color.

Other Italian church-music composers of the early seventeenth century worked out different solutions to the problem of adding voices and instruments without multiplying parts and choirs. In his *Salmi concertati* of 1609 Girolamo Giacobbi, *maestro di cappella* at San Petronio in Bologna, calls for a solo choir (*coro ordinario*) of five voices, plus a second choir of one voice and three instruments—either trombones or bowed strings (*viole*) will do. In big churches, he continues, "where there are large numbers of singers and instrumentalists," the maestro can add more choirs, according to the acoustics (*qualità*) of the room and the number of performers. He will have to copy out extra parts for the extra performers, but he need only copy those passages marked "R" ("ripieni") in the print, because these are the only places that the additional choirs will sing.[64]

Monteverdi, in the seven-part Gloria he composed for St. Mark's in 1631, arranges his singers in a single choir, with "solo" and "tutti" instructions. In addition to two solo violin parts, he calls for four violin-family instruments (*viole da brazzo*) or four trombones, but these instruments can be omitted. Monteverdi does not provide parts for the violin or trombone ensembles—presumably they double the singers in tutti passages. In all of these schemes, polychoral organization has been replaced by what might be called concertato organization, in which singers and instrumentalists are consolidated into two groups, one large and one small, and the contrast of several choirs is replaced by the contrast of soloists and ripienists.

For festive events at the cathedral of San Petronio in Bologna in the 1680s singers were divided into one or more choirs of soloists in one choir loft and a group of vocal

---

[63] Translated in Jerome Roche, *North Italian Church Music in the Age of Monteverdi* (Oxford, 1984), 118–19. Quoted in full in Jerome Roche, "North Italian Liturgical Music in the Early 17th Century: Its Evolution around 1600 and its Development until the Death of Monteverdi" (Ph.D. diss., Cambridge, 1967), 191–93. See also Wielakker's introduction to Lodovico Grossi da Viadana, *Salmi a quattro chori* (Madison, 1998).

[64] Gaetano Gaspari, *Catalogo della biblioteca musicale G. B. Martini di Bologna* (Bologna, 1961), ii. 233–34.

ripienists in the opposing loft. Most of the instrumentalists, however, were placed together at the back of the apse, organized as a single ensemble instead of being dispersed among multiple choirs.[65] This organization can be seen in depictions of performances in San Petronio (see Pl. IV). It is reflected in the scores of Cazzati, Colonna, and other seventeenth-century Bolognese composers, who use the instrumental ensemble itself as a kind of ripieno. In their works the contrast of choirs is replaced by the contrast between voices and instruments.[66] The use of an instrumental ripieno is also seen in works by seventeenth-century Venetian composers such as Rovetta, Cavalli, and Chinelli.[67]

Roman churches retained polychoral organization longer than the churches of northern Italy. The ideology of the Counter-Reformation and the wealth of the Americas forwarded to Rome by the Spanish and French governments combined to create a style that Bukofzer calls "the colossal baroque."[68] To increase the magnificence of festivities in their churches, Romans added instruments and multiplied choirs with abandon: three choirs at St. Peter's in 1599, accompanied by 10 instruments; four choirs and 19 instruments at San Luigi dei Francesi in 1628; seven choirs and "a multitude of sweet instruments" at the Gesù in 1639.[69] At St. Peter's in 1628 the Feast of Peter and Paul was celebrated with a vespers for 12 choirs (representing the 12 apostles), "each with an organ and other musical instruments"—150 performers in all.[70] André Maugars, a French musician who visited Rome in 1634, attended a performance in the Church of Santa Maria sopra Minerva, where there were choirs in the organ lofts on either side of the altar, then eight more choirs installed on platforms on both sides of the nave, each with its own organ. Maugars mentions "two or three violins with an organ and several archlutes," which played "excellent symphonies," but he does not say how the instruments were divided among choirs. The choirs were coordinated by the same method as in St. Mark's and at Salzburg: "The *maestro* [*maistre Compositeur*] gave the principal beat in the first choir, accompanied by the best voices. In each of the other choirs there was a man who did nothing else but watch

---

[65] Giovanni Paolo Colonna, *Messa a nove voci concertato con stromenti*, ed. Anne Schnoebelen (Madison, 1974), p. x; Anne Schnoebelen, "The Role of the Violin in the Resurgence of the Mass in the 17th Century," *EM* 18 (1990), 537–42.

[66] Roche, *North Italian Church Music*, 154.

[67] See *Masses by Giovanni Rovetta, Ortensio Polidori, Giovanni Battista Chinelli, Orazio Tarditi*, ed. Anne Schnoebelen (New York, 1996).

[68] Manfred Bukofzer, *Music in the Baroque Era from Monteverdi to Bach* (New York, 1947), 69.

[69] Jean Lionnet, "La Musique à Saint-Louis des Français de Rome au XVIIème siècle," *Note d'archivio per la storia musicale*, NS, Supplement III–IV (1985–86), ii. 28–29, 60–61; Graham Dixon, "The Origins of the Roman 'Colossal Baroque,'" *PRMA* 106 (1979–80), 115–29 at 125. See also Noel O'Regan, "The Performance of Roman Sacred Polychoral Music in the Late Sixteenth and Early Seventeenth Centuries: Evidence from Archival Sources," *Performance Practice Review*, 8 (1995), 107–46.

[70] Hammond, *Music and Spectacle*, 143. 24 instruments were distributed among the 12 choirs: five cornetts, six trombones, seven violins, a contralto violin, a contralto viola, two tenor violas, a violone, and a bassoon. One is tempted to hypothesize an even distribution of two instruments per choir. See Frederick Hammond, *Girolamo Frescobaldi* (Cambridge, Mass., 1983), 64.

TABLE 2.2. *Organization of oratorios at San Marcello in Rome, 1664–90*

Date	Rubric	Singers	Keyboard and plucked instruments	Bowed strings	Source
1664, 7 Mar.	1° choro	5	1 organ		Liess, "Materialien," 142
	2° choro	4	1 organ		
	3° choro	4	1 organ		
	choretto sopra l'altare	2	1 organ		
	Istromenti		2 lutes	2 violins	
			1 spinet		
1674, 16 Feb.	1° choro	8	1 organ	2 violins	Ibid. 149
			1 harpsichord	1 violone	
			2 lutes		
	2° choro	4	1 organ		
	3° choro	4	1 organ		
	Istromenti			1 violin	
				3 violas	
				1 violone	
1677, 12 Mar.	1° coro	8	1 organ	2 violins	Ibid. 156
			1 harpsichord		
			2 lutes		
	2° coro	5	1 organ		
	3° coro	4	1 organ		
	2° coro di strumenti		1 mandora	5 violins	
				3 violas	
				4 violoni	
1682, 20 Feb.	1° coro	9	1 organ	2 violins	Ibid. 160
			1 harpsichord	3 violoni	
			2 archlutes	1 double bass	
	2° coro di voci	5	1 organ		
	3° coro	5	1 organ		
	2° coro di strumenti			7 violins	
				3 violas	
				[1 violone]	
				[1 double bass]	
1690, 4 Apr.		6	1 organ	6 violins	Ibid. 163
			1 harpsichord	2 violas	
				1 violone	
				2 double basses	

this beat and match his own beat to it. Thus all the choirs sang to the same beat without dragging."[71]

Outdoor celebrations of civic and political events in Rome also used multiple choirs during much of the seventeenth century. In 1650 at the Feast of the Resurrection in the Piazza Navona, four choirs were placed in towers around the square; in 1662 four choirs were distributed around the same square to celebrate the birth of the heir to the Spanish throne. Not all Roman ensembles were polychoral, however. Already in 1644, the musicians who performed in the Piazza Navona to celebrate the accession of Innocent X to the papacy were organized as a single choir: 30 singers, plus an ensemble of six trombones, two cornetti, four violins, a violone, and an organ, all crowded into one balcony.[72] In the second half of the seventeenth century polychoral organization became less prevalent in Rome. Records of the Lenten oratorio performances at the Church of San Marcello in the second half of the seventeenth century document this transition, as shown in Table 2.2.[73] In the 1660s the singers were divided into three choirs, each with its own organ. The placement of the instruments is not recorded, but it can be assumed that they were distributed among the choirs. The records for 1674 assign seven instruments to the first choir, while five more instruments are listed at the end as "istromenti." Choirs 2 and 3, and a small "choretto" above the altar, have organs but no other instruments. By 1677 the instrumental ensemble has grown larger and is explicitly designated as a "coro di strumenti"—evidently it occupied a place of its own in the church.[74] By 1682 this choir of instruments has grown larger still: 13 instruments, all bowed strings. A mixed ensemble of keyboards, plucked, and bowed strings continues to accompany the first choir. Finally, in 1690 polychoral organization has disappeared. Now there are only six singers in a single choir, listed as soloists. The instruments are listed at the end in sections: six violins, two violas, a violone, and two double basses—in essence a small orchestra.

FRENCH STRING BANDS

At the Louvre in Paris on Sunday, 29 January 1617, the young Louis XIII danced in a new *ballet de cour, La Délivrance de Renaud*. The Salle des machines had been transformed into a verdant landscape with groves of trees on either side, and in this forest

---

[71] Ernest Thoinan, *Maugars: célèbre joueur de viole . . . suivie de sa Response faite à un curieux sur la sentiment de la musique en Italie . . . 1639* (London, 1865), 27.

[72] *L'effimero barocco: strutture della festa nella Roma del '600*, ed. Maurizio Fagiolo Dell'Arco and Silvia Carandini (Rome, 1977–78), 136.

[73] The figures in Table 2.2 are based on Andreas Liess, "Materialien zur römischen Musikgeschichte des Seicento: Musikerlisten des Oratorio San Marcello 1664–1725," *Acta musicologica*, 29 (1957), 137–71.

[74] Among the members of this choir of instruments was "Arcangelo del violino," i.e. Arcangelo Corelli. See Ch. 4.

was concealed a large chorus of voices, plus 14 lutenists and 28 viol players.[75] The lute band accompanied the singers in a five-part song. Then the curtain fell to reveal the King and 12 of his courtiers, dressed as fiery demons watching over Renault (the Duke of Luynes). The King descended to the front of the stage "to the sound of the Vingt-quatre Violons, dressed as spirits (*esprits*) and placed in a gallery off to one side so as to be available for the different acts of the ballet."[76] Later another lute ensemble appeared, again hidden in a forest but somewhat smaller than in the opening scene. An engraving (Fig. 2.5) shows 10 lutes of various sizes, as well as two viols and several players whose instruments cannot be made out. The Vingt-quatre Violons and the lute ensembles alternated throughout the ballet, the violins playing music for the dances, the lutes accompanying songs. At the end violins and lutes together played "une grande Musique du concert," with 64 vocalists, 28 "violles," and 14 lutes.[77]

Instrumental ensembles for the *ballets de cour* were similar in several respects to those of the Italian intermedii. In both genres large numbers of instruments were organized into separate sub-ensembles. Instrumentalists appeared onstage in costume, and they often participated in the dances. At the end of the ballet or intermedio, the sub-ensembles came together for a grand finale. The *ballet de cour* also adopted some of the instrumental symbolism of the intermedii. In the *Nymphes bocagères de la forêt sacrée* (1627) shepherds danced to the sound of three flutes. In the final scene of the *Balet comique de la royne* (1581) Jupiter descended from the golden vault of the heavens, to the sound of 40 voices and instruments—a French version of the Olympian ensemble.[78]

There were three important differences, however, between intermedio and *ballet de cour* ensembles. Where the intermedii featured a kaleidoscope of ensembles assembled according to the symbolic, musical, and dramatic requirements of each number, the *ballets de cour* alternated between two more or less fixed ensembles: a lute band and a violin band. In general the strings played for dancing; lutes and viols accompanied vocal music. Each ensemble had an institutional identity: the lutes and viols were members of the King's Musique de chambre; the violin-family instruments belonged to the Vingt-quatre Violons du Roy. Occasionally players from the Écurie (the stables, outdoor music) added ensembles of flutes, shawms (hautbois), or cornetts. Although instruments in the *ballet de cour* could be symbolic, the composition of the standing ensembles tended to determine the instrumentation of most numbers. Martial music in the *Ballet de quatre monarchies chrestiennes* (1635) was played by the violins, with a fife and two drums added

[75] *Discours au vray du ballet dansé par le Roy le dimanche 29. jour de Janvier, 1617* (Paris: 1617), fol. 3[r].

[76] Ibid., fol. 6[r].

[77] Ibid. fol. 22[v]. See also Henry Prunières, *Le Ballet de cour en France avant Benserade et Lully* (Paris, 1914), 115 ff., 253; Margaret M. McGowan, *L'Art du ballet de cour en France, 1581–1683* (Paris, 1963); and Kate Van Orden, *Music, Discipline, and Arms in Early Modern France* (Chicago: University of Chicago Press, forthcoming), ch. 2.

[78] Prunières, *Le Ballet de cour*, 181 ff.; Baltasar de Beaujoyeulx, *Le Balet comique de la royne* (Paris, 1582), 49.

QUATRIEME DECORATION, OÙ L'ON
VOIT LE PALAIS D'ARMIDE DÉTRUIT,
ET UN BOIS REMPLI DE MUSICIENS
POUR CHANTER LE TRIOMPHE DE RENAULT.

FIG. 2.5. *La Délivrance de Renaud* (ballet de cour), Paris, 1617

for color. Maritime music for the tritons in the *Ballet de Madame* (1615) was played by shawms.[79] Meanings were expressed more by the the content of the music than by which instruments played. Finally, the ensembles of the *ballet de cour*, unlike intermedio ensembles, customarily played with several instruments on each part. And they did not follow the intermedio principle of equal distribution. According to Mersenne in 1636, the Vingt-quatre Violons distributed themselves on unequally five parts: six instruments on the treble, six on the bass, but only four on each of the middle parts.[80]

Ensembles of many lutes, like the one hiding in the forest in Fig. 2.5, were common in the *ballets de cour*. Usually they also included one or more viols, which were tuned like lutes, and played by the same personnel. The use of lute ensembles to accompany singers is also documented in the *Ballet de la Reine* of 1601 and the *Grand Ballet de Nemours* (1604). How 12 or more lutenists played in an ensemble is not known. Clearly they did not all play continuo, because they used lutes of different sizes and also small viols. Most likely they distributed themselves in some fashion across all the parts.[81]

Large string bands with several violin-family instruments on each part were not unique to the *ballets de cour*. From the early sixteenth century on, Parisian notarial records document associations of three to 15 instrumentalists who joined together to play for weddings, festivals, serenades, and aubades. By the 1580s these ensembles had become violin bands with several players on each part. For example, a contract of 1585 established an association consisting of: three violinists (dessus), two performers on high viola (haute contre), two low violas (taille), four bass violins (basse contre), plus some string-wind doublers—one on cornett and viola, another on bass cornett, viola, and flute, and one on bass violin and alto cornett.[82] In a contract of 1607 with the ribbon-makers' guild a band of 14 musicians promises to "play . . . 92 serenades on their violins and cornetts in the usual fashion outside of the buildings that will be indicated to them . . . beginning at eight in the evening . . . and continuing until 7 the next morning."[83] Their fee for the entire job was 75 livres.

The King employed members of these bands on an occasional basis during the second half of the sixteenth century and began putting them on his payroll in the 1580s.[84]

---

[79] Prunières, *Le Ballet de cour*, 185, 187.

[80] Mersenne, *Harmonie universelle*, iii. 185.

[81] François Lesure, "Le Recueil de ballets de Michel Henry," in Jean Jacquot (ed.), *Les Fêtes de la Renaissance* (Paris, 1956), 205–11 at 209–10; Prunières, *Le Ballet de cour*, 187. Since a lute can play more than one polyphonic part, it is possible that each lute took several parts in the texture. This is the opinion of Paul O'Dette, based on two 16th-c. intabulations of vocal works for multiple lutes. See Paul O'Dette, "Plucked Instruments," in Jeffery T. Kite-Powell (ed.), *A Performer's Guide to Renaissance Music* (New York, 1994), 139–53 at 143–44.

[82] François Lesure, "Les Orchestres populaires," 39–43, 51.

[83] Madeleine Jurgens (ed.), *Documents du minutier central concernant l'histoire de la musique, 1600–1650* (Paris, 1967), i. 420.

[84] François Lesure, "Die 'Terpsichore' von Michael Praetorius und die französische Instrumentalmusik unter Heinrich IV," *Die Musikforschung*, 5 (1952), 7–17 at 11–12. See Ch. 3.

By about 1620 the Vingt-quatre Violons had become a standing ensemble, playing for the *ballets de cour* and other court functions as well as for public events and festivities. The Vingt-quatre Violons continued to work outside the court, around the city of Paris, as the largest, most stable and most prestigious among several string bands.

Most of the repertory played by the violin bands seems to have been composed by the violinists themselves and preserved either in violin tablature or in staff notation. Members of the bands pledged to rehearse their repertory and fined themselves for not knowing their parts.[85] The stability of part assignments, the simplicity of the repertory, and the insistence on rehearsal might suggest that violin bands played from memory. Indeed, most pictures of dances depict the instrumentalists playing without music. A description in a novel published in 1626 of the Vingt-quatre Violons at a *ballet de cour* in the Palais Bourbon seems to contradict this notion, however. The hero has gained access to the ballet, but the room is so crowded that he has to take refuge on the bandstand:

Just as I settled down there, the Violins arrived. Each one was holding onto his tablature, and having no music stands, they assumed that I had been put there for the purpose. One detached a pin from his ruff, another from his collar, and then all came over to attach their pages to my coat. I had music on my back; I had music on my arms; I even had music in my hatband. . . . The violins began tuning up all around me, when . . . I started to scramble down from the bandstand. You should have seen how the players tried to catch me—one with his hand, another with the scroll of his bass, most of them with their bows—in order to retrieve their music.[86]

It is hard to know what to make of the information in this satirical report. If the violins played from music, why hadn't anyone thought to provide stands? Still, the story suggests that the Vingt-quatre Violons lived and worked in a musically literate environment. The reader of the novel could imagine them playing from music, even if they may seldom have done so in performances at Court.

Violin bands—ensembles of violin-family instruments playing several on a part—spread from Paris to the French provinces and to other parts of Europe. Sebastiano Locatelli, an Italian traveler, reported from Lyons in 1664 that "the music in this region is made by what I can only call an assembly [*radunanza*] of violin, viola, and violone players, up to 40 or 50 at a time."[87] It was not just the size of the ensemble that impressed Locatelli. He also seems to have been surprised that, in contrast to Italian practice, the entire group consisted of violin-family instruments organized as a single choir rather than polychorally.

---

[85] François Lesure, "Les Orchestres populaires," 46–47.

[86] Charles Sorel, *Histoire comique de Francion (Livres I à VII)*, ed. Yves Giraud (Paris, 1979), 400–1.

[87] Sebastiano Locatelli, *Viaggio di Francia: costume e qualità di quei paesi (1664–1665)*, ed. Luigi Monga (Moncalieri, 1990), 169.

Several European courts established violin bands in imitation of the Vingt-quatre Violons of the French king. In England the "Violins," which had existed as an ensemble since the early sixteenth century, were expanded during the early years of James I's reign from seven to 12.[88] By the time of *The Triumph of Peace* in 1634, the King's Violins numbered 14 and functioned as an independent standing ensemble with several players on each part. In Germany Pierre Caroubel and other French violinists migrated to the Court of Brunswick in Wolfenbüttel during the early years of the seventeenth century, taking with them a large repertory of dances, which Michael Praetorius published under the title *Terpsichore* in 1612.[89] The Swedish court, under Queen Christina, imported French violinists in 1647 and set up a violin band.[90] At its height, however, the ensemble numbered only eight players.

In Italy too, the French practice of doubling the string parts with large numbers of instruments began to turn up during the seventeenth century. Already at the Medici wedding in 1608, a band of twelve French violinists played for the equestrian ballet and for dancing as well. As late as the middle of the century, however, violin bands and part doubling were still considered a French import. A manuscript note at the beginning of a Serenata by Cesti, written in Florence in 1662 to celebrate the birth of a new Medici duke, specifies: "The *sinfonie* should be played with doubling in the manner of the French bands [*raddopiate all'uso de concerti di Francia*], as follows: six violins, four alto violas, four tenor violas, four bass violins, one contrabass viol, one small spinet, one large spinet, a theorbo, and an archlute."[91] Singers in Cesti's serenade were accompanied by the keyboards and plucked strings, with two violins added in some arias.

TOWARD THE ORCHESTRA

Most sixteenth- and seventeenth-century instrumental ensembles were not orchestras. They can be considered "pre-orchestral" in the sense that they preceded orchestras in time, not that they were earlier forms of the same institution. Large numbers of instrumentalists were assembled for special occasions—coronations, royal marriages, the anniversary of a church, or the festival of a patron saint. For the most part these ensembles were put together on an ad hoc basis, starting with a core of players

---

[88] Peter Holman, *Four and Twenty Fiddlers: The Violin at the English Court, 1540–1690* (Oxford, 1993), 173–75.

[89] Lesure, " 'Terpsichore.' "

[90] *Seventeenth-Century Instrumental Dance Music in Uppsala Univ. Library Instr. mus. hs. 409*, ed. Jaroslav Mrácek (Stockholm, 1976), 9.

[91] Quoted in Egon Wellesz, "Zwei Studien zur Geschichte der Oper im XVII. Jahrhundert," *Sammelbände der IMG*, 15 (1913–14), 124–33 at 125. The manuscript, in the Staatsbibliothek in Vienna, is attributed to Cesti in a different hand from the copyist's hand, and the instructions for instrumentation are written not on the score but on the wrapper. Nevertheless the instructions are almost surely contemporary with the piece.

on the payroll of a church or a court, hiring additional musicians according to the importance of the event and the available budget. Instrumentalists were not organized as a single ensemble but instead were divided into sub-ensembles, typically organized into consorts or choirs according to the principle of equal distribution of parts. In polychoral music the choirs functioned as autonomous ensembles, each with its own continuo, coordinated by a system of relaying a beat from the *maestro di cappella* to the various choirs. For entertainments like intermedii, banquets, or masques, separate ensembles followed one another in succession, combining only for a grand finale at the end of the show. Although the ensembles for events like these were often modeled on ensembles at earlier events, the patterns of organization were not normative, that is, each event usually had its own particular combination of instruments and organizational plan.

During the seventeenth century, however, three developments began to point the way toward the orchestra. In Italian churches polychoral organization was gradually displaced by the concertato principle, in which instrumentalists and vocalists were consolidated into two choirs: a small choir of soloists and a large choir of ripienists in which the performers played and sang several on a part. In some churches the instrumentalists constituted a choir of their own—in effect, an instrumental ripieno with several on each part. In theaters in Italy, France, England, and Germany standing ensembles came into being, hired for the season and playing with the same configuration of instruments night after night. Theater ensembles were initially divided into sub-ensembles of bowed strings vs. plucked strings and keyboards vs. winds; but toward the end of the seventeenth century composers began increasingly to ask these sub-ensembles to play at the same time or to use elements of them in combination. Rather than seeing these sixteenth- and seventeenth-century ensembles as the ancestors of the orchestra, it is better to view them as different approaches to the problem of organizing large numbers of instruments to play at the same occasion. The ensemble that perhaps most clearly began to point in the direction of an orchestra was the French string band. Already in the late sixteenth century French string players organized themselves into large, standing ensembles of violin-family instruments in which all parts were doubled. Royal patronage at the beginning of the seventeenth century gave one of these ensembles an institutional identity as the Vingt-quatre Violons du Roy, an organization whose repertory and performance practices were soon to become decisive in the development of European music.

Chapter Three

Lully's Orchestra

THE LULLY MYTH

In a treatise on tuning keyboard instruments published in Paris in 1650 Jean Denis reports a curious and touching story. A beloved wife had fallen into profound melancholy. Her husband, in despair and having exhausted all known remedies, decided to follow the advice of a friend and hired the King's famous string band, the Vingt-quatre Violons du Roy. Following a previously agreed-upon plan, the members of the King's band tuned their instruments in advance, entered the house, and crept noiselessly behind a tapestry suspended in the bedroom where the wife was sleeping:

The violins all began together. The force of these instruments, which twenty-four men made to sound with all their strength and with great intensity, surprised the lady utterly, for it was the last thing she expected. This harmony made such an impact that it instantly banished her baleful melancholy. She recovered her former health and her merry disposition.[1]

Beyond any insights this anecdote may provide into the treatment of depression, it is important to the history of the orchestra, for it confirms that by the 1640s at the latest the Vingt-quatre Violons played as a unified ensemble with several on a part and that they were valued for their ability to play powerfully and with unanimity. The musical gesture that effects the cure beginning a piece with a simultaneous downbow in all the parts is the *premier coup d'archet*, for which Parisian orchestras continued to be famous well into the eighteenth century. The anecdote attests to the exceptional reputation of the Vingt-quatre, while also demonstrating that the royal band was available, like other Parisian string bands, for serenades and freelance work around town.

---

[1] Jean Denis, *Traité de l'accord de l'espinette* (1650), ed. Alan Curtis (New York, 1969), 25; trans. Panetta (1987), 82–83, slightly modified.

What is most interesting, perhaps, about Jean Denis's tale is its date of publication—1650—three years before Jean-Baptiste Lully entered the King's service and more than a decade before Lully assumed control of the Vingt-quatre Violons. The strength, the uniformity, the discipline, the *premier coup d'archet*, all of which have been considered as Lully's innovations, seem to have been characteristic features of performance practice among the King's Violins before Lully came on the scene. Histories of music, beginning with Le Cerf de la Viéville in 1705, traditionally assign Lully a central place in the story of the orchestra.[2] It was Lully, the story goes, who brought together large numbers of violin-family instruments into a single ensemble with several on a part, who taught a rag-tag band of dance musicians to bow together and to play with the same ornamentation, who added new wind instruments like oboes and flutes to the orchestra, and whose overture and dance suites constituted the first repertory of truly orchestral music.

A 1715 version of the melancholy wife anecdote transfers credit for the miracle cure from the King's Violins to Lully's music:

A famous court doctor reported to me that he had cured a high-born lady, who had been driven mad with grief over the faithlessness of her lover. He had an alcove built in the chamber of this lady, and there he placed musicians, who without her being able to see them, played three concerts every day, and at night they sang airs . . . from the most beautiful moments in the operas of Sieur de Lully. After six weeks of this her wits were restored . . .[3]

The Vingt-quatre Violons are no longer mentioned. Lully alone gets credit for the success of the music therapy, which is brought about by his orchestral music and his songs.

Born in Florence, Giovanni Battista Lulli (1632–87) came to France at the age of 14 to serve as Italian tutor to the King's cousin, Anne-Marie-Louise d'Orléans, Duchesse de Montpensier, known as the Grande Mademoiselle. Soon he began to style himself Jean-Baptiste Lully. His cleverness and talent for the violin, guitar, singing, and dancing gained him instruction in music and dance and brought him to the attention of the young King Louis XIV. In 1652 Mlle de Montpensier was banished to the provinces for choosing the wrong side in the failed rebellion known as the Fronde. By then, however, the 20-year-old Lully had made himself indispensable. The King kept him in Paris, appointed him *Compositeur de la musique instrumentale* in 1653, and placed him at the head of the Petits Violons, the King's private violin band. In 1661 he appointed Lully *Surintendant de la musique de la chambre du roi*, which brought the Vingt-quatre Violons under Lully's command, along with the singers and

---

[2] See Jean-Laurent, Le Cerf de la Viéville, *Comparaison de la musique italienne et de la musique françoise*, 2nd edn. (Brussels, 1705); Hawkins, *General History*, ii. 646 ff.; Henry Prunières, "Notice historique: Les premiers ballets de Lully," in *Œuvres complètes de J.-B. Lully*, i (Paris, 1931), pp. xiii–xxiii; Spitzer and Zaslaw, "Orchestra," in *NG II*, xviii. 557.

[3] Pierre Bourdelot and Jacques Bonnet, *Histoire de la musique et de ses effets* (1715) (Amsterdam, 1725), i. 48–49.

accompanists of the King's household, the Musique de la chambre. Finally, in 1672 Lully consolidated his control over French musical life by purchasing the bankrupt Académie Royale de Musique. With Louis XIV's support, he created a brand new instrumental ensemble, the orchestra of the Opéra, which became the largest, best disciplined, and most renowned orchestra of the day.

Lully perhaps does deserve a good deal of credit for the birth of the orchestra, but the Lully legend needs closer scrutiny. Lully did not invent the orchestra: all the ensembles at the French court were in place before he arrived there. The only ensemble he created was the orchestra of the Opéra. Nor did he invent new wind instruments: he continued to use recorders in preference to the newer transverse flute, and the "hautbois" he used in his orchestra were transitional instruments, somewhere between shawms and so-called Baroque oboes. Finally, an international repertory of French string-band music circulated already in the 1640s and 1650s, a generation before Lully's music became famous. On the other hand, Lully did in fact play a crucial role in synthesizing, consolidating, and disseminating orchestral organization, scorings, performance practices, and repertory. If Lully was not the orchestra's biological father, he was at least its godfather.

ORGANIZATION AND INSTITUTIONS

The Vingt-quatre Violons du Roy

At the court of François I (r. 1515–47) and the succeeding Valois kings the violins formed part of the royal cavalry, at least administratively. There were positions on the payroll of the Grande Écurie ("royal stables"), for six double-handed performers, who played violins, oboes, sackbuts, and other instruments as well.[4] Under the Bourbon kings dance became an increasingly important part of court entertainment and ceremonial. By the end of the sixteenth century a group of string players had been shifted from the Écurie to the Chambre, joining the singers, viol, and keyboard players already employed there for the diversion of the King and his inner circle. In 1609 there were 22 violins on the payroll; by 1614 there were 24. In 1618 a ledger entry mentions by name "the Twenty-four Violins in ordinary," suggesting that the band had acquired a distinct administrative existence within the royal establishment.[5] At the court of Louis XIII the Vingt-quatre were indispensable for the *ballets de cour*, where they often had an *entrée* of their own at the beginning, playing their instruments as they marched into the hall and onto a bandstand erected for them.[6] They also played for court balls, receptions of important visitors, and state banquets. The

---

[4] Bernard Bardet, "Violons, Vingt-quatre," in *Dictionnaire de la musique en France aux XVIIe et XVIIIe siècles*, ed. Marcelle Benoit (Paris, 1992), 724.

[5] "Vingt-quatre violons ordinaires." Ibid.　　　[6] Prunières, *Le Ballet de cour*, 100, 140. See above, Ch. 2.

violins remained part of the Chambre and their official number remained at 24 until the group's dissolution in 1761.[7] Their proud title, Les Vingt-quatre Violons du Roy or simply Les Vingt-quatre, became an emblem of instrumental organization and practice at the Bourbon court.

In addition to their status as officers of the King's Chambre, the Vingt-quatre maintained an independent professional existence as members of the Confrérie de St-Julien des ménestriers, the Parisian instrumentalists' guild. Records from the first half of the seventeenth century document bands of three to 14 members that the Confrérie provided for the yearly festivals of other Parisian guilds. Often there were at least two, sometimes more, players on each part. In 1642 a group of 12 agreed to meet once a week in the winter and twice a week in the summer to give concerts at the Louvre, at the Petit-Bourbon palace, "or in whatever other place is most convenient to play our royal concert."[8] Such concerts allowed persons who did not have access to court to hear the music of the Vingt-quatre.

Occasionally the entire band of Twenty-four Violins hired themselves out for engagements outside Paris. In a letter written in the 1630s the poet Vincent Voiture describes a visit to the country estate of Mme du Vigean just north of Paris, for a party in honor of one of the royal princesses:

Mme la Princesse wanted to have a look at the garden walkways before dinner . . . At the end of a grand allée, hidden from view, we found a fountain that by itself spouted more water than all the fountains of Tivoli. Around it stood twenty-four violins, who had difficulty making themselves heard over the noise of the water.

The company dances to the sound of the violins, then returns to the château to find an extravagant repast.

As we rose from the table, the sound of the violins enticed us upstairs, where we found a room so brilliantly lit that it seemed as though daylight had been brought back from the other side of the planet. There the dancing resumed, better organized and more beautiful than it had been around the fountain . . .[9]

Late that night on the way back to Paris, M. Voiture's carriage overtakes the Vingt-quatre Violons, who are also returning home. The revelers ask the Vingt-quatre to serenade them back to town. But the Violons have left their instruments behind in La Barre—evidently a porter will bring them along later—so they turn down the request. This anecdote, like Jean Denis's story of the melancholy wife, shows that the Vingt-quatre Violons sometimes worked outside the immediate confines of Paris and the court. Wherever the Violons played, however, their positions as employees of the royal Chambre and their identification as the Violons du Roy assured that their

[7] Between 1655 and 1697 the Vingt-quatre Violins had an extra, 25th member. See below.

[8] Jurgens (ed.), *Documents du minutier central*, 123, 420 ff.

[9] Vincent Voiture, *Lettres*, in *Oeuvres de Monsieur de Voiture* (Paris, 1654), 32–35.

performance would add to the prestige of the King and his court, while reflecting some royal glory upon their employers of the moment.

During the years of Louis XIV's minority (1643–52), the Vingt-quatre Violons became yet more important to life at court. They played for ceremonial dinners, like the one at the Palais-Royal for the wedding of the King and Queen of Poland in 1645. On religious holidays they set up on outdoor bandstands and played as processions filed by. They played for public functions in the city of Paris, such as a reception in 1649 for the young King and his mother the Queen, who were "received in the courtyard by trumpets, drums, and fifes, at the base of the staircase by the oboes, and in the Salle des gardes by the King's Twenty-four Violins." Most of all they played for the King and his court to dance: at a reception for the King and Queen at Fontainebleau, at a reception for the King at the Maltese ambassador's palace, at a ball for the King and Queen in the Grande salle of the Hôtel de Ville.[10]

When Louis XIV appointed Jean-Baptiste Lully *Surintendant de la musique de la chambre* in 1661, the Vingt-quatre Violons came under the administrative supervision of the Florentine composer. It does not seem as though Lully directed the string ensemble in person, however, for the day-to-day director of the Vingt-quatre was still Guillaume Dumanoir, head of the Parisian violinists' guild. By special order of the King in 1655, Dumanoir had been appointed as the "twenty-fifth" violin, "to direct the band . . . because his ability, his loyalty, and his diligence are considered necessary to maintain this ensemble in its state of perfection."[11] He remained the group's administrative and musical director throughout Lully's tenure and beyond. For Lully's own *Ballet des ballets* in 1671, Dumanoir was in charge of the Vingt-quatre's rehearsals.[12] Lully directed the group personally only for important events. On most occasions the Vingt-quatre continued to perform autonomously without him.

The functions of the Vingt-quatre at court were described in 1663, two years after Lully took control: "They serve whenever the King commands them: when a ballet is given, etc. At certain ceremonies, a coronation or the King's entry into a city, for [royal] marriages and other solemnities or festivals, they play along with the violins of the Écurie, the oboes, fifes, etc."[13] Twenty-four years later, in 1687, the last year of Lully's life, a description of their duties reads somewhat differently: "The Grande bande of twenty-four violins, always so called even though at present they are twenty-five . . . plays for the King's dinner, for ballets, for stage works [*comédies*], and for operas."[14] The latter description seems to place less emphasis on public and ceremonial functions, more on private entertainments, like the operas that Lully staged at

[10] Norbert Dufourcq, "En parcourant la 'Gazette' 1645–1654," *RMFC* 23 (1995), 176–202 at 185, 187, 191, 193, 195.

[11] Bernard Bardet, "Dumanoir (les)," in *Dictionnaire de la musique en France*, ed. Benoit, 251.

[12] Marcelle Benoit, *Musiques de cour: Chapelle, chambre, écurie, 1661–1733* (Paris, 1971), 36.

[13] *État de la France, ou l'on voit tous les princes, ducs & pairs, maréchaux de France . . .* (Paris, 1663), 83.

[14] Ibid. (1687), 176.

court. Overall, however, the duties and functions of the Vingt-quatre Violons remained much the same after 20 years of Lully's administration as they had been before he took control.

Membership in the Vingt-quatre was an "office" in the household of the King, what today might be called a civil service position. The office holder received wages, plus additional sums for food and transportation, as well as payments in kind of candles and cloth.[15] A violinist, like all officers of the King, was exempt from the *taille*, the national head tax. The salary of a member of the Vingt-quatre in the second half of the seventeenth century was 365 livres per year, considerably less than the other members of the Chambre—the singers, keyboardists, and lutenists.[16] Membership in the Vingt-quatre bestowed considerable prestige, however, in the world of French music. It gave a musician the titles "honorable homme" and "bourgeois de Paris" and entitled him to wear a sword in public. It also opened doors to a multitude of possibilities for performance, teaching, and musical commerce, possibilities that the limited number of engagements at court allowed ample time to pursue.[17]

A violinist's position could be bought and sold, like every other office in France. A fiddler who aspired to become a member of the Vingt-quatre had to find an incumbent member of the band who wanted to sell his position, and the two men negotiated a deal. The price in the late seventeenth century ranged from 2,000 to 3,000 livres.[18] In addition the new violinist had to pay several fees and grease a number of palms: "pin" money to the incumbent's wife, a payment to the notary to record the sale, a fee to the court bureaucracy to agree to the sale, plus a ceremonial dinner for his 23 new colleagues.[19] The total cost could rise to half again the price of the office. Still, a position among the Vingt-quatre was relatively cheap compared with other offices in the King's service, probably because the post offered only limited opportunities for personal enrichment and graft.

Given that an instrumentalist gained entry into the Chambre by purchasing the office, quality control was a nagging problem. In principle the King (or his representative) could refuse to acknowledge the sale if the purchaser was judged to be incompetent, but there is no record of this ever happening. Usually the incoming violinist was already well known to his fellows, either because he was the son or the nephew of a current member of the ensemble or because he had already been playing with the Vingt-quatre as a supernumerary or an interim replacement.[20] Competitive auditions were sometimes held for high-level positions in the Chambre or the Chapelle, but

[15] Catherine Massip, *La Vie des musiciens de Paris au temps de Mazarin (1643–1661): Essai d'étude sociale* (Paris, 1976), 43–44.

[16] Marcelle Benoit, *Versailles et les musiciens du roi, 1661–1733: Étude institutionelle et sociale* (Paris, 1971), 203; Massip, *La Vie des musiciens*, 34.

[17] See Massip, *La Vie des musiciens*, 109 ff.

[18] Benoit, *Versailles*, 110–11. Prices around 1650 had been somewhat lower: 1200–2400 livres (Massip, *La Vie des musiciens*, 34–35).

[19] See Benoit, *Versailles*, 114–15.   [20] Ibid. 112, 141 ff.

the practice did not extend to the Vingt-quatre. Presumably Dumanoir had to give his assent to a new appointment, and after 1661 perhaps Lully's approval was required too, but the stories about Lully auditioning violinists with passages from his music refer to the orchestra of the Opéra, not to the Vingt-quatre.[21]

Except for the presence of a 25th violin from 1654 to 1697, the number of players in the Vingt-quatre Violons remained constant at 24 from the early seventeenth century until the dissolution of the ensemble in 1761. The distribution of instruments on the various parts also remained relatively constant until the 1690s, as shown in Table 3.1. According to Mersenne, in 1636 the instruments were almost equally distributed, with six violins and six basses de violon on the outer parts and four players apiece on three viola parts in the middle. An archival record from around 1650 shows the same distribution.[22] Unfortunately, no documentation of this sort survives from the period during which Lully was in charge of the ensemble (1661–87). In 1692, however, the *État de la France* began to publish a complete roster of the Vingt-quatre. There is an extra dessus—Guillaume Dumanoir, the 25th violin—and one of the quintes has been replaced by a basse de violon. Otherwise the distribution has not changed since 1636. These, then, must have been the balances of the Vingt-quatre in Lully's day: relatively equal distribution of instruments on five parts, with a slight emphasis on the highest and lowest parts.[23] After Lully's death and under the influence of Italian music, which used more violins and fewer violas, the distribution of the Vingt-quatre began to change. The number of violins increased, the number of viola parts decreased, and the number of players on those parts was reduced. This evolution, shown in Table 3.1, resulted in a texture with fewer parts and a stronger treble-bass polarity.

TABLE 3.1. *Les Vingt-quatre Violons du Roy, 1636–1718*

Date	Dessus	Haute contre	Taille	Quinte	Basse	Total	Source
1636	6	4	4	4	6	24	Mersenne, *Harmonie*, iii. 185
c.1650	6	4	4	4	6	24	Benoit, *Versailles*, 204
1692	7	4	4	3	7	25	*État* (1692), 215
1702	9	3	4	2	6	24	*État* (1702), 232
1708	10	2	3	2	7	24	*État* (1708), 234
1718	11	3	2	0	8	24	*État* (1718), 220

[21] Le Cerf, *Comparaison*, ii. 228.　　[22] Benoit, *Versailles*, 204.
[23] See La Gorce, "Some Notes," 110.

The Petits Violons

When in 1653 the 20-year-old Lully was appointed the King's *Compositeur de la musique instrumentale,* he was also made leader of another court string band, Les Petits Violons. The standard account of the origins of this ensemble is that of Charles Perrault, who claimed in 1696 that the ensemble had been called into being specifically for Lully:

the King . . . commanded [Lully] to take charge of his violin band, since he played that instrument in a way that no one else had come close to before; and his Majesty even created a new ensemble for him, dubbed the Petits Violons. Under his direction it soon equaled and even surpassed the Vingt-quatre, the most famous band in all of Europe. It is true that the Petits Violons had the advantage of playing pieces composed by M. Lully—pieces entirely different from anything heard before.[24]

Perrault's account, written forty years after the event and a decade after Lully's death, has provided the basis for almost everything subsequently written about the Petits Violons. It contains some problematic assertions, for instance that Lully took charge of the Vingt-quatre Violons immediately in 1653, whereas, in fact, there was a lapse of eleven years before he gained control of that group. It also claims that the Petits Violons were created especially for Lully but, according to one contemporary witness, the group was already in existence when Lully arrived at court. Monsieur Dubois of Rouen, a gentleman servant at the French court, recorded in his memoirs that in 1648 the King, then all of 10 years old, wished to present a serenade to his mother the Queen and her ladies. He ordered Guillaume Dumanoir "to compose several pretty pieces and include some bizarre instruments in them." According to Dubois, it was not the Vingt-quatre but the Petits Violons who presented themselves to the Queen and performed three pieces entitled "Charivaris,"

in which mingled with the violins were hurdy-gurdies, recorders, castanets, penny whistles, a Persian organ, a little terra-cotta nightingale filled with water, and a wooden saltbox, which one of them attached to his waistband and struck with drumsticks . . . The whole thing was lovely and gave the audience much pleasure.[25]

If this account can be taken at face value, the Petits Violons were created around 1648, perhaps as a kind of toy orchestra for the young King—"petit" because they had fewer players than the Vingt-quatre Violons, but perhaps also because the King himself was *petit*.[26] The fact that Dumanoir, who had been a member of the

---

[24] Charles Perrault, *Les Hommes illustres qui ont paru en France pendant ce siècle avec leurs portraits au naturel* (Paris, 1696–1700), i. 181–82. Perrault's account is elaborated in Le Cerf, *Comparaison,* ii. 171.

[25] Léon Arbinau, "Fragments des mémoires inédits de Dubois, Gentilhomme servant du Roi," *Bibliothèque de l'École des Chartes—Revue d'Érudition,* 9 (II/4) (1847–48), 1–45 at 6. A "Persian organ" was a mouth organ made of reed tubes, a relative of the Chinese *sheng.* We have been unable to locate the original memoir, which is partly quoted and partly paraphrased in the 1847 edition.

[26] Bardet states that the Petits Violons began in 1648 with 10 members, but does not cite a source for this information (Bardet, "Violons, Petits," in *Dictionnaire de la musique en France,* ed. Benoit, 724).

Vingt-quatre since 1639, led the Petits Violons in their serenade suggests that membership in the two ensembles overlapped at first.

In their early years the Petits Violons, also known as the Petite Bande, led a somewhat shadowy existence. The *État de la France* does not mention them until the 1660s, and the earliest roster of their members dates from the 1680s. At first they may have been called together somewhat intermittently, unlike older court ensembles that formed part of the court hierarchy, had regularly assigned duties, and occupied permanent lines in the budget. Another name for the ensemble, the Violons du Cabinet, suggests that they performed at private functions for select audiences.

Under Lully the Petits Violons took on an institutional identity distinct from and to some extent in competition with the Vingt-quatre. The Petite Bande enabled him to navigate around the guild structure, archaic performance practices, and repertory of the Vingt-quatre. In the masquerade *La Galanterie du temps* (1656), the first *ballet de cour* for which he composed the music without collaborators, Lully employed the Petits Violons rather than the Vingt-quatre.[27] In the *Ballet de l'impatience* of 1661 Lully used 14 violins, all of them members of the Petite Bande, along with lutes, viols, and flutes.[28] The Petits Violons were more closely tied to the court than the Vingt-quatre, who were based in the world of the Paris guilds. Whereas members of the Vingt-quatre tended to live in the musicians' quarter of Paris, the Petits Violons had lodgings in the King's palace at Saint-Germain-en-Laye until 1680, at Versailles thereafter.[29] The Petite Bande accompanied the King when he traveled; the Vingt-quatre welcomed him back when he returned.

The Petite Bande seems always to have had fewer members than the Vingt-quatre, but just barely. An account of the *Plaisirs de l'isle enchantée* in 1664 suggests that at that time the Petits Violons numbered 19 or 20 (Table 3.2). In 1690 the *État de la France* reported that the Petite Bande comprised 21 members and that each of them was paid 600 livres per year, which was almost twice the salary of a member of the Grande Bande. Beginning in 1692 the *État de la France* regularly reported not only the size but also the composition of the Petite Bande. Compared with the Vingt-quatre Violons the balances of the Petite Bande seem slightly more Italianate, with proportionately more violins and fewer violas and basses. The most striking difference between the two ensembles is that, by the 1690s, the Petits Violons included winds as well as strings. The *État* of 1692 lists two "dessus de cromorne" and two bassoons among the Violons du Cabinet. The former were oboes of some sort, not the obsolete crumhorn, which in France was known as a "tournebout."[30] In any case, the *État* of

---

[27] James R. Anthony, *French Baroque Music from Beaujoyeulx to Rameau*, 2nd edn. (Portland, Ore., 1997), 21; Henry Prunières, "Les Petits Violons de Lully," *L'Écho musical*, 5/4 (30 Apr. 1920), 125–31 at 127.

[28] Rebecca Harris-Warrick, "Magnificence in Motion: Stage Musicians in Lully's Ballets and Operas," *Cambridge Opera Journal*, 6 (1994), 189–203 at 196.

[29] Massip, *La Vie des musiciens*, 94 ff.; Bardet, "Violons, Petits," 724.

[30] Haynes, *The Eloquent Oboe*, 37–45.

TABLE 3.2. *Les Petits Violons du Roy, 1664–1712*

Date	Dessus	Haute contre	Taille	Quinte	Basse	Winds	Total	Source
1664	—	—	—	—	—	—	19–20	Lemaître, "Sources," 200
1681	—	—	—	—	—	—	22	Tessier, "Document," 888
1690	—	—	—	—	—	—	21	Benoit, *Versailles*, 233
1692	7	2	3	2	4	2 dessus de cromorne 2 bassons	22	*État* (1692), 227
1698	7	2	3	2	5	2 dessus d'hautbois 2 bassons	23	*État* (1698), 229
1702	7	2	3	2	5	2 hautbois 2 bassons	23	*État* (1702), 232
1712	8	2	3	2	5	3 hautbois 2 bassons	25	*État* (1712), 228

1698 lists the same men as playing "dessus de hautbois." With the addition of a third oboe in 1712, the Petite Bande numbered 25 musicians, at last overtaking the Vingt-quatre Violons in size. Created as a plaything for the young Louis XIV, the Petits Violons were disbanded at the grand monarch's death in 1715.

The Chapelle

Every day at 10:00 AM Louis XIV attended mass, usually in the chapels attached to his residences in the Louvre, at Saint-Germain-en-Laye, or at Versailles.[31] On holidays and special occasions he often made a more public appearance at the Sainte Chapelle or the Convent of the Feuillants in Paris. The Chapelle, that is, the court's religious music establishments, had grown from modest medieval beginnings to carry out these religiously and politically indispensable ceremonies.[32] An appointment to the Chapelle was the most prestigious and most lucrative of all the musical offices in

[31] Béatrix Saule, *Versailles triomphant: Une journée de Louis XIV* (Paris, 1996), 62 ff.

[32] On the organization of the Chapelle, see Benoit, *Versailles*, 179 ff. In general see Alexandre Maral, *La Chapelle royale de Versailles sous Louis XIV* (Sprimont, Belgium, 2002).

the royal service. More than 60 singers—men and boys, ecclesiastics and laymen, even a few castrati—were on the payroll, but for the most part they sang in rotation by semester rather than as a single large ensemble. The singers were accompanied by four organists, organized again in rotation, with each man serving for a quarter of the year.

In the early seventeenth century the Chapelle contained only a few instrumental-ists—mainly serpent players, who accompanied plainchant and doubled the bass line in polyphonic music.[33] Around the middle of the century bowed-string players were added in order to perform concerted music, especially motets, which were multi-sectional sacred cantatas with instrumental accompaniment. By 1702 there were 15 instrumentalists in the Chapelle, enough to constitute a small ensemble.[34] Compared with the Vingt-quatre Violons or the Petite Bande, however, the instrumental forces of the Chapelle were far from orchestral. For everyday services, even "grands motets" for two choirs with instrumental "symphonies" were performed with one or two players on the string parts.[35] Descriptions of motet performances in the 1650s and 1660s mention keyboards, lutes, and viols, not bowed strings.[36]

On occasions of state—royal births, coronations, weddings, military victories, funerals, and the like—instrumentalists were brought into the Chapelle from other departments to mount large-scale performances of concerted music. In 1668 for example, the Vingt-quatre Violons joined musicians from the Chapelle and accom-panists from the Chambre at the feast of St. Joseph. Robinet, who chronicled the event in verse, considered this combination of forces to be an innovation:

> The band, surely the most refined
> That anyone could call to mind,
> Was made up not of lutes, nor yet
> of mandoras or theorbos; instead
> The Violons, the four and twenty
> Performed by expert hands aplenty,
> Delighted all who heard them play
> The office of the mass that day.[37]

---

[33] *Anthologie du motet latin polyphonique en France (1609–1661)*, ed. Denise Launay (Paris, 1963), p. xxxiii.

[34] Benoit, *Versailles*, 188. Four violins, three violas (1 haute-contre, 1 taille, 1 quinte), three basses de vio-lon, and one theorbo, plus two transverse flutes, a bassoon, and a cromorne.

[35] Surviving sets of parts for grand motets usually comprise one for each melody instrument plus a larger number of bass and continuo parts. See Jean-Paul C. Montagnier, "The Problems of 'Reduced Scores' and Performing Forces at the Chapelle Royale of Versailles during the Tenure of Henry Madin (1738–1748)," *Journal of Musicological Research*, 18 (1998), 63–93. Montagnier analyzes the transmission of parts from a some-what later repertory. See also *Actes du colloque international de musicologie sur le grand motet français 1663–1792*, ed. Jean Mongédien and Yves Ferraton (Paris: Presses de l'Université de Paris-Sorbonne, 1986).

[36] Yolande de Brossard, "La Vie musicale en France d'après Loret et ses continuateurs, 1650–1688," *RMFC* 10 (1970), 115–73 at 138, 141, 144, 145.

[37] Ibid. 147. "Ce Concert, des plus délicas, / Dont on a fait beaucoup de cas, / Etoit non de Luths ou Mandores / Et ni de Théorbes encores, / Mais de vingt-et-quatre Violons / Touchez par autant d'Apollons, / Qui ravirent chacun, sans cesse, / Pendant l'Office de la Messe."

Yet more musicians were involved in a 1679 performance of Lully's *Te Deum* at Versailles to celebrate the marriage of Marie-Louise d'Orléans, the King's niece, to Charles II of Spain in 1679. According to the *Mercure galant*:

The musicians were placed in a gallery that formed part of a large stage, reaching up almost to the ceiling. Those from the Chambre were at the right, those from the Chapelle on the left. There were oboes, flutes, trumpets, and drums, along with the Vingt-quatre Violons. At least 120 persons sang or played instruments.[38]

Such orchestral performances of sacred music were reserved for special occasions and required the participation of instrumentalists from outside the Chapelle.

The Grande Écurie

From the mid-seventeenth to the late eighteenth century, the French court had exactly 35 positions for woodwind players.[39] Most of these players of oboes, flutes, recorders, bassoons, shawms, cromornes, serpents, and yet more exotic instruments, held positions in the Grande Écurie, the royal stables. This large corps of wind players was divided administratively into five groups: the Trompettes; the Violons, Hautbois, Saqueboutes et Cornets; the Hautbois et Musettes de Poitou; the Fifres et Tambours; and the Cromornes et Trompettes Marines. Each group functioned as an independent ensemble, with its own characteristic duties, venues, and repertory. The instruments they played, however, did not always correspond to what their names implied. By the second half of the seventeenth century, sackbuts and cornetts were no longer in use, and the violins had been transferred to the Chambre, so the Violons, Hautbois, Saqueboutes et Cornets consisted mainly of double-reed players. They were usually referred to as the Douze Grands Hautbois. Each of the 12 players, however, was listed in the accounts as playing a violin-family instrument as well as a double reed, so appparently the Douze Grands Hautbois could also muster a string band when the occasion demanded.[40] The Hautbois et Musettes de Poitou had become an ensemble of flute and recorder specialists.[41] The Fifres et Tambours comprised four drummers and four oboists. They supplied music for the King's public appearances and accompanied the public reading of royal decrees. The cromorne had become old-fashioned and the marine trumpet obsolete by the mid-seventeenth century: the Cromornes et Trompettes Marines served as a source of supplementary oboe and bassoon players.[42]

Besides their traditional duties, the ensembles of the Grande Écurie could be called upon for special occasions—to receive foreign dignitaries, to celebrate a military victory—for which they received extra pay.[43] Selected players from the Écurie

---

[38] Quoted in *Jean Baptiste Lully, Œuvres complètes,* ed. Henry Prunières (Paris, 1930–39), ii, "Notice."

[39] Haynes, *The Eloquent Oboe,* 49.

[40] Benoit, *Versailles,* 221–22.

[41] Haynes, *The Eloquent Oboe,* 53; Benoit, *Versailles,* 223 ff.

[42] Benoit, *Versailles,* 225–28.

[43] Ibid. 222, 227.

ensembles appeared in ballets and theatrical music at court, usually onstage and in costume.[44] Their members, like the Vingt-quatre Violons, also took on work outside of court. In 1658, for instance, six members of the Hautbois et Musettes de Poitou banded together to perform concerts around Paris.[45] Finally, the musicians of the Écurie served as a reservoir of wind players who could be added to the string ensembles of the Chambre to create combined ensembles that increasingly resembled orchestras.

Combined ensembles at court

For many years before Lully's time, the Vingt-quatre Violons, the lute, and keyboard players of the Chambre, and the various wind ensembles from the Écurie had been combined for special performances. In Rossi's *Orfeo* of 1640 the Vingt-quatre Violons, plus harpsichords, theorbos, lutes, and guitars all played together before the curtain was raised.[46] In 1650, when the King returned to Paris from a trip to Burgundy, he was greeted by "the King's hautbois, arrayed on the stairs of the palace . . . and the trumpets, who had marched in front of his Majesty, wedded their tones with the sound of the Vingt-quatre Violons, who were making a most agreeable harmony."[47] Here it seems as though oboes, trumpets, and violins, although assembled for the same event, are not playing together, but instead are playing different pieces in succession or perhaps even simultaneously.

When Lully took over as *Surintendant de la musique* in 1661, he increased the practice of combining the court ensembles in performance. Figure 3.1 shows the first day of *Les Plaisirs de l'isle enchantée*, a multi-day entertainment at Versailles in 1664. The instrumentalists, elaborately costumed, participate—along with elephants, dromedaries, and servants carrying plates piled high with food—in a tableau representing the four seasons. Three distinct ensembles are seen. On the left is an ensemble of lutes, guitars, and viols from the Chambre; in the center are 14 wind players from the Écurie; to the right is a 12-man violin band. Curiously, a written list of the performers contradicts the picture.[48] It says that the tableau was accompanied by a single large string band, composed of 20 Grands Violons plus 14 Petits Violons. The wind players, it says, accompanied a different tableau; the guitar and viol players are not mentioned at all.[49] On the next day, however, bowed and plucked strings were indeed combined—the picture and the lists agree. For a performance of Molière and Lully's *comédie-ballet, La Princesse d'Élide,* in a specially constructed open-air theater, 19

---

[44] Harris-Warrick, "Magnificence"; La Gorce, "Some Notes."   [45] Haynes, *The Eloquent Oboe*, 53.

[46] Hammond, "Orpheus," 118. See above, Ch. 1.   [47] Dufourcq, "En parcourant la 'Gazette,'" 192.

[48] Edmond Lemaître, "Les Sources des *Plaisirs de l'Isle enchantée*," *Revue de Musicologie,* 77 (1991), 187–200 at 197–98.

[49] Perhaps the artist, Israël Silvestre, has "telescoped" successive tableaux into a single picture. On "telescoping," see Ch. 4, n. 48, and Ch. 10, p. 345.

Premiere Journée.

FIG. 3.1. *Les Plaisirs de l'isle enchantée*, first day (1664)

Grands Violons, 11 Petits Violons, and six keyboards, lutes, and viols were placed together in a single box in front of the stage (Fig. 3.2).[50] In addition, eight wind players from the Écurie and eight members of the Petits Violons joined one another in an elaborate machine on the stage. The official description emphasizes how instruments of different sorts were combined:

During the dances there rises from beneath the stage the machine of a great tree with sixteen fauns in it, eight of whom play on the flute, and the others the violin, with the most agreeable concert in the world. Thirty violins answer them from the orchestra, with six other instruments—harpsichords and theorboes.[51]

The third and final day of the festivities featured an aquatic ballet accompanied by 20 Grands Violons, 19 Petits Violons, and 8 wind players, combined once again into a

[50] Lemaître, "Sources," 198–99.

[51] André Félibien, *Les Plaisirs de l'isle enchantée, ou, Les festes et divertissements du Roy à Versailles diviséz en trois journées et commencéz le 7me. jour de may de l'année 1664* (Paris, 1673), 79, 180–81.

FIG. 3.2. *Les Plaisirs de l'isle enchantée*, second day, Princesse d'Elide (1664)

single ensemble.[52] The pictures and documents from *Les Plaisirs de l'isle enchantée* show how Lully combined and coordinated all available ensembles in a magnificent entertainment. Winds, lutes, viols, and violins were joined in large, mixed ensembles, seated together and playing the same music.

Ten years later in 1674, to celebrate the conquest of the Franche-Comté, Louis XIV ordered another lavish entertainment at Versailles. For it Lully produced his opera *Alceste*, introduced earlier that year at the Opéra, along with a revival of Molière and Charpentier's *comédie-ballet*, *Le Malade imaginaire*. Now the integration of ensembles went even further. An engraving of the *Alceste* performance, outdoors in the Marble Courtyard, shows a large ensemble of bowed and plucked strings placed

[52] Lemaître, "Sources," 199–200. For a picture of this ensemble, see Neal Zaslaw, "Lully's Orchestra," in *J.-B. Lully, Actes du Colloque/Kongressbericht, 1987*, ed. Jérôme de La Gorce and Herbert Schneider (Heidelberg, 1990), 539–79 at 566.

in two boxes in front of the stage, not in costume but in livery (Fig. 3.3). At the stage apron a man with a short baton, presumably Lully, beats time for the singers and instrumentalists. Wind instruments are missing from the representation. The score to

Premiere Journée.

Alceste, Tragedie en musique, ornée d'entrées de Ballet, representée à Versailles dans la cour de marbre du Chasteau éclairé depuis le haut jusqu'en bas d'une infinité de lumieres.

Dies primus.

Alcestis Tragœdia, perpetuo cantu et variis Saltationibus decorata, in marmoreo Palatij Versaliarum cavaedio, undequaque facibus accensis illuminati, acta.

FIG. 3.3. Lully's *Alceste* performed in the Marble Courtyard at Versailles, 1674, and details of the instrumentalists

Alceste calls for flutes, oboes, trumpets, and drums, but perhaps they appeared on stage rather than being placed with the other instruments.[53] The engraving of the *Malade imaginaire* (Fig. 3.4) does show wind instruments: an oboist and two flutists can be discerned just below the armed guard to the left of the stage. Here the ensemble, about 40 strong, has been consolidated into a single box. In the center stands a timebeater (Charpentier?) with both arms raised.[54] Strings, winds, and continuo are combined in a single ensemble, led by a single director, playing a single piece of music. This looks, and perhaps it sounded, a lot like an orchestra. In Lully's and Charpentier's scores the bowed strings play for overtures, dances, and choruses, and they occasionally accompany the singers in airs and récits as well. In one comic scene from the first Intermède in *Le Malade imaginaire* the violins engage in a running battle with Pulcinello, interrupting him as he tries to sing a serenade.

FIG. 3.4. *Le Malade imaginaire* (Molière/Charpentier), Versailles, 1674

[53] See Harris-Warrick, "Magnificence," 191.

[54] A third picture from the festivities of 1674, a concert in the gardens of the Trianon palace, depicts bowed strings in two tribunes to the left, and to the right an oboe and two flutes in a tribune and lute, harpsichord, and a female singer in another, and again a timebeater. See Zaslaw, "Lully's Orchestra," 553–55.

Even larger numbers of instrumentalists were assembled for the *Triomphe de l'Amour*, a ballet given in the newly built Salle de Comédie at Saint-Germain-en-Laye in 1681 to celebrate the marriage of the dauphin. A provisioner hired to supply food and drink at rehearsals sent the court an invoice in which he named everyone involved in the production—a cast of nearly 150 persons, including 76 instrumental-ists.[55] Nine keyboard and plucked string players from the Chambre are listed as "Musitiens," along with a larger number of singers. Then come the Vingt-cinq Grands Violons du Roy and 22 Petits Violons du roy, plus two porters to transport the instruments. Finally, 21 wind players from the Écurie are listed as "Fluttes et aulbois." Most likely the Petits and Grands Violons played together in a single ensem-ble, perhaps with the addition of some of the winds. Keyboards and plucked strings probably constituted a separate ensemble for vocal accompaniment. The organiza-tion of the provisioner's bill makes it clear that Lully's instrumental forces in the *Triomphe de l'Amour* were still conceived as four separate groups, temporarily com-bined for a lavish entertainment.

The orchestra of the Opéra

Under the patronage of Giulio Mazzarini, who as Jules Mazarin became a French car-dinal and government minister, seven Italian operas were produced in Paris between 1645 and 1662. All of them used instrumentalists from the existing court ensembles. For Rossi's *Orfeo* in 1647 the Vingt-quatre Violons were pressed into service, along with theorbos and lutes from the Chambre and trumpets and drums from the Écurie. The Petits Violons probably performed in Cavalli's *Serse* at the Louvre in 1660, because the overture and six ballets were by Lully. For Cavalli's *Ercole amante* in 1662 Lully composed spectacular ballets at the ends of the acts in which members of the nobility danced. Both Grands and Petits Violons were probably involved, as well as continuo players from the Chambre and wind players from the Écurie.

Alongside these Italian operas, several operas and opera-like entertainments sung entirely in French were staged between 1647 and 1661. The most successful of these were by the poet Pierre Perrin and the composer Robert Cambert. The instrumen-tal requirements of Perrin and Cambert's operas seem to have been modest compared with Mazarin's Italian extravaganzas. Their first collaboration, entitled *Pastorale*, pre-miered at a country estate in Issy, near Paris, and was then performed for the King at Vincennes in April 1659.[56] The music is lost, but the *livret* says that each of the five acts opened and closed with an instrumental *symphonie* and that short instrumental *ritournelles* linked the scenes.[57] Since it was staged outside Paris and did not have

---

[55] André Tessier, "Un Document sur les répétitions du *Triomphe de l'Amour*," in *Actes du Congrès d'Histoire de l'art, Paris, 26 Sept.–5 Oct. 1921*, iii (Paris, 1924), 874–94; La Gorce, "Some Notes."

[56] Anthony, *French Baroque Music*, 86.

[57] Louis E. Auld, *The Lyric Art of Pierre Perrin, Founder of French Opera* (Henryville, Pa., 1986), iii. 82.

ballets, the little opera probably used a small instrumental ensemble and did not involve the court musicians. For their next opera, *Ariane, ou le mariage de Bacchus*, commissioned in 1659 by Mazarin, Perrin and Cambert envisioned more ambitious instrumental resources. The *livret* says that Acts I and III should be introduced by "a symphony of stringed instruments," Act II by a ensemble of musettes, Act IV by a band of oboes, and Act V by a "grand symphony of violins."[58] Perhaps Perrin and Cambert believed they could obtain the services of the Vingt-quatre Violons, the Hautbois et Musettes de Poitou, and the Douze Grands Hautbois for their opera. However, Mazarin's death and chaos in the company's affairs caused the enterprise to collapse before the opera could be performed.[59]

In 1669 Perrin and Cambert obtained a royal privilege to found an Académie Royale de Musique, which would establish a repertory company and produce French operas on a regular basis. The privilege gave them permission to hire singers and actors and to purchase stage machinery and costumes, but it did not mention instrumentalists.[60] Clearly, however, an instrumental ensemble was involved in the enterprise. *Pomone*, the Academy's first production in March 1671, and *Les Peines et les plaisirs de l'amour* (January–February 1672), its second, require continuo accompaniment for the airs and *récits*, plus a four-part string band for overtures and dance music. Wind instruments are specified for the *ritournelles* of a few numbers. Although the Academy enjoyed a royal privilege and royal support, it probably did not use either of the King's string bands. Both the Petits Violons and the Grande Bande were controlled by Lully, who kept them busy with the *comédie-ballets* that he and Molière were staging at court.[61] Besides, Cambert's four-part scoring indicates that he was not writing for the court ensembles, both of which divided the strings into five parts. Very likely he recruited modest-sized ensembles from the ranks of the Confrérie de St-Julien and instrumentalists who played in the Paris theaters.

Les Peines et les plaisirs de l'amour looked set for a long run when general mismanagement, including embezzlement by the director, Sablières, threatened the whole enterprise with financial ruin. On 1 April 1672, the Académie Royale de Musique was closed by royal edict. Lully purchased the privilege from its former owners, and Louis XIV issued a new royal privilege, which tried to fix the Academy's problems by strengthening its monopoly. Lully was given exclusive rights to produce sung plays, in French or in any other language, and to charge for admission. The new privilege

---

[58] Ibid. 100 and *passim*.

[59] *Ariane* was revived and put into rehearsal in 1669–70 for the Académie de Musique, but again not performed. It finally reached the stage in London in 1674 in a third version, with additional music (or perhaps entirely new music) by Louis Grabu. See Ch. 8; also Christina Bashford, "Perrin and Cambert's *Ariane, ou Le Mariage de Bacchus* Re-examined," *M & L* 72 (1991), 1–26, and J. S. Powell, *Music and Theatre*, 46.

[60] Benoit, *Musiques de cour*, 24.

[61] Performances of Molière and Lully's *comédie-ballets* in the public theaters did not use the court ensembles either. *La Princesse d'Élide* in 1664, which had been performed with a large ensemble at Versailles (Fig. 3.2), was given at the Palais-Royal Theater that same year with an ensemble of eight strings, three oboes, and continuo (Powell, *Music and Theatre*, 37).

explicitly recognized the importance of instrumental music to opera: "To make this enterprise a success we entrust its management to a person whose experience and abilities are well known to us and who has the resources to train pupils in dancing and acting and also to assemble bands of violins, flutes, and other instruments . . ."[62] When Molière, who was now working with Marc-Antoine Charpentier rather than Lully, hired an ensemble of 12 violins for *comédie-ballets* at the Palais-Royal Theater, the King issued yet another *ordonnance*.[63] This one gave Lully exclusive rights to use large instrumental ensembles in the theater:

His Majesty has been informed that the permission he had given actors to make use of up to six singers and up to 12 violins or other instrumentalists threatens to inhibit the success of the-atrical works by Sr. Jean-Baptiste de Lully . . . His Majesty therefore revokes the permission he had formerly given to these actors . . . and henceforth allows them to have only two singers and six violins or other instrumentalists. His Majesty expressly forbids all troupes of actors, French or foreign . . . to make use of supernumerary singers or a greater number of violins in the entr'actes, or any additional dancers, or to have any orchestra [*orquestre*] whatsoever, under penalty of law.[64]

This amounted to a monopoly not just over sung entertainment but over orchestras and orchestral music in the theater. The monopoly over the orchestra was a vital component of Lully's success at the Opéra, and he defended it fiercely and for the most part effectively. Other Parisian theaters could hire a handful of instrumentalists to accompany the singers and entertain the audience between the acts, but only Lully had an orchestra. In provincial cities impresarios were allowed to put on operas and ballets with orchestral accompaniment, but they were required to pay Lully a signif-icant fee for permission.

The same privilege that gave Lully control of the Académie Royale de Musique forbade him to use the Vingt-quatre Violons or other court musical ensembles at the Opéra. "We grant him permission," the King's decree said, ". . . to present to the pub-lic all the works that he shall compose, even those which have been performed for Us [at court]; but in the performance of such pieces, he may not make use of musicians who are in our employ . . ."[65] This clause guaranteed that the King could command the services of his own musicians whenever and wherever he pleased. Its consequence was that Lully was obliged to create a new orchestra for the Opéra. Presumably he recruited his instrumentalists from the ranks of the Confrérie St-Julien, as well as among the sons and nephews of court musicians. Whatever difficulties this may have

---

[62] Pierre Mélèse, *Le Théâtre et le public à Paris sous Louis XIV, 1659–1715* (Paris, 1934), 415.

[63] Catherine Cessac, *Marc-Antoine Charpentier*, 1988, trans. E. Thomas Glasow (Portland, Ore., 1995), 50–56.

[64] Mélèse, *Le Théâtre et le public*, 417–18.

[65] Ibid. 416. The prohibition against double employment remained in force until the 1690s when Mme de Maintenon persuaded Louis XIV to allow her to use court musicians for theatrical productions at the girls' school in Saint-Cyr, near Versailles (Anne Piéjus, *Le Théâtre des demoiselles: Tragédie et musique à Saint-Cyr à la fin du grand siècle* (Paris, 2000), 590). By 1704 several court musicians played in the Opéra orchestra.

caused Lully in the beginning, it proved an advantage in the long run. The Opéra orchestra combined strings, harpsichord, theorbos, and winds on the same payroll for the first time. Unlike the court instrumentalists, who were divided into administratively distinct bands, the players at the Opéra were organized as a standing ensemble with invariant forces. Players did not hold offices but rather positions, which they earned by audition and appointment rather than by purchase.[66] With fixed personnel and a single composer-director, the Opéra orchestra could function in a more integrated and consistent manner than the fiefdoms and kaleidoscopic arrangements among the several groups of court musicians had previously allowed.

Surprisingly little information has survived about the makeup of the Opéra orchestra during Lully's lifetime. Since the instrumentalists did not hold offices and were not on the royal payroll, they did not leave as many bureaucratic traces as the court musicians. In 1704, however, the faltering Opéra was reorganized under royal supervision, and the legal documents thus generated include a list of musicians, their instruments, and their salaries.[67] Because the Opéra had experienced a period of stagnation after Lully's death in 1687, this list probably gives a reasonable idea of what the orchestra was like at the end of his tenure:

> Orquestre
> M[rs] du petit choeur
>   1 [batteur de mesure]
>   1 [clavecin]
>   2 [theorbes]
>   2 [dessus de violon]
>   2 [basses de violon]
>   2 [basses de viole]
>
> Mrs Les Fluttes
>   2 Hautbois et flûtes
>   2 Flûtes allemandes
>   2 [Flutes, hautbois, bassoon]
>   2 Bassons
>
> [Grand choeur]
>   9 Mrs Les Dessus [de violon]
>   3 Mrs Les Hautecontres
>   3 Mrs Les Tailles
>   2 Mrs Les Quintes
>   8 Mrs Les Basses [de violon]

[66] According to Le Cerf, the piece that Lully used to audition players for the Opéra orchestra was the "Entrée des songes funestes" from *Atys* (Le Cerf, *Comparaison*, 209). The passage, which features dotted notes and tirades in all the parts, is given as Ex. 13.13 below.

[67] Jérôme de La Gorce, "L'Académie royale de Musique en 1704, d'après de documents inédits conservés dans les archives notariales," *Revue de musicologie*, 65 (1979), 160–91. The following list is adapted from this source.

The 42 instrumentalists plus a conductor (*batteur de mesure*) would have been the largest standing orchestra in Europe in the 1680s—indeed, it was still the largest in 1704.

The 1704 list shows that although the Opéra orchestra was a single administrative entity, it was subdivided into two groups reflecting its performance practice: a *grand choeur*, consisting of a large number of stringed instruments of all sizes plus oboes and bassoons, and a *petit choeur*, which filled the double function of continuo group and concertino. This division into large and small "choirs" was a way of dealing with the differing requirements of vocal and dance music. The *petit choeur* accompanied solo vocalists in recitatives, *récits*, and airs, while the *grand choeur* accompanied choral numbers and played overtures, *ritournelles*, *symphonies*, and the dance music that Lully introduced into each act of every opera. The divisions in the list seem to represent vestiges of the court organization: the *petit choeur* corresponds to the keyboards, lutes, and viols of the Chambre, the *grand choeur* to the Grands and Petits Violons, while "Messieurs Les Fluttes" are the heirs of the Écurie. Drum parts were played by one of the violinists, but who played trumpet remains something of a mystery.

Lully's opera orchestra was not exactly a novelty. Large numbers of bowed strings, winds, and continuo instruments had already played together for more than a century—in the final scenes of intermedii and masques, in festival productions of Italian operas, in Lully's own extravaganzas at the French court. But all of these were one-of-a-kind productions, which took administratively and musically distinct ensembles, combined them for a few gala performances, and then sent them on their separate ways. The orchestra of the Opéra was the first large, integrated, standing orchestra under a single administration and a single leadership.

SCORING AND INSTRUMENTATION

Contracts of association between Parisian string players in the late sixteenth century document a transition from ensembles in which players were assigned to four parts (*dessus, haute-contre, taille,* and *basse*) to ensembles that included players for a fifth part (designated *quinte*).[68] In 1636 Marin Mersenne described the French string scoring. The upper part, the *dessus*, was played by violins. The three middle parts, *haute-contre, taille,* and *quinte*, were played by small, medium-sized, and large violas, tuned in unison with *c* as their lowest note, like modern violas.[69] The *basse* part was played by an 8-foot instrument somewhat larger than a modern cello and tuned a whole step

---

[68] Lesure, "Les Orchestres populaires," 51–52.

[69] Mersenne claimed that the Vingt-quatre Violons named the middle parts differently from regular ensembles, calling the one played by the smallest viola the *quinte*, the next *haute-contre*, and the lowest part *taille* (*Harmonie universelle*, iii. 189). By Lully's time Mersenne's "regular" terminology prevailed everywhere.

lower.[70] The Vingt-quatre Violons distributed themselves almost evenly across the five parts, with extra players on the *dessus* and *basse* parts, and a total of 12 violas in the middle (see Table 3.1). This distribution still obtained in the middle of the century, when Lully took over the Vingt-quatre. The balance of players on parts in the Petits Violons and the orchestra of the Opéra in Lully's time is not known. By the 1690s and 1700s the balances in all three ensembles had shifted toward slightly more polarized textures, with extra violins on the *dessus* part and fewer violas in the middle.

Le Cerf de la Viéville claimed—and other authors have repeated—that Lully composed only the *dessus* and *basse* parts, leaving the three *parties de remplissage* (the middle voices) to his assistants.[71] It is difficult to know how to interpret this. In the early stages of his career Lully would not have had assistants at his beck and call, and furthermore, according to Charles Perrault, Lully had actually made the inner parts a bit of a specialty:

Before him people cared only about the melody in the treble part, while the bass line and inner parts were mere accompaniment and a rough sort of counterpoint, which the players on those parts most often improvised in performance. . . . M. Lully made all the inner parts sing almost as agreeably as the treble; he inserted into those parts admirable fugal passages, and especially some completely novel tempos and rhythms previously unknown to most composers.[72]

Perrault's description contradicts Le Cerf's claim that Lully farmed out the writing of his inner parts and suggests that unlike earlier composers who wrote music for the Vingt-quatre Violons, Lully actually wrote out all five parts himself. Given his reported abhorrence of free ornamentation, this is believable.

For the works he staged at court, Lully could potentially draw wind players from any or all five of the ensembles in the Écurie. Most often he called on the services of the Douze Grands Hautbois to play double reed parts and the Hautbois et Musettes de Poitou to play recorders and transverse flutes. These ensembles performed sometimes alone, sometimes in alternation with the string band, sometimes doubling the strings. As the violins were divided into five parts, the Grands Hautbois were divided into four, played by instruments of different sizes. The instruments on the top and bottom parts—dessus de hautbois and basse de hautbois—may be considered early forms of the oboe and bassoon. The middle parts were played by what might be described as alto and tenor oboes, designated haute-contre and taille de hautbois.[73] A few numbers in Lully's ballets and operas are scored in four parts and designated "pour les hautbois."[74] He occasionally scored for flutes too as a four-part ensemble. The

---

[70] Jürgen Eppelsheim, *Das Orchester in den Werken Jean-Baptiste Lullys* (Tutzing, 1961), 40–41.

[71] Le Cerf, *Comparaison*, ii. 119; Eppelsheim, *Das Orchester*, 40–41.

[72] Perrault, *Les Hommes illustres*, 181. See also Le Cerf, *Comparaison*, ii. 119.

[73] Rebecca Harris-Warrick, "A Few Thoughts on Lully's *Hautbois*," *EM* 18 (1990), 97–106 at 102 ff.; Haynes, *The Eloquent Oboe*, 373 ff. The haute-contre de hautbois was pitched in A, the taille de hautbois in F. Haynes also mentions a five-part double reed scoring (p. 60).

[74] "Marche de Hautbois pour le Dieu Pan" in *Les Plaisirs de l'Isle enchantée* (1664); "Symphonie pour les hautbois et les musettes" in *Festes de l'Amour et de Bacchus* (1672).

parts for the "Concert de flustes" that accompanies a dance of cherubs in *Les Amours déguisés* (1664) are designated *dessus, haute-contre, taille*, and *basse de flûte*, that is alto, tenor, bass, and contrabass recorders.[75] In the "Prélude pour l'Amour" from *Le Triomphe de l'Amour* (1681), the upper part is taken by a transverse flute (flûte d'Allemagne), the lower three parts by recorders.

To create contrast with the five-part texture Lully often reduces his scoring to a trio of two *dessus* and *basse*. The two *dessus* usually share the same range and have similar melodic material, although imitation is rare. The *basse* part tends to be considerably slower, more like a continuo part than the bass in five-part texture. Sometimes Lully scores an entire movement in reduced texture; sometimes he alternates within a movement between five- and three-part textures. How these trios were executed is not entirely clear. It seems as though the parts could have been rendered by strings, by winds, or by both together. And they could have been doubled or played one on a part, like the concertino in Italian string music of the same period.[76] In a single instance Lully used a solo violin in alternation with five-part scoring, namely in the *Ballet des muses*, where he himself played a violin solo to represent Orpheus' lyre (see above, Ex. 1.2).

Lully's most common trio scoring for winds, and one that remained popular well into the eighteenth century, is two oboes and bassoon, perhaps doubled, perhaps not. For a flute trio he could put either two alto recorders or two transverse flutes on the *dessus* parts; for the bass part it seems that he used a viola da gamba or basse de violon or perhaps a theorbo.[77] The *livret* to *Atys* (1676) says that the trio passages in the famous "Sommeil" scene in Act III were played by six recorders, three on each of the *dessus* parts.[78] Surviving performance materials from Lully's operas suggest that oboes or recorders sometimes played along with the *dessus de violon* part, even though this was not explicitly indicated in the score.[79] Bassoons played along on the *basse* part in the same fashion, while the three parts in the middle were left to the violas. This added double-reed sonority to the sound of the string band and tended to emphasize the outer voices above the inner. Over the course of Lully's works, there seems to be a trend away from four-part wind-band textures toward wind-trio textures. Partly this may have been due to the decline in popularity of flutes and oboes in the *haute contre* and *taille* registers. It may also have been a concession to Italian trio-sonata textures.

Lully is often given credit for introducing new "Baroque" woodwind instruments into the orchestra. This notion can be traced in part to a statement by the flutist Michel de la Barre, who, half a century after Lully's death, wrote:

[75] Eppelsheim, *Das Orchester*, 89 ff.; Jean-Baptiste Lully, *Ballet des Saisons, Les Amours déguisés, Ballet royal de Flore*, ed. Rebecca Harris-Warrick (Œuvres Complètes, 1/vi (Hildesheim, 2001)), pp. xxxiv, 134.

[76] Caroline Wood, *Music and Drama in the* Tragédie en Musique*, 1673–1715: Jean-Baptiste Lully and his Successors* (New York, 1996), 173. Occasionally the concertino in Italian concerti grossi was performed with two players on a part. See Ch. 4.

[77] See Eppelsheim, *Das Orchester*, 200 ff. For an instance of flute trio scoring, see Ex. 13.39.

[78] Anthony, *French Baroque Music*, 127.   [79] Eppelsheim, *Das Orchester*, 197–98.

His rise to power caused the utter downfall of all the old instruments except for the oboe—thanks to the labors of the Philidors and the Hotteterres, who whittled away at their wood and practiced their instruments until they had succeeded in rendering them suitable for use in ensembles.[80]

But certain "old instruments" like cornetts and sackbuts had disappeared from all but religious music before Lully arrived in France, whereas others, like recorders, remained in use throughout his career.[81] Still, as La Barre correctly stated, double-reed instruments did undergo significant design changes. The Philidors and Hotteterres were families of wind players, instrument makers, and composers, several generations of whom were members of the Douze Grands Hautbois. No instruments have survived from Lully's lifetime that can be attributed to members of either family, but iconographical evidence suggests that the external form and playing characteristics of French oboe-family instruments changed considerably during the seventeenth century.

In the 1630s and 1640s hautbois were shawm-like instruments constructed from a single piece of wood, with a broad reed that the player placed inside his mouth, not between his lips. By the end of the century they were oboe-like instruments, divided at three joints, with two or three keys, and with a narrower reed that the player controlled with his lips. This transition from shawm to "Baroque oboe" probably began before Lully came to power. Already in Mersenne's day, shawms were being built with keys, and players were putting their lips on their reeds. And the transition was not complete by the time Lully died. The earliest descriptions of three-joint, prototypical Baroque oboes date from 1688, the year after his death.[82] "Baroque" recorders, flutes, oboes, and bassoons resulted from decades of changes in the instruments and the way they were played by many instrumentalists, not all of them located in Paris or Versailles.

Bruce Haynes has noticed something interesting about the chronology of hautbois parts in Lully's works: at almost the exact moment that Lully became *Surintendant*, he stopped calling for oboes in his ballets and dramatic works.[83] He continued to score for flutes (recorders), but for the double-reed ensemble all he composed were some *Trios pour le coucher du Roy*.[84] When he resumed writing hautbois parts in his dramatic works, with *Le Bourgeois gentilhomme* in 1670, Lully began to coordinate his double reeds more closely with the string ensemble, and he began to score more often for winds in trio texture. Haynes speculates that the hiatus in Lully's use of the oboe was designed to give the players in the Écurie a "grace period," during which they

---

[80] Quoted in Bruce Haynes, "Lully and the Rise of the Oboe as Seen in Works of Art," *EM* 16 (1988), 324–38 at 324.

[81] The only instrument whose use declined at the French court during the Lully period was the basse de cromorne, which was gradually replaced by the bassoon.

[82] Haynes, "Lully," 325, 330; id., *The Eloquent Oboe*, 12 ff., 121–23.

[83] Haynes, *The Eloquent Oboe*, 56.   [84] Also called *Trios de la chambre* (LWV 35).

worked out reeds, fingerings, and playing techniques on their new instruments. No documentary or material evidence supports this theory, but it fits well with the contemporary perception of a revolution in instrument design at the French court.

Lully does deserve credit in any case for integrating the wind instruments into the string orchestra. Before he asssumed control of the royal musical establishment, the winds almost always performed as a distinct and self-contained band—at the King's supper, at outdoor events, or in the *ballets de cour*. Lully, too, began by using the winds as a separate band, for example in the *Ballet de l'amour malade* (1657), where the groom at a peasant wedding in the last entrée dances to the sound of a "country band [*concert champêtre*]" of hautbois. Soon, however, he began to find new ways to combine winds and strings. In the *symphonie* at the beginning of *Les Amours déguisés* (1664) wind and string bands engage at closer quarters: a four-part flute ensemble accompanying the "Graces and Pleasures" alternates with a five-part string band that accompanies the "Arts and Virtues."[85] In *Alceste* (1674) oboes and strings are combined into a single band and play in unison, the oboes marked *fort*, the violins *doux*.[86] In the "Sommeil" of *Atys* (1676) Lully alternates and combines recorders and violins: sometimes a recorder trio, sometimes five-part violins, sometimes recorders and violins together.[87] In *Persée* (1682) he writes several passages in the *passacaille* for oboes, flutes, and violins, all playing at the same time.[88]

Scorings like these were new and in a sense experimental. Between 1672 to 1687 Lully had the orchestra of the Opéra at his disposal, the same instruments and the same players, both strings and winds, year after year. The availability and stability of instruments and personnel allowed him to try new combinations, new textures, and new effects. He experimented with combinations of strings and winds as described above.[89] He experimented with reduced scorings, especially trio textures, but also some four-part textures and textures in which the violas take over the bass line.[90] He also experimented with combinations of instruments and voices, in which the orchestra continued to play while a soloist sang recitatives and airs. Occasionally he allowed five-part strings to accompany a solo voice.[91] But more often he lowered the volume of the orchestra in such passages by reducing the texture to a string trio, played sometimes by the members of the *petit choeur*, sometimes by all the violins and basses. He even experimented with passages in which winds provided vocal accompaniment, for example the pair of flutes that accompany the end of the "Sommeil" scene in *Atys* (1676), or the trio of oboes that plays as Proteus sings in *Phaëton* (1683).[92]

[85] Lully, *Ballet des Saisons*, etc., 77 ff., 306–7.   [86] See Ex. 13.29.   [87] Act IV, scene i.
[88] Act V, scene viii.
[89] Lully also experimented with combinations of trumpets and strings. See Ch. 13.
[90] In the passacaille from *Persée* (Act V, scene viii), where the violins, oboes, flutes double on two *dessus* parts, a note in the score reads: "the *hautes contres* and the *quintes* should play the bass in the trio passages."
[91] Examples of five-part strings accompanying solo singers: *Bellérophon*, Act II, scene vi; *Armide*, Act III, scene iv; *Phaëton*, Act III, scene ii.
[92] *Atys*, Act III, scene iv; *Phaëton*, Act I, scene v.

For Lully the orchestra of the Opéra must have been something like a laboratory, in which he could try out increasingly adventurous orchestral combinations. And he may not have been the only experimenter: perhaps the players in the Opéra orchestra tried out new combinations and new sounds and brought their best discoveries to Lully for him to incorporate in his works.

PERFORMANCE PRACTICE

The year after Lully's death a tribute was published by Antoine Bauderon de Sénecé. In it the author imagines Lully arriving in the Elysian Fields and leading a group of musician-shades in a concert of his music:

One of the violinists of the late King [Louis XIII] joined the band and tried to call attention to himself above the others by playing a certain passage in his part with lots of variations and embellishments, imagining, in accordance with the taste of his time, that this was the most exquisite refinement of his art and that his performance practice would endow his playing with great elegance. Lully, losing all patience, picked up . . . the fattest stick he could find and fetched the fellow five or six blows about the ears. "You there!" he said, "Hit the road. Take your embellishments to a tavern—if there is a tavern in these parts—and let the barmaids dance to them. Don't come back to ruin the best harmonies of my instrumental music [*symphonie*] with your monkeyshines."[93]

This entertaining anecdote is a literary fiction, but its implications are clear: the string bands of the generation before Lully had ornamented their parts profusely; when Lully took over the Petite Bande and then the Vingt-quatre Violons, he suppressed improvised ornamentation and insisted that the musicians play only the written music.

There is little question that French string bands of the generations before Lully engaged in improvised ornamentation. In his *Harmonie universelle* of 1636 Mersenne published a Fantasia by Jean Henry the Younger (1560–1635), a member of the Vingt-quatre Violons. All five parts are fully notated, and alongside the text of the Fantasia, Mersenne included diminutions for the *dessus*, "so that you can see the way in which violinists are accustomed to ornament all kinds of melodies."[94] To modern eyes and ears Henry's elaborate paraphrase of the melodic line may seem appropriate only for a soloist, yet Mersenne is clearly talking about the performance practices of the Vingt-quatre Violons. The explanation of this apparent contradiction may lie in a kind of heterophony in which a melody is heard simultaneously ornamented and plain.[95] Michael Praetorius, who arranged and published music from the repertory of

---

[93] Antoine Bauderon de Sénecé, "Lettre de Clément Marot à M. de ★★★ touchant ce qui s'est passé à l'arrivée de Jean Baptiste de Lulli aux Champs Elysées (1688)," in *Œuvres choisies de Sénecé* (Paris, 1855), 299.

[94] Mersenne, *Harmonie universelle*, iii. 189.

[95] See John Spitzer and Neal Zaslaw, "Improvised Ornamentation in Eighteenth-Century Orchestras," *JAMS* 39 (1986), 524–77.

the Vingt-quatre Violons for performance in Germany, seems to be advocating this sort of playing in his *Syntagma Musicum* (1615). When several violinists play on the same part, says Praetorius, they must not all ornament at the same time "like a flock of sparrows," but should take turns embellishing the melody, "each awaiting his turn to show off his runs, trills, and ornaments."[96]

Lully, according to accounts published after his death, undertook to eliminate this sort of heterophony from his orchestra. Le Cerf de la Viéville paints a vivid picture of the process by which this was accomplished:

[Lully] had such an acute ear that from the back of the theater he picked out a violinist who played a wrong note, ran up to him and said, "You! That's not in your part." . . . The instrumentalists would never have taken it upon themselves to ornament their parts. [Lully] would not have allowed them to do this any more than he allowed it with his singers. He did not think it was right when they imagined they knew more than he did and added graces to the written music. When this happened, he grew angry and quickly set them straight.[97]

Michel Pignolet de Montéclair, who arrived in Paris in the year of Lully's death, gave an aesthetic justification for Lully's campaign to eliminate improvised ornamentation from performances by his ensembles:

The incomparable Lully, that superior genius, whose works will always be admired by true connoisseurs, preferred melody, beautiful modulation, pleasant harmony, accurate expression, naturalness, and noble simplicity to the absurdities of free ornamentation and heterophony [*musiques heteroclites*] . . .[98]

These latter-day anecdotes should be taken with a grain or two of salt. None of them dates from Lully's lifetime; all of them cast his music in an austere, classicizing light. The nearest thing to contemporary testimony is provided by the German composer Georg Muffat, who spent six years in Paris from 1663 to 1669 studying Lully's music and the French style. In the preface to his *Florilegium secundum* (1698), Muffat paints a rather different picture of the role of ornamentation in Lully's music. Ornaments, he says, are essential to the Lully style. They "enrich, soften, and enliven the music, creating activity in all the parts."[99] Muffat catalogues the musical situations in which the addition of ornaments is appropriate: when a melodic line descends by step, when the line rises by third, and so on. He makes it clear in his presentation that "Lullist" string players must know when and where to add these ornaments, whether or not they see a sign for an ornament in the music.

Muffat's testimony does not necessarily mean that Lully's musicians were playing improvised heterophony like violinists in the first half of the century. Lully rehearsed his operas extensively before they were performed in public, and one of the purpos-

[96] Michael Praetorius, *Syntagma Musicum* (Wolfenbüttel, 1619), ii. 148.
[97] Le Cerf, *Comparaison*, ii. 208–9.
[98] Michel Pignolet de Montéclair, *Principes de musique* (Paris, 1736), 86–87.
[99] Georg Muffat, *Florilegium secundum* (1698), ed. Heinrich Rietsch (Vienna, 1895), 49.

es of rehearsal may have been to coordinate the ornamentation added to each part. Le Cerf recounts an alarming anecdote about Lully's rehearsal techniques;

It is a true story that more than once in his life [Lully] broke a violin across the back of a musician who was not playing the way he wanted. When the rehearsal was finished, Lully summoned the violinist, paid him three times what his violin was worth, and took him to dinner. The wine dispelled the ill feelings. In this way Lully set an example [for the other musicians] while the violinist received some extra money, a meal, and a good warning.[100]

The theme of violence and its use to enforce correct performance practice runs through the literature of Lully anecdotes—the violinist beaten with a stick, the violin broken across a fiddler's back. These stories convey the same message as do the armed guards posted prominently in Figs. 3.1–3.4: the discipline and unanimity of orchestral performance, like the grandeur and magnificence of royal absolutism, can only be achieved and maintained by the threat of violence.

Besides the suppression of free ornamentation, Lully has been credited with other innovations in performance practice, including the *premier coup d'archet* and the "rule of the downbow," which enabled the entire orchestra to bow up and down in perfect agreement. But as Jean Denis's story of the melancholy wife shows, the *premier coup* was already a specialty of the Vingt-quatre Violons 15 or 20 years before Lully took control of the ensemble. Similarly, Mersenne in 1636 had already articulated the rule of the downbow:

one should always bow down on the first note of the measure and up on the following note. For example, if the measure contains eight eighth notes, one bows down on the first, third, fifth, and seventh and up on the second, fourth, sixth, and eighth, so that one bows down on the first note of every measure containing an even number of notes.[101]

If an ensemble follows this rule (along with a few modifications that Mersenne also explained), then all the string players on each part will bow their parts in unison. Uniform bowing, like the *premier coup*, seems to have been another performance practice of the Grande Bande that Lully adopted, generalized, and made the basis of his orchestral style.

In sum, it seems reasonable to suggest that Lully reformed and restrained the performance practices of the Vingt-quatre Violons and other string players at the French court. He did not, however, end ornamentation altogether, nor did he invent the *premier coup d'archet* or uniform bowing. What he did do was to refine and develop these practices and integrate them into a system of training and performance. He articulated the performance practices of French string bands as a set of rules and norms, inculcated them into the ensembles that he led at the French court and the Opéra, and turned them into an ideology of orchestral discipline that could be exported to other ensembles. The ideology behind his performance practices

---

[100] Le Cerf, *Comparaison*, ii. 208–9.   [101] Mersenne, *Harmonie universelle*, 185.

reflected the values of the French court and of autocratic absolutism in general. Under Lully's system the Vingt-quatre, the Petits Violons, and the orchestra of the Opéra became disciplined, hierarchical, polished ensembles, simulacra of a well-functioning autocratic society.

REPERTORY

Historical circumstances have conspired to make the music of the generation before Lully relatively inaccessible. What music does survive from the repertories of Parisian string bands prior to his time is mainly dance music, much of it composed for the *ballets de cour*, which were a central institution of court life under Louis XIII. Little of this music is transmitted in French sources. One reason for this may be that the string bands learned their music by heart, using scribbled staff or tablature notation as an aide-mémoire when necessary, but otherwise playing without music.[102] Another reason may have been the constant desire for fashionable new music: since much music became obsolete soon after it was first performed, there was little reason to preserve it. On the other hand, when French violinists traveled abroad and taught their music in other countries, the need for notation and preservation was stronger. Consequently, four foreign sources—manuscript anthologies from Kassel and Stockholm, and printed collections from Wolfenbüttel and Amsterdam—preserve at least some of the repertory of the French string bands in more or less authentic forms.[103]

Only two sources closer to Paris survive. The first is a volume from the large collection of French royal music assembled at the beginning of the eighteenth century by André Danican Philidor, the royal music librarian.[104] It contains music attributed to Louis Constantin (1619–55), Michel Mazuel (1643–76), and Lazarin (Lazzarini Salami, d. 1653), all members of the Vingt-quatre. As a witness to music of half a century or more earlier, Philidor's collection has problems. He sometimes edited or modernized notation, voice-leading, and harmony, supplied missing parts, and perhaps other features. The second Parisian source is a publication by the King's official music printer, Robert Ballard, entitled *Pièces pour le violon à 4 parties* (1665).[105] This

---

[102] See Lesure, "Les Orchestres populaires." Also see above, Ch. 2.

[103] Kassel: *Vingt suites d'orchestre du XVIIe siècle français*, ed. Jules Écorcheville (Paris, 1906); Amsterdam: *'T Uitnement Kabinet—Vol Paduanen, Allmanden, Sarbanden, Couranten, Balletten, Intraden, Airs &c . . . Amsterdam 1646, 1649*, ed. Rudi Rasch (Amsterdam, 1973–); Stockholm: *Seventeenth-Century Instrumental Dance Music*, ed. Mrácek; Wolfenbüttel: Michael Praetorius, *Terpsichore* (1612), ed. Günther Oberst (Wolfenbüttel, 1929). The Amsterdam source, which was intended for use by amateurs, omits two of the five parts. The Stockholm anthology had to be hypothetically rescored from a source written in German organ-tablature notation. Isolated pieces survive in a few other sources.

[104] See David Buch, *Dance Music from the Ballets de Cour, 1575–1651: Historical Commentary, Source Study, and Transcriptions from the Philidor Manuscripts* (Stuyvesant, NY, 1995).

[105] *Pièces pour le violon, à 4 parties, de differents autheurs, 1665*, ed. Martine Roche (Paris, 1971).

volume is nearly contemporaneous with the music it contains, but because it was intended for the use of amateurs and dilettantes, it may provide only an indirect view of the activities of the professional violin bands.

These six principal sources of French string-band music, most of it composed during the first half of the seventeenth century, contain a two-tiered repertory. Each source preserves some music unique to itself, often anonymous, which apparently originated in the immediate vicinity of the compiler of that particular anthology and which may be described as a local repertory. Each also preserves works found in more than one source, sometimes attributed to members of the Vingt-quatre Violons, which may be described as a common international repertory. This music seems to have been anthologized for use at balls, concerts, theaters, and as dinner music.

It would be hard to claim that this pre-Lully string-band repertory is "orchestral." Some of it may have been conceived with the idea of part doubling, some for single players on the parts, but no clear differentiation in style suggests which is which. The writing does not seem particularly idiomatic for the violin, and the works could, without difficulty or rearrangement, be played by wind instruments or mixed consorts of strings and winds. Indeed, accounts of *ballets de cour* and entertainments at foreign courts where these works were played describe wind instruments and bands of lutes playing dance music.[106]

Lully's early ballets share features with the music preserved in these anthologies of music that the Vingt-quatre played before he arrived at the French court. They are in five parts; the *dessus* carries the melody throughout; the textures tend to be non-imitative and homophonic; suspensions are rare; rhythms are contained within the bar lines. Like the dances of Constantin, Mazuel, and Henry, many of Lully's dances could be played by strings one on a part. Yet already there seem to be some orchestral features. Lully occasionally scores for a string trio as a contrast to the five-part texture, a scoring that is more effective when the full texture has several players on the parts. He also writes parts specifically for flutes and oboes, not only as separate ensembles, but occasionally mixed with the strings.

Another proto-orchestral feature in Lully's early ballets is the overture, in which the unanimity and the execution of the ensemble were displayed to the audience before the actors and dancers appeared. Opera overtures from Venice and elsewhere in Italy in the mid-seventeenth century frequently consisted of a slow section in duple meter followed by a faster section in triple meter. Lully used this binary, duple–triple layout in several of his early ballets, but starting with *Alcidiane* (1658) he began to develop a more elaborate structure.[107] In making the transition from Italy to France and from string band to orchestra, he standardized the style so that the first repeated section was always a stately march, prominently featuring dotted rhythms and ending

---

[106] Prunières, *Le Ballet de cour*; Bowles, *Musical Ensembles*.

[107] Henry Prunières, "Notes sur les origines de l'ouverture française," *Sammelbände der IMG*, 12 (1910–11), 565–85.

on a half cadence, while the second repeated section always began with a point of imitation in the dominant, beginning in the treble and echoed by each of the four other parts in fugal fashion (see below, Ex. 13.3). This seemingly unremarkable formulation, which later became known as the French overture, proved to have remarkable staying power and potential for further development. Several subsequent generations of composers in many European countries wrote overtures in Lully's style to preface church, chamber, and theater music, gradually expanding upon his pattern by means of greater length, sometimes adding a third section, employing more elaborate instrumentation, or introducing concertante elements.

It was not the style of the music alone that caused Lully's French overture to be so widely admired and imitated. The special mode of performance—a large orchestra suddenly beginning together and executing with precision the dotted rhythms and tirades of the first section and the points of imitation and carefully rehearsed ornaments of the second—made it sound much more impressive than a similar piece played one on a part. Evidently the style and the performance practice struck listeners as an innovation, because Vivaldi and other Italian composers labeled pieces featuring double dotting, tirades, and other written-in ornamentation as "alla francese," even when they lacked fugal sections (see below, Ex. 13.14).

After the overture, which was usually repeated as an entr'acte between the prologue and Act I, the opportunities for purely orchestral music were limited in a Lully opera. There were four more entr'actes played by the orchestra. There were also the three-part *ritournelles* (often labeled *préludes*) that introduced the first vocal item of the prologue and each act.[108] Lully wrote *ritournelles* in five parts only when the character introduced was a god or a king, like Juno descending from heaven in a cloud in Act II of *Isis* (1677) or the entrance of King Iobates in the prologue of *Bellérophon* (1679).

Perhaps Lully's most striking orchestral passages occur in the so-called *symphonies dramatiques*, in which the orchestra conveys in sound the spectacle that the audience sees on the stage.[109] In some of these "symphonies" he employed colors familiar from Renaissance intermedii and from festival operas, for example oboes to evoke pastoral settings, or trumpets and drums for warfare. But he also created more innovative orchestral textures. In the "Prélude pour la nuit" in *Le Triomphe de l'Amour* (1681) and in the "Sommeil" in Act II of *Armide* (1674) Lully has the string section play with mutes. In the Delphic oracle scene in Act III of *Bellérophon* (1679) he uses the orchestra to evoke wind, thunder, and an earthquake. In *Proserpine* (1680) he paints a picture of the Elysian Fields by doubling flutes and violins in an ethereal four-part texture.[110]

Lully's greatest international fame, however, was based on his dance music, found not only in his ballets but in the prologue and all five acts of his operas. In each act he

---

[108] Wood, *Music and Drama*, 173 ff.
[109] See Ch. 13 and Wood, *Music and Drama*, 285 ff.   [110] Act IV, Scene i.

and his librettist find a more or less plausible dramatic excuse for a *fête* or *divertissement*, in which a large cast sings and dances in a series of numbers. The dances are frequently organized in pairs, the first played by the large five-part ensemble with the winds doubling some of the string parts, the second by a trio of strings or winds. Many of these dances became classics and were disseminated to the far corners of Europe during Lully's lifetime and for several decades afterward, not only in their orchestral guise but in a wide variety of arrangements.

For French spectators and perhaps for European audiences in general it was the orchestral music—overtures, descriptive symphonies, and most of all dance music—that distinguished French opera from Italian. Writing in the 1670s, the French soldier and amateur musician Saint-Évremond commented on the mutual incomprehension of the Italians and the French for each other's operas:

The Italians, who interest themselves entirely in the action and in the particular care taken to convey things by words or gestures, cannot bear the fact that we will call "opera" a series of dances and instrumental numbers, which have neither a genuine connection to nor a tolerably natural link with the plot. The French, accustomed to the beauty of their overtures, to the agreeableness of their airs, to the charm of their orchestra [*symphonie*], endure with misery the ignorant or paltry employment of instruments in Venetian opera, and lose interest in lengthy recitative that becomes boring because it lacks any variety.[111]

Although opera in Germany and England tended to imitate Italian models rather than French, Lully's operas were occasionally performed outside the borders of France and the Low Countries in the seventeenth century. *Isis* was produced in Regensburg in 1683; *Psyché* was mounted in Wolfenbüttel and *Cadmus* in London in 1686. *Acis et Galathée* was produced at the court of Hesse-Darmstadt in 1687 and *Psyché* in Modena in the same year, sung in French with Italian interpolations. *Acis* was done in Hamburg in 1689, *Armide* in Rome (in Italian) in 1690, and so on.[112] Foreign cities and courts, however, generally lacked the large numbers of disciplined orchestral musicians and the highly trained dancers that Lully's operas required, and such performances remained exceptions.

Lully's orchestral music, nonetheless, was widely popular and influential outside of France, in arrangements. Overtures and dances were extracted from his ballets and operas, arranged into suites, disseminated around Europe, and performed wherever a string band could be assembled. Beginning in Lully's lifetime and increasingly in the decades immediately following his death, there was a steady trade in such suites, which circulated in various formats: in keyboard arrangements, intabulated for lute or guitar, arranged for one or two violins and basso continuo, as full sets of five manuscript parts issued by Parisian music-copying establishments, or as reduced arrangements of four

---

[111] Charles Saint-Évremond, *Sur les opéra*, in *Œuvres meslées*, xi (Paris, 1684), 96–98.

[112] See Carl B. Schmidt, *The Livrets of Jean-Baptiste Lully's* Tragédies Lyriques: *A Catalogue Raisonné* (New York, 1995).

printed parts published in Amsterdam.[113] Dozens of composers, many of whom had never been to Paris and had never seen a work by Lully staged, were kept busy writing such suites themselves. Suites of Lully's music and suites of French dances introduced by an overture in his manner became the first international repertory of orchestral music.

THE LULLY MYTH (2)

In all four areas considered in the preceding discussion—organization, instrumentation, performance practices, and repertory—the innovations in orchestras and orchestral practices attributed to Lully turn out to have predated him. The Vingt-quatre and the Petits Violons played large-ensemble music with several players on each part before Lully took them over. The wind instruments that Lully supposedly introduced into the orchestra were already in use before he arrived at the French court. Orchestral performance practices like the *premier coup d'archet* and the rule of the downbow were established among French string-band players already in the 1630s and 1640s. And some of the music of an earlier generation of string-band composers—Michel Henry, Louis Constantin, and Guillaume Dumanoir—had already been widely disseminated.

Triumphalist accounts of Lully's activities and accomplishments require a bit of qualification, it seems. While Lully was undoubtedly a "great" man, the great-man approach to writing history has distorted subsequent understanding of the nature and extent of his contribution to the history of the orchestra. He was certainly an innovator, but much more an organizer and synthesizer. He took ideas, instruments, performance practices, and musical styles that already existed and combined them in an institutional form. His synthesis was embodied in the orchestra of the Paris Opéra and in the repertory of orchestral music that it played. Lully also cemented the link between the orchestra and royal absolutism. Only a great prince like Louis XIV had the resources to sponsor an instrumental ensemble as large as Lully's orchestra, and that orchestra in turn reflected and broadcast the glory of the French monarch. Any foreign prince who wanted to imitate Louis XIV had to have an orchestra.

Given that the elements of the orchestra were already in place in the generation before Lully, what could have caused the historical amnesia by which the activities and achievements of Lully's predecessors were forgotten and their innovations attributed to him? We see four possible answers to this question. First, the great-man

---

[113] Herbert Schneider, "The Amsterdam Editions of Lully's Orchestral Suites," in Heyer (ed.), *Jean-Baptiste Lully . . . Essays in Honor of James Anthony*, 113–30; David Fuller, "Les Arrangements pour clavier des oeuvres de Lully," in *Jean-Baptiste Lully: Actes du colloque / Kongressbericht, Saint-Germain-en-Laye—Heidelberg 1987*, ed. Jérôme de La Gorce and Herbert Schneider (Heidelberg, 1990), 471–82; Monique Rollin, "Les Oeuvres de Lully transcrites pour le luth," ibid. 483–94.

narrative, with its associated cult of originality and genius, privileges a few leading figures, placing them in the spotlight and moving others into the shadows at the back of the stage. If Lully had not been the godfather of the orchestra, historians would have had to find another great man to fill the role. Second, the royalist propaganda machine during and after Louis XIV's lifetime extended to all aspects of courtly life and society. The regime's brilliant manipulation of its own image tended to make what had preceded it seem faint by comparison. Lully's power, not only over music at court but also over opera and theater music throughout France, emanated directly from the King, and his music in turn reflected the power of the King. Third, the elaborate bureaucracy that developed under Louis XIV left extensive records. It is much easier to document the activities of Lully and his musicians than those of his predecessors at the court of Louis XIII, whose careers and whose music have sunk into obscurity for lack of adequate documentation.

Fourth and finally, much more of Lully's music was preserved in written notation than the music of the men who composed for French string ensembles in the generation before his. In the musical culture of the Vingt-quatre Violons and the Confrérie St-Julien scores were virtually unknown. The guild fiddlers were required to learn their music by heart. Once a piece had been memorized and was being used as the basis for improvised group performance, the written parts were no longer needed. And as musical styles changed, older music tended to be discarded and forgotten. At the end of the seventeenth century, perhaps in homage to French musicians of the past, perhaps as an act of royalist piety, one of the King's musicians, André Danican Philidor, undertook the ambitious project of collecting and preserving the court's vanishing musical repertories. Into a series of nearly 50 thick folio volumes he copied all the French court music of the sixteenth and seventeenth centuries that he could locate, creating a monumental historical anthology. In its original form this collection included two volumes containing music for court ballets danced between 1582 and 1649, which are still extant, plus three volumes containing dances and other compositions composed by more than three dozen members of the Vingt-quatre Violons and dating mainly from the first half of the seventeenth century. In the late 1820s, however, an assistant librarian at the Paris Conservatoire, thinking perhaps that the music and the composers of these old ballets de cour were so obscure that no one would notice their absence, dismembered two of the three volumes and sold their deluxe paper and bindings for his own profit.[114] He was apprehended and prevented from embarking on further acts of vandalism, but the music was forever lost.

---

[114] François-Joseph Fétis, "Notice d'une collection manuscrite d'ancienne musique française, recueillie par Michel Danican Philidor, en 1690," *Revue musicale*, 1/2 (1829), 9–13 at 12.

Chapter Four

Corelli's Orchestra

Rome in the seventeenth century resembled Paris in several respects. Like Paris, it was a capital city. The Pope ruled as temporal and absolute sovereign over the Papal States, stretching from Rome and the Campagna across the Apennines to Bologna and on to the Adriatic. In addition, Rome functioned as the capital and administrative center for the worldwide operations of the Catholic Church. Rome, like Paris, was a magnet for wealth. Money flowed into the papal coffers from taxes and duties within the Papal States and also from the sale of ecclesiastical offices and papal dispensations.[1] Besides the income of the Pope, money came to Rome from the religious orders, whose headquarters were located in the city, and from foreign countries that maintained embassies there. The cardinals, most of them drawn from the Italian nobility and almost all of them living in Rome, were entrusted with the upper administrative positions in the Papal Curia and played the role of courtiers at the papal court.[2] Local landed gentry and foreign dignitaries also swelled the ranks of the aristocracy. Rome in the seventeenth century, like Paris, had become the site of an aristocratic culture, centralized in a capital city under autocratic rule.

Differences between seventeenth-century Rome and Paris were also significant. In Paris there was essentially a single patron, the King. He or his ministers sponsored and paid for a great part of the theater, dance, painting, music, and literature in Paris. The Popes did not maintain this kind of cultural monopoly. They sponsored painting, architecture, devotional literature, and vocal music, but they avoided arts that were perceived as excessively secular, like theater, dance, and instrumental music. In addition, the succession to the papacy by election rather than by inheritance meant that several Italian families nurtured papal ambitions and maintained papal pretensions

---

[1] Jean Delumeau, *Rome au XVIe siècle* (Paris, 1975), 189 ff.
[2] Laurie Nussdorfer, *Civic Politics in the Rome of Urban VIII* (Princeton, 1992), 41–43.

during the seventeenth century. Consequently, patronage in Rome was more diffuse than in Paris. Wealthy, ambitious cardinals competed with one another to sponsor literature, architecture, art, and music. Foreign legates sought to advance the interests of their governments by cultural as well as political means.[3] Churches and charitable foundations, many with substantial endowments, constituted further centers of patronage for the arts.[4]

These differences between the character of patronage in Rome and in Paris led Roman orchestras toward organizational forms quite different from the Vingt-quatre Violons du Roy and musical results different from Lully's ballets and operas. Whereas in Paris the orchestra came into being as a "court orchestra," a part of the royal household, the Roman orchestra developed in the context of a city-wide market for instrumentalists and instrumental music. The Popes' hostility to secular entertainments meant that resources that in Paris went into opera and ballet, in Rome were funneled into cantatas, oratorios, and instrumental music.[5] Because of the diffuseness of patronage in Rome, instrumentalists could find work in many venues for many employers.[6] Roman churches often kept a pair of violinists and a bass player on the payroll to play at Mass and Vespers; for feast days and special occasions they hired additional string players. Other instrumentalists found positions in the households of cardinals, foreign dignitaries, or Roman nobility. Thus, a pool of instrumentalists formed in Rome over the course of the seventeenth century, performing in a variety of contexts for a variety of patrons.

ROMAN ENSEMBLES BEFORE CORELLI

Instrumental ensembles in Rome did not look much like orchestras until the last three decades of the seventeenth century. Although violin-family instruments became more common over the course of the century, they were not organized into large ensembles with several on a part but into multiple choirs with singers and instrumentalists one on a part (see Ch. 2). However, beginning around mid-century four new trends began to manifest themselves: instrumental ensembles got larger; they were dominated increasingly by violin-family instruments; instrumentalists separated themselves from singers; and multiple choirs were consolidated into unitary groupings.

The growth in size and the increasing importance of bowed strings can be traced in the ensembles for the annual Feast of St. Louis at the Church of S. Luigi dei Francesi, the French church in Rome. Lists of musicians for this event are summarized in Table 4.1. In 1660 four violins and two violone players were hired for the

---

  [3] Ibid. 39 ff.   [4] Delumeau, *Rome*, 68–69.
  [5] Popes Innocent XI (1676–89) and Innocent XII (1691–1700) repeatedly closed Roman theaters; indeed Innocent XII ordered the Tordinona destroyed in 1697.
  [6] Peter Allsop, *Arcangelo Corelli: New Orpheus of our Times* (Oxford, 1999), 29.

TABLE 4.1. *Orchestras for the feast of St. Louis at the church of San Luigi dei Francesi, 1660–90*

Date	Keyboards	Plucked strings	Bowed strings	Winds	Source
1660	4 organs	3 lutes	4 violins 2 violoni		Lionnet, "La Musique," ii. 118–19
1665	7 organs 1 spinetta	2 lutes 2 theorbos	4 violins 1 viola da braccio 4 violoni		Ibid. 126–27
1670	3 organs	1 archlute 1 guitar	2 violins 1 violone	1 trumpet	Ibid. 134–35
1675	3 organs	1 archlute	3 violins [1 cello] 2 violoni	2 trumpets	Ibid. 139–40
1680	[3] organs		8 violins 3 violas [1 cello] 3 double basses		Ibid. 145
1685	3 organs		10 violins 2 violoni 3 double basses		Ibid. 150
1690	3 organs		10 violins 2 violoni 3 double basses		Ibid. 171

festival, along with three lutenists and four organs. In 1665, for what was apparently an especially lavish celebration, there were nine bowed-string players, balanced by four lutes and eight keyboards. In 1675 a single archlute was the only plucked instrument in the ensemble, and two trumpets had been added. By 1680 the number of bowed strings at the festival had reached 15; there were still four organists but no plucked strings at all.[7]

The lists from S. Luigi also demonstrate the separation of instrumentalists from singers and the decline of polychoral organization. Documents 4.1 and 4.2 are transcriptions of the lists from 1660 and 1680.[8] In the earlier list instrumentalists are arranged along with the singers into three choirs. At the head of the list come the nine singers of the first choir. Each name is followed by an indication of that musician's regular employment: Domenico Palombo sings in the papal Cappella; Giuseppe Fede is employed by the Colonna household; Senesino sings at the Chiesa Nuova, and so on. Each man's salary is recorded in scudi. After the singers are listed the instruments of the first choir (1 violone, 2 lutes, 2 violins), then the organist ("sr. Mutij"), and a rented organ. Next come 10 singers in the second choir, followed by an organist, a lutenist, two violinists, and another organ. The third group, a ripieno choir, contains 17 singers, but the only instruments are an organ and a violone ("Matteo" and "Gio. Battista"). The arrangement on the list probably mirrors the spatial arrangements in the church, with singers and instrumentalists mixed together in lofts next to the organs that accompanied them. In the list dated 1680 (Doc. 4.2) the singers are still arranged according to the polychoral principle (four choirs now instead of three), but the instruments are listed separately at the end as "Strumenti": nine violins, three violas, and three double basses (plus three organs, rented for the event). There should have been 10 violins, but one of them, a fellow from Modena ("Sr Modanese"), missed the performance. Some of the instrumentalists played at three services, some at two. The separation of instrumentalists from singers on the list of 1680 does not necessarily mean that the instruments were spatially separate from the choirs of singers, although this may well have been the case. But it does suggest that the sponsors of the event had begun to think of the instrumentalists as an ensemble of their own, conceptually distinct from the singers.

The four trends evident in the lists from S. Luigi dei Francesi can also be seen in pictures from seventeenth-century Rome.[9] Plate II is a watercolor by Pierre Paul Sevin, a French artist in the entourage of Queen Christina of Sweden. Evidently the picture represents a performance sponsored by the Queen, most likely during the

---

[7] Compare Table 2.2 above, which shows a similar evolution at the church of San Marcello, also in Rome.

[8] Lionnet, "La Musique à Saint-Louis." We wish to thank Mgr Max Cloupet of the Church of Saint-Louis des Français in Rome for providing us with copies of these documents.

[9] See Spitzer, "The Birth of the Orchestra in Rome."

DOCUMENT 4.1. *List of musicians for the Feast of St. Louis at San Luigi dei Francesi in 1660*

Musici forastieri presi in San Luigi nel giorno della sua festa li 25 Agosto 1660

Sr Domenico Palombo di Cappella	sc. 3	Sr Fabbritio org.ta di S Pietro	1.50
Sr Giuseppe Fedi di Colonna	2	Sr Ant.o Leuto	1.50
Sr Senesino della Chiesa Nova alla messa	–.60	Sr Jacomuccio Violino	1.50
Sr Gio Batta Vulpio di Cappella	2	Sr Bocci Violino	1.50
Sr Christofano di Capp.a	2	Sr Vincenzo org.ta di Capp.a di S Lorenzo	1.50
Sr Francesco Vulpio dell'Apolinare	1.50	organo	
Sr Giovanni Ricchi della Chiesa Nova	1.50		
Sr D. Girolamo Navarra di Capp.a	2	Sr Domenico Ricciardi di S Pietro per vespro	1
Sr Isidoro di Cappella	2	Soprano del Sr Durante nella vespro	1
Sr Michele Violone	1.50	Sr Giuseppe Alto di San Pietro	1.50
Sr Arcangelo Leuto	1.50	Sr Gio. Francesco di San Lorenzo	1.50
Sr De Petris Leuto	1.50	Sr D. Oratio Trastevere	1.50
Sr Gio. Antonio Violino	1.50	Sr D. Ant.o Tubij della Chiesa Nova	1.50
Sr Carlo Caproli Violino	1.50	Sr Basselli del Giesù	1.50
Sr Mutij org.ta di S. Mar. Mg.re	1.50	organo	
organo		Sr Michelangelo di S. Lorenzo	1.50
		Sr Pavolo Felice di S Gio. Laterano	1.50
Sr Checchino di S Pietro	1.50	Sr Paganelli di S. Lorenzo per vespro	1
Figlio del Sr Matteo Simonelli per il vespro	–.50	Sr Costantino di S Pietro	1.50
Sr Francesco Flaminj di Cappella messa e vespro	1.20	Sr Matteo Buonavera di S Mar. Mgg.re	1.50
Sr Coilozzi di Cappella	2	Sr Pietro Pavolo di S Mar. Magg.re	1.50
Sr Ferrotti di S Mar. Mg.re	1.50	Sr Bernardino di San Pietro	1.50
Sr Borgiani di S Pietro	1.50	Sr Gabbrini di S Pietro	1.50
Sr D. Giovanni di Cappella	2	Sr Ghirighella di S Gio. Laterano	1.50
Sr Fra Pavolino di Cappella	2	Sr D. Gio. Batt.a di S Lorenzo	1.50
Sr D. Michele di Cappella	2	Sr Matteo org.ta di Capp.a di S Gio. dei Fiorentini	1.50
Sr Domenico Rosa di S Pietro	1.50	Sr Gio. Batt.a Violone	1.50
			81.80

Source: Archive of St. Louis des Français, Carton 60b, 1660

1660s.[10] The performers are grouped into choirs around four organs, with singers, organs, bass violins, and plucked strings in an upper tier, other instruments in a lower tier. Bowed strings constitute only about a third of the instruments. In the center of the upper tier a singer beats time with a rolled up sheaf of paper. In lofts on either side stand two vocal soloists, each of them accompanied by a violinist. Most of the players in the upper tier have instruments like lutes and violoni that can play the continuo part along with the organs. The instruments in the lower tier seem to be melody instruments, arranged by timbre, so that each of the four choirs has a distinctive sound—trombones in the leftmost choir, cornetts in the second choir from the left, violins and flutes in the third choir, trumpets and a serpent in the choir on the far right. The four choirs are minimally separated in space, however, and they are depicted as all playing and singing together.

Polychoral organization is no longer seen in Fig. 4.1, which depicts the performance in 1687 of a serenata in honor of Maria Luisa, the Queen of Spain.[11] The large ensemble is composed almost entirely of bowed strings: 46 violins and violas can be counted in the upper three tiers, and 11 violoni or basses in the front row. To the left, on a raised platform, stand two violinists who lead the ensemble. The instruments are not arranged in choirs but rather in sections of similar instruments, and there are no singers among the instrumentalists. Five solo singers are placed in front, along with two harpsichords and two lutes. Presumably the continuo instruments accompanied the singers during arias and recitatives, while the strings played during what a contemporary account of the event calls various *sinfonie*, that is instrumental numbers.[12] The differences between these two pictures may represent differences between the performance practice of sacred and secular music. But they also represent general trends seen in other pictures and archival records. In the last quarter of the seventeenth century Roman instrumental ensembles got larger, violin-family instruments displaced plucked strings, and instrumentalists distanced themselves spatially and organizationally from singers.

As Roman instrumental ensembles changed, the old polychoral system evolved into what can be called "concerto grosso" organization. The concerto grosso technique emerged from the distinction that composers and *maestri di cappella* in the early seventeenth century made between the first choir or *coro favorito*, a choir of the best voices, singing one on a part, and the second choir, the *cappella* or *ripieni*, with several singers on each part (see Ch. 2). Adapting instruments to this system, Roman choir

[10] Hans Joachim Marx says that Sevin's picture was painted in the late 1660s and represents the performance of a four-choir mass ("The Instrumentation of Handel's Early Italian Works," *EM* 16 (1988), 496–505 at 497). The concert setting makes this interpretation unlikely. The picture is discussed in Per Bjurström, *Feast and Theatre in Queen Christina's Rome* (Stockholm, 1966), 55–60, and Spitzer, "The Birth of the Orchestra in Rome," 19–20.

[11] The serenata performed was very likely an *Aplauso musicale a 5. voci* by Bernardo Pasquini. See Thomas Edward Griffin, "The Late Baroque Serenata in Rome and Naples: A Documentary Study with Emphasis on Alessandro Scarlatti" (Ph.D. diss., University of California, Los Angeles, 1983), 120–27.

[12] *Avvisi di Rome* (Munich), quoted ibid. 120–21.

DOCUMENT 4.2. *List of musicians for the Feast of St. Louis at San Luigi dei Francesi in 1680*

Lista delli Sig.ri Musici straordinarij che sono stati a cantare p. la festività di S Luigi in sua chiesa. 1680

Sr Bernardo Org.ta	sc.	3	Sr Basso di S Tivoli		1.50
Sr Fedi		2	Sr Tobbia		1.50
Sr Fedino		3	Sr Pietro Ant.o Org.ta		1.50
Sr Paoluccio		3	4°		
Sr Dom.co Rietino		1.50	Sr Bastiano		1.50
Sr Giuseppe di Loreto		1.50	Sr Severo		1.50
Sr Tiburtio		1.50	Sr Pietro Paulo		1.50
Sr Siface		3	Sr Paolo Felice		1.50
Sr di Facchinetti		1.50	Sr Lodovico		1.50
Sr Gio.		1.50	Sr Filippo Coresi		1.50
Sr Gio Matteo		3	Sr Girolimo Lucchese		1.50
Sr Paulo		2	Sr Girolimo di S Pietro		1.50
Sr Verdoni		3	Sr Luca Organista		1.50
Sr Checco		1.50	Strumenti		
Sr di Andrea		2	*per tre servitij*		
Sr di Benedetto		1.50	Sr Gio. Viola		1.80
2° Choro			Sr Simone Contrabasso		2
Sr Petrignani		1.50	Sr Teodosio Contrabasso		2
Sr Sop.o del Giesù		1.50	Sr Carlo Mannelli		1.50
Sr dei [illegible]		1.50			
Sr di Felice		1.50	*per due servitij*		
Sr Niccolo		1.50	Sr Checco		1
Sr Gio Ant.o		1	Sr Vacarini		1
Sr Girolimo		1.50	Sr Matteo		1
Sr di Tommaso Tizzi		2	Sr Dom.co Todesco		1
3°			Sr Paolo Maria		1
Sr Leoni		1.50	Sr Gio Carlo		1
Sr Salina		1.50	Sr Luigi		1
Sr Besci		1.50	Sr ~~Modanese~~ manco		
Sr Manni		1.50	Sr Carlo Violetta		1
Sr Martinelli		1.50	Sr Pertica Violetta		1
Sr Natalino		1.50	Sr Bart.o Violetta		1
Sr Pietro		1.50	Sr Ant.o Contrabasso		1.20
Sr Carlo d'Avalo		1.50	Tre organi forestieri		4.50
					100.

Fig. 4.1. Serenata in the Piazza di Spagna, Rome, 1687

masters of the second half of the seventeenth century characteristically placed two violins and a violone with the first choir, additional instruments of various kinds with the ripieno choir.[13] The spatial separation and timbral contrast of multiple choirs were replaced by a new contrast of few vs. many and soft vs. loud. Document 4.3, the transcription of a list of instrumentalists hired at the church of San Giovanni dei Fiorentini in a series of festive oratorios in 1675, makes the new organizational principle explicit. The work they performed was *San Eustachio*, an oratorio by Antonio Masini. At the head of the list and designated as "concertino" are two violins (Manelli and Giuseppe), a lute (Colista), a harpsichord (Pasquini), and two violoni (Contarelli and Benedettini). Under the rubric "concerto grosso" are listed six violins, four alto violas, four tenor violas, and four basses. A note at the end of the list says that the players rehearsed the oratorio twice before the performance.

[13] Franco Piperno, " 'Concerto' e 'concertato' nella musica strumentale italiana del secolo decimo settimo," *Recercare*, 3 (1991), 169–202.

DOCUMENT 4.3. *Instrumental ensemble for* San Eustachio *by Masini at San Giovanni dei Fiorentini in 1675*

Nota degli Istromenti adoprati nell'Oratorio del Consolato nella Quarta Domenica

    Concertino
Sr Carlo Mannelli
Sr D. Giuseppe
Sr Lelio Colista
Sr Bernardo Pasquini
Sr D. Gasparo Contarelli
Sr Francesco Maria Benedettini

    Violini del Concerto Grosso
Sr Giocomo Branchi
Sr Federico Generali
Sr Antonino di Venetia
Sr Gio. Pavolo
Sr Il Bolognese
Sr Gio. Antonio Modanese

    Contralti
Sr Antonio Ferrini
Sr Gio. Carlo
Sr Gio. Batta discepolo del Sr Mannelli
Sr Gio. Batta Gasparini

    Tenori
Sr Giuseppe Piccini
Sr Francesco del Sr Mannelli
Sr Bartolomeo di Pamfilio
Sr Il Canonico di Ronciglione

    Bassi
Sr Fabritio Fontana
Sr Il Padre di S Agostino
Sr Teodosio
Sr Antonio Garuffi

Si deve avvertire che furno fatte due buone prove del detto Oratorio con gl'Istromenti, che perciò si devono pagare nella conformità come è esposto che è quanto etc.

Source: Casimiri, "Oratorii."

How concertino and concerto grosso were put to musical use may be seen in the score of *San Giovanni Battista* by Alessandro Stradella, performed at S. Giovanni dei Fiorentini in the same year as Masini's *San Eustachio* and with approximately the same numbers of singers and instrumentalists.[14] Stradella designates the small and large groups of instrumentalists in his score as "concertino" and "concerto grosso delle viole." The concertino consists of two violins and bass; the concerto grosso is scored for violins, violas in two parts, and basses.[15] Assuming the same distribution of instruments as in *San Eustachio*, this would make six violins on the top part, four violas on each of the two middle parts, and four violoni or contrabasses on the bottom, a middle-heavy scoring that recalls the equal distribution of instruments on parts characteristic of sixteenth-century ensembles and also of contemporary French string bands. Stradella deploys concertino and concerto grosso flexibly in *San Giovanni Battista*, but he does not exploit the possibilities for contrast between the two. Some arias are accompanied by continuo only, some by the concertino alone, some by concerto grosso alone, some by concertino and concerto grosso playing together. The *sinfonia* is played by the concerto grosso from beginning to end.

Stradella used the concerto grosso technique in several other works he composed in Rome during the 1670s. In the serenata "Qual prodigio è ch'io miri" he employs three groups: a concertino, a concerto grosso, and a "concertino della dama," which accompanies one of the three singers. Here the first concertino is also designated "primo cocchio" (first carriage) and the concerto grosso "secondo cocchio." Evidently "Qual prodigio" was written for an outdoor performance, perhaps a serenade, with singers and instrumentalists placed in separate carriages—two singers and a concertino in one carriage, the "lady" and her concertino in another carriage and the concerto grosso in a third carriage.[16] During most of "Qual prodigio" large and small groups play the same or similar material in antiphonal fashion. In the opening *sinfonia*, however, Stradella uses concertino vs. concerto grosso for dynamic and registral contrast, and in one aria he contrasts simple material in the concerto grosso parts with more virtuosic material in the concertino.[17] Thus, Stradella began to extend concerto grosso technique beyond its initial functions of spatial separation and differentiation of accompaniment toward new possibilities of dynamic and textural contrast within the instrumental ensemble itself.[18]

[14] Carolyn Gianturco, *Alessandro Stradella, 1639–1682: His Life and Music* (Oxford, 1994), 189. See also Owen Jander, "Concerto Grosso Instrumentation in Rome in the 1660's and 1670's," *JAMS* 21 (1968), 168–80.

[15] David W. Daniels, "Alessandro Stradella's Oratorio 'San Giovanni Battista': A Modern Edition and Commentary" (Ph.D. diss., University of Iowa, 1963).

[16] See Owen Jander, "Alessandro Stradella and his Minor Dramatic Works" (Ph.D. diss., Harvard University, 1962), 124 ff.; Gianturco, *Alessandro Stradella*, 121.

[17] The aria with concertino vs. concerto grosso contrast is "Basilisco allor che dorme." Handel borrowed several passages from "Qual prodigio è ch'io miri" for use in *Israel in Egypt*.

[18] Jander, "Concerto Grosso Instrumentation," 179–80.

The other composers who wrote oratorios for S. Giovanni dei Fiorentini in 1675 had the same string ensemble at their disposal as Stradella had used in *San Giovanni Battista*, but the scores of their oratorios have not been preserved, so there is no way to tell whether they used concerto grosso techniques. *Sinfonie* by Lelio Colista, a lutenist and composer active in Rome in the mid-seventeenth century, with their slow harmonic rhythms and homophonic passages, look as though they might have been composed for string ensembles with several players on a part, but they do not call explicitly for part doubling, nor for a concertino and a concerto grosso.[19] Violinist-composers, such as Carlo Ambrogio Lonati and Carlo Manelli, led string ensembles in Rome during the 1670s, but their *sinfonie* emphasize melody and violin virtuosity rather than exploiting the power of an ensemble of massed strings.[20] By the 1670s, then, the elements for an orchestra and an orchestral style of composition and performance were in place in Rome, but the orchestra had not yet emerged as an institution.

CORELLI'S CAREER

The birth of the orchestra in Rome was closely linked to the career and the compositions of Arcangelo Corelli.[21] From about 1680 until his retirement in 1709 Corelli organized orchestras, directed orchestras, and composed music for orchestras to play. "He was the first," wrote Crescimbeni,

to introduce Rome to ensembles [*sinfonie*] of so large a number of instruments and of such diversity that it was almost impossible to believe that he could get them to play together without fear of discord, especially since wind instruments were combined with strings, and the total very often exceeding one hundred . . .[22]

Corelli's achievement in Rome was similar to Lully's in Paris. Like Lully, Corelli used the patronage of the wealthy and powerful to dominate the musical life of his generation. Like Lully, he organized and led his own orchestra and composed music for that orchestra to play. Corelli, in addition, played in his orchestra as violin soloist. Corelli's orchestra, like Lully's, was based on a pre-existing tradition of string ensembles, and his musical style was based on the procedures of his predecessors (including Lully). He synthesized these procedures into a successful style of composition for orchestral ensembles that, like the Lully style, served as a model for several generations to come.

[19] See Peter Allsop, *The Italian Trio Sonata* (Oxford, 1992), 310; id., "Problems of Ascription in the Roman *Sinfonia* of the Late Seventeenth Century: Colista and Lonati," *Music Review,* 50 (1989), 39.

[20] For examples of works by Lonati and Manelli, see Allsop, *Italian Trio Sonata,* 315–19.

[21] For Corelli's biography, see Allsop, *Corelli.*

[22] G. M. Crescimbeni, *Notizie istoriche degli Arcadi morti* (Rome, 1720), i. 250. Quoted in Mario Rinaldi, *Arcangelo Corelli* (Milan, 1953), 132.

Born in the small town of Fusignano near Ravenna, Corelli was trained as a violinist in Bologna, and during the first part of his career in Rome he was known as "Arcangelo Bolognese" or simply "il Bolognese." Much has been made of Corelli's background, since Bologna in the seventeenth century was a center of instrumental music, particularly of music for large ensembles. However, the search for Bolognese antecedents may be misdirected. Roman ensembles were already incipient orchestras, and concerto grosso techniques had appeared in Rome before Corelli arrived there in the 1670s.[23] Unlike almost all other composers of his time, Corelli did not compose vocal music.[24] He concentrated his energies as a performer and composer entirely on instrumental music—music for solo violin, music for string trio, and music for orchestra.

The first mention of Corelli's presence in Rome occurs on the list of performers for Masini's *San Eustachio* in 1675 (see Doc. 4.3): "Il Bolognese," near the bottom of the "Violini del Concerto Grosso" is almost certainly the 22-year-old Corelli. Most likely he also played in Stradella's *San Giovanni Battista* later that spring in the same series at S. Giovanni dei Fiorentini. Thus, from the beginning of his career Corelli was involved in the proto-orchestral activities characteristic of Roman instrumental music. He was acquainted with Stradella, Colista, Manelli, and other composers working in this milieu, and he played the music they wrote for string ensembles. Other places where he played during the 1670s include the church of San Marcello (again as a member of a string ensemble with several on a part), San Luigi dei Francesi, Santa Maria Maggiore, and the Capranica theater in a small ensemble for opera.[25]

Building his reputation as a violinist with freelance jobs like these, Corelli soon garnered aristocratic patronage. In a letter of 1679 he reports that he has "entered into the service" of Queen Christina and that he is composing sonatas for academies at her palace.[26] Sometime in the mid-1680s Corelli entered the service of Cardinal Benedetto Pamphili, nephew of Pope Innocent X and one of the outstanding musical patrons of his time. By 1688 Corelli was listed among the Cardinal's "famiglia della casa" with a monthly salary of 10 scudi. Another member of the Cardinal's

[23] Peter Allsop argues cogently against the significance of Bolognese "influences" on Corelli (*Italian Trio Sonata*, 227 ff.; *Corelli*, 143 ff.)

[24] Franco Piperno believes that Corelli may have composed a cantata called "La Fama" for the first festival of the Academy of Design in 1702 (Franco Piperno, " 'Anfione in Campidoglio': presenza corelliana alle feste per i concorsi dell'Accademia del Disegno di San Luca," in *Nuovissimi studi corelliani: Atti del Terzo Congresso Internazionale*, ed. Sergio Durante and Pierluigi Petrobelli (Florence, 1982), 151–208 at 164). The evidence for this intriguing hypothesis is circumstantial.

[25] Liess, "Materialien," 155 ff.; Lionnet, "La Musique à Saint-Louis," ii. 143 ff.; Luca Della Libera, "La musica nella basilica di Santa Maria Maggiore a Roma, 1676–1712: nuovi documenti su Corelli e sugli organici vocali e strumentali," *Recercare*, 7 (1995), 87–157 at 108 ff.; Allsop, *Corelli*, 27 ff., 42 ff. Corelli did *not* travel to France during the 1670s, as Rousseau mistakenly reported, nor did he travel to Germany (Allsop, *Corelli*, 5–6).

[26] Letter of 13 May 1679 to Fabrizio Laderchi, quoted in Adriano Cavicchi, "Corelli e il violinismo bolognese," *Studi corelliani* (Fusignano, 1968), 33–47 at 39. The sonatas presumably became Corelli's Opus 1 trio sonatas, published in 1681 and dedicated to the Queen.

household was Matteo Fornari, Corelli's student and intimate friend, who played second violin to Corelli's first in nearly every documented performance by Corelli from the 1680s on. As a member of Pamphili's household, Corelli not only composed music and performed on the violin, he organized ensembles for musical events that the Cardinal sponsored, and he led these ensembles in performance.[27]

When Pamphili moved to Bologna in 1690, Corelli, along with Matteo Fornari, entered the service of Cardinal Pietro Ottoboni, nephew of Pope Alexander VIII. From 1690 until the end of his life, Corelli remained a member of Ottoboni's household; during much of that time he lived in an apartment in the Cardinal's palace, the Cancelleria. Ottoboni presided over a small but wealthy court, where there was continual demand for instrumental ensembles. At the Cardinal's titular church, S. Lorenzo in Damaso, adjacent to the Cancelleria, large ensembles were required for the feast of San Lorenzo in August, as well as for the "40 Hours" at the beginning of Lent and midnight mass on Christmas Eve.[28] Ottoboni also put on oratorios in the Cancelleria, at the Chiesa Nuova, and at the Seminario Romano. In addition, the regular Monday "academies" that the Cardinal gave at his palace sometimes involved instrumental ensembles that were orchestral in size and scope.[29] Corelli was responsible for recruiting instrumentalists, arranging for their transportation, composing music for them to play, rehearsing and leading them, and paying them their wages.[30] Thus, he was not simply a composer or simply a violin virtuoso. He was composer, conductor, contractor, soloist, orchestra leader, and musical personality all rolled up in one—the seventeenth-century equivalent of a modern bandleader.

Corelli's activities were not restricted to events sponsored by Cardinal Ottoboni. He provided orchestras and orchestral music for feast days at Roman churches, for outdoor public celebrations and festivities, and for other patrons, including Queen Christina, Cardinal Pamphili, and Prince Ruspoli. From the early 1680s through the first decade of the eighteenth century just about every performance in Rome by an ensemble of 10 or more instruments documented in surviving records was led by Corelli. Whether by virtue of his talent, his position, his reputation, or some other means, he was the only person who could recruit, organize, and lead a Roman orchestra, and in most cases the orchestra played at least some music that he had composed. In a real sense, all Roman orchestras from 1680 to 1713 were "Corelli's orchestra."

[27] Hans Joachim Marx, "Die 'Giustificazioni della Casa Pamphilj' als musikgeschichtliche Quelle," *Studi musicali*, 12 (1983), 121–87, *passim*.

[28] Id., "Die Musik am Hofe Pietro Kardinal Ottobonis unter Arcangelo Corelli," *Analecta musicologica*, 5 (1968), 104–77 at 107–10.

[29] Examples of academies that involved large orchestras: 2 May 1694, 13 June 1694, 27 Mar. 1695 (Marx, "Kardinal Ottoboni," 142, 147).

[30] Marx, "Kardinal Ottoboni," *passim*. Corelli customarily countersigned the paylists for the instrumentalists. Often he signed for receipt of the money, indicating that he functioned as paymaster.

VENUES AND PERFORMANCES

Contemporary records document performances by Corelli's orchestra in a variety of contexts. It played for private and semi-private entertainments given by patrons in their palaces and gardens. In February 1687, for example, Queen Christina held a gala "academy" in her palace to celebrate the ascension of James II, a fellow Catholic, to the English throne:[31]

When the signal was given, the royal festival began with a grand symphony comprising one hundred and fifty instruments of all sorts, played by master musicians, and directed and led by the famous Arcangelo Corelli, the Bolognese. . . . When [the overture] had finished, there began the most beautiful music that has ever been heard, composed by Bernardo Pasquini in alternation with Corelli and divinely sung by the excellent members of the choir of the Queen's Academy . . .[32]

During the long conclave of cardinals that followed the death of Alexander VIII in February 1691, Cardinal Ottoboni provided entertainment in the form of a "bellissima serenata," which was performed in the Belvedere courtyard immediately outside the Vatican walls. Pay records show that Ottoboni's serenade was accompanied by a small orchestra of six violins, two violas, two violoni, and lute, led, as usual, by Corelli.[33] As secular music, the serenata was not performed inside the Vatican proper, but it aroused opposition nonetheless:

Prince Savelli, Marshall of the conclave . . . spoke from the little window and complained about the serenata, saying that if he had been informed of it in advance, he would have had all the singers and instrumentalists thrown in prison. The performers were greeted with volleys of stones thrown from the windows of the Conclave. A stone hit one of the instrumentalists in the leg, and he was the last to return home.[34]

For a cantata in the garden of the Ruspoli palace in August 1694, Corelli put together a considerably larger orchestra: 38 violins, five violas, and 26 violoni, cellos, and double basses.[35]

Corelli's orchestra often performed in churches, usually for special occasions like the festival of a patron saint or a votive mass. When Queen Christina celebrated her recovery from a serious illness in 1689 with a Te Deum at the church of S. Maria di Loreto,

---

[31] The celebration was belated. James II became King in Feb. 1685. He ruled until Dec. 1688, when he fled to France.

[32] Quoted in Andreas Liess, "Neue Zeugnisse von Corellis Wirken in Rom," *Archiv für Musikwissenschaft*, 14 (1957), 130–37 at 133–34. The figure of 150 instrumentalists seems inflated, but it is repeated in a second account (ibid. 131).

[33] Marx, "Kardinal Ottoboni," 128.

[34] *Avvisi Marescotti*, 26 May 1691, quoted in Griffin, "The Late Baroque Serenata," 179–80.

[35] Marx, "Kardinal Ottoboni," 143.

The celebrated Signor Arcangelo Corelli, Virtuoso of her Majesty, also made an appearance and played a newly composed symphony with trumpets. It was played by a large number of the most accomplished string players [*professori di arco*] of this city.[36]

At the Feast of San Lorenzo at Cardinal Ottoboni's church of S. Lorenzo in Damaso each August, the orchestra played "symphonies" during the mass. In 1699, for example,

Cardinal Ottoboni, always the creator of novel and beautiful things, . . . had mass sung by a large number of singers . . . and to the mass two fine motets were added, as well as a grand symphony by Arcangelo [Corelli].[37]

The orchestra for this event numbered over 35, including two trumpets.[38] An English visitor, who attended midnight mass on Christmas eve at S. Lorenzo in 1699, reported that he heard "Paluccio, an admired young eunuch, singing, and Corelli, the famous violin, playing in concert with at least 30 more; all at the charge of Cardinal Ottoboni."[39] The estimate is a little low. Records show that 53 instrumentalists, all string players, were engaged for the performance.[40] At other occasions in church Corelli's orchestra was smaller. For the Festival of St. Louis at S. Luigi dei Francesi the orchestra usually numbered 15–20, sometimes with trumpets, sometimes without. At S. Maria Maggiore, on the other hand, Corelli played in the old non-orchestral style, as one of a pair of solo violins, assigned to the first choir in a polychoral setting.[41]

Corelli assembled his largest orchestras for the oratorios given by Pamphili, Ottoboni, and other Roman patrons. *Santa Beatrice d'Este* by Giovanni Lorenzo Lulier was commissioned by Cardinal Benedetto Pamphili to honor a visit of Cardinal d'Este to Rome in 1689. An account of its performance at the Pamphili palace conveys an idea of the level of magnificence at such events:

The great hall in which the oratorio was given was hung with shiny brocade, richly worked with gold embroidery . . . One part of the room was taken up by a stage as in a theater, on which there was a broad stairway covered with Turkish-style silk carpets. Here eighty musicians [*suonatori*] with their instruments were artfully displayed.

Columns rose from the stairs, shaped like lilies and like eagles, allusions to the house of Este. They supported the lights and also served as stands for the music of the instrumentalists. At the foot of the stairway was a platform . . . for the singers and the harpsichords and other instruments necessary for accompaniment. . . . At the other end of the room a structure was erected for another group of twenty instruments, raised six feet above the floor and decorated in a similar fashion. . . . The fullness of the instrumentation, with so many contrabasses for

---

[36] Quoted in Liess, "Materialien," 136.   [37] Quoted in Griffin, "The Late Baroque Serenata," 295.

[38] Marx, "Kardinal Ottoboni," 155 (18 vn, 5 vla, 7 violoni, 6 cb, 2 trpt).

[39] Samuel Pepys, *Private Correspondence and Miscellaneous Papers of Samuel Pepys, 1679–1703*, ed. J. R. Tanner (London, 1926), i. 257–58. The visitor was John Jackson, Pepys's nephew.

[40] Marx, "Kardinal Ottoboni," 155 (32 vn, 6 vla, 8 violoni, 6 cb, 1 lute).

[41] See Della Libera, "Santa Maria Maggiore."

a foundation and with trumpets too, created such a resonance [*rimbombo*] that the whole room seemed to echo.[42]

The Pamphili account books pertaining to this performance show that 79 instrumentalists were paid a total of 279.50 scudi for four rehearsals and a performance.[43] Corelli played solo violin, led the orchestra, and composed an instrumental *sinfonia* for Lulier's oratorio.[44]

Handel's *La Resurrezione*, commissioned by Prince Francesco Maria Ruspoli for Palm Sunday in 1708, was produced on an equally grand scale. A *teatro* was built in the great hall of the Palazzo Bonelli, with four rows of curved risers for the orchestra and a special raised podium for the "Concertino de' Violini."[45] The orchestra numbered approximately 45, with Corelli leading the violins and Handel playing one of the two harpsichords.[46] Handel's score made extreme demands on Corelli's ensemble, with solos for violin, oboes, recorders, flute, viola da gamba, and theorbo, as well as tutti–solo alternation in both the strings and the oboes.[47]

Finally, Corelli's orchestra played for many of the public festivities and outdoor events that enlivened civic life in Baroque Rome. In 1687, for example, Cardinal d'Estrées, the French ambassador, staged a festival in the Piazza di Spagna to celebrate the recovery of Louis XIV from a severe illness. Figure 4.2, an engraving by Vincenzo Mariotti, depicts the proceedings. Where the Spanish steps are now, a wooded path leads up to the Trinità dei Monti, whose façade is elaborately decorated for the occasion. Above the church burst fireworks. Corelli's orchestra appears in the middle of the picture, seated on risers on a large platform, labeled with the letter "K," which, an accompanying legend explains, indicates the "stage for the instrumentalists and singers, where they performed a grand concerto and cantata." Wind instruments and drums were placed apart from the other instruments on the rooftops of neighboring buildings (labeled "P" in the engraving). According to a contemporary account,

The fireworks were accompanied by the sound of drums, trumpets, and wind instruments [*pifferi*]. Opposite the two galleries where those instruments were placed, there was a large platform for the singers and instrumentalists, who began with a beautiful *sinfonia* for concerted instruments composed by the famous Arcangelo Bolognese, who had assembled together all the best string players in Rome. Then two vocalists, accompanied by the orchestra

---

[42] Quoted by Cavicchi, "Prassi esecutiva," 116–17.

[43] Marx, "'Giustificazioni," 157–58 (43 vn, 10 vla, 17 violoni, 7 cb, 1 lute, 1 hpschd).

[44] Corelli's sinfonia for *Santa Beatrice d'Este* survives in a single manuscript. It is printed in Arcangelo Corelli, *Werke ohne Opuszahl*, ed. Hans Oesch and Hans Joachim Marx (*Historisch-kritische Gesamtausgabe*, 5; Cologne, 1976).

[45] Ursula Kirkendale, "The Ruspoli Documents on Handel," *JAMS* 20 (1967), 222–73 at 234. For depiction of such a podium, see Fig. 4.1.

[46] Ibid. 256–57 (22 vn, 4 vla, 6 violoni, 6 cb, 4 ob, 2 trpt, 1 trb).

[47] Ibid. The pay records for *La Resurrezione* do not include performers on flute, bassoon, theorbo, or viola da gamba, all required by the score.

FIG. 4.2. Festival in the Piazza di Spagna, Rome, 1687

[*sinfonia*], sang a poem in praise of the King [Louis XIV]. The audience listened in profound silence.[48]

The serenata in the Piazza di Spagna in honor of the Queen of Spain, also in 1687 (Fig. 4.1 above), was the Spanish Ambassador's response to these French festivities. Neither the engraving nor the contemporary accounts mention Corelli, but given his preeminent position, it is hard to imagine that anyone else in Rome could have organized an orchestra as big as the one in Fig. 4.1. If this is a depiction of Corelli's orchestra, then the two violinists standing on the raised platform to the left of the ensemble must be Corelli and Matteo Fornari.

Corelli was documentably the leader of "more than 100 instrumentalists, the most distinguished in Rome on both strings and trumpets and other wind instruments," who played for an outdoor public performance of Alessandro Scarlatti's oratorio *Il regno di Maria assunta in cielo* in August 1705.[49] In the courtyard of his palace, the Cancelleria, Cardinal Ottoboni had erected a large stage [*teatro*] with painted back-drops, a platform for the singers, and seven risers for the instrumentalists. Stage and courtyard were brilliantly illuminated with torches, chandeliers, and colored lights. Carriages had been drawn into the courtyard, unhitched, and packed side by side to serve as boxes for the cardinals, princes, ecclesiastical dignitaries, and noble ladies in attendance. Behind them masses of ordinary Romans stretched through the palace gates all the way to the Piazza de' Pollaroli. Even with an orchestra of 100, the music could not be heard this far away, but the account reports that people could at least see the lights.[50] The performance was repeated the following night, with even more lights and even larger crowds.

Another example of performances by Corelli's orchestra at public festivities was the Accademia del Disegno di San Luca, held each spring in the Capitoline Palace. This celebration, at which prizes were awarded for architecture and design, was attended by the nobility and "a great multitude of common people."[51] Each year from 1702 to 1709 Corelli assembled and directed an orchestra for the Accademia del Disegno, and after Cornelli's retirement, Matteo Fornari continued the tradition for several years.

---

[48] Anon., *Raguaglio dele sontuose feste* . . . (Rome, 1687), quoted in Renato Bossa, "Corelli e il Cardinal Benedetto Pamphilj," in *Nuovissimi studi corelliani: Atti del Terzo Congresso Internazionale*, ed. Sergio Durante and Pierluigi Petrobelli (Florence, 1982), 211–23 at 222. Although the account makes it clear that the fire-works were accompanied only by trumpets and drums, not by strings, the engraving shows fireworks bursting overhead and Corelli's orchestra playing at the same time. This seems to be an example of the "telescoping" typical in 17th- and 18th-c. engravings of official spectacles and festivities. In order to include all significant aspects of the event in a single picture, the artist depicts events that take place one after another as happening simultaneously. See Barbara Russano Hanning, "The Iconography of a Salon Concert: A Reappraisal," in Georgia Cowart (ed.), *French Musical Thought, 1600–1800* (Ann Arbor, 1989), 129–48.

[49] The event is described in a contemporary manuscript account (I-Rvat Urb. Lat 1706) transcribed in Gioia Sofia Serafina Brunoro, "The Life and Works of Giovanni Lorenzo Lulier" (Ph.D. diss., Victoria University of Wellington, 1994), 555 ff.

[50] Ibid. 560.   [51] Piperno, " 'Anfione in Campidoglio,' " 154.

The orchestra opened the festivities with a *sinfonia* to accompany the ceremonial entrance of the cardinals; it also played after the oration of the principal speaker.

At all these venues—private entertainments, churches, oratorios, and public festivities—the role of Corelli's orchestra was limited. It did not play throughout, and in particular it seldom accompanied singers.[52] In an oratorio, for example, the orchestra usually played a *sinfonia* at the beginning and another *sinfonia* to open the second half. When there were instrumental interludes between arias, these may also have been played by the full ensemble.[53] The rest of the oratorio seems to have been accompanied by a reduced ensemble. The *sinfonie* that the orchestra played were usually composed by Corelli, rather than by the composer of the oratorio. Thus, for *Santa Beatrice d'Este* at the Pamphili palace in 1689, Giovanni Lorenzo Lulier composed the oratorio, but Corelli composed the *sinfonia*, and Corelli's name was featured prominently on the title page of the libretto printed for the occasion. Similarly, for a performance during Holy Week 1702 of Alessandro Scarlatti's setting of the Lamentations of Jeremiah the orchestra played a "superb concerto for basses, contrabasses, violas, and violins, composed by Arcangelo."[54] Another example is the pastorale *Amore e gratitudine*, with text by Ottoboni and music by Flavio Lanciani (1690).[55] According to Ottoboni pay records, the pastorale was performed 10 times, accompanied by an ensemble of five violins, two violas, two violoni, a bass, and a harpsichord.[56] During the prologue two trumpets also played. Two of the performances were enhanced by an additional "sinfonia nella pastorale," probably composed by Corelli, for which a large number of bowed strings and a trombone were added to the ensemble: 21 violins, six violas, nine violoni, five double basses, and a trombone.

In these examples as well as others like them, Corelli's orchestra—that is, the massed strings of the concerto grosso—was idle during most of the performance. Rather than accompanying the piece, the orchestra framed it—highlighting the extraordinary character of the occasion, setting the featured text and/or composition apart from its surroundings, and providing a visual backdrop for singers, orators, and other performers. The sudden entry, the full sound, and the unified execution of so large a group of instruments was a glorious special effect, like the fanfares and the fireworks at some of the same events.

---

[52] The only suggestion that the full orchestra accompanied singers is the account of the festival for Louis XIV in 1687 mentioned earlier, where two vocalists were accompanied by the *sinfonia*.

[53] Gloria Staffieri, "Arcangelo Corelli compositore di 'sinfonie': nuovi documenti," in *Studi corelliani IV: Atti del Quarto Congresso Internazionale*, ed. Pierluigi Petrobelli and Gloria Staffieri (Florence, 1990), 335–57 at 344.

[54] *Avvisi di Roma* (Munich), 11 Apr. 1702. Quoted in Griffin, "The Late Baroque Serenata," 359–60.

[55] See Franco Piperno, "Le orchestre di Arcangelo Corelli. Pratiche musicali romane. Lettura dei documenti," in Giovanni Morelli (ed.), *L'invenzione del gusto: Corelli e Vivaldi* (Milan, 1982), 42–48 at 47–48.

[56] Marx, "Kardinal Ottoboni," 126.

INSTRUMENTATION AND BALANCES

Preserved in the archives of Roman churches and of the great Roman families are personnel records that document players, instruments, and wages for many of the orchestras that Corelli assembled and led between 1680 and 1713. The size of his orchestra varied considerably from one performance to another. A Te Deum at S. Luigi dei Francesi in 1686 used only 10 violins, violas, and violoni; the Feast of St. Louis at the same church in 1682 required an orchestra of 20.[57] In 1692 for the Feast of San Lorenzo at Cardinal Ottoboni's church of S. Lorenzo in Damaso, Corelli assembled an orchestra of 40, including lutes and trumpets. The orchestra for the celebration there of the Quarant'ore required 46 instrumentalists, including five archlutes and two trumpets. A cantata sponsored by Cardinal Ottoboni at his palace, the Cancelleria, in 1690 used an orchestra of 25 strings; another cantata, given by the Cardinal in 1694, this time in the garden of the Ruspoli palace, employed an orchestra of 69.[58] There is considerable consistency, however, in the size of the orchestra at the same event from one year to the next. The orchestra for the Feast of St. Louis hovered between 15 and 20 during the 1680s, then rose gradually during the 1690s and 1700s. The orchestra for the feast of San Lorenzo numbered 40 to 50, and usually included two trumpets. The Accademia del Disegno began ambitiously with an orchestra of 23 in 1702, then cut back during succeeding years, presumably to save money.[59]

Although the size of Corelli's orchestra varied from event to event, its balances remained consistent. Whether the orchestra was large or small, whether it was playing in church or at a civic festival, violins made up about half of the total number of instruments and bass instruments (cellos, violoni, double basses) from a third to a fourth.[60] Only the violas varied noticeably as a proportion of the ensemble—from a fourth of the total in small ensembles to an eighth, a ninth, or less in large ensembles.[61] These balances moved decisively away from the earlier ideal of equal distribution on parts, still evident in the balances for Masini's *San Eustachio* and Stradella's *San*

[57] Lionnet, "La Musique à Saint-Louis," ii. 151 (6 vn, 4 violoni, 1 org); ii. 147 (10 vn, 4 vla, 6 violoni, 4 org).

[58] Marx, "Kardinal Ottoboni," 124 (18 vn, 7 vla, 7 violoni, 7 cb, 2 trpt, 5 archlutes); 125 (12 vn, 4 vla, 6 violoni, 3 cb); 143 (38 vn, 5 vla, 25 violoni and cb, 1 lute).

[59] A memorandum by G. Ghezzi, the organizer of the Academy, reviews the expenses for 1702, looking for ways to cut the budget. Some expenses are fixed, but he guesses that the outlay for music can be cut by two-thirds (Piperno, "'Anfione in Campidoglio,'" 173).

[60] The balance among cellos, violoni, and contrabasses varied considerably. The players of these instruments overlapped, and often it is hard to tell who was playing which instrument.

[61] The variability in the proportion of the violas is something of an artifact: since there are relatively few violas, their proportion is strongly affected by the addition or subtraction of one or two players.

Giovanni Battista in 1675. The preponderance of violins also reflects the fact that Corelli wrote two violin parts, unlike Stradella, who used the older scoring with only one violin part and two parts for viola. There may have been a tendency, when Corelli's orchestra got very large, for the proportion of violins to rise even further. Overall, however, the consistency of proportions of instruments in the orchestra, in a variety of venues over a period of almost 30 years, suggests that Corelli had a clear idea of the acoustical balance he wanted in his orchestra and that he was able to recruit instrumentalists as needed to obtain this balance, no matter how large or small the ensemble.

Another striking feature of Corelli's orchestra is that it did not include keyboards. Personnel records show that organs and harpsichords were indeed present at many of Corelli's performances. The keyboards are not listed with the orchestra, however, but by themselves or among the singers. In Rome as elsewhere, organists and harpsichordists were associated conceptually and practically with the vocal rather than the instrumental aspects of the performance. When a choir or soloists sang, they were almost always accompanied by one or more keyboards. When an orchestra played— that is, the entire orchestra with concertino and concerto grosso together—harpsichords and organs were usually silent.[62] This division between the orchestra on the one hand and a smaller ensemble for vocal accompaniment on the other can be seen in pictures like Fig. 4.1, where harpsichords and lutes accompany the singers, but the orchestra is led by the pair of concertino violinists.

Was the bass line realized by any continuo instruments at all in Corelli's sinfonias and concertos? Lutes and archlutes appear on many of the paylists for his orchestras. Often there are two lutenists; sometimes there are as many as five.[63] Unlike keyboard players, the lutenists are always listed among the instrumentalists. Plucked strings might have been used in the concertino, as an alternative to the cello or violone on the bass part.[64] They might also have played along with the concerto grosso, though it would have been hard for them to make themselves heard, particularly outdoors. In the one surviving Corelli autograph—a draft of the Pastorale from Concerto Grosso, No. 8, and the Corrente from No. 6—the bass line of the Corrente is figured, the bass of the Pastorale is not.[65] This suggests that Corelli may have expected that a lute would play with the concerto grosso, at least in the Corrente.[66]

Although Crescimbeni praised Corelli for getting strings and wind instruments to play together "without discord," winds were scarce in Corelli's orchestra. Pairs of trumpets were included in the ensembles for outdoor performances, like the

---

[62] Piperno, "Le orchestre di Corelli," 47.   [63] Ibid.   [64] Ibid.
[65] Photographs of these two movements appear in Hans Joachim Marx, "Ein neuaufgefundenes Autograph Arcangelo Corellis," *Acta musicologica*, 41 (1969), 116–18.
[66] A lutenist could easily have played the Pastorale too, from the bass line without figures.

Scarlatti oratorio in 1705, for festive occasions in church, and occasionally for oratorios. However, only one surviving composition attributed to Corelli contains a trumpet part, a Sonata a Quattro for trumpet, two violins and basso (WoO 4).[67] If trumpets played in other extant pieces by Corelli, their parts must have been improvised or produced on an ad hoc basis.[68] The account of the celebration in the Piazza di Spagna for Louis XIV, where the trumpets were placed on rooftops and played before the orchestra rather than with it, suggests that trumpets, even when they were present at an event, did not necessarily play in the orchestral *sinfonie* and concertos. Trombones appear on Corelli's paylists only rarely.[69] There is no clue as to what their role might have been in the music. The first documented participation of oboes in Corelli's orchestra was at the Feast of San Luigi dei Francesi in 1704.[70] There were four oboes in the orchestra that he put together for Handel's *Resurrezione* in 1708. Oboes joined the orchestra for the Academy at the Campidoglio in 1709, the last year that Corelli led that ensemble.[71] Two "additional flutists" were added to the list for the Academy of 1704, but crossed off again.[72] All in all, winds were used sparingly and mainly toward the end of the period in question. Corelli's orchestra was overwhelmingly based on bowed strings.

THE ORGANIZATION OF CORELLI'S ORCHESTRA

Corelli's orchestra was not a standing ensemble, like a modern symphony or opera orchestra. Its size varied from day to day, from event to event, according to the demands of the occasion. Beneath this variability, however, lay a stable and efficient system.

Table 4.2 takes a sample period beginning in February 1702 and ending in August 1705 and analyzes the personnel at 16 performances of instrumental ensembles led by Corelli for which paylists have been preserved. These well-documented events were sponsored by several different patrons: an oratorio staged by Cardinal Pamphili, feast

---

[67] Peter Allsop calls this sonata "apocryphal" (Allsop, *Corelli*, 51); Hans Joachim Marx says the objections to its authenticity are "baseless" (Hans Joachim Marx, "Unveröffentlichte Kompositionen Arcangelo Corellis," in *Studi corelliani*, 53–69 at 58). See also Corelli, *Werke ohne Opuszahl*, 20.

[68] H. J. Marx and Franco Piperno both speculate that trumpet parts may have been added on occasion to the concertos of Opus 6. See Marx, "Instrumentation," 503; Piperno, "Le orchestre di Corelli," 42. Allsop speculates that a few movements from Opus 6 might originally have been composed for trumpets. This theory is intriguing, but he offers no evidence save for the trumpet-like character of the violin parts (*Corelli*, 151).

[69] Marx, "Kardinal Ottoboni," 126; id., "'Giustificazioni,'" 130, 152, 157; Kirkendale, "Ruspoli Documents," 256–57.

[70] Lionnet, "La Musique à Saint-Louis," 193–94.   [71] Piperno, "'Anfione in Campidoglio,'" 193.

[72] Ibid. 179. Both flutists were evidently Frenchmen: Monsù Giovanni (Jean) and Monsù Valentino (Valentin). Monsù Nicolò and Mengone, elsewhere an oboist, played flute at the Campidoglio in 1711 (Piperno, "'Anfione in Campidoglio,'" 199).

days and lesser celebrations at Ottoboni's Church of S. Lorenzo in Damaso, processions and festivals at the Church of S. Luigi dei Francesi, and performances for the Accademia del Disegno at the Campidoglio. The 16 documented performances may be considered as representative of a larger set of performances during this period by Corelli and his orchestra, for which documentation does not survive.

According to Table 4.2, 57 different instrumentalists played in Corelli's orchestra between February 1702 and August 1705—29 violinists, four violists, 12 cello or violone players, six bassists, a lutenist, four trumpeters, and a drummer. Several of the players were well-known virtuosos or composers. Giuseppe Valentini, nicknamed "Straccioncino" (Tatters), was a virtuoso violinist, a composer, and also a poet, whom Francesco Geminiani mentions as a rival to Corelli.[73] Filippo Amadei ("Pippo del violoncello"), recognized as one of Rome's leading cellists, emigrated in 1719 to London, where he played in the orchestra of the opera.[74] Some of the players switched instruments from one performance to another—violin to viola (Petruccio), cello to bass (De Carolis, Laurelli, Bandiera), violone to lute to violin (G. A. Haym).

Only a few of these instrumentalists enjoyed positions on the house payroll of a Roman patron. Fornari was a member of the Pamphili household, then transferred with Corelli to Ottoboni's establishment. Giovanni Lorenzo Lulier, cellist and composer, was also on the Pamphili payroll and later worked sporadically for Cardinal Ottoboni.[75] The rest of Corelli's orchestra were essentially freelancers. Most of them had steady but low-paying jobs at one or more Roman churches. Some of them held positions in Rome's civic band, the Concerto del Campidoglio, not as string players but as cornett players and trombonists.[76] A significant part of their income must have come from freelance activity, much of it in Corelli's orchestra.[77]

Some members of Corelli's orchestra were better paid than others. At the Campidoglio Academy in 1702, for example, most of the musicians were paid 1.5 scudi. Giuseppe Valentini and Paolomaria Ceva, however, received 2 scudi apiece, Matteo Fornari received 3 scudi; Filippo Amadei, the cellist, was paid 9 scudi, and Corelli himself was paid 15 scudi.[78] Perhaps the elevated payments to Amadei and

---

[73] Michael Talbot, "A Rival of Corelli: The Violinist-Composer Giuseppe Valentini," in *Nuovissimi studi corelliani: Terzo Congresso,* 347–65; also Enrico Careri, "Giuseppe Valentini (1681–1753)," *Note d'archivio per la storia musicale,* NS 5 (1987), 69–125.

[74] Stefano La Via, "Il violoncello a Roma al tempo del Cardinale Ottoboni: ricerche e documenti" (diss., Università di Roma, 1983), 119 ff.

[75] Ibid. 109–19; Brunoro, "Lulier."

[76] Alberto Cametti, "I musici di Campidoglio ossia il 'concerto di cornetti e trombone del senato e inclito popolo romano' (1524–1818)," *Archivio della R. Società Romana di Storia patria,* 48 (1925), 95–135.

[77] There was also freelance work in smaller ensembles outside Corelli's orbit. For example, some of the instrumentalists in Table 4.2, including Andrea di Luigi and Giovanni Travaglia, played for a series of oratorios at San Girolamo della Carità in 1704 and 1705. See Careri, "Giuseppe Valentini."

[78] Piperno, "'Anfione in Campidoglio,'" 171.

Table 4.2. *Personnel of Corelli's orchestra, 1702–5*

Players	25 Feb. 1702	18 June 1702	25 Aug. 1702	Feb. 1703	10 June 1703	25 Aug. 1703	17 Apr. 1704	18 July 1704	10 Aug. 1704	10 Aug. 1704	25 Aug. 1704	19 Feb. 1705	7 May 1705	10 Aug. 1705	10 Aug. 1705	25 Aug. 1705
Violin																
Andrea di Luigi	x		x			x		x	x		x	x				x
Antoniuccio	x		x	x		x		x	x			x	x			x
Batistino				x			x		x	x		x				
Bernardino Bonazzi			x			x					x	x		x		
Giuseppe Budassi						x					x					x
Giov. Batt. Carpani	x		x	x		x	x		x		x	x	x	x		x
Pietro Castrucci	x		x	x				x				x	x	x	x	
Prospero Castrucci	x								x							
Paolo Maria Ceva	x		x			x										
Mennicuccio [Colista]	x		x			x					x	x	x			
Arcangelo Corelli	x	x	x	x	x	x	x	x	x	x	x	x	x	x	x	x
Domenico [Lucchese]	x	x		x		x	x		x		x	x	x	x		x
Carlo Ferrini	x								x		x			x		
Matteo Fornari	x	x	x	x	x	x	x	x	x	x	x	x	x	x	x	x
Giov. Batt. Gasparini											x					
Giovannino			x				x	x			x	x	x	x		x
Carlo Guerra	x										x	x		x	x	x
Pietro Antonio Haym							x						x			
Lamberto									x			x				
Frances. Maria Massa	x								x							
Peppino									x		x	x			x	x
Perugino									x							
Petruccio (Petruccino)	vla								vla			x	x			
Monsu Pietro			x													
Prospero Pittore												x		x		
Alfonso Poli	x		x			x			x	x	x	x				x
Silvestro Rotondi						x		x								
Tibaldi	x										x		x		x	x
Giuseppe Valentini	x	x	x	x	x	x	x		x			x	x	x	x	x
Viola																
Giuseppe Barbosi	x		x			x			x	x						x
Bartolomeo di Panfili	x		x	x		x	x	x	x	x		x	x	x		x
Lorenzo Gasparini			x	x		x	x		x	x		x	x			x
Giov. Maria Pertica	x		x			x			x	x		x		x		x
Cello-violone																
Filippo Amadei (Pippo)	x	x	x	x	x	x	x			x			x			x
Collodi	x		x						x	x						cb

Table 4.2. (*Cont.*)

Players	25 Feb. 1702	18 June 1702	25 Aug. 1702	Feb. 1703	10 June 1703	25 Aug. 1703	17 Apr. 1704	18 July 1704	10 Aug. 1704	10 Aug. 1704	25 Aug. 1704	19 Feb. 1705	7 May 1705	10 Aug. 1705	10 Aug. 1705	25 Aug. 1705
Giuseppe De Carolis	x		x			cb										
Francese			x													
Giov. Ant. Haym			x	lt		x		lt		x		vn	lt			x
Domenico Laurelli	x								x			cb		cb		
Lazzaro												x		x		
Giov. Lorenzo Lulier									x							
Bartolomeo Mazarini			x				x	x	x	cb		x	x			cb
Peppino						x				x						x
Perroni	x		x			x	x	x	x	x		x	x	x		x
Pietruccio						x										
Double Bass																
Almerico Bandiera	x			x		x			x	x	vne	x	x	x	x	
Bartolomeo Cimapane	x	x	x	x		x	x	x	x	x	x	x	x	x	x	x
Giovan Pietro Franchi	x											x				
Petrino Specchi						x			x	x						x
Giovanni Travaglia	x		x	x	x	x	x		x	x		x	x	x	x	x
Marcello Valenti	x		x													
Lute, Archlute																
Memmo [Furloni?]	x															
Trumpet																
Camillo	x			x		x	x		x				x			x
Francese									x							
Gaetano	x			x		x	x		x				x			x
Girolamo									x							
Timpani																
Filippo									x							

Sources: Piperno, "Anfione"; Marx, "Die Musik"; Marx, " 'Giustificazioni' "; Lionnet, "La Musique," ii.

Corelli mean that they composed music in addition to playing. The higher payments to Valentini, Ceva, and Fornari suggest that they, along with Corelli and Amadei, played concertino parts.[79] Similarly in the paylists for the festivals at S. Luigi dei Francesi in 1702, 1703 and 1704, most of the musicians are paid 1.5 scudi, while Amadei and Fornari are paid 2 scudi and Corelli 6.[80] Again, Corelli and Fornari must have played the concertino violin parts and Amadei the concertino cello part. In addition Corelli seems to have been paid for providing music and organizing the orchestra.

Based on Table 4.2, Corelli's orchestra can be depicted as a set of concentric circles (Fig. 4.3). In the center is a "core" group of 11 instrumentalists who played at 10 or more events between 1702 and 1705. Moving outward, the next group of musicians can be called "regulars," 19 musicians who played at between 5 and 9 events during the period. Then come 17 musicians who played two to four services and who can be thought of as "occasional" musicians. Finally, in the outermost circle are 10 instrumentalists each of whom made a single appearance between 1702 and 1705. The "core" musicians got the most work and were most likely to play concertino parts and to be paid more. For small events like a procession at S. Luigi the core group was enough, plus perhaps one or two regulars. For larger events, like the Feast of St. Louis, most of the regulars were added, plus occasional musicians as needed. Many of the musicians who put in single appearances seem to have been foreigners, like the "Francese" who played violone at the Feast of St. Louis in 1702 or the "Perugino" who played violin at the Feast of San Lorenzo in 1704. The system displayed in Fig. 4.3 is an early version of the modern world of studio musicians in Los Angeles, Nashville, or London—a city-wide network of freelance musicians organized in concentric circles, with those at the center getting the most work, those on the periphery the least. And Corelli's orchestra was, in fact, perceived in just this way by contemporaries. A list of Roman church musicians drawn up in 1694 arranges the singers by church, but places the instrumentalists together at the end under the rubric "Sig.ri Stromenti di Roma," arranged according to instrument. Corelli's name stands at the head of the list, followed by Fornari, Valentini, and most of the other names in Fig. 4.3.[81] Moreover, the names on the list seem to follow the same concentric logic as the figure—the core group comes first, then the regulars, with the occasional musicians at the end.

[79] This would imply a concertino with two rather than one on a part, something that Georg Muffat, in his report on the performance style of Corelli's concerti grossi, says should not be done, "except in a very large space and when the concerto grosso has many players on each part" (*Sechs Concerti Grossi I: Auswahl aus Armonico tributo* (1701), ed. Erwin Luntz (Vienna, 1904), 13). The Capitoline Palace is a large space, and the concerto grosso in 1702 had eight first and eight second violins.

[80] Lionnet, "La Musique à Saint-Louis," ii. 190–93.

[81] Oscar Mischiati, "Una statistica della musica a Roma nel 1694," *Note d'archivio per la storia musicale*, NS 1 (1983), 209–27.

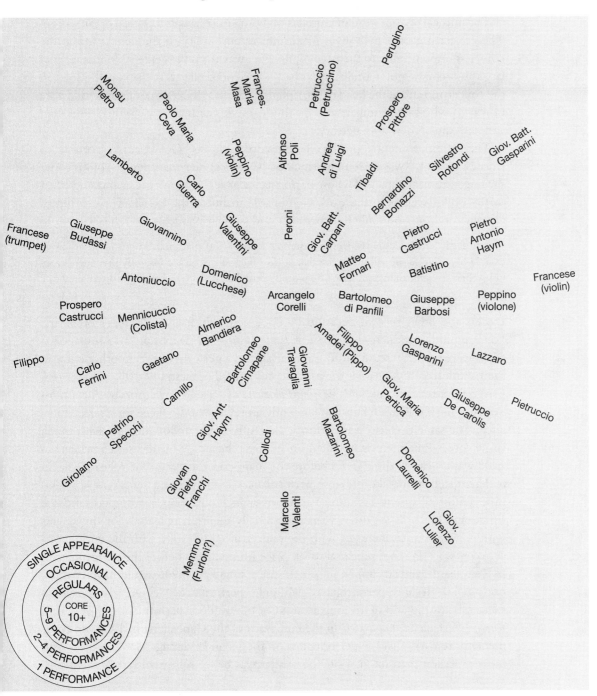

IG. 4.3. The structure of Corelli's orchestra (1702–5)

The musical organization of Corelli's orchestra mirrored its logistical organization. The concerto grosso style gives maximum responsibility to the concertino at the core, less responsibility to the ripieno, further away from the center. No matter how large his orchestra got, Corelli always had experienced players in the key positions, in the concertino and at the head of the ripieno sections. He could count on a solid core of players who were familiar with his musical style, with the style of his leadership, and with the orchestra's repertory.

The system evidently produced noteworthy results. Geminiani, according to Burney's report, "was extremely struck by [Corelli's] nice management of his band, the uncommon accuracy of whose performance gave the concertos an amazing effect to the eye as well as to the ear." Geminiani attributed the excellent execution of Corelli's orchestra not only to experience and familiarity but also to rehearsal:

Corelli regarded it as essential to the ensemble of the band that their bows should all move exactly together, all up, all down; so that at his rehearsals, which constantly preceded every public performance of his concertos, he would immediately stop the band if he discovered one irregular bow.[82]

Paylists and other records occasionally document rehearsals of Corelli's orchestra. For Pamphili's production in 1689 of *Santa Beatrice d'Este* by Lulier 78 instrumentalists were paid 279 scudi for four rehearsals and a performance.[83] Another entry in the Pamphili archives names the members of a small orchestra (9 string players) that played for a rehearsal of *Santa Maria Maddalena de Pazzi*, an oratorio by Alessandro Scarlatti, in July 1704.[84] This was evidently a preview of the piece for a select audience. The same oratorio was performed in April of the following year with much larger forces, but there is no mention of any rehearsal.[85] Handel's *Resurrezione* in 1708 was rehearsed three times before the main concert. Again the rehearsals seem to have been more like preview performances than working rehearsals, and this time almost all of the orchestra participated, including oboes, trumpets, and the trombone. Records for other years occasionally mention rehearsals for the singers with continuo instruments or with the concertino, but rarely with the entire concerto grosso.[86] Perhaps rehearsals took place immediately before the performances, as Geminiani seems to imply, in which case a single payment would have covered both rehearsal and performance. Multiple performances could also serve as rehearsals. At the end of his long account of the outdoor performance of Scarlatti's *Il regno di Maria assunta in cielo* in the courtyard of the Cancelleria in 1705 the commentator remarks that the performance on the second evening "was executed with more precision than the first one because it was better rehearsed [*per haverla meglio considerata*]."[87]

[82] Burney, *A General History of Music*, ed. Mercer, ii. 443.
[83] Marx, " 'Giustificazioni,' " 158.   [84] Ibid. 167–68 (6 vn, 1 vla, 1 vc, 1 cb, 1 lute, 1 hpschd).
[85] Ibid. 169.   [86] See Brunoro, "Lulier," 277.   [87] Ibid. 561.

THE REPERTORY OF CORELLI'S ORCHESTRA

For almost thirty years Corelli organized and led orchestral performances in Rome. At many, perhaps most, of these events the orchestra performed compositions by Corelli himself: a "sinfonia di novo concerto" during a mass at Santa Casa di Loreto in 1689; a "concerto" before a cantata at the Vatican Palace in 1690; a "sinfonia grande" for a Good Friday performance at the Cancelleria in 1692; "una di quelle bellissime Sinfonie" for a meeting of the Arcadian Academy in 1708; a "sinfonia stra-ordinaria" for the Academia del Disegno in 1709 to honor the presence of the King of Denmark.[88] Yet the only extant compositions by Corelli written for orchestra are the 12 concerti grossi of Opus 6, plus the *sinfonia* for Lulier's *Santa Beatrice d'Este* (WoO 1). Did Corelli's orchestra play these same thirteen pieces at the same events, for the same people, month after month, year after year?

It is likely that Corelli's orchestra sometimes repeated a piece that had been heard before. Crescimbeni, referring to a performance at the Arcadian Academy, remarks that "Corelli began the musical portion of the entertainment by directing one of those magnificent *sinfonie* that he has composed at the Ottoboni palace."[89] Crescimbeni's remark implies that he was familiar with several Corelli *sinfonie* and perhaps had heard the same ones in a variety of contexts. On the other hand, accounts of Corelli performances often refer to "new *sinfonie*" or "newly composed *sinfonie*."[90] In all likelihood, Corelli kept composing new music for his orchestra to play from the beginning of his career until his retirement or close to it.[91] The identity and fate of all these new *sinfonie* and concertos that Corelli's orchestra performed between 1680 and 1709 remain a mystery.

One possibility is a massive loss of repertory. "In the course of nearly 40 years of artistic activity in Rome," says Hans Joachim Marx, "Corelli wrote a large number of compositions that we know about only through contemporary accounts. The great bulk of these unpublished compositions disappeared after Corelli's death."[92] Marx has identified 10 of these unpublished compositions, argued in each case for Corelli's authorship, and published them in the *Gesamtausgabe* as "works without opus number."[93] To account for the missing repertory, however, requires many more than 10 compositions. Extrapolating from the figures in Table 4.2, which covers three and a half years, it seems as though Corelli's orchestra played at least 200

---

[88] Marx, "Unveröffentlichte Kompositionen," 55; Marx, "Kardinal Ottoboni," 123; Piperno, "'Anfione in Campidoglio,'" 192.

[89] Quoted in Rinaldi, *Arcangelo Corelli*, 149. Rinaldi does not give a source for this quotation.

[90] Griffin, "The Late Baroque Serenata," 552; Marx, "Unveröffentlichte Kompositionen," 55.

[91] Hans Joachim Marx, *Die Überlieferung der Werke Arcangelo Corellis: Catalogue raisonné* (Cologne, 1980), 41.

[92] Ibid. 40.

[93] Corelli, *Werke ohne Opuszahl*. Of the 10 works that Marx includes among the "Works without opus number" only one is for orchestra, the Sinfonia to Lulier's *Santa Beatrice d'Este* (WoO 1). The others are sonatas à 3 and à 4.

and probably more performances over the course of his career, from 1680 to 1709. If he composed new music for even half of these performances, this implies that there are something like 100 missing works by Corelli. Given Corelli's reputation, the prestige of his music, and the number of people who had access to the parts, it is hard to imagine that the bulk of the music he wrote for his orchestra has vanished without a trace.

Another solution that has been proposed to the mystery of the missing repertory is that, like Poe's purloined letter, it is lying in plain sight. Before Corelli published his Op. 6 Concerti Grossi, he published four sets of works scored for two violins and bass: Opus 1 and Opus 3, later designated "sonate da chiesa," and Opus 2 and Opus 4, designated "sonate da camera" by Corelli himself. Several commentators have suggested that Italian trio sonatas, particularly church sonatas, may have been performed in Corelli's day with more than one on a part.[94] There is no direct evidence that Opus 1 and Opus 3 were performed in this manner. A Sonata a Quattro by Corelli (WoO 2) is transmitted in a seven-part version with a concertino and a concerto grosso and also in a version in which "solo" and "tutti" indications have been written into the parts.[95] Francesco Geminiani, Corelli's student, published arrangements of Corelli's Opus 3 as concerti grossi, with the original trio as the concertino and ripieno parts added.[96] It is hard to know, however, whether these later arrangements represent the Roman practice of Corelli's day, much less of his orchestra.

There is in addition the evidence of Georg Muffat, the German organist and composer sent by his patron to Rome around 1680 to study with Bernardo Pasquini.[97] Muffat met Corelli and was so impressed by the master's "concertos, performed with the greatest exactness by a large number of instrumentalists,"[98] that he composed his own pieces in imitation of Corelli's style. Muffat's sonatas were premiered at Corelli's home, presumably by musicians from Corelli's orchestra. Published in 1682 as *Armonico Tributo*, these sonatas are scored for strings in five parts, but Muffat explained in an introduction that they could be played as trio sonatas in three parts, as quartets, as quintets, or "in concerti pieni" with a three-part concertino and a concerto grosso.[99] In the partbooks Muffat inserts "S" for solo and "T" for tutti to indicate where the concertino should play alone and where the concerto grosso should join in. His statement about large ensembles playing Corelli's concertos has been interpreted to mean that Corelli's Opus 6 concertos were already written and were being performed when Muffat was in

[94] Stephen Bonta, "The Church Sonatas of Giovanni Legrenzi" (Ph.D. diss., Harvard University, 1964), 207; John Daverio, "In Search of the Sonata da camera before Corelli," *Acta musicologica*, 57 (1985), 195–214 at 204; Sandra Mangsen, "The Trio Sonata in Pre-Corellian Prints: When Does 3 = 4?," *Performance Practice Review*, 3 (1990), 138–64 at 161. Peter Allsop criticizes this view (*Italian Trio Sonata*, 43).

[95] Marx, "Unveröffentlichte Kompositionen," 62–63.

[96] Geminiani's arrangements are reprinted in Arcangelo Corelli, *Sonate da chiesa: Opus I und III*, ed. Max Lütolf (Laaber, 1987).

[97] Georg Muffat, *Armonico tributo: 1682 . . . concerti grossi, zweiter Teil*, ed. Erich Schenk (Vienna, 1953), p. viii. This is the same Georg Muffat who studied with Lully in Paris in the 1660s. See Ch. 3.

[98] Georg Muffat, *Sechs Concerti Grossi*, 8.   [99] Muffat, *Armonico tributo*, p. xxv.

Rome (1680–82).[100] But in 1682 Corelli was just coming into his own as a bandleader and had only recently published his Opus 1 trio sonatas. It seems more likely that Muffat's sonatas and their instructions represent the performance practice of Corelli's Opus 1 or, perhaps, Opus 3 trio sonatas "in concerti pieni."[101] It is possible, then, that some of the Corelli's trio sonatas or movements from these trio sonatas represent part of the missing repertory of his orchestra.

A third possible solution to the mystery of the missing repertory is that the twelve concerti grossi of Corelli's Op. 6 represent more than twelve pieces—that the "concerti" and "sinfonie" that Corelli and his orchestra performed in many of their engagements were individual movements or movement pairs from Op. 6. According to this hypothesis, Corelli developed his orchestra's repertory gradually over the period 1680–1705, then, toward the end of his life, selected, revised, and combined pieces for publication in twelve homogeneous sets.[102] Some diplomatic evidence supports this selection–revision hypothesis. The single surviving Corelli autograph is a double sheet with the Pastorale from Op. 6 No. 8 on one side and the Corrente of Op. 6 No. 10 on the other.[103] These two pieces, then, were composed at about the same time, possibly for the same purpose, and independently of the concerti grossi with which they were eventually published. The same manuscript also provides evidence of revision: the corrente in the autograph is in D major, but when Corelli included the piece in Concerto Grosso No. 10, he transposed it to C. Another example of selection and revision comes from the introductory sinfonia that Corelli composed for Lulier's *Santa Beatrice d'Este* in 1689. The second movement of the sinfonia, a largo, turns up, with extensive revisions in scoring and voice leading, as the third movement of Op. 6 No. 6. The other movements from the sinfonia do not appear in the Concerti Grossi. Corelli himself, in a letter to a German prince who had asked him for a "concertino da camera," complained that he could bring himself to publish his music only after a long process of revision ("doppo molte, e lunghe correzzioni").[104] Perhaps the largo from the *Santa Beatrice* sinfonia was tried out in performance several times and revised before Corelli considered it ready for Op. 6. Peter Allsop, on the other hand, argues that the concertos of Corelli's Opus 6 show many signs of having been conceived and composed as unified works rather than being anthologies of a preexisting repertory.[105] Some of them seem to have

[100] Marc Pincherle, *Corelli: His Life, his Work,* trans. Herbert Russell (New York, 1956), 120–22.

[101] John Daverio, considering the same evidence, believes that Muffat probably heard Corelli trio sonatas in orchestral scorings ("In Search of the Sonata da camera," 204).

[102] Piperno, "Le orchestre di Corelli," 46. See also id., "Corelli e il 'concerto' seicentesco: lettura e interpretazione dell'opera VI," in *Studi Corelliani IV,* ed. Petrobelli and Staffieri, 359–80 at 364.

[103] See above. Corelli ran out of room for the Pastorale, so he put the last few bars on the other side of the page, after the Corrente. Thus the Corrrente must have been composed first. Marx believes that the Pastorale was written for Christmas 1689. See Hans Joachim Marx, "Römische Weihnachtsoratorien aus der ersten Hälfte des 18. Jahrhunderts," *Archiv für Musikwissenschaft,* 49 (1992), 163–99 at 193.

[104] Letter to Kurfürst Johann Wilhelm of Pfalz-Neuburg, quoted in Rinaldi, *Arcangelo Corelli,* 444.

[105] Allsop, *Corelli,* 150–51.

thematic links between movements (Concertos 3, 12); in others the movements have similar formal plans (Concertos 3, 6).

Perhaps all three solutions to the mystery of the missing repertory are correct. Corelli's orchestra may well have played some works by Corelli that are now lost. The orchestra may also have performed pieces that Corelli published as trio sonata movements; and if so, the trios were most likely turned into concerti grossi by adding the full ensemble in loud passages. Finally, Corelli's orchestra almost certainly played individual movements or pairs of movements from Op. 6 as independent works in separate performances.

Chapter Five

The Orchestra in Italy

By the time of Corelli's death in 1713 many Italian instrumental ensembles had taken on attributes of an orchestra. They were based on violin-family instruments; they used several players on each part; they played as unified ensembles. A distinctive repertory of music was beginning to emerge for such ensembles—concertos, *sinfonie*, and concerted sacred music—and instrumental ensembles were beginning to assume their own identities, distinct from singers and other musical personnel. Corelli's ensembles in Rome had been pioneers and leaders in these developments, but they were not alone. Ensembles with some or all of these characteristics could be found in Bologna, Turin, Venice, and several other Italian cities.

VOICES AND INSTRUMENTS IN ITALIAN OPERA

The ensembles that played in the theater for operas underwent striking changes during the first half of the eighteenth century. Perhaps the most important change lay in the relation between voices and bowed stringed instruments. In seventeenth-century Italian opera bowed strings rarely played when anyone sang. Singing was usually accompanied by a continuo of plucked strings and keyboards—the "mean symphony" of lutes, theorbos, and harpsichords that Saint Didier heard in Venetian theaters in the 1670s (see Ch. 2). Example 5.1 shows a passage from Act I of *Orfeo* by Antonio Sartorio (Venice, 1673), one of the Orpheus operas discussed in Chapter 1. At the beginning of the scene keyboard and plucked-string continuo accompanies the singer's recitative. Next the bowed strings play a short introduction in five parts presenting the tune of the following aria. When the voice enters, the bowed strings fall silent and the continuo instruments alone play along with the singer. This is a so-called continuo aria, accompanied by keyboards and plucked strings, all playing from

Ex. 5.1. A. Sartorio, *L'Orfeo*, Act I, Scene iv ("Poor Aristeo burns for Euridice, but she won't even discuss the subject of love. Either she doesn't hear, or she doesn't want to understand. If I could return to the flower of my youth. . . .")

the bass part. In Sartorio's opera the bowed strings accompany arias directly only at emotional high points, like Orfeo's lament for Euridice in Act III (Ex. 5.2). In this "accompanied" aria the string band enters at the ends of phrases and echoes Orfeo's words, falling silent again when the voice enters.[1] Only at the words "uccidami il duol" ("may sorrow kill me") do the strings play while Orfeo is singing. Accompanied arias like this one were rare in seventeenth-century Italian operas. For the most part the bowed strings served purposes other than vocal accompaniment: they introduced the acts with *sinfonie*; they marked the beginnings and ends of arias with ritornellos; they accompanied dances; and they attempted to cover up the noise of the stage machinery between scenes.

Beginning in the 1680s, the nascent orchestra encroached more and more on the domain of the voice in Italian opera. Bowed strings accompanied more arias, and they accompanied more insistently. The decisive period was from 1690 to about 1730. Harris Saunders, in his study of the Grimani theater in Venice, shows that the proportion of accompanied arias began to climb around 1690, until by 1710 accompanied arias outnumbered continuo arias by a considerable margin. Not only did the string ensemble accompany more arias, it accompanied more actively, overlapping the last few beats of the singer's phrase—sometimes the last few bars. The orchestra began to play along with the voice for entire phrases, sometimes adding a countermelody, sometimes a rhythmically active accompaniment.[2]

By 1730 continuo arias had practically disappeared from Italian opera, and instruments overlapped voices ever more closely. Michael Collins traces this development in a series of operas by Alessandro Scarlatti.[3] In Scarlatti's earlier operas half or more of the arias are accompanied by continuo without bowed strings. The percentage decreases gradually from 1679 to 1697, rapidly thereafter: in *Eraclea* (1700) 28 percent of the arias are continuo arias, in *Mitridate* (1707) only 7 percent. In his last two operas, *Marco Attilio Regolo* (1719) and *Griselda* (1721) Scarlatti eliminates continuo arias altogether: all arias are accompanied by the full orchestra. Handel and Vivaldi, Scarlatti's younger contemporaries, still wrote occasional continuo arias, but the percentage decreased over the course of their careers too. In operas by the generation of composers that came to prominence in the 1720s and 1730s—Vinci, Leo, Hasse, and others—continuo arias are rare: most arias are accompanied by full strings. Sometimes the violins simply double the voice part. Alarmed by this trend, Pietro Francesco

---

[1] Ellen Rosand explains how these string echoes function rhetorically: "Their immediate reiteration of a vocal phrase reinforces the meaning of that phrase without actual text repetition. Thus the composer can use them to intensify an affect without resorting to unnatural rhetoric" (Antonio Sartorio, *L'Orfeo*, ed. Rosand, p. xl).

[2] Harris Sheridan Saunders, "The Repertoire of a Venetian Opera House (1678–1714): The Teatro Grimani di San Giovanni Grisostomo," (Ph.D. diss. Harvard University, 1985), 182, 229, 280, 290.

[3] Michael Collins, "L'orchestra nelle opere teatrali di Vivaldi," in *Nuovi studi vivaldiani*, ed. Antonio Fana and Giovanni Morelli (Florence, 1988), 285–312.

Ex. 5.2. A. Sartorio, *L'Orfeo*, Act III, Scene iii ("Euridice is dead; never again will I see the rays of the sun. Sorrow is killing me")

Tosi, in his vocal treatise of 1723, complained that the voice now has "the Mortification to resign its Place to the Violins."[4]

Wind instruments too began to join aria accompaniments in the late seventeenth century. Trumpets, which in the stereotyped martial ensembles of intermedio and court opera had played fanfares and symphonies for battle scenes, now sometimes accompanied arias along with the strings. Often these were calls to arms or arias in which the trumpet was mentioned by name.[5] By the third decade of the eighteenth century the trumpet had become an equal partner in these arias, sometimes a rival to the singer. Charles Burney transmits an anecdote about the great castrato Farinelli, singing in Rome in 1722:

During the run of an opera, there was a struggle every night between him and a famous player on the trumpet, in a song accompanied by that instrument. This, at first, seemed amicable and merely sportive, till the audience began to interest themselves in the contest, and to take different sides . . .[6]

The aria ended with a cadenza in which Farinelli and the trumpeter had a long trill together in thirds. "The trumpeter," continues Burney, "gave it up, thinking . . . his antagonist as much tired as himself." Farinelli, however, "broke out all at once in the same breath, with fresh vigor, and not only swelled and shook the note, but ran the most rapid and difficult divisions, and was at last silenced only by the acclamations of the audience."[7]

Oboes and flutes, like trumpets, joined aria accompaniments initially for their extra-musical associations, in this case pastoral and rustic. Flutes kept their pastoral associations throughout the eighteenth century and beyond. Oboes, however, soon shed their stereotypical role. Composers began to use them to reinforce the violin parts or to provide contrast to the violin sound.[8] Oboes also found a new role in arias expressing strong emotions. Whereas in the mid-seventeenth century the addition of string accompaniment had been enough to mark an aria as special, by the eighteenth century string accompaniment had become routine, and it took the pathos of a wind soloist to suggest the same level of emotion.

Besides its incursions on the voice in arias, the nascent orchestra began to encroach on recitative as well. Already in the mid-seventeenth century composers like Cavalli occasionally used bowed strings to enhance the recitative at climactic moments in the drama. By the 1720s such episodes of accompanied recitative had become a standard

---

[4] Pietro Francesco Tosi, *Observations on the Florid Song*, trans. Galliard (London, 1743), 73, 116.

[5] For a comprehensive survey of trumpet accompaniments in 17th-c. Italian opera, see Tarr and Walker, "'Bellici carmi, festivo fragor.'"

[6] Charles Burney, *The Present State of Music in France and Italy* (London, 1773), 213–14. This anecdote is fantastically re-created in the opening scene of the film *Farinelli* (1994).

[7] For further accounts of contests between singers and wind soloists, see John Spitzer, "Improvized Ornamentation in a Handel Aria with Obbligato Wind Accompaniment," *EM* 16 (1988), 514–22.

[8] Saunders, "Repertoire," 232.

feature of *opera seria*, with the orchestra adding its voice to threats, promises, expressions of despair, and invocations to the gods. As Metastasio explained in a letter to the composer Hasse on the subject of accompanied recitative, the instruments should vary the tempo and the harmonies, "not merely to express and enforce the words or sentiments . . . but to paint also the situation of mind of him who pronounces these words and sentiments."[9] In operas by mid-eighteenth-century composers like Hasse, J. C. Bach, and Jommelli, bowed strings and sometimes the full orchestra accompanied more and more of the recitative, until in Gluck's *Orfeo* (Vienna, 1762) the orchestra accompanied not only the arias but all the recitatives as well.[10]

The changes in the role of the orchestra over the course of the eighteenth century were noted by critics and commentators, often with disapproval. Burney, describing the opera at Milan in 1770, complained on acoustical grounds: "In the opera-house little else but the instruments can be heard, unless when the baritoni or base voices sing . . . a delicate voice is suffocated: it seems to me as if the orchestra not only played too loud, but that it had too much to do."[11] Arteaga (1785) objected for aesthetic reasons: instruments, unlike singers, could not speak and thus could not convey human emotions, "which are not expressed in man by the sound of an oboe or a violin."[12] Burney and Arteaga's critiques (like much music criticism) came after the fact. By their day the orchestra had long since consolidated its position in opera as a intimate collaborator, sometimes an equal partner, with the voice.

THE SIZE AND SHAPE OF OPERA ORCHESTRAS

The trend toward more pervasive orchestral accompaniments in Italian opera stimulated larger orchestras. Larger orchestras in turn appropriated for themselves an ever more important role in the theater. The growing importance of the orchestra in Italian opera over the course of the eighteenth century can be seen in personnel records from selected Italian theaters, summarized in Table 5.1. The Teatro Ducale in Milan and the Teatro Regio in Turin were the two largest theaters in northern Italy. Both were sponsored and subsidized by courts—the Teatro Ducale by the Austrian governor's court in Milan, the Teatro Regio by the court of Savoy. The orchestras at both theaters grew steadily larger during the eighteenth century. Already in 1707 the strings of the Milan orchestra were copiously doubled, with 18 violins, eight violas, three violoni, and 3 double basses—and the number of violins continued to increase: 22 in 1747, 30 in 1778. The orchestra in Turin, which was initially somewhat small-

[9] Charles Burney, *Memoirs of the Life and Writings of the Abate Metastasio* (London, 1796), i. 326.

[10] In its exclusive use of accompanied recitative, Gluck's *Orfeo* was exceptional for its time. Not until the second decade of the 19th c. did orchestral accompaniment throughout become the norm.

[11] Burney, *Present State of Music in France and Italy*, 108.

[12] Esteban de Arteaga, *Le rivoluzioni del teatro musicale italiano della sua origine fino al presente* (Venice, 1785), 47.

er than in Milan, caught up around about the middle of the century. As the number of violins increased, other instruments did not keep up. Instead, the principle of unequal doubling became ever more pronounced. The proportion of violas to violins declined steadily in both orchestras, from almost half as many violas as violins at the beginning of the period to about a fifth by 1770. The proportion of lower strings (violoni, cellos, double basses) in the orchestra remained about the same in Milan, but in Turin it declined, from nine cellos and basses vs. 17 violins and violas in 1736 to nine cellos and basses vs. 30 violins and violas in 1780. Both orchestras used only two cellos during most of the century. Thus, Italian opera orchestras of the period tended to be polarized, with ever-increasing numbers of violins on top, little sound in the alto and tenor range, then a strong bass in the 16' register. The number of wind instruments was not large, but the winds maintained themselves in proportion to the strings during most of the period, then increased in the last quarter of the century. Players listed in the rosters as "oboes" doubled on flutes, sometimes also on bassoons and, toward the end of the century, on clarinets as well. Horns and trumpets were played by the same personnel during much of the period.

The development of the orchestra at the San Carlo theater in Naples took a somewhat different course from those in Milan and Turin. Where the northern orchestras enjoyed more or less steady growth during the eighteenth century, the San Carlo orchestra showed a pattern of fluctuation according to the finances of the opera house, which was administered by the court. It grew to 70 members in 1741, but the next year a new impresario took over with a mandate to downsize, and the orchestra was cut back to 53, over the protests of the furloughed instrumentalists.[13] Around 1780 it reached another maximum, then declined gradually in the final decades of the century. Nonetheless, the balances of the San Carlo orchestra were similar to those in Milan and Turin: the growing numbers of violins were not matched by the basses, and the middle parts (violas and cellos) grew proportionately weaker. As in northern Italy, the winds at first merely kept up with the increase in violins, then increased proportionately in the last quarter of the century. Flutes are not distinguished from oboes, nor horns from trumpets on the Neapolitan payrolls, but operas staged in Naples contained flute parts as early as 1700 and horn parts from the 1720s.[14]

The orchestras of Naples, Milan, and Turin were the largest standing theater orchestras in all of Italy, because they were located in cities with important and relatively prosperous courts. The court in each case underwrote the opera with large annual subsidies, and the personnel of the Naples and Turin orchestras overlapped with the membership of the court *cappelle*.[15] The size of the orchestra, like the

---

[13] Ulisse Prota-Giurleo, *La grande orchestra del R. Teatro San Carlo nel Settecento* (Naples, 1927), 12.

[14] Helmut Hell, *Die neapolitanische Opernsinfonie in der ersten Hälfte des 18. Jahrhunderts* (Tutzing, 1971), 47–48, 55–57.

[15] See Marie-Thérèse Bouquet, *Il Teatro di Corte dalle origini al 1788* (Turin, 1976), 168; Dennis Libby, "Italy: Two Opera Centres," in Neal Zaslaw (ed.), *The Classical Era* (Englewood Cliffs, NJ, 1989), 15–60 at 23–24.

TABLE 5.1. *Representative Italian opera orchestras, 1707–99*

City, date, venue	Keyboard and plucked strings	Bowed strings	Winds	Brass and percussion	Source
Bologna, 1778, Teatro Comunale	2 harpsichords	25 violins 8 violas 2 cellos 7 double basses	2 flutes 2 oboes 1 English horn 2 bassoons	4 horns 4 trumpets 4 trombones 1 timpani	Ricci, *Teatri*, 654
Cremona, 1759, Teatro Nazari	1 harpsichord	10 violins and violas 1 cello 2 double basses	2 oboes	2 horns	Santoro, *Teatro*, 239
Cremona, 1797, Teatro della Società	1 harpsichord	13 violins 2 violas 1 cello 2 double basses	2 oboes	3 horns	Ibid. 203
Faenza, 1788, Teatro Comunale	[1 harpsichord]	16 violins 2 violas 1 cello 3 double basses	2 oboes 1 clarinet 1 bassoon	2 horns 1 trumpet 1 trombone	Tampieri, "Orchestre," 460
Florence, 1767, Teatro della Pergola	2 harpsichords	19 violins 4 violas 2 cellos 4 double basses	2 flutes 2 oboes 1 bassoon	2 horns 2 trumpets 1 timpani	Weaver and Weaver, *Chronology*, 88

Location	Keyboard	Strings	Winds	Brass	Source
Milan, 1707, Teatro Ducale	2 harpsichords	18 violins 8 violas 3 violoni 3 violoni gross	6 oboes 2 bassoons	1 horn	Schnoebelen, "Performance," 45
Milan, 1747, Teatro Ducale	[2 harpsichords]	22 violins 6 violas 2 cellos 5 double basses	2 oboes 2 bassoons	5 trumpets [and horns]	Barblan, "Musica," 627
Milan, 1778, La Scala (opening)	2 harpsichords	30 violins 8 violas 13 cellos and basses	2 flutes 6 oboes [and clarinets] 2 bassoons	4 horns 4 trumpets	Ibid. 654
Naples, 1737, Teatro San Carlo	2 harpsichords	24 violins 6 violas 3 cellos 3 basses	2 oboes 3 bassoons	2 trumpets	Prota-Giurleo, *Grande orchestra*, 7–8
Naples, 1741, Teatro San Carlo	2 harpsichords	38 violins 8 violas 2 cellos 4 basses	6 oboes 4 bassoons	6 trumpets [and horns]	Ibid. 11
Naples, 1796, Teatro San Carlo	2 harpsichords	25 violins 4 violas 2 cellos 6 double basses	2 oboes 2 clarinets 4 bassoons	4 horns [and trumpets]	Ibid. 53

TABLE 5.1. (*Cont.*)

City, date, venue	Keyboard and plucked strings	Bowed strings	Winds	Brass and percussion	Source
Naples, 1799, Teatro Nuovo	1 harpsichord	14 violins and violas 2 cellos 2 double basses	2 oboes 1 bassoon	2 trumpets	Robinson, "Late 18th-Century," 161
Piacenza, 1752, Ducal theater	1 harpsichord	10 violins 4 violas 1 cello 3 double basses		2 horns	Rabitti, "Orchestre," 37
Reggio Emilia, 1759, Teatro dell'illustrissimo publico	1 harpsichord	17 violins 3 violas 2 cellos 3 double basses	[2 oboes] 2 bassoons	2 horns 1 trumpet 1 timpani	Fabbri and Verti, *Due secoli*, 73
Rome, 1758, Teatro Argentina	[2 harpsichords]	16 violins 4 violas 2 cellos 4 double basses	2 oboes	2 horns 2 trumpets	Rostirolla, "Professione," 168

Trieste, 1793, Teatro San Pietro	1 harpsichord	10 violins 2 violas 1 cello 2 double basses	2 oboes	2 horns	Curiel, *Teatro*, 481
Turin, 1736, Teatro Regio	2 harpsichords	12 violins 5 violas 2 cellos 7 bassi	2 oboes 2 bassoons	2 horns 2 trumpets [?]	Bouquet, *Teatro*, 133
Turin, 1755, Teatro Regio	2 harpsichords	21 violins 4 violas 2 cellos 6 bassi di ripieno 2 double basses	3 oboes	4 horns	Ibid. 172
Turin, 1780, Teatro Regio	2 harpsichords	26 violins 4 violas 3 cellos 6 contrabassi	4 oboes 2 clarinets 3 bassoons	4 horns 2 trumpets 1 timpani	Ibid. 388

lavishness of the sets, the opulence of the decor, and the reputation of the singers, reflected the wealth, power, and prestige of the court.

Theater orchestras in cities where opera was a purely commercial undertaking tended to be smaller than the orchestras of Milan, Turin, and Naples. Unfortunately, few records have survived from such theaters, not even from Venice, where four or five theaters maintained orchestras during most of the eighteenth century. The largest of these commercial theater orchestras in Table 5.1 is an orchestra of 58 at the opening of the Teatro Comunale in Bologna in 1763. However, only 37 of these players were members of the standing orchestra; the rest were brought from neighboring cities for the gala event.[16] Representative orchestras in Florence, Reggio Emilia, and Rome number from 30 to 40 players; orchestras in smaller cities (Cremona, Piacenza, Trieste) number around 20. The string proportions of all these orchestras resemble those of the court-sponsored orchestras: heavy on violins, light on violas and cellos. The winds, however—except for the gala ensemble in Bologna—tend to be more sparse than in Turin, Milan, and Naples: just pairs of horns and oboes in many cases. Orchestras for comic opera were smaller than orchestras for *opera seria*, but hardly any records have survived.[17]

The changes in musical style that took place between 1690 and 1730 greatly enhanced the role of bowed strings in Italian opera, but the continuo ensemble retained primary responsibility for vocal accompaniment. In arias it shared accompaniment duties with the bowed strings and sometimes with the winds as well; in simple (*secco*) recitative only the continuo accompanied. The continuo players rehearsed the singers in advance of general rehearsals; they guided (or followed) the singers in performance.

The make-up of the continuo ensemble changed significantly during the late seventeenth and early eighteenth centuries. Cello, violone, and double bass, which had originally belonged to the string band rather than the vocal accompaniment, were introduced into the continuo group, perhaps during the last decade of the seventeenth century.[18] Pictures of operas in Turin and Venice in the 1680s and 1690s show continuo groups comprising keyboards and plucked strings only, no bowed bass instruments.[19] In depictions of eighteenth-century opera orchestras, on the other hand, cellos and double basses sit next to the keyboard players, evidently playing along on the continuo part.[20] The orchestras in Table 5.1, all from the eighteenth

---

[16] Piero Mioli, "Il Teatro Communale: centottanta anni di presenza," in Conati and Pavarani (eds.), *Orchestre in Emilia-Romagna nell'Ottocento e Novecento*, 325–42 at 327.

[17] At the Teatro Nuovo in Naples the orchestra numbered about 25 in 1799; at the Teatro dei Fiorentini, another Neapolitan comic opera venue, the orchestra numbered 23 in 1799 (Michael F. Robinson, *Naples and Neapolitan Opera* (Oxford, 1972), 161). When comic operas were given in Turin during the 1760s, only half as many parts were copied out for the instrumentalists as were copied for serious operas (Bouquet, *Il Teatro di Corte*, 194).

[18] Tharald Borgir, *The Performance of the Basso Continuo in Italian Baroque Music* (Ann Arbor, 1987), 31–35.

[19] See Pl. XV.   [20] See Pl. III and below, Figs. 10.2, 10.3.

century, contain no plucked strings at all. Lutes, archlutes, and theorbos must still have been available, though, because opera scores occasionally call for them in the accompaniments.[21] On the whole, however, lutenists, guitarists, and theorbo players, who had been common on the personnel lists of seventeenth-century opera orchestras, disappeared from eighteenth-century rosters. The decline of plucked strings may have been due to the soft dynamics of lute-family instruments and their inability to project in the new, larger theaters constructed in the first half of the eighteenth century.[22]

Another reason for the disappearance of plucked strings from the continuo may have been intonation. Lutes and other fretted instruments in the seventeenth and eighteenth centuries were customarily tuned in something approximating equal temperament, with half-steps equal or nearly equal to one another. Harpsichords, on the other hand, tended to be tuned in meantone tuning, where whole steps were equal but the size of half-steps varied.[23] In consequence, keyboards and plucked strings were chronically out of tune with one another, a problem that contemporary critics often complained about.[24] Given a choice between lutes and keyboards for the continuo ensemble, Italian opera chose keyboards. Cellos and basses, since they were unfretted instruments, could adapt themselves to either tuning system. One or two bassoons were added to the continuo in the larger theaters, but smaller theaters usually got along without them.

The continuo ensemble in eighteenth-century Italian opera was often divided into two sub-ensembles. Francesco Galeazzi described the system in 1791: "there are usually two harpsichords, one at the head of the orchestra, one at the foot, each one of which is surrounded by a group of bass instruments. In this all the orchestras of Italy agree."[25] By the "head" of the orchestra, Galeazzi means the left-hand side—that is, stage right—which was considered the more "noble" side of the theater. The instrument in this position was the first harpsichord, from which the composer led the first three performances of an opera. After that the local *maestro di cappella* took over. The harpsichord at the "foot" of the orchestra was played by a second cembalo player—first the local maestro, then, from the fourth performance on, his assistant. Next to each harpsichordist were a cellist and a bassist, who read the bass line from the score on the harpsichord.

---

[21] 18th-c. operas that specify plucked strings as members of the continuo group include: Feo, *Amor tirannico* (1712), lute; Vinci, *Farnace* (1724), bass lute; Handel, *Giulio Cesare* (1724), theorbo and harp; Handel, *Partenope* (1730), theorbo; Hasse, *Cleofide* (1731), archlute (Hell, *Die neapolitanische Opernsinfonie*, 47).

[22] A new Teatro Ducale opened in Milan in 1717; the San Carlo theater in Naples was built in 1737; the Teatro Regio in Turin was inaugurated in 1740. On the musical building boom in 18th-c. Europe, see Ch. 10.

[23] Patrizio Barbieri, "Conflitti di intonazione tra cembalo, liuto e archi nel 'concerto' italiano del Seicento," in *Studi corelliani IV*, ed. Pierluigi Petrobelli and Gloria Staffieri (Florence, 1990), 123–53 at 125, 128–38; Mark Lindley, *Lutes, Viols, and Temperaments* (Cambridge, 1984), 19–42, 43 ff. Lindley believes that some lutenists and viol players used meantone tunings but acknowledges that they were exceptions (p. 50).

[24] Bruce Haynes, "Beyond Temperament: Non-keyboard Intonation in the 17th and 18th Centuries," *EM* 19 (1991), 357–81 at 361 ff.

[25] Francesco Galeazzi, *Elementi teorico-pratici di musica* (Rome, 1791–96), i. 221.

The two-continuo system can be seen clearly in many pictures. Plate III is a painting of the orchestra at the opening of Teatro Regio, Turin, in 1740. The first harpsichordist sits on the left flanked by a cellist and a bassist. The second harpsichordist is on the right with a second continuo group. Additional cellists and bassists stand farther back on either side, reading not from the score but from their own parts. Bassoonists stand next to the ripieno basses on both sides, presumably playing along with the continuo. Other pictures of eighteenth-century orchestras for Italian opera, not just in Italy but elsewhere in Europe, show the same configuration with two harpsichords and two continuo groups.[26]

The purpose of the two-continuo system is imperfectly understood. A few extant parts for eighteenth-century Italian operas are labeled "2° cembalo"; they contain arias and *sinfonie*, but no recitatives.[27] This implies that the first cembalo player accompanied recitative by himself, perhaps along with the cellist and bassist who read from his score.[28] In arias first and second continuo groups both played. Pasquale Cafaro, maestro at the San Carlo theater in Naples in 1773, explains one reason for this practice: "The second harpsichord, along with a violoncello and a double bass in the same location, is very necessary for the convenience of the singers whenever they find themselves far from the first [harpsichord] to prevent them from straying from the path of perfect intonation."[29] The orchestral enclosure in an eighteenth-century opera house was long and narrow, and the theater was often noisy. Placing a continuo group at either end of the orchestra made the bass line, the beat, and the harmony audible to the singers, no matter where they stood on the stage. It also helped the long rows of instrumentalists stay together and perhaps to find their places when they got lost.[30]

Occasionally composers took advantage of the two-continuo system to create special effects. Bononcini, in an accompanied aria from *Il trionfo di Camilla* (Naples, 1696), has cembalo 1° and cembalo 2° play in unison during the ritornello, but when the voice enters, the first harpsichord plays with the singer, while the second plays

[26] See Figs. 10.2, 10.3.

[27] See Curtis Price, Judith Milhous, and Robert D. Hume, *Italian Opera in Late Eighteenth-Century London*, i: *The King's Theatre, Haymarket, 1778–1791* (Oxford, 1995), 118; Reinhard Strohm, *Italianische Opernarien des frühen Settecento (1720–1730)* (Analecta Musicologica, 16/1–2; Cologne, 1976), i. 83; Hell, *Die neapolitanische Opernsinfonie*, 35. The first harpsichordist played from a full score of the opera, often the only full score available to any of the performers. The second harpsichordist usually read from a *basso* part, sometimes with figures, often unfigured. See Patrick J. Rogers, *Continuo Realization in Handel's Vocal Music* (Ann Arbor, 1989), 61 ff.

[28] That the first cello played along in recitatives can be deduced from Benedetto Marcello's sarcastic suggestion (*c*.1720) that the cellist should accompany recitatives an octave above the written bass line, particularly when the singer is a tenor or a bass (Benedetto Marcello, *Il teatro alla moda* (*c*.1720) (Udine, 1992), 54). See also Spitzer and Zaslaw, "Improvised Ornamentation in Eighteenth-Century Orchestras," 534–35, 564–65.

[29] Quoted in Prota-Giurleo, *La grande orchestra*, 27.

[30] In some cases it seems as though the second harpsichord may have played in only the ritornello of an aria, then dropped out when the singer entered. Two insertion arias for the 1736 revival of Handel's *Poro* in London have second cembalo parts containing only ritornelli (George Frederick Handel, *Poro*, ed. Friedrich Chrysander (Leipzig, 1880), Preface, 102, 107).

with the violins.[31] In one aria from Alessandro Scarlatti's *Il prigioniero fortunato* (Naples, 1698) the first harpsichord plays with the first violins, *sempre forte*, the second harpsichord with the second violins, *sempre piano*, thereby creating an echo effect that Scarlatti maintains for the entire aria.[32] In a duet from *Sosarme* (1732), an Italian opera written for London, Handel lets one continuo group accompany the *prima donna*, while the other group (which includes a theorbo) accompanies the male lead.[33] Leonardo Leo in the *sinfonia* to *Lo matrimonio annascuso* (Naples, 1727) divides the entire orchestra into two halves, each with its own harpsichord.[34]

Smaller theaters and theaters that played mainly comic operas normally used only a single harpsichord. Here the harpsichord could be heard by the singers no matter where they stood. By the beginning of the nineteenth century the second harpsichord had begun to disappear from large theaters, as more and more of the opera was accompanied by the orchestra.

In seventeenth-century Italian operas one of the principal roles of the bowed-string ensemble had been to accompany dances. As dance was formalized in the eighteenth century and turned into ballets at the ends of the acts or at the end of the opera as an afterpiece, dance music remained distinct from the rest of the opera. Ballets were usually composed by a different person than the composer of the opera, often by one of the violinists in the orchestra.[35] Harpsichords and plucked strings did not play during the dances, and some of the other instrumentalists were permitted to take a break as well. Regulations from the Teatro di Corte in Turin in 1747 state that the two harpsichords, the concertmaster (*capo d'orchestra*), the principal second violin, and the first-chair oboe, bassoon, cello, and bass players are excused from ballet rehearsals and from playing the ballets during the opera.[36] A later set of regulations (1768) exempts the same players, except for the first bassoonist, who is obliged now to play for both opera and ballet.[37] In Turin as elsewhere a violinist other than the concertmaster was designated as leader "per i balli," a designation that continued to appear in Italian orchestra lists and libretti well into the nineteenth century. Accompanying the dance

[31] Giovanni Bononcini, *Il Trionfo di Camilla, Regina de' Volsci*, ed. Howard Mayer Brown (New York, 1978), 117.

[32] See below, Ex. 13.25.

[33] George Frederick Handel, *Sosarme*, ed. Friedrich Chrysander (Leipzig, 1880), 102 ff. See Dirk Möller, "Zur Generalbassbesetzung in den Opern Georg Friedrich Händels," *Göttinger Händel-Beiträge*, 2 (1986), 141–54 at 148–49; also Friedrich Chrysander, "Zwei Claviere bei Händel," *Allgemeine musikalische Zeitung*, 12/13 (1877), cols. 177–80, 193–98.

[34] Hell, *Die neapolitanische Opernsinfonie*, 59. "Torbido in volto e nero," an aria in Pergolesi's *Adriano in Siria* (Naples, 1734), is likewise accompanied by two orchestras.

[35] Kathleen Kuzmick Hansell, "Il ballo teatrale e l'opera italiana," in *Storia dell'opera italiana*, v, ed. Lorenzo Bianconi and Giorgio Pestelli (Turin, 1987), 175–302 at 211.

[36] Bouquet, *Il Teatro di Corte*, 175. The exemptions for one oboist and one bassoonist show that the dance orchestra at Turin, although based on violin-family instruments, also included winds. Scores for ballets performed at Turin in the mid-18th c. and preserved at the Conservatorio di S. Cecilia in Rome include wind parts (Hansell, "Il ballo teatrale," 212–13, and personal communication).

[37] Bouquet, *Il Teatro di Corte*, 177.

was less prestigious than accompanying voices, and players shirked the task when they could. A memorandum from the management of the San Carlo theater in Naples dated 1742 warns that all the violinists must play in all the ballets, so that no one can complain that some players are receiving special treatment. The warning seems to have fallen on deaf ears: a memorandum of 1772 complains that out of 54 instrumentalists, only 20 play the ballets.[38] The 1747 Turin regulations, although they exempt the first violinist from playing in dances, instruct him to remain in the orchestra and "watch to see that the other *virtuosi* perform their parts."[39]

Besides accompanying ballets danced by professionals between the acts of operas, Italian orchestras played for social dancing. Dances were held after the end of the opera, sometimes in the theater itself, with music provided by the same ensemble that had played the dances in the opera. The orchestra was moved to the stage, and the theater was transformed into a ballroom. More often, dances were held in palaces or private residences, using an orchestra assembled for the occasion. Aristocratic social dancing in Italy is not well documented: surprisingly little music is transmitted, and there are few pay records for the musicians. There are, however, many pictures. Figure 5.1 depicts a masked ball given in the royal palace in Naples in 1747 as part of the festivities to celebrate the birth of a male heir to the Bourbon throne. Most of the guests are seated to the sides of the dance floor. Chairs for the king and queen have been placed directly in the center. A very large orchestra is installed in tiers on the stage, dressed, according to a contemporary account, in pink satin uniforms "all'eroica."[40] Almost 60 bowed strings can be seen, plus eight oboes, two flutes, four horns, and an archlute. There are no keyboard instruments nor any sign of a continuo group. In the center of the front and back rows stand two men with raised sticks in their right hands. Presumably these are drummers, keeping the beat for the orchestra and the dancers.[41] This orchestra is considerably larger than the orchestra of the San Carlo theater during the same period. Very likely it represents both the theater orchestra and the court *cappella*, augmented by local musicians. Except for the lack of keyboards and a continuo group, and the addition of drums, the instrumentation and balances for Italian dance orchestras were similar to those of opera orchestras.

Another distinct ensemble in seventeenth- and eighteenth-century Italian operas was the stage band, that is, instrumentalists who appeared onstage in costume as part of the action. Stage bands, which could include strings or winds or both, appeared most often in festive scenes. Already in Pallavicino's *Nerone* (Venice, 1679) an ensemble of forty instruments, including "flutes, trumpets, drums, viols, and violins,"

---

[38] Prota-Giurleo, *La grande orchestra*, 14, 21.   [39] Bouquet, *Il Teatro di Corte*, 176.

[40] *Narrazione delle solenne reali feste fatte in Napoli di sua Maestà il Re delle due Sicilie Carlo Infante di Spagna per la nascita del suo primo genito Filippo, reale principe delle Due Sicilie* (Naples, 1749), 7.

[41] Drummers are common in pictures of 18th-c. dance orchestras, particularly large ones. Keyboards are extremely rare.

Fɪɢ. 5.1. Masked ball in the royal palace, Naples, 1747

played onstage for a dance and in a triumphal procession.[42] In the last act this stage band was broken into smaller groups to accompany a banquet, then reassembled on platforms at the back of the stage surrounded by clouds, a reminiscence of the Olympian tableaux of the sixteenth century. Occasionally stage bands accompanied arias. In *Arsace* by Domenico Sarro (Naples, 1718) the comic bass declares his love for his sweetheart to the accompaniment of a stage band of oboes and bassoons.[43] In many

[42] *Mercure de France* (Apr. 1679), pp. 75 ff. Text in Eleanor Selfridge-Field, *Pallade Veneta: Writings on Music in Venetian Society, 1650–1750* (Venice, 1985), 340–43. Viols were unusual in the Italian theater. Perhaps the French reporter was confused about Italian instrument terminology.

[43] Domenico Sarri, *Arsace* (New York, 1978), 265 ff.

cases the players for the stage band did not come from the regular theater orchestra; instead supernumeraries were hired for the occasion. In Naples at the San Carlo theater a wind band from the Swiss guards provided onstage music for Sarro's *Ezio* (1741) and *Tigrane* by Hasse (1746).[44] For a dance scene in Hasse's *Ipermestra* (Naples, 1746), students from the Conservatorio della Pietà dei Turchini were placed in two bandstands on the stage. They played dance music together with the dance ensemble from the regular orchestra.[45] Unlike the other sub-ensembles, which tended to merge more and more into a single opera orchestra, the stage band became more distinct during the course of the eighteenth century, leading toward the nineteenth-century *banda sul palco*, made up exclusively of wind instruments.

Two overall trends can be discerned in Italian opera orchestras during the eighteenth century: growth and integration. Opera orchestras got larger, especially the orchestras for *opera seria* in the large theaters, but also orchestras for comic opera and orchestras in smaller theaters. Growth at first emphasized the violins, later the winds. It de-emphasized plucked strings, violas, and cellos, so that by the end of the eighteenth century the sound of Italian opera orchestras was not only louder but more treble dominated than it had been at the beginning of the period. Integration took two related forms. The continuo ensemble and the bowed string ensemble, which at the beginning of the period had distinct identities and roles, tended to merge more and more into a single unified orchestra. At the same time this emerging orchestra was increasingly integrated into the texture of the opera, playing more music in more contexts, and assuming an ever more central role.

ORCHESTRAS FOR ORATORIOS AND SERENATAS

As large-scale works, sung in Italian, featuring solo singers, and accompanied by an instrumental ensemble, oratorios and serenatas were close in style to opera. But whereas most operas received five to 20 or more performances during the course of a season, serenades and oratorios were one-time affairs. Oratorios were customarily performed once or maybe twice during Holy Week or at Christmas; serenatas were occasional works, written and performed for the birthday of a prince or princess or for some other political, dynastic, or social occasion.[46] In Italy the venue for oratorios was usually a church, although performances in seminaries and private theaters were not uncommon. Serenatas were most often performed outdoors and usually in the evening, but sometimes they took place in a theater. Serenades and oratorios used sets, often elabor-

---

[44] Prota-Giurleo, *La grande orchestra*, 14; Libby, "Italy," 24.   [45] Prota-Giurleo, *La grande orchestra*, 15.

[46] Howard Smither, *A History of the Oratorio*, i: *The Oratorio in the Baroque Era: Italy, Vienna, Paris* (Chapel Hill, 1977), 258 ff.; Michael Talbot, "The Serenata in Eighteenth-Century Venice," *RMA Research Chronicle*, 18 (1982), 1–40.

ate, and the singers wore costumes. However, there were no scene changes or stage effects, and the singers sang from music rather than memorizing their parts.[47]

Because they entailed only a single performance and because they were usually sponsored by a wealthy patron, serenatas and oratorios tended to use big orchestras. For serenatas performed outdoors, large numbers of instruments were desirable for acoustical reasons too. The orchestra for serenatas and oratorios was usually displayed on a stage or on a structure built specially for the occasion. Figure 5.2 depicts the performance of a Christmas oratorio in Rome, sponsored by Cardinal Ottoboni and staged in January 1728 at the private theater in his palace.[48] A large orchestra is deployed onstage and also in front of the stage. On semicircular risers, which fit into the vanishing-point perspective of the scenery, sit 35 violinists and violists, plus two bass players. In the enclosure in front of the stage a harpsichordist can be seen on either side, just as in an opera orchestra. Horns, trumpets, and bassoons are placed behind the harpsichords; the instruments between the harpsichords cannot be identified. Sheets of music can be seen on the rails in front of the first row of instrumentalists, and indeed a copyist's bill has been preserved from this very performance: there are 14 violin parts, two viola parts, five basso parts, two parts each for oboes, trumpets, and horns.[49] Assuming that strings played two on a part, winds one on a part, this is just about the right amount of music for the 56 instrumentalists depicted in Fig. 5.2. Such a large orchestra displayed in so ostentatious a manner does not merely accompany the three singers who sit center stage; it frames them and shares the spotlight.

Italian oratorio orchestras do not show the same pattern of long-term growth as Italian opera orchestras. Instead, oratorio orchestras seem to have been larger or smaller according to the size of the venue, how much of an impression the sponsor needed to make, and how much money was available. Christmas oratorios in the Vatican Palace and oratorios performed in the palaces of wealthy patrons like Cardinal Pamphili, Cardinal Ottoboni, and Prince Ruspoli used orchestras of 50 to 80.[50] In smaller venues, like the church of San Marcello, the same patrons sponsored less ambitious oratorios with smaller orchestras.[51] Oratorios put on by the oratorian churches and confraternities were yet more modest. The Confraternity of San Girolamo della Carità made do with orchestras of one or two on a part.[52] Oratorios

---

[47] Talbot, "The Serenata," 7; Griffin, "The Late Baroque Serenata," 38; Howard E. Smither, "Oratorio and Sacred Opera, 1700–1825: Terminology and Genre Distinction," PRMA 106 (1980), 88–104.

[48] The oratorio was the *Componimento sacro per la festività del S. Natale*, text by Metastasio, music by G. B. Costanzi. Properly speaking this was a Christmas cantata rather than an oratorio. See Stefano La Via, "Il Cardinale Ottoboni e la musica: nuovi documenti (1700–1740), nuove letture e ipotesi," in Albert Dunning (ed.), *Intorno a Locatelli* (Lucca, 1995), 319–526 at 336, 379.

[49] Ibid. 339.

[50] Kirkendale, "The Ruspoli Documents on Handel"; Marx, "Die Musik am Hofe Pietro Kardinal Ottobonis"; id., " 'Giustificazioni' "; Agnese Pavanello, "Locatelli e il Cardinale Camillo Cybo," in Dunning (ed.), *Intorno a Locatelli*, 749–92.

[51] Marx, " 'Giustificazioni' "; La Via, "Il Cardinale Ottoboni."

[52] Eleonora Simi Bonini, *Il fondo musicale dell'Arciconfraternità di S. Girolamo della Carità* (Rome, 1992), *passim*; Careri, "Giuseppe Valentini," 108–9.

FIG. 5.2. Oratorio at the Palazzo della Cancelleria, Rome, 1727

performed at Santa Maria in Vallicella during the eighteenth century employed similarly modest orchestras.[53]

Oratorios were performed in other Italian cities, but the orchestras for them were seldom as large as those for the biggest Roman oratorios. Partly this was because in these cities opera satisfied the demand for spectacle, partly because the pool of available instrumentalists was not as large as it was in Rome. In Modena, where the pious Duke Francesco II d'Este (r. 1660–94) sponsored oratorios not only at Christmas and Easter but also for occasions of state, the orchestra was provided by the ducal *cappella*, which consisted of about 15 bowed-string players plus theorbo, cornetts, and organ.[54] Oratorio flourished also in Florence, especially during the reign of Cosimo III de' Medici (1670–1723). A contemporary account of an Easter oratorio in 1712 at the church of San Jacopo reports that the performance attracted such a large crowd that people had to stand in an anteroom and in the sacristy. The source describes the orchestra in detail:

Three harpsichords, two contrabasses, and in place of the third contrabass, a bassoon played by a German; then three bass viols, the first of them played by Sig. Dr. . . . Salucci, a celebrated player; the theorbo was played by Gio. Filippo Palafuti, our brother. There were also 16 violins including violas, the first of which was played by Sig. Martino Bitti, Genovese . . . a most celebrated player and famous throughout the world . . . When, in the course of the oratorio, Sig. Martino Bitti, the first violinist, as well as Sig. [Lodovico Erdtman], the oboe player, played things to arouse admiration, the people responded by crying *viva* in loud voices.[55]

The writer mentions the singers by name but does not comment on their performance. Evidently the orchestra made a bigger impression on both the commentator and the audience.

Oratorios were introduced to Venice at the oratorian church of Santa Maria della Fava, beginning in the 1660s. Initially the forces were modest. Acounts from the Lenten series in 1672 list payments mainly to continuo instruments—just a theorbo, a spinet, and a violone for most performances. The performance of oratorios was taken up in the 1680s by the *ospedali*, the famous Venetian orphanages that specialized in musical performances by female singers and instrumentalists.[56] Because the performers were wards of the institution and did not have to be paid, the instrumental ensembles at the *ospedali* tended to be larger and more diverse than those at the Fava.[57] The score to Vivaldi's *Juditha triumphans*, performed at the Ospedale della

[53] Joyce L. Johnson, *Roman Oratorio, 1770–1800: The Repertory at Santa Maria in Vallicella* (Ann Arbor, 1987), 187–90.

[54] Victor Crowther, "A Case-Study in the Power of the Purse: The Management of the Ducal *Cappella* in Modena in the Reign of Francesco II d'Este," *PRMA* 115 (1990), 207–19; Rodolfo Baroncini, "Organici e 'orchestre' in Italia e Francia nel XVII secolo: differenze e omologie," *Studi musicali*, 25 (1996), 373–408 at 400. In the 1680s the instruments in the ducal *cappella* in Modena were distributed as follows: 5 vn, 2 alto vla, 2 tenor vla, 3 vc, 2 cb, 2 cornetts, 1 thrb, 1 org, 1 hpschd (Baroncini, 400).

[55] Translation in Smither, *History of the Oratorio*, i. 286–87, slightly altered.

[56] Denis Arnold and Elsie Arnold, *The Oratorio in Venice* (London, 1986), 2, 10 ff.

[57] There are no rosters for oratorios at the *ospedali*. The hypothesis that they used large orchestras is based on the scores of works performed there.

Pietà in 1716, requires a four-part string ensemble, plus a remarkable procession of obbligato instruments: viola d'amore, five viole all'inglese, mandolin, four theorbos, chalumeau, and two clarino trumpets, as well as solo violins and oboes.[58] The Fava responded to the competition from the *ospedali* with grander oratorios, but its orchestras remained relatively modest: 10–12 string players plus oboes, and occasionally horns or trumpets.[59]

Orchestras for serenatas vied with the largest oratorio orchestras in size. The serenata described in the previous chapter, which the Spanish ambassador staged in Rome to celebrate the Queen of Spain's name day in 1687, featured an orchestra of over 60 performers, mainly string players, led by Arcangelo Corelli (Fig. 4.1 above). An account of the serenata for the same occasion the following year provides an amusing insight into the politics and finances of the serenade in Italy:

The Signor Ambassador of Spain, without paying out any money in advance, put together a magnificent festival for the birthday of her majesty the Queen. The whole Piazza was illuminated by torches and candles and in the middle there was a large structure [*teatro*] . . . In this theater was performed a Serenata with the principal parts sung by two ladies and with a large number of singers and instrumentalists accompanying. This Serenata, however, did not please most people. And although the staging was very beautiful, people found grounds for criticism . . . because the singers and instrumentalists appeared before the eyes of the whole populace dressed in their own clothes. This was thought to be very improper, since his Excellency should have outfitted them all in uniforms. It would have put no strain on his pocketbook, since he was financing the whole affair on credit anyway. The next morning the following *bon mot* made the rounds: "The Marquis of Coccogliudo does all he must do, until payment comes due." [*Il signor Marchese di Coccogliudo fa tutto quello che deve e deve tutto quello che fa.*][60]

The commentator does not remark on how the orchestra sounded but rather on how it looked. Where theater orchestras dressed in everyday clothes, the orchestra for a serenade was on display and ought properly to be in uniform.

The French ambassador, engaged in an ongoing political and cultural competition with the Spanish ambassador, also sponsored serenatas in Rome. The birth of the Dauphin in 1729 was celebrated by turning the courtyard of the ambassador's palace into a giant theater, with a stage on which "130 players were arranged with all sorts of instruments, dressed like spirits, with laurel wreaths on their heads, and rhinestone-

---

[58] Eleanor Selfridge-Field, "Vivaldi's Esoteric Instruments," *EM* 6 (1978), 332–38; ead., "Italian Oratorio and the Baroque Orchestra," *EM* 16 (1988), 506–13.

[59] Arnold and Arnold, *Oratorio*, 37, 55. Estimates for the size of these orchestras are based on sets of parts.

[60] Letter of 18 Aug. 1688 from Paolo Negri, quoted in Alessandro Ademollo, *I teatri di Roma nel secolo decimosettimo* (Rome, 1888), 171–72. Mario Rinaldi quotes another manuscript account of what purports to be the same event. The description differs from Negri's, particularly on the question of uniforms (Rinaldi, *Arcangelo Corelli*, 129). This account says that the instrumentalists appeared in blackface (!) and were dressed in silver lamé uniforms. It seems impossible to reconcile the two versions. Perhaps one of the accounts should be assigned to another year. See Griffin, "The Late Baroque Serenata," 151.

studded belts and bracelets . . . When the audience was in place, a curtain was drawn to reveal the stage, and everyone broke into applause."[61] Occasionally a Roman serenade had a religious rather than a political theme. For the vigil of San Lorenzo in 1694, the *Avisi di Roma* reports, Cardinal Ottoboni "gave a magnificent serenata in his garden with one hundred stringed instruments. Singers and instrumentalists were placed in tiers on a high platform, brightly lit, in front of a picture of San Lorenzo."[62] The account books for the event record a total of 71 instrumentalists, led by Corelli.[63]

Serenatas were as important politically in Naples as in Rome. Figure 5.3 shows a performance of *Il genio austriaco* by Alessandro Scarlatti, staged in the royal palace in

FIG. 5.3. Serenata at the Royal palace in honor of Empress Elisabetta, Naples, 1713.

[61] *Mercure de France* (Dec. 1729), 3128. [62] Quoted in Griffin, "The Late Baroque Serenata," 212.
[63] Marx, "Kardinal Ottoboni," 143.

Naples to celebrate the birthday in 1713 of Elizabeth, the wife of Emperor Charles VI of Austria. The Hapsburg Emperor had only recently taken control of Naples, and the Austrian viceroy lost no opportunity to put on a public show of the new regime's power and authority. The orchestra is displayed onstage, flanking a giant portrait of the Empress. In the center are the singers plus a continuo group consisting of a single harpsichord, a lute, and two cellos. An account of the performance in the *Gazzetta di Napoli* claims that "the musical instruments included innumerable drums, trumpets, and horns, as well as flutes, all sorts of stringed instruments, and an organ."[64] Neither wind instruments nor drums are visible in the engraving, and the keyboard in the center is clearly not an organ. Winds are better documented in the orchestra for a serenata given at the Neapolitan palace in 1732. Six oboes, four horns, two trumpets, and a bassoon joined forty-six bowed strings in *Giasone* by Nicola Porpora.[65]

In Bologna, where there was no court, serenades were occasionally sponsored by the local nobility. In July 1706, for example, Count Pirro Albergati staged a serenata at his palace for an unknown occasion featuring an orchestra of over 70.[66] Two singers and a group of continuo players were placed on a platform in the center, with the rest of the instrumentalists arranged in rows on either side, a layout similar to that of the Neapolitan serenata depicted in Fig. 5.3. In Venice serenatas tended to be performed in private homes or for academies, and orchestras tended to be rather small. The largest orchestra recorded for an eighteenth-century Venetian serenata comprised only 30 instrumentalists, for an academy in 1735.[67]

CHURCH ORCHESTRAS

Despite complaints by ecclesiastical conservatives, instrumental music played an important role in Italian churches during the seventeenth and eighteenth centuries. From the sixteenth century on, Italian churches began to add instrumentalists to their payrolls: organists, trombonists, cornettists; then violinists, violists, and violone players during the second half of the seventeenth century and the first half of the eighteenth. By 1749 Pope Benedict XIV was obliged to acknowledge in a papal bull, *Annus qui*, that orchestras had made themselves indispensable in churches: "Finally We speak of orchestral music [*symphonias*]. Where it has been introduced, it may be tolerated, as long as it is serious and does not because of its length cause boredom or

---

[64] Quoted in Griffin, "The Late Baroque Serenata," 647.

[65] Porpora's serenade was performed on 23 and 24 Apr. 1732. Pay records list the following forces: 32 vn, 6 vla, 2 vc, 4 cb, 6 ob, 1 bn, 4 hrn, 2 trpt, 2 hpschd, 2 lutes (Dennis Libby, "Introduction," in *Giovanni Battista Pergolesi: Salustia* (Complete Works, 1, forthcoming).

[66] Victor Crowther, *The Oratorio in Bologna (1650–1730)* (Oxford, 1999), 17–18. The paylist for the orchestra shows: 31 vn, 12 vla, 11 vc, 14 cb, 4 ob, 2 trpt, 4 trb, 3 thrb, 2 hpschd.

[67] Talbot, "The Serenata," 4.

serious inconvenience to those in the choir or the celebrants at the altar during Vespers and Mass."[68]

Just as the instrumental ensemble in opera increasingly encroached upon the voice, so the instruments in church assumed a more and more active role in the service, at first framing the vocal music, then overlapping, then accompanying throughout.[69] Independent instrumental compositions, like sonatas and concertos, were added to the service, as preludes, interludes, or postludes to sung sections or as substitutions for parts of the proper. Chants for the gradual, the offertory, and the elevation of the host were often replaced with instrumental music.[70] During the seventeenth century these instrumental selections were often trio sonatas, performed by two solo violins plus continuo or in more orchestral fashion with several players on the parts (see Ch. 4). In the eighteenth century sonatas were superseded by music for full orchestra: whole violin concertos and symphonies, or single movements, were inserted into the liturgy of the Mass and Vespers at every opportunity.

Instrumental music, along with vocal numbers in operatic style, constituted a chief attraction of the service, drawing fashionable and wealthy people to church. Mass and vespers often took on the character of concerts, with the liturgy incidental to the music. Pierre Jean Grosley, a French visitor to Venice in 1758, attended such a performance at the Church of San Lorenzo on the name-day of that saint:

Four hundred voices and instruments, selected from the best virtuosos of Italy, who flock to Venice for this festival . . . filled the bandstand [*l'orchestra*]. This bandstand was built at the main entrance, at the other end of the nave from the altar, and it occupied the entire width of the church . . . which became a sort of great hall, wider than it was long. [The bandstand] was raised about 12 feet above floor level, divided into symmetrical compartments and decorated tastefully . . . with ribbons, garlands, and flounces of cloth. The church was filled with row upon row of chairs, set up with their backs to the altar, and they remained in this singular position even during the grand mass, which lasted for five long hours, hot as only Venice can be in the month of August.[71]

Galeazzi, writing in 1791, condemns the practice of placing the orchestra in a loft above the main entrance, because it encourages "indecency and irreverence."[72]

The number of instrumentalists on the payrolls of Italian churches grew over the course of the seventeenth and eighteenth centuries, but not nearly as much as opera orchestras grew. Table 5.2 presents selected examples from the well-preserved records of the Church of San Petronio in Bologna. The number of players on the

---

[68] *Bullarii Romani continuatio, Summorum Pontificum Benedicti XIV. . . . Pii VIII* (Prati, 1840–), i. 21–22; Robert F. Hayburn, *Papal Legislation on Sacred Music, 95 A.D. to 1977 A.D.* (Collegeville, Minn., 1979), 104.

[69] Schnoebelen, "The Role of the Violin in the Resurgence of the Mass," 541.

[70] Stephen Bonta, "The Uses of the *Sonata da Chiesa*," *JAMS* 22 (1969), 54–84 at 57 ff.; Allsop, *The Italian Trio Sonata*, 63–65.

[71] Pierre Jean Grosley, *Observations sur l'Italie et sur les italiens*, 2nd edn. (London, 1774), 55–56.

[72] Galeazzi, *Elementi teorico-pratici*, i. 216–17.

TABLE 5.2. *The orchestra at San Petronio, Bologna, 1660–1786*

Date	Keyboard and plucked strings	Bowed strings	Winds	Brass	Source
1660	2 organs 1 theorbo	1 violin 2 alto violas 1 tenor viola 2 violoni		2 trombones	Gambassi, *Cappella musicale*, 134
1663	regulars 2 organs 1 theorbo extras[a] 1 organ 1 theorbo	regulars 3 violins 1 alto viola 1 tenor viola 2 violoni extras[a] 11 violins 1 alto viola 1 cello 3 violoni		regulars 2 trombones extras[a] 1 trombone	Gambassi, 136; Schnoebelen, "Performance," 43
1687	regulars 2 organs 1 theorbo extras[a] 2 organs 2 theorbos	regulars 3 violins 1 viola 1 tenor viola 2 cellos 2 violoni extras[a] 7 violins 3 violas 2 cellos 1 violone		regulars 1 trombone extras[a] 1 cornett 4 trumpets 8 trombones	Gambassi, 150; Schnoebelen, 43
1694	regulars 2 organs 1 theorbo extras[a] 2 organs 4 theorbos	regulars 3 violins 1 viola 1 cello 1 violone extras[a] 7 violins 6 violas 2 cellos 5 violoni		regulars 2 trombones extras[a] 2 cornetts 2 trumpets 8 trombones	Gambassi, 155; Schnoebelen, 43

	2 organs 1 theorbo	3 violins 3 violas 1 cello 1 violone		1 trombone	Sambassi, 186
1761	2 organs 1 theorbo	9 violins [and violas] 1 cello 1 violone	2 oboes 1 bassoon	2 trumpets 1 trombone	Ibid. 192
1776	2 organs	11 violins [and violas] 1 cello 1 violone 1 double bass	2 oboes	2 trumpets 1 trombone	Ibid. 201
1786	2 organs	11 violins 2 violas 1 cello 1 violone 1 double bass	2 oboes	2 trumpets 1 trombone	Ibid. 207

[a] Extras hired for the feast of San Petronio (4 Oct.)

permanent payroll of the church is never large, the instrumentation is rather conservative, and growth is modest. Bowed strings increase only gradually; plucked strings persist in the continuo group until the 1760s; there are no winds except for trombones until the second half of the eighteenth century. For the feast of San Petronio each October, however, the church orchestra was considerably expanded. Most of the instrumentalists available in Bologna were engaged for the occasion, and additional players were brought in from neighboring towns, especially violins, bowed bass instruments, and trombones. This yearly expansion of the San Petronio orchestra is seen in Pl. IV, which depicts the festival of 1722, a particularly lavish occasion because it was attended by James III, pretender to the English throne.[73] In the painting the perspective has been opened out to a wide angle to show the choir lofts filled with singers and instrumentalists. Two organs and continuo instruments can be seen among the singers on the right and on the left. Most of the instrumentalists, however, are located in the center, on a platform at the rear of the chancel, arranged in tiers, facing the audience, and illuminated by tall candles. Violins, violas in several sizes, cellos, basses, and theorbos can be made out, but no wind instruments.[74] Pay records from 1722 show that 141 musicians in all (singers and instrumentalists) participated in this event—34 on the regular payroll, 107 engaged for the occasion. The picture, grand though it is, probably underrepresents the number of players in the orchestra.

The church of St. Mark's in Venice had more instrumentalists on its regular payroll than did San Petronio, but the ensemble followed a similar pattern of development. It grew rather rapidly at the end of the seventeenth century—from 26 members in 1680 to 48 in 1690—only to be cut back at the beginning of the eighteenth century for lack of funds.[75] Instrumentation at St. Mark's, as at San Petronio, was conservative. Cornetts remain in the ensemble until after 1710, theorbos until the 1740s. A modern wind section with oboes and horns was not added until the orchestra was reorganized in 1766.[76] The strings at St. Mark's tended to be more evenly distributed than in opera orchestras. In the 1680s there were still as many bowed strings on the middle parts as on the treble; and in 1766 there were still more violas and cellos at St. Mark's than in an opera orchestra of comparable size. As in Bologna, the orches-

---

[73] Plate IV comes from a series of miniatures called the *Insignia degli Anziani*, which depict important civic events in Bologna. The Insignia are catalogued and described in Giuseppe Plessi, *Le insignia degli anziani del comune dal 1530 al 1796: catalogo-inventario* (Rome, 1954).

[74] For further discussion of this picture, see Anne Schnoebelen, "The Concerted Mass at San Petronio in Bologna: c. 1660–1730," (Ph.D. diss., University of Illinois, 1968), 39 and Eugene Enrico, *The Orchestra at San Petronio in the Baroque Era* (Washington, DC, 1976), 40.

[75] 1680: 5 vn, 2 vla, 1 viola da braccio, 3 violoni, 1 cb, 2 bn, 3 cornetti, 4 trb, 4 thrb, 1 hpschd; 1690: 17 vn, 5 vla, 4 viole da braccio, 2 violoni, 1 cb, 2 bn, 5 cornetti, 1 trpt, 5 trb, 5 thrb, 1 hpschd; 1700: 12 vn, 4 vla, 3 viole, 4 violoni, 1 cb, 1 ob, 2 cornetti, 2 trpt, 5 trb, 4 thrb, 1 hpschd. (Francesco Caffi, *Storia della musica sacra nella già cappella ducale di San Marco in Venezia* (Venice, 1855), 60–61; Selfridge-Field, "The Viennese Court Orchestra in the Time of Caldara," 119; ead., *Venetian Instrumental Music*, 19–20).

[76] Denis Arnold, "Orchestras in Eighteenth-Century Venice," *GSJ* 19 (1966), 3–19 at 6–9.

tra was enlarged by hiring freelancers for special occasions.[77] Eleanor Selfridge-Field has suggested that there was a sort of "platoon system" at St. Mark's in which half of the musicians played one day and the other half another day, with the two platoons playing together only for important feasts.[78] However, a calendar published in 1761 of the duties of musicians at St. Mark's shows that there were only 19 days in the entire year on which instruments were used at all in the service at St. Mark's.[79] Evidently a position in the orchestra at St. Mark's had become something of a sinecure. Singers, the calendar shows, were occasionally split into two groups so that they could participate in simultaneous services at different churches. The calendar says nothing, however, about dividing the orchestra. Nor is there evidence of such a system in any other Italian churches.

Although the general tendency in Italian church music was toward consolidation into a single orchestra, the old tradition of polychorality persisted through the eighteenth century. Singers and instrumentalists were often divided, usually into two groups, and placed in choir lofts facing one another across the chancel or on two specially built platforms. Burney, touring Italy in 1770, heard music arranged in this fashion in Milan, Padua and Venice. In Padua, he reports: "the bases are all placed on one side, the violins, hautbois, french-horns, and tenors on the other, and the voices half in one organ-loft, and half in another; but, on account of their distance from each other, the performers were not always exact in keeping time."[80] Similarly in Venice at the convent church of Santa Maria della Celestia on the eve of the Assumption "there was a long symphony in dialogue, between the two orchestras."[81] Galeazzi, writing in 1791, deplored polychoral arrangements of church orchestras, because it took something like an eighth of a beat for the sound to travel from one orchestra to the other. "Anyone who has even a modicum of experience with music," said Galeazzi, "knows what disorder, what confusion, what anarchy can arise in music when there is a discrepancy of an eighth of a beat."[82]

Divided ensembles, small size, and archaic instruments were symptomatic of the conservatism of Italian church orchestras in the eighteenth century. Where seventeenth-century church ensembles had taken the lead in the development of the *concertato* style, eighteenth-century church orchestras lagged behind opera and oratorio ensembles. Church orchestras remained important, however, because they provided instrumentalists with year-round employment in an environment where there were

---

[77] Selfridge-Field, *Venetian Instrumental Music*, 19–20.

[78] Eleanor Selfridge-Field, "Venice in an Era of Political Decline," in George J. Buelow (ed.), *The Late Baroque Era* (Englewood Cliffs, NJ, 1993), 66–93 at 69–70.

[79] Reproduced in J. H. Moore, *Vespers at St. Mark's*, 301 ff.

[80] Burney, *Present State of Music in France and Italy*, 143.

[81] Ibid. 178. Two-orchestra music may have been a specialty at the feast of the Assumption. Vivaldi composed at least two concertos "in due Cori per la Santissima Assontione di Maria Vergine," both for solo violin and two orchestras (RV 581 and RV 582).

[82] Galeazzi, *Elementi teorico-pratici*, i. 217–18.

few court *cappelle* and where opera seasons lasted only a few weeks out of the year. Famous composers and virtuosos, like Sammartini, Tartini, and Valentini, relied on their positions as church musicians for an important part of their incomes. Performances at mass and vespers amounted to public concerts at which they and their fellow instrumentalists displayed their talents.

CONCERT ORCHESTRAS

Orchestral performances in venues other than theaters and churches became increasingly common in eighteenth-century Italy, particularly in Lombardy, which was under Austrian administration from 1706 to 1796. Orchestra concerts were also an important part of musical life in other regions of northern Italy, including Venice, Mantua, and Bologna. Some were private concerts, sponsored by an individual patron or an academy, with access limited to a small, select group.[83] A few, especially outdoor concerts, were free and open to the public. Concerts could be put on in connection with a festive event, a royal birthday, a visit by an important person, or the installation of an official—but often they were given simply for entertainment. Private concerts and academies were aimed primarily at the nobility, while outdoor concerts seem to have attracted a mixture of social classes. Compared to operas, oratorios, or serenatas, concerts were a relatively inexpensive form of recreation and cultural display. Concerts did not need a dedicated facility like a theater, and they did not involve elaborate sets or machinery. However, they did require an orchestra. Displayed on a platform or surrounded by the audience, the orchestra became the aural and visual focus of the event.

The concerts sponsored by Count Pallavicini, the Austrian Governor of Milan in 1746–47 and again from 1750 to 1753, provide an example of the north Italian concert milieu. These outdoor concerts were given during the summer months in a plaza next to the moat of the Castello Sforzesco.[84] Figure 5.4, a detail from an engraving dated 1751, shows the castle wall, the moat, and the bandshell (labeled "Y") where the orchestra played. The orchestra is not seen, but contemporary reports say that it was large and that it included winds as well as strings.[85] The Count explained the purpose of his concerts in a letter: "I redoubled the musical concerts, which, at my orders, take place three times a week during the summer toward evening in the plaza

---

[83] An academy (*accademia*) was a club or a society with restricted membership devoted to intellectual or artistic pursuits (Michael Talbot, "Musical Academies in Eighteenth-Century Venice," *Note d'archivio per la storia musicale*, NS 1 (1983), 21–65 at 21). During the 18th c. the word "academy" and its cognates in other European languages took on the meaning of "concert."

[84] Newell Jenkins and Bathia Churgin, *Thematic Catalogue of the Works of Giovanni Battista Sammartini* (Cambridge, Mass., 1976), 11.

[85] Ibid.; Guglielmo Barblan, "La musica strumentale e cameristica a Milano nel '700," in *Storia di Milano* (Milan, 1962), 619–60 at 633.

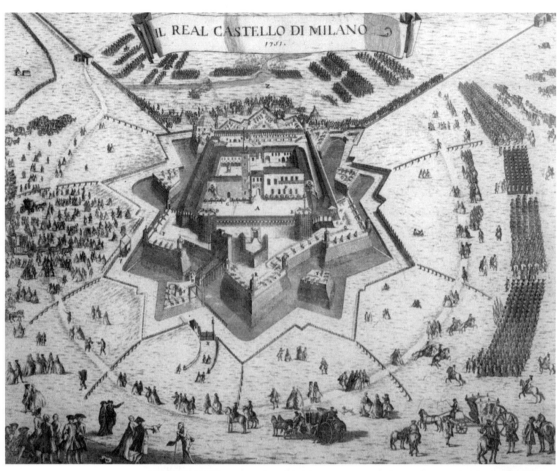

FIG. 5.4. View of the Castello Sforzesco, Milan, 1751, and detail showing the bandshell outside the moat

of the Royal Castle, to provide entertainment for the nobility and for the people, who come there to promenade in the evening air."[86] On Fridays, when the opera house was closed, the Count gave indoor concerts for the nobility at the ducal palace, followed by dancing and gambling.[87]

The unseen orchestra in Fig. 5.4 was led by Giovanni Battista Sammartini, who seems to have played the role of composer-contractor-director in Milan parallel to Corelli's role in Rome half a century before, providing orchestras and orchestral music for the Governor's concerts, for Milanese academies, and for public events. Sammartini and his orchestra became the object of local pride and boosterism. "For a long time now," wrote Giovenale Sacchi, a mathematician and musical amateur, "the Milanese orchestra has been among the most famous in Italy, and the longer we maintain such a reputation, the more we must cultivate it diligently, lest it diminish and disappear."[88] Sammartini and his orchestra provided music for other north Italian cities as well as Milan. In 1765, for example, when the Austrian Archduke Leopold and his wife visited Lombardy, Sammartini took 32 players from Milan to Cremona and to Padua to play concerts and also to provide music for balls.[89] In each city local musicians were added to the Milanese contingent to make the orchestra larger.

Sammartini's orchestra was not the only concert orchestra in Milan. Charles Burney heard an orchestra of Milanese amateurs, playing indoors:

A private concert in Italy is called an *accademia*; the first I went to was composed entirely of *dilettanti*; *il padrone*, or the master of the house, played the first violin, and had a very powerful hand [i.e. a good technique]; there were twelve or fourteen performers, among whom were several good violins; there were likewise two German flutes, a violoncello, and small double base.[90]

Burney found the performance of these Milanese amateurs "much upon a level with our own private concerts among gentlemen in England." The social level of the participants is not made explicit in his account. These do not seem to be aristocratic circles, because Burney does not mention the name of his host, calling him "the master of the house" without any other title.

The participation of amateurs in concert orchestras was not unusual in northern Italy. In 1758 Sammartini, along with several aristocratic music lovers, founded the Accademia Filarmonica, an amateur orchestra, which met once a week.[91] To join the Academy, dilettante instrumentalists had to play an audition—evidently more than a pro forma exercise, for one amateur violinist, Doctor Faccioli, petitioned repeatedly

---

[86] Ibid. 86. See also Gaetano Cesari, "Giorgio Giulini musicista," in *Opera inedita di Giorgio Giulini* (Milan, 1916), 157–59.

[87] Barblan, "La musica strumentale," 633.

[88] Giovenale Sacchi, *Della divisione del tempo nella musica nel ballo e nel poesia* (Milan, 1770), 26.

[89] Jenkins and Churgin, *Thematic Catalogue*, 13; Barblan, "La musica strumentale," 644.

[90] Burney, *Present State of Music in France and Italy*, 94–95. [91] Barblan, "La musica strumentale," 635.

to join and was turned down each time by Sammartini and the president of the Academy. Faccioli finally took his case to Count Firmian, the Austrian administrator, who decreed that the doctor must be allowed to join the violin section.

The Reale Accademia in Mantua also sponsored a dilettante orchestra, the Colonia Filarmonica. Members were divided into three classes: performing amateurs, non-performing amateurs, and paid professionals. The professionals (*professori*) were theater and church musicians, recruited to raise the artistic level of the ensemble. In 1770, when Mozart visited Mantua, there were 18 professionals and an unknown number of amateurs.[92] The Colonia Filarmonica had its own problems with would-be virtuosos. The Marquis Cavriani, a flutist and one of the participating amateurs, demanded in a letter of 1770 to the Academy Directorate that he be allowed to play all the flute solos. The Directors responded that "when members are at the Academy, they lay aside differences of birth, talent[!], and rank and consider themselves equal to one another."[93] Moreover, the rules called for the solo parts to be played by professionals. The Marquis took his case to the Prefect, who, unlike Count Firmian in Milan, declined to intervene. Cavriani continued to make a nuisance of himself for several decades.

Little documentation has turned up so far on the size and balances of northern Italian concert orchestras. For the concerts that he put on in Cremona and Padua in 1765, Sammartini fielded orchestras of about 35: four-part strings plus oboes and horns.[94] The orchestra of the Reale Accademia in Mantua, where Mozart attended a concert in 1770, was somewhat smaller: six violins, two violas, one cello, two double basses, one bassoon, and pairs of oboes and horns.[95] Strikingly, these documented Italian concert orchestras all lack keyboard instruments. Perhaps Sammartini, who was an accomplished organist, led from the harpsichord. But when there was no singer, it is more likely that the ensemble was led from the violin and that keyboards were not used. Orchestras for private academies were probably smaller, like the ensemble of 12 to 14 at the home that Burney visited in Milan. Even when ensembles were larger, the emphasis in such concert orchestras does not seem to have been on size and grandeur but rather on entertainment and social participation.

With the popularity of concert orchestras in northern Italy in the eighteenth century, there arose a distinctive repertory of music for orchestra suitable for performance in informal settings by dilettante ensembles. Music designed for very large ensembles, like Corelli's Concerti Grossi, or for very proficient ensembles, like Vivaldi's concertos, was problematic under these circumstances. Opera arias and opera *sinfonie* were easier to play and more accessible; they served as staples of the

[92] Gian Giuseppe Bernardi, *La musica nella Reale Accademia Virgiliana di Mantova* (Mantua, 1923), 18–19. See also Leopold Mozart's letter of 11 Jan. 1770, in Wolfgang Amadeus Mozart, *Briefe und Aufzeichnungen*, ed. Wilhelm A. Bauer and Otto Erich Deutsch (Kassel, 1962–75), i. 303.

[93] Bernardi, *La musica*, 37.   [94] See Barblan, "La musica strumentale," 651.

[95] Otto Erich Deutsch (ed.), *Mozart und seine Welt in zeitgenössischen Bildern* (Kassel, 1961), 97.

concert repertory. In addition, north Italian composers like Vivaldi, Giulini, Lampugnani, Chiesa, Brioschi, and above all Sammartini wrote concertos and symphonies aimed directly at concert performance. Such pieces needed to be adaptable for ensembles of different sizes; they needed to be easy enough that amateurs could play them at sight; and they needed to sound good without much interpretation or ornamentation. The demand for such pieces was vigorous. Count Giantomaso Calvi wrote from Parma to his niece in 1730:

I have an Academy of dilettantes in my house three times a week, and knowing that you are often at the house of Giorgio Giulini, I would like you to see if you can obtain sonatas by him, as well as some concertos with violin obbligato and also *Ouvertures*, a dozen in all if you can manage it.[96]

Orchestra music was almost never printed in Italy, although ensemble music by Italian composers was printed in Paris, London, and Amsterdam. Instead, it circulated in sets of manuscript parts, produced by professional copyists. Nevertheless, concertos and symphonies by north Italian composers achieved wide distribution during the first half of the eighteenth century, particularly in Germany, where they contributed to the development of an orchestral style of composition and performance.

INSTRUMENTS FOR ORCHESTRAS

The development of orchestras in Italy as elsewhere during the seventeenth and eighteenth centuries was constrained but also stimulated by two factors: the availability of instruments and the availability of players. When players and instruments were plentiful, orchestras could grow. When players and instruments were scarce, the growth of orchestras was limited.

The technical development of violin-family instruments and their production in Italy from the sixteenth through the eighteenth century were crucial to the growth of the orchestra. The center of stringed-instrument manufacture was Lombardy: Milan, Brescia, and especially Cremona. North Italian violin makers—including the Amati family, the Guarneri family, Antonio Stradivari (1644–1737), and scores of lesser-known craftsmen in workshops throughout northern Italy—improved the design and the production techniques of violins, violas, and cellos, and they built thousands of instruments that made their way into the hands of orchestral players throughout Italy and the rest of Europe as well. Other regions of Italy also manufactured stringed instruments. Workshops in Venice, Bologna, Rome, and Naples produced instruments that, although not as prized as those of Amati and Stradivari,

---

[96] Quoted in Cesari, "Giorgio Giulini musicista," 1, 149–50.

were considered adequate for orchestral playing.[97]

Seventeenth-century Italian violins and violas resembled later instruments in overall shape and design, but they came in several sizes. Paylists and scores refer to piccolo violins, violette, alto, and tenor violas, and pictures of ensembles show instruments of many different sizes. Toward the end of the century, the Cremonese makers, particularly Antonio Stradivari and Giuseppe Guarneri del Gesù, developed a new violin design with a flatter body, which increased the brilliance and carrying power of the instrument.[98] The Stradivari design was widely imitated, both in Italy and elsewhere in Europe. In the early decades of the eighteenth century a longer, straighter bow, with more weight at the tip, gradually came into general use, first by soloists but eventually by ripienists as well.[99] This so-called long or Tartini bow remained in use during most of the century. Violins and violas were strung with gut throughout the period, and in Italy the strings seem to have been thick and raised to relatively high tension, again to increase the volume and brilliance of the sound.[100] The center of the Italian string-making industry was Rome; there were also workshops in Naples and Padua.[101]

François Raguenet, a French visitor to Rome in 1702, commented on the superiority of Italian stringed instruments, particularly for orchestral use:

Their violins are mounted with strings much larger than ours; their bows are longer, and they can make their instruments sound as loud again as we do ours. The first time I heard our band in the [Paris] Opera after my return out of Italy, my ears had been so used to the loudness of the Italian violins that I thought ours had all been bridled.[102]

Italian instruments and strings were exported and imitated throughout Europe.

The cello emerged in the second half of the seventeenth century, again from the workshops of north Italian craftsmen. Around 1650 the standard bass instrument was still the violone, a long-necked, somewhat unwieldy bass violin tuned at 8-foot pitch, used for playing bass lines. A smaller version of the violone was the violoncino or violoncello, which was easier to play in the tenor and alto registers, but which did not project very well, particularly in the lower register. Sixteen-foot contrabassi, shaped like viols rather than violin-family instruments, were also widely used.[103] The cello

[97] Roberto Regazzi, "The Situation of Violin Making in Bologna in the Eighteenth Century," paper read at the Fourth Tiverton Violin Conference (1989); Seymour Benstock, "Venice: Four Centuries of Instrument Making," *Journal of the Violin Society of America*, 8 (1984), 41–56; Patrizio Barbieri, "Cembalaro, organaro, chitarraro e fabbricatore di corde armoniche nella 'Polyanthea technica' di Pinaroli (1718–32). Con notizie sui liutai e cambalari operanti a Roma," *Recercare*, 1 (1989), 123–209.

[98] W. Henry Hill, Arthur F. Hill, and Alfred E. Hill, *Antonio Stradivari, his Life and Work (1644–1737)*, 2nd edn. (London, 1909), 152 ff.

[99] Boyden, *History of Violin Playing*, 206–7.

[100] Ephraim Segerman, "Strings Through the Ages," *The Strad*, 99 (Jan., Mar., Apr. 1988), 52–55, 195–200, 295–98; Mimmo Peruffo, "Italian Violin Strings in the Eighteenth and Nineteenth Centuries: Typologies, Manufacturing Techniques and Principles of Stringing," *Recercare*, 9 (1997), 155–201.

[101] Peruffo, "Italian Violin Strings," 167 ff.   [102] Raguenet, *A Comparison*, 49.

[103] Bonta, "From Violone to Violoncello," 68 ff.

was created, according to Stephen Bonta, by Bolognese craftsmen and performers who wound the lowest string on the violoncello with thin silver wire, to create an instrument whose neck was short enough to be convenient for the left hand, but whose lower register was powerful enough to project outdoors or in a large room.[104] Although the cello quickly became important as a solo instrument and as a member of the continuo group, the violone and the contrabasso remained as the standard bass instruments of Italian orchestras during much of the eighteenth century.

It is impossible to estimate how many stringed instruments were produced in Italy during the seventeenth and eighteenth centuries. Something like 600 to 700 Stradivari instruments survive today; the total number of instruments the master produced over the course of his career has been estimated at over 1,100.[105] Stradivari seems to have been a fast worker, and he continued making instruments past the age of 80, but his was just one workshop out of scores of establishments in Lombardy. No one has attempted to estimate the production of other famous violin makers or workshops. The manufacture of violas seems to have been less vigorous than the production of violins and cellos, judging from the smaller number of eighteenth-century violas that survive.[106] This is almost certainly related to the shrinking proportion of violas in eighteenth-century ensembles. Overall, the supply of stringed instruments in Italy seems to have been adequate to the demand during the eighteenth century. Lalande, a French visitor, remarked in 1769 that Italian orchestras were larger than French "because instruments are neither scarce nor expensive in Italy."[107] Although large numbers of Italian instruments were purchased for export in the eighteenth century, foreigners did not complain that instruments were hard to buy, nor did Italians complain about instruments being exported. Evidently Italian workshops were producing enough violins and cellos in the eighteenth century to furnish instruments to larger and larger orchestras, and to musical amateurs and foreigners as well.

Wind instruments seem to have been harder to come by. Trombones and cornetts had been manufactured in Italy since the fifteenth century, especially in Siena and Venice, to provide instruments for churches and for civic bands.[108] However, these ensembles generally did not use woodwinds, and thus there was no similar tradition of production of woodwind instruments. The manufacture of woodwinds is documented in Venice as early as the sixteenth century. When the newer types of oboes

[104] Ibid. 95. In the late 17th c. gut-core strings overwound with metal began to be used for the lowest strings on violins and violas too (Peruffo, "Italian Violin Strings," 159).

[105] Hill, Hill, and Hill, *Antonio Stradivari*, 234 ff.; Herbert K. Goodkind, *Violin Iconography of Antonio Stradivari, 1644–1737* (Larchmont, NY, 1972), 723 ff.

[106] See Boyden, *History of Violin Playing*, 315.

[107] Joseph Jérôme de Lalande, *Voyage d'un françois en Italie, fait dans les années 1765 et 1766* (Paris, 1769), vi. 354.

[108] Edward H. Tarr, "Ein Katalog erhaltener Zinken," *Basler Jahrbuch für historische Musikpraxis*, 5 (1981), 11–232 at 13–16; Renato Meucci, "On the Early History of the Trumpet in Italy," *Basler Jahrbuch für historische Musikpraxis*, 15 (1991), 9–34 at 24 ff.

and transverse flutes were first being introduced to Italy from France, the players often brought their instruments with them. After a while the instruments were copied, and local players were trained.[109] Unlike string instrument makers who were organized into a guild of luthiers, Italian wind instrument makers did not have a guild of their own. According to Renato Meucci, they led an unincorporated, marginal existence under constant pressure from the turners and joiners' guild, with whom they shared tools and techniques.[110] Not until the breakdown of the guild system in the late eighteenth century did the manufacture of woodwind instruments emerge as an industry in Italy. The first Venetian craftsman officially authorized to make woodwind instruments was Andrea Fornari in 1792.[111]

What wind instruments were manufactured in Italy were not always of the highest quality. A bassoonist in Lisbon who made the mistake of ordering an instrument from Carlo Palanca in Turin complained that the bassoon he received was a patchwork of old and new parts.[112] Surviving instruments attributed to Palanca give evidence of poor materials and shoddy workmanship. The document authorizing Fornari to open his shop in Venice notes that wind instruments "ordinarily come from outside the [Venetian] State."[113] The lack of instruments may have been one reason that Italian orchestras tended to have proportionately fewer wind players than French or German orchestras in the eighteenth century.

TRAINING ORCHESTRA MUSICIANS

Instruments by themselves do not make an orchestra. For Italian orchestras to grow and prosper, they needed skilled instrumentalists, used to playing in an orchestral setting. Some orchestra musicians were trained at conservatories; the majority learned on the job.

The conservatories of Naples and Venice were a uniquely Italian institution. There were four conservatories in Naples, each attached to a charitable foundation whose chief business was running an orphanage.[114] Instruction in vocal and instrumental music supplied the musical needs of the foundation and prepared the orphans for

[109] Renato Meucci, "La costruzione di strumenti musicali a Roma tra XVII e XIX secolo, con notizie inedite sulla famiglia Biglioni," in *La musica a Roma attraverso le fonti d'archivio—Atti del convegno internazionale, Roma 4–7 giugno, 1992,* ed. Bianca Maria Antolini, Arnaldo Morelli, and Vera Vita Spagnuolo (Lucca, 1994), 581–93 at 587; Alfredo Bernardini, "Carlo Palanca e la costruzione di strumenti di fiato a Torino nel Settecento," *Il flauto dolce,* 13 (1985), 22–26; Haynes, *The Eloquent Oboe,* 401 ff.; Federico Maria Sardelli, *La musica per flauto di Antonio Vivaldi* (Florence, 2001), 3–38.

[110] Meucci, "La costruzione," 588–89.

[111] Alfredo Bernardini, "Woodwind Makers in Venice, 1790–1900," *JAMIS* 15 (1989), 52–73.

[112] Bernardini, "Carlo Palanca," 23.   [113] Quoted in Meucci, "La costruzione," 589.

[114] The Neapolitan conservatories were Sant'Onofrio, S. Maria della Pietà dei Turchini, S. Maria di Loreto, and the Conservatorio dei Poveri di Gesù Cristo. See Helmut Hucke, "Verfassung und Entwicklung der alten neapolitanischen Konservatorien," in Lothar Hoffmann-Erbrecht and Helmut Hucke (eds.), *Festschrift Helmuth Osthoff zum 65. Geburtstag* (Tutzing, 1961), 139–54 at 140–41.

gainful employment. Music performance was also a source of revenue for the conservatories. The boys were hired out for parades, church services, festivals, and special events at the Royal Palace.[115] Finally, the conservatories took paying students: promising singers and instrumentalists who were not orphans and whose musical education was financed by a relative or a wealthy sponsor.[116] So great was the demand for instruction that the conservatories grew severely overcrowded. At the Conservatorio della Pietà dei Turchini, according to a memorandum of 1746, "the violin class is to be held in the lower corner of the Senior Dormitory, the oboe class in the detention room, the class for cellos and double basses in the passage of the upper cloakroom, and the class of trombones and trumpets in the lower cloakroom."[117] Burney described vividly the results of this overcrowding at the Conservatorio of Sant'Onofrio:

On the first flight of stairs was a trumpeter, screaming upon his instrument till he was ready to burst; on the second was a french-horn, bellowing in the same manner. In the common practising room there was a *Dutch concert*, consisting of seven or eight harpsichords, more than as many violins, and several voices, all performing different things, and in different keys.

Despite the overcrowding and the cacophony, he acknowledged that "this constant perseverance, for a number of years, with genius and good teaching, must produce great musicians."[118]

Many famous singers and composers emerged from the conservatories of Naples. It is hard to tell, however, how important the conservatories were in staffing Italian orchestras. Samuel Sharp, an English visitor to Naples in 1765, identified the conservatories as the training place of "hundreds" of young Italian musicians.[119] Many of the players in the orchestra of the San Carlo theater were indeed trained at one of the conservatories, and Neapolitans occasionally turn up on the rosters of orchestras in Rome and elsewhere in Italy.[120]

Venice also had four conservatories, called *ospedali*, similar in many ways to the Neapolitan conservatories.[121] They were not a source of instrumentalists for most

---

[115] Denis Arnold, "Instruments and Instrumental Teaching in the Early Italian Conservatoires," *GSJ* 18 (1965), 72–81; Hucke, "Verfassung und Entwicklung," 143. Robinson gives details of some contracts between Neapolitan churches and the Conservatory of S. Maria di Loreto (Michael F. Robinson, "The Governors' Minutes of the Conservatory S. Maria di Loreto, Naples," *RMA Research Chronicle*, 10 (1972), 1–97 at 63).

[116] At S. Maria di Loreto paying students received considerably better treatment than the orphans. They were given more food, and they were not required to participate in money-making performances. The governors of the Conservatory made efforts during the 18th c. to equalize the conditions of the two groups of students (Robinson, *Naples and Neapolitan Opera*, 52–56).

[117] Translated in Arnold, "Instruments," 80.

[118] Burney, *Present State of Music in France and Italy*, 336, 338–39.

[119] Samuel Sharp, *Letters from Italy, Describing the Customs and Manners of that Country, in the Years 1765 and 1766*, 3rd edn. (London, 1767), 81.

[120] Arnold, "Instruments," 78.

[121] The four *ospedale* were the Ospedale della Pietà, the Ospedale degli Incurabili, the Ospedale dei Derelitti (Ospedaletto), and the Ospedale di San Lazaro e dei Mendicanti.

orchestras, however, because the resident musicians were all women. Like the Neapolitan conservatories, the Venetian *ospedali* were orphanages that had undertaken music teaching and music making as a way of raising money and also to make their girls, who were provided with dowries, more attractive candidates for marriage. All but one of them (the Pietà) took both male and female orphans. However, only the women were trained as musicians.[122] These *figlie di coro* (choir girls) included not just orphans but scholarship students selected by audition and also paying students, sponsored by their families or a patron.[123] The girls were trained to sing and to play instruments by older *figlie* who had not married, and also by male *maestri* employed as instrument teachers and composers. The list of *maestri* employed at the Pietà and the Incurabili in the eighteenth century is impressive: Vivaldi, Porpora, Sarti, Galuppi, Hasse, and Jommelli, among others.

The *ospedali* were organized and run like convents: the *figlie di coro* lived in isolation, dressed in uniforms, and were subject to quasi-monastic rules.[124] Each *ospedale* maintained what amounted to a *cappella*: a chorus and an orchestra, as well as vocal and instrumental soloists, all of them women. In the churches associated with their *ospedali* the choir girls performed at mass and at vespers, they produced oratorios, and they put on special performances for Venetian nobility and foreign visitors.[125]

By the eighteenth century the *ospedali* had become an international tourist attraction. Their orchestras came in for special mention. Visitors were astounded to see women playing instruments that elsewhere were reserved for men. "They play the violin, the flute, the organ, the oboe, the violoncello, the bassoon," reported Charles de Brosses, who heard the *figlie* in 1739, "in brief, there is no instrument large enough to frighten them."[126] Visitors were also surprised at the skill of the instrumentalists. Because their membership was stable and rehearsal time was abundant, the orchestras of the *ospedali* were able to attain an impressive level of execution.

It is hard to tell how large the orchestras were at typical *ospedale* performances or how the instruments were distributed. A smattering of eighteenth-century rosters from the *ospedali* list 15 to 20 instrumentalists, most of them string players.[127] Nevertheless, travelers' reports, instrument inventories, and surviving repertory all indicate that the orchestras included winds. The girls performed in lofts behind a

---

[122] Boys were sometimes accepted as day students in music at conservatories other than the Pietà.

[123] Jane Baldauf-Berdes, *Women Musicians of Venice: Musical Foundations, 1525–1855* (Oxford, 1993), 116–17.

[124] Ibid., ch. 5.

[125] Denis Arnold, "Orphans and Ladies: The Venetian Conservatoires (1680–1790)," *PRMA* 89 (1963), 31–47; Libby, "Italy," 41.

[126] Charles de Brosses, *Lettres familières*, ed. Giuseppina Cafasso (Naples, 1991), i. 333.

[127] Pietà, 1707: 4 vn, 2 violette, 3 viole, 1 violone, 3 org, 1 thrb; Ospedaletto, 1743: 8 vn, 2 vla, 4 viole, 3 violoni; Derelitti, 1770: 7 vn, 3 vla, 4 vc, 3 violoni. See Giancarlo Rostirolla, "L'organizzazione musicale nell'ospedale veneziano della Pietà al tempo di Vivaldi," *Nuova rivista musicale italiana*, 13 (1979), 168–95 at 189; *Arte e musica a l'ospedaletto: schede d'archivio sull'attività musicale degli ospedali dei Derelitti e dei Mendicanti di Venezia (Sec. XVI–XVIII)* (Venice, 1978); Baldauf-Berdes, *Women Musicians*, 126.

choir screen for modesty's sake; there they could be glimpsed as if through a veil. For visits of foreign dignitaries to Venice, singers and instrumentalists from all four conservatories were combined into a grand chorus and orchestra for a private concert. A painting by Francesco Guardi (Pl. V) shows the performance of a cantata in honor of the Crown Prince of Russia, who visited Venice in 1782. Twenty female instrumentalists, all string players, all in plain view, are seen in Guardi's picture. The account books, however, say that the orchestra numbered 43.[128] Although the records show that a harpsichord accompanied the performance, there is no keyboard in the picture. There are two basses or violoni in the center of the front row, and a singer in the top row center beats time with a rolled up piece of paper. The *figlie di coro* are dressed in basic black uniforms, but with white collars and significant decolletage.

Through the descriptions of the all-girl orchestras of the Venetian conservatories runs an undercurrent of prurience. Performances by the *figlie di coro* were staged as spectacles for the aural and visual pleasure of the audience, and the sight of women engaged in musical activities ordinarily forbidden to them was more than a little titillating for male guests. Charles de Brosses expressed himself in typical fashion:

I swear to you that there is nothing as pleasant as to see a young and pretty nun in a white habit, with a bouquet of gardenias tucked behind her ear, playing and beating time with consummate grace and exactness. . . . The conservatory out of all the four to which I go the most often and where I am entertained the best is the *Ospedale de la Pietà*, which has the reputation for the best orchestral music. What strength of execution! Here is the only place that one can hear the premier *coup d'archet* for which the Paris Opéra so vainly prides itself.[129]

De Brosses speaks as though the choirgirls were in plain sight. When P. J. Grosley attended a concert (he does not say at which conservatory) the girls were behind a metal screen. This only whetted his appetite:

The most brilliant music . . . is executed here, both the voice and the instrument parts, by the girls from the conservatory, who can be glimpsed through a grillwork draped with gauze, as they flutteringly abandon themselves to all the movements that the performance of lively music requires . . .[130]

Sound, sight, and the male imagination combined to generate an atmosphere of voluptuousness, which Guardi captures in his painting.

The Venetian conservatories, because they trained only women, did not contribute to the supply of orchestra musicians in Italy, and the four Naples conservatories alone probably did not come close to meeting the demand. The large and increasing number of Italian instrumentalists in the eighteenth century must have

---

[128] Denis Arnold and Elsie Arnold, "Russians in Venice: The Visit of the *Conti del Nord* in 1782," in Malcolm Brown and Roland John Wiley (eds.), *Slavonic and Western Music: Essays for Gerald Abraham* (Ann Arbor, 1985), 123–30 at 125.

[129] Brosses, *Lettres familières*, i. 334.

[130] Arnold and Arnold, *Oratorio*, 61; Grosley, *Observations*, ii. 54.

been educated privately and trained on the job, playing in orchestras. There was no formal system of musical apprenticeship in Italy as there was in northern Europe.[131] Aspiring instrumentalists attached themselves to a teacher, paid him for lessons, and played alongside him in orchestras. The records of Roman orchestras in the late seventeenth and early eighteenth centuries contain many entries for an established instrumentalist followed by an entry for his pupil: *scolaro di Silvestro, scolaro d'Ippolito*, etc.[132] Often the student was a son or a nephew of the teacher. The rosters of orchestras in Milan, Florence, and Turin are filled with names of instrumentalists from the same families, who played together and succeeded one another decade after decade, some families specializing in stringed instruments, others in winds.[133] When a student had attained a certain level, the teacher would begin to send him to play as a deputy, often because the teacher had another job to play at the same time. This practice of substitutes was a perennial source of dispute between instrumentalists and theater managements throughout the eighteenth century. In a report to the governing board of the San Carlo theater, Naples, in 1773 the *maestri di cappella* complained that

Most evenings at the opera the majority of the violinists in the orchestras absent themselves and send others in their place. This gives rise to two great problems. The first is that adding seven or eight entirely new violinists, who have never rehearsed the music, inevitably creates disharmony in the orchestra; the second is that they usually send very poor players.[134]

The Neapolitan *maestri* recommended that no more than two substitutes be allowed to play in the orchestra on a given night. The Teatro Regio in Turin in 1768 attempted to enforce an even stricter standard:

None of the players [*Virtuosi*], no matter who, will be permitted to send another in his place because of sickness or for any other reason. It is the prerogative of the Director to make whatever arrangements he deems appropriate and to be sure that the [absent] player is paid only for as much as he has worked.[135]

Despite official attempts to create tighter discipline, the practice of substitutes was often tolerated because it served at least two useful purposes: it gave young players experience in orchestras, and it increased the pool of instrumentalists available for orchestral performances.

---

[131] Unlike other Venetian guilds, the guild of instrumentalists (Arte dei Suonatori) had no apprentices or journeymen, but only the single rank of "master." If a player passed his audition and paid his membership fee, he was thereby a *maestro*. See Thomas Bauman, "Musicians in the Marketplace: The Venetian Guild of Instrumentalists in the Later 18th Century," *EM* 19 (1991), 345–55.

[132] Kirkendale, "Ruspoli Documents," 256; Marx, "'Giustificazioni,'" 158. For a discussion of student–teacher relations in Rome, see Giancarlo Rostirolla, "La professione di strumentista a Roma nel Sei e Settecento," *Studi musicali*, 23 (1994), 87–174.

[133] Rosy Moffa discusses several Turinese musician families: *Storia della regia cappella di Torino dal 1775 al 1870* (Turin, 1990), 36 ff. For Milanese families, see Barblan, "La musica strumentale"; for Florence, see John Walter Hill, "Veracini in Italy," *M & L* 56 (1975), 257–76 at 257.

[134] Prota-Giurleo, *La grande orchestra*, 23–24.   [135] Quoted in Bouquet, *Il Teatro di Corte*, 176.

If the available instrumentalists did not suffice to provide orchestras for theaters, churches, and academies, then players had to be imported from elsewhere. Musicians enjoyed considerable freedom of movement between Italian cities during the seventeenth and eighteenth centuries. Large cities, which had many venues for orchestras, attracted the most instrumentalists. Rome, where few native players were trained, but where a great many events required big orchestras, had an almost insatiable demand for instrumentalists. Roman pay records are full of designations like Genovese, Napolitano, Bolognese, Todesco, Spagnoletto, etc.[136] Many of these players stayed in Rome and made careers for themselves. Venice seems to have trained more native instrumentalists than Rome, but Venetian orchestras still relied on immigrants, particularly on German wind players.[137] The instrumentalists' guild responded by charging considerably higher membership fees for non-Venetians.[138] For the opera season or for gala performances, smaller cities routinely brought in out-of-towners (*forestieri*), who were paid not only a wage but also their expenses for the duration of the festival or the opera. They returned home when the job was over.

In large cities like Naples, Rome, Venice, and Milan, a pool of instrumentalists developed that could be called upon to form larger or smaller orchestras as necessary. These musicians held down jobs at theaters, churches, and conservatories and supplemented this income with related activities like music copying and teaching. In these major centers, most orchestra musicians seem to have been full-time professionals. Enough young players were trained and enough trained musicians migrated from smaller to larger towns that there were adequate numbers of instrumentalists during the eighteenth century to make up orchestras of appropriate size and shape for theater, church, concerts, and special events. In smaller towns like Piacenza or Ravenna, many instrumentalists were part-timers who pursued another trade alongside music—barbers, in particular, often moonlighted in orchestras (see Ch. 12).

Wind players, like wind instruments, seem to have been in shorter supply than strings. J. J. Quantz, who heard an orchestra in Milan in the 1720s, complained that "here as in all of Italy," there was a lack of wind players.[139] Wind instruments, he said, are less used in Italy than in other countries "and consequently people do not have such good taste in this regard as they have for other things in music."[140] North Italian orchestras imported wind players from across the Alps: the rosters of orchestras in Turin, Milan, and Venice teem with French and German names.[141] Rome and Naples in turn imported wind players from Venice, Turin, and Milan.[142]

---

[136] See Rostirolla, "La professione," 156 ff.

[137] Alfredo Bernardini, "The Oboe in the Venetian Republic, 1692–1797," *EM* 16 (1988), 373–87 at 374.

[138] Bauman, "Musicians," 347. In 1783 the guild attempted to exclude foreigners altogether, but the regulation was struck down by the courts (p. 351).

[139] Willi Kahl, *Selbstbiographien deutscher Musiker des XVIII. Jahrhunderts* (Cologne, 1948), 143.

[140] Johann Joachim Quantz, *Versuch einer Anweisung die Flöte traversiere zu spielen* (Berlin, 1752), 243.

[141] Bouquet, *Il Teatro di Corte*; Barblan, "La musica strumentale"; Bernardini, "The Oboe."

[142] Prota-Giurleo, *La grande orchestra*, 12–13; Rostirolla, "La professione," 156 ff.

String players, on the other hand, were an Italian export. Italian violinists and cellists staffed orchestras throughout Europe. Orchestras in London, Dresden, Stuttgart, Lisbon, and St. Petersburg hired large numbers of Italian string players throughout the eighteenth century. How does it happen, asked Samuel Sharp, traveling in Italy in 1765, that Italy furnishes all Europe with musicians?

The answer is, that the infinite quantity of musick exhibited in their churches and chapels, provides bread, though the wages be small, for a prodigious number of performers; and, as trade is despicable, and laborious employments are held in detestation, parents are induced to bring up their children to this profession, which they can do at small expence: for there are several hundred youths brought up to musick, in their Conservatories, or charitable foundations. Now where there are so many hundreds in continual practice, it is not strange that emulation and genius should every now and then, produce an excellent performer, who, if he be well advised, will certainly set out for England, where talents of every kind are rewarded tenfold above what they are in Naples . . .[143]

Thus, conservatory education and on-the-job training combined to create a supply of instrumentalists adequate not only for Italian orchestras but for England and much of the rest of Europe as well.

[143] Sharp, *Letters from Italy*, 81.

Chapter Six

The Orchestra in France

In France the orchestra began in the seventeenth century as a de facto royal mono-poly. Only Louis XIV, the Sun King, had the resources to combine string bands, winds, keyboards, and lutes into large, unified ensembles on an ongoing basis. The orchestra at the Académie Royale de Musique was an explicit monopoly: by the King's edict of 1672, only the Opéra was allowed to have an orchestra containing "more than six violins or other instrumentalists" (see Ch. 3). As a royal monopoly, the orchestra represented and symbolized the French monarchy and the absolutist system to the world—not only through its size, but also by its variety, discipline, repertory, and performance practices. Lully, when he died in 1687, bequeathed the Opéra and its orchestra to his heirs. Even before the death of Louis XIV in 1715, however, the monopoly had begun to erode. Over the course of the eighteenth century more people and more organizations laid claim to the orchestra—theaters, noble patrons, government officials, parvenu financiers, concert societies, and provincial academies. As new orchestras were created in new social contexts, the link between the orches-tra and royal absolutism was attenuated. No longer did the orchestra symbolize just the King and the monarchy; it took on new and various meanings: cosmopolitanism, sociability, sensuality, urban fashion, and local pride. By the time the Revolution came in 1789, the orchestra already belonged to the nation.

THE DECLINE OF ORCHESTRAL MUSIC AT COURT

In the 1690s, with the depredations of old age and under the influence of the pious Marquise de Maintenon, Louis XIV took less interest in dance, spectacle, and theater. Orchestral activities continued at court, but in an increasingly pro forma manner. At Versailles and the other royal residences concerted masses and motets were still performed in the royal chapels on occasions of state and major feasts of the Church calendar, Te Deums were sung to celebrate victories, and Requiems memorialized public figures. Theatrical entertainments involving orchestral forces were produced from time to time, but multi-day spectacles and large-scale theatrical works were a thing of the past.

Public music at court was de-emphasized, while private or semi-private entertainments open only to an inner circle received renewed attention. In his quarters at Versailles the King put on "divertissements" for his intimates. These became known by metonymy as "appartements." *Appartements* were held most Mondays, Wednesdays, and Thursdays. According to court protocol, the Salle de la Paix in the Queen's apartments was used for billiards, but other activities took place in the King's quarters: the Salle d'Apollon for concerts and dancing, the Salle de Mercure for gaming by the royal family alone, the Salle de Mars for gaming by others, and the Salle de l'Abondance for a buffet and drinking.[1] In 1694 Antoine Trouvain produced six engravings collectively entitled *Appartemens ou amusemens de la Famille Roiale à Versailles*, which portray members of the royal family and the inner court circle gambling, playing billiards and cards, drinking coffee, dancing, and listening to a concert. Figure 6.1, the "Fourth room of the apartments," shows a dancing couple on the right—the Duke of Chartres and his sister—a small group of onlookers on the left, and an even smaller band of musicians.[2] Only two violins, two oboes, and a basse de violon can be seen, although a few more musicians may be cut off at the left border. The musicians are installed in a raised niche built into a wall, an arrangement motivated not solely by visual and acoustical considerations but also by concerns of etiquette. A character in a novel by Mme de Scudéry published some years earlier remarks that instrumentalists were "placed in a tribune so that the auditors can avoid being encumbered by the musicians and having to praise them, which one is obliged to do when they are situated any closer."[3] The intimacy of this scene and the small number of participants constitute a striking contrast to the engravings of 1664 and 1674 (see above, Figs. 3.1–3.4), where large numbers of dancers are accompanied by large instrumental ensembles.

The combination of instruments that accompanies the dance in Fig. 6.1—two pairs of treble instruments and one bass—cannot be playing the five-part dance music of the Vingt-quatre Violons and of Lully's ballets and operas. Much more likely, they are performing music in the three-part trio texture that became increasingly popular around the turn of the century, for example Lalande's *Simphonies pour les soupers du Roy* (1703, 1713) and François Couperin's *Concerts royaux* (c.1713–15). Couperin says in the introduction to the *Concerts royaux* that he and other court musicians performed them at "the little chamber concerts to which Louis XIV summoned me

---

[1] Marie-Christine Moine, *Les Fêtes à la cour du Roi Soleil (1653–1715)* (Paris, 1984), 61–64.

[2] Rebecca Harris-Warrick, "Ballroom Dancing at the Court of Louis XIV," *EM* 14 (1986), 41–63 at 43.

[3] Madeleine de Scudéry, *Artamène; ou, Le Grand Cyrus* (Paris, 1656), vii. 1211.

QUATRIEME CHAMBRE DES APARTEMENS.

Fig. 6.1. Dance ensemble at Versailles, 1696

nearly every Sunday of the year."[4] Although not intended for massed instruments, this repertory probably accommodated part doubling when the necessary resources were at hand.[5] When French symphonies first started to appear in the 1730s, their most common instrumentation was not the traditional five-part textures of Lully's orchestra but rather the trio texture of two trebles and bass, with winds, if any, doubling or alternating with the strings.[6]

After Louis XIV's death, in the more informal, pleasure-seeking atmosphere of the regency, this more intimate approach to music continued. Official musical activities at court went on as before, but the court's musical institutions regained neither their

---

[4] François Couperin, *Musique de chambre I* (Œuvres complètes de François Couperin, 7; Paris, 1933), 9.

[5] Anthony, *French Baroque Music*, 362.

[6] Barry S. Brook, *La Symphonie française dans la seconde moitié du XVIIIᵉ siècle* (Paris, 1962), i. 93–94.

former brilliance nor their role as an internationally emulated model. When Louis XV took control of government in 1723, the structure and functions of the court music establishment were much the same as they had been in the seventeenth century. The division into Chapelle, Chambre, and Écurie still obtained; positions in the King's music were still offices that could be bought and sold; some of the same families still monopolized the same offices. The duties of instrumentalists in the King's service were relatively light. The Vingt-quatre Violons were officially obligated to play only eight or nine times a year; the instrumentalists of the Chapelle played as a group only on special occasions. Many of the King's musicians held multiple offices from which they drew multiple incomes; others had purchased only a part of an office, which meant they served only a few days per year. The old separation of the Opéra from the King's music had fallen by the wayside. Many, perhaps most, of the King's musicians derived a good deal of their income from playing in the Paris theaters, especially the Opéra.[7] During the course of the reign, and particularly with the Seven-Year War, which began in 1756, the King and his ministers found themselves constrained to cut back on the expenses of the bloated royal bureaucracy. Music, it seemed, was dispensable.

In 1761 Louis XV announced an extensive reorganization of his musical establishment. "We have fixed now and for all time," he decreed, "the expenditure of our Music at the sum of 320,000 livres, which includes wages, appointments, and pensions of those who now serve and will serve in the future."[8] A sum of 10,000 livres per year was set aside for the purpose of gradually buying back offices from musicians and their heirs. With fewer offices and fewer officeholders each year, the drain on the treasury would gradually be reduced. The Chapelle and the Chambre were merged into a single unit with about half as many instrumentalists as before, who were designated to serve at all court functions, both sacred and secular. The Vingt-quatre Violons du Roy, the fount and origin of the orchestra in France, indeed in all of Europe, simply ceased to exist. Those of their number who did not retire were absorbed into the King's "Musique Instrumentale," without special privileges or special duties. The leader of the Vingt-quatre, Jean-Pierre Guignon, an Italian virtuoso whose original name was Giovanni Pietro Ghignoni, continued for a few years as "roy et maître" of the Confrérie St-Julien, the Paris musicians' guild, but the position had become meaningless. In 1773 Guignon submitted a letter of resignation to the King, who accepted it and abolished the post.[9]

The reform of 1761 brought the orchestra at Versailles into line with international eighteenth-century musical practices, with strings in four parts, pairs of winds, trumpets, drums, and even a harp. Compared with the orchestras of the German

---

[7] Roberte Machard, "Les Musiciens en France au temps de Jean-Philippe Rameau d'après les actes du Secrétariat de la Maison du Roi," *RMFC* 11 (1971), 5–177 at 29.

[8] Ibid. 147.

[9] Lionel de La Laurencie, *L'École française de violon de Lully à Viotti* (Paris, 1922–24), ii. 49–60.

courts, however, or the large Italian opera houses, or to those in the Paris theaters, the French King's orchestra was rather modest. In an edict of 1782 the next King, Louis XVI, under pressure of an ever-worsening financial crisis, cut back yet further on the size of his orchestra: "Our Instrumental Music shall be fixed at the number of forty-two performers: namely 16 violins, four violas, five cellos, four flutes, one oboe, four bassoons, two double basses, two clarinets, two horns, and two organists, each serving a half year."[10] Rather than creating prestige, the King's orchestra now had to buy it. A number of famous performers were recruited, like Rodolphe Kreutzer (violin), Pierre Berton (cello), Gaetano Besozzi (oboe), and Étienne Ozi (bassoon). These men, who had established themselves already at the orchestras of the Opéra, the Concert Spirituel, and in the salons of Paris, brought virtuosity and modernity to the rather sleepy musical precincts of Versailles. Other famous musicians were not interested. Offered the post of Court Organist in 1778, Mozart turned it down, saying: "Whoever enters the King's service is forgotten in Paris."[11]

THE ORCHESTRA AT THE OPÉRA

In 1715 the orchestra at the Académie Royale de Musique was the most prestigious orchestra in France, indeed in all of Europe. Its prestige stemmed in part from the fact that it had been Europe's first orchestra, that is, the first to combine strings, winds, and continuo in a permanent ensemble. It was also Europe's largest orchestra, at least the largest that was free-standing and independent of any court Kapelle. The Opéra enjoyed royal sponsorship, noble patronage, and a legal monopoly on orchestral performance in the theater. Despite various vicissitudes, the prestige and high standing of the Opéra orchestra were maintained all the way to the Revolution.

At the same time the orchestra of the Opéra was a profoundly conservative institution. Lully's operas, composed between 1672 and 1687, formed the core of the repertory well into the eighteenth century. As the years passed they were revised: prologues were omitted; repeats were eliminated in airs, instrumental numbers, and choruses; unpopular numbers and scenes were cut; the orchestration was modernized; and newly composed, up-to-date arias and dances were added.[12] New operas were modeled on Lully's style. A statute of 1704 provided that one of Lully's operas should always be prepared in parallel with any premiere, to be held in reserve in case

---

[10] Brigitte François-Sappey, "Le Personnel de la musique royale de l'avènement de Louis XVI à la chute de la monarchie (1774–1792)," *RMFC* 26 (1988–90), 133–72 at 165.

[11] Letter of 3 July 1778, in Mozart, *Briefe*, ii. 390.

[12] Herbert Schneider, *Die Rezeption der Opern Lullys im Frankreich des Ancien Régime* (Tutzing, 1982), 75–122; Lois Rosow, "How Eighteenth-Century Parisians Heard Lully's Operas: The Case of *Armide's* Fourth Act," in Heyer (ed.), *Jean-Baptiste Lully and the Music of the French Baroque*, 213–37.

the new work failed.[13] Plate VI, a watercolor by Gabriel de Saint-Aubin, depicts a revival at the Opéra of Lully's *Armide* in 1747 in the presence of Louis XV and the Dauphin, who occupy the first box next to the stage on the right.[14] The orchestra is crowded into an enclosure in front of the stage. The only instruments that can be made out are four cellos of the *grand choeur* on the far right, plus another cello on the far left, and the double bass of the *petit choeur*, which rises up directly below the figure of Armide onstage. In the very center the *batteur de mesure* with a baton in his raised hand directs the show. This performance took place 60 years after *Armide* was first introduced at the Opéra, yet it still presented and affirmed the monarchy to the nobility, the nation, and the world.

Instrumentation at the Opéra was just as conservative as repertory. The Opéra retained five-part scoring with three viola parts until at least 1720.[15] When the *quinte* was eliminated, Lully's operas were simply played with four instead of five parts.[16] Many composers of the 1720s and 1730s continued to write in five parts: now first and second *dessus, haute-contre, taille,* and *basse.* Not until the 1740s did four-part scoring become common at the Opéra. The Opéra retained the division into *petit choeur* and *grand choeur* until the 1790s—a last vestige of the vocal accompaniment and dance ensembles that Lully had combined in the 1670s. The orchestra was led by a *batteur de mesure* rather than by a violinist.

There were periodic attempts to update the repertory, instrumentation, and performance practices of the Opéra orchestra, but they always seemed to lag behind the curve. Bass viols dropped out of the orchestra at the end of the 1720s; basses de violon were replaced by cellos beginning perhaps in the 1720s.[17] Horns were added to the roster in 1760, clarinets in 1770—long after these instruments had become standard in other European orchestras.[18] The *petit* vs. *grand choeur* organization was modified in the 1730s to integrate the violin and flute soloists into the rest of the orchestra, while the harpsichord, several cellos, and a double bass remained as a *petit choeur* for vocal accompaniment.[19] The combination of prestige and conservatism made the Opéra orchestra a broad target for critics who argued that its reputation and its monopoly were undeserved.

[13] Jacques-Bernard Durey de Noinville, *Histoire du théâtre de l'Académie Royale de Musique en France* (Paris, 1757), 128.

[14] See Neal Zaslaw, "Observations: At the Paris Opéra in 1747," *EM* 11 (1983), 515–16; Lois Rosow, "Lully's *Armide* at the Paris Opéra: A Performance History: 1686–1766" (Ph.D. diss., Brandeis University, 1981), 367.

[15] La Gorce, "L'Orchestre de l'Opéra," 29–30.

[16] Rosow, "Armide," 219. A few passages had to be rewritten, where the *quinte* had an imitative entrance.

[17] La Gorce, "L'Orchestre de l'Opéra," 27; Cyr, "Basses and *basse continue*," 158 ff.

[18] Hornists and clarinetists had been hired earlier at the Opéra as supernumeraries to play scores that required these instruments, for example, Rameau's *Zoroastre* (1749) and *Acante et Céphise* (1751).

[19] In the revival of Rameau's *Zoroastre* that opened the new opera house in 1770, an attempt to eliminate the harpsichord failed, because without it the singers had intonation problems. The harpsichord was reinstated (Baron Friedrich Melchior von Grimm, "Correspondance," in *Correspondance littéraire, philosophique et critique,* ed. Maurice Tourneux (Paris, 1879), viii. 451).

In part the criticism had its roots in politics. As disaffection grew with royalty, the nobility, and the ancien régime, opponents of the system, like the Encyclopedists and their sponsors among the liberal nobility, rather than criticizing the monarchy directly, found it more prudent to criticize the Opéra and its orchestra. In January 1752 the Encyclopedist Baron von Grimm took the occasion of a revival of Destouches's *Omphale* (1701) to publish a fierce diatribe, in which he excoriated the Opéra's repertory (with the exception of Rameau's music), its singers (with the exception of two beloved stars, Mlle Fel and Pierre Jélyote), and its orchestra (no exceptions made).[20] By August, when an Italian troupe presented Pergolesi's comic intermezzo *La serva padrona* between the acts of a *tragédie lyrique* at the Opéra, the *Querelle des bouffons* had come to dominate Parisian cultural life. Italian opera became a symbol for all that was progressive and forward-looking, French opera a symbol for all that was wrong with French politics and society. In the years 1752–54 more than sixty pamphlets and related items were published attacking and defending either French or Italian music or trying to mediate between the two camps.[21] At the Opéra itself supporters of French music gathered at the side of the auditorium where the King's and Mme de Pompadour's box was situated (the "coin du roi"), supporters of Italian music on the other side near the Queen's box ("coin de la reine").

The Opéra orchestra and its leaders were subjected to particularly harsh criticism. The management of the Opéra, the repertory, the singers, and the dancers had all changed over the years; the orchestra remained the one constant, and its defects—real or imagined—came to symbolize the defects of French music (and French politics) in general. The criticisms of the orchestra can be summarized under three headings: a low standard of performance, obsolete performance practices, and finally, bad faith.

The members of the orchestra, says Rousseau in his *Lettre à M. Grimm* (1752), "claim that nowadays their performance is at a high standard, but I myself say that those people will never have either taste or soul."[22] The Opéra orchestra, Rousseau goes on, lacks all nuance. "To supplement, to soften, to support, to inflect sounds according to the requirements of good taste and expression, to understand the spirit of an accompaniment, to support the voices and set them off to advantage, every orchestra in the world has these skills, except that of our Opéra."

The Opéra orchestra neither understands nor has the training to perform "modern" Italian music to good effect. "In the accompaniments," complains Holbach, "they sometimes drag; other times they rush the tempos; they almost always play the opposite of what the music calls for. They play out of tune, their tempos are shaky. This is the sum total of their art."[23] "Rinforzando, dolce, risoluto, con gusto,

---

[20]　Friedrich Melchior von Grimm, *Lettre de M. Grimm sur Omphale* (1752).

[21]　Most of these pamphlets have been republished in *La Querelle des bouffons: Textes des pamphlets avec introduction, commentaires et index* (1752–54), ed. Denise Launay (Geneva, 1973).

[22]　Jean-Jacques Rousseau (attrib.), *Lettre à M. Grimm au sujet des Remarques ajoutées à sa Lettre sur Omphale* (1752), 25.

[23]　Baron d'Holbach, *Lettre à une dame d'un certain âge, sur l'état présent de l'Opéra* (1752), 8.

spiritoso, sostenuto, con brio," says Rousseau, "these terms do not even have syn-onyms in their language, and the word 'expression' signifies nothing to them."[24]

Finally, the critics accused the Opéra orchestra and its leaders of bad faith. The management of the Opéra, acquiescing at last to popular pressure and modern taste, had programmed Pergolesi's *La serva padrona* and other Italian intermezzi between the acts of French operas. However, according to Rousseau, the orchestra deliberately sabotaged these Italian operas by refusing to master their style and performance prac-tices. Rousseau's imaginary *symphoniste* learns that Jommelli's *Uccellatrice* has been scheduled for performance, and he obtains a copy of the score. "I am not very skilled at score-reading," he says,

. . . but I understood enough to know that the overture is entirely suitable for our undertaking, for the parts are highly coordinated, highly varied, full of shadings and rapid interchanges among diverse instruments, which enter one after another—in a word it demands great pre-cision in performance. Consider how easily we can make a big mess of the whole thing by just doing what comes naturally.[25]

The critics of the Opéra orchestra saved their harshest criticism for the noisy baton of the *batteur de mesure*, whom Grimm satirized as a "wood-chopper."[26] Italian orches-tras, the critics claim, have no need for a timebeater, because they feel the beat instinc-tively. French orchestras need to have the beat dictated to them. "The Paris Opéra," says Rousseau, "is the only theater in Europe where they beat time but don't keep it. Elsewhere they keep time, but don't beat it."[27] Here the political agenda of the Opéra's critics emerges clearly. The orchestra of the Opéra is inferior because it is ruled by tradition and by force—the same things that are wrong with the government of France. To reform the Opéra orchestra would be to challenge not only French music but the French monarchy as well. "All liberties," says d'Alembert in his essay *De la lib-erté de la musique* (1759), "stand together and are equally dangerous. Freedom of music implies freedom to feel, freedom to feel implies freedom to think, freedom to think implies freedom to act, and freedom to act is the ruin of nations. If we wish to preserve the kingdom," he concludes ironically, "let us preserve the Opéra just as it is."[28]

Actually the Opéra had changed a good deal between Lully's death and the *Querelle des bouffons*, and it changed even more in the second half of the century. Table 6.1 traces the size and balances of the Opéra orchestra over the eighteenth century, begin-ning in 1704, when an administrative reorganization generated the earliest extant ros-ter and paylist.[29] The most obvious change in balances was the gradual elimination of

---

[24] Jean-Jacques Rousseau, *Lettre sur la musique françoise* (1753), 14.

[25] Jean-Jacques Rousseau (attrib.), *Lettre d'un symphoniste de l'Académie Royale de Musique à ses camarades de l'orchestre* (1753), 366.

[26] Friedrich Melchior von Grimm, *Le Petit Prophète de Boehmischbroda* (Paris, 1753), 9–11.

[27] Jean-Jacques Rousseau, *Dictionnaire de musique* (Paris: Duchesne, 1768), 53.

[28] Jean Le Rond d'Alembert, *De la liberté de la musique* (Amsterdam, 1759), 397.

[29] See Ch. 3; La Gorce, "L'Orchestre de l'Opéra."

TABLE 6.1. *The orchestra of the Opéra, 1704–89*

Date		Keyboard and plucked strings	Bowed strings	Winds	Brass and percussion	Total	Source
1704:	Petit choeur	1 clavecin 1 *batteur* 2 theorbos	2 dessus de violon 2 basses de violon 2 basses de viole	—	—	43	La Gorce, "L'Académie," 178
	Grand choeur	—	9 dessus de violon 3 hautes contres 3 tailles 2 quintes 8 basses de violon	2 oboes and flutes 2 flutes allemandes 2 flute/bassoon 2 bassoons			
1713:	Petit choeur	1 harpsichord 1 *batteur* 2 [theorbos]	2 [dessus de violon] 2 [basses de violon] 2 [basses de viole] 2 flutes allemandes	2 flutes allemandes		48	Durey, *Histoire*, 121
	Grand choeur	—	12 dessus 2 tailles 3 hautes contres 2 quintes 8 basses	8 oboes, flutes, bassoons	1 drum		
1729:	Petit choeur	[1 *batteur*] 1 harpsichord 1 theorbo	[2 dessus de violon] 3 cellos and basses de violon 1 double bass	[2 flutes allemandes]		45	La Gorce, "L'Orchestre," 25–6
	Grand choeur	—	14 dessus de violon 3 hautes contres 3 tailles 6 basses de violon	3 oboes and flutes 5 bassoons			

Year		Direction	Strings	Winds	Brass/Percussion	No.	Source
1738:	Petit choeur	1 *batteur* 1 harpsichord	4 violins 3 cellos 1 double bass			47	Sauer, "Rameau's Singers," 462–64
	Grand choeur	—	12 violins 3 tailles 3 hautes contres 8 cellos and basses 1 double bass	5 flutes and oboes 5 bassoons			
1751		2 *batteurs* 1 harpsichord	16 violins 6 violas (quintes) 3 cellos (petit choeur) 1 double bass (p.c.) 8 cellos and basses (grand choeur)	10 oboes, flutes, and bassoons	2 drums	49	*Almanach* (1752), 100; La Gorce, "L'Orchestre," 25
1764		1 maître 1 harpsichord	17 violins 6 violas (parties) 3 cellos (p.c.) 1 double bass (p.c.) 8 cellos and basses (g.c.)	4 flutes and oboes 5 bassoons	2 horns 1 trumpet 1 musette	50	*Almanach* (1765), 14; La Gorce, 25
1776		1 maître 1 aide	25 violins 5 violas 4 cellos (p.c.) 1 double bass (p.c.) 11 cellos (g.c.) 5 basses (g.c.)	1 solo flute 7 flutes and oboes 2 clarinets 8 bassoons	2 horns 3 trumpets 1 drum	77	*Almanach* (1777), 21
1789		1 maître 1 sous-maître	28 violins 6 violas 4 cellos (p. c.) 8 cellos (g. c.) 5 double basses	2 flutes 4 oboes 2 clarinets 5 bassoons	4 horns 3 trumpets and trombones 1 drum	74	*Almanach* (1790), 21

the multiple parts in the middle of the texture. The *quintes* disappeared around 1720; *hautes-contres* and *tailles* were consolidated into a single viola section in the 1740s. The total number of players remained more or less constant during the first half of the century, then increased rapidly between 1764 and 1770, so that by 1776 the orchestra was half again as large as it had been in 1764. The old theater of the Académie de Musique had burned in 1763, and the Opéra performed until 1770 in the Salle des Machines at the Tuileries, a large room in which neither voices nor instruments could be heard clearly.[30] The augmentation of the orchestra may have been an attempt to counteract the poor acoustics of this venue. The new theater at the Palais Royale, to which the Opéra moved in 1770, was considerably larger than the original theater at the same location, and the orchestra remained at its larger size.

The orchestra of the Opéra continued to draw top-quality instrumentalists in the eighteenth century, as it had in Lully's day. "To avoid any favoritism," the *Almanach des spectacles* reported in 1780,

. . . positions in the orchestra can only be gained by means of competition. Aspiring instrumentalists should present themselves to M. Francoeur, Director of the Orchestra, who will bring them before a committee. The committee will listen to an audition and rank the applicants. Positions will be awarded by a plurality of votes. The Director gets two votes.[31]

The *Almanach* went on to explain that a musician's position in the section was determined by seniority, except the first chair, which was assigned by another competition. Despite these safeguards, and even though a post at the Opéra could not be sold or inherited, a few families of musicians—Caraffe, L'Abbé, Dun, Sallaentin, Plessis, Despreaux—established and maintained themselves in the Opéra orchestra during the eighteenth century.[32] These families were less numerous than the families that dominated the court music offices, and they did not own their positions. Over the course of the century the social and geographical background of the Opéra orchestra seems to have broadened, as instrumentalists migrated to Paris from the provinces, from Italy, and increasingly after 1750 from Germany and Bohemia.

---

[30] Soufflot tried to improve the acoustics of the Salle des Machines by building what amounted to a theater within the theater. Evidently this did not work (Rebecca Harris-Warrick, "Paris (3) 1725–89," in *GroveO*, 861).

[31] *Almanach des spectacles de Paris . . .* (1780), 18–19.

[32] Sylvette Milliot, "Vie de l'orchestre de l'Opéra de Paris à travers les documents du temps," in *L'Opéra au XVIIIᵉ siècle: Actes du Colloque, les 29, 30 avril et 1ᵉʳ mai 1977*, ed. André Bourde (Université de Provence, 1982), 263–85 at 276–77. For the crises experienced by the Opéra orchestra in the 1790s under the Revolution, Terror, and Directorate, see Alexandre Dratwicki, "La Réorganisation de l'orchestre de l'Opéra de Paris en 1799: de nouvelles perspectives pour le répertoire de l'institution," *Revue de musicologie*, 88 (2002), 297–325.

ORCHESTRAS IN THE THEATERS OF PARIS

Besides the Opéra there were two other "official" theaters in Paris, the Comédie-Italienne and the Comédie-Française. Like the Opéra they held monopolies—to spoken drama in Italian and French respectively—and like the Opéra they received royal subsidies. According to Lully's royal privilege of 1672, neither theater was allowed to have an orchestra or to use more than two singers. Eighteenth-century audiences, however, expected and demanded singing and specially dancing when they went to the theater. The Comédie-Française and the Comédie-Italienne felt compelled to offer singers and dancers in their productions and to enlarge their orchestras, thus challenging the Opéra and its monopoly.[33] Their orchestras never came near the size of the orchestra at the Opéra, but they often exceeded the legal limit of six instrumentalists. Table 6.2 shows the size and make-up of some typical eighteenth-century Paris theater orchestras.

The Académie Royale did not hesitate to take its competitors to court and demand the fines stipulated in the royal *ordonnance* of 1672 as the penalty for infractions against Lully's privilege. In 1717, for example, the Opéra complained to the King's Council of State that a play called *Les Dieux comédiens* was running at the Comédie-Française, in which songs and dances were accompanied by "nine instruments in the orchestra, namely four violins, two basses, two oboes, and one bassoon."[34] Not only that, but there was a *batteur de mesure* leading the performance. The Council acknowledged that the privilege had been violated and moreover that this was not the first time. However, they let the Comédie-Française off with a warning that if it happened again the *ordonnance* would be enforced. The directors of the Opéra were back in court again in 1725, claiming that the Comédie-Française was violating their privilege on a daily basis. For its current production it had constructed "a space for the orchestra in front of the stage" in which it had placed nine instrumentalists (Table 6.2).[35] Once again the Council declined to take action.

The Italian theater too enlarged the orchestras that accompanied its productions. For a play in 1733 called *Le Temple du goût* an orchestra of 14 played an overture, and an Italian singer was accompanied by a trumpet, violins, and two flutes.[36] Two plays at the Comédie-Italienne in 1742 featured "an orchestra of 12 instruments, violins, basses, bassoons, flutes, and flageolets," which accompanied an elaborate series of ballets.[37] And in 1745 the Italiens presented *La Fille, la veuve et la femme*, which was sung all the way through "without a single word of prose," and accompanied by an orchestra of 11.[38]

[33] See Henri Lagrave, *Le Théâtre et le public à Paris de 1715 à 1750* (Paris, 1972), 364 ff.

[34] Émile Campardon, *Les Comédiens du Roi de la troupe française* (Paris, 1879), 282–83.

[35] Ibid. 287–88.

[36] Émile Campardon, *Les Comédiens du Roi de la troupe italienne* (Paris, 1880), ii. 247. The source insists that there were two different types of flute: "deux flûtes, l'une allemande et l'autre traversière." By "flûte allemande" the writer, a police investigator, seems to mean a recorder, although this contradicts ordinary parlance.

[37] Ibid. ii. 253.   [38] Ibid. 261–62.

TABLE 6.2. *Orchestras in the Paris theaters, 1704–87*

COMÉDIE-ITALIENNE

Theater and date	Keyboard and plucked strings	Bowed strings	Winds	Brass and percussion	Total	Source
1733	—	6 violins 3 basses [de violon]	1 recorder 1 transverse flute 1 musette	1 trumpet 1 drum	14	Campardon, *Comédiens . . . italienne*, ii. 247
1751	—	7 violins 1 cello	1 flute 1 oboe 1 bassoon	2 horns 1 drum	14	*Almanach* (1752), 73
1754	—	9 violins 2 cellos	1 flute/musette 2 flutes and oboes 1 bassoon	1 drum	16	*Almanach* (1755), 78
1762 (merged with Opéra comique)	—	9 violins 2 violas (quintes) 2 cellos and basses	2 oboes 2 bassoons	—	17	*Almanach* (1763), 89
1769	—	10 violins 2 violas 3 cellos 2 double basses	2 flutes and oboes 2 bassoons	2 horns 1 timpani	24	Barnes, "Instruments," 148
1772	—	11 violins 2 violas 3 cellos 2 double basses	2 flutes and oboes	2 horns 1 drum	22	*Almanach* (1773), 88
1787	?	18 violins 2 violas 5 cellos 2 double basses	3 flutes and oboes 2 bassoons	2 horns 1 drum	35	*Almanach* (1788), 116

Year		Strings	Winds	Horns/Percussion	Total	Reference
1717	1 timebeater 2 basses de violon	4 violins	2 oboes 1 bassoon	—	10	Campardon, *Comédiens . . .française*, 283
1725	—	4 violons 2 basses de violon	2 oboes 1 bassoon	—	9	Ibid. 288
1752	—	5 violins and violas 2 cellos and basses	1 bassoon	—	8	*Almanach* (1752), 23
1762	—	7 violins 1 viola 2 cellos	2 oboes 1 bassoon	2 horns	15	*Almanach* (1763), 65
1773	—	11 violins 2 violas 3 cellos and basses	2 oboes 2 bassoons	3 horns	23	*Almanach* (1774), 52
1786	?	14 violins 2 violas 4 cellos 1 double bass	3 oboes 2 bassoons	1 horn 1 drum	28	*Almanach* (1787), 63

THÉÂTRE DE LA FOIRE

Year		Strings	Winds	Horns	Total	Reference
1704 (Alard)	—	5 violins 1 basse de violon	1 oboe 1 bassoon		8	Cucuel, *Créateurs*, 45
1711 (Baron)	—	3 violins 2 basses de violon	1 oboe		6	Campardon, *Spectacles*, i. 91
1715 (Lesage: *Télémaque*)	1 harpsichord	8 violins 1 double bass	1 flute 1 oboe 1 bassoon	2 horns	14	Barnes, "Instruments," 146

TABLE 6.2. (*Cont.*)

Theater and date	Keyboard and plucked strings	Bowed strings	Winds	Brass and percussion	Total	Source
1720 (Francisque)	—	4 violins 2 basses de violon		[2] trumpets 1 drum	9	Campardon, *Spectacles*, i. 340
1721 (Antony)	—	6 violins 3 basses de violon	1 bassoon		10	Ibid. 16
OPÉRA COMIQUE						
1744	?	6 violins 3 cellos 1 double bass	2 flutes and oboes 2 bassoons	2 horns	16	Cucuel, 50
1753	—	9 violins and violas 2 cellos 1 double bass	1 oboe 2 bassoons	2 horns	17	*Almanach* (1754), 173
1761	—	9 violins and violas 2 cellos 1 double bass	2 flutes and oboes 1 bassoon	1 horn	16	*Almanach* (1762), 99

This amounted to an opera, a flagrant violation of the Académie's privilege. The King's Council banned it and ordered the Italiens to pay a fine of 10,000 livres to the Opéra. There is no record, however, of whether the fine was ever paid.

The Opéra's battle to preserve its orchestral monopoly was a losing cause. The Académie complained to the authorities, it obtained judgments against the other theaters, perhaps it even collected some fines. Yet the Comédie-Française and the Comédie-Italienne continued to have orchestras; indeed their orchestras grew larger (Table 6.2). An orchestra had become a necessity in the theater, not only to accompany songs and dances, but also as an attraction of its own, playing music before the show and between the acts. An orchestra was a mark of luxury in the theater, a sign that management had spared no expense to give the public what it wanted.

The orchestras at both the Comédie-Italienne and the Comédie-Française were organized differently from the Opéra orchestra. By the middle of the century, when the *Almanach des spectacles* began to publish their rosters, there were four string sections, there was no division between *petit* and *grand choeur*, and the orchestras were led by the first violinist rather than by a timebeater. Thus they resembled Italian orchestras more than they did the orchestra of the Opéra, and mid-century critics of the Opéra orchestra sometimes pointed to the other theaters as examples of what a good orchestra ought to be.

The three "official" theaters were not the only shows in town. The so-called Fair theaters (*Théâtre de la foire*) operated without royal privilege. The Foire St-Germain ran for two months in the spring; the Foire St-Laurent took place from July through September. Besides shops and booths that sold merchandise, food, and drink, entertainment was an important attraction at both fairs. Buskers sang, fiddled, danced on ropes, did acrobatics, and put trained animals through their paces. Theater troupes set up temporary theaters for the duration of each season.[39] They offered comedies, vaudevilles, and parodies of works recently seen at the official theaters—always something new, usually topical, and often scandalous. To accompany dancing and for entr'actes the Fair theaters employed bands of musicians, sometimes only the "six violins or other instrumentalists" prescribed by the Opéra privilege, sometimes more, as shown in Table 6.2. The Opéra and even more often the Comédie-Française attempted to enforce their privileges against violations by the Fair theaters, often quite vigorously. Police inspectors were sent to report on the shows, and in particular to see whether they had spoken dialogue (a violation against the Comédie-Française) or an orchestra (a violation against the Opéra). Inspector Joseph Aubert dropped by the theater run by Antoine Francisque at the Foire St-Laurent in 1720 and reported:

when the curtain rose we saw a theater outfitted with painted sets representing a solitary place, [with] a mausoleum and several chandeliers. There was an orchestra with four violins and two basses, which played a sad air. The actors, both men and women, declaimed a prologue in loud

---

[39] See Lagrave, *Le Théâtre et le public*, 94 ff.; Clifford R. Barnes, "Instruments and Instrumental Music at the 'Théâtres de la foire' (1697–1762)," *RMFC* 5 (1965), 142–68.

voices and spoke to and answered one another. . . . Afterwards the same actors played another act of a comedy called "The Black Head," where the decor represented a room and the same four violins and two basses played between the acts.[40]

Four violins plus two basses make six, so Francisque was safe from the wrath of the Opéra, but not from the Comédie-Française, which objected to the spoken dialogue.

Antony de Sceau's theater at the Foire St-Germain in 1721, on the other hand, did violate the Opéra's monopoly. According to Inspector Daminois:

In the first act a boy and a girl danced, together, then in alternation, then together again, to the sound of a bassoon and nine stringed instruments, three of them basses, all in the orchestra. . . . In the second act there was a dance of four savages . . . and in the third act a dance of four moors. . . . The last act ended with a chaconne in which all the actors and actresses . . . danced together, all to the sound of the same instruments, which also played incessantly between the acts, playing different pieces of music from written-out parts.[41]

This was too much for Louis-Antoine-François Duchesne, one of the directors of the Académie Royale, who attended the show. Duchesne complained to the authorities that Sceau was violating the Opéra's privilege and demanded legal action. If there was a judgment against his theater, however, no record of it has survived.

Records have survived for a succession of cases brought against Louis and Marie St-Edme, who ran theaters at both fairs from 1712 to 1718. The St-Edme theater was reported to have had an orchestra of ten in 1714, and in 1716 the police reported that "St-Edme has an orchestra filled with 20 musicians, who play together, each with a different musical instrument."[42] Legal actions were brought repeatedly against St-Edme by the Opéra. In 1714 the troupe was assessed a fine of 10,000 livres, which apparently went unpaid. Having failed to get its way by force, the Académie Royale tried negotiations. In 1716 M. and Mme St-Edme agreed to pay the Académie for the privilege of having an orchestra and presenting sung drama at the Fairs. The yearly payments were set at 35,000 livres, a preposterous sum that a seasonal theater could not come close to paying. In 1718 the St-Edmes went bankrupt, and their theater was closed.[43]

Chronically short of money, the Académie continued to seek an accommodation with the Fair theaters, judging perhaps that its monopoly on the orchestra had eroded to the point where, rather than defend it wholesale, it was better to sell it piecemeal. In 1724 a group of promoters negotiated a viable agreement with the Opéra and opened a long-term Fair theater under the name "Opéra Comique," the ancestor of the later institution of that name. The Opéra Comique agreed to make yearly payments to the Opéra in return for permission to employ singers and an orchestra and to present songs and dances on the stage. A permanent theater was built at the Foire St-Germain, and the Opéra Comique began to give vaudevilles, parodies, and

---

[40] Émile Campardon, *Les Spectacles de la foire* (Paris, 1877), i. 340–41.
[41] Ibid. i. 16.   [42] Ibid. ii. 349, 355–56.   [43] Ibid. ii. 344–45.

other plays to the accompaniment of a standing orchestra, reported as having 16 members in 1744 (Table 6.2). According to Ancelet's *Observations sur la musique* the orchestra at the Opéra Comique in 1757 sounded better than the orchestra at either the Comédie-Française or the Italiens, because of the quality of the musicians and even more because of the superior acoustics of its theater.[44]

In 1762 the Opéra Comique merged with the Comédie-Italienne, becoming in the process an "official" theater. The two orchestras, as well as the rest of the personnel of the two theaters, were combined. Plate VII shows the merged Italiens and Opéra Comique orchestra in their theater at the Hôtel de Bourgogne in 1772. About 17 musicians can be seen in front of the stage, which is slightly fewer than the 22 listed in the *Almanach des spectacles* for that year (Table 6.2).[45] Many of them are violinists. In addition a double bass and two bassoons stick up above the lip of the stage—although the roster lists two double basses and no bassoons at all. There is no sign of any keyboard, and indeed a keyboardist never appears on the roster of either the Italiens or the Opéra Comique. The man in the center looks like a timebeater, but he is much more likely a prompter, since the orchestra was led by Le Bel, the first violinist. All the musicians face the stage, which helps them coordinate with the singers in the absence of a keyboard.

Toward the end of the eighteenth century still more theaters sprang up around Paris outside the official system, each with its own orchestra. These included the Théâtre de l'Ambigu Comique, the Théâtre des Variétés, Théâtre du Vaudeville, and others. Because these were unofficial theaters, they left little information about their orchestras. During the Revolution, however, the system of theatrical privileges was abolished, and the *Almanach des spectacles* began to publish rosters for all the theaters in the "République Théâtrale."[46] The Théâtre de la Rue Feydeau, it turned out, had an orchestra of 40, the Théâtre de la République an orchestra of 23, the Théâtre de Mlle Montansier 41, the Théâtre de l'Ambigu Comique 21, and so on. According to the *Almanach* of 1793, twelve Parisian theaters had orchestras, and the total number of instrumentalists in them came to almost 400. Unmentioned in official reports, a whole world of orchestras and orchestra musicians had come into being in Paris, to be revealed at last in the new, anti-monopolistic atmosphere of the Revolution.

THE CONCERT SPIRITUEL

By law both spoken theater and opera were forbidden throughout France on the great religious holidays: during Lent and the Easter season, at Pentecost, Christmas, and several other feast days. During the Regency a socially acceptable way was found

---

[44] Ancelet, *Observations sur la musique, les musiciens et les instruments* (Amsterdam, 1757), 11.
[45] *Almanach des spectacles* (1773), 88.   [46] Ibid. (1792).

to offer entertainment for music lovers on these holy days. Beginning in 1725, a series of concerts was organized at the Salle des Cent Suisses at the Tuileries. The room was provided free of charge by the Court, but beyond this the concerts depended on receipts to survive. The series was called the "Concert Spirituel," and it featured a large orchestra—almost as large as that of the Opéra. Indeed, the orchestra overlapped extensively with the personnel of the Opéra orchestra, because it provided employment for the musicians during days when the theater was shuttered. In deference to the Opéra's monopoly on orchestras of more than six, the Concert Spirituel paid the directors of the Opéra 10,000 livres per year for many years. The Concert Spirituel endured from 1725 until 1790 and rivaled the Opéra in prestige.

Fairly complete programs for the entire span of 65 years have been reconstructed.[47] Occasionally there were as few as eight concerts a year (1740); exceptionally one year there were 87 (1729); but most years offered roughly 20 to 30 concerts. In its first two years, the Concert Spirituel's contract with the Opéra allowed only sacred Latin motets and purely instrumental music, but in 1727 that constraint was lifted. Latin motets continued to be performed, however, particularly those by Michel-Richard de Lalande. His *Confitebor* was included on the Concert Spirituel's very first concert (18 March 1725); the last performance of a Lalande motet, *Dominus regnavit*, took place in 1770. On that occasion Charles Burney, on the Continent to undertake research for his history of music, was in the audience. Burney was deeply committed to the latest musical styles, genres, and performance practices from Italy, Germany, and England, and had limited patience for most older styles. To his surprise the audience still loved this work, composed over 65 years earlier:

Though this wholly stunned me, I plainly saw, by the smiles of ineffable satisfaction visible in the countenance of ninety-nine out of a hundred of the company, and heard by the most violent applause a ravished audience could bestow, that it was quite what their hearts felt, and their souls loved. *C'est superbe!* was echoed from one to the other through the whole house.[48]

At the Concert Spirituel these motets were removed from the anonymity of the church choir loft and placed on a specially constructed bandstand, which held the instrumentalists, the vocalists, and, in the center at the back, a handsomely displayed organ. No longer accessories to worship, the motets were now objects of aesthetic contemplation.

The Church, since at least the time of St. Augustine, had worried that music could bring sensuality rather than spirituality to its sacred texts. That this last fear was not entirely idle is suggested by a recollection from the adolescence of Michel de Chabanon, author of the *Éloge de M. Rameau* (1764), as well as of other essays, plays, and music:

---

[47] By Antoine Bloch-Michel in Constant Pierre, *Histoire du Concert spirituel 1725–1790* (Paris, 1975), 227–370.

[48] Burney, *Present State of Music in France and Italy*, 27.

Very early I displayed a rather marked talent for the violin. My extreme piety caused me to neglect it, however. One All Saints Day . . . the great Leclair, who had ceased to perform in public, made his reappearance [?1 November 1745]. I received an express command from my parents to go to hear him at the Concert Spirituel. I felt as though they had asked me to commit a crime. Me, set foot in a performance? I ran to my confessor to confide my uneasiness and seek his wise advice. From him I received an order even more specific than the first, to attend this innocent (even pious) spectacle. . . . My first impression on walking in was of a whirlwind of delicious scents, which completely enveloped me. I seemed to breath another kind of air, to be living in another element. My next impression was the sound of the organ, which practically lifted me out of my seat. Finally, when the music began, I was overcome by a giddiness that my scruples made seem like a crime: I was unable to imagine I could reach this height of sensual pleasure without offending God. . . . I attempted to close my ears to the music's charms by stuffing them with wads of paper, which I pushed in with all my might. This obstruction was hardly effective, however, against the noise of an entire orchestra.[49]

Chabanon's mini-drama, with himself cast as straight man, offers a layered critique of Western society's love–hate relationship with music. He mocks the hypocrisy of the Concert Spirituel, which dresses up sensual enjoyment as spirituality and sells it to the public on holy days. Of all the attractions at the concert, it is the orchestra that Chabanon cannot resist and that catapults the prudish adolescent into the orbit of worldly pleasures.

As the years went by, secular and instrumental music assumed an ever-greater role in the Concert Spirituel's repertory. By the 1740s concerts almost always began with a symphony. On 2 February 1753, the program began with the sonata from Mondonville's *Pièces de clavecin*, arranged for full orchestra. This was followed by sacred motets by Giraud and Gilles, alternating with arias and instrumental selections by Hasse and Grassy, a flutist. The concert ended with *Nisi Dominus*, a motet by Mondonville. Two decades later secular music had come to predominate over sacred. The concert of 2 February 1779, for instance, began with a symphony by Haydn, M. Moreau from the Opéra sang a motet by M. Candeille, M. Voundelich [Wunderlich] performed a flute concerto, Mme Todi sang a new aria by Piccinni, and Messrs Pals and Tierschmiedt presented a concerto for two horns. *Samson*, a new oratorio with words by Voltaire and music by Cambini, was sung. M. Chartrain then performed a new violin concerto of his own, and the concert finished with an Italian aria by Guglielmi, sung by Mme Todi.[50]

The transition from sacred to secular and from Lalande to Haydn, Mozart, and Piccinni was not smooth. An orchestra conceived and trained for the earlier repertory was badly equipped for the later one. The issues were amply debated in the press. In 1771 the *Journal de musique* complained about the old-fashioned placement of the instruments:

[49] Michel-Paul-Guy de Chabanon, *Tableau de quelques circonstances de ma vie* (Paris, 1795), 12–13.
[50] Pierre, *Histoire du Concert Spirituel*, 264, 310.

The poor disposition of the orchestra . . . hinders performance. The first and second violins neither see nor hear each other; consequently they often lack good ensemble. The flutes and oboes are buried among the bass instruments and lose their effect; the horns are no better placed, and the miserable organ, which is in the midst of the violas, divides and destroys all the harmony.[51]

The orchestra was rearranged, placing instruments by section instead of by function, and the bandstand was elevated—to good effect, judging from the press notices:

We notice that the orchestra was raised higher than on the previous Thursday, rendering the effect of the instruments more salient. The orchestra's seating plan was also better.[52]

The Concert Spirituel has a much greater following since the new arrangement. They have nearly Italianized it, and people agree that, as far as the instrumental portions are concerned, it is at present the best regulated concert in all of Europe.[53]

The directors also experimented with eliminating the *batteur de mesure* and having the orchestra led by two violinists: "By placing M. Gaviniès at the head of the first violins and M. Capron at the head of the seconds, they have (as in Italy) dispensed with beating time with a baton in all the instrumental music."[54] A timebeater and his assistant continued to be listed on the roster of the Concert Spirituel until 1770, but after that they disappeared, and the two violinists were clearly in charge:

A numerous orchestra [was] directed by Messrs Gaviniès and Leduc, excellent violinists, who were at the head of the first and second violins respectively. The section leaders, closer together and more prone to hear one another, were able to put more precision and better ensemble into the performances.[55]

Finally, the Concert Spirituel adapted itself to the performance practices of orchestras in the rest of Europe:

Not for a long time have we heard a Concert Spirituel as brilliant as that of the day before yesterday. Mr. La Houssaye's taste and intelligence were remarked by the audience. This able musician spent 15 years in Italy and seven in London. The first symphony [by Gossec] produced the greatest effect. We especially admired a crescendo that produced an entirely new impression.[56]

The international experience of Pierre La Houssaye, the new concertmaster, was evidently essential to his success in leading the performance of modern symphonies and concertos, which required instrumental effects and even an occasional crescendo. In 1784 Louis XVI and Marie Antoinette moved their residence to the Tuileries palace, and the Concert Spirituel was forced to remove to the Salle des Machines. For its final

---

[51] *Journal de musique* (Paris), 1771, 208–9.   [52] *Mercure de France* (1773), i. 169–70.
[53] Louis Petit de Bachaumont, *Mémoires secrets pour servir à l'histoire de la république des lettres en France . . .* (London, 1780–89), xxiv. 260.
[54] *Mercure de France* (1762), ii. 184.   [55] Ibid. (1773), i. 169–70.
[56] *Journal de Paris*, 25 Mar. 1777, 3.

concert in the Salle des Cent Suisses the orchestra played Haydn's Farewell Symphony.[57]

PRIVATE AND PUBLIC CONCERT ORCHESTRAS

At the beginning of the eighteenth century, the only individual in France who possessed an orchestra was Louis XIV. The orchestras that played at official festivities and special occasions at court were assembled from instrumentalists in the King's employ; it was the King who sponsored the orchestra at the Opéra. The orchestra was a symbol of royal power and privilege, and for another man to sponsor an orchestra would have been something approaching *lèse majesté*. Under the Regency and the reign of Louis XV, as court music declined and as orchestras spread through French musical life, a few wealthy individuals presumed to sponsor orchestras and to give private or semi-private concerts.

The best known of the private orchestras was that of Alexandre Jean-Joseph Le Riche de La Pouplinière (1693–1762).[58] "Le Riche," Pouplinière's family name, was an appropriate coincidence: he was a so-called tax farmer, one of the lucky few commissioned by the Crown to collect France's taxes, skim off a generous percentage, and give the remainder to the treasury. Beginning around 1731, La Pouplinière maintained an orchestra at his Paris home that was directed by Jean-Philippe Rameau. Around 1748, however, when his patron went through a scandalous and well-publicized divorce, Rameau found himself on the wrong side of the dispute and had to leave. La Pouplinière remarried and launched his orchestra anew, with F.-J. Gossec as its director from 1751. In 1754 Johann Stamitz was guest director of the ensemble, which included pairs of clarinets and horns and performed an up-to-date international repertory.

According to rosters of 1762 and 1763, the orchestra consisted of 15 instrumentalists.[59] La Pouplinière treated them as part of his household, just as if he had been a king or a prince. According to Marmontel,

He lodged the performers at his house, and every morning they rehearsed the symphonies they were to play that evening—and with what marvelous execution. . . . All the excellent musicians who came from Italy—violinists and singers—were received, lodged, and fed at his house; and they took turns shining at these concerts. . . . Never did a bourgeois live more like a prince, and princes came to share in his pleasures.[60]

---

[57] Michel Brenet [Marie Bobillier], *Les Concerts en France sous l'ancien régime* (Paris, 1900), 338.

[58] Georges Cucuel, *La Pouplinière et la musique de chambre au XVIIIe siècle* (Paris, 1913).

[59] Ibid. 336–39. 5 vln, 1 vc, 1 fl, 1 ob, 2 cl, 1 bn, 2 hn, 1 harp, 1 hpschd.

[60] Jean-François Marmontel, *Mémoires* (1804), ed. Jean-Pierre Guicciardi and Gilles Thierriat (Paris, 1999), 140.

Rather than coming from the Court, the Opéra, or the Paris theaters, La Pouplinière's musicians tended to be outsiders and newcomers, ambitious young instrumentalists from the provinces, or virtuosos from Italy or Germany. Of the 15 musicians on the roster in 1763, only five had French surnames; the rest were Italians and Germans.[61] Besides his house orchestra, he engaged many soloists and supernumeraries on a per-concert basis.

When La Pouplinière died in 1762, his orchestra was disbanded, and many of the musicians transferred to another private ensemble, the orchestra of the Prince de Conti.[62] A member of the royal family and a successful general, the Prince had managed to offend both Mme de Pompadour, the King's mistress, and Turgot, the prime minister; he was forced to resign his commission and leave the Court. The Prince's private orchestra, which he established in 1757, like his patronage of Rousseau, Beaumarchais, and Diderot, was perceived at the time as political opposition to the power and prerogatives of the King. It is not clear how large an orchestra he employed at any given moment, but some of the foremost musicians of the time were members of his household, including Gossec and Johann Schobert. Conti, like La Pouplinière, offered concerts free of charge to invited guests, guests of guests, and others who managed to procure introductions. Such private concerts amounted to salons whose focus was music rather than conversation.[63]

Other members of the French nobility did not support house orchestras on this scale. Instead they employed a core of professional instrumentalists who provided chamber music on a regular basis, and who, when orchestral forces were desired, could organize and lead students, amateurs, and professionals from the theater orchestras. The Baronne d'Oberkirch in her *Mémoires* mentions the Comte d'Albaret: "He is Piedmontese, very rich, and has his own musicians, who live at his house and never leave without his permission. He is crazy about music, and gives musical salons that last the entire day. Also his concerts are excellent. They have a reputation as the best in Paris."[64]

Other Parisian nobles who employed house musicians and gave concerts on a similar basis included the Duke d'Orléans, the Prince de Condé, the Duke de Noailles, Baron de Bagge, the Marquise de Montesson, Prince de Guéméné, the Count d'Artois, the Duke d'Aiguillon, the Baron d'Ogny, and the Duchess de Bourbon.[65] Some of these people were amateur instrumentalists of considerable talent, and occasionally they ran what amounted to amateur orchestras. The Duke de Luynes in 1746 described a performance at the home of Mme de la Marck, an excellent harpsichordist and good singer, whose husband played the bass viol:

[61] Cucuel, *La Pouplinière*, 339.

[62] Herbert C. Turrentine, "The Prince de Conti: A Royal Patron of Music," *MQ* 54 (1968), 309–15; David Hennebelle, "Nobles, musique et musiciens à Paris à la fin de l'Ancien Régime: Les transformations d'un patronage séculaire (1760–1780)," *Revue de musicologie*, 87 (2001), 395–417 at 404.

[63] Richard J. Viano, "Salons," in *Dictionnaire de la musique en France*, ed. Benoit, 631–33.

[64] Quoted in Hennebelle, "Nobles, musique et musiciens," 399.   [65] Ibid. 406.

Madame de la Marck has taken a notion to have operas performed at her house without making use of any of the singers from the Opéra but only her friends of both sexes. Among them are the Duchess de Brancas, the Duke d'Ayen, M. de la Salle, [and] the Duke d'Autin. Even the orchestra is composed of her acquaintances, except for two or three violinists from the Opéra to lead the amateurs. Royer, the famous music master, beats time. . . . There are costumes and machines at these operas, and the expenses are met in common: all the singers on the stage and the musicians in the orchestra contribute.[66]

The Marquise de Montesson, morganatic wife of Louis Philippe, Duc d'Orléans, had a theater built in her mansion on the Chaussée d'Antin and engaged an orchestra led by the Chevalier de Saint-Georges, the Black violinist-composer. There members of the nobility took roles in plays by the Marquise herself and operas by Saint-Georges and others.

Enthusiasm for maintaining private orchestras subsided during the 1770s and 1780s. Baron d'Ogny terminated his orchestra in 1769. The Prince de Conti disbanded his orchestra in 1771. Baron de Bagge spent much less time in Paris after 1778. In 1785 the Duke d'Orléans died and his orchestra was disbanded; the Marquise de Montesson closed her theater and dismissed her orchestra in the same year. The decline of private orchestras was due in part to the financial crises of the 1780s and the growing indebtedness of the French nobility. David Hennebelle shows, however, that this cannot have been the only reason.[67] As the musical market expanded, and as orchestras became more common in the theaters and ballrooms of Paris, possessing an orchestra no longer made the same statement that it had in the 1750s. The orchestra had long since ceased to be the exclusive property of royalty; now it was not exclusive to a few grand noblemen either.

The French nobility continued to patronize orchestras in the 1770s and 1780s, but now as a class rather than as individuals. The period during which the private orchestras began to decline was also the period in which concerts and concert societies flourished to an astonishing extent. There was the Concert des Amateurs (1769–81), the Concert des Associés (1770–?), the Concert de l'École Graduite de Dessein (1770–72), the Concert des Amis (1772–?), the Société du Concert d'Émulation (1781–86), and the Concert de la Loge Olympique (1783–89). Men like the Baron d'Ogny and the Duke de Noailles, who had formerly sponsored private orchestras, now devoted themselves to organizing, financing, and promoting concert societies. Most of these were organized as private societies with limited membership, financed by donations and subscriptions. A hall was rented, or in some cases provided gratis by one of the wealthy sponsors. A music director was engaged, who in turn hired an orchestra for the season and engaged composers and soloists. Some concert societies were set up to encourage amateur participation; others hired orchestras made up

---

[66] Norbert Dufourcq, *La Musique à la cour de Louis XIV et de Louis XV d'après les Mémoires de Sourches et Luynes, 1681–1758* (Paris, 1970), 105.

[67] Hennebelle, "Nobles, musique et musiciens," 413 ff.

entirely of professionals. A concert society was not usually a professional musician's principal employment. The players tended to be instrumentalists from the theater orchestras.

The most famous of these orchestras was the Concert des Amateurs, which performed in the Hôtel de Soubise under the direction first of Gossec (1769–73) and then the Chevalier de Saint-Georges (to 1780). Its leading patrons were Count Claude François Marie Rigoley d'Ogny and the tax farmer Charles Marin de La Haye des Fosses. Another series, the Concert de la Loge Olympique, was organized as a Masonic lodge. For 120 livres a year subscribers not only got to hear 12 concerts, they were also admitted to the first-degree rites of the lodge. The orchestra in 1786 comprised 17 violins, four violas, six cellos, four double basses, pairs of flutes, oboes, and bassoons, a clarinet, three horns, a trumpet, and a drum.[68] Of these 45 musicians, 12 were identified as amateurs. A roster shows that amateur and professional violinists were paired, so that there would be a strong player at each stand. This was the orchestra for which Haydn composed his "Paris" symphonies.

Anton Rosetti, who visited Paris in 1781–82, recorded his impressions of three private orchestras and the Concert Spirituel in a letter to Prince Öttingen-Wallerstein, his patron. "The best and largest orchestra," Rosetti writes,

is maintained by Prince de Guéméné. It consists of the foremost musicians of Paris—virtuosos who are everywhere in demand. . . . For the most part their playing is very quick and very accurate, although I must say that the Wallerstein orchestra is superior in decreasing or increasing expression on individual notes, in playing softly, and in unity. The Concert Spirituel plays fast and riotously; for a visitor it is more frightening than ingratiating. . . . The Concert des Amateurs no longer exists, but it is said to have been the best. At the Concert d'Émulation I heard much that was very beautiful. It is small but good—the only place where the players all strive for expression.[69]

ORCHESTRAS IN THE FRENCH PROVINCES

Historians of France have tended to focus their attention on events at the centers of wealth, power, and culture in Paris and Versailles. Activities in the provinces often seem of secondary importance and shrouded in obscurity. Yet the biographies of numbers of eighteenth-century French composers highlight the musical significance of the provincial cities: Blavet was from Besançon, Colasse from Reims, Corrette and Dagincourt from Rouen, Gossec from Vergnies, Grétry from Liège, Leclair and Marchand from Lyons, Mondonville from Narbonne, Rameau from Dijon, and so on. Besides the centripetal forces that attracted talented musicians to Paris, there were

---

[68] Jean-Luc Quoy-Bodin, "L'Orchestre de la Société Olympique en 1786," *Revue de musicologie*, 70 (1984), 95–107 at 97, 104.

[69] Anton Rosetti, *Ausgewählte Sinfonien*, ed. Oskar Kaul (Leipzig, 1912), p. xxii.

also centrifugal forces at work, dispatching music, musicians, and musical institutions to the provinces in a complex web of reciprocal relationships.

From the Middle Ages onward, there were three main musical patrons in the French provinces: the Catholic church, local theaters, and the noble families of each region. The French cathedrals and the larger monasteries maintained *maîtrises*, choir schools that trained musically talented boys in music and school subjects, fitting them for careers in the Church, as teachers, as civil servants, or as musicians. In the Renaissance over half of all "known" French composers were trained in *maîtrises*.[70] By the seventeenth century only approximately 25 percent of "known" composers issued from those institutions; in the eighteenth century that number fell to 10 percent. This decline illustrates the fall of sacred music from a position of dominance to one of mainly secondary interest to composers, patrons, and society in general.

In the course of the eighteenth century many French cathedrals followed the Court's lead and used motets written for Versailles by Lully, Lalande, Campra, and others.[71] However, provincial *maîtres de chapelle* also composed a large number of motets modeled on the Versailles style. This provincial sacred music soon made its way back to Paris. The Concert Spirituel, where motets from the Court repertory formed the core of the repertory in the 1720s and 1730s, began in its second season (1726) to program motets by provincial composers. These works had been conceived for the instrumental forces available in the provinces, but their composers understood orchestras and orchestral style well enough that the music worked well with the large chorus and orchestra at the Concert Spirituel.

The Catholic Church supported another type of education for youths besides the *maîtrises*: the Jesuit *collèges*.[72] These were mostly not universities but secondary schools, ancestors of the present-day *lycées*. It was a basic tenet of Jesuit schools in all parts of the world that music and theater were key elements in successful education. In seventeenth- and eighteenth-century France this was understood to include ballet. There were "salles des actions" in the colleges of more than 50 French cities. But even though it can be demonstrated that the performance of opera, oratorio, and ballet was a regular part of the curriculum of the Jesuit colleges in the French provinces, details about the instrumental accompaniments are lacking.

Theatrical productions at the Jesuit colleges were frequently fully staged, with machines for instantaneous changes of scene, flying machines, sung airs, soloists, corps de ballet, and instrumental forces of some sort. The ballets were often performed as

---

[70] François Lesure, *Dictionnaire musicale des villes de province* (Paris, 1999), 15. By "known" composer Lesure means one who has been deemed important enough for there to be an article about him in at least one recent dictionary or encyclopedia of music.

[71] Pierre, *Concert Spirituel, passim.*

[72] These paragraphs on Jesuit education in France are informed by the following: Ernest Boysse, *Le Théâtre des Jésuites* (Paris, 1880); François de Dainville, *L'Éducation des Jésuites (XVIᵉ–XVIIIᵉ siècles)* (Paris, 1978); Charles Muteau, *Les Écoles et collèges en province depuis les temps les plus reculés jusqu'en 1789* (Dijon, 1882); Pierre Peyronnet, "Le Théâtre d'éducation des Jésuites," *Dix-huitième siècle*, 8 (1976), 107–21.

entr'actes to spoken Latin tragedies. In 1695 at the Jesuit college in Langres, the subject of the tragedy was the biblical story of Belshazzar.[73] The ballet after the first act represented a banquet in Belshazzar's palace; after the second act came a ballet of soothsayers; the ballet after the third act depicted Persian soldiers; and so on. Ballets on this scale must have been accompanied at least by string bands, but no documentation about them has been reported. If these ensembles followed the patterns usual in the provinces all over Europe, they would have been staffed by students and local amateurs and led by local professionals.[74]

During the seventeenth century, theater was provided to provincial cities by itinerant troupes of actors, often under the protection of some noble personage. Such troupes spent anywhere from a few months to a year or two in one town, then moved on to another.[75] Very likely the companies included musicians, but probably the instrumentalists appeared onstage and one on a part. It is unlikely that a troupe could have traveled with anything like an orchestra.

An orchestra was required, however, for the operas of Lully, which began to be performed in provincial cities during the 1680s. While the terms of Lully's privilege forbade any other opera whatsoever in Paris, operas could be staged in the provinces by negotiating a contract and paying a fee to the Académie Royale. In 1684 Pierre Gautier journeyed from Marseilles to Paris, met the great man, and struck a deal that gave him exclusive rights to stage operas, not only in Marseilles but in a number of nearby towns as well. His first production, in January 1685, was not a Lully opera, but one of his own called *Le Triomphe de la paix*, followed by an unnamed Lully opera in October. There is no record of what Gautier used for an orchestra in either production, but a visitor from Paris, who was impressed by the quality of the singing and dancing, complained that "the orchestra [*symphonie*] was not very full and [played] much worse than I had been led to expect."[76] Gautier and his successors staged several more Lully operas between 1685 and 1704, not only in Marseilles but also in Avignon, Aix-en-Provence, Toulon, and Montpellier.

Other provincial cities soon joined Marseilles in obtaining privileges and mounting productions of Lully's operas: Lyons from 1688, Rouen from 1688, Rennes from 1689, and in a later period, Lunéville from 1706, Lille from 1718, and Dijon from

[73] Dainville, *Éducation*, 498–99.

[74] In Paris at the Jesuit Collège Louis-le-Grand, which enjoyed extraordinary patronage, productions sometimes involved singers from the Opéra and, presumably, instrumentalists of similar stature (Robert W. Lowe, *Marc-Antoine Charpentier et l'opéra de collège* (Paris, 1966)).

[75] See Georges Mongrédien and Jean Robert, *Les Comédiens français du XVIIe siècle, suivi d'un inventaire des troupes, 1590–1710* (Paris, 1981); Max Fuchs, *Lexique des troupes de comédiens au XVIIIe siècle* (Paris, 1944); Henri Lagrave, Charles Mazouer, and Marc Regaldo, *La Vie théâtrale à Bordeaux* (Paris, 1985), 95 ff., 133 ff.

[76] Jeanne Cheilan-Cambolin, "La Première Décentralisation des opéras de Lully en province: La création de l'Opéra de Marseille au XVIIe siècle," in *J.-B. Lully, Actes du Colloque/Kongressbericht, 1987*, ed. Jérôme de La Gorce and Herbert Schneider (Heidelberg, 1990), 529–38 at 531.

1729.[77] Presumably all of these productions had orchestras of one sort or another, but hardly any trace of them survives. An anonymous priest, who wrote an attack on the performance of *Phaëton* in Lyons in 1688, fumed that "this representation . . . contains nothing but evil: the words, the costumes, the processions, the songs, the glances, the gestures, the dances, the sounds of the instruments, even the subjects of these tragedies—everything is full of poison, everything reeks of impurity."[78] This diatribe proves that there were instruments of one sort or another, but it can hardly be considered a critique of the orchestra's performance.

Many provincial cities and towns built theaters during the eighteenth century, put together theatrical troupes, and presented operas, comedies, and other entertainments. Occasional comments reveal that many of these theaters had standing orchestras, but details are hard to come by. Plate VIII shows the orchestra of the theater in Lille at a gala performance to celebrate the birth of the dauphin in 1729. Despite the significance of the event, the orchestra numbers only seven: an oboe on the left, a bassoon on the right, two violins, a cello (perhaps a basse de violon), and two unseen instruments. In the center a *batteur de mesure* leads the ensemble, just as at the Paris Opéra.[79] Provincial orchestra rosters remain scarce for most of the century. Table 6.3 presents a few available figures. A roster from the Lyons theater in 1764 documents 17 instrumentalists; in Lille in 1767 there were 18. In 1792, however, when the *Almanach des spectacles* began listing the personnel of all the Parisian theaters, it also began publishing rosters for several theaters in the provinces, and, as in Paris, a world of orchestral activity was suddenly revealed. There were two theaters in Bordeaux, one with an orchestra of 20, the other with an orchestra of 32; two theaters in Marseilles; a theater in Rouen, in Toulouse, in Nantes—all of them with orchestras of 15 to 30 (Table 6.3).

For the most part these orchestras were staffed by professional musicians, although some of the players probably had other occupations on the side. The *Almanach* of 1793 notes that at the Théâtre de Molière in Bordeaux six out of 11 violinists are amateurs who play in the orchestra for pleasure rather than for pay. The best and brightest of the professionals had been making their way from provincial theaters to Paris for many years. Still, the standard in many provincial orchestras does not seem to have been very high. A report drawn up by the management of the Lyons theater in 1786 has nothing good to say about anyone in the orchestra. Kautz, the first violinist, "lacks intelligence and is a sloppy player." Le Couteux, another violinist, is "weak

---

[77] See Carl B. Schmidt, "The Geographical Spread of Lully's Operas during the Late Seventeenth and Early Eighteenth Centuries: New Evidence from the *Livrets*," in Heyer (ed.), *Jean-Baptiste Lully . . . Essays in Honor of James R. Anthony*, 183–211.

[78] Quoted in Léon Vallas, *Un Siècle de musique et de théâtre à Lyon, 1688–1789* (Lyons, 1932), 30.

[79] Another watercolor from the same series depicts a slightly larger orchestra playing for a dance in the same theater. This dance band consists of: 3 vn, 2 vc, 3 ob, 2 bn. Both pictures are found in a portfolio at the Bibliothèque municipale de Lille entitled "Description des réjouissances que se sont faites en la ville de Lille le 29 septembre 1729 et jours suivants pour la naissance de Monseigneur le Dauphin."

TABLE 6.3. *Orchestras in French provincial theaters, 1764–93*

Date and theater	Keyboard, plucked strings, etc.	Bowed strings	Winds	Brass and percussion	Total	Source
Bordeaux, 1792 Grand Théâtre National	2 maîtres	13 violins 2 violas 5 cellos 2 double basses	2 flutes and oboes 2 bassoons	2 horns 1 trumpet 1 drum	32	*Almanach* (1793), 336
Bordeaux, 1792 Théâtre de Molière	1 maître	11 violins 1 viols 2 cellos 1 double bass	1 flute 1 clarinet 1 bassoon	1 horn	20	*Almanach* (1793), 342
Lille, 1767	1 maître / 1 harpsichord	6 violins / 2 violas 2 cellos	2 oboes / [2] bassoons	[2] horns	18	Duhamel, *Musique*, 337
Lyons, 1764	1 maître 2 cellos 1 double bass	7 violins and violas	2 oboes 2 bassoons	2 horns	17	Vallas, *Un Siècle*, 309
Lyons, 1784	2	2	2	2	24	ibid., 422

	maîtres	strings	winds	brass/percussion	number	source
Théâtre de Marseilles		2 violas 4 cellos 2 double basses	2 oboes 2 bassoons	1 trumpet 2 trombones 1 drum		
Marseilles, 1792 Théâtre national	2 maîtres	8 violins 2 violas 5 double basses	3 flutes and oboes 2 bassoons	2 horns 1 trumpet or trombone	25	Almanach (1793), 352
Nantes, 1792 Grand Théâtre	?	?	?	?	15	Almanach (1793), 355
Rouen, 1791	1 maître	8 violins 2 violas 1 cello 1 double bass	2 bassoons	2 horns	17	Almanach (1792), 74
Rouen, 1793	1 maître	10 violins and violas 2 cellos 2 double basses	2 oboes 1 clarinet 2 bassoons	2 horns	22	Almanach (1794), 61
Toulouse, 1793 Grand Théâtre	1 maître	10 violins 2 violas 4 cellos 2 double basses	2 flutes 2 oboes 2 bassoons	2 horns	27	Almanach (1794), 57

and incapable of improvement given his nonchalant attitude and limited intelligence." Demaki, the oboist, "doesn't bother playing the overture and often lays out in the entr'actes as well." The first bassoonist, Garnier, "only shows up when he has a solo: during one stretch he was absent for eight nights in a row", and Backoffen, the second, "imitates his example".[80]

Besides theater orchestras, many provincial cities and towns also had orchestras for concerts. Important citizens, both noble and bourgeois, wanted to create settings in which they could hear the music that was fashionable in the capital without incurring the expense of full-scale theatrical productions and without opening the venue to a wider public.[81] Until the middle of the eighteenth century the most common name for such institutions in provincial towns was "Académie" and after that time either "Concert" or "Société." In eastern France, where French and German, Catholic and Protestant cultures overlapped, they were sometimes called "Collegium musicum." The earliest group of provincial academies—Orléans, Dijon, Lyons, and Toulouse—were founded in the 1670s and 1680s in imitation of Lully's Académie in Paris. Most of them obtained privileges and staged operas. The next big group of academies were formed between 1710 and 1730. These tended to be more like concert societies than theatrical ventures. By the 1740s the movement had spread to smaller towns (Nîmes, Colmar, Moulins, Amiens, Annecy, etc.), and many of them were calling their series "concert" instead of "academy," perhaps in imitation of the Concert Spirituel in Paris. Most of these societies were somewhat intermittent. In Dijon, for example, Claude Rameau (brother of Jean-Philippe) founded an "Académie des concerts" in 1725 with municipal sponsorship. Soon, however, he quarreled with the other participants, and the venture collapsed.[82] This first attempt was followed by an "Académie de musique," sponsored by the governor of Burgundy, an enterprise that lasted until 1734. In 1748 Charles de Brosses, president of the Parliament of Burgundy and an enthusiastic music lover, started a "Concert" that met once a week and that, like its predecessor, fell victim to chronic disputes.

The Dijon orchestra seems to have revived again by the 1760s, because when Wolfgang and Nannerl Mozart passed through in 1766, the 10-year-old composer was invited to have his works performed at the Hôtel de Ville. In his diary Leopold Mozart entered the names of the orchestral musicians, accompanied by a variety of epithets in French, Italian, and English:

---

[80] Vallas, *Un siècle*, 432.

[81] The information in the remainder of this paragraph is drawn from Lesure, *Dictionnaire musicale* and *Dictionnaire de la musique en France*, ed. Benoit.

[82] Lesure, *Dictionnaire*, 144; Joëlle Doussot, "Dijon," in *Dictionnaire*, ed. Benoit, 240.

Violinists:	Sotrau	*Très mediocre.*
	Fantini	*Un miserable italien detestable.*
	Paquet	
	Lorenzetti }	*Asini tutti.*
	Mauriat	
Viola:	Le Brun	*Un racleur.*
Cello and Bass:	Du Chargé	
	Amidey	*Miserable.*
Bassoon:	Le Maire	
Oboe:	Two brothers	Rotten.

At this point Leopold had reached the end of a page; the next page is missing from his diary, so we are spared his disparaging remarks about the Dijonnais horn players.[83]

A successful concert society depended on the sponsorship of a noble patron or a town government, on the willingness of local music lovers to subscribe and attend concerts, on the energy and expertise of the professional musician who took charge of organizing and leading the orchestra, and on the availability of a critical mass of instrumentalists. If enough players were not available from the local theaters, then the orchestra had to be filled out with amateur instrumentalists. The statutes of the Concert in Lille in 1733 provide a typical example of how such societies were organized.[84] "Director" of the concert was the Duke de Boufflers, who had recently conquered the city of Lille for France; however, management was left to three "subdirectors." The number of members was fixed at 150, each of whom subscribed 100 livres for the season, payable in two installments. Each subscriber received two tickets to the concerts, which were to take place twice a week during the season. "The music," said the regulations, "shall be partly French and partly Italian, and whenever possible, the concert will end with a motet."[85] The Concert society hired a Music Master, who not only led the orchestra but was also available to give music lessons three mornings a week to the children of Lille. The idea seems to have been to have an orchestra made up mainly or entirely of professional musicians, which means it must have overlapped to a considerable extent with the theater orchestra (Pl. VIII). The statutes stipulate that the instrumentalists must be present in the orchestra half an hour before the beginning of the concert—otherwise their wages will be withheld.

The musical academies, concerts, and societies of provincial cities have customarily been portrayed as country-bumpkin knock-offs of the institutions in Paris and at the French court, featuring weak performances of second-hand repertory. This portrayal could use additional nuance. Not all performances in Paris and Versailles were first rate. Many provincial towns and cities had their own composers who wrote

---

[83] R. Thiblot, "Le Séjour de Mozart à Dijon en 1766," *Mémoires de l'Académie des sciences, arts et belles-lettres de Dijon* (1937), 139–43; Mozart, *Briefe*, i. 227.

[84] See Jean-Marie Duhamel, *La Musique dans la ville de Lully à Rameau* (Lille, 1994), 327 ff.

[85] Ibid. 329.

works for local performance, and sometimes provincial orchestras were ahead of those in Paris in matters of repertory, organization, and performance practices. As the international prestige of French music declined during the eighteenth century, the location of several of these cities near the borders with Italy or Germany proved to be an advantage. As private orchestras began to die away in Paris during the 1770s, the Parisian nobility turned to the model of provincial concert societies to found the Concert des Amateurs, the Concert de la Loge Olympique, and other Parisian concert series.

Chapter Seven

The Orchestra in Germany

The orchestra was born in Germany into a political and social environment quite different from that of Italy or France. The German-speaking lands in the seventeenth and eighteenth centuries were a patchwork of principalities: kingdoms, dukedoms, free cities, ecclesiastical states, and others—over 300 distinct political entities in all.[1] Except for the free cities, each of these principalities was ruled by an individual sovereign—an emperor, king, prince, duke, or bishop—surrounded and assisted by family, nobility, bureaucrats, artisans, soldiers, and servants, organized into a court (*Hof*). A large court, like the Imperial court at Vienna in the mid-eighteenth century, could encompass as many as two thousand people; a middle-sized court, like Mannheim during the same period, numbered five hundred to a thousand; a small court a few hundred.[2] Unlike Italy, where patronage was relatively diffuse and where patrons competed with one another to sponsor orchestras, and unlike France, where patronage was centralized at a single court, the German political system created musical patronage that was centralized and diffuse simultaneously. In each principality the ruler was the primary, often the only, patron of instrumental ensembles. But there were many principalities, and their rulers competed with one another to see who could maintain the biggest and best orchestra. The German courts did not engender the birth of the orchestra as an institution—the orchestra in Germany was copied from earlier models in France and Italy—but German court culture proved highly favorable to the orchestra's growth and development.

[1] Walter Bruford, *Germany in the Eighteenth Century: The Social Background of a Literary Revival* (Cambridge, 1935), 7; Rudolf Vierhaus, *Germany in the Age of Absolutism*, trans. Jonathan B. Knudsen (Cambridge, 1988), 33.

[2] Vierhaus, *Germany*, 34.

COURTS AND KAPELLEN

German orchestras grew up as part of Kapellen, that is, the music establishments of the German courts. Along with instrumentalists a Kapelle included singers, organists, harpsichord tuners, copyists, and other musical personnel. In the sixteenth and early seventeenth centuries, Kapellen were composed mainly of singers, plus an organist or two and a smattering of plucked strings and wind instruments. During the period from 1670 to 1750 German Kapellen increasingly took on the character of orchestras, with large numbers of instrumentalists, particularly bowed-string players. Not every German court had a Kapelle, and not every Kapelle got more orchestral. But by the 1770s at least 60 German courts could boast of Kapellen with 20 or more instrumentalists.[3]

A court was simultaneously the household of the ruler and the administrative mechanism of the state. Nobles, clergy, commoners, administrators, bureaucrats, artisans, cooks, and personal servants—everyone required to serve the needs of the prince and his affairs—were arranged in a hierarchy according to function and rank. These hierarchies are documented in *Staats-Kalender*, directories of court events and personnel that many courts published during the eighteenth century. In the *Staats- und Addresse-Calender* of the court of Baden at Rastatt (Fig. 7.1) the Kapelle (*Cammer-, Hof-, und Kirchen-Music*) and the court trumpeters (*Hof-Trompeter*) are tucked in between the table servants (silver polishers, waiters, linen maids) and the court gardeners (*Hof-Gärtnerey*). This position is typical. To be a member of a court Kapelle in seventeenth- and eighteenth-century Germany was like being a state employee or civil servant; but at the same time it was like being a family retainer or personal servant of the Prince.

German courts formed a network of courts, connected to one another by relations of kinship and marriage, by territorial ambitions and alliances, by wars and peace treaties. Relations between courts, like relations within courts, were hierarchical: rulers with more territory, more subjects, and more money took precedence over rulers with less. Central to the ethos of German courts was display, the external manifestation of social relations. In order to maintain the allegiance and acquiescence of his subjects and to assert his position in the hierarchy of courts, a sovereign needed to display his status and his power in visible, palpable, and audible forms. He built palaces in which he lodged his family, court officials, servants, artisans, and any number of visitors, all at his own expense and the expense of the state. His kitchens fed the members of his court, court officers, servants, and visitors. For special events, like a royal

---

[3] Based on tabulations in the following sources: Julia Moore, "Beethoven and Musical Economics" (Ph.D. diss., University of Illinois, Urbana-Champaign, 1987); Zaslaw, "Toward the Revival of the Classical Orchestra"; Carse, *The Orchestra in the XVIIIth Century*; and Schreiber, *Orchester und Orchesterpraxis in Deutschland zwischen 1780 und 1850.*

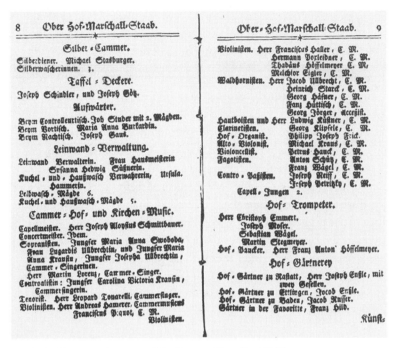

Fig. 7.1. Personnel roster of the Rastatt Kapelle, 1768

birthday or wedding, the birth of an heir, or a visit by another sovereign, he put on entertainments that lasted for days or weeks and included banquets, hunts, parades, fireworks, operas, plays, balls, and church services. Courtly display was communicated to other courts by means of reciprocal visits, *Staats-Kalender*, prints, engravings, and commemorative books that describe and depict the splendor of the court and its celebrations.[4]

Music played an important part in display at seventeenth- and eighteenth-century German courts. Trumpets and drums marched in parades and announced the sovereign at ceremonial and festive occasions. In church instruments accompanied mass and vespers on feast days and holidays. Many courts had theaters, either temporary or permanent, where instruments accompanied plays, operas, and ballets. Singers and instruments provided table music for banquets and background music for social gatherings. Instrumental ensembles played for court balls and masquerades. The bigger the court, the more ambitious the prince, the more important the event—the bigger the instrumental ensemble needed to be. The Kapellmeister of the Württemberg court in 1714 argued for an increase in the size of his rather small Kapelle in the following terms:

[4] On these so-called 'festival books,' see Bowles, *Musical Ensembles in Festival Books*.

Of course it is possible to play music with an ensemble of two or three people—any burgher can do that; but for a Most Serene reigning Duke of Württemberg to provide princely church and court music in accordance with the style and honor of his princely house, for that an ensemble needs to have at least eight musicians, or more.[5]

German Kapellen grew and turned themselves into orchestras because of the need for an aural component in courtly display and because of competition and rivalry between courts.

Competition and display were not the sole reasons that German princes maintained Kapellen. Music was a part of aristocratic education in the seventeenth and eighteenth centuries, and many German sovereigns, as well as their brothers, sisters, children, cousins, and wives, were accomplished musicians. In the seventeenth century these aristocratic amateurs were trained as singers, lutenists, viol players, and keyboardists; in the eighteenth they learned violin, flute, and cello, as well such exotic instruments as the baryton and lira organizzata.[6] Some of them were composers as well, whose works were performed at court and occasionally published.[7] Such rulers took a close personal interest in the staffing and management of their Kapellen, and they often played along with or led performances. German princes built up orchestras not only for display but out of personal predilection as well.

THE GERMAN LULLISTS

German Kapellen at the beginning of the seventeenth century were dominated by singers. Most contained few instrumentalists; the instruments consistently represented were organs and plucked strings.[8] Court records frequently mention trumpets, although administratively they did not usually form part of the Kapelle but rather of the palace guards or the army. Violins and other bowed strings are seldom mentioned by name. Most instrumentalists are designated generically as *Instrumentisten*, suggesting what is confirmed by other sorts of evidence: that they were generalists, who switched from one instrument to another as the occasion demanded. Descriptions

---

[5] Quoted in Owens, "The Württemberg Hofkapelle," 92.

[6] Prince Nicholas Esterházy played the baryton, a viola da gamba with metal sympathetic strings; Ferdinand IV of Naples played the lira organizzata, a hurdy-gurdy with strings and small organ pipes. Both men commissioned music for their instruments from Haydn.

[7] Frederick the Great of Prussia (r. 1740–86) was a flutist and a composer. Duchess Sophie-Elisabeth of Braunschweig-Wolfenbüttel (1613–76) played viols and keyboards and composed prolifically. Duke Ernst Ludwig of Hesse-Darmstadt (r. 1688–1739) played viola da gamba and composed; Ludwig X of Hesse (r. 1790–1830) was a violinist who often led the court Kapelle in performance. Emperor Leopold I of Austria (r. 1658–1705) played harpsichord, violin, and flute; he composed arias and scenes that were inserted into the operas of Viennese court composers. Joseph I, his son (r. 1705–11) also played and composed; Leopold II (r. 1790–92) was an avid performer and patron of music.

[8] Martin Ruhnke, *Beiträge zu einer Geschichte der deutschen Hofmusikkollegien im 16. Jahrhundert* (Berlin, 1963), *passim*.

and depictions of German instrumental ensembles from the early seventeenth century show that their most common venues were in church and at banquets, and that they usually played one on a part, sometimes divided into multiple choirs.

These shifting groupings of small ensembles, mixed with vocalists and playing one on a part, were transformed in the last quarter of the seventeenth century into larger, violin-based ensembles, sometimes with two or more players on a part. One cause for the change was the end of the Thirty Years War, marked by the Treaty of Westphalia in 1648, which consolidated the power of German territorial rulers and led to slowly increasing prosperity and rapidly increasing display at German courts. Another factor was the influence in Germany of the court of Louis XIV, which extended to architecture, gardens, fashion, theater, dance, and music.

Louis XIV and his handlers went to great lengths to impress the other courts of Europe with the greatness of the Sun King and the splendor of his court. The French government minted coins, printed books, published engravings, and staged public festivities aimed at the courts of other European countries, particularly the German-speaking lands on France's eastern border. Foreign ambassadors, many of them Germans, formed an important part of the audience for French court festivals, ballets, and operas.[9] In addition, many German princes made personal visits to Paris and Versailles in order to see with their own eyes the splendor of the Sun King and his entourage. Anton Ulrich, heir to the Duchy of Braunschweig-Wolfenbüttel, spent over six months in Paris in 1655–56. He was received by Louis XIV, attended 20 comedies and ballets, and frequently visited the Palais Royal, the home of the Opéra, where, he said, "all the best musicians congregate."[10] Ernst Ludwig of Hesse-Darmstadt, along with his younger brother and several musicians from the Darmstadt Kapelle, visited Paris in 1685.[11] The young princes paid weekly visits to the opera and the spoken theater and were honored with an invitation to the premiere of Lully's *Acis et Galatée* at court. The Darmstadt musicians were encouraged to take lessons on the violin and in theater craft, and at the end of his stay Ernst Ludwig engaged four French musicians—two violinists, an oboist, and a bassoonist—to return with him to Darmstadt.

The music of Lully and the violin-based ensembles that played this music became first a fad, then a fashion, then a standard against which German Kapellen were measured. German musicians were sent to Paris to learn the new music and its performance practice. Courts all over Germany—Dresden, Stuttgart, Eisenach, Sorau, Wolfenbüttel, and others—hired French string players to form bands of "Violinisten"

---

[9] Peter Burke, *The Fabrication of Louis XIV* (New Haven, 1992), 162.

[10] Quoted from a letter of Anton Ulrich in Gerhard Gerkens, *Das fürstliche Lustschloss Salzdahlum und sein Erbauer Herzog Anton Ulrich von Braunschweig-Wolfenbüttel* (1974), 19. See also James Leonard Brauer, "Instruments in Sacred Vocal Music at Braunschweig-Wolfenbüttel: A Study of Changing Tastes in the Seventeenth Century" (Ph.D. diss., City University of New York, 1983), 247.

[11] Kaiser, *Barocktheater in Darmstadt*, 68–69.

or "Französische Geiger" and to train German musicians in the French style. In addition German musicians composed their own suites in imitation of the Lully style—an overture followed by a series of French dances. Many of these collections mention "France" or "French" in their titles, for example:

> Georg Bleyer, *Lust-Music nach ietziger frantzösischer Manier gesetzet, bestehend von unter-schiedlichen Airn, Bourreen, Gavotten, Gagliarden, Giquen, Chansons, Allemanden, Sarabanden, Couranden &c.* . . . (Leipzig, 1670)
>
> Johann Sigismund Kusser, *Composition de musique suivant la Méthode Françoise* (Stuttgart, 1682)
>
> Philip Heinrich Erlebach, *VI Ouvertures begleitet mit ihren darzu schicklichen Airs nach Französischer Art und Manier* (Nürnberg, 1693)

Others, like Georg Muffat's *Florilegium Secundum* (Passau, 1698) and J. C. F. Fischer's *Journal du Printems* (Augsburg, 1695), have lengthy prefaces that explain the conventions of French tempos, French-style notation, and French performance practice to German musicians.[12]

"France," "French," "Lully," and "Lullist" became buzzwords, evoking all that was modern and fashionable in German court music of the late seventeenth century. J. S. Kusser, in the flowery dedication of his collection to the regent of Württemberg, emphasizes the link between the Lully style and the prestige of the French court:

Monseigneur, in recognition of the favors that Your Serene Highness has bestowed upon me, I am obliged to seek out everything that can add to your diversion, and in this I cannot do better than attempt to imitate that renowned BAPTISTE [i.e. Lully], whose works today contribute to the entertainment of all the courts of Europe. I have set myself the task of following his Method and of replicating his refined manner to the extent that I can.[13]

Kusser had spent several years in Paris learning the French style first hand. P. H. Erlebach, who had not visited Paris, sounds somewhat defensive in the introduction to his own set of French overtures:

I myself was never in France . . . [but] just as one learns from travel accounts and maps the customs and geography of foreign peoples, so too through diligent examination, listening, practice, and consideration of the works of art they transmit to us, we can learn to appreciate their style, understand their artistic intent, and make use of what we have learned from them.[14]

---

[12] Other German collections with explanatory introductions include Johann Caspar Horn, *Parergon musicum, oder Musicalisches Neben-Werck* . . . (Leipzig, 1663–76); Rupert Ignatz Mayr, *Pythagorische Schmids-Fünklein* . . . (Augsburg, 1692); Georg Muffat, *Florilegium I* (Augsburg, 1695); Benedikt Anton Aufschnaiter, *Concors discordia amori et timori* . . . (Nuremberg, 1695); Johann Abraham Schmierer, *Zodiaci musici in XII Partitas balleticas* (Augsburg, 1698). See Rüdiger Pfeiffer, "Der französische, inbesondere Lullysche Orchesterstil und sein Walten in der deutschen Musikkultur des ausgehenden 17. Jahrhunderts," in *Der Einfluss der französischen Musik auf die Komponisten der ersten Hälfte des 18. Jahrhunderts: Blankenburg/Harz, Juni 1981*, ed. Eitelfriedrich Thom (Michaelstein, 1982), 15–20.

[13] Johann Sigismund Kusser, *Suiten für Orchester* (1682), ed. Rainer Bayreuther (Mainz, 1994), modern edn. of *Composition de musique suivant la Methode Françoise* (Stuttgart, 1682), unpaginated.

[14] Philipp Heinrich Erlebach, *Harmonische Freude musikalischer Freunde—Erster und Anderer Teil* (1693), ed. Otto Kinkeldey (Leipzig, 1914), p. xxxvi.

Erlebach and other German Lullists refer in their introductions not only to Lully but also to one another, giving the impression that they saw themselves as a new and self-conscious musical movement, seeking to transplant the French instrumental style to Germany.

One of the most impressive and influential features of Lully's ensembles in Paris was their size, achieved by putting several violin-family instruments on each part. Size, however, does not seem to have been the central issue for Lully's German disciples. Georg Muffat, in the long preface to his *Florilegium secundum* (1698), says nothing about how big a Lully-style ensemble should be or the number of players to put on each part—a contrast to his preface in an earlier publication on the Corelli style, where he gives elaborate instructions about the distribution of players on parts and the balance between concertino and concerto grosso.[15] Other German Lullists say similarly little on the subject of orchestra size and part doubling. The exception is Schmierer, who discusses unequal part doubling in the introduction to his *Zodiaci musici* (1698):

It should be particularly observed that the violins and the violoni need to be more heavily manned and doubled than the other two middle parts (called the violetta and Alt-viola). If there are enough amateurs [*Liebhaber*] present, all these stringed instruments can be tripled or even quadrupled, so long as the violins are always manned by one more person than the violoni.[16]

If not enough string players are available, however, then one on a part will have to do:

On the other hand, if a large number of performers is lacking, then ultimately it will suffice if only the violin is doubled, along with one good, strong violone . . . Or, finally, these pieces can be played one on a part, as they say, *alla camera*.

Performances of music by German Lullists must often have been one on a part, because most of these men worked at small courts where the Kapelle records document only four or five bowed-string players. Muffat, for example, was employed at Salzburg, where the Kapelle records list one violin, one viola da gamba, and four unidentified instrumentalists.[17] Then he worked at Passau in Bavaria, where in 1700 there were only eight "Hofmusiker" plus trumpets and drums.[18] J. C. F. Fischer worked at Schlackenwerth, then at Rastatt, both small courts with small Kapellen.[19] Kusser had larger ensembles available at Stuttgart, where he lived as a young man and to which he returned from 1700 to 1704. At Ansbach, however, where he was

---

[15] Muffat, *Sechs Concerti Grossi.*

[16] Johann Abraham Schmierer, *Zodiaci musici, in XII Partitas balleticas . . . Pars I* (1698), ed. Ernst von Werra (Leipzig, 1902), 90.

[17] Chafe, *The Church Music of Heinrich Biber*, 39. These figures date from shortly after Muffat's departure from Salzburg.

[18] Inka Stampfl, *Georg Muffat: Orchesterkompositionen* (Passau, 1984), 14–15.

[19] Rudolf Walter, *Johann Caspar Ferdinand Fischer, Hofkapellmeister der Markgrafen von Baden* (Frankfurt, 1990), 19–20; Klaus Häfner, "Johann Caspar Ferdinand Fischer und die Rastatter Hofkapelle: Ein Kapitel südwestdeutscher Musikgeschichte im Zeitalter des Barock," in *J. C. F. Fischer in seiner Zeit—Tagungsbericht Rastatt 1988*, ed. Ludwig Finscher (Frankfurt, 1994), 137–79.

employed at the time he published his *Composition de musique*, only four members of the eight-man Kapelle were designated as bowed-string players.[20] The previous Ansbach Kapellmeister had already complained about the inadequacy of the Kapelle for French-style music:

The performance of French partitas—since the violin or discant part needs to be played by six persons, and the viola, bass, and bassoon need to be doubled—requires a good number of subjects, and these days (as all the Duke's musicians well know) such people are not available within the Court's instrumental music; indeed there has often been a severe lack of performers.[21]

At Ansbach as at other courts, singers, trumpeters, and musical amateurs may have filled in on stringed instruments. On the whole, however, large ensembles and part doubling do not seem to have been defining features of the Lullist movement in Germany.

Style was more important than size to the German Lullists. A crucial ingredient of the Lully style was orchestral discipline, that is, the ability of a group of instrumentalists to play together as a unified ensemble rather than an aggregation of individuals. Muffat, in the preface to his *Florilegium secundum*, points to uniform bowing as one of the hallmarks of the French style:

It is well known that the Lullists, whom the English, the Dutch and many others already imitate, . . . all observe the same way of bowing. Gentlemen returning from these lands fail to find this uniformity among our German violinists, no matter how excellent; they remark upon and wonder at the difference this makes in the sound, and they frequently complain about the incorrect rhythm of the dance.[22]

He also stresses the importance of playing in tune and of applying ornamentation in a correct and consistent manner. Achieving this discipline seems to have required more rehearsal than previous musical styles. Duchess Magdalena Sibylla of Württemberg admonished her Kapelle in 1684: "a great deal depends on the rehearsal of the music, especially for the French pieces popular these days, which particularly require daily practice . . ."[23]

At Ansbach Kusser's demand for daily rehearsal aroused the opposition of violinist Johann Mayer, who asked to be exempted, complaining in a letter to the Duke that rehearsals and French-style playing ruined his technique:

young Kusser from Stuttgart has now proposed that rehearsals in the French style take place daily. . . . I learned what little science I have in violin playing at the Viennese court from one of the foremost masters in the world and at rather high cost. Up until now your Serene Highness has been content with my insignificant person, and has even requested me several times to play a solo in the presence of one or another visiting Lord; but if I adopt the short

---

[20] Günther Schmidt, "Die Musik am Hofe der Markgrafen von Brandenburg-Ansbach" (Diss., Ludwigs-Maximilians-Universität, Munich, 1953), 63.

[21] Quoted in Schmidt, "Die Musik am Hofe," 61. The Kapellmeister, G. H. Künstel, recommends that the problem be addressed by training two young choirboys as string players, a half-measure at best.

[22] Muffat, *Florilegium secundum* (1698), ed. Rietsch, 21.

[23] Quoted in Owens, "The Württemberg Hofkapelle," 14.

[French] bow stroke, I will have to give up playing any kind of decent solo—indeed I will no longer be able to accompany in church and for other vocal pieces.[24]

The anecdote suggests that the novelty (and the danger) of the French style lay in the technical details of bowing and also in the ideology of rehearsal and group discipline, which ran counter to the individualistic ethos of seventeenth-century German violin playing.

THE TRANSFORMATION OF GERMAN KAPELLEN

Along with the rage for Lully and French-style music, orchestral traits increasingly began to appear in German Kapellen at the end of the seventeenth century. There were more string players, particularly violinists, suggesting both part doubling and unequal balances. The new French oboes, flutes, and bassoon were added, supplanting cornetts, shawms, dulcians, and trombones. In paylists and other court records players are designated as specialists on particular instruments rather than simply as "Musiker" or "Instrumentisten." Occasionally, at one or another German court, these new traits emerge so rapidly and so distinctly that a modern observer seems once again, as in Lully's Paris or Corelli's Rome, to witness the birth of the orchestra.

At the Saxon court in Dresden, for instance, the orchestra was born during a short period between 1691 and 1709. Dresden was one of the largest German courts and had long maintained one of the biggest Kapellen. During the seventeenth century the Kapelle was typically divided into two or more ensembles (Table 7.1). In 1691, for example, there was a first choir for Italian-style *concertato* music in the princely chapel and for Italian opera, plus a second choir for everyday music in church. Both choirs contained only a few instrumentalists, and the German church music lacked strings entirely. Besides the instruments listed in Table 7.1, the Dresden court maintained an ensemble of "French violins" (all of them Frenchmen) from 1675 on.[25] There were also ensembles of shawm players, of bagpipers, and of hammered dulcimers, as well as a large corps of trumpets and drums. This proliferation of separate ensembles was typical of late seventeenth-century German Kapellen.

The modernization of the Dresden Kapelle seems to have begun with the accession of Friedrich August I (August der Starke) in 1694. As a youth he had visited the French court at Versailles, where he was received twice by Louis XIV and where he attended both opera and spoken theater.[26] He also traveled to Venice, where

---

[24] Quoted in Curt Sachs, "Die Ansbacher Hofkapelle unter Markgraf Johann Friedrich (1672–1686)," *Sammelbände der IMG*, 9 (1909–10), 105–37 at 131.

[25] Moritz Fürstenau, *Zur Geschichte der Musik und des Theaters am Hofe zu Dresden* (Dresden, 1861), i. 201. See also Michael Walter, "Italienische Musik als Representationskunst der Dresdener Fürstenhochzeit von 1719," in Barbara Marx (ed.), *Elbflorenz—Italienische Präsenz in Dresden 16.–19. Jahrhundert* (Amsterdam and Dresden, 2000), 177–202.

[26] Karl Czok, *Am Hofe Augusts des Starken* (Stuttgart), 29–30.

TABLE 7.1. *The transformation of German Kapellen, 1671–1721*

Place and date	Keyboard and plucked strings	Bowed strings	Winds	Unidentified	Source
DRESDEN					
1691					Fürstenau, *Zur Geschichte*, i.3 09
Choir 1	1 organ	3 violins	1 bassoon 2 trumpets		
Choir 2	1 organ		2 cornetts 3 trombones		
1697					
Catholic	2 organs 1 theorbo	[2 violins] [2 violas] [1 violone]	6 oboes 3 bassoons 2 trumpets 1 timpani	6 *Instrumentisten*	Ibid. ii. 18–19
Protestant	2 organs	2 violins 2 violas 1 violone			Ibid. ii. 13–14
1709	2 organs 2 theorbos	6 violins 1 haute contre 1 taille 2 violas 5 cellos 1 contrabass	2 flutes 4 oboes 2 bassoons		Ibid. ii. 50
1728	1 harpsichord 2 theorbos	7 violins 4 violas 5 cellos	1 flute 5 oboes 3 bassoons		Landmann, "Dresdener Hofkapelle," 9

1671	1 organ 1 lute	2 violins		4 *Instrumentisten*	Noack, *Musikgeschichte*, 126
1687	1 kbd. 1 lute	7 violins 1 viola 2 viole da gamba 1 violone	1 oboe 1 bassoon		Ibid. 158
1712	1 kbd.	6 violins 2 viole da gamba 1 violone	2 oboes 1 bassoon	11 unidentified	Biermann, "Darmstadter Hofkapelle," 60 ff.
BERLIN					
1681	2 organs			7 *Instrumentisten*	Sachs, *Musik*, 61
1708	1 organ	6 first violins 3 second violins 4 violas 4 cellos	4 oboes 4 bassoons		Ibid. 66–67

TABLE 7.1. (*Cont.*)

Place and date	Keyboard and plucked strings	Bowed strings	Winds	Unidentified	Source
VIENNA					
1685	[harpsichord] 1 theorbo	8 violin/viola 3 cellos 1 viola da gamba	1 bassoon 1 cornett 3 trombones		Selfridge-Field, "Viennese," 119
1712	[harpsichord] 1 theorbo 1 lute	22 violin/viola 6 cellos 2 violoni 2 viole da gamba	6 oboes 3 bassoons 2 horns 1 cornett 3 trombones		
STUTTGART					
1684	2 organs	1 violin 1 basse de violon	1 oboe	6 *Hofmusici*	Owens, "Württemberg Hofkapelle," 102
1714	1 organ 1 lute	9 violins 1 cello 1 basse de violon 2 violoni	2 oboes 1 flute 2 horns		Ibid. 443
KOBLENZ					
1711	1 organ 1 lute	12 violins 1 bass		1 *Konzertmeister* 10 *Instrumentisten*	Bereths, *Musikpflege*, 139
1721	1 organ 1 theorbo		1 flute 1 oboe 2 horns	1 *Konzertmeister*	Ibid. 140

he acquired a lifelong taste for Italian opera. Succeeding his brother in 1694, he embarked on a campaign of courtly display and cultural exhibitionism modeled upon and even rivaling Louis XIV's. A roster of 1697 shows the Dresden Kapelle still divided into two ensembles—one for the chapel of the now-Catholic Friedrich August, the other for services in the Protestant church that the Elector still maintained (Table 7.1).[27] However, both ensembles now had a core of five-part bowed strings, and cornetts and shawms had been replaced by oboes and bassoons. Soon Friedrich August began to shape the Kapelle along yet more orchestral lines. He engaged new instrumentalists, particularly string players and performers on the French winds: transverse flutes, recorders, oboes, and bassoons. French and Italian players were brought to Dresden and put at the head of the violin, cello, and wind sections. By 1709 something very much like an orchestra had emerged. All the Kapelle instrumentalists had been consolidated into a single ensemble, based on a core of bowed strings, still laid out in five-part scoring, but now with several on a part. Rather than being musical generalists with skills on several instruments, Dresden musicians now specialized on particular instruments.[28] The young J. J. Quantz, who arrived in Dresden in 1716, was much impressed by these instrumental virtuosi:

The Royal Orchestra . . . boasted of various famous instrumentalists such as: Pisendel and Veracini on the violin . . . Sylvius Leopold Weiss on the lute and theorbo, Richter on the oboe, Buffardin on the transverse flute, not to speak of the good violoncellists, bassoonists, horn players, and bassists. . . . I wanted to prepare myself so that in time I too could become a fair member of this excellent company.[29]

The new Dresden orchestra is depicted in an engraving of a performance in the newly built Zwinger opera house around 1728 (Fig. 7.2).[30] The orchestra sits in facing rows in front of the stage. With their backs to the stage can be seen (from the right) five violins, three flutes (one of whom watches the action rather than playing), a bassoon, a lute, a theorbo, an oboe, and a recorder. To the far right and far left sit more cellos and bassoons. The instruments of the players with their backs to the audience are hard to see: a cello can be distinguished near the center, oboes toward the right. In the center a harpsichordist leads the performance. The size and the instrumental balances of the orchestra in the picture approximate rather closely the roster of instrumentalists in the Dresden Kapelle in 1728 (Table 7.1).

[27] Fürstenau, *Zur Geschichte*, ii. 13, 18.

[28] Ortrun Landmann, "Die Dresdener Hofkapelle zur Zeit Johann Sebastian Bachs," *Concerto*, 51 (1990), 7–16 at 8.

[29] Quantz in Paul Nettl, *Forgotten Musicians* (New York, 1951), 287. See also Kahl, *Selbstbiographien deutscher Musiker*, 113–14.

[30] This often-reproduced drawing has traditionally been identified as representing Antonio Lotti's *Teofane*, which was performed at the Zwinger in 1719. According to Michael Walter, however, the sets do not correspond to those for *Teofane*, which are depicted in a different set of engravings, and the picture does not represent the opera house in 1719 but must date from 1728 or later ("Italienische Musik," 193). Perhaps it depicts an imaginary rather than a real opera in the Zwinger theater (pers. comm.).

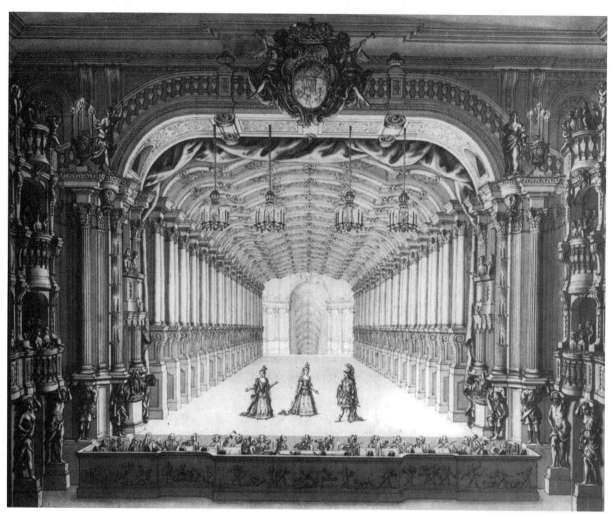

Fig. 7.2. Opera performance at the Zwinger Theater, Dresden, *c.*1728

Another example of the rapid emergence of an orchestra within a German Kapelle during the first decade of the eighteenth century is provided by the court of Hesse-Darmstadt. The pattern is similar to that of Dresden, although Darmstadt was a much smaller court, ruled by a Landgrave (*Landgraf*). From 1688 to 1739 the Landgrave was Ernst Ludwig, a francophile and musicomane, who played viola da gamba and composed instrumental suites.[31] Already under his predecessors Darmstadt had been a center for court ballets and theater. Instrumentally, however, these remained in the

---

[31] Elisabeth Noack, *Musikgeschichte Darmstadts vom Mittelalter bis zur Goethezeit* (Mainz, 1967), 186.

tradition of Renaissance entertainments, with one-on-a-part instrumentalists in costume or concealed behind the scenes.[32]

Ernst Ludwig's trip to Paris in 1685 inspired and informed the transformation of the Darmstadt Kapelle. With the violinists and wind players he had brought back from Paris, he mounted a production in 1687 of *Acis et Galatée*, the opera that had made such an impression on him at Versailles. The Kapelle was doubled in size and modernized by adding violins and French-style wind instruments (Table 7.1). In 1709 Christoph Graupner was brought to Darmstadt as Vice-Kapellmeister with a mandate to introduce Italian-style opera, and the Kapelle was expanded further to 22 instrumentalists.[33] The Landgrave kept his new orchestra extremely busy. In a little over two years, between January 1713 and March 1715, it played for 153 theatrical performances, 33 public rehearsals, and two masked balls, plus its regular duties at church services.[34]

Ernst Ludwig's modernization of the Kapelle coincided with the escalation of other sorts of display at Darmstadt. A French theater troupe was engaged. The French architect Louis Rémy de la Fosse was hired to build a hunting lodge, to plan a new palace for the Landgrave's residence, and to turn the riding school into an opera house.[35] Display on this scale could not long be sustained in a state as small as Hesse-Darmstadt. Ernst Ludwig supplemented his income from crown lands and taxes by renting out his army to the Duke of Braunschweig, who was embroiled in the War of the Spanish Succession. The Treaty of Rastatt in 1714 brought an end to these subsidies, which precipitated a financial crisis in Hesse-Darmstadt. In 1717 Ernst Ludwig, much against his will, was forced to cut back on the extravagance of his court.[36] The French theater troupe was dismissed, and in 1722 the opera house was shuttered. The Kapelle too was reduced, but not drastically—from 28 members in 1718 to 21 members in 1720. It fluctuated between 20 and 40 members for most of the eighteenth century.[37]

The transformation of the Dresden and the Darmstadt Kapellen took place during almost exactly the same period, between 1685 and 1715, and the emerging orchestras resembled each other closely. The number of string players increased to the point where there were enough to have several players on each part, with violins doubled more heavily than the other strings. Transverse flutes, oboes, and bassoons were

[32] Kaiser, *Barocktheater in Darmstadt*.

[33] Oswald Bill, "Dokumente zum Leben und Wirken Christoph Graupners in Darmstadt," in id. (ed.), *Christoph Graupner, Hofkapellmeister in Darmstadt 1709–1760* (Mainz, 1987), 82–181 at 113.

[34] Kaiser, *Barocktheater*, 110.

[35] Ekhart G. Franz and Jürgen Rainer Wolf, "Hessen-Darmstadt und seine Fürsten im Zeitalter des Barock und Rokoko (1678–1780)," in Eva Huber (ed.), *Darmstadt in der Zeit des Barock und Rokoko* (Darmstadt, 1980), 13–19 at 17; Carl Horst Hoferichter, "Der Hofstaat Ernst Ludwigs," ibid. 69–79 at 77.

[36] Joanna Cobb Biermann, "Die Darmstädter Hofkapelle unter Christoph Graupner, 1709–1760," in Bill (ed.), *Christoph Graupner, Hofkapellmeister in Darmstadt 1709–1760*, 27–72 at 48.

[37] Ibid. 32.

introduced; cornetts and shawms disappeared. Rather than being generalists, players began to specialize on particular instruments. These same changes took place at several other German courts at more or less the same time. Table 7.1 gives "before and after" figures for selected German Kapellen. In Berlin a Kapelle that in 1681 contained seven instrumentalists and two organists had expanded by 1708 to 25 members, now identified by instrumental specialty. The Imperial Kapelle in Vienna already contained a substantial number of violin-family instruments in 1685, but between that date and 1712 it was massively expanded, chiefly by the addition of violins and the introduction of French winds. In Stuttgart these same changes took place at just the same time (1684–1714) but on a smaller scale. At the Bishop-Elector's court in Koblenz, they came somewhat later (1711–21). The figures in Table 7.1 must be viewed with caution, because they are derived from different types of sources and because they represent Kapellen at arbitrary moments in time. Still, the same pattern can be discerned in so many different places that it seems reasonable to propose that the orchestra in Germany was born between the years 1685 and 1715 in the context of German court culture.

COURT ORCHESTRAS—DUTIES AND VENUES

The Stuttgart court Kapelle, according to a memo dated 1684, was required to play "in church, as table music, and for other princely entertainments; in addition it is expected to participate in comedies, ballets, and dances."[38] This list of duties and venues can probably be interpreted as a ranked hierarchy: the Kapelle's original and primary duty was to sing and play in church, then came music for the princely table, court entertainments and other festivities, then the theater, and finally the dance. By 1711, when a similar memorandum was written for another Kapellmeister, the list has been changed to read: "all court musicians, both instrumentalists and singers, shall be present in the church or in the princely chambers or at balls whenever they are required, and also for operas and their rehearsals, both public [*Proben*] and private [*Exercitien*], always punctually and at the appointed place."[39] Church music retains priority but table music has disappeared; operas have replaced "princely entertainments" and comedies; and a new category, "chamber," has been added to designate musical performance in the private quarters of the Prince. This list—church, chamber, theater, dance—is repeated in many other instructions for other Kapellmeisters and parallels the classification of musical styles into church, chamber, and theater that became normative in the eighteenth century.[40]

---

[38] Quoted in Owens, "The Württemberg Hofkapelle," 279.   [39] Quoted ibid. 434.

[40] Similar lists of duties are preserved in contracts from Rudolstadt (Erlebach, *Harmonische Freude*, p. xx); Eszterháza (Landon, *Haydn: Chronicle and Works*, i. 350–51); Rastatt (Walter, *J. C. F .Fischer, Hofkapellmeister*, 121 ff.); and Braunschweig-Wolfenbüttel (Brauer, "Instruments," 163).

At both Protestant and Catholic courts instrumental music in church was an important part of princely display. By celebrating mass and the offices on lavish scale, princes advertised that they were doing their duty to God, and at the same time they appropriated some of God's authority. Daily mass was usually performed with only singers and continuo instruments, but for Sundays and feast days instruments were added in profusion. Some courts had two chapels: one Catholic and one Protestant (e.g. Dresden), or one for the King and one for the Queen (e.g. Stuttgart); and here the Kapelle had to be divided or had to alternate between one location and the other.

Figure 7.3 shows the musical forces for a particularly magnificent church service— at the coronation of the Elector of Brandenburg as King Friedrich I of Prussia in 1701.[41] The engraving, a detail from a panoramic view, shows the Kapelle gathered in two lofts above the altar. The organ loft on the left is filled with singers; the instrumentalists occupy a larger loft to the right. In the front left corner of the instrumentalists' loft stands a timebeater, flanked by plucked strings. Across the front row can be seen, from left to right, six violins or violas, three oboes, and three violoni. In back of them stand about 30 more people. If these are meant to be instrumentalists, then this would be one of the largest ensembles documented for Germany in the early eighteenth century. On the other hand, the instrumentalists actually seen correspond approximately to the players listed in court records for the Prussian court at a slightly later date (Table 7.1), so perhaps the extra people are spectators. Unlike earlier depictions of sacred music, where instrumentalists are divided along with singers into multiple choirs in separate lofts, here the separation is between singers in the organ loft and instrumentalists, united into a single ensemble, in their own loft. Trumpets and timpani, not shown in this detail, are found in yet another loft along the nave of the church.

In the courtly ethos of the seventeenth and eighteenth centuries great symbolic importance was placed on eating. A ruler had an obligation to feed his household, that is, the entire court. Some princely employees and retainers received cash payments in lieu of meals, but many actually dined at the palace, seated in hierarchical order at a series of tables: the Prince's table, the Marshall's table, the Officers' table, etc.[42] Those at the higher-ranking tables received better food and more attentive service. Thus, eating at court was both a display and an enactment of hierarchical social order. At special occasions, like a wedding or a state banquet, the princely table and the accompanying ceremony had to be especially grand, because the display of wealth and paternalistic obligation were aimed not only at the prince's own subjects but at other princes and other courts as well.

---

[41] The coronation took place in Königsberg on 18 Jan. 1701. For documentation of the engraving and the ceremonies, see Bowles, *Musical Ensembles*, 405 ff.

[42] See Uta Lowenstein, "Voraussetzungen und Grundlagen von Tafelzeremoniell und Zeremonietafel," in Jörg Jochen and Thomas Rahn Berns (eds.), *Zeremoniell als höfische Ästhetik in Spätmittelalter und früher Neuzeit* (Tübingen, 1995), 266–79 at 267.

FIG. 7.3. Coronation of Elector Friedrich III of Brandenburg as King Friedrich I of Prussia, Königsberg, 1701 (detail)

Music was a standard concomitant of dining at German courts during the seventeenth and eighteenth centuries. Trumpets announced the entry of the prince, instrumental and vocal music accompanied the meal. To be heard above the din of serving, eating, drinking, and conversation, the music needed to be as full and loud as possible. In a large room, says J. A. Scheibe in 1739, "with a well-stocked banquet table surrounded by a large number of people, a symphony will never have much of an effect unless it is amplified by a full and loud harmony as well as lively, forceful activity in the middle voices."[43] At large courts with large Kapellen, table music became increasingly orchestral. As early as 1672 at a banquet given by Count Zinsendorf in Vienna for the Emperor and Empress, "the Royal Couple were treated to a lavish meal and table music performed by twenty-four violins."[44]

Theater at German courts in the first half of the eighteenth century was dominated by French spoken theater and Italian opera.[45] Instrumentalists seldom appeared onstage or in costume any more. Now they were placed in front of the stage as in the Italian theater, separated from the audience by a barrier. Both spoken theater and opera used instrumentalists from the court Kapelle to provide music, but documentation of musical practices in the spoken theater is scarce. It is also hard to know how large or small German orchestras for Italian opera may have been during this period. Since the instrumentalists were on the payroll in any case, it is possible that most or all the Kapelle played; Fig. 7.2, for instance, shows what seems to be the entire Dresden Kapelle of about 40 musicians accompanying an opera. From the beginning of the eighteenth century on, most operas in Germany were accompanied by instrumental ensembles that were "orchestral" in the sense that they were unified ensembles, placed in the pit rather than onstage, based on violin-family instruments playing several on a part, and usually including flutes, oboes, and bassoons.

The "princely chamber" mentioned in the 1711 instruction for the Stuttgart Kapellmeister was a new venue for an instrumental ensemble. As at Versailles, "Chamber" (*Kammer*) meant the private quarters of the prince and his family, as opposed to the public precincts of the court (*Hof*). In reality the "chamber" was a thoroughly public place, since it was open to members of the court, guests, and often many onlookers as well. During the seventeenth century the instrumentalists who played in the "chamber" tended to be lutenists, gambists, and keyboardists. In the early eighteenth century lists of court musicians began to designate a certain number of violinists, cellists, flutists, and others as "chamber" musicians (*Kammermusiker*). Music in the chamber functioned both as entertainment and as accompaniment to social activities like card playing and conversation. If the prince and his family were musicians, they often took part themselves. Burney's account of the Dresden court in 1772 gives the flavor of this milieu:

At eight o'clock the Elector's band assembled, for his private concert. The . . . ladies of the court were at cards, in the music room: the concert was begun by two symphonies of Schwindl. . . . The first song was sung by Signor Panzachi. . . . After this song, the Electress

---

[43] Johann Adolf Scheibe, *Critischer Musikus. Neue, vermehrte und verbesserte Auflage* (Leipzig, 1745), 620–21.

[44] Paul Nettl, "Die Wiener Tanzkomposition in der zweiten Hälfte des siebzehnten Jahrhunderts," *Studien zur Musikwissenschaft*, 8 (1921), 45–175 at 103. For a depiction of festive table music at the Saxon court in 1718, see below, Fig. 10.1.

[45] German opera, which had enjoyed a vogue during the late 17th and early 18th c. at the courts of Halle, Stuttgart, Baden-Durlach, Gotha, Rudolstadt, and Wolfenbüttel, was replaced by Italian opera at German courts in the first half of the 18th c. See Renate Brockpähler, *Handbuch zur Geschichte der Barockoper in Deutschland* (Emsdetten, 1964).

dowager of Saxony sung a whole scene in her own opera of *Talestri*; M. Naumann accompanied her on the harpsichord, and the Elector played the violin with Kröner. She sung in a truly
fine style; her voice is very weak, but she never forces it, or sings out of tune.... Though there
were but few violins, in this concert they were too powerful for the voice ... After this the
Elector played one of Schwindl's trios on his Viol da gamba.[46]

It is hard to tell how large these ensembles for the chamber were at any given court
or how "orchestral" they may have been in terms of organization and playing style.
In Burney's account the "Elector's band" seems to have consisted of just the
"Kammermusiker" of the Dresden Kapelle, since there were "but few violins."[47]
Frederick the Great's chamber music at Rheinsberg in the 1730s numbered 17,
including six violins, two flutes (one of them Frederick himself), and two horns. After
he became King of Prussia in 1740, Frederick continued to play regularly in his chamber, accompanied by many of the same players, now members of the Berlin Kapelle.[48]
Figure 7.4, attributed to Peter Haas, depicts such a concert at Sans Souci in the
1770s.[49] The King, dressed in his military uniform, is accompanied by ten musicians:
seven violins or violas, cello, bass, and harpsichord. The configuration is typical of
"chamber" ensembles, with the soloist in front, cello and bass reading from the keyboard part, and rows of violinists facing one another across the harpsichord. Burney,
who attended one of these performances in 1772, commented that the King's performance on the flute "surpassed, in many particulars, any thing I had ever heard
among *Dilettanti*, or even professors."[50]

At many courts by the 1730s and 1740s "chamber" music had turned into regularly scheduled performances by a large ensemble. The instructions for the Kapelle at
Rastatt in 1737, for example, call for "Music at the court every Sunday and every
Thursday: full music on Sunday and chamber music on Thursday."[51] Some types of
music performed in the chamber, for example symphonies and overtures, probably
called for larger ensembles; others, like concertos and vocal music, for smaller ensembles. Variability seems to have been the rule, according to the size of the Kapelle, the
size of the room, the kind of music played, and the interests and taste of the sovereign.

Music for the dance was similarly variable. From the mid-seventeenth century on
most German courts had a dancing master, usually a Frenchman, who taught the royal

[46] Charles Burney, *The Present State of Music in Germany, the Netherlands and United Provinces* (London, 1775),
i. 140–41. The Elector was Kurfürst Friedrich August III of Saxony (r. 1763–1827). The Electress Dowager
was Maria Antonia Walpurgis (1724–80), wife of the recently deceased Elector Friedrich Christian. Maria
Antonia studied singing with Porpora and composition with Hasse. She composed several operas, among them
Talestri, regina delle amazoni (1763). She was also a painter. Domenico Panzacchi, a tenor, and Franz Kröner
[*recte* Croemer], a violinist, were members of the Bavarian Kapelle in Munich; Johann Gottlieb Naumann
belonged to the Dresden Kapelle. Friedrich Schwindl (1737–1786), who lived in Switzerland, composed symphonies and instrumental music.

[47] The Dresden Kapelle numbered at least 40 in 1772 (Mahling, "Orchester und Orchestermusiker").

[48] Eugene Helm, *Music at the Court of Frederick the Great* (Norman, Okla., 1960), 88–89, 119–20.

[49] Figure 7.4 is not Haas's original etching, but a redrawn version published in 1840.

[50] Burney, *Present State of Music in Germany*, ii. 153.   [51] Häfner, "J. C. F. Fischer," 154.

FIG. 7.4. Music in the chambers of Frederick the Great

children, the pages, and others, and who was often responsible for providing dance music for court balls and sometimes for ballets in the theater as well. Almost invariably the dancing master played violin. J. B. Volumier, a Flemish violinist, studied in Paris, went to Berlin as a dancing master, then in 1709 to Dresden, where he retrained the Kapelle in the French style of playing.[52] At Darmstadt a procession of French violinists—J. B. Tayault, P. F. Demoll, F. J. Etienne, F. Dubois—served as dancing masters and played with the court orchestra.[53] When dances were incorporated into Italian operas as ballets, the ensemble was led by a violinist, who often composed the music for the ballet as well. Ballets in the theater were apparently accompanied by the full orchestra; there is no sign in Germany of the Italian custom of excusing the principal players from the ballet (see Ch. 5). Often the Kapelle remained after the opera was over to accompany the court ball that followed.

[52] Fürstenau, *Zur Geschichte*, ii. 289.   [53] Biermann, "Die Darmstadter Hofkapelle," 62.

Fig. 7.5. A dress ball, *c.*1750

　　Court balls were held according to a yearly schedule and also for special occasions—weddings, christenings, state visits, etc. The more important the occasion, the more musicians were required for the dance orchestra. Figure 7.5, engraved by G. B. Probst of Augsburg, is a *vue optique*, designed to be viewed through the lens-and-mirror setup of a zograscope, where it appears to be three-dimensional. The engraving depicts an imaginary court ball around the middle of the eighteenth century. As in other pictures of eighteenth-century balls, the orchestra is placed in balconies so that the music, reflecting off the ceiling and walls, can be heard clearly, while the floor remains free for the dancers. Here the dance band numbers over 20, with strings in the lower balcony, winds in the upper.

COURT ORCHESTRAS—ORGANIZATION

Eighteenth-century German Kapellen included both singers and instrumentalists. The Kapelle was subject to the authority of the Kapellmeister, whose musical and administrative duties are laid out in many surviving contracts from the seventeenth and eighteenth centuries. He composed music; he trained musicians (especially singers); he looked after instruments and written music, printed or manuscript; he led the Kapelle in performance, in most cases from the keyboard; and he was responsible for the good behavior of the musicians. He did *not* have the power to hire or fire. This was the prerogative of the ruler, who issued separate contracts to each musician. Many Kapellen also had a concertmaster (*Konzertmeister*), who was responsible specifically for instrumental music, while the Kapellmeister retained responsibility for vocal music, especially church music and opera. Where there was a concertmaster, he was usually considered the leader of the orchestra. At some courts a Vice-Kapellmeister was responsible for instrumental music.

Beyond the Kapellmeister, Vice-Kapellmeister, and Concertmaster, there was relatively little administrative hierarchy within eighteenth-century Germany orchestras. However, differences between instrumentalists' salaries suggest that there were differences in status nonetheless. At Dresden in 1709, for example, the highest-paid regular instrumentalist, the violinist Carlo Fiorelli, earned 600 Thalers per year, while the lowest-paid, the cellist (Houlondel), made 200 Thalers.[54] A paylist from Baden-Durlach in 1715 shows the same 3 to 1 differential between the top and bottom of the salary scale, as do lists from Darmstadt in 1740 and Stuttgart in 1745.[55] At Mannheim in 1745 the differential was a little steeper: 3.5 to 1.[56] These differentials, strikingly consistent among German orchestras, may reflect differences in ability among the musicians, or they may reflect age and seniority.

Over the course of the eighteenth century, more explicit markers of differentiation developed within German orchestras. Lists of musicians increasingly distinguished a few *Kammermusiker*, who played in the prince's chambers, from a larger number of *Hofmusiker*, that is, ordinary instrumentalists. The designation *Kammermusiker* could also signify a specialist on a single instrument, as opposed to a *Hofmusiker*, who was expected to play several instruments.[57] *Kammermusiker* generally received higher salaries, which reflected their higher status but may also have compensated them for a greater number of services. By the mid-eighteenth century, the word "Kammermusiker," along with "soloist" (*Solist*), seems to have acquired the meaning of "first-chair player," as opposed to section players, who came to be called ripienists (*Ripienisten*). A memorandum from Darmstadt in 1758 explains that "among vocalists and instrumentalists a Soloist or Virtuoso always takes precedence over a Ripienist

[54] Fürstenau, *Zur Geschichte*, ii. 50. These and subsequent figures leave out the Kapellmeister and the Konzertmeister. For more on the salaries and living standards of 18th-c. orchestra musicians, see Ch. 12.

[55] Baden-Durlach: Ludwig Schiedermair, "Die Oper an den badischen Höfen des 17. u. 18. Jahrhunderts," *Sammelbände der IMG*, 13 (1912–13), 191–207, 369–449, 510–50 at 374–75; Darmstadt: Noack, *Musikgeschichte Darmstadts*, 218; Stuttgart: Josef Sittard, *Zur Geschichte der Musik und des Theaters am württembergischen Hofe* (Stuttgart, 1891), 29–30.

[56] Friedrich Walter, *Geschichte des Theaters und der Musik am kurpfälzischen Hofe* (Leipzig, 1898), 102.

[57] See Owens, "The Württemberg Hofkapelle," 126.

or section player [*Ausfüllungs Geiger*]. This is aside from any consideration of seniority."[58] In addition, orchestra lists began to record the presence of "Accessisten" (trainees), young musicians who played for free or for a minimal wage while they waited for a regular position to open up.[59]

Trumpeters and drummers, as a rule, were administratively separate from the Kapelle. Usually they belonged to the marshall's staff or to the stable. Trumpets and drums were an essential concomitant of royalty, and they were required in large numbers. The Dresden court at one time employed 20 trumpeters and two drummers; at Mannheim during most of the eighteenth century there were 13 trumpets and two drums; the Archbishop of Passau needed six trumpets, the Archbishop of Salzburg 10 or 11.[60] At many courts the trumpeters contributed to the orchestra not only on their main instrument but also as doublers, usually on violin or viola. At Salzburg in 1757, for example, according to Leopold Mozart's report, "There is not one of the trumpeters or kettledrummers in the princely service who does not play the violin well. For performances of large-scale concerted music at court, all of them must appear and join in playing second violin or viola."[61] In the second half of the eighteenth century, when trumpets had become necessary for operas, symphonies, and even some dance music, adminstrators began transferring a pair of trumpeters to the Kapelle, where their duties were somewhat lighter than those of the court and military trumpeters. Another separate ensemble at many courts was the "Hautboistencorps," a wind band composed of oboes in various sizes and bassoons.[62] Later the Hautboisten were expanded to include horns and sometimes clarinets. They performed as a distinct ensemble at table or even for dances, but their members could also be added to orchestras as necessary, either on wind instruments or as string players.

The musical instruments that Kapelle members played were owned in most cases by the sovereign, who lent them to the musicians. Already in 1700, for example, the Bishop of Kremsier owned some 58 instruments, including violins made by Stainer and Amati.[63] A Stuttgart inventory of 1718 records 36 stringed and eight wind instruments in good condition, plus 24 stringed and eight wind instruments in need of

---

[58] Noack, *Musikgeschichte Darmstadts*, 242.

[59] See Mahling, "The Origin and Social Status," 242–43; also Wolf, "On the Composition of the Mannheim Orchestra," 116.

[60] Dresden: Fürstenau, *Zur Geschichte*; Mannheim: Wolf, "On the Composition"; Passau: Gottfried Schäffer, *Das fürstbischöfliche und königliche Theater zu Passau (1783–1883)* (Passau, 1973); Salzburg: Ernst Hintermaier, "Die salzburger Hofkapelle von 1700 bis 1806, Organisation und Personal" (Diss., Universität Salzburg, 1972).

[61] Leopold Mozart (attrib.), "Nachricht von dem gegenwärtigen Zustande der Musik Sr. Hochfürstlichen Gnaden des Erzbischoffs zu Salzburg im Jahr 1757," in *Historisch-kritische Beyträge zur Aufnahme der Musik*, ed. Friedrich Wilhelm Marpurg, iii (Berlin, 1757), 197. Trans. in Zaslaw, *Mozart's Symphonies*, 550–57 at 556.

[62] See Werner Braun, "The 'Hautboist': An Outline of Evolving Careers and Functions," in Salmen (ed.), *The Social Status of the Professional Musician*, 123–58 at 128 ff.

[63] Jiri Sehnal, "Die Musikkapelle des Olmützer Bischofs Karl Liechtenstein-Castelcorn in Kremsier," *Kirchenmusikalisches Jahrbuch*, 51 (1967), 79–123 at 98.

repair but still playable. Finally, 79 more instruments—32 cornetts, 10 crumhorns, four bass recorders, etc.—are designated as "old stuff, useless and not worth repairing."[64] These large collections of instruments represented significant investments of princely capital. The prince assumed the costs of keeping the instruments in repair as well as buying strings, reeds, rosin, etc. At Stuttgart in 1699 musicians were not allowed to take instruments home with them; if they wanted to practice at home, they had to use their own instruments.[65] The Rastatt regulations of 1747 insist: "it is our express command that all instruments, except those that our trumpeters and hunting hornists use every day, be kept . . . in a special room and in locked cabinets. No one is to have the key but the Kapellmeister and the Konzertmeister."[66]

At many German courts instrumentalists held appointments not only as members of the Kapelle but at other positions as well, sometimes a job in the court bureaucracy—secretary, accountant, schoolteacher—sometimes as a lackey or personal servant. When in 1765 the violinist and composer Dittersdorf took a job as Kapellmeister for the Bishop of Grosswardein, he found that his orchestra "consisted of 34 persons, among them nine servants in livery, one chamber servant, and a confectioner."[67] In some cases these joint appointments may have been sinecures. In other cases it is clear that the person was expected to do both jobs, a situation that could lead to conflict. An instruction from the Margrave of Baden to his Kapelle in Rastatt in 1747 stipulates:

[For] musicians who are also liveried servants, namely the lackeys, we have already issued the most gracious decree that, without neglecting their service or obtaining any special dispensation, they should [nonetheless] be present at all musical occasions described above. Any absence will be punished harshly.[68]

The overlap of instrumental music with other types of court service persisted at smaller courts throughout the eighteenth century.

Another kind of overlap in eighteenth-century German Kapellen was double-handedness, that is, performers who played two or more instruments in the orchestra. This was a holdover from pre-orchestral Kapellen, where all musicians were expected to be generalists. A roster of the Stuttgart Kapelle in 1717 describes the abilities of each of the 21 members. A few are listed only on one instrument; seven play two instruments; seven play three, two play four, and one plays five. The champion is Stephan Freudenberg, who "is best on the violin and viola d'amore, plays recorder nicely and also oboe, transverse flute, and bassoon. And he can also play harpsichord

---

[64] Owens, "The Württemberg Hofkapelle," 476 ff. The inventory also records 13 keyboard instruments. For more inventories of 18th-c. instrument collections see Gustav Bereths, *Die Musikpflege am kurtrierischen Hofe zu Koblenz-Ehrenbreitstein* (Mainz, 1964), 144; Shelley Davis, "The Orchestra under Clemens Wenzeslaus: Music at a Late-Eighteenth-Century Court," *JAMIS* 1 (1975), 86–112 at 97–100; Sehnal, "Die Musikkapelle," 96 ff.

[65] Owens, "The Württemberg Hofkapelle," 127.   [66] Walter, *J. C. F. Fischer, Hofkapellmeister*, 134.

[67] Dittersdorf, *Lebensbeschreibung*, 141.   [68] Walter, *J. C. F. Fischer, Hofkapellmeister*, 135.

well."[69] Doublers are similarly prominent in Leopold Mozart's 1757 report on the Salzburg Kapelle. Wenzl Sadlo, the hornist, also plays the violin, while Joseph Hölzel, the violinist, plays the horn. Andreas Mayr, a violinist, "also plays the cello well"; J. A. Marchall, a cellist, "also plays the violin well." Franz Schwarzmann, a violinist, "plays concertos on the bassoon, and no less beautifully on the oboe, flute, and horn."[70]

Double-handedness was essential to the functioning of eighteenth-century German orchestras, because it allowed a limited number of Kapelle musicians to provide appropriate music in a variety of contexts. The 1747 regulations of the Rastatt Kapelle called on the court trumpeters, "when they have nothing of their own to play, to help reinforce the music by playing other instruments they have learned."[71] In many orchestras flutes and oboes overlapped completely: the same players played both instruments, switching back and forth according to the demands of the music. A letter to the Elector of Dresden in 1789 pleads the case of a young Kapelle oboist who also plays flute in the wind band (*Jagd-Pfeifern*):

he is required sometimes to play the oboe, sometimes the flute. But since each instrument requires a different embouchure, in the long run his tone and his lip will suffer from this. Consequently it would be advisable to remove this young man as soon as possible from the wind band and let him devote himself exclusively to the oboe . . .[72]

Over the course of the eighteenth century, double-handedness seems to have declined, or at least become less essential to the operation of German orchestras. By the end of the eighteenth century flute specialists and also clarinetists had established themselves in most German Kapellen, and Kapelle regulations encouraged musicians to be specialists rather than generalists.

CIVIC ORCHESTRAS

Courts were the not the only places where orchestras developed in Germany during the late seventeenth and the first half of the eighteenth centuries. Many German cities had no court—either because they were free Imperial cities, like Hamburg, Nuremberg, and Frankfurt, or because they held charters from the territorial ruler (e.g. Leipzig, Erfurt, Rostock). Cities in general did not provide as favorable an environment as courts for the birth and growth of orchestras. Instrumental ensembles played in church, in the theater, if there was one, for dancing (mainly at weddings), and occasionally for civic banquets. Musical amateurs organized themselves into clubs to play for their own

---

[69] Owens, "The Württemberg Hofkapelle," 464.   [70] Zaslaw, *Mozart's Symphonies*, 551 ff.

[71] Walter, *J. C. F. Fischer, Hofkapellmeister*, 135.

[72] Ortrun Landmann, "Die Entwicklung der Dresdener Hofkapelle zum 'klassischen' Orchester: Ein Beitrag zur Definition dieses Phänomens," *Basler Jahrbuch für historische Musikpraxis*, 17 (1993), 175–90 at 186.

amusement and for others. However, wealth and patronage were less concentrated in cities than they were at German courts: no burgher had pockets as deep as those of a prince. Cities and city residents competed with one another in commerce, civic buildings, and churches, but not in hospitality, luxury, or display. Moreover, the formation of orchestras in German cities was inhibited by the system of guilds and civic music left over from the Middle Ages. Cities had only a limited number of positions for instrumentalists on the municipal payroll as *Stadtpfeifer* or *Ratsmusikanten*, and the holders of these offices and the town council that paid their salaries had a common interest in keeping the number of town musicians at a minimum. Few German cities were capable of maintaining a large standing ensemble like a princely Kapelle.

Hamburg, a thriving seaport and the second largest city in Germany, had more instrumentalists on the civic payroll than any other German city. To eight *Ratsmusikanten* were added two *Expectanten* (assistants) and 15 *Rollbrüder* (supplementary musicians).[73] The *Rollbrüder* were not on the city payroll but were paid per service—either by the city or by private employers. *Ratsmusikanten* and *Rollbrüder* were generalists who learned multiple instruments in the course of their apprenticeship. Hamburg musicians, however, were noted for their competence on stringed instruments, and their leader was traditionally a violinist.[74] In addition, Hamburg had city trumpeters and, beginning in the late seventeenth century, a band of Hautboisten.[75] The principal functions of Hamburg civic musicians were to provide instrumental music at the city's four large churches and to play at weddings, for which they held a monopoly by law. Church services tended to overlap with one another, so instrumentalists were spread thin on Sunday mornings.[76] For most events Hamburg instrumentalists did not play as a single ensemble but worked in smaller groups, often one on a part.

There were some occasions, however, when most or all of Hamburg's civic instrumentalists played as a single group. Beginning in the 1660s, a collegium musicum met on Thursday evenings in the refectory of the Domkirche. The collegium was an independent organization of music professionals and amateurs who played and sang for their own enjoyment and edification. According to Johann Mattheson, local composer and critic, the Hamburg collegium, "brought together up to 50 persons, all of whom participated," playing "the best pieces from Venice, Rome, Vienna, Munich, Dresden, and elsewhere."[77] These collegium meetings quickly took on the

---

[73] Max Seiffert, "Matthias Weckmann und das Collegium Musicum in Hamburg," *Sammelbände der IMG*, 2 (1900–1), 76–132 at 93–95.

[74] Liselotte Krüger, *Die hamburgische Musikorganisation im 17. Jahrhundert* (Strassburg, 1933), 206; George J. Buelow, "Protestant North Germany," in Curtis Price (ed.), *The Early Baroque Era* (Englewood Cliffs, NJ, 1993), 185–205 at 194.

[75] Krüger, *Die hamburgische Musikorganisation*, 196–97.

[76] Johann Mattheson, *Der musicalische Patriot* (Hamburg, 1728), 64.

[77] Johann Mattheson, *Grundlage einer Ehren-Pforte* (Hamburg, 1740), 397–98.

character of public concerts, and visitors to Hamburg often attended, both to listen and to participate. A regulation from the 1720s subjected the collegium to the restrictions of the guild system by specifying that only the *Ratsmusikanten* and *Rollbrüder* should play the instrumental parts. However, with 25 members the civic musicians could provide the collegium with a relatively large orchestra.[78]

Once a year, on 24 August, the captains of Hamburg's civil guard (*Bürgerkapitäne*) met for a festive banquet at which they celebrated their solidarity, inducted new members, and drank a great deal of beer.[79] The ceremonies at the armory (*Drillhaus*) ended with concerted music for voices and instruments, newly composed each year for the occasion. Telemann, who was Kantor and director of music in Hamburg from 1721 to 1767, composed some 40 oratorios and serenatas for these banquets. The instrumentalists, once again, were the *Ratsmusikanten* and the *Rollbrüder*, sometimes in small one-on-a-part ensembles, sometimes in large orchestras.[80] Figure 7.6 shows the Captains' banquet of 1719 in an engraving by Christian Fritzsch. Singers and instrumentalists are placed in a gallery at one end of the hall, designated in the artist's caption as "*Orchestre* with 40 musicians." The ensemble is just as large as table music ensembles at princely courts during the same period: violins, cellos, oboes, bassoons, lutes, and a harpsichord (at the far end). Similarly large ensembles may have been assembled in Hamburg for other civic festivities like the feast days for the patron saints at the Peterskirche and the Michaeliskirche, which were sponsored by the town council.

Finally, orchestra-like ensembles developed in Hamburg at the public opera, which opened at the theater in the Gänsemarkt in 1678. No records survive to indicate the size or makeup of these opera orchestras. McCredie notes that scores from Hamburg operas sometimes divide the violins into three or four parts, the violas into three, and the cellos into solo and ripieno. Based on this he posits an orchestra of at least eight violins, three violas, two cellos and basses.[81] Oboes had been added by the 1690s, also transverse flutes and bassoons. Once again the *Ratsmusikanten* and *Rollbrüder* formed the basis of the orchestra, but musicians not on the civic payroll played as well. In 1703 one of the violinists was the young George Frederick Handel, who, according to Mattheson, played "the second of the doubled violin parts." This suggests that the opera may have used only four violins that year: two on the first part and two on the second.[82]

Hamburg's instrumental ensembles transformed themselves into orchestras during just about the same period as this transformation took place at German court

---

[78] Sittard, *Zur Geschichte der Musik und des Theaters*, 63.

[79] See Willi Maertens, *Georg Philipp Telemanns sogenannte hamburgische Kapitainsmusiken (1723–1765)* (Wilhelmshaven, 1988).

[80] Ibid. 75.   [81] McCredie, "Instrumentarium and Instrumentation," 303 ff.

[82] See Donald Burrows, *Handel* (New York, 1994), 16; John Mainwaring, *Georg Friedrich Händel: Biographie*, trans. Johann Mattheson, ed. Hedwig Mueller von Asow and E. H. Mueller von Asow (Lindau, 1949), 32. Mattheson's phrase in his translation of Mainwaring's *Memoirs* is "die andre oder zwote, doppeltbesetzte Violin."

Fɪɢ. 7.6. Banquet of the Hamburg Civil Guards, 1719

Kapellen. As Germany's leading seaport and commercial center, Hamburg had an interest in maintaining its image in the world of court culture. Ostentation on the scale of the German courts, however, could not be contemplated in the city. The opera went bankrupt repeatedly and closed its doors in 1738. Within the framework of the civic music system it was impossible to create and maintain an orchestra that could compete with those of Dresden or Darmstadt.

At Lübeck, another northern German port, city music was organized in a manner similar to that in Hamburg but on a more modest scale, with seven *Ratsmusikanten* plus two trumpeters, a city piper, and a city drummer.[83] From 1668 until 1710 Dietrich Buxtehude served as organist at the Marienkirche and leader of the city's music. Beginning in the 1670s he organized the *Abendmusiken*, a series of concerts given on successive Sunday evenings during the winter months at the Marienkirche. The Abendmusiken were sponsored not by the city but by a consortium of merchants. In addition to whatever entertainment these concerts provided for the local audience, they were also meant to enhance the city's reputation, and there may have been at least some notion of competition with court music. When Buxtehude bought two new trumpets for the Abendmusik in 1673, he noted in his account book that "their like . . . has not been heard even in princely Kapellen, where otherwise everything noble in music is put on display."[84] The music that Buxtehude composed for the Abendmusiken makes considerable use of instruments, particularly violins. Nevertheless, as Kerala Snyder shows, most of it was performed one on a part.[85] A few cantatas have parts marked "ripieno" or "complemento" that double other parts; others have extra violin parts but no violas.[86] Evidently, Buxtehude was tailoring his music for the available *Ratsmusikanten*. In *Die Hochzeit des Lamms*, however, a lost oratorio of 1678, the soprano was accompanied in one aria by 11 violins. A wedding cantata, composed in 1705 for the senior Bürgermeister, began with a "Sonatina forte con molti Violini all unisono."[87] Scorings like this seem to lie beyond the capabilities of the seven *Ratsmusikanten*. Perhaps students, amateurs, and apprentices were recruited to create a violin section. Finally, for an "extraordinary" Abendmusik to celebrate the accession in 1705 of Joseph I as Emperor, Buxtehude composed *Templum honoris*, a festive cantata, which opened with a "Sinfonia all'unison 25. Violin."[88] Martin Heinrich Fuhrmann, in his *Musikalischer Trichter* published the next year, seems to be referring to this performance when he says: "The incomparable Herr Buxtehude at Lübeck . . . staffs the violins not with two or three

---

[83] Kerala J. Snyder, *Dieterich Buxtehude: Organist in Lübeck* (New York, 1987), 51.

[84] Quoted ibid. 60, 472.

[85] Ibid. 382 ff.; also Dietrich Buxtehude, *Sacred Works for Four Voices and Instruments—Part 2*, ed. Kerala Snyder (New York, 1987), pp. xiv–xv.

[86] Ibid. 15.   [87] Snyder, *Dieterich Buxtehude*, 383.

[88] *Templum honoris*, BuxWV 135, was published in 1705. See facsimile in Georg Karstädt, *Thematisch-systematisches Verzeichnis der musikalischen Werke von Dietrich Buxtehude: Buxtehude-Werke-Verzeichnis (BuxWV)*, 2nd edn. (Wiesbaden, 1985).

persons but with twenty or thirty or even more. But all these players must take care not to change a single note or dot or play anything different than what is written in the music."[89]

Buxtehude's 25 massed violins in *Templum honoris* seem to have been an experiment. Subsequent Abendmusiken returned to one-on-a-part practice. Whatever ambitions Buxtehude may have had to compete with court music, there was not enough patronage in Lübeck to support the formation of a real orchestra in the early eighteenth century. Indeed, Buxtehude complained repeatedly to the authorities that support for the Abendmusiken was inadequate and that more money was required to maintain them as an "incomparable ornament" of the city.[90] Although the Abendmusiken continued throughout the eighteenth century, there was no standing orchestra in Lübeck until the nineteenth century.

Circumstances in other German cities during the seventeenth and eighteenth centuries were no more favorable to the development of orchestras than they were in Hamburg and Lübeck. Usually the most orchestra-like ensembles were collegia musica. As in Hamburg, these were gatherings of musicians on a regular basis for their own enjoyment. Often they were connected with universities in some way. Most of the participants were amateurs, often students, sometimes merchants, and, so far as can be ascertained, always men. The city musicians (*Ratsmusikanten*, etc.) usually participated as well. They met in private houses, civic buildings, coffee houses, or other public places. Collegia musica are documented in Leipzig, Rostock, Ulm, Frankfurt, Augsburg, Jena, and other German cities.[91] They tended to form and dissolve according to the energy and enthusiasm of their members. Telemann started or revived collegia musica wherever he went: in Leipzig (1702), Frankfurt (1713), and Hamburg (1721). During the eighteenth century collegia musica began to take on the character of public concert series, with regular schedules, increased participation of professionals, and paying audiences. Many began to call themselves "Konzert."

Many, probably most, performances by German collegia musica were one on a part until well into the eighteenth century. However, there are some earlier suggestions of part doubling and more orchestral performance practices. The elaborate instructions quoted above from the introduction to Schmierer's *Zodaici musici* (1698) may have been aimed at the Augsburg collegium and similar ensembles in other German cities. Figure 7.7, probably painted in Jena in the 1730s or 1740s, depicts an ensemble that is very likely a collegium musicum. There are 29 instruments in all, including oboes, bassoons, trumpets, and drums. In the center four singers are gathered around a harpsichord. The instrumentalists are arranged to face one another rather than facing an audience, and indeed there is no audience: the members of the

[89] Martin Heinrich Fuhrmann, *Musikalischer-Trichter* (Frankfurt an der Spree, 1706), 77–78.
[90] Snyder, *Dieterich Buxtehude*, 66.
[91] Emil Platen, "Collegium Musicum," in *MGG²*, Sachteil 2, cols. 943–51 at 946.

FIG. 7.7. Jena collegium musicum, *c.*1740

collegium are either rehearsing or playing for their own pleasure. Spare instruments, evidently part of the collegium's collection, hang on the wall to the left.

Neither the city music guilds nor the collegia musica could compete with the orchestras of the princely Kapellen. Charles Burney in 1772 explained the problem with a bit of socio-political analysis:

I stayed but a short time at Augsburg; for to say the truth, I was somewhat tired of going to imperial cities after music . . . These cities are not rich, and therefore have not the folly to support their theatres at a great expense. The fine arts are children of affluence and luxury: in despotic governments they render power less insupportable, and diversion from thought is perhaps as necessary as from action. Whoever there seeks music in Germany, should do it at the several courts, not in the free imperial cities.[92]

[92] Burney, *Present State of Music in Germany*, i. 118.

BACH'S ORCHESTRAS

Johann Sebastian Bach held a succession of jobs in a series of German towns, cities, and courts: Arnstadt (1703–7), Mühlhausen (1707–8), Weimar (1708–17), Cöthen (1717–23), and Leipzig (1723–50). Only in Leipzig can he be said to have had anything like an orchestra at his disposal.

At Arnstadt Bach was not a Kapellmeister or Kantor but the organist at the Neukirche, and he pointedly refused to organize cantata performances by the students.[93] He does not seem to have composed or produced any music requiring an instrumental ensemble during his Arnstadt years. At Mühlhausen Bach was again appointed as organist, but here he composed and led a number of cantatas with instrumental accompaniment, including Cantata 71 ("Gott ist mein König"), a festive cantata that calls for a rich instrumental accompaniment, including trumpets and drums. The six *Stadtpfeifer* on the Mühlhausen town payroll could not have covered the 15 instrumental parts in this large score. Terry speculates that students and amateur members of the local "Musical Society" may have helped out.[94] A large score, however, does not necessarily imply orchestral performance. The original Mühlhausen parts of Cantata 71 have been preserved, and they correspond exactly to the number of lines in the score—that is, there are no duplicate parts (doublets) to enable additional instrumentalists to play on a line.[95] Two violinists or two violists could have read from the same part, but if the ensemble were any larger, more parts would have had to be copied. Thus, in "Gott ist mein König," as in his other pre-Leipzig cantatas, Bach seems to be working within the seventeenth-century tradition of expanding a piece by multiplying lines rather than by adding several players to the same line.

With his appointment in 1708 as organist to Duke Wilhelm Ernst of Weimar, Bach became a member of a typical small-time Hofkapelle. His initial appointment was as *Kammermusicus*; from 1714 on he was *Konzertmeister*. During his tenure at Weimar, there were six instrumentalists in the ducal Kapelle.[96] In addition one of the singers may have been available as a string player. As Table 7.2 shows, the available instruments were keyboard, four violins or violas, a violone, and one woodwind. Several of the players were double-handed, so the wind player could switch to a stringed instrument when necessary, or a singer could be used as an instrumentalist. On festive occasions trumpets could be added from the Duke's six-man trumpet and drum corps. These configurations account for the scoring of all cantatas that Bach composed at

---

[93] Terry, *Bach*, 70–71; *Bach-Dokumente* (Kassel, 1963–72), ii. 20.   [94] Terry, *Bach's Orchestra*, 3.

[95] The only duplicate part in the set is one marked "tromba," which contains the first trumpet part plus a bass line. This part was probably intended for a timebeater placed in a separate loft with the trumpets and drums. See *Ratswahlkantaten I*, ed. Christiane Fröde (NBA I/32.1; Kassel, 1992); Joshua Rifkin, "More (and Less) on Bach's Orchestra," *Performance Practice Review*, 4 (1991), 5–13 at 8.

[96] See *Bach-Dokumente*, i. 62.

TABLE 7.2. *J. S. Bach's "orchestras," 1714–46*

Place and date	Keyboard and plucked strings	Bowed strings	Winds	Trumpets and drums	Unidentified	Source
WEIMAR, 1714	1 organ	4 violins/viola 1 singer/violin 1 violone	1 bassoon	5 trumpets 1 drum		Cowdery, "Early," 139
CÖTHEN, 1717	1 kbd.	3 violins 1 cello 1 viola da gamba	2 flutes 1 oboe 1 bassoon	2 trumpets 1 drum	2 *Hofmusici* 1 *Stadtpfeifer*	Smend, *Bach*, 166 f.
LEIPZIG, 1730 "Entwurf" actual	[1 organ]	2 violins	2 oboes 1 bassoon	2 trumpets		*Bach-Dokumente*, i. 61
"Entwurf" ideal	[1 organ]	2–3 violin I 2–3 violin II 2 viola I 2 viola II 2 cellos 1 violone	2–3 oboes 1–2 bassoons	3 trumpets 1 drum		Ibid. 60–61
LEIPZIG, 1746 "Grosse Konzert"	1 harpsichord	5 violin I 5 violin II 1 viola 1 cello 3 violoni	1 flute 2 oboes 2 bassoons 2 horns			Schering, *Musikgeschichte*, i. 264

Weimar.[97] The important point, once again, is that the number of parts corresponds to the number of players. Each of the five string players was given his own part to play—switching from violin to viola to viola d'amore as necessary, according to the tessitura Bach wanted for the piece. Similarly, the bassoonist could play flute or oboe if needed, and one of the string players seems to have been able to play a treble wind in a pinch (Cantata 12). In Weimar Bach was again working with a pre-orchestral ensemble.[98]

Cöthen, Bach's next stop, was another court Kapelle. Bach wrote a considerable amount of instrumental music for the Cöthen performers, including the violin partitas and sonatas, the cello suites, several concertos for one and two violins, and some or all of the Brandenburg Concertos.[99] The Cöthen Kapelle included five string and four wind players, plus three unspecified *Hofmusici* and *Stadtpfeifer* (Table 7.2). When necessary, the Prince's trumpeters could be drafted to play stringed instruments; Bach's students and the apprentices of other Kapelle members could help out; Bach could play violin, viola, or harpsichord; and the Duke himself could join in on violin or viola da gamba.[100] The scorings of the Brandenburg Concertos, according to Heinrich Besseler, correspond to the instrumentalists available in the Cöthen Kapelle, with one player for each part.[101] The Fifth Concerto, for example, lacks a second violin part, Besseler proposes, because Bach played the virtuoso harpsichord part and thus was unavailable to play the violin. The Third Concerto—with three violin, three viola, and three cello parts—would have required some of the wind players to play stringed instruments. The unusual scoring of the Sixth Concerto, with two violas, two viole da gamba, cello and bass, probably signals the participation of the Duke on viola da gamba. Only the first concerto is anomalous, since the Cöthen Kapelle lacked horns; however, court documents record the presence of two visiting hornists from September 1721 to 1722.[102] Once again at Cöthen, then, Bach was working in the old tradition of one-on-a-part instrumental ensemble performance.[103]

[97] William Cowdery, "The Early Vocal Works of Johann Sebastian Bach: Studies in Style, Scoring, and Chronology" (Ph.D. diss., Cornell University, 1989), 178 ff., 198.

[98] To say that all Bach's Weimar cantatas were originally performed with singers and instrumentalists one on a part is not to say that these works *must* be performed in this fashion. When Bach revived Weimar cantatas for performance in Leipzig, he had additional string parts copied out so that he could put more players on the parts.

[99] The assignment of the Brandenburg Concertos to the Cöthen years has been challenged by Martin Geck, who argues on stylistic grounds that Concertos 1, 3, and 6 were written in Weimar (Martin Geck, "Gattungstraditionen und Altersschichten in den Brandenburgischen Konzerten," *Die Musikforschung*, 23 (1970), 139–52). One problem with this theory is that the six instrumentalists in the Weimar Kapelle would not have sufficed to cover the horn parts of Concerto 1, the nine string parts of Concerto 3, or the viola da gamba parts in Concerto 6. Weimar versions of these concertos may possibly have existed, but the the concertos that were delivered to the Margrave of Brandenburg in 1721 were almost certainly conceived for Bach's Cöthen Kapelle.

[100] Ernst König, "Die Hofkapelle des Fürsten Leopold zu Anhalt-Köthen," *Bach-Jahrbuch*, 46 (1959), 160–67; Friedrich Smend, *Bach in Köthen*, trans. John Page, ed. and revised with annotations by Stephen Daw (St. Louis, 1985), 40.

[101] Heinrich Besseler, *Sechs Brandenburgische Konzerte: Kritischer Bericht* (NBA VII/2; Kassel, 1956), 18 ff.

[102] Ibid. 21. On the visiting hornists, see Smend, *Bach in Köthen*, 190.

[103] Christoph Wolff presents an account of the Cöthen Kapelle somewhat different from Besseler's (*Bach:*

At Leipzig Bach held a municipal, not a court position. His principal duties were to provide instrumental and vocal music for Leipzig's four churches and to supervise the education of the pupils at the Thomasschule. Officially, the instrumentalists for his church music were the Leipzig civic musicians: four *Stadtpfeifer* and three *Kunstgeiger* plus one apprentice, an ensemble even smaller than the Kapellen at Cöthen or Weimar. Bach's predecessor Johann Kuhnau had complained already in 1709 about the inadequacy of this ensemble for orchestral music:

In particular, since the Stadtpfeiffer, Kunstgeiger, and apprentices together are only eight persons, and barely enough to cover all the necessary wind instruments (namely, two or more trumpets, two oboes or cornetts, three trombones or other similar winds, one German Fagott, and a French bassoon), it is hard to see how a string band, which is so agreeable, can be assembled, because throughout Europe and here too a string band requires many players: at least eight persons on the two violin parts, and furthermore violas two on a part and violoni, cellos, colascioni, timpani, and more, and these people are tied up in the Neue Kirche.[104]

Bach voiced the same complaint in his much-quoted "Memorandum for a well-appointed church music" of 1730. To his Leipzig ensemble of eight city musicians, alternating on violins, oboes, bassoon, and trumpets, he contrasts an ideal orchestra of 18 to 22 instrumentalists, with string parts doubled and a full complement of winds (Table 7.2).[105] To realize that such an orchestra is possible, Bach says, one has only to go to nearby Dresden and hear the "outstanding and excellent" court Kapelle, whose members are professionals and specialists on their instruments.[106] Bach in fact heard the Dresden orchestra many times. He knew Volumier and Pisendel, the concert-masters, and other musicians, and he traveled to Dresden to hear the opera.[107]

Bach's situation in Leipzig was not quite as desperate as he made it out to be. He admitted in his "Memorandum" that it was usually possible to supplement his orchestra with present and past Thomasschule students. He also put his sons to work in the orchestra along with the private students who lived at his house.[108] The original parts for many of Bach's Leipzig cantatas have been preserved; typically they contain doublets for violin 1 and violin 2, suggesting that he often succeeded in rounding up three

---

Essays on his Life and Music (Cambridge, Mass., 1991), 8–9). He does not, however, disagree with the characterization of Cöthen performances as one on a part.

[104] Quoted in Philipp Spitta, *Johann Sebastian Bach* (Leipzig, 1921), ii. 859. Kuhnau's list of wind instruments reads in German: "2 oder mehr Trompeten, 2 Hautbois, oder Cornetten, 3 Trombonen oder andern dergleichen Pfeiffen, 1 Fagott, und einem Basson."

[105] In his "Memorandum" Bach lists only seven rather than eight municipal instrumentalists. One *Kunstgeiger* position was vacant at the time he wrote the memo (Terry, *Bach*, 14; Ulrich Siegele, "Bachs Endzweck einer regulierten und Entwurf einer wohlbestallten Kirchenmusik," in Thomas Kohlhase and Volker Scherliess (eds.), *Festschrift Georg von Dadelsen Zum 60. Geburtstag* (Stuttgart, 1978), 313–51 at 333).

[106] *Bach-Dokumente*, i. 63.

[107] Johann Nikolaus Forkel, *Ueber Johann Sebastian Bachs Leben, Kunst und Kunstwerke* (Leipzig, 1802), 47–48.

[108] Siegele, "Bachs Endzweck," 336 ff.

or four players for each of the violin parts.[109] When Bach revised his Weimar cantatas for Leipzig performance, he characteristically had duplicate parts copied to accommodate this larger orchestra.[110] Similarly, when he revised the first Brandenburg concerto as the first movement of Cantata 174, he added second and third copies for the strings.[111] Despite his complaints in the "Memorandum," it is clear that Bach had a more "orchestral" ensemble at his disposal in Leipzig than he had enjoyed at any of his earlier positions. And it is clear that he took advantage of the available players by doubling the string parts, particularly the violins. His instrumental ensemble for sacred music in Leipzig was far smaller than the Dresden Kapelle, but in size and shape it was an incipient orchestra.

Besides music in Leipzig's churches, Bach was involved with the collegium musicum, which met twice a week at Zimmermann's coffee house and which he led from 1729 to 1737 and from 1739 until perhaps 1744.[112] The size of the collegium musicum can be estimated from sets of parts for the Extraordinary Concerts that it put on when the Elector visited Leipzig from Dresden. Bach's secular cantatas for these occasions typically have one or two doublets for the violin parts, as well as for the continuo.[113] The cantatas that he composed for special occasions at the university, again played by the collegium, are transmitted with parts similarly doubled.[114] Thus in secular contexts as well as sacred Bach could assemble enough instrumentalists to make a small orchestra.

Not all Bach's music for the collegium was orchestral. Christoph Wolff has shown that many of his concertos and suites, long thought to have been composed for Cöthen, were probably composed for the Leipzig collegium. None of the concertos, however, has been transmitted with doublets for the ripieno parts. Of course, ripienists might have read two or three to a part; but it seems equally likely that the collegium followed a tradition of one-on-a-part concerto performance. Even more striking are Bach's four *Ouvertüre*, often called "orchestral suites," all composed during the Leipzig years and most likely for the collegium.[115] Again these are transmitted with the minimum number of parts. Overtures 3 and 4 sound particularly grand and "orchestral," but Bach achieves this by multiplying parts rather than multiplying players and by writing orchestral effects into the music, so that his one-on-a-part ensemble sounds more orchestral than it actually is.[116]

[109] Examples of this configuration of parts in Leipzig cantatas include BWV 6, 13, 16, 24, 110, 136, 176, and 187.

[110] Examples of Weimar cantatas with Leipzig doublets include BWV 63 and 185.

[111] See Besseler, *Kritischer Bericht*, 80–81.

[112] Werner Neumann, "Das 'Bachische Collegium Musicum,'" *Bach-Jahrbuch*, 47 (1960), 5–27 at 10.

[113] Examples of secular cantatas with extra parts include BWV 193a, 198, 205a, 206, 207a, 208a, 213, 214, and 215.

[114] Examples include BWV 30a, which was expanded from an earlier cantata, and BWV 207, which opens with a reworking of the third movement of the first Brandenburg Concerto.

[115] Christoph Wolff, "Bach's Leipzig Chamber Music," *EM* 13 (1985), 165–75; Wolff, *Bach: Essays*, 237.

[116] Concerning "orchestral effects," see Ch. 13.

THE STUTTGART ORCHESTRA

The orchestra of the Dukes of Württemberg in Stuttgart provides a vivid example of how the court culture of competitive display brought an orchestra into being and turned that orchestra into one of the most famous ensembles in Europe. It also shows the financial strain that the orchestra and the court music establishment placed on state finances.

An orchestra emerged within the Kapelle at Stuttgart at almost exactly the same moment as it appeared at Dresden and Darmstadt: in the last two decades of the seventeenth century. Again, French influence led the way. A French string band was engaged in 1683 to play for the dance lessons of 7-year-old Duke Eberhard Ludwig and his two sisters.[117] When he assumed personal power in 1693 at the age of 16, Eberhard Ludwig set about building up a Kapelle that could compare with those of his German neighbors and rivals. By 1714 Kapellmeister Johann Pez could boast:

Your Royal Highness . . . will find that all [the musicians] are experienced on 3 or 4 or 5 different types of instruments, and that they also bow in a neat French style, so clear and so unified that I would challenge any other Kapelle in the entire Holy Roman Empire, even one five times bigger than ours, to play any better than we do.[118]

Pez's Kapelle may have been small compared with ensembles at the French court, but by German standards it was relatively large. Table 7.3, based on research by Samantha Owens, shows that by 1714 the Stuttgart Kapelle could field an instrumental ensemble of 19 members, with violins and violas doubled, oboes, a flute, and a pair of horns. In addition, several singers, a court trumpeter, and the court portrait painter could be added to the ensemble when necessary on stringed instruments. Another roster, compiled by Theodore Schwartzkopff in 1717, lists 20 instrumentalists, almost all of them multi-handed, plus 10 trumpeters, many of whom could play stringed instruments as needed (Table 7.3). One of the trumpeters is Elisabeth Schmid, who entered court service at the same time as her father, also a trumpeter. Elisabeth, says Schwartzkopff, "knows how to play a good many pieces on the trumpet, but otherwise understands almost nothing about music."[119]

These multi-handed instrumentalists could be combined into a variety of ensembles to suit any and every occasion. In another memo dated 1717, J. G. C. Störl, the new Kapellmeister, describes different ways in which this Kapelle can be deployed (Table 7.3). "Complete church music" requires 16 instruments: strings plus bassoon, organ, *and* harpsichord.[120] However, notes Störl, for daily services one can get by with

---

[117] Owens, "The Württemberg Hofkapelle," 15.   [118] Quoted ibid. 26–27.

[119] Ibid. 467. Clearly, a female trumpeter was exceptional in 17th- and 18th-c. Germany.

[120] On the simultaneous use of organ and harpsichord in 18th-c. German church music, see Laurence Dreyfus, *Bach's Continuo Group: Players and Practices in his Vocal Works* (Cambridge, Mass., 1987), 68–71.

just strings plus an organ—10 instruments in all.[121] Table music requires 20 instruments, the maximum number, with the violins tripled or quadrupled, two pairs of violas, and pairs of winds.

The buildup of the Kapelle was just one aspect of Eberhard Ludwig's campaign of cultural one-upsmanship. He greatly increased the size of his army. He engaged a troupe of actors to give French comedies. He rebuilt his hunting lodge at Ludwigsburg into one of the largest castles in Europe. There, in imitation of Louis XIV at Versailles, he moved his seat of government, his mistress, and his orchestra.[122] The size of the Württemberg court—ministers, bureaucrats, professionals, craftsmen, servants, et al.—increased geometrically, and so did the cost of their maintenance. Between 1693 and 1718 allowances to members of the Duke's family increased by 63 percent, salaries for court staff (the *Hofstaat*) increased 71 percent, and the expenses of the stable and the hunt increased 136 percent.[123] The cost of the Kapelle rose even more rapidly. Total salaries paid to instrumentalists ballooned from 1,383 Gulden in 1684 to 7,969 Gulden in 1717—an increase of 576 percent.[124]

Expenses far exceeded available income. The court's deficit for 1716 was estimated at 350,000 Gulden; the 1717 deficit was 450,000 Gulden. By 1718 the cumulative deficit had reached 3 million Gulden.[125] Eberhard Ludwig acknowledged the deficit but insisted that it was not his fault. In a memo to the privy council he wrote:

If you had got the treasury office in better order we would never have had this confusion and lamentable administration of our royal finances. . . . We have considered various policies of retrenchment compatible with our royal dignity and great reputation and find nothing more that we can cut back on.[126]

At base, Eberhard Ludwig's argument boiled down to the claim that the demands of cultural competition and the courtly ethos made it intrinsically impossible for a German prince to balance a budget. Modern music demanded larger and larger ensembles, and as the Kapellen of his neighbors grew to meet the demand, Eberhard Ludwig felt he had no choice but to expand his orchestra. By 1731 there were over 30 instrumentalists on the payroll (Table 7.3).

All this changed with the death in 1734 of Eberhard Ludwig and the accession of his cousin Carl Alexander to the throne. A military man, who had served as Prince Eugene of Savoy's assistant, then as governor of newly conquered Serbia, Carl Alexander was determined to bring the costs of cultural competition under control and to introduce efficient adminstration to Württemberg.[127] He suspended Eberhard Ludwig's lavish construction projects and moved the government from the palace at

---

[121] Owens, "The Württemberg Hofkapelle," 290, 469.

[122] James Allen Vann, *The Making of a State: Württemberg, 1593–1793* (Ithaca, NY, 1984), 190.

[123] Ibid. 205.   [124] Figures from Owens, "The Württemberg Hofkapelle," 102, 112, 451.

[125] Vann, *The Making of a State*, 206.   [126] Translated ibid. 207.

[127] Ibid. 216 ff. For a revisionist account of Carl Alexander's character and administration, see Peter H. Wilson, *War, State and Society in Württemberg, 1677–1793* (Cambridge, 1995), 165 ff.

TABLE 7.3. *Instrumentalists in the Stuttgart Kapelle, 1684–1780*

Date	Keyboard and plucked strings	Bowed strings	Winds	Trumpets and drums	Unidentified	Source
1684	2 organs	1 violin 1 basse de violon	1 oboe	4 trumpets 1 drum	6 *Hofmusici*	Owens, "Württtenberg," 102
1702	1 organ	2 violins 1 basse de violon	1 oboe 1 flute 1 bassoon	5 trumpets	12 *Instrumentalisten*	Ibid. 86
1714	1 organ 1 lute	9 violins and violas 1 cello 1 basse de violon 2 violoni	2 oboes 1 flute 2 horns	[trumpets] 1 drum		Ibid. 443 ff.
1717 Personnel Report	3 keyboards 1 theorbo/lute	5 violins 3 violas 1 cello 1 viola da gamba 1 basse de violon 1 violone	3 oboes 2 horns	10 trumpets		Ibid. 462 ff.
1717 Complete Church Music	1 organ 1 harpsichord	6 violins 4 violas 1 cello 1 basse de violon	1 bassoon			Ibid. 288

	Keyboard/continuo	Strings	Winds	Brass/percussion	Other	Source
Table Music	1 harpsichord	4 First violins 3 second violins 2 first violas 2 second violas 1 basse de violon 1 viola da gamba 1 violone	2 oboes 2 horns 1 bassoon			Ibid. 296
1731	1 organ 1 lute	10 violins 1 cello 1 viola da gamba 1 violone	5 oboes 1 flute 1 bassoon 2 horns	7 trumpets 1 drum	4 choirboys	Sittard, *Geschichte . . . würt.*, i. 123
1736	3 organs	6 violins 2 violas 1 cello 1 bass	1 flute 1 oboe 4 horns	8 trumpets 1 drum	9 *Hautboisten* 2 unknown	Owens, "Württenberg," 100
1751	2 organs 1 harpsichord 1 lute	8 violins/violas 2 cellos 3 violoni	1 flute 2 oboes 3 horns	7 trumpets 1 drum		Mahling, "Orchester"
1764	2 organs	21 violins 2 violas 4 cellos 3 double basses	2 flutes 4 oboes 3 horns	8 trumpets 2 drums		Ibid.
1776	1 organ	14 violins 4 violas 5 cellos 4 double basses	4 oboes 3 flutes 2 bassoons 4 horns	4 trumpets 2 drums		Ibid.
1780	2 organs 1 harpsichord	26 violins 5 violas 4 cellos 5 double basses	3 flutes 4 oboes 2 bassoons 4 horns	4 trumpets 2 drums		Ibid.

Ludwigsburg back to Stuttgart. He dissolved the Italian opera company and also the French theater troupe. In April 1734 he gave orders that the entire "church, chamber, and table music" should be dismissed.[128] Somehow, though, nothing much happened. A roster dated 1736 shows that not only did the Kapelle continue to exist, but it contained almost as many instrumentalists as it had in 1731 (Table 7.3).[129] True, the musicians complained in 1737 that their pay had been canceled for two quarters in a row, but they thanked the Duke for keeping them in court service, and they comforted themselves with a promise of payment for the last quarter of the year.[130] When Carl Alexander died suddenly in 1737, most of the instrumentalists who had been on the payroll when he came to power were still members of the court Kapelle.

Carl Alexander was succeeded by his son, Carl Eugen, who inherited his title at the age of 9 and assumed personal power in 1744 at the age of 16. Duke Carl Eugen became one of the great patrons of his age—sponsoring art, architecture, education, theater, dance, and above all music. He also became a symbol for the excesses of absolutism. He imprisoned his political opponents, his critics, and even a few musicians who thwarted his wishes.[131] Carl Eugen's notoriety, although surely deserved, was increased by the fact that Württemberg, unlike other Germany states, had an active Landtag (state assembly), which opposed the Duke's Catholic religion, his lavish lifestyle, his extramarital affairs, and his incessant demands for money. The propaganda of the Landtag served to blacken Carl Eugen's reputation in his own time and for many years to come.

Carl Eugen had spent his teenage years (1741–44) in Berlin at the court of Frederick the Great, where he heard the King's excellent orchestra and acquired a taste for Italian opera. In 1748 he visited Paris, where he was greatly impressed by the court of Louis XV, particularly the redecorated palace at Versailles and the ballet at the Opéra.[132] As his regime got underway, Carl Eugen imitated and even surpassed these models. He hired the French architect Philippe de la Guêpière to build a new palace in Stuttgart, and then to design and build two pleasure retreats: "Solitude" and "Mon Repos." A French theater troupe was engaged, and an Italian opera company was formed with some of the biggest names in Europe, including Francesca Cuzzoni and Giuseppe Aprile. In 1753 Carl Eugen engaged Niccolò Jommelli to be his *maestro di cappella*; in 1760 he hired Jean Georges Noverre to create a *corps de ballet*. In each area of the arts Carl Eugen sought out the best and the brightest and brought them to Stuttgart with promises of high salaries and the prospect of a stimulating artistic environment.

---

[128] Sittard, *Zur Geschichte der Musik und des Theaters*, ii. 4.

[129] Owens, "The Württemberg Hofkapelle," 100.

[130] Sittard, *Zur Geschichte der Musik und des Theaters*, ii. 5.

[131] The soprano Marianne Pirker, a confidante of the Duke's estranged wife, was locked up for eight years (1757–65). C. D. F. Schubart, composer, poet, and journalist, was imprisoned for 10 years.

[132] Adrien Fauchier-Magnan, *Les Petites Cours d'Allemagne au XVIIIème siècle* (Paris, 1947), 169–70.

The opera opened in 1750 on the Duchess's birthday in the old *Lusthaus* in Stuttgart, remodeled to hold 4,000 spectators. The Stuttgart Kapelle, still about the same size as it was when Carl Eugen became Duke, was too small for the hall; extra players had to be brought in from Bayreuth.[133] Carl Eugen set about building up the court Kapelle by his characteristic method of importing star performers. Pasquale Bini, a pupil of Tartini, was brought in as first violin, followed by two more Italian virtuosos, Antonio Lolli and Pietro Nardini. Other violinists included Pietro Martinez, Florian Deller, who composed most of the ballets for Jommelli's operas, and Luigi Baglioni. Wind players included (at various times) the Plà brothers, oboists from Madrid, the Besozzi brothers from Parma, likewise oboists, and J. F. Daube, a flutist and theorbo player. These star performers were designated *Kammervirtuosen*, while long-time Stuttgart instrumentalists remained *Hofmusiker*. The Duke's orchestra garnered praise as one of the best in Europe, but the star system also had its drawbacks. C. D. F. Schubart, who was court keyboardist until the Duke imprisoned him in 1777, commented:

The orchestra at the court of Württemberg was composed of some of the greatest virtuosos in the world—and indeed that was its problem. Each player constituted his own little circle, and conformity to any system was anathema to them all. In ordinary passages one would often hear ornamentation that did not fit in with what the others were playing. An orchestra composed of virtuosos is a world of kings without kingdoms.[134]

By the time a new opera house opened in 1764, the Kapelle numbered 41 members, twice as large as it had been when Carl Eugen became Duke in 1737. The combined salaries of the instrumentalists had increased fivefold, with virtuosos like Lolli and Plà receiving as much money as singers.[135]

This large, modern orchestra, along with the singers, actors, dancers, designers, artisans, costumes, sets, and all the other expenses of Carl Eugen's artistic ambitions, cost much more money than the Duke's private income plus annual subventions from the Landtag could provide. Carl Eugen was obliged to resort to extraordinary measures to raise money: sale of offices, forced loans from government officials, a state lottery with compulsory tickets, and expropriation of the property of political opponents.[136] He mortgaged crown properties to outside lenders, among them the philosopher Voltaire, from whom the Duke borrowed 700,000 Gulden.[137] Another source of money was Louis XV. Under the terms of a treaty signed in 1752, the French king paid Carl Eugen a subsidy of 520,000 Florins per year, in return for which the Duke agreed to equip and maintain 3,000 soldiers to be available to France

---

[133] Alan Yorke-Long, *Music at Court: Four Eighteenth-Century Studies* (London, 1954), 48.

[134] Christian Friedrich Daniel Schubart, *Ideen zu einer Aesthetik der Tonkunst*, ed. Ludwig Schubart (Vienna, 1806), 156.

[135] See Sittard, *Zur Geschichte der Musik und des Theaters*, ii. 10, 194–95.

[136] See Vann, *The Making of a State*, 277.   [137] See ibid. 266.

in the event of war.[138] So long as France remained at peace with her neighbors, the Duke could spend the money as he liked. But when the Seven Years War broke out in 1756, he was forced to enter the war on the side of Austria and France against Frederick the Great. Despite the war and the financial stresses it generated, Carl Eugen maintained his lifestyle for several more years over the increasingly bitter opposition of the Landtag. By 1767, however, Carl Eugen was obliged to begin retrenching. Noverre was dismissed, along with many of the dancers and the entire French theater company.[139] In 1768 several of the principal singers left, and yet more actors and dancers were dismissed. In 1769 Jommelli requested his discharge.

The orchestra too felt the budget-cutter's knife. Burney, who visited Ludwigsburg in 1772, observed the process firsthand:

At present his highness seems oeconomising, having reformed his operas and orchestra, and reduced a great number of old performers to half pay: but, as most musicians have too great souls to live upon their whole pay, be it what it will, this reduction of their pensions is regarded, by the principal of those in the service of this court, as a dismission; so that those who have vendible talents, demand permission to retire, as fast as opportunities offer, for engaging themselves elsewhere.[140]

Several star performers left Stuttgart in this fashion, including the oboist Plà and the violinist Deller. The overall size of the Kapelle was reduced, particularly the violin section, which shrank to 14 by 1776 (see Table 7.3). But once again the Stuttgart Kapelle proved resistant to downsizing. Lolli, Martinez, and many others stayed, and by 1780 the orchestra was as large as it had ever been.

The story of the Stuttgart orchestra shows once again how the orchestra was a product of the politics of absolutism and the culture of competitive display. It also shows what a burden the orchestra and the rest of the Kapelle could be on the finances of the state and ultimately on the populace. Finally, the Stuttgart Kapelle demonstrates the inertia of the orchestra as an institution. Over the course of repeated budget crises, reductions in pay, late wages, and dismissals, the orchestra held its own. Its numbers shrank only to grow again a few years later. And despite the comings and goings of star performers, the same instrumentalists, along with their brothers, sons, and nephews, formed the core of the Stuttgart orchestra for much of the eighteenth century.

THE MANNHEIM ORCHESTRA

The Mannheim orchestra was the most famous German orchestra of its time. Charles Burney, who heard it in 1773, pronounced it "deservedly celebrated throughout

---

[138] See Wilson, *War, State and Society*, 206.   [139] Yorke-Long, *Music at Court*, 64.
[140] Burney, *Present State of Music in Germany*, i. 101.

Europe"; Leopold Mozart called it "indisputably the best in Germany."[141] Other German Kapellen—Dresden, Stuttgart, Berlin—enjoyed high reputations, but Mannheim was the first to become famous specifically as an orchestra rather than as part of a larger musical establishment. The Mannheim orchestra was the creation of two music-loving Electors, Carl Philipp (r. 1716–42) and his nephew Carl Theodor (r. 1742–99). It had a relatively short existence—from 1720, when Carl Philipp established his Residence at Mannheim, until 1778, when Carl Theodor inherited the Electorship of Bavaria and moved the court and much of the orchestra to Munich. The earliest roster of the Mannheim Kapelle, a report from 1723, already shows a modern ensemble based on a large number of violin-family instruments (Table 7.4).

Mannheim was a classic *Residenzstadt*, a town whose principal purpose was the upkeep of the sovereign and the court. The palace was one of the largest in Europe. Streets and houses, newly constructed, were laid out in blocks following a symmetrical plan.[142] Rather than trade or manufacture, most of the town's commerce involved luxuries aimed at the court: textiles, buttons, jewelry, paper, gold and silver, powder and wigs. A large number of soldiers were quartered in town. Burney, accustomed to life in a real city like London, was simultaneously impressed and dismayed: "The expence and magnificence of the court of this little city are prodigious; the palace and offices extend over almost half the town; and one half of the inhabitants, who are in office, prey on the other, who seem to be in the utmost indigence."[143]

That a small principality was able to sustain this level of display for over 50 years without the financial crises typical of other German states may have been due to the fertility and general prosperity of the Palatinate. It can also be attributed to extremely vigorous tax collection by the Electoral bureaucracy. Property tax, inheritance tax, personal tax, excise tax, Jew's tax, fines, tolls, transit tax, and a quasi-compulsory lottery all helped fill the coffers of the state.[144] Adequate revenues, prudent fiscal administration, and vigorous enforcement enabled the Electors of Mannheim to maintain the appearances and the amenities of court life.

For Carl Theodor, a good flutist and occasional cellist, music was among the most important amenities, "the chief and most constant of his electoral highness's amusements," as Burney put it.[145] The Kapelle played for mass and other services in the electoral chapel; it played at the Elector's table; it played for opera at the theater built into the west wing of the palace; it played for spoken theater and ballet; it played for dancing at court balls; it played in the Elector's "cabinet," i.e. his private quarters, and

---

[141] Ibid. 94; Mozart, *Briefe*, i. 79.

[142] Christel Hess, "Mannheimer Alltagsleben im 18. Jahrhundert: Impressionen jenseits höfischer Kultur," in Karin von Welck and Liselotte Homering (eds.), *176 Tage: W. A. Mozart in Mannheim* (Mannheim, 1991), 100–10.

[143] Burney, *Present State of Music in Germany*, i. 83.

[144] Günther Ebersold, *Rokoko, Reform und Revolution: Ein politisches Lebensbild des Kurfürsten Karl Theodor* (Frankfurt am Main, 1985), 32–33.

[145] Burney, *Present State of Music in Germany*, i. 99.

it played more public "chamber" music at "academies" usually held in the Rittersaal, a large, ornate room in the center of the palace.[146] Academies featured vocal and instrumental soloists—sometimes members of the Kapelle, sometimes visitors like Mozart—but they also highlighted the Mannheim orchestra itself, which played opening and closing symphonies, usually composed by orchestra members. The importance of these academies seems to have increased as the years went by. During the early years of Carl Theodor's reign, they seem to have been occasional and held at the Elector's pleasure, but by around 1768 they had increased to a regular, twice-a-week schedule: Wednesdays or Thursdays and Saturdays. Mannheim, notes Eugene Wolf, distinguished itself from other courts of the time by "the emergence of the orchestra as a status symbol comparable to the opera."[147]

This does not mean that the orchestra was the only or even the principal attraction at a Mannheim academy. A report by a traveler in 1785 gives the flavor of the occasion:

This evening these was an academy, or, to use a more appropriate term, a concert at court. . . . Above us and to the right of the windows card tables had been set up, and to the left was the space for the orchestra, raised somewhat off the floor and encircled with a railing. After six o'clock the court entered, the elector and electress, the dowager electress of Bavaria, and the ladies-in-waiting and cavaliers. Then the music began and at the same time everyone began to play cards. . . . There was such a crush of people that I at first despaired of getting through to see their Highnesses up close. But then I decided, together with some *abbés*, to endure and also mete out some elbows in the ribs, and in this manner we finally came close to the two princely tables. And what did I see there? The Kurfürst, and he was wearing a new suit of clothes. . . . The Electresses, who were my real object, were seated so that I was unable to see their faces. . . . So I waited patiently and listened in the meantime to the orchestra.[148]

The Mannheim orchestra was an important part of the event for this anonymous traveler; but the display of the court to the public was the real show.

Table 7.4, based on the research of Eugene Wolf, shows the development of the Mannheim orchestra over almost the entire term of its existence. Eliminating pensioners, who appeared on the roster but did not play, and musicians known to be on leave, Wolf's figures represent the number of instrumentalists actually available for performance in a given year.[149] The most obvious change in the orchestra is its

---

[146] Eugene K. Wolf, "The Mannheim Court," in Neal Zaslaw (ed.), *The Classical Era* (Englewood Cliffs, NJ, 1989), 213–39.

[147] Ibid. 220.

[148] Original in Bärbel Pelker, "Musikalische Akademien am Hof Carl Theodors in Mannheim," in Ludwig Finscher (ed.), *Die Mannheimer Hofkapelle im Zeitalter Carl Theodors* (Mannheim, 1992), 49–58 at 54 ff. Translation adapted from Wolf, "On the Composition," 226 ff. This description dates from a time after the court had moved to Munich and most of the orchestra had been transferred. The court was in Mannheim on a visit.

[149] See Wolf, "On the Composition," 115 ff. Most of Wolf's adjustments decrease the size of the orchestra. He notes, however, that he does not count trumpeters, who, he says, played stringed instruments when necessary and could have increased the number of available musicians. Trumpeters paid as members of the Kapelle are listed in both the "trumpet and drum" and "winds" columns in Table 7.4.

growth over time. After a dip in the 1730s and 1740s, the numbers increase rapidly during the 1750s, then more gradually to the end of the period. The decrease in the 1730s and 1740s was due perhaps to Carl Philipp's preoccupation with the construction of the new palace, perhaps also to the War of the Austrian Succession (1740–48). The growth in the 1750s seems to reflect Carl Theodor's effort to increase the importance of music in his court. Just as significant as the rise in numbers, Wolf shows, is the increase in the number of violins as a proportion of the ensemble. Wolf suggests that this change in balances may have been the result of Johann Stamitz's visit in 1754–55 to Paris, where he heard large orchestras at the Opéra and the Concert spirituel.[150]

These numbers and these proportions represent instrumentalists available in the Kapelle, not the orchestra as it appeared at any actual performance. The size of the orchestra in performance was a function of the venue and the character of the event. For church music in the Elector's chapel on important feast days the orchestra seems to have consisted of the full Kapelle or close to it. Mozart, in a letter of 4 November 1777, described the orchestra for mass on All Saints' Day: "The orchestra is very good and large. There are 10 or 11 violins on either side, four violas, two oboes, two flutes, and two clarinets, two horns, four cellos, four bassoons, and four double basses, also trumpets and drums."[151] These numbers correspond closely to the entire Kapelle in the rosters of 1777 and 1778. Only a few winds, notably horns, seem to have been left out. Surviving sets of parts for masses by Ignaz Holzbauer and Carlo Grua composed during the 1750s suggest that they were performed by orchestras that included most of the instrumentalists in the Kapelle. On the other hand, sets of parts for symphonies by Cannabich, performed at academies, suggest somewhat smaller orchestras: 10 to 16 violins, two or three on the remaining string parts, and pairs of winds. This amounts to something like 70–80 percent of the full Kapelle, playing in the Rittersaal. Other venues—for example daily church services—may have used much smaller ensembles, but records have not survived. There is no evidence at Mannheim—nor indeed anywhere else in Germany during the eighteenth century—of anything like a *Dienstplan* or systematic rotation where half of the orchestra played one day, the other half another.[152]

Like Carl Eugen's Stuttgart Kapelle, the Mannheim orchestra included a number of star instrumentalists, players who had achieved international reputations as soloists and virtuosos. Some of them were recruited to Mannheim from other Kapellen. But many of the stars came up through the ranks of the Mannheim Kapelle itself. Christian Cannabich, whose father played flute at Mannheim, joined the orchestra as a violinist at age 13 and took over from Stamitz as Konzertmeister in 1757. Violinists Ignaz Fränzl and Friedrich Johann Eck both began playing in the orchestra (without

---

[150] See Wolf, "On the Composition," 124.   [151] Mozart, *Briefe*, ii. 101.
[152] Wolf, "On the Composition," 124–25, 136.

TABLE 7.4. *Instrumentalists in the Mannheim Kapelle, 1723–78*

Date	Keyboard and plucked strings	Bowed strings	Winds	Trumpets and drums	Source
1723	2 organs 1 theorbo 2 lutes	12 violins 3 violas 2 cellos 3 double basses	9 *Hautboisten* 2 bassoons 3 horns	11 trumpets 2 drums	Wolf, "On the Composition," 118
1736	2 organs 1 theorbo 1 lute	6 violins 2 violas 3 cellos 2 double basses	5 *Hautboisten* 3 bassoons 5 horns	13 trumpets 2 drums	Ibid.
1744	2 organs 2 lutes	9 violins and violas 2 cellos 2 double basses	2 flutes 2 oboes 1 bassoon 5 horns	13 trumpets 2 drums	Ibid.
1748	2 organs 1 lute	15 violins 2 violas 5 cellos 2 double basses	2 flutes 2 oboes 2 bassoons 3 horns	13 trumpets 2 drums	Ibid.
1756	2 organs	11 first violins 9 second violins 4 violas 4 cellos	2 flutes 2 oboes 3 bassoons 4 horns	[13 trumpets] [2 drums]	Marpurg, *Beyträge*, ii. 567

Year		Strings	Winds	Brass/Percussion	Source
1763	2 organs	24 violins 4 violas 4 cellos 2 double basses	3 flutes 3 oboes 2 clarinets 3 bassoons 6 horns [4 trumpets]	13 trumpets 2 drums	Wolf, 118
1770	2 organs	19 violins 4 violas 3 cellos 3 double basses	3 flutes 3 oboes 4 clarinets 4 bassoons 7 horns [4 trumpets]	13 trumpets 2 drums	Ibid.
1778	2 organs	25 violins 3 violas 4 cellos 3 double basses	4 flutes 3 oboes 3 clarinets 4 bassoons 6 horns	13 trumpets 2 drums	Ibid.

pay) at age 11. C. J. Toeschi and Wilhelm Cramer, also violinists, likewise joined the orchestra as children and came up through the ranks to become virtuoso performers. Elector Carl Theodor gave stipends to promising young players to study in Italy and elsewhere, and he sponsored virtuoso tours by his star instrumentalists. Unlike the Stuttgart stars, whose wages were often in arrears and who moved on to other courts when times got tough, the careers of most of the Mannheim virtuosos seem to have been relatively stable. Roland Würtz argues that Mannheim musicians had it better than members of other German Kapellen: their salaries were relatively high; they were paid on time; they received pensions when they retired; many of them owned their own homes.[153]

Because many of the string players were trained at Mannheim and because most of them remained in the orchestra for long periods, the Mannheim Kapelle achieved a level of execution that seems to have been unusual among German orchestras. C. D. F. Schubart credited it to Cannabich's leadership: "He . . . has the ability to keep even the largest orchestra in order with a mere nod of his head or a gesture of his elbow. Really, it is he who has created the evenness of execution that prevails in the Mannheim orchestra."[154] Charles Burney, in an oft-quoted passage, attributed good execution to orchestral discipline, which enabled a large number of instrumentalists to play together with both strength and subtlety:

I cannot quit this article, without doing justice to the orchestra of his electoral highness, so deservedly celebrated throughout Europe. I found it to be indeed all that its fame had made me expect: power will naturally arise from a great number of hands; but the judicious use of this power, in all occasions, must be the consequence of good discipline; indeed there are more solo players and good composers in this, than perhaps in any other orchestra in Europe; it is an army of generals, equally fit to plan a battle, as to fight it.[155]

Among the "good composers" who were members of the Mannheim orchestra were Johann Stamitz, Christian Cannabich, C. J. Toeschi, Anton Fils, Ignaz Fränzl, Anton and Carl Stamitz. Together they created a repertory designed specifically to be played by the Mannheim orchestra, mainly symphonies for the Elector's academies, but also concertos, chamber music, operas, and church music. Their music, exploiting the discipline, balance, dynamic range, and virtuoso abilities of the orchestra, was much published, much played, and much imitated. Symphonies by Mannheim composers exerted a strong influence on the development of a specifically orchestral compositional style.

---

[153] Roland Würtz, "Die Organisation der Mannheimer Hofkapelle," in Finscher (ed.), *Die Mannheimer Hofkapelle im Zeitalter Carl Theodors*, 37–48 at 46. On home ownership by Mannheim musicians, see Gabriele Busch-Salmen, " '. . . Auch Unter dem Tache die feinsten Wohnungen': Neue Dokumente zu Socialstatus und Wohnsituation der Mannheimer Hofmusiker," in Finscher (ed.), *Die Mannheimer Hofkapelle im Zeitalter Carl Theodors*, 21–35.

[154] Schubart, *Ideen zu einer Aesthetik der Tonkunst*, 137.

[155] Burney, *Present State of Music in Germany*, i. 95.

Chapter Eight

The Orchestra in England

PATRONAGE AND THE PUBLIC

The orchestra in England, as elsewhere in Europe, arose in the second half of the seventeenth century in the context of a royal court. But in England the orchestra was far less a creature of the court and of aristocratic culture than it was in Italy, France, or Germany. The English court and its culture were decisively interrupted by the Puritan revolution and the Commonwealth. When the King returned and the court resumed in 1660, he was constrained by the continuing divisions between Catholic and Protestant, Whig and Tory, City and Court, and by the continuing vigilance that Parliament exercised over the budget. King Charles II, like his mentor and financial backer, Louis XIV, had Twenty-Four Violins, but they played in the theaters and at public concerts as well as at court. With the Glorious Revolution in 1688, the role of the Court in the development of the orchestra became even less important. No longer was the orchestra's primary function to display the power of the King and the glamor of his court. In the eighteenth century orchestras in England came to be patronized by and to express the values of a broad public, made up of people from several social classes.

Aristocratic patronage too was less important to the orchestra in England than it was in continental Europe—or at least it took different forms. Unlike German princes or Italian cardinals, few English aristocrats maintained private orchestras. James Brydges, Earl of Carnarvon and later Duke of Chandos, who made his fortune as army paymaster during the wars of the Spanish Succession, maintained a music establishment on a Continental scale on his estate at Cannons for a few years around 1720, hiring leading singers and instrumentalists of the time as members of his "household."[1] Brydges's

---

[1] Graydon Beeks, "Handel and Music for the Earl of Carnarvon," in Peter Williams (ed.), *Bach, Handel, Scarlatti: Tercentenary Essays* (Cambridge, 1985), 1–20. For the composition of the orchestra at Cannons, see Table 8.1.

most famous employee was Handel, who was in the Duke's service from 1718 to 1720 and composed the Chandos Anthems, *Acis and Galatea,* and the oratorio *Esther* for performance at Cannons. A musical establishment on this scale was unusual for an English aristocrat. Other English lords maintained one or two performers as their guests for limited periods of time. Lord Burlington, for example, brought Pietro Castrucci to England from Rome in 1715 and launched the Italian violinist on an English career. The Duke of Rutland brought Carbonelli, another Roman violinist, to England in 1719.[2] In 1766–67 Peter Beckford, the heir to a West Indies sugar fortune, heard the 14-year-old Muzio Clementi play the harpsichord brilliantly in Rome and bought him from his father for seven years' indentured service, during which period he kept the talented lad as his private musician on his country estate. None of these patrons, however, except for Brydges, maintained anything like an orchestra. When they wanted music on an orchestral scale, they hired instrumentalists for the occasion.

More important to the development of the orchestra than individual patronage was patronage by the aristocracy as a class. Groups of aristocrats formed joint stock companies to build theaters, like Dorset Garden, Drury Lane, and the King's Theatre in the Haymarket. The Royal Academy of Music, which reestablished Italian opera in London in 1720, was set up as a joint stock venture that pooled (and eventually lost) the money of its aristocratic directors.[3] The "Opera of the Nobility" in 1733 and Lord Middlesex's operatic venture in 1739 were funded in a similar manner.[4] The most important mechanism of aristocratic patronage was the subscription system, in which a number of patrons paid in advance for an opera season or a series of concerts, providing up-front capital in return for future admission. During the eighteenth century the Italian opera and many concerts were financed by subscription. The King himself subscribed to the opera, the oratorios, and sometimes to concert series.[5] The King usually subscribed at a higher rate than other patrons, but unlike Continental monarchs, he did not own the theater or the concert hall or the orchestra. He paid for music just like other people.

To hear an orchestra in seventeenth- and eighteenth-century England one did not have to invest in a joint stock company or subscribe to the opera. In most cases one could simply buy a ticket—to the theater, to a benefit concert, or to one of London's pleasure gardens, several of which had standing orchestras. Music formed an import-

[2] Philip H. Highfill Jr. et al., *A Biographical Dictionary of Actors, Actresses, Musicians, Dancers, Managers and Other Stage Personnel in London, 1660–1800* (Carbondale, Ill., 1973–93), iii. 104, 54.

[3] Elizabeth Gibson, "The Royal Academy of Music (1719–28) and its Directors," in Stanley Sadie and Anthony Hicks (eds.), *Handel Tercentenary Collection* (Ann Arbor, 1985), 138–64; Judith Milhous and Robert D. Hume, "New Light on Handel and the Royal Academy of Music in 1720," *Theatre Journal,* 35 (1983), 149–67.

[4] Robert D. Hume, "Handel and Opera Management in London in the 1730s," *M & L* 67 (1986), 347–62; Carole Taylor, "From Losses to Lawsuit: Patronage of the Italian Opera in London by Lord Middlesex, 1739–45," *M & L* 68 (1987), 1–25.

[5] See Donald Burrows and Robert D. Hume, "George I, the Haymarket Opera Company and Handel's Water Music," *EM* 19 (1991), 323–41.

ant part of the process that J. H. Plumb has called the "commercialisation of leisure."[6] Leisure activities in England were increasingly set apart from work activities and marketed as fashion, pleasure, sport, or entertainment, to be consumed by an ever broader public. To the extent that access to orchestral music could be had for the price of a ticket, orchestras became one more leisure commodity, competing with other commodities for the consumer's discretionary income.[7] Thus, patronage for orchestras in England extended beyond the royalty and aristocracy to include people whom Daniel Defoe in 1709 called "the middle sort": gentry, merchants, professionals, tradesmen, and others.[8] Increasingly over the course of the eighteenth century theater managers, concert promoters, and pleasure garden proprietors marketed orchestras to this broader public, advertising their product in the press, selling tickets by subscription, at shops, or even at the door.

The breadth of patronage for the orchestra and the orchestra's integration into a culture of commercialized leisure were unique in the eighteenth century to England. There was public opera in Italy; there were subscription concerts in Germany; there were concert societies in France. On the Continent, however, the bulk of patronage, the enduring and decisive patronage, came from the court and from the upper aristocracy, and the orchestra expressed and reflected the values of this class. In England orchestras depended on the public and the market. Yet despite this difference in social basis, English orchestras resembled their Continental cousins in all essential respects. They came into being at the same time as orchestras in the rest of Europe; they used the same instruments; they played the same music; performance practices were similar or identical. Yet although the orchestra in England looked the same as it did in the rest of Europe, it meant something different. In England the orchestra signified the access that wealth and prosperity could provide to the finer and grander things in life.

THE KING'S MUSICK

Before the middle of the seventeenth century large instrumental ensembles in England existed mainly at court. Records from the early sixteenth century document large numbers of singers and trumpeters in the King's employ, plus a few "Sackbuts and Shalmeys." By Henry VIII's reign an ensemble of "Fluttes" had been added, as well as two string ensembles, the "old vialles," who had been on the payroll since perhaps as early as 1515, and the "newe vialles," Italian Jews recruited from Venice in 1540. These ensembles worked for a succession of Tudor monarchs, performing at

---

[6] John H. Plumb, *The Commercialisation of Leisure in Eighteenth-Century England* (Reading, 1973). See also Peter Burke, "The Invention of Leisure in Early Modern Europe," *Past and Present*, 146 (1995), 136–50.

[7] Deborah Rohr, *The Careers of British Musicians, 1750–1850: A Profession of Artisans* (Cambridge, 2001), 53.

[8] Daniel Defoe, *The Review* (25 June 1709), quoted in George Rudé, *Hanoverian London: 1714–1808* (Berkeley, 1971), 37.

meals, for dancing, for theatricals, and at coronations, weddings, and funerals. The "new viols" may have performed on violins as well. Already under Queen Elizabeth they were referred to as "the violins" in court records, and the size of the group increased somewhat during her reign—from six at her coronation in 1558 to nine in 1598.[9]

Under Charles I an order of 1631 "concerning the musicians for the violins" divided 14 players as follows:

3 Trebles
2 Contratenor
3 Tenor
2 Low tenor
4 Basso.[10]

This looks very much like the five-part string bands at the French court during the same period (see Ch. 3). Indeed, several French violinists came to work at the English court, in the 1620s and 1630s. In addition to the Violins, the King's Musick under Charles I included the "Trumpets," the "Lutes, Violls, and Voices," who played in the King's chambers, and the "Winds," which included shawms, sackbuts, curtals, flutes, and other instruments. A roster of 1641 lists a total of 85 instrumentalists on the royal payroll, plus an instrument maker, an organ tuner, a virginal tuner, and a lute stringer.[11]

For dinner music and for services in the King's Chapel, the Winds were organized in 1633 into a rotation, so that six musicians played one week, another six the next week.[12] This strongly suggests one-on-a-part performance. The Violins, on the other hand, seem to have played with several on a part. Pay records from masques put on between 1611 and 1613 suggest that an ensemble of 10 violins played at rehearsals. For performances, even more players were added, making the ensemble considerably larger and implying heavy, perhaps unequal, part doubling. Orazio Busino, a Venetian diplomat, reported that "violins to the number of twenty-five or thirty" accompanied Ben Jonson's *Pleasure Reconciled to Virtue* in 1618.[13]

The growth of instrumental ensembles at Court was interrupted by the Puritan Revolution of 1640, the ensuing Civil War (1642–48), and the Commonwealth (1649–60). The King's Violins, along with the Chapel Royal and the rest of the King's Music, were dissolved and their members forced to find other employment. The Interregnum, however, did not stop all development of the orchestra. Oliver

---

[9] Henry Cart de LaFontaine, *The King's Musick* (London, 1909), 2–3, 5–8, 12–13; Holman, *Four and Twenty Fiddlers*, 75, 78 ff., 89, 110.

[10] Andrew Ashbee, *Records of English Court Music* (Aldershot, 1986–96), iii. 59.

[11] LaFontaine, *The King's Musick*, 110–11; Ashbee, *Records*, iii. 112–14.

[12] LaFontaine, *The King's Musick*, 87; Ashbee, *Records*, iii. 74. For "solemne feasts and collar days of the yeere" the entire wind band played together.

[13] Quoted in Holman, *Four and Twenty Fiddlers*, 182–84.

Cromwell, as Lord Protector, maintained a court at Whitehall and kept several violinists on his payroll.[14] When he wanted larger ensembles, he hired extra musicians, probably former members of the King's violins, many of whom still lived in London. A report on the wedding of Cromwell's daughter in 1658 says that "they had 48 violins, 50 trumpets and much mirth with frolics, besides mixt dancing (a thing heretofore accounted profane) till 5 of the clock."[15] If there really were 48 violins, it seems unlikely that they all played in a single ensemble; but even assuming a division into two bands of 24, these would have been ensembles that rivaled those of the Stuart court.

The masque tradition also continued, now no longer at court but in private venues. *Cupid and Death*, a masque by James Shirley with music by Christopher Gibbons and Matthew Locke, was performed for the Portuguese ambassador in 1653 and again on the Military Ground in Leicester Fields in 1659.[16] The instrumental ensemble that played is not recorded, but the score contains dances in two and in three parts that seem intended for violin-family instruments. For Davenant's *Siege of Rhodes* (1656/1659), more of an opera than a masque, the instruments are documented: three violins or violas, a bass viol, a theorbo, and a harpsichord.[17]

The most enduring effect of the Interregnum on the development of the orchestra in England was that it prevented instrumental music from establishing itself in church. By an ordinance of 1644 Parliament ordered church organs destroyed (although by no means all were); organists, singers, and church musicians were dismissed from their jobs. Concerted sacred music with winds and strings, which was just becoming fashionable on the Continent, was not introduced in England until after the Restoration, and even then it was performed mainly for ceremonial occasions at Court. Throughout the eighteenth century instrumental music remained relatively unimportant in English churches. The Anglican Church, even the cathedrals and the Chapel Royal, maintained only small instrumental ensembles; Presbyterian and Nonconformist churches discouraged instruments. Churches in England never provided the training or steady employment for instrumentalists that they did on the Continent.

In Charles Burney's view it was Charles II at the Restoration who laid the foundation for the orchestra in England:

The use of the violin and its kindred instruments, the tenor and the violoncello, in court, was doubtless brought from Italy to France to England; for Charles II, who, during the Usurpation, had spent a considerable time on the Continent, where he heard nothing but French Music, upon his return to England, in imitation of Lewis XIV, established a band of

---

[14] Ibid. 267; Percy A. Scholes, *The Puritans and Music in England and New England* (London, 1934), 148–49.

[15] Letter of 14 Nov. 1658 from William Dugdale to John Langley, quoted ibid. 144.

[16] Matthew Locke and Christopher Gibbons, *Cupid and Death*, ed. Edward J. Dent (London, 1951).

[17] Holman, "Thomas Baltzar," 5.

violins, tenors and basses, instead of the viols, lutes and cornets, of which the court band used to consist.[18]

Peter Holman has shown convincingly that violin-family instruments were established well before the English Revolution and that French violinists and the French style of playing were already familiar in England.[19] Contemporary commentators agreed with Burney, however, that the Restoration brought a decisive change in instrumental music at the English Court. Roger North, a young law clerk in the 1670s, complained that Charles II "after the manner of France . . . set up a band of 24 violins to play at his dinners, which disbanded all the old English musick at once."[20] Anthony Wood, amateur musician and diarist at Oxford, observed that viols fell out of fashion after the return of Charles II because "the king according to the French mode would have 24 violins playing before him, while he was at meales, as being more airie and brisk than viols."[21] In fact nine new violinists were appointed in 1660 "by his Majesty to increase the number of his violins."[22] Added to the 15 members of the pre-war King's Violins, this made twenty-four, the number enshrined by the practice of the French court. The Twenty-four Violins, as they were now called in court records, began to encroach on the duties and the prerogatives of the other branches of the King's Musick. Violins instead of wind instruments played at the King's dinners; bowed-string instruments began to accompany the singers at the King's Chapel. Budget lines of the Musick were taken away from lutes, viols, and voices to fund positions for the Violins.[23] Although the old ensembles survived until the reign of James II, they were increasingly displaced in day-to-day service and in public perception by the Twenty-four Violins.

At important state occasions the Twenty-four Violins played together as a single unit. In the elaborate pageant that welcomed Charles II to London in 1661 the "Band of twenty four violins" was placed atop a triumphal arch representing a "Temple of Concord."[24] The Violins then moved to Westminster Abbey, where they played at the coronation service, and to Westminster Hall, where they accompanied a banquet.[25] Samuel Pepys, who was a spectator at the banquet, reports that there was "Musique of all sorts; but above all the 24 viollins."[26] At the next coronation, that of James II in 1685, there were 35 instrumentalists, the 24 violins, plus some retirees and a few wind and keyboard players. An engraving of the event (Fig. 8.1) shows about

[18] Burney, *A General History of Music*, ii. 407.   [19] Holman, *Four and Twenty Fiddlers*, 230–36.

[20] Roger North, *Roger North on Music*, ed. John Wilson (London, 1959), 300.

[21] Anthony Wood, *The Life and Times of Anthony Wood, Antiquary, of Oxford, 1632–1695, Described by Himself*, ed. Andrew Clark (Oxford, 1891), i. 212.

[22] Ashbee, *Records*, i. 29. Holman notes that one of the nine newly appointed violinists, the composer Matthew Locke, may not have played the violin (Holman, *Four and Twenty Fiddlers*, 284).

[23] Holman, *Four and Twenty Fiddlers*, 286.

[24] Eric Halfpenny, "The 'Entertainment' of Charles II," *M & L* 38 (1957), 32–44 at 34. Other arches along the parade route were staffed by musicians from the King's trumpets, the King's Winds, and the City waits.

[25] Ashbee, *Records*, i. 15–16.

[26] Samuel Pepys, *The Diary of Samuel Pepys*, ed. Robert Latham and William Matthews (Berkeley, 1970–74), ii. 86.

FIG. 8.1. The coronation of James II at Westminster Abbey, 1685 (detail)

twenty musicians, most of them string players, squeezed into a gallery high on the wall of Westminster Abbey. A single oboist (or shawm player) can be seen in the front row. In another gallery on the opposite side (not shown) several singers with part-books are led by a timebeater. An engraving of the banquet that followed depicts about 20 musicians, all of them playing violin-family instruments.[27]

One of the most magnificent and best-documented performances by the King's Musick during the Restoration was *Calisto; or, The Chaste Nymph*, a masque given at Whitehall in 1675, with music by Nicholas Staggins. It seems as though there were two instrumental ensembles in *Calisto*. Onstage a series of old-fashioned, symbolic ensembles appeared in costume: a band of violins and guitars, a martial ensemble of trumpets and drums, and a pastoral ensemble of oboes. In front of the stage was a newer, more "orchestral" ensemble, consisting of violins, recorders, harpsichords, and theorbos. Of players identified as "violins" in the two ensembles, about half were members of the King's 24; the rest must have been hired for the occasion.[28]

In other performance contexts the 24 Violins were broken down into smaller ensembles. In 1662 the King ordered John Banister "to instruct and direct twelve persons . . . chosen by him out of the 24 of the band of violins, for better performance of service, without being mixed with the other violins, unless the King orders the 24."[29] Banister's Select Band may be regarded as an English cousin of Lully's "Petite Bande," except that it was formed by splitting the 24 Violins rather than setting up a parallel ensemble.[30] When two patent theater companies were created in the 1660s, 12 of the 24 Violins were designated to play at the King's Theater in Bridges Street, Drury Lane, the other 12 to play for the Duke of York's company at Lincoln's Inn Fields. In 1668 this platoon principle was extended to all aspects of the Violins' service. Two lists were drawn up of 12 musicians each, and they were instructed to "wayt and attend upon his Ma[jes]ty as they are here sett down, twelve one month and twelve ye other till further ord[e]r."[31] Thus, although the 24 Violins existed official-ly as one administrative and performing unit, it seems that in most situations they per-formed as two ensembles of 12.

One reason for the rotation of the violins may have been lack of money.[32] The King's violins, like Continental Kapellen, received both yearly wages and in-kind payments of food and clothing. However, because Parliament controlled his budget, Charles II was chronically short of money, and the wages of his musicians fell further and further in arrears. State papers from the 1660s are filled with remonstrances from

---

[27] Francis Sandford, *The History of the Coronation of the Most High, Most Mighty, and Excellent Monarch, James II* (London, 1687), 30.

[28] Andrew W. Walkling, "Masque and Politics at the Restoration Court: John Crowne's *Calisto,*" EM 24 (1996), 27–62.

[29] Ashbee, *Records*, viii. 152. [30] On Lully's Petite Bande, see Ch. 3.

[31] Ashbee, *Records*, i. 59, 61, 83; Locke, *The Rare Theatrical*, ed. Holman, pp. xvii–xviii; Holman, *Four and Twenty Fiddlers*, 297–98.

[32] Holman, *Four and Twenty Fiddlers*, 352 and *passim*.

the 24 Violins individually and as a group for back wages. "Yo[u]r Ma[jes]ties Musitians for the Violins, whose names are subscribed," reads a petition of 1666

are in Arreare of their Sallaryes at the Treasury Chamber fower yeares and three quarters. And . . . severall of your Ma[jes]ties pet[itione]rs have had their houses and Goods burnt by the late Fire [the Great Fire of 1666], which hath reduced them to great misery and want.[33]

In the absence of regular wages, the musicians supplemented their incomes by playing in the theaters, giving concerts, and playing for dances. John Banister, leader for a time of the 24 Violins, presented concerts at his house in Whitefriars and elsewhere beginning in 1672, for which he charged one shilling admission.[34] Thomas Britton, a coal merchant, offered concerts at his shop from 1678 until 1714. Banister's and Britton's concerts regularly featured members of the 24 Violins, as did the "Musick Meetings" at the York Rooms beginning in the 1680s. By the 1690s the London papers were full of advertisements for concerts, many of them featuring performances by the King's musicians.[35] In almost all cases, however, they played as soloists, in small ensembles, or as accompaniment for singers, not as a band. The only concert that featured a large instrumental ensemble was John Banister's "Parley of Instruments" at Lincoln's Inn Fields in 1676. The Parley featured songs accompanied by harp, lutes, and guitars as well as consorts of viols, violins, and winds, and concluded with "one great Compound" in which all the instruments played together. After the show there was a ball, where "persons of Quality . . . shall have twenty Violins to attend them." So large a band must have consisted of all or most of the 24 Violins, augmented perhaps by other members of the King's Musick in what Holman calls "a mass exercise in moonlighting by court musicians."[36]

The theaters too provided employment for the King's musicians. The lutenists, trumpeters, and fiddlers who appeared onstage seem to have been actors and other members of the theater companies.[37] However, the theaters also used bands of professional musicians, mostly string players. Samuel Chappuzeau, a French visitor in 1667, reported that London playhouses usually had "no less than 12 violins for the opening music and between the acts."[38] This report matches the groups of 12 from the 24 Violins assigned to play in the theaters in 1665.[39]

---

[33] Ashbee, *Records*, viii. 177. See also 171, 173, 191, 198, and *passim*.

[34] Robert Elkin, *The Old Concert Rooms of London* (London, 1955), 18–22.

[35] See Michael Tilmouth, "A Calendar of References to Music in Newspapers Published in London and the Provinces, 1660–1719," *RMA Research Chronicle*, 1 (1961), 1–107.

[36] Holman, *Four and Twenty Fiddlers*, 351–52.

[37] Price, "Restoration Stage Fiddlers and their Music," 72 ff.

[38] *L'Europe vivante* (1667), 215, quoted ibid. 267.

[39] It is not known how long the King's Violins continued to staff the theaters on an official basis. By the 1690s the theaters were evidently hiring standing ensembles of their own, although members of the King's Music still moonlighted in the theaters on occasion. See Peter Holman, "Purcell's Orchestra," *MT* 137 (1996), 17–23 at 22.

Plays acted at Court required a larger ensemble. An order from the Lord Chamberlain in 1676 stipulates that "his Majesty's four and twenty violins should attend his Majesty every night that a play is acted at Court." Musicians who ignored the order were threatened with suspension. But some of the King's Violins seem to have had more pressing engagements, for later that year Jeffrey Ayleworth and three other musicians had their wages stopped "for neglecting their duty in attending at the play acted before his Majesty at Whitehall on Tuesday night last." Perhaps the four wayward musicians were moonlighting at the theater or at a concert that night. Suspension of wages was something of an idle threat, since, as the musicians complained earlier that same year: "warrants belonging to them remain unsatisfied in the Exchequer." At the end of James II's reign back wages were due to all 24 of the King's Violins.[40]

THE BIRTH OF THE ORCHESTRA

The orchestra was "born" in England between about 1685 and 1715. This was the period during which the traits that came to characterize the orchestra took hold, in particular the multiplication of violins, the substitution of cellos and double basses for bass violins and bass viols, the integration of winds into the ensemble, and the consolidation of the ensemble in a single location. The orchestra was born in other European countries during just the same period—in Rome, in northern Italy, in Germany and Austria, and (slightly earlier) in France. To a certain extent the birth of the orchestra in England can be considered as the result of Continental "influence." French, Italian, and German musicians came to England during these years, bringing their compositions, styles, and performance practices with them. However, the violin band tradition was already strong in England, and the personnel and repertory of the emerging orchestra were largely English.

One Continental influence was the introduction from France of newly redesigned wind instruments: recorders, oboes, and bassoons, with narrower bores, separate joints, larger ranges, and more flexible intonation than the old shawms and curtals. In 1673 four French wind players arrived in England with the composer and producer Robert Cambert, whose ambition was to found an English Royal Academy of Music.[41] In *Ariane ou le mariage de Bacchus*, the Academy's first and last production, the four instrumentalists appeared onstage as "several hoboyes belonging to Bacchus."[42] Cambert returned to France, but the "hoboyes" stayed in England, where they played in several more dramatic productions, eventually turning up on the payroll of

---

[40] Ashbee, *Records*, i. 182, 196; ii. 202; viii. 224.

[41] Christina Bashford, "Perrin and Cambert's *Ariana, ou Le Mariage de Bacchus* Re-Examined," M&L, 72 (1991), 1–26.

[42] Lasocki, "Professional Recorder Playing," 183. On Cambert's career in France and the earlier history of *Ariane*, see Ch. 3.

the King's Musick, and also at theaters and in concerts, playing oboes, recorders, and bassoons.[43] At first the winds seem to have played as a separate ensemble, often onstage and in costume as in *Ariane*. By the 1680s, however, the new winds were playing alongside the strings in the main ensemble, either doubling the violins and basses or playing obbligato parts.[44] The original immigrants were joined in the following decades by other French wind players and also by Englishmen, probably converted shawm players from the City waits.[45] From the 1690s on the orchestras in the patent theaters included at least two oboists (doubling on recorders) and one or more bassoons. The transverse flute did not arrive in England (as the "flûte allemande") until around 1700.

The cello and the double bass were also introduced to England by Continental musicians. The standard bass instrument in English string bands during most of the seventeenth century was probably a bass violin tuned a step below the modern cello, the equivalent of the French basse de violon.[46] The first mention in England of the cello—a smaller bass violin, tuned C–G–D–A—seems to be a list of instrumentalists proposed for the Haymarket theater in 1707, which mentions four "violoncelli."[47] Perhaps some of the four actually played the bass violin or violone, but Nicola Haym, at the head of the list, was a well-known cellist, a Roman who had been brought to England by the Duke of Bedford in 1702. Other Italian cellists who came to London in the early eighteenth century included Filippo (Pippo) Amadei, Charles Pardini, and Pietro Chaboud. The first double bass player in London was also an Italian: Giuseppe Saggione, who arrived in England around 1702 and is listed in the orchestras at the Queen's Theatre as playing "double base."[48] By the 1720s the double bass was usually played by English performers, though many cellists were still Italians.

One more instrument that became a regular part of the English orchestra at the end of the seventeenth century was the trumpet. Here most of the players were Englishmen. Trumpets had been an important part of the King's Musick since the fifteenth century. But their primary functions were ceremonial and heraldic. When the trumpets played at the same event as the King's Violins, they were placed in a separate location and they played at different moments. The development of upper-partial clarino technique, however, made it possible to integrate the trumpet into

---

[43] The four players who came in 1673 were Jacques Paisible, Maxant De Bresmes, Pierre Guiton, and Jean (?) Boutet. Boutet may have returned to Paris by the 1690s. The others remained in England. See David Lasocki, "The French Hautboy in England, 1673–1730," *EM* 16 (1988), 339–57 at 351 ff.; Haynes, *The Eloquent Oboe*, 145 ff.

[44] Lasocki, "The French Hautboy," 342–43; Haynes, *The Eloquent Oboe*, 149 ff.

[45] Haynes, *The Eloquent Oboe*, 148.   [46] Holman, *Four and Twenty Fiddlers*, 318–19.

[47] Judith Milhous and Robert D. Hume, *Vice Chamberlain Coke's Theatrical Papers, 1706–1715* (Carbondale, Ill., 1982), 31.

[48] Highfill et al., *Biographical Dictionary*, vii. 209; xiii. 169–70; Milhous and Hume, *Vice Chamberlain Coke's Theatrical Papers*, 30–31. Earlier references to the double bass (e.g. in the score to Blow's anthem *Lord, Who Shall Dwell*) probably designate a double bass viol, pitched a fourth lower than a normal bass viol, but still an 8-foot rather than a 16-foot instrument (Holman, *Four and Twenty Fiddlers*, 410).

ensembles with other instruments.[49] The music that Nicholas Staggins composed for the coronation of James II in 1685 was scored for "trumpetts, hautboyes, violins, tennors [violas], [and] bases."[50] This may be the earliest English example of a piece combining oboes, trumpets, and strings in full scoring.[51] By the 1690s trumpets were used in the theaters, not only in combination with strings but also with voices.

Another aspect of the emergence of the orchestra between 1685 and 1715 was spatial consolidation, especially in the theater. In the 1660s and 1670s theater musicians were placed in a "Musick room," usually a loft or gallery like those built for musicians in churches and banqueting halls. In other theaters the music room was located at the back of the stage, sometimes built into clouds or other scenery.[52] In still others it was a gallery on one side, next to the spectator's boxes.[53] A large orchestra for John Eccles's setting of *The Judgement of Paris* at Dorset Garden in 1701 was displayed onstage in a sort of bandshell made of tin, which projected the sound.[54]

These changes in instrumentation, balances, and location took place relatively rapidly in England—at least in London—so that when Handel arrived in 1710, he found an up-to-date orchestra already in place at the Italian opera in the Haymarket.[55] It was organized as a single unit; the violins were doubled more heavily than the other strings; cellos and basses had replaced violoni and bass viols; it included modern winds and trumpets; and the orchestra had a place of its own in front of the stage. Reports that have been transmitted about orchestras that performed Handel's works with participation of the composer are summarized in Table 8.1. The entry for 1710 represents the orchestra at the Queen's Theatre on the eve of Handel's arrival. The bass part is heavily manned, with seven cellos, four bassoons, and a double bass.[56] Two of the cellos are entered separately with the harpsichord at the head of the list, suggesting that this group accompanied the singers in continuo arias. Two violinists, a cellist, and a bassoonist are marked on the personnel list as "excluded." Evidently they began the season with the orchestra but were let go midway through, perhaps to save money.[57]

[49] Peter Downey, "Performing Mr. Purcell's 'Exotick' Trumpet Notes," in Michael Burden (ed.), *Performing the Music of Henry Purcell* (Oxford, 1996), 49–60.

[50] Ashbee, *Records*, ii. 12.

[51] Staggins had his piece copied "into forty several parts," which implies that extra string players were probably used beyond the 24 or so on the royal payroll (Ashbee, *Records*, ii. 12). None of Francis Sandford's pictures of the Coronation of James II shows trumpets playing together with the King's violins, and none shows an ensemble of more than 20.

[52] Eleanore Boswell, *The Restoration Court Stage (1660–1702)* (Cambridge, Mass., 1932), 250.

[53] Price, "Restoration Stage Fiddlers," 83–84.

[54] William Congreve, *Letters and Documents*, ed. John C. Hodges (New York, 1964), 20 (letter of 26 Mar. 1701).

[55] The Queen's Theatre orchestra had been assembled by Vanbrugh for the opera seasons of 1708 and 1709. See Milhous and Hume, *Vice Chamberlain Coke's Theatrical Papers*.

[56] Some of the players listed as cellists in 1710 may have played an older type of bass instrument.

[57] Milhous and Hume, *Vice Chamberlain Coke's Theatrical Papers*, 160.

TABLE 8.1. *Handel's English orchestras, 1710–58*

Date and place	Keyboard and plucked strings	Bowed strings	Winds	Brass	Source
1710: Queen's Theatre, Haymarket	2 harpsichords	5 first violins 5 second violins 2 violas 7 cellos 1 double bass	2 oboes/flutes 4 bassoons	1 trumpet	Milhous and Hume, *Coke's Theatrical Papers*, 159–61
1720: Cannons	1 harpsichord	7 violins 1 viola 3 cello/basses	2 oboes 1 bassoon	1 trumpet	Beeks, "Handel," 17
1720: King's Theatre, Haymarket (Royal Academy)	[2 harpsichords] 1 theorbo	16 violins 2 violas 4 cellos 2 double basses	4 oboes/flutes 2 bassoons	1 trumpet	Milhous and Hume, "New Light," 160–61
1728: King's Theatre, Haymarket	2 harpsichords 1 archlute	24 violins/violas 3 cellos 2 double basses	? oboes/flutes 3 bassoons	? trumpets/horns	Dean, "French," 177 (Fougeroux)
1733: King's Theatre, Haymarket (*Orlando*)	2 harpsichords 1 theorbo	24 violins/violas 4 cellos 2 double basses	2 oboes 4 bassoons		Dean and Knapp, *Handel's Operas*, 22 (Sir John Clerk)
1754: Foundling Hospital (*Messiah*)	1 organ/harpsichord	14 violins 6 violas 3 cellos 2 double basses	4 oboes/flutes 4 bassoons	2 horns 2 trumpets 1 drum	Deutsch, *Handel*, 751
1758: Foundling Hospital (*Messiah*)	[1 organ/harpsichord]	12 violins 3 violas 3 cellos 2 basses	4 oboes/flutes 4 bassoons 1 drum	2 horns 3 trumpets	Ibid. 800

The first orchestra listed for 1720 is the Earl of Carnarvon's private orchestra at Cannons, smaller than a theater orchestra, but with much the same proportions. The second entry for 1720 is the orchestra projected for the first season of the Royal Academy of Music. Here, violins are more heavily doubled than in the opera orchestra of 1710, and there are fewer cellos and bassoons, making for a more treble-oriented sound. Now there are four oboists, making it possible for oboes and flutes or recorders to play at the same time, a scoring that Handel used, but rarely.[58] The Royal Academy list is arranged into five salary classes: those in the first class are projected to receive 80 or 100 pounds for the season; those in the fifth class get only 30.[59] The figures from 1728 and 1733 come from reports by travelers who attended the opera at the Haymarket, so they are less explicit and probably less accurate than reports based on rosters. Neither author distinguishes between violins and violas, but both reports still seem to show continued expansion of the violin section compared with the rest of the orchestra. The Italian two-harpsichord system is firmly in place now: both reports mention a continuo group of two harpsichords and theorbo, plus, perhaps, two of the cellists. The final two reports document orchestras for Handel oratorios. These performances took place at the Foundling Hospital rather than at the King's Theatre or Covent Garden, which were the two most common venues for Handel's oratorios in London. The Foundling Hospital orchestras were pick-up groups made up of performers from the various London theaters, and they may have been somewhat smaller than the orchestras that performed the oratorios in the theaters themselves.[60] Horns have now been added, and the violas are more strongly represented compared with the violins. This last feature may be characteristic of oratorios, where each string section often doubles a voice part in the choruses, and the strings, thus, need to be more evenly distributed than in the two- or three-part textures characteristic in operas.

THE DECLINE OF THE KING'S MUSICK

Shortly after his accession in 1685, James II undertook a reorganization of the King's Musick. What had been an aggregation of separate ensembles and separate payrolls was consolidated into a single ensemble of 31 members under the rubric "Private Music."[61] Dr. John Blow was the "Composer"; Nicholas Staggins was "master of the Musick"; Henry Purcell played the "harpsicall." Even under James II, however, the

---

[58] In Act II, Scene i of *Alessandro* two flutes trade phrases with two oboes. In Act III, Scene v of *Tamerlano* Handel scores for two flutes and two recorders. Further examples may be found in *Alcina* (1736 version), *Solomon*, and *Joshua*.

[59] Milhous and Hume, "New Light on Handel," 158. These pay differentials, presumably based on skill level and responsibility, resemble the 3 to 1 differentials typical of 18th-c. German Kapellen. See Ch. 7.

[60] Winton Dean, *Handel's Dramatic Oratorios and Masques* (London, 1959), 104–5.

[61] Ashbee, *Records*, ii. 122.

role of the Private Musick was modest. Its members played at the Chapel Royal and also in the short-lived Catholic chapel.[62] The full ensemble, now known as the "King's Band of Musick," played as a unit primarily in the "court odes" that celebrated the King's and Queen's birthdays, New Year's Day, St. Cecilia's Day, and military victories. Since court duties were relatively light, members of the King's Musick were free to play in the theaters and at concerts, which they did as individuals, not as a group.

With the accession of William and Mary in 1688 the role of the King's Musick receded further. After 1689 the King's musicians no longer played for services in the Chapel Royal.[63] In 1690 as part of a general cutback in the size of the royal Household, the King's Musick was reduced to 24 members, where it remained through most of the eighteenth century.[64] Wages were set at a modest £40 per year, far less than a professional instrumentalist could earn in a theater orchestra.[65] Another factor in the decline of the King's Musick was the Settlement Act of 1701, which besides settling the royal succession on the House of Hanover, also stipulated that "no person born out of the kingdoms of England, Scotland, or Ireland . . . shall enjoy any office . . . either civil or military."[66] This meant that foreign musicians could no longer serve in the Chapel Royal or the King's Band, not even after they were naturalized as English citizens. The King's Band was thus deprived of the services of some of London's foremost musicians, like the Italian violinists and cellists who came around the turn of the century, or George Frederick Handel, who, though patronized steadfastly by the Hanoverian kings, was never appointed to any official position.[67]

By the reign of George II (1720–60), the King's Band was playing only about 10 to 15 performances per year: New Year's Day, Twelfth Night, the King's and Queen's birthdays, installations of Knights of the Garter, royal balls, and occasional special events like weddings and funerals.[68] For really festive performances the 24-man orchestra did not suffice and additional instrumentalists were hired, like the "Fifty Seven Supernumerary Performers of Musick" who were engaged to play Handel's anthems at the coronation of George II in 1727.[69] Although the workload was light, an appointment to the King's Band was not a sinecure: all members of the band were professional musicians. The bulk of their musical life, however, took place outside the

---

[62] Holman, *Four and Twenty Fiddlers*, 413.

[63] Nicholas Temperley, "Music in Church," in *The Eighteenth Century*, ed. H. Diack Johnstone and Roger Fiske (The Blackwell History of Music in Britain, 4; Oxford, 1990), 357–96 at 366.

[64] Ashbee, *Records*, viii. 282; Peggy Ellen Daub, "Music at the Court of George II (r. 1727–1760)," (Ph.D. diss., Cornell University, 1985), 306–7.

[65] Ashbee, *Records*, ii. 128. [66] *Encyclopaedia Britannica*, 11th edn. (Cambridge, 1911), xxiv. 706.

[67] Handel held positions as Music Master to the royal princesses and as Composer to the Chapel Royal. From an administrative standpoint these were not government offices. See Burrows, *Handel*, 117–18, 122–24.

[68] Daub, "Music at the Court of George II," 188. Court records do not specify who played what instrument in the King's Band, but sets of parts for court odes by William Boyce written in the 1750s suggest a distribution something like: 10 vln, 2 vla, 2 vc, 1 cb, 2 ob/fl, 2 bn, 2 tpt, 1 timp.

[69] Daub, "Music at the Court of George II," 209.

context of the court.[70] In the theaters or the concert rooms the King's musicians typically played toward the back of their sections, relinquishing the first chairs to younger and to foreign-born instrumentalists.

THEATER ORCHESTRAS

In the eighteenth century only the theaters in Drury Lane and Covent Garden were licensed to give public dramatic entertainments and designated as "Theatres Royal" or "patent theaters." In addition, the King's Theatre in the Haymarket had a license for the performance of sung dramas, that is operas.[71] Each of the three theaters had its own orchestra, and since their performances often overlapped, a musician could play in only one of them.[72] Instrumentalists signed contracts for one season at a time, but players tended to remain at the same theater year after year, so that the orchestras at the three patent theaters constituted three standing professional orchestras. In addition, smaller theaters in the Haymarket, in Goodman's Fields, and outside city limits had orchestras of their own. Counting only theater orchestras, London had more professional standing orchestras in simultaneous operation than any other European city.

The orchestra was just as necessary at Covent Garden and Drury Lane as it was for opera at the King's Theatre. English-language opera and oratorio constituted a large proportion of the season at both theaters, and spoken dramas were filled with songs and dances. Before the performance started, as the audience found its seats and ordered refreshments, the orchestra played instrumental selections, called "First music" and "Second music," followed by an overture.[73] Between the acts it played "act music," often concertos or solo turns of some other sort. London publishers found it profitable to issue sets of theater overtures and airs, scored for four-part string ensemble. These ready-made suites enabled London and also provincial theaters to put together an evening of music quickly and relatively inexpensively.[74]

Songs, which were almost as frequent in spoken theater as in opera, were sometimes accompanied by onstage musicians but more often by the orchestra. The orchestra also accompanied dances, which were inserted into many spoken dramas.[75] In addition, the orchestra was used to create atmosphere—nightfall, a pastoral scene,

---

[70] Ibid. 294.

[71] *The London Stage, 1660–1800*, ed. William Van Lennep et al. (Carbondale, Ill., 1960–68), iii, pp. xix ff. The Covent Garden patent was at Lincoln's Inn Fields from 1714 to 1732. The Little Theatre in the Haymarket had the status of a patent theater from 1766 to 1777.

[72] Beginning in 1748 Covent Garden and Drury Lane agreed to play on alternate nights (*The London Stage*, v, p. cxxxi). However, the tradition of separate orchestras was already well established.

[73] Price, "Restoration Stage Fiddlers," 53.

[74] Roger Fiske, *English Theatre Music in the Eighteenth Century*, 2nd edn. (Oxford, 1986), 591 ff.

[75] *The London Stage*, iii, pp. clv–clvii.

sleep, and dreams, etc.—with "symphonies" of instrumental music. In spoken theater the orchestra did not play while the actors spoke, whereas in opera the orchestra accompanied both song (aria) and speech (recitative) as well as playing overtures, act music, dances, and "symphonies."

At all the theaters the orchestra and its music constituted one of the principal attractions drawing the audience to the show. The names of the leader of the orchestra and the soloists scheduled to play between the acts were advertised in the newspapers, as were the works they planned to perform. A notice for *Perseus and Andromeda* at Covent Garden in 1735 advertised: "For the First Musick, a Concert for Hautboys; for the Second Musick, A concerto of Geminiani; and for the Third, The Overture of Ariadne. The Act Tunes for French Horns, and Trumpets."[76]

Music lovers came early so as not to miss the first and second music and the overture.[77] Indeed, if they left before the curtain rose, they could get their money back at the box office, a custom that persisted until the late eighteenth century.[78] Between orchestra and audience in English theaters a direct, almost intimate relationship grew up. The denizens of the gallery applauded their favorite performers and called out for their favorite tunes. If the orchestra did not oblige, they threw oranges and other debris into the pit.[79] Certain instrumentalists became audience favorites, like Jacob Cervetto (Cervetto the elder), principal cellist at Drury Lane, a Venetian immigrant with a particularly prominent nose, who was greeted with cries of "Nosey" every evening as he walked into the pit.[80] Anecdotes like these suggest that the audience in the eighteenth-century English theater considered itself the orchestra's patron. Just as a King could tell his Kapelle what to play, the folks in the gallery had paid their shilling, and they wanted their money's worth from their orchestra.

Scattered reports have survived of the size and composition of London theater orchestras, as shown in Table 8.2. Orchestras at Covent Garden and Drury Lane numbered from 19 to 25, and during the entire period they remained about the same size. The orchestra for the Italian opera was significantly larger, and it grew from 32 in 1720 to 39 in 1790, mainly through the addition of wind instruments.[81] The opera orchestra was also more violin-dominated than the orchestras at the English-language theaters. There was a certain amount of double-handedness in all the orchestras: oboists standardly doubled on flutes and occasionally on clarinet; two of the violinists at Drury Lane in 1778 played clarinet as needed and a violist doubled on trumpet. By the 1790s, however, at least in the opera orchestra, flutes, clarinets, horns, and trumpets were all played by specialists. Additional players were occasionally hired,

---

[76] *The London Stage*, iii. 467.   [77] Price, "Restoration Stage Fiddlers," 53.

[78] *The London Stage*, iv, p. xlviii; v, p. xxix.

[79] Allardyce Nicoll, *The Garrick Stage: Theatres and Audience in the Eighteenth Century*, ed. Sybil Rosenfeld (Manchester, 1980), 86.

[80] Highfill et al., *Biographical Dictionary*, iii. 131.

[81] The King's Theatre burned in 1789, and the Italian opera performed at the Pantheon until 1792. Orchestra personnel remained the same.

TABLE 8.2. *London theater orchestras, 1708–1818*

Date: theater	Keyboard and plucked strings	Bowed strings	Winds	Brass and drums	Unidentified	Source
1708: Queen's Theatre Haymarket	[2] harpsichords	11 violins 2 violas 6 cellos/violoni 1 double bass	2 oboes 3 bassoons	1 trumpet		Milhous and Hume, *Coke's Theatrical Papers*, 78–9
1720: King's Theatre, Haymarket	[2 harpsichords] 1 theorbo	16 violins 2 violas 4 cellos 2 double basses	4 oboes/flutes 2 bassoons	1 trumpet		Milhous and Hume, "New Light," 160–1
1760: Covent Garden	1 harpsichord	2 violins 1 viola 2 cellos	3 oboes/flutes 1 bassoon	1 horn	9 musicians	*London Stage*, iv. 815
1778: Drury Lane	1 harpsichord (organ)	5 first violins 4 second violins 3 violas 4 cellos/basses	3 oboes 2 bassoons (2 clarinets)	2 horns (1 trumpet)		Ibid. iv, p. cxxvii
1782: King's Theatre, Haymarket	1 harpsichord	14 violins 3 violas 5 cellos 1 bass	2 flutes 2 oboes 2 bassoons	3 trumpets/horns 1 timpani		Price et al., *Italian Opera*, 286

	Harpsichord	Strings	Woodwinds	Brass & timpani	Source
Haymarket		8 second violins 4 violas 4 cellos 3 basses	clarinet 2 bassoons	[3 trumpets] 1 timpani	
1790: Pantheon (Italian opera)	1 harpsichord	8 first violins 8 second violins 4 violas 4 cellos 3 double basses	2 oboes 2 flutes 2 clarinets 2 bassoons	2 horns 2 trumpets 1 timpani	Milhous et al., *Italian Opera*, 424
1791: Drury Lane	[1 harpsichord] 1 harp	7 violins and violas 3 cellos 1 double bass	2 oboes 2 bassoons	2 horns and trumpets	*London Stage*, v. 1358
1818: Covent Garden	[1 harpsichord]	8 violins 1 viola 2 cellos	2 oboes 1 flute 2 bassoons	1 horn 2 trumpets 1 trombone 1 timpani	Rohr, *Careers*, 123

sometimes on special instruments like harp or mandolin, sometimes to augment the size of the orchestra.

Pictures of English theater orchestras are not as common as those for opera on the Continent, perhaps because an English orchestra did not advertise the grandeur of a king or a prince. Plate IX, an aquatint by Rowlandson and Pugin published in 1808, shows the orchestra for Italian opera at the King's Theatre. The shadowy orchestra stretches across the entire width of the stage. It numbers almost 50 players, even larger than the 40 members on the roster in 1790 (Table 8.2). There is only one harpsichord rather than two as in Handel's day, but it is still surrounded by a continuo of cellos and basses. A harp can be seen on the left, directly behind the harpsichord. The winds have been divided from the strings and placed together on the right, facing center, with a row of basses behind them. In Rowlandson's picture the orchestra accompanies a ballet rather than a singer.

Playing together night after night, year after year, musicians in each theater orchestra developed a good deal of group solidarity and esprit de corps. To a considerable extent the orchestras operated as autonomous entities. At the King's Theatre the first violinist-leader—Felice Giardini in the 1750s and 1760s, then William Cramer until 1796—exercised both musical and administrative control over the orchestra, and management customarily addressed the players through the leader. The power to hire and fire resided with management, but when Le Texier, the manager, in 1779 threatened to dock the salaries of the wind players, the musicians called a general meeting and shouted him down.[82] Theater orchestras rehearsed regularly, particularly when they performed new music. Rehearsals seem to have been lubricated with alcoholic beverages: payments for "negus" and "rehearsal wine" turn up occasionally in the Covent Garden account books.[83] Italian operas were rehearsed in private with the singers, continuo, and perhaps a few violins, then publicly in the theater with the full orchestra. A public rehearsal is portrayed vividly by Susan Burney, daughter of Charles, who recorded a visit to the King's Theatre in 1779 in her diary:

the Wind instruments were all out of tune, & tho' I pit[i]ed poor Cramer 'twas impossible not to laugh—After repeatedly desiring the French Horn Players to make their Instruments sharper, at last he called out . . . with his foreign accent—"Gentlemen . . . You are not in tune at all?"—"Its [not] a very sharp Morning Sir," said one of them—"We shall do better another time."[84]

---

[82] Curtis Price et al., *Italian Opera in Late Eighteenth-Century London*, i. 189, 187.

[83] Laura Alyson McLamore, "Symphonic Conventions in London's Concert Rooms, circa 1755–1790," (Ph.D. diss., University of California, Los Angeles, 1991), 193; *The London Stage*, iv, p. cxxviii.

[84] Quoted in Price et al., *Italian Opera*, 191.

ORCHESTRAS AT THE PLEASURE GARDENS

The pleasure gardens were a distinctive and characteristically English institution, a paradigm of the commercialization of leisure. Amenities and luxuries of life that on the Continent were available to the aristocracy alone—shaded walks, beds of flowers, lamps, statuary, grottos—in England were sold to the public for a relatively low admission price. Music was one more piece of the good life that the gardens offered, particularly orchestral music, which was more expensive to produce than songs or instrumental solos and which thus served as a symbol of affluence. Already in the late seventeenth century Epsom Wells advertised "eight MUSITIANS and a TRUMPET," and at Lambeth Wells in 1697 there was a "consort of vocal and instrumental musick, consisting of about thirty instruments and voices."[85] At Vauxhall, Marlybone, and Ranelagh special pavilions called "orchestras" were built for the musicians, and daily orchestral performances became a major attraction. A picture by Rowlandson (Fig. 8.2) shows the "orchestra" at Vauxhall in 1784. Fredericka Weichsel, who sang at Vauxhall from 1766 until 1786, stands at the front of the balcony. Behind her a band of about 15 instrumentalists arranged on risers play violins, cellos, oboes, bassoon, trumpets, and timpani. At the back of the orchestra an organ is visible. Many of the audience members can be identified. Directly underneath the singer, Admiral Paisley, with the eyepatch and wooden leg, ogles the Duchess of Devonshire and Lady Bessborough (white dressses), while on the right the Prince of Wales, in a tall beaver hat, whispers into the ear of his mistress, Mary Robinson.[86] In rainy weather Vauxhall concerts were held indoors at the Great Room, also called "the Umbrella." At Ranelagh, although there were gardens, the principal feature was an immense circular amphitheater or "Rotunda." In the center an elaborate structure of columns and arches contained an open fire; against the wall stood a large "orchestra" with an organ.[87] The Ranelagh orchestra accompanied diners, just like the Vingt-quatre Violons at a *souper* of Louis XIV. They also played for evening concerts and dances.

Since the season for the pleasure gardens ran from May to September, it did not overlap the theatrical season, and instrumentalists from the theaters staffed the orchestras of the gardens. In size and composition these orchestras were probably similar to those at the theaters. A painting by Canaletto of the Rotunda at Ranelagh in the

[85] Michael Tilmouth, "Some Early London Concerts and Music Clubs, 1670–1720," *PRMA* 84 (1957–58), 13–26 at 24; Warwick Wroth, *The London Pleasure Gardens of the Eighteenth Century* (London, 1896), 279.

[86] See John Hayes, *Rowlandson: Watercolours and Drawings* (London, 1972), 80; John Riely, *Rowlandson Drawings from the Paul Mellon Collection* (New Haven, 1978), 4–6.

[87] The orchestra at Ranelagh was initially placed in the central structure, but this proved to be an acoustical disaster, and it was moved to the side (Wroth, *The London Pleasure Gardens*, 202).

Fig. 8.2. The orchestra at Vauxhall Gardens, 1784

1750s shows about 30 to 35 players in the orchestra.[88] Parts for an ode by Boyce performed at Ranelagh in 1752 suggest that it was played by an orchestra of 25–30.[89]
Boyce's Ode, composed to celebrate the 14th birthday of Prince George, later
George III, was performed not at court but at Ranelagh, that is, in a public venue for
a general audience. Already in the eighteenth century the English royal family was
being marketed to the public—at the pleasure gardens, as they are today on television.

[88] Reproduced in Katherine Baetjer and J. G. Links, *Canaletto* (New York, 1989), 249. Canaletto produced
several versions of this subject, all with orchestras about the same size.

[89] William Boyce, *Three Birthday Odes for Prince George*, ed. Robert J. Bruce (New York, 1987), p. xii. Parts
for songs by James Hook performed at Vauxhall imply an orchestra of about the same size in the 1780s (Charles
Cudworth, "The Vauxhall 'Lists,'" *GSJ* 20 (1967), 24–42 at 27).

ORCHESTRAS IN CONCERT

"The public concert," states Peter Holman, "was an English invention."[90] As early as the 1670s John Banister and Thomas Britton were organizing events at which several instrumentalists joined together "in concert" and performed for auditors who paid for the pleasure of listening. However, the ensembles that played at these seventeenth-century concerts do not seem to have been orchestral. Usually they were pick-up groups assembled for just one occasion, and in most instances they played one on a part. Roger North's description of the concerts at the York Buildings make them sound rather chaotic:

not under the rule or order of any person, and every one forward to advance his owne talents and spightfull to each other, . . . one master brings a consort with fuges, another shews his guifts in a solo upon the violin, another sings, and then a famous lutinist comes forward, and in this manner changes followed each other, with a full cessation of the musick between every one, and a gable and bustle while they changed places.[91]

The only really large ensemble that has been documented was the "great Compound" that concluded John Banister's Parley of Instruments in 1676.

Concerts with large, standing orchestras seem to have grown not from professional ventures but rather from musical societies organized by a mixture of amateur and professional instrumentalists. In 1724 a notice in *The Daily Post* announced that "near one hundred gentlemen and merchants of the City have lately form'd themselves into a musical society, the one part Performers the other auditors."[92] The society met initially at the house of Talbot Young, a member of the King's Band, later at the Castle Tavern, from which it took the name "Castle Concerts."[93] Members paid a subscription of two guineas per year for the privilege of playing; performances took place every Wednesday evening. There do not seem to have been rehearsals. Violinist-members took turns leading the ensemble, with the leader for the night picking the repertory. According to bylaws published in 1731, double-handedness was discouraged:

Every Performer shall provide his own Instrument, (except the harpsichord and Double Bass), and shall play in the Concert on the same Instrument which he play'd on for his approbation, and on no other . . . unless he be desired by the President, or first Fiddle for the Night, to play on some other Instrument.[94]

---

[90] Peter Holman, "The British Isles: Private and Public Music," in Julie Ann Sadie (ed.), *Companion to Baroque Music* (New York, 1990), 261–69 at 266.

[91] North, *Roger North on Music*, 353. See also p. 305.

[92] Highfill et al., *Biographical Dictionary*, xvi. 358. Apparently these same musical gentlemen had been meeting for several years before 1724 (Rosamond McGuinness and H. Diack Johnstone, "Concert Life in England I," in *The Eighteenth Century* (ed. Johnstone and Fiske), 31–95 at 36).

[93] Hawkins, *General History*, ii. 808.

[94] Quoted in McLamore, "Symphonic Conventions," 148.

At the Castle Concerts music lovers could hear or perform the same concertos and overtures that they heard orchestras play at the theaters. There seem to be no extant reports on the size and composition of this ensemble, but the large membership of the society suggests that the strings were heavily doubled.

Other musical societies came into being during the first half of the eighteenth century along the same lines as the Castle Concerts. There were concerts at the Swan Tavern, the Ship Tavern, the Union Coffee House, the King's Arms Tavern, the Devil Tavern, and other public places, most of them catering to "gentleman performers."[95] Most societies also admitted professional musicians, who might be paid to participate, as well as auditors, who paid a subscription but did not play.

The first concerts that employed a standing orchestra of professional musicians were probably the subscription series at Hickford's Rooms beginning in the late 1720s. At Hickford's the "subscribers" were all auditors rather than amateur performers, while the orchestra was made up of the "best Masters," i.e. professionals from the theater orchestras.[96] Other subscription series were organized during the 1740s and 1750s at Hickford's and at the Great Rooms in Dean Street by entrepreneurs and performers, including the keyboardist Ogle, the singers Giuseppe and Christina Passerini, and the violinist Felice Giardini. These were series of 12 to 20 concerts, and they probably engaged orchestras for the season. In 1760 Teresa Cornelys, singer, promoter, and mistress to the rich and powerful, bought the Carlisle House in Soho and offered a series of 12 Thursday evening entertainments. A visitor reported: "The vocal and instrumental music, by an orchestra at the end of the room, begins at seven o'clock and lasts until nine; dancing afterwards goes on until one or two."[97] In 1764 Mrs. Cornelys engaged the opera composer Gioacchino Cocchi as musical director of her concerts; in 1765 she replaced him with J. C. Bach and C. F. Abel.

The Bach–Abel concerts, which ran from 1765 until 1782, marked a new stage in the development of the orchestra in England.[98] They featured a standing professional orchestra, and they were built around orchestral music. Although every concert offered vocal selections, equal or greater weight was given to concertos, overtures, and symphonies. The Bach–Abel concerts programmed orchestral music in the new, Continental style, by composers such as Sammartini, Jommelli, Maldere, Toeschi, and Stamitz—and of course by Bach and Abel themselves—with cantabile instrumental melodies, prominent use of wind instruments, and orchestral effects like

---

[95] See Simon McVeigh, *The Violinist in London's Concert Life, 1750–1784* (New York, 1989), 28. Also Elkin, *Old Concert Rooms*, 50 ff.

[96] McGuinness and Johnstone, "Concert Life in England," 42.

[97] Baron Kielmansegge's diary entry 26 Nov. 1761. Quoted in McVeigh, *The Violinist in London's Concert Life*, 18.

[98] Bach and Abel's connection with Mrs. Cornelys ended in 1768. From 1768 to 1782 they managed the concert series jointly. After Bach's death in 1782 Abel continued briefly on his own.

crescendo and subito piano. Soon the Bach–Abel concerts moved to their own venue, specifically designed for orchestral music—the Hanover Square Rooms, built in 1775 by the two composers in partnership with Sir John Gallini, with seating for 500 or 600 auditors and a raised platform for the orchestra at one end.[99] About the orchestra itself and its members, not much is known. Burney states that "the best performers of all kinds which the capital could supply, enlisted under their banners."[100] Since the concerts took place on Wednesdays, many of the instrumentalists probably came from the orchestra at the King's Theatre, which had Wednesday nights off.[101] These were subscription concerts: the subscription list was socially exclusive, ticket prices were high, applicants were screened, and the very few advertisements were so discreet that they usually did not mention performers' names or repertory.

The success and the prestige of the Bach–Abel concerts soon inspired competing ventures. Giardini organized a "Musical Academy" at Mrs. Cornelys's house in 1770.[102] John Parry, a harpist, ran a morning subscription series at Hickford's Rooms. Violinist Franz Lamotte ran a series at Tottenham Street in 1777, then with Rauzzini, a singer, at Hanover Square. The Pantheon, built in 1772, presented Monday subscription concerts featuring an orchestra of "eminent performers" led by Giardini. "Should the Nobility and Gentry form any Parties for Dancing," the management announced, "proper Bands of Music will be ready for this Purpose."[103] Dancing afterward was featured at many concerts to attract additional subscribers.

By the 1780s London had become the scene of a veritable battle of the bands, with several orchestras offering subscription concerts in competition with one another. The Bach–Abel concerts were replaced at Hanover Square by the Professional Concert, organized as a musicians' cooperative, with the players sharing profits at the end of the season.[104] At the Pantheon John Peter Salomon led another orchestra in a concert series that featured Mme Mara, the great German soprano. The Professional Concert endeavored to maintain its status by forbidding its members to play at other subscription concerts. Its personnel overlapped heavily, however, with the orchestra at the King's Theatre.[105] The orchestra for the Pantheon Concerts was drawn in a similar manner from the orchestras at the other theaters and the pleasure gardens. London concert orchestras in the late eighteenth century resembled the opera orchestra in size and composition. All had 12–16 violins, 3–5 each of violas, cellos, and basses, pairs of woodwinds, horns, and trumpets.[106] By the last quarter of the

---

[99] Elkin, *Old Concert Rooms*, 93; McVeigh, *The Violinist in London's Concert Life*, 3.

[100] Burney, *General History*, ii. 1017.

[101] *The London Stage*, v, pp. cxxxi–cxxxiii. Drury Lane was also closed on Wednesday nights.

[102] See McLamore, "Symphonic Conventions," 113 ff.; McVeigh, *The Violinist in London's Concert Life*, 278 ff.

[103] *Morning Chronicle* (30 Dec. 1773), quoted in McLamore, "Symphonic Conventions," 136–37.

[104] McVeigh, "The Professional Concert,", 6–7, 39.　　[105] Ibid. 40, and Price et al., *Italian Opera*, 321.

[106] McVeigh reproduces the rosters of the Professional Concert for several years in the 1780s ("The Professional Concert," 39 ff). For example: 1785: 12 vn, 3 vla, 3 vc, 3 cb, 2 fl, 3 ob, 2 bn, 2 hn, 1 piano; 1786: 13 vn, 4 vla, 3 vc, 3 cb, 2 fl, 3 ob, 2 bn, 2 hn, 1 piano.

eighteenth century the orchestra in England had become to a considerable extent standardized and institutionalized.

Concerts competed with one another to attract the most fashionable audience, to program the newest music, to engage the most popular vocalists, and to offer the most "complete" orchestra. The height of the spirit of competition came in the 1790s with the rivalry between the Professional Concert at the Hanover Square Rooms on Mondays and Salomon's concerts in the same hall on Fridays. The Professional Concert was generally acknowledged to have the better orchestra. Salomon, however, had Europe's greatest composer, Joseph Haydn, who arrived in London in January 1791 and presided at the keyboard over 12 subscription concerts, each featuring a Haydn symphony immediately after the intermission. In the spring of 1793 the Professional Concerts suspended its series, conceding victory to Salomon, whose concerts went on for three more seasons. The "professors" continued to play, however, at the "Opera Concert" which began in 1795 in a newly constructed music room in the King's Theatre. Salomon led the Opera Concert during its opening season, and Haydn composed his Symphonies 102–104 for this orchestra.

The Opera Concerts ended in 1798, but there were still plenty of orchestras and plenty of work for London's instrumentalists. Competition may have brought the end of one or another series, but in the long run it expanded the market for orchestras and orchestral music. Doane's *Musical Directory for the Year 1794* lists 1,333 "composers and professors of music," the great majority of them living in London.[107] Not all of them played in orchestras by any means, but they formed a pool of professional instrumentalists from which a large number of orchestras could be constituted. There were standing orchestras not only the three patent theaters but also at suburban theaters Goodman's Fields, Sadler's Wells, and Clerkenwell. The pleasure gardens and several of the subscription series also had standing orchestras. Ad hoc orchestras were organized for benefits and for special events. A good performer could put together a living by playing in several orchestras, as well as giving lessons and perhaps selling sheet music or musical instruments on the side.[108] The world of orchestras in London was not a single set of concentric circles, like Corelli's Rome a century earlier, but a complex network with multiple nodes and intricate interconnections.

AMATEUR ORCHESTRAS

Samuel Sharp, an Englishman visiting Italy in 1765, was surprised to find that "very few Gentlemen here practise the fiddle, or any other instrument . . ." and that instrumental ensembles were composed almost entirely of professionals.[109] In

---

[107] Joseph Doane, *A Musical Directory for the Year 1794* (London, 1794).   [108] See below, Ch. 12.
[109] Sharp, *Letters from Italy*, 79. On Italian amateur performers in the 18th c., see above, Ch. 5.

eighteenth-century England the "gentleman amateur" was a familiar figure in musical circles. He was a "gentleman" because he made his living from land ownership, civil or military office, or a profession, rather than from a trade or from labor; he was an "amateur" because he played music for love rather than for money. As a young man he had taken lessons on a stringed or keyboard instrument or perhaps the flute; for years thereafter he kept his hand in by playing ensemble music on a regular basis with other amateurs. A few gentleman amateurs achieved a rather high level on their instruments, for example John Blathwayt, son of a cabinet minister and a child prodigy on the harpsichord, who was said to have studied with Alessandro Scarlatti in Rome.[110] Blathwayt became a major, then a colonel, in the army, but he kept up his harpsichord playing in amateur orchestras around London, and he was one of the first directors of the Royal Academy of Music. Most gentleman amateurs played at a more modest level, good enough to play the ripieno parts but not the solos in the concertos of Corelli or Geminiani. Gentlemen amateurs were more common in England than on the Continent partly because music was a more acceptable leisure activity for men and partly because the entry into the class of "gentlemen" was so much easier in England than elsewhere.

Organized into musical societies, gentleman amateurs played an important role in the development of the orchestra in England. Henry Angelo estimated that in the second half of the eighteenth century "there were, perhaps ten or a dozen musical meetings, private and public, held weekly" in the City of London.[111] These included the Castle Concerts, the Crown Concert, the St. Cecilian Concert, the Anacreontic Society, and several others. The Castle Society, discussed above, was made up of "gentlemen and merchants of the City" along with professional musicians drawn from the King's band and the theater orchestras. Its bylaws attempted to restrict membership to "gentlemen" by excluding vintners, victuallers, tailors, wig makers, and barbers, as well as apprentices, journeymen, and bankrupts.[112] Women were not permitted to play at "gentlemen's concerts," although many societies admitted women as guests or as non-performing subscribers. Interaction between amateurs and professionals in the musical societies was intimate and vigorous. John Marsh (1752–1828), gentleman violinist and composer, visiting London from Chichester in 1779, reported that he attended "the weekly morning concert at the Thatched House Tavern, led by Cramer, where I took a fiddle in the full pieces," that is in music where the strings played several on a part.[113] Then the performers did Marsh the favor of reading through one of his string quartets, with "Cramer and Shields taking the

---

[110] Hawkins, *General History*, ii. 806, 860. See also William Weber, *The Rise of Musical Classics in Eighteenth-Century England* (Oxford, 1992), 72.

[111] Henry Angelo, *Reminiscences, with Memoirs of his Late Father and Friends* (London, 1828–30), i. 278.

[112] McGuinness and Johnstone, "Concert Life in England," 38.

[113] John Marsh, *The John Marsh Journals: The Life and Times of a Gentleman Composer (1752–1828)*, ed. Brian Robins (Stuyvesant, NY, 1998), 197–98. On the Thatched House Tavern, also called "Almack's" after its proprietor, see Elkin, *Old Concert Rooms*, 74 ff.

fiddle parts, myself the tenor and Cervetto the bass." Cramer, Shields, and James Cervetto (son of "Nosey" Cervetto) were first-chair players in London theater orchestras. "With 3 out of 4 such capital performers," writes Marsh, "the piece went off as might be expected to my utmost satisfaction."

One of the longest lived concert societies was the Academy of Ancient Music, which was founded in the 1720s and continued to meet until 1792. The Academy, composed of both amateurs and professional musicians, met every other week, directed by the members in turn. It declared its mission to be: "searching after, examining, and hearing performed Works of the Masters, who flourished before and about the Age of Palestrina: however not neglecting those who in our Time have become famous."[114] Many of the violinists at the Academy were amateurs; for example, Henry Needler, an official in the Excise Office, who managed the organization's affairs, often led the orchestra, and was much praised as a performer of Corelli's works.[115] Oboes, bassoons, and brass instruments, less fashionable among gentleman performers, were usually played by professionals from the theaters or military bands. Normally only members were admitted to the concerts, but at the end of the season there was a public meeting to which guests, in particular ladies, were admitted.[116] From 1780s on ladies were admitted as guests to all meetings, and in 1788 ladies were permitted to become subscribers (though not performers). In addition, the Academy began to engage professional performers on the string parts, and the whole enterprise took on the character of a public concert series, though amateurs remained involved. A list of performers for the Academy season of 1787–88 documents an orchestra of 36 players, almost all of them professionals, with strings heavily doubled plus winds and brass.[117]

Amateur orchestras were especially important outside London in provincial towns, where gentleman amateurs abounded but professional instrumentalists were scarce. Instrumental ensembles developed first in cathedral towns, like Winchester, Canterbury, Salisbury, and Chichester, and the university towns of Oxford and Cambridge, where a critical mass of singers, church musicians, and amateur instrumentalists was available.[118] Neighboring towns often shared the services of professional musicians who traveled from one town to the next to fortify amateur musical societies. William Herschel, an immigrant German musician, finding London "so overstocked with musicians that we had but little chance of any great success," set out for the north of England, where he commuted between Halifax, Leeds, Sunderland, all the way to Newcastle. Along the way Herschel gave lessons to the gentry and their

---

[114] *Letters from the Academy of Ancient Music* (1732), quoted in Weber, *The Rise of Musical Classics*, 62.

[115] Ibid. 72.   [116] McVeigh, *The Violinist in London's Concert Life*, 32.

[117] 16 vn, 4 vla, 4 vc, 3 cb, 4 ob, 3 bn, 2 hn, 2 tpt, 1 timp, 1 organ. The list is written by hand into the front of the Library of Congress copy of John Hawkins, *An Account of the Institution and Progress of the Academy of Ancient Music* (London, 1770) [ML 28 L8 A2].

[118] Stanley Sadie, "Concert Life in Eighteenth-Century England," *PRMA* 85 (1958–59), 17–30 at 18–19.

daughters, and played in musical societies and at concerts in private homes.[119] Plate X, a painting dated 1734, shows a house concert at Melton Constable, about 30 km northwest of Norwich. The performers all seem to be gentleman amateurs. Three of the violinists have been identified as clergymen; the harpsichordist is a captain in the Army. Sir Jacob Astley, proprietor of the estate, plays the cello.[120] With four violins, a viola, a cello, two flutes, and a harpsichord, this ensemble would have been adequate to play much of the orchestral music of the 1730s.

The journals of John Marsh paint a vivid picture of the musical milieux in eighteenth-century English provincial towns and of provincial music meetings and societies.[121] Marsh was a lawyer, but the bulk of his income came from land holdings, and he was able devote himself passionately to music without needing to make a living from it. He learned the violin and viola as a teenager, later harpsichord, organ, and kettle drums. Wherever his business and family interests took him—mainly in the south of England—he participated in musical activities, playing violin in local concerts and musical societies. In each of the towns where he established himself— Salisbury, Nethersole, Canterbury, Chichester—he organized and led orchestras. For these amateur orchestras Marsh composed over 30 symphonies, plus concertos and other works.

All the orchestras in which Marsh participated were organized as music meetings or concert societies. The arrangements in Chichester, where he moved in 1787, were typical.[122] Amateur musicians who wished to participate in the concerts paid one guinea to play in a series of 12 fortnightly concerts, which took place in the assembly rooms owned by the city. Concerts were alternately private and public: to the public concerts non-performers, principally ladies, were admitted. The orchestra was led by Marsh or by Giovanni Salpietro, a violinist in the King's Theatre orchestra who visited Chichester frequently. Amateur participants included a couple of military officers, a schoolmaster, a surgeon, a bookseller, and several landed gentlemen. In addition, several members of the Chichester cathedral choir played instruments at the concert. The orchestra was augmented by professionals from the Sussex Militia Band, who played stringed as well as wind instruments and who were paid 4 shillings apiece plus a free meal for playing at the concerts.[123] Women participated in the Chichester concerts only as singers and listeners. When Marsh was at Canterbury, however, he

---

[119] Sir William Herschel, *The Scientific Papers of Sir William Herschel* (London, 1912), pp. xvii–xix; Constance A. Lubbock, *The Herschel Chronicle* (Cambridge, 1933), 13–19. As well as being an oboist, violinist, keyboardist, and composer, Herschel was an amateur astronomer. After his discovery of the planet Uranus in 1781 and his appointment as Royal Astronomer in 1782, he gave up music as a profession and devoted himself to science.

[120] Duleep Singh, "Portraits in Norfolk Houses," *Volumes of the Walpole Society*, 46 (1978), 71–90.

[121] Marsh's journals cover the period 1765–1801.   [122] Marsh, *John Marsh Journals*, 414 ff.

[123] The Sussex Band was maintained by the Duke of Richmond, whose estate was near Chichester, both as a military band and as a sort of personal Kapelle. The Duke hired Salpietro to come to Chichester and give lessons to the bandsmen on stringed instruments (*John Marsh Journals*, 404).

encountered a young blind girl who played harpsichord and organ. "As on account of her blindness music was her only amusement," Marsh writes, "the gentlemen of the Concert were so good as to let her always have a place at the back of the orchestra both at the Subscription Concerts & at the annual Music Meeting."[124]

Marsh's largest orchestras numbered 18 or 19 performers, with 6–8 violins, a pair of violas, a cello or two, and a double bass. The lack of winds was a nagging problem for English concert societies. Only the flute was considered suitable for a gentleman amateur to learn: oboes, bassoons, horns, and trumpets were left to professionals. For Marsh the best solution was to hire wind players from a regimental band, but when bandsmen were unavailable (as in Romsey or Canterbury), he had recourse to less satisfactory expedients, such as playing the oboe parts on violin or on flute, or writing the wind parts out for organ or even piano.[125] In 1793 the Sussex Militia Band declared that if their wages of 4s. per service were not raised they would secede from the Chichester concert. Unwilling and perhaps unable to give in to their demands, Marsh managed to hire two or three members of a Marine Band to replace the mutinous militiamen.[126]

Marsh's orchestras were based overwhelmingly on amateur performers. The only professionals needed, he said, looking back in 1821 on the eighteenth-century amateur musical scene, were

a leader and principal violoncello, and sometimes a principal second violin; as the ripieno violins and bass, which might all be doubled or tripled at pleasure, and the tenor might all be taken by amateurs, who many of them being men of business, or not having much leisure for practise, were thus not only furnished with an agreable recreation for themselves, but were enabled occasionally to entertain and gratify their friends and neighbours, upon very easy terms.[127]

The increasing professionalization that marked London's concert societies in the second half of the eighteenth century did not take place in Salisbury, Canterbury, or Chichester, first because audiences were not large enough to support a professional concert series, second because these towns had no theaters or other venues that could provide the core of a living for professional instrumentalists. As musical styles changed around the middle of the eighteenth century from the "ancient" works of Corelli, Geminiani, and Handel to the "modern" music of Stamitz, Abel, and J. C. Bach, the lack of professionals became more and more of a problem. As Marsh explained:

the amateur violin and violoncello players, unless able to play from the principal parts, were thus thrown out; not but that many of them could manage to take a duplicate first, or second violin, or bass part of the symphonies of those days. But this not being the case with the more elaborate symphonies of Haydn, Mozart, Beethoven &c., . . . these permanent subscription concerts therefore gradually dropped, the expence of supplying an orchestra with so many

[124] Ibid. 180.   [125] Ibid. 145, 300, 48, 354, 564, 619.   [126] Ibid. 334–35.
[127] John Marsh, *Instructions and Progressive Lessons for the Tenor* (1821), quoted in Charles Cudworth, "John Marsh on the Subscription Concert," *GSJ* 19 (1966), 132–34 at 133.

Pl. I. Festive music in the Salzburg Cathedral, 1682

Pl. II. Concert in a Roman church, *c.* 1660

Pl. III. Opera at the Teatro Regio, Turin, 1740

Pl. IV Festival at the church of San Petronio, Bologna, 1722 (detail)

Pl.V.   Concert for the "Counts of the North" at the Casino filarmonico, Venice, 1782

Pl. VI. Revival of Lully's *Armide* at the Paris Opéra, 1747

Pl.VII. Opéra Comique at the Hôtel de Bourgogne, 1772

Pl.VIII. Opera in Lille, 1729

Pl. IX. Ballet at the King's Theatre, c. 1808

Pl. X. Amateur orchestra at Melton Constable (East Anglia), 1734

Pl. XI. The Orchard St. Theatre, Bath, late eighteenth century

Pl. XII. Giostra dei caroselli, Rome, 1656

Pl. XIIa. Detail showing
instrumental ensemble

Pl. XIII. Serenata in the Teatro Argentina, Rome, 1747

Pl. XIV. Masked ball, Madrid, 1767

Pl. XV. G. M. Pagliardi, *Lisimaco*, Turin, 1681

Pl. XVI. Concert in the Sala d'Ercole, Bologna, 1705

professional performers, being greater than their funds would allow of, and they were succeeded by occasional concerts upon a larger scale . . . For want of this rallying point, or periodical assemblage of amateurs, it is now difficult, except in the larger provincial cities, or towns, to meet with four gentlemen capable of making up a Quartetto.[128]

By the end of the eighteenth century, amateur orchestras, the institution to which Marsh had devoted his life, were no longer viable in most English provincial towns.

PROVINCIAL ORCHESTRAS

A few provincial towns followed London toward the professionalization of orchestras. Although no provincial town enjoyed anything approaching London's rich network of venues, instrumentalists, and orchestras, the musical life in commercial towns, administrative centers, and resorts grew increasingly vigorous during the second half of the eighteenth century, as prosperity increased and communications improved. Provincial orchestras were based initially on the participation and leadership of gentleman amateurs, but with improving transportation they were drawn more and more into the network of London's musical life. By the end of the century several provincial towns had professional orchestras of their own.

In larger towns, like Norwich, amateur orchestras gave way to professionals around the middle of the eighteenth century. From 1724 on Norwich had a "Musick Meeting," at Mr. Freemoult's Long Room. "Any Gentlemen that are Lovers of Harmony," read the newspaper announcement, "may next Thursday Night be admitted into the said Musical and Friendly Society . . . either as Members, or Clubbers," that is, auditors.[129] By the late eighteenth century there were several concert societies in Norwich, including the Anacreontic Society, where the vocal performers were amateurs, but the instrumentalists were professionals from the theater orchestra. The White Swan, Norwich's first theater, was superseded by the New Theatre, which opened in January 1758 with "a compleat and regular Band of Musick."[130] "Regular" meant that it was a standing orchestra of professionals engaged for the season. There is no indication of how large an orchestra was considered "compleat" in Norwich in the 1750s; it needed to be big enough, however, to perform the symphonies by Pasquali, Giuseppe Sammartini, and Stamitz that were advertised as overtures and act music. During the plays themselves, it seems, the instrumentalists were free to come and go. A newspaper article of 1782 complained that "instead of entering the orchestra in a silent and becoming manner, they jostle together without the least order, and not only disturb the audience by tuning their instruments, but are equally or almost as vociferous as the actors."[131]

[128] Cudworth, "John Marsh," 133–34.
[129] Quoted in Trevor Fawcett, *Music in Eighteenth-Century Norwich and Norfolk* (Norwich, 1979), 4.
[130] Ibid. 8, 23.   [131] Ibid. 27.

Norwich also had not one but two pleasure gardens: Quantrell's, and Bunn's Rural Pavillion, each with its own orchestra. By the second half of the eighteenth century Norwich had reproduced in miniature most aspects of London's musical life, including standing orchestras, competing concerts, and a thriving market for orchestral music and musicians.

One reason for the vigor of Norwich orchestras was that the town was relatively close to London and transportation between Norwich and the metropolis improved considerably during the eighteenth century. Orchestra musicians from London made occasional appearances in Norwich, often in the summer and usually as soloists. As London to Norwich, so Norwich was to its smaller neighbors, like Fakenham, Bury St. Edmunds, Melton Constable, and King's Lynn. Gentleman amateurs organized musical societies, reinforced with Norwich professionals, who led the concerts and took the solo parts.[132] Norwich musicians also gave lessons in the surrounding countryside and played in private house concerts.

Bath was a special case among provincial towns, because the market for music there was much the same as the market in London. The same people, nobility and gentry, who came to London for the season also went to Bath to take the waters and to participate in the social whirl. As a resort town, Bath was the epitome of commercialized leisure, and many of its leisure activities—theater, dancing, dining, concerts, even drinking the mineral waters that gave the town its name—involved orchestras. There were standing orchestras at the Pump Room, at the New Assembly Rooms, at the Orchard Street Theatre, and also for the balls, each of them offering its players a contract for the duration of the season.[133] Plate XI depicts the Orchard Street Theatre in the last quarter of the eighteenth century. There seem to be about 20 musicians in front of the stage, playing violins, cellos, double bass, and harpsichord.[134] A roster from the Orchard Street Theatre in 1774 documents a somewhat smaller orchestra— 13 musicians in all, with only one of each wind instrument (Table 8.3). Orchestras in Bath were smaller than London orchestras, but they competed with one another just as vigorously. In the 1770s the old Pump Room orchestra, led by William Herschel (who had moved to Bath in 1767) and the orchestra of the New Assembly Rooms, led by Thomas Linley, were locked in bitter struggle in the concert rooms and in the press. Since there were only 15 or 20 professional instrumentalists altogether in Bath, competing orchestras had to be staffed by the same personnel. The musicians played concerts on alternate Tuesdays at the New Rooms and the Old, at the Orchard Street Theatre on Thursdays, and for dances at both rooms on a revolving

[132] Ibid. 37–38. See Pl. X.

[133] Kenneth Edward James, "Concert Life in Eighteenth-Century Bath" (Ph.D. diss., Royal Holloway College, University of London, 1987), 57. Jenny Burchell, *Polite or Commercial Concerts? Concert Management and Orchestral Repertoire in Edinburgh, Bath, Oxford, Manchester, and Newcastle, 1730–1799* (New York and London, 1996), 103–7. Some representative Bath orchestras are shown in Table 8.3.

[134] The ensemble in Pl. XI is larger than any recorded for the Orchard St. theater during this period. See Table 8.3; also Burchell, *Polite or Commercial Concerts?*, 115.

TABLE 8.3. *British provincial orchestras, 1757–1818*

City and date Venue	Keyboard and plucked strings	Bowed strings	Winds	Brass and drums	Unidentified	Source
BATH, 1767 Pump Room band					9 musicians	James, "Concert Life," 1047
BATH, 1771 New Assembly Rooms		6 violins 2 cellos	1 oboe		3 musicians	Ibid. 1051
BATH, 1774 Orchard St. Theatre	1 harpsichord	3 violins 1 viola 1 cello	1 oboe 1 bassoon	1 horn 1 trumpet	3 musicians	Ibid. 1050
CANTERBURY, 1783 Subscription concert	1 harpsichord	8 violins 2 violas 3 cellos 1 double bass	2 clarinets 1 bassoon			Marsh, *Journals*, 300
CHICHESTER, 1783 Music meeting	1 harpsichord	4 violins 2 violas 2 basses	2 flutes			Ibid. 402
DUBLIN, 1748 Smock Alley Theatre	1 harpsichord	10 violins 1 viola 1 cello 2 double basses	2 oboes 2 bassoons	2 horns 1 trumpet		Walsh, *Opera*, 74
EDINBURGH, 1757 Canongate Theatre		2 violins 1 viola 1 cello			4 musicians	Burchell, *Polite*, 58
EDINBURGH, 1817 New Theatre Royale	[1 keyboard]	4 violins 1 viola 1 cello 1 bass	1 flute 1 oboe 1 bassoon	2 horns		Ibid. 47

TABLE 8.3. (*Cont.*)

City and date Venue	Keyboard and plucked strings	Bowed strings	Winds	Brass and drums	Unidentified	Source
SALISBURY, 1776 Gentleman's concert	1 harpsichord 1 organ	6–8 violins 2 violas 1 cello 1 double bass	1–2 flutes 1 oboe	2 horns		Marsh, *Journals*, 145
PHILADELPHIA, 1794 Chestnut St. Theater	1 piano	"several violins"	2 flutes/oboes 2 bassoons	2 horns	[20 musicians in all]	Sonneck, *Early Opera*, 117
PHILADELPHIA, 1796 Oeller's Hotel	1 harpsichord	5 violins 1 viola 1 cello 1 bass	1 oboe 1 bassoon	2 horns (1 trumpet)		Sonneck, *Early Concert-Life*, 102
PHILADELPHIA, 1797 Bush Hill Gardens	1 organ	2 violins 1 viola 1 cello	1 clarinet	1 horn	4 musicians	Ibid. 102
CHARLESTON SC, 1783 "concerts"	1 harpsichord	4 first violins 3 second violins 2 violas 2 cellos	2 flutes 2 oboes/clarinets 2 bassoons	2 horns		Sonneck, *Contemporary*, 98
CHARLESTON SC, 1796 Grand Musical Festival	1 organ	12 violins 5 violas 3 cellos/basses	6 oboes/flutes/ clarinets 1 bassoon	2 horns 1 timpani		Sonneck, *Early Concert-Life*, 34
NEW YORK, 1798 Park Theater	[1 keyboard]	5 violins 1 viola 1 cello	1 oboe/clarinet 1 bassoon	2 horns		Odell, *Annals*, 38

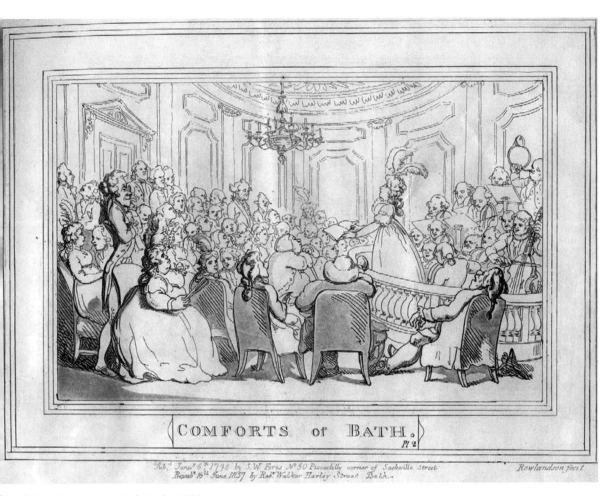

COMFORTS of BATH.

FIG. 8.3a. A concert at Bath in the 1790s

schedule.[135] The resident Bath musicians were augmented by a steady stream of virtuosos from London, some of whom appeared as soloists for a few concerts, others of whom stayed for an entire season. A visitor who attended a concert by the oboist J. C. Fischer in 1779 was dazzled by "the most brilliant Assembly my Eyes ever beheld. The Elegance of the room, illuminated with 480 wax Candles, the prismatic colours of the Lustres, the blaze of Jewels, and the inconceivable Harmony of near 40 Musicians, some of whom are the finest hands in Europe."[136]

Figures 8.3(*a–b*), caricatures by Thomas Rowlandson from the 1790s, give some sense of the Bath milieu. "The Concert" in Fig. 8.3(*a*) seems to be set in the Tearoom

[135] This account simplifies a situation that was in flux for most of the 1770s and that aroused a great deal of bitterness and controversy in the press. See James, "Concert Life", 191–229; also Ian Woodfield, *The Celebrated Quarrel between Thomas Linley (senior) and William Herschel: An Episode in the Musical Life of 18th-Century Bath* (Bath, 1977).

[136] Journal of Edmund Rack, quoted in James, "Concert Life," 226.

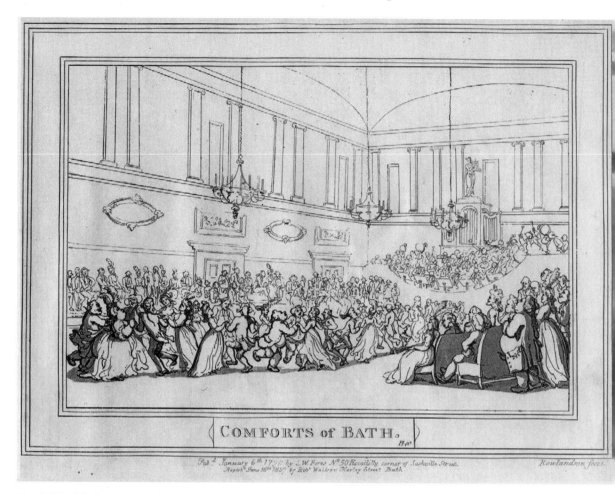

FIG. 8.3*b*. A ball at Bath in the 1790s

at the New Assembly Rooms. The orchestra, in a bandstand behind the singer, is closer to the 12 to 15 musicians in the records than the 40 in the account above. The orchestra in the ballroom at the New Assembly Rooms (Fig. 8.3(*b*)) contains about 20 instruments, including an organ, which is probably not being played, since the orchestra is accompanying a dance.

Edinburgh and Dublin, as historic capitals, tried to maintain musical institutions modeled on those of London. Dublin had two standing orchestras, the Lord Lieutenant's orchestra, whose members held government appointments like the King's Band, and a theater orchestra in Smock Alley, later at the Crow Street theater. The leader of the Lord Lieutenant's orchestra from 1716 to 1727 was J. S. Kusser, one-time Kapellmeister at Stuttgart and Lullist apostle in Germany (see Ch. 7).

Anglicized now as John Cousser, he composed an ode each year for the birthday of the English monarch. In addition he led the theater orchestra, whose personnel overlapped with that of the Lord Lieutenant's orchestra. Cousser at one point seems to have been in charge of the theater's finances too, for in his commonplace book he projected expenses and income in charmingly phonetic English:

1. The nights charge of yᵉ Playhouse in Dublin, is about five pounds odd money.
2. A weeks Salary for their Servants, &c: is three pounds ten or twelfe Shillings.
3. Boxes therein keeps at yᵉ most 80. Tikets. The Pit 150. Tikets: The Gallerie 200 Tikets.

There were also seats backstage, but "tikets" for them proved impossible to control:

4. Behind yᵉ Stage, suppose, there should be five pounds, which is impossible because yᵉ players lett inn, a whole trieb of perrewig makers, with their wifes, Daughters & friends, & several others of their own acquaintance upon written Tikets for yᵉ Use of Perewigs & other necessairies for yᵉ play.[137]

By 1748 Smock Alley boasted an orchestra of 22, larger than any other English provincial town (Table 8.3).

Many of the Dublin instrumentalists came from London, usually for only a season or two, arousing a certain degree of resentment from Dublin's resident musicians.[138] Dublin's pleasure gardens, the Rotunda Gardens, were owned and operated by the Lying-In Hospital and employed a standing orchestra of 18–20 musicians, which gave three concerts a week from April to September.[139] During the winter months, the Charitable Musical Society for the Release of Imprisoned Debtors put on a series of subscription concerts, which in some years employed the entire orchestra of the Smock Alley Theatre.[140] Finally, there were the orchestras of amateur musical societies, which in Dublin seem to have operated without the aid of professionals. Lord Mornington's Musical Academy, founded in 1757, stipulated in its bylaws: "No public mercenary performer, professor, or teacher of music shall ever be admitted into any rank of the Academy on any account whatsoever."[141]

In Edinburgh the Musical Society was composed of both amateurs and professionals, and for much of the eighteenth century it constituted the center of the town's elegant musical activities. Founded in 1728, the Society limited its membership at first to 70; later the enrollment was increased to 100, then to 130, finally in the 1770s to 170.

---

[137] New Haven, Yale University, Beinecke Library, Osborn Music MS 16, p. 409.

[138] Brian Boydell, "The Dublin Musical Scene 1749–50 and its Background," *PRMA* 105 (1978–79), 77–89 at 81.

[139] Brian Boydell, "Music at the Rotunda Gardens in Dublin, 1771–91," *Irish Musical Studies*, 1 (1990), 99–116.

[140] Boydell, "Dublin Musical Scene," 80.

[141] Quoted in Brian Boydell, "Music in Eighteenth-Century Dublin," in id. (ed.), *Four Centuries of Music in Ireland* (London, 1979), 34.

It gave weekly concerts and maintained a large music library.[142] Because Edinburgh was far from London, professional instrumentalists were not so readily available as in other provincial towns, and the Musical Society engaged "Masters" on salary for the season to raise the level of their concerts. Violinists Francesco Barsanti, Giuseppe Passarini, and John Collett all journeyed to Edinburgh as Masters of the Musical Society. The Society also hired several local professionals (at considerably lower wages than the "Masters") to reinforce the efforts of the amateurs. At the end of each concert members of the Society conferred to decide what music should be performed the next week and also who should play the "Leading Fidle."[143] By the 1790s the Musical Society had entered a period of decline, for reasons very much like those that John Marsh described in his post mortem on provincial subscription concerts: gentlemen amateurs found it hard to participate in the concerts, and subscriptions could not cover the expense of hiring professionals.[144] At the end of 1798 the Society was dissolved.

In Presbyterian Scotland the theater was the target of constant hostility, so Edinburgh's Canongate Theatre operated under the law as a concert hall. It sold tickets for "Concerts of Vocal and Instrumental Musick," after which the actors gave a free performance of a play.[145] Despite its legal status as the main attraction, the orchestra at the Canongate Theatre and in the Theatre Royal, which replaced it in 1769, was never large. In 1757 there were only eight instrumentalists in the pit (Table 8.3), and even in the nineteenth century the orchestra had only about 12 members. Edinburgh also had a succession of pleasure gardens, each with an orchestra but none of them particularly successful. A visitor to Comely Gardens in 1770 described it as "a wretched attempt to imitate Vauxhall."[146] Another visitor gave a lugubrious description of the instrumental ensemble:

I then approached the orchestra [i.e. the bandstand], which was in the ruins of an old pigeon house, with no other alteration, but that of removing the pigeons, and making room for four or five musicians, who were playing a composition, most musical, most melancholy, out of one of the windows. They continued thus for some time, but finding there was no one to listen to them . . . they gave over playing, and retired for the evening.[147]

Either there was not that much interest in pleasure, or Edinburgh residents found their pleasures somewhere other than the pleasure gardens.

Orchestras in the American colonies resembled those in the English provinces. Because America was a two to four months' journey from London, visiting stars

---

[142] David Johnson, *Music and Society in Lowland Scotland in the Eighteenth Century* (London, 1972), 33 ff.; Burchell, *Polite or Commercial Concerts?*, 31 ff. Although the Edinburgh Musical Society was formally organized in 1728, predecessor societies had been in operation since the 1690s.

[143] Minutes of 28 Jan. 1736, quoted in Johnson, *Music and Society*, 35.

[144] Burchell, *Polite or Commercial Concerts?*, 55.

[145] Burchell, *Polite or Commercial Concerts?*, 55–56

[146] H. Arnot, *The History of Edinburgh from the Earliest Accounts to the Present Time* (Edinburgh: William Creech, [1788]), quoted in Burchell, *Polite or Commercial Concerts?*, 59.

[147] E. Topham, *Letters from Edinburgh; Written in the Years 1774 and 1775* (London, 1776), quoted ibid. 50.

could not drop by to play a concerto or to lead the band. In other respects, however, musical life in Philadelphia, New York, and Charleston resembled that of other provincial towns. And the American Revolution of 1776–81 did little to alter the resemblance. American musical life in the Federal period was still very much that of an English province.

The largest city in the American colonies was Philadelphia, which with 17,000 inhabitants in 1760 could claim to be one of the largest English-speaking cities in the world. By the end of the eighteenth century Philadelphia had theaters, pleasure gardens, subscription concerts, and amateur musical societies, all of them with orchestras. Subscription concerts began in 1757. In 1771 a newspaper advertised a benefit concert, "commencing and ending with favourite Overtures, performed by a full Band of Music, with Trumpets, Kettle Drums, and every Instrument that can be introduced with Propriety."[148] In 1796 a benefit concert by Raynor Taylor at Oeller's Hotel featured an orchestra of 13 professional musicians (Table 8.3).

Religious restrictions hampered the development of Philadelphia theaters in the first half of the eighteenth century: as late as the 1760s plays and operas were being presented in Philadelphia, as in Edinburgh, disguised as "concerts." The Southwark Theatre, however, opened in the 1760s, and by the 1769 it had assembled the core of a professional orchestra, "assisted by some musical Persons who . . . have no View but to contribute to the Entertainment of the Public," that is, amateurs who performed in the theater for their own amusement and perhaps also as a sort of public service.[149] When the Chestnut Street Theater opened in 1794, however, it boasted a professional orchestra of "twenty accomplished musicians, many of them of great notoriety as concert players on their respective instruments."[150] By the 1790s Philadelphia also had pleasure gardens, indeed several competing gardens, Gray's, Harrowgate, and Bush Hill, each with an orchestra of about 10 instrumentalists (see Table 8.3). In Philadelphia, as in other English towns, a small number of instrumentalists served in a large number of venues. The same names turn up at the theater, at the subscription concerts, and at the pleasure gardens.

Charleston, South Carolina, had subscription concerts already in the 1730s, just about the time such concerts appeared in other provincial towns. The Santa Caecilia Society, founded in 1762, sponsored concerts by a mixed orchestra of gentleman performers and professionals. As in Edinburgh, the professionals were recruited to come to Charleston for the season. In 1771 the Society inserted an advertisement in the Boston Evening Post:

The St. Caecilia Society give notice that they will engage with, and give suitable encouragement to musicians properly qualified to perform at their Concert. . . . The performers they are

---

[148] *Pennsylvania Gazette* (29 Nov. 1771), quoted in Oscar Sonneck, *Early Concert-Life in America* (Leipzig, 1907), 75.

[149] Oscar Sonneck, *Early Opera in America* (New York, 1915), 25.

[150] Charles Durang, *History of the Philadelphia Stage* (manuscript), quoted in Sonneck, *Early Opera*, 117.

in want of are, a first and second violin, two hautboys, and a bassoon, whom they are willing to agree with for one, two, or three years.[151]

Evidently their recruiting campaign was successful, for a visitor to Charleston in 1773 reported hearing a concert that featured two bass viols (possibly cellos) and French horns, plus "one Abbercrombie, a Frenchman just arrived [who] played a first fiddle and solo incomparably, better than any I ever had heard."[152] "Abbercrombie," he continued, "can't speak a word of English and has a salary of 500 guineas a year from the St. Cecilia Society." In 1783 another visitor heard music by Corelli, Bach, Abel, Stamitz, and Haydn played by an orchestra of 20 (Table 8.3).[153] The orchestra was still led by Abercrombie, whom this writer identified as a Scotsman. Perhaps the earlier visitor mistook Abercrombie's Scottish burr for French. The St. Cecilia performers played in the theater as well and also in Charleston's very own "Vauxhall Garden."

New York too had a "Vauxhall Garden," indeed a succession of Vauxhall Gardens, which competed with a succession of "Ranelagh Gardens," each offering "a complete band of music." There were also competing concert series in the 1790s put on by professional musicians, some of whom had just come from London's rival orchestras. Gentleman performers participated in these concerts too. A performance in 1770 of Handel's *Messiah* was accomplished with "the kind assistance of gentlemen, who are lovers of music and performers on instruments."[154] When the Park Street Theater opened in 1798, the orchestra numbered 14 (Table 8.3). New York theater musicians, like their English cousins, came and went during the performance. An observer at the John Street Theater in 1787 complained that "The musicians . . . instead of performing between the play and the farce are suffered to leave the orchestra to pay a visit to the tippling houses, and the ladies in the meantime, must amuse themselves by looking at the candles and empty benches."[155]

In English industrial cities and towns of the Midlands and the North, the development of orchestras took a somewhat different course. Birmingham had a "Musical and Amicable Society" that gave a subscription series beginning in 1762, and it had both a "Vauxhall" and an "Apollo" garden already in the 1750s.[156] Manchester had a musical society that sponsored sporadic concerts as early as 1748 and a regular series from 1770.[157] More characteristic of the Midlands, however, were the "music

---

[151] *Boston Evening Post* (17 June 1771). Quoted in Sonneck, *Early Concert-Life*, 18.

[152] Journal of Josiah Quincy, quoted in Robert J. Bagdon, "Musical Life in Charleston, South Carolina, from 1732 to 1776, as Recorded in Colonial Sources" (Ph.D. diss., University of Miami, 1978), 179.

[153] Oscar Sonneck, "A Contemporary Account of Music in Charleston, S.C., of the Year 1783," in William Lichtenwanger (ed.), *Oscar Sonneck and American Music* (Urbana: University of Illinois Press, 1983), 94–99 at 98–99.

[154] Sonneck, *Early Concert-Life*, 166–67, 180–81, 191. This was not a performance of the entire *Messiah* but of "the overture and sixteen other pieces. . . . Never performed in America."

[155] Quoted in George Odell, *Annals of the New York Stage*, ii: *1798–1821* (New York, 1927), i. 254.

[156] J. Sutcliffe Smith, *The Story of Music in Birmingham* (Birmingham: Cornish Brothers, 1945), 10–14.

[157] Burchell, *Polite or Commercial Concerts?*, 244 ff.; Sadie, "Concert Life," 20.

festivals" that took place in the summer and often involved strikingly large orchestras.[158] Festivals typically lasted two or three days and featured both morning and evening concerts, as well as public breakfasts, glee and catch singing, and dances after the evening concerts. The repertory of the festivals was built around large-scale works for voices and orchestra, above all the oratorios and anthems of Handel. Festivals represented an enormous outlay of organizational energy and money, so towns staged them every third year at most. They were financed both by subscription and by ticket sales, sometimes for a charitable purpose, sometimes as a kind of civic speculation. Liverpool had a festival as early as 1740, Birmingham from 1768, Newcastle from 1778, York from 1791. Festivals were not confined to the Midlands and the North. Oxford and Cambridge held sporadic festivals, as did some cathedral towns like Salisbury and Winchester.

Festival orchestras, as shown in Table 8.4, were much larger than other provincial orchestras. Local theaters and concert societies could not furnish nearly enough professional instrumentalists, so players were brought in on contract from London. A sort of "festival circuit" grew up in which the same London instrumentalists played at Birmingham one summer, at Liverpool the next, at Manchester the next, and then back to the beginning of the circuit, with stops along the way at Newcastle, York, and elsewhere. Rather few of the players at the festivals were local musicians; most of them came from the theaters and concert orchestras of London. The festival circuit was formalized by John Ashley and his sons, who organized "Grand Musical Festivals" and "Festival Tours" of London-based performers in the 1790s and 1800s.[159] Balances in these provincial festival orchestras were similar to those of London oratorio orchestras, with middle parts more heavily staffed than in theater orchestras and with the wind parts heavily doubled. The Handel commemoration at Westminster Abbey in 1784 was modeled, then, on provincial music festivals, not the other way round.[160] The musical forces in London, however, were much larger than what was possible in the provinces (Table 8.4).

The size and strength of the orchestra was a point of special pride for festival organizers: "The Band will be more numerous than on any former Occasion"; "The band was more numerous and select, and the power and choral effect greater than on any former occasion"; "some of the best Voices, and . . . some of the most finely touched

---

[158] Information on the music festivals is taken from the series of studies by Reid and Pritchard: Douglas J. Reid, assisted by Brian W. Pritchard, "Some Festival Programmes of the Eighteenth and Nineteenth Centuries—1. Salisbury and Winchester," *RMA Research Chronicle*, 5 (1965), 51–60; Douglas J. Reid, "Some Festival Programmes of the Eighteenth and Nineteenth Centuries—2. Cambridge and Oxford," *RMA Research Chronicle*, 6 (1966), 3–22; Brian W. Pritchard, "Some Festival Programmes of the Eighteenth and Nineteenth Centuries—3. Liverpool and Manchester," *RMA Research Chronicle*, 7 (1969), 1–25; Brian W. Pritchard and Douglas J. Reid, "Some Festival Programmes of the Eighteenth and Nineteenth Centuries—4. Birmingham, Derby, Newcastle Upon Tyne and York," *RMA Research Chronicle*, 8 (1970), 1–22.

[159] Brian W. Pritchard, "The Provincial Festivals of the Ashley Family," *GSJ* 22 (1969), 58–77.

[160] Dean, *Handel's Dramatic Oratorios*, 105.

TABLE 8.4. *Orchestras for English music festivals, 1759–1805*

City and date	Keyboard and plucked strings	Bowed strings	Winds	Brass and drums	Unidentified	Source
Birmingham, 1759	[1 organ]	16 violins 4 violas 4 cellos [1] double bass	[2] oboes 4 bassoons	[2] horns [2] trumpets timpani		Pritchard and Reid, "Some Festival Programmes," 5
Birmingham, 1767	1 organ 1 harpsichord	16 violins 4 violas 5 cellos 2 double basses	4 oboes 4 bassoons	2 horns 2 trumpets timpani		Ibid. 6
Gloucester, 1763	[keyboard]	16 violins 4 violas 4 cellos 2 double basses	4 oboes 3 bassoons 2 clarinets	2 horns 3 trumpets 1 timpani		Dean, *Handel's Dramatic Oratorios*, 104
Liverpool, 1787	1 organ	6 violins 1 viola 2 cellos 1 double bass	4 oboes 1 flute 4 bassoons	1 horn 2 trumpets 1 trombone 1 timpani	4 musicians	Pritchard, "Some Festival Programmes," 4
Liverpool, 1805		23 violins 6 violas 6 cellos 4 double basses	2 flutes 4 oboes 2 clarinets 4 bassoons	2 horns 4 trumpets 3 trombones 1 timpani		Ibid. 7–8
London, 1784 (Handel Commemoration)	1 organ 1 harpsichord	48 first violins 47 2nd violins 26 violas 21 cellos 15 double basses	13 first oboes 13 2nd oboes 6 flutes 26 bassoons 1 double bassoon	12 horns 21 trumpets 6 trombones 4 drummers		Burney, *Account*, 17–19
Manchester, 1785	[1 organ]	9 violins 2 cellos 1 double bass	1 flute 1 oboe 1 bassoon	1 trumpet	10 musicians	Pritchard, "Some Festival Programmes," 16
Manchester, 1792	[1 organ]	13 violins 2 violas 5 cellos 1 double bass	1 flute 3 oboes 3 bassoons	2 horns 1 trumpet	8 musicians	Ibid. 17

Instruments that this Country could boast of."[161] For the local gentry and for the merchants and manufacturers of these northern towns, having the biggest and best orchestra in England was a point of civic pride. The festival and its orchestra represented not just the purchasing power of new money, but the cultural aspirations and pretensions of the entire community. This was a new meaning for the orchestra, one that would become more important during the nineteenth century, not only in England but in America and on the Continent as well.

[161] Pritchard, "Festival Programmes . . . 3," 5, 6, 15.

Chapter Nine

The Classical Orchestra

Which was the best orchestra in Europe in the second half of the eighteenth century? Every critic, commentator, and musical tourist seemed to have an opinion. "The first orchestra in Europe, for the number and intelligence of symphonists," says Jean-Jacques Rousseau in 1754, "is that of Naples; but the best distributed . . . is the orchestra at the opera house of the King of Poland, at Dresden."[1] Not so, says Louis Petit de Bachaumont, publicist and chronicler, in 1773: "as far as the instruments are concerned," everyone agrees that the Concert Spirituel in Paris "is at present the best regulated concert in all of Europe."[2] Leopold Mozart (1763) declares that the orchestra at Mannheim is the best, if not in all of Europe, at least in Germany.[3] A critic at the London *Advertiser* in 1778 casts his vote for the home team: the orchestra of the King's Theatre in the Haymarket, he says, is "infinitely superior to any other in Europe."[4] Finally, Francesco Galeazzi in 1791 does not hesitate to assert that the orchestra of the Teatro Regio in Turin is "indisputably the finest in Europe."[5]

Evidently the question of "which is the best orchestra" could not be resolved in the eighteenth century any more satisfactorily than it can be today. What is more important than who is right is that so many writers presumed to make such a comparison at all. All seem to accept the premise that the instrumental ensembles at theaters and concert halls in France, Germany, Italy, and England have enough in common that ranking them is a meaningful exercise. This had not always been the case. When Sebastiano Locatelli visited Lyons in 1664, he found ensembles of massed strings so different from what he was accustomed to in Bologna that he did not have a name for

---

[1] Jacques Rousseau, *Dictionnaire de musique*, 354.   [2] Bachaumont, *Mémoires secrets*, xxiv. 260.

[3] Letter of 19 July 1763; Mozart, *Briefe*, i. 79.

[4] Quoted in Theodore Fenner, *Opera in London: Views of the Press, 1785–1830* (Carbondale, Ill., 1994), 248.

[5] Galeazzi, *Elementi teorico-pratici*, i. 222.

them and resorted to calling them "an assembly [*radunanza*] of instrumentalists."[6] When François Raguenet went to Rome at the beginning of the eighteenth century, he found the orchestras of Rome similarly incommensurate with those of Paris. Roman violins had thicker strings and longer bows, Italians used a 16-foot double bass, and Roman orchestras played so much more loudly than French that when he returned to Paris, it seemed to him as though the orchestra at the Opéra were playing with mutes.[7] At the end of the eighteenth century Friedrich Nicolai, visiting Vienna from Berlin, had the opposite experience. He expected Viennese orchestras to sound considerably different from what he was used to; instead he found that they sounded very similar. The Viennese musicians lifted their bows off the strings more than the Berliners did, and they did not lengthen dotted notes in slow overtures. However, symphonies by Haydn and Vanhal, he reported, "sound almost exactly the same as when I heard them in Berlin."[8] What for Locatelli and Raguenet were differences in kind between instrumental ensembles have become for Nicolai differences in degree between orchestras.

The transformation of instrumental ensembles into orchestras, which began in France around the middle of the seventeenth century, spread rapidly to the rest of Europe, so that by 1740 almost every large city and every important court had an ensemble that called itself, or could be called, an orchestra. The ensuing period— from about 1740 to about 1815—was a time of consolidation. The instrumentation, organization, social roles, and performance practices of the orchestra changed comparatively little during this period. In retrospect the orchestras of the second half of the eighteenth century and the early nineteenth century can be referred to collectively as the "classical orchestra"—classical in that they represented the first orchestral configuration that was both stable and normative. In addition, these were the orchestras for which Haydn, Mozart, and Beethoven composed their symphonies, concertos, and operas; as their works were turned into "classics," their orchestra became "classical." The classical orchestra had three relatively stable aspects:

1. Instruments. The classical orchestra typically included violins, violas, cellos, and double basses, flutes, oboes, horns, and bassoons, and keyboard continuo. Trumpets and timpani were optional. Clarinets were added toward the end of the period.

2. Internal organization. Four-part scoring was the norm: two sections of violins and one of violas, plus a *basso* group consisting of cellos, double basses, bassoons, and keyboard. Winds were added as pairs of players, usually one on a part, although in larger orchestras the parts could be doubled.

3. Balances and proportions. The size of the classical orchestra varied greatly from one place and one venue to another. However the balances between instruments var-

---

[6] Locatelli, *Viaggio di Francia*, 169.   [7] Raguenet, *Parallele des Italiens et des François*, 104.

[8] Friedrich Nicolai, *Beschreibung einer Reise durch Deutschland und die Schweiz, im Jahre 1781* (Berlin, 1783–96), iv. 542.

ied much less. Whether an orchestra was large or small, violins typically comprised 50 to 70 percent of the string section, violas 10 to 15 percent, cellos and double basses 20 to 30 percent. The proportion of winds in the orchestra varied considerably: from 20 percent in large orchestras to over 50 percent in smaller orchestras.

Recent historians have tended to emphasize the particularities of local traditions and the differences between orchestras used for different kinds of music in the eighteenth century.[9] Orchestras that played oratorios tended to be larger than orchestras that played symphonies, orchestras that played symphonies larger than orchestras for concertos. Italian orchestras used three-string double basses during most of the period, while German and French orchestras tended to use four- or even five-string instruments. English amateur orchestras preserved concertino–ripieno organization long after it had been abandoned elsewhere. French orchestras tended to have more cellos than basses, Italian orchestras more basses than cellos. Despite these and other differences between particular orchestras, a broad consensus obtained during much of the eighteenth century about what an orchestra was, what instruments it comprised and in what proportions, and how those instruments were organized. There was also general agreement about the venues and social situations in which orchestras performed, how orchestras should be administered, what orchestral music should look like, and how instrumentalists should comport themselves in an orchestra.

These areas of consensus about the "classical" orchestra made it possible for orchestra musicians and orchestral repertory to circulate with great freedom during much of the eighteenth century. German musicians played in French, English, and Italian orchestras, Italian musicians in English, French, and German orchestras. Musicians from theater orchestras played in church orchestras; musicians from church orchestras played for dances. German symphonies were heard in London and Paris, French dances were played in Copenhagen and Vienna, and Italian opera was staged in all the capitals of Europe. The circulation of musicians and repertory among eighteenth-century orchestras suggests that local traditions and performance practices formed part of an overarching trans-national culture of the orchestra.

Not every eighteenth-century instrumentalist or instrumental ensemble participated in this culture of the orchestra. Civic musicians and town waits in Germany and England operated for the most part in a different world—of music for processions and public ceremonies, of wedding and dance music played one on a part. Trumpet and drum corps, military bands, and the *Harmonie* bands that played outdoor serenades and dinner music operated in distinct, non-orchestral musical cultures. Musicians did circulate between these ensembles and orchestras, but not nearly so frequently or so freely as from one orchestra to another. Similarly, orchestral and non-orchestral

---

[9] See e.g. Zaslaw, *Mozart's Symphonies*, 450, or Dexter Edge, "Mozart's Viennese Orchestras," *EM* 20 (1992), 64–88 at 65. For a view more like ours, see George Stauffer, "The Modern Orchestra: A Creation of the Late 18th Century," in Joan Peyser (ed.), *The Orchestra: Origins and Transformations* (New York, 1986), 37–68.

ensembles could share repertory, but only on the basis of extensive rescoring—for example, symphonies arranged for string quartet or opera arias arranged for *Harmonie* band. By the mid-eighteenth century the boundaries between orchestral and non-orchestral ensembles had become relative clear, and they served to emphasize the distinctiveness of orchestras and orchestral culture.

ORCHESTRAL INSTRUMENTS

The instrumentation of the classical orchestra remained stable from about 1740 until the end of the eighteenth century—both the types of instruments used and the design of those instruments. Only one new instrument, the clarinet, was introduced into the orchestra during this period. Stringed instruments hardly changed at all. Instrument makers experimented with added keys on woodwinds and with devices that enabled horn and trumpet players to alter the sounding lengths of their instruments, but none of these instruments was fundamentally redesigned. The models of instrument prevalent at the beginning of the period were still the most widespread at the end. With a few exceptions (double basses, horns), orchestras in different countries used instruments of similar design.

Standard tunings for violins and violas had been established in the seventeenth century; dimensions became standard in the first quarter of the eighteenth century.[10] The large violas that had been used for the lower middle parts (*taille, quinte*) in seventeenth-century orchestras went out of fashion in the first half of the eighteenth century.[11] Strings were gut, but the lowest string (G on the violin, C on the viola) was overspun with silver or copper wire.[12] This pattern, which originated in Italy, became universal by the last quarter of the eighteenth century.[13] Contemporary writers say little about the bows that orchestral violinists and violists used in the second half of the eighteenth century. Judging from pictures, orchestral players may have continued to use the short bows of seventeenth-century string bands for some time after soloists had adopted longer Italian bows. Perhaps both types were in simultaneous use in some orchestras. Beginning around the 1780s the Tourte-style bow, with its hatchet head and concave stick, and other similar bows, began to make their way among violin soloists, and within a generation they started to turn up in orchestra violin and viola sections, gradually displacing older models.

---

[10] Peter Walls, "The Violin Family," in Howard Mayer Brown and Stanley Sadie (eds.), *Performance Practice: Music after 1600* (New York, 1989), 44–67 at 46.

[11] Grétry complained that the violas in French orchestras of the late 18th c. were too small, "violins strung with viola strings." He advocated a return to the larger violas of the beginning of the century (quoted in Maurice Riley, *The History of the Viola* (Ann Arbor, 1980), 152).

[12] Boyden, *The History of Violin Playing*, 321; Peruffo, "Italian Violin Strings," 159.

[13] Segerman, "Strings through the Ages," 54.

The situation with respect to orchestral bowed bass instruments was more complex than that of the upper strings. Four principal types of bowed bass instruments could be found in eighteenth-century orchestras: (1) the bass viol—a viola da gamba in the 8-foot register with six or more strings and a fretted fingerboard; (2) a large 8-foot violin-family instrument with four to six strings and a long neck, that went by the names basse de violon, violone, Bassgeige, and others; (3) the violoncello, a smaller 8-foot instrument—essentially the modern cello; (4) a 16-foot viol-like instrument with three or four strings, called violone, contrebasse, contrabasso, or double bass. By 1740 the first two types had pretty much disappeared from orchestras, although an occasional gambist can still be found on personnel rosters, and some older musicians played 8-foot violoni past mid-century.[14] Because of terminological overlap— "violone" can be either a 8-foot or a 16-foot instrument and "basse" can be either a cello or a basse de violon—it is often difficult to ascertain just which bass instruments were present in a given orchestra. In principle the "classical" orchestra contained both cellos and double basses, although many individual orchestras lacked cellos, and a few had no double basses. Three-string, unfretted double basses were the rule in Italy, four-string fretted basses in France; German players used three-, four- and five-string models.[15]

Oboes and bassoons had been part of the orchestra since the end of the seventeenth century. Alto and tenor oboes, which sometimes played the middle parts in Lully's orchestra, were sparingly used in Italy and England. In Germany the hautbois d'amour, pitched in A, and the oboe da caccia, pitched in F, enjoyed a vogue as obbligato soloists in the early eighteenth century, but had passed out of fashion by 1740.[16] Already at the beginning of the eighteenth century the most common scoring in France as well as the rest of Europe was a pair of treble oboes, who could either play solo parts or double the violin parts.

Transverse flutes, which entered the orchestra as specialty instruments in opera scores around the beginning of the eighteenth century, had replaced recorders almost entirely by the 1740s.[17] At first most orchestras used the same performers to play both flutes and oboes, but in the 1740s and 1750s orchestras began to hire flute specialists, and by the 1770s most larger orchestras included one or two flutes alongside the oboes. Circular "hoop" horns with one or two coils and no valves, which had been used as hunting instruments in the second half of the seventeenth century, became increasingly common in orchestras during the 1720s and 1730s—except in France,

[14] The orchestra of San Petronio Cathedral in Bologna lists a violone player alongside a cellist and a double bassist as late as 1807 (Osvaldo Gambassi, *La cappella musicale di S. Petronio* (Florence, 1987), 310).

[15] Cyr, "*Basses* and *basse continue*"; Rodney Slatford and Alyn Shipton, "Double Bass," in *NG II*, vii. 519–25.

[16] See Haynes, *The Eloquent Oboe*, 367–83. In several cantatas Bach calls for a "taille," a tenor oboe, e.g. BWV 140, 146, 169, 186.

[17] Simpson, "The Orchestral Recorder."

where they were not introduced until the late 1740s.[18] Horn players specialized either on high (*alto*) or low (*basso*) parts, played on the same instruments but with a different technique and possibly different mouthpieces. By the 1750s most symphonies published in Paris, London, and Amsterdam were scored for four string parts plus two oboes and two horns, suggesting that horns and oboes were available in most orchestras. This *à 8* scoring, which could accommodate flutes alternating with oboes as well as bassoons playing along on the bass line—remained standard for published symphonies until the 1780s.

Trumpets, and the timpani which usually accompanied them, occupied a peculiar position in the instrumentation of the classical orchestra. Essential to ceremony and display, trumpeters and drummers were organized into guilds or trumpet corps and were seldom listed on orchestra personnel rosters or payrolls until the latter part of the century. However, trumpets were usually available to orchestras when needed—for royal entrances in the theater, for the Te Deum in church, for festive symphonies on important occasions. Published symphonies occasionally include parts for trumpets and drums; just as often, trumpet and drum parts were added to symphonies *ad lib*. Many symphonies circulated both with and without trumpet and drum parts.

The only new instrument added to the orchestra between 1740 and 1815 was the clarinet. During the first half of the eighteenth century the clarinet was a novelty instrument, a woodwind that could imitate a trumpet.[19] Technical improvements that enabled the clarinet to play in its lower (chalumeau) register as well as the upper made it more useful to ensembles, and in the 1730s German Kapellen began to acquire pairs of clarinets, usually played by oboists.[20] Clarinet specialists do not turn up on Kapelle rosters until decades later: Mannheim, 1759; Koblenz, 1769; Munich, 1774; Berlin, 1786; Dresden, 1795.[21] La Pouplinière's orchestra in Paris included a pair of clarinet players in 1763; the Opéra added clarinetists to its payroll in 1770.[22] The first Italian orchestra to list clarinets as regular members seems to have been the Turin Teatro Regio in 1779.[23] Other wind instruments were less successful at making their way into the orchestra. Oboe d'amore, English horn, chalumeau, basset horn, flageolet, and musette all made appearances at one time or another during the eighteenth century as solo instruments and in opera accompaniments but never acquired a permanent role or a place on orchestra rosters.

The design of wind instruments changed more during the period of the classical orchestra than stringed-instrument design. Orchestral wind players seem to have been rather slow, however, to adopt redesigned instruments. In the last decades of the eighteenth century, for example, many players continued to use one- or two-key

[18] R. Morley-Pegge, *The French Horn*, 2nd edn. (London, 1973), 16–17.
[19] See Rice, *The Baroque Clarinet*, 143 ff.   [20] Ibid. 151 ff.
[21] Mahling, "Orchester und Orchestermusiker," *passim*.   [22] Cucuel, *La Pouplinière*, 1771.
[23] Moffa, *Storia della regia cappella di Torino*, 63. The Teatro Regio roster for 1773–74 lists six "Oboè e Clarinette," of which two were very likely already clarinet specialists (Bouquet, *Il Teatro di Corte*, 171).

wooden flutes, even though models with additional keys had long been available.[24] The oboe was a two-key instrument throughout the period. In the 1730s and 1740s German and Italian makers began to make a new kind of oboe with a narrower bore and a sweeter sound.[25] This was the instrument favored by famous players like Besozzi and Fischer, but is hard to tell how quickly it replaced older models in general orchestral use. Four- and five-key clarinets were the prevalent models in orchestras until the second or third decade of the nineteenth century.[26] They were usually played with the reed against the upper rather than the lower lip. The standard orchestral horn during the entire period was a natural horn fitted with a set of crooks that could transpose the instrument into as many as eight or nine different keys. In the second half of the century other systems were developed, the Inventionshorn and the cor solo, where the extra tubing was added in the middle of the horn rather than next to the mouthpiece, but these seem to have been primarily solo instruments, not widely used by orchestral horn players.[27]

It is possible, indeed likely, that there were systematic differences during the period under consideration between the design of wind instruments in use in different regions of Europe. Shackleton suggests that Austrian and Bohemian clarinets of the late eighteenth century had larger holes and a fuller tone in the lower register than French and English instruments.[28] Bowers distinguishes between "English style" flutes with metal-lined head joints and a bright, open sound vs. "German style" flutes with smaller embouchure holes and no metal, which produced a more veiled sound.[29] However such differences are hard to document, and regional differences were balanced by the international market for wind instruments and the movement of players from one country to another.

The keyboard instrument most widely used in the classical orchestra was the harpsichord. When an orchestra accompanied a singer, in the theater or in concert, a harpsichord usually realized the bass line in order to keep the singer on pitch and to coordinate between the singer and the instrumentalists. In *secco* recitative the harpsichord, often along with the first cello and first bass, provided the entire accompaniment. In church orchestras the organ was the primary keyboard continuo instrument, but solo singers were often accompanied by harpsichord.[30] On the other hand, some

---

[24] John Solum, *The Early Flute* (Oxford, 1992), 50; Ardal Powell, *The Flute* (New Haven, 2001), 111–12.

[25] Haynes, *The Eloquent Oboe*, 396–401.

[26] Nicholas Shackleton, "Clarinet," in *The New Grove Dictionary of Musical Instruments*, ed. Stanley Sadie (London, 1984), i. 389–403 at 393; Albert Rice, "A History of the Clarinet to 1820" (Ph.D. diss., Claremont Graduate School, 1987), 243 ff., 265 ff.

[27] Morley-Pegge, *The French Horn*, 22.   [28] Shackleton, "Clarinet."

[29] Jane Bowers, "Mozart and the Flute," *EM* 20 (1992), 31–42 at 39. These differences parallel the preference for high-arched Stainer violins in central Europe and for flatter Stradivari and Amati instruments in Italy, France, and England, and also between Viennese and English fortepianos. See Neal Zaslaw, "Mozart's Instruments," *EM* 20 (1992), 5–6.

[30] Johann Mattheson, *Der vollkommene Capellmeister* (Hamburg, 1739), 484; Dreyfus, *Bach's Continuo Group*, 23–25, 32 ff.

theater and concert orchestras used the organ in place of the harpsichord. Handel, for performances of his oratorios at the King's Theatre in the Haymarket, played both harpsichord and organ—harpsichord for recitatives and arias, organ for choruses and for the concertos he played as entr'actes.[31] The orchestra of the Concert Spirituel in Paris was arranged around an organ; it listed a harpsichordist among its personnel in 1752, but an organist for many years thereafter. Very likely both instruments were available, once the management had negotiated with the Opéra for permission to include French and Italian arias in the programs (see Ch. 6). After 1774 there was no keyboardist at all on the Concert Spirituel roster, although vocalists continued to appear at the concerts.

A harpsichord might also play in purely instrumental works like symphonies and concertos, but here there was great variability in practice. Over half of the symphonies published or copied in France between 1733 and 1756 were provided with a figured bass, presumably to help a harpsichordist play along. After that the percentage declined steadily, so that during the last decade of the century, according to Barry Brook's survey, not a single symphony was published with a figured bass.[32] Charles Avison, in the preface to his Concertos Op. 3 (1751), calls explicitly for a harpsichord, but he warns the harpsichordist to play only in tutti sections and to take care that "no jangling Sound, or scattering of the Notes" is heard in the pauses after cadences.[33] Some symphonies composed at Mannheim in the 1760s have figures under the bass line in the manuscript parts, suggesting that a harpsichord might have been a regular member of the orchestra for symphonies at that time.[34] Haydn, on the other hand, did not use a harpsichord in the orchestra that played his symphonies at Eszterháza and Eisenstadt.[35] By the second half of the eighteenth century south German orchestras in general did not use a harpsichord for symphonies or on other occasions when there was no vocalist. At the Paris Opéra in Rameau's time the harpsichord accompanied recitatives, arias (*airs, ariettes*), duets, and other solo vocal numbers but did not play in overtures, *symphonies,* and dances, nor in the choruses.[36] Whether orchestras included a keyboard instrument when there was no vocalist seems to have been a matter of regional preference or custom. English and north German orchestras were more likely to use a harpsichord for symphonies and concertos;

[31] Dean, *Handel's Dramatic Oratorios*, 110. In 1738 Handel acquired a claviorgan, an instrument on which the same keyboard operated both a harpsichord and an organ. For it he wrote the organ concerto inserted into his oratorio *Saul*.

[32] Brook, *La Symphonie française*, i. 467–72.

[33] Charles Avison, *Six Concertos in Seven Parts, Op. 3* (London, 1751), p. iii.

[34] Robert Münster, "Die Sinfonien Toeschis" (Diss., Munich: Ludwig-Maximilians-Universität, 1956), 120–21.

[35] Webster, "On the Absence of Keyboard Continuo"; see also Sonja Gerlach, "Haydns Orchesterpartituren: Fragen der Realisierung des Textes," *Haydn-Studien*, 5 (1984), 169–83 at 175.

[36] Graham Sadler, "The Role of the Keyboard Continuo in French Opera 1673–1776," *EM* 8 (1980), 148–57.

in France, southern Germany, and Italy the harpsichord was rare in purely orchestral music.

INTERNAL ORGANIZATION

The classical orchestra was founded on the principle of four-part string scoring. "The instruments that accompany the solo part," says J. A. Scheibe in 1739, "consist of two violins, a viola, and the thoroughbass; however, these can be doubled or increased further in performance according to preference and also depending on how many musicians are available."[37] Georg von Unold, 60 years later in 1802, says almost exactly the same thing: "the quartet (first and second violins, violas, basses, and keyboard), needs to be placed together [because] all compositions really have only four parts; other instruments, no matter how necessary, are really just filler and doubling."[38] In four-part scoring the number of parts in the music corresponds in a stable way to the grouping of instruments and players in the orchestra. String players are divided, conceptually and physically, into four groups, with cellos and double basses combined as a single "basso." Each part in the score represents a cohesive group of instrumentalists who play that part together in movement after movement, piece after piece.

In its application, however, the four-part principle was far from rigid. Composers often combined first and second violins for entire movements—particularly in Italian opera arias. Violas could be omitted to reduce the texture; the violas could also double the violins an octave lower or the basso an octave higher. If violas were unneeded for long stretches, violists could play violins.[39] On the other hand, a composer might call for the violas to play divisi, creating a temporary five-part texture.[40] Solo–ripieno scorings also persisted during much of the period, overlapping standard four-part scoring. In England orchestras continued to differentiate between principal and ripieno violinists and continued to perform the concerti grossi of Corelli, Geminiani, and Handel. As late as 1802 H. C. Koch still says that when an orchestra accompanies a soloist and there are many players on the four principal parts, then it is customary for some of the ripienists to stop playing during solo passages and to reenter when they see "Tutti" written in their music.[41] And indeed, sets of manuscript

---

[37] Scheibe, *Critischer Musikus*, 631.

[38] Georg von Unold, "Einige Bemerkungen über die Stellung der Orchester und Einrichtung der Musiksäle," *AMZ* 4 (Aug. 1802), cols. 782–83.

[39] For examples of entire operas without violas, see David Guion, "The Instrumentation of Operas Published in France in the 18th Century," *Journal of Musicological Research*, 4 (1982), 115–43 at Table IX.

[40] In sacred music from Dresden the violas are often divided into two parts marked "alto" and "tenore" (Thomas Kohlhase, "Anmerkungen zur Generalbasspraxis der Dresdener Hofkirchemusik der 1720er bis 1740er Jahre," in id. (ed.), *Zelenka Studien I* (Kassel, 1993), 233–40 at 234). Mozart wrote divisi viola parts in a number of his symphonies, e.g. K. 84, K. 139.

[41] Heinrich Christoph Koch, *Musikalisches Lexikon* (Frankfurt am Main, 1802), col. 1610.

parts for Viennese concertos in the second half of the eighteenth century sometimes include ripieno violin parts, which contain music for the tutti sections but not for accompanying the solos.[42]

The *basso* in four-part scoring differed from the upper three parts in that it could include instruments of different types: cellos, double basses, keyboards, and bassoons.[43] The balance of the different types of instruments in the *basso* varied from one place to another—some orchestras had more cellos than basses, some more basses than cellos; some had only one or two bassoons, others had four or five.[44] In principle all the *basso* instruments played from the same bass line, with the keyboard adding improvised harmonies. However, the presence of instruments of several types in the *basso* created possibilities for micro-scoring within the *basso* group. For example *secco* recitative was usually accompanied by a reduced *basso*, often a keyboard and a double bass and/or a cello. Composers sometimes created special textures in arias by indicating that only certain *basso* instruments should play. If they wanted the 8-foot register only, they could write "senza contrabasso" or simply shift from bass to tenor clef, which signaled the double basses to drop out. Indications of "senza cembalo" and "senza fagotto" are also common in eighteenth-century orchestral *basso* parts, as is "tasto solo," which told the keyboard player to play the bass line as written and not to realize the harmonies.

The wind instruments of the classical orchestra were not generally conceived of in four parts on the model of string scoring. Instead they were organized into pairs of similar instruments: two oboes, two flutes, two horns, etc. This seemingly obvious fact requires explanation, because in Lully's orchestra, where wind instruments were first combined with strings in orchestral fashion, the winds had been scored in four parts—*dessus de hautbois*, *haute-contre de hautbois*, *taille de hautbois*, and *basse de hautbois*. But Lully in his later works preferred to write for winds in trio rather than four-part texture, and French orchestras had abandoned the middle wind parts by the second decade of the eighteenth century. For the most part orchestras in other countries had never used them. Why did winds abandon four-part scoring in the eighteenth century, just as stringed instruments were adopting it? One possible explanation is that the winds, unlike orchestral strings, came from several different families of instruments. It was economically impractical to hire enough wind players to constitute four-part flute, clarinet, or horn choirs. Pairs of flutes, oboes, horns, and/or bassoons could function as a single mixed wind choir, offering one another adequate timbral support at relatively low cost. Thus, during the first half of the

---

[42] Edge, "Manuscript Parts,", 435–41.

[43] Lutes and theorbos had become unusual in French, English, and Italian orchestras by 1740, and they soon disappeared in Germany as well.

[44] On the role of the bassoon in the basso, see Christoph-Hellmut Mahling, "Con o Senza Fagotto? Bemerkungen zur Besetzung der 'Bassi' (1740 bis ca. 1780)," in id. (ed.), *Florilegium Musicologicum: Hellmut Federhofer zum 75. Geburtstag* (Tutzing, 1988), 197–207.

eighteenth century the undifferentiated "oboes" on earlier orchestra rosters were replaced by pairs of specialists on the various wind instruments.

Although the basic organization of the classical orchestra remained pretty much stable between 1740 and 1815, a trend can be discerned toward increased differentiation of instrumental groups. Oboes, flutes, and clarinets were separated into sections, each with pairs of specialist performers. While this variegated wind group continued to function as a choir, doubling string parts and sustaining harmonies, increasingly during the second half of the eighteenth century its constituent instruments served, separately and in various combinations, to add coloristic highlights to orchestral palettes. Cellos and bassoons were differentiated from the *basso* and increasingly received their own parts, cellos as an obbligato voice in the tenor register, bassoons as tenor soloists or as the bass of the wind choir. Various reduced scorings became familiar, for example three-part string scorings that combined first and second violins or omitted the violas, or scorings in which the *basso* dropped out and the violas or even the second violins took the bass line.[45] Four-part scoring remained the norm, but the other instruments were no longer "filler and doubling": they were an essential and indispensible part of the orchestra.

THE SIZE OF THE CLASSICAL ORCHESTRA

A great many reports have been preserved that purport to represent the number of instruments or instrumentalists in various orchestras between 1740 and 1815. We have assembled well over 1,000 discrete reports of orchestras and their balances between 1740 and 1815. To present and analyze all these reports would be impractical. Instead we have chosen four sub-periods for detailed analysis: 1754–59, 1773–78, 1791–96, 1808–18.[46] Reports from these sub-periods, offering data on orchestras in different countries and in various venues, are summarized in Appendices A–D. The 127 orchestras cover a geographical area extending from Naples to Edinburgh, Trieste to Madrid. They include theater orchestras, church orchestras, dance orchestras, orchestras assembled for concerts and special events, and the rosters of princely Kapellen and other musical establishments. The Appendices do not present all available reports for each sub-period. Our aim was to get a representative cross-section and not to let a few orchestras with well-preserved records overwhelm the sample. The Appendices are designed to give a good idea of the range of sizes and the balances between instruments in a cross-section of classical orchestras.

Classical orchestras came in all sizes. The smallest orchestras in the sample number just 10 players; the largest comprise over 100. The distribution of orchestra sizes is

---

[45] For examples of reduced scorings, see Ch. 13.

[46] Each of the sub-periods encompasses six years, except the last, which covers 11 years (1808–18), because reports on orchestras become rather scarce during the first two decades of the 19th c.

analyzed in Table 9.1, which divides the orchestras in the Appendices into four categories: small (25 players or fewer), medium (26–50 players), large (51–75 players), and huge (76 or more). The great majority of the orchestras in Table 9.1 fall into the small or medium categories. Only about a sixth are large; only a handful are huge. The sample is rather heavy on German orchestras, light on English, and very light on orchestras outside the four central areas. English orchestras in the sample are all small or medium sized. The majority of German orchestras are medium sized. French and Italian orchestras are fairly evenly distributed among small, medium, and large categories. Huge orchestras seem to be a German specialty.

Analysis of the orchestras in Table 9.1 by date reveals a clear trend: orchestras seem to be getting bigger over time. Large orchestras do not appear in the sample until the second period (1773–78), huge orchestras not until the third (1791–96). Conversely, small orchestras, which are common in the earliest period, have become relatively rare in the last. Even in the second decade of the nineteenth century, however, "medium"-sized orchestras, with 26 to 50 members, still constitute over half of the total. Analyzed by venue, the trends are similarly clear: church orchestras and dance orchestras tend to be small; concert orchestras and Kapellen tend to be medium

TABLE 9.1. *The size of classical orchestras, 1754–1818*

	Small (<25)	Medium (26–50)	Large (51–75)	Huge (76+)
Number of orchestras	43	60	18	6
By country				
England	6	9	0	0
France	11	9	7	0
Germany	14	32	6	6
Italy	11	8	5	0
Other	1	2	0	0
By date				
1754–59	11	12	0	0
1773–78	13	13	7	0
1791–96	15	20	5	3
1808–18	4	15	6	3
By venue				
Concert	2	17	4	4
Church	5	2	0	0
Kapelle	9	18	4	2
Theater	24	23	10	0
Dance	3	0	0	0

TABLE 9.2. *The size of selected orchestras, 1741–1815*

Orchestra[a]	1741–45	1746–50	1751–55	1756–60	1761–65	1766–70	1771–75	1776–80	1781–85	1786–90	1791–95	1796–1800	1800–5	1806–10	1811–15	Source
Paris: Opéra	43		45	46	50	52	66	**74**	63	71	68		74		71	La Gorce, "L'Orchestre"; *Almanach*
Paris: Concert Spirituel			34	38	42	41	40	55	53	**57**	53					*Almanach*
Paris: Comédie-Italienne			13	16	20	22	23	24	25	35	38	**54**	45		48	Charlton, "Orchestra"; *Almanach*
Turin: Teatro Regio	37	36	43				**60**	55		57						Bouquet, *Teatro*; Moffa, *Storia*
Naples: S. Carlo	**68**	[53]		49				56	56	56		49			[59]	Prota-Giurleo, *Grande orchestra*; *AMZ*
Bologna: S. Petronio	10	10	9	10	18	17	16	20	17	**21**	21	21	16	16	18	Gambassi, *Cappella musicale*
Esterházy Kapelle					14	14	18	19	**24**	24	24		20			Bartha & Somfai, *Haydn als Opernkapellmeister*; Gerlach, "Haydns Orchestermusiker"; Landon, *Haydn*
Salzburg Kapelle	19	22	28	30	28	27	26	24	**34**	26	26	20	22			Hintermaier, "Die salzburger Hofkapelle"
Dresden Kapelle	42	46	45	49	41	44	45	47	46	44	**53**	53	52	52	52	Mahling, "Orchester"
Munich Kapelle		25	35	45	41	44	41	62	**88**	86	81	82	84			Ibid.
Stuttgart Kapelle			25	33	43	39	46	43	55	**57**	43	44	35	33	40	Ibid.

[a] Boldface indicates the maximum size of the orchestra.

sized.[47] Theater orchestras come in small, medium, and large sizes. Most of the huge orchestras were one-time affairs, organized for special concerts.

Table 9.1 suggests that orchestras on the whole tended to get larger between 1740 and 1815, but it does not say anything about the growth patterns of specific orchestras. For a few orchestras records have been preserved that extend over all or most of the period from 1740 to 1815. Table 9.2 shows the total number of instrumentalists in eleven of these orchestras by five-year intervals from 1741 to 1815.[48] Empty cells indicate either that the orchestra did not exist during the indicated years or that no data are available. Violin-playing concertmasters are included in the totals, as are listed supernumeraries. Keyboard players, Kapellmeisters, and directors (*chefs d'orchestre*) are not counted.[49]

Every orchestra in the table save one is larger at the end of the series than it was at the beginning. The exception is the San Carlo Theater in Naples, which had 68 members in 1741 but no more than 59 thereafter. In no case, however, is the orchestra biggest at the end. The maximum size for most orchestras (indicated by boldface in Table 9.2) comes in the 1770s or 1780s. After their maxima the orchestras shrink slightly (Munich, San Petronio) or even considerably (Salzburg, Stuttgart). In some cases the decrease was abrupt: the San Carlo orchestra was reduced by a reform in 1742, the Stuttgart orchestra by the collapse of State finances in 1767–69.[50] For almost every orchestra in Table 9.2 the average size was larger during the second half of the period (1775–1815) than during the first, and in this sense the classical orchestra did grow over the period 1741–1815. For the most part, however, the growth within individual orchestras seems to have been complete by the 1780s: from then to the end of the period most orchestras remained the same size or shrank slightly. This leveling off may have been connected with the French Revolution, the Napoleonic wars, and accompanying social and economic disruptions.

BALANCES AND PROPORTIONS—IDEAL ORCHESTRAS

Although the size of classical orchestras varied from one orchestra to another, their balances—that is, the proportions of the various instruments to one another—

---

[47] Because court Kapellen played in each of the other venues—church, concert, theater, and dance—they have been considered as a "venue" of their own.

[48] When possible, figures were taken from the first year of the indicated span; if no roster was transmitted for that year, the first available number was taken instead. The figure for Eszterháza, 1790 was entered for 1791. The figure for Naples, 1742 was entered in the column for 1746 in order to show the reduction in the size of the orchestra brought about by the reforms of 1742. A figure from a Naples report of 1818 was entered for 1815.

[49] If a court had a trumpet and drum corps separate from the Kapelle, three musicians (2 trumpets, 1 drum) were added to the Kapelle total, because they were available as needed for the orchestra.

[50] For Naples see Ulisse Prota-Giurleo, *La grande orchestra del R. Teatro San Carlo nel Settecento* (Naples, 1927), 12 ff.; on Stuttgart, see Ch. 7.

remained relatively stable. This stability is reflected in contemporary discussions about what orchestral balances ought to be. It can also be seen in the proportions of instruments in actual orchestras.

Several eighteenth-century commentators articulated their ideas about orchestral balances in the form of descriptions of well-proportioned imaginary ensembles. These "ideal orchestras" are analyzed in Table 9.3. The earliest, from an essay in J. A. Scheibe's *Critischer Musikus*, dates from 1740; the latest comes from an encyclopedia article by Gottfried Weber in 1822.[51] Some of the authors give an example of a single ideal orchestra. Charles Avison, for example, in the Preface to his *Six Concertos in Seven Parts,* Op. 3 (London, 1751), thinks simultaneously in terms of four-part scoring and concerto grosso organization:

exclusive of the four principal Parts, which must be always complete, . . . the *Chorus* of other Instruments should not exceed the Number following, viz. Six *Primo,* and four *secondo Ripienos*; four *Ripieno Basses,* and two Double *Basses,* and a *Harpsichord.*[52]

He recommends against wind instruments altogether because of "irremediable" poor intonation, "unless we admit of the *Bassoon,* which if performed by an expert Hand, in a soft and ready Tone . . . may be of singular Use, and add Fullness to the Harmony." Avison's ideal orchestra consists then of:

  7 First Violins
  5 Second Violins
  1 Viola
  5 Cellos
  2 Double basses
  1 Bassoon
  1 Harpsichord.

Other authors lay out a series of ideal orchestras of different sizes. "Observe," says Galeazzi in his *Elementi* of 1791, "how to arrange the parts of an orchestra in good proportion":

In an orchestra with 4 violins, one cello and a viola are sufficient (unless there are two obligato parts). With 4 to 8 [violins] it is necessary to add a double bass and another viola; from 8 to

---

[51] Sources for the ideal orchestras are: Johann Adolf Scheibe, *Critischer Musikus* (Leipzig, 1745); Charles Avison, *Six Concertos in Seven Parts,* Op. 3 (London, 1751); Johann Joachim Quantz, *Versuch einer Anweisung die Flöte traversiere zu spielen* (Berlin, 1752); Johann Samuel Petri, *Anleitung zur praktischen Musik* (1st edn.) (Lauban, 1767); id., *Anleitung zur praktischen Musik* (2nd edn.) (Leipzig, 1782); Francesco Galeazzi, *Elementi teorico-pratici di musica* (Rome, 1791); Anton Stadler, "*Musick Plan* (1800)," in Ernst Hess, "Anton Stadlers 'Musick Plan,'" *Mozart-Jahrbuch* (1962–63), 37–52; Heinrich Christoph Koch, *Musikalisches Lexikon* (Frankfurt am Main, 1802); Georg von Unold, "Einige Bemerkungen über die Stellung der Orchester und Einrichtung der Musiksäle," *Allgemeine musikalische Zeitung,* 4 (1802), 782–84; Giuseppe Scaramelli, *Saggio sopra i doveri di un primo violino direttore d'orchestra* (Trieste, 1811); Gottfried Weber, "Besetzung," in *Allgemeine Encyclopedie der Wissenschaften und Künste,* ed. Ersch and Gruber (Leipzig, 1822), 284–85. See also Zaslaw, "Toward the Revival of the Classical Orchestra," 181, and id., *Mozart's Symphonies,* 462.

[52] Avison, *Six Concertos,* pp. ii–iii.

12, you need to add two more basses, one of them a cello, the other a double bass, but 2 violas are still enough . . .[53]

For every additional six violins, he goes on, you need to add a viola and another bass instrument, alternating cellos and double basses. As for winds, "as these are highly audible [*sensibilissimi*], two of each kind will be enough for any orchestra, until the number of violins exceeds 16, at which point the winds may be doubled."[54] Galeazzi's ideal orchestra may be represented as follows:

Bowed strings	Winds and brass	Orchestra Size
4 violins		
1 viola		
1 cello		6
5–8 violins	[6 pairs]	
2 violas		
1 cello		
1 double bass		21–24
. . . etc.		
17–22 violins	[6 double pairs]	
5 violas		
3 cellos		
4 double basses		53–58
. . . etc.		

To the extent that the authors agree, their ideal orchestras may be taken to express principles that lay behind the balances of real classical orchestras.

The balances of the ideal orchestras are analyzed in the right-hand portion of Table 9.3. The relative size of the violin and viola sections are gauged by showing them as a proportion of all strings. The balance of winds to strings is measured by calculating winds as a percentage of all instruments (excluding keyboards). The strength of the *basso* group is represented by the sum of cellos, basses, and bassoons divided by all instruments. Finally, a ratio is calculated of cellos to double basses.

The number of violins as a proportion of total strings varies from ideal orchestras where violins comprise only about half the strings to orchestras in which the strings are over two-thirds violins. Opinions seem to divide into two groups: authors who think that violins should comprise 55–60 percent of the strings (Quantz, Petri, Koch), and another group that calls for 65–70 percent violins (Galeazzi, Unold, Scaramelli, Weber). This may reflect a preference in Italian orchestras for relatively more violins (*pace* Unold and Weber), or it might be a chronological trend: later orchestras become more violin-heavy (*pace* Koch). The proportion of violas as a percent of strings varies

---

[53] Galeazzi, *Elementi teorico-pratici*, i. 214–15.

[54] When an author, like Galeazzi, says "pairs" of winds, we assume pairs of flutes, oboes, clarinets, and bassoons, plus horns and trumpets.

TABLE 9.3. *Ideal orchestras, 1745–1822*

| Author | Orchestra size (exc. kbd) | % of strings | | | % of total | | Ratio of cellos to basses |
		Violin	Viola	Basso	Winds	
J. Scheibe, *Critischer Musicus* (1745)	23–26	0.50–0.53	0.13–0.11	0.34–0.36	0.15–0.17	1.0–1.33
C. Avison, *Six Concertos, Op. 3* (1751)	21	0.60	0.05	0.38	—	2.5
J.J. Quantz, *Versuch* (1752)	7	0.57	0.14	0.29	—	1.0
	13	0.50	0.17	0.38	—	1.0
	22	0.57	0.14	0.27	0.36	1.0
	25	0.58	0.12	0.28	0.32	1.5
	34	0.57	0.14	0.26	0.38	2.0
J. S. Petri, *Anleitung zur praktischen Musik* (1st edn., 1767)	5–7	0.50–0.66	0.17–0.25	0.43	—	—
	8–10	0.40–0.57	0.14–0.20	0.30–0.38	0.30–0.38	1.0
	22–25	0.60–0.61	0.11–0.13	0.23–0.24	0.28–0.32	3.5–4.0
J. S. Petri, *Anleitung* (2nd edn., 1782)	18	0.68	0.11–0.13	0.23–0.24	0.55	—
	23	0.54	0.08	0.30	0.43	1.5
	31–32	0.55–0.57	0.09–0.10	0.26–0.28	0.31–0.32	1.0–1.3

1. Galeazzi, Elementi teorico-pratici						
(1791)	27–30	0.60–0.67	0.11–0.13	0.40–0.44	0.20–0.22	1.0
	35–38	0.57–0.62	0.15–0.17	0.32–0.34	0.21–0.23	1.0
	53–58	0.59–0.65	0.15–0.17	0.41–0.45	0.19–0.21	0.75
	61–66	0.62–0.67	0.14–0.16	0.36–0.40	0.18–0.20	1.0
	69–74	0.64–0.68	0.14–0.15	0.32–0.35	0.18–0.19	0.80
A. Stadler, "Musick Plan" (1800)	20–21	0.50–0.57	0.13–0.14	0.57–0.60	0.19–0.20	1.0
	28–29	0.50–0.53	0.20–0.25	0.41–0.43	0.21	1.0
H. C. Koch, *Musikalisches Lexikon* (1802)	14	0.57	0.14	—	—	1.0
	18	0.55	0.17	—	—	1.5
G. von Unold, "Einige Bemerkungen" (1802)	24	0.69	0.15	0.42	0.17	1.0
G. Scaramelli, *Saggio* (1811)	43	0.67	0.13	0.28	0.19	0.5
G. Weber, "Besetzung" (1822)	28–31	0.61–0.67	0.13–0.17	0.39–0.42	0.18–0.19	1.0–2.0
	45–48	0.67	0.11–0.12	0.25–0.27	0.20–0.21	1.0–1.3

within a narrower range than the violins. With a couple of exceptions (Stadler, Petri 1782), most authors recommend 11–17 percent violas in their orchestral strings—something like one viola for every five or six violins. Although contemporaries complained that Italian viola sections were understaffed, this is not evident in the ideal orchestras of Galeazzi or Scaramelli. Indeed, no national preferences whatsoever are evident in the strength of the viola section, nor does there seem to be any particular trend over time.

Most of the authors agree that every orchestra needs pairs of wind instruments, including flutes and (after 1790) clarinets. In consequence, the percentage of winds rises above 50 percent in some of the smaller ideal orchestras. H. C. Koch, in his lexicon article on "Accompaniment," makes it clear that such wind-heavy orchestras were not just hypothetical:

When a composer works with an orchestra in which there are 16 to 20 violinists and a corresponding number of violas and basses, he composes parts for oboes, bassoons, flutes, horns, and trumpets, and doubtless calculates to what extent he can assign the harmony and the melody to all these instruments without disrupting the balance between them and the principal parts. When this composition is played in public, it is usually performed with all the wind instruments, even in orchestras so tiny that one needs opera glasses [*eine Lorgnette*] to locate the string players who carry the principal parts.[55]

Some authors, however, seem to advocate precisely the wind-heavy balances that Koch deplores. Petri (1782) recommends that orchestras, whatever their size, should use pairs of winds throughout. Wind players in smaller orchestras, he says, should correct the balance by blowing half as hard.[56] Quantz recommends that all the winds should be doubled if the number of violins exceeds 12; Galeazzi wants doubled winds after 16 violins. On the other hand, both Scaramelli and Weber say that there is no need for doubled winds no matter how large the rest of the orchestra gets. The percentages of winds in Table 9.3 rise a bit toward the end of the period, as flutes and clarinets became permanent members of the orchestra.

Looking at the *basso* group as a proportion of all instruments, a clear trend emerges: earlier authors prefer a stronger bass than later authors. Scheibe, Avison, Quantz, and Petri all advocate balances in which cellos, basses, and bassoons comprise over a quarter of the orchestra. Galeazzi, Unold, Scaramelli, and Weber, writing after 1790, recommend a *basso* that makes up only about 20 percent of the orchestra. In part the decline in the *basso* results from the increasing numbers of wind instruments, but it also seems to reflect a decline in basso continuo practice in the late eighteenth century, particularly since bassoons and cellos were increasingly assigned tenor obbligato rather than *basso* parts. The ratio of cellos to basses seems to indicate a regional preference rather than a chronological trend: German (and English) writers prefer more

---

[55] Koch, *Musikalisches Lexikon*, cols. 235–36.
[56] Petri, *Anleitung* (2nd edn.), 187. In the first edition of his book (1767), Petri had recommended that smaller orchestras use fewer wind players.

cellos, Italians more basses. The ideal orchestra with the greatest preponderance of 8-foot over 16-foot instruments is Petri's 1767 ensemble, which includes both viole da gamba and cellos in the 8-foot register. Scaramelli, at the other extreme, asks for twice as many double basses as cellos.

BALANCES AND PROPORTIONS—REAL ORCHESTRAS

Do the balances of the ideal orchestras in Table 9.3 correspond to the balances of actual orchestras between 1740 and 1815? To answer this question the orchestras in Appendices A–D were analyzed in the same way as the ideal orchestras, calculating violins as a percentage of all strings, violas as a percentage of all strings, winds as a percentage of all instruments, *basso* instruments as a percentage of all instruments, and the ratio of cellos to double basses. The results are presented in Tables 9.4–9.8, broken down by country, by venue, and by size. The Spanish, Portuguese, and Dutch orchestras in Appendices A–D have been left out of the analysis by country because there are not enough reports to permit meaningful analysis. Orchestras for dancing have been omitted from the analysis by venue for the same reason. The aim of the analysis is to ascertain whether differences in balances in classical orchestras can be explained by country, venue, or orchestra size, and to what extent the balances changed over time.

Tables 9.4–9.8 should be regarded with caution. Unlisted performers, supernumeraries, absentees, etc. can affect balances considerably. So can double-handed players: a couple of trumpeters who play viola when there is no trumpet part can turn a seemingly small viola section into a large one. When there are only two or three reports available within a cell, then an atypical orchestra can skew the average. In Table 9.4, for example, the average proportion of violins in church orchestras during the period 1773–78 is unduly influenced by the large and violin-heavy orchestra at a mass in Mannheim in 1777 that Mozart attended and reported on. Despite these deficiencies, the tables suggest several interesting hypotheses about balances in classical orchestras.

The average proportion of violins as a percentage of all strings (Table 9.4) varies from 53 to 68 percent, almost exactly the same range as in the ideal orchestras. In all four sub-periods Italian orchestras tend to be a little heavier on violins than orchestras in other countries, corresponding to the ideal orchestras of Italian commentators like Galeazzi and Scaramelli. French orchestras tend to be light on violins, but the averaged figures conceal significant differences among French orchestras. For instance, the table says that in French orchestras between 1754 and 1759 the violins constituted on average 58 percent of all strings. But the Opéra had only 46 percent violins, while the Comédie-Italienne had 60 percent (see App. A). Venue does not seem to have made much difference to string balances: the average strength of violin sections

TABLE 9.4. *Classical orchestra balances: violins as a percentage of all strings*

	1754–59	1773–78	1791–96	1808–18
Country				
England	62	61	58	61
France	58	61	58	54
Germany	59	62	59	58
Italy	65	62	63	61
Venue				
Concert	60	62	57	58
Church	—	68	58	—
Kapelle	60	64	61	58
Theater	61	60	59	58
Size				
Small	60	64	62	58
Medium	59	60	59	60
Large	—	60	53	55
Huge	—	—	62	58

in concert orchestras, theater orchestras, and Kapellen is almost the same in the first sub-period and identical in the last. Orchestra size, on the other hand, seems to have a modest effect on the proportion of violins. In the first three sub-periods small orchestras tend to have proportionately more violins than larger orchestras, but the difference seems to disappear in the final sub-period. There are no strong trends over time in any of the categories. If anything, the proportion of violins may decline slightly from the beginning to the end of the period.

The proportion of violas as a percentage of all strings (Table 9.5) shows a distinct effect by country. In each sub-period English orchestras have higher averages of violas than orchestras in other countries. French orchestras have the lowest proportions of violas in the first three sub-periods, Italian in the last. Overall there seems to be a tendency for the proportions in different countries to become more similar over time. The differences in the average strength of viola sections between English, French, German, and Italian orchestras are greatest in the first two sub-periods, less in the later sub-periods, suggesting that national differences are disappearing. Concert orchestras have proportionately larger viola sections than other types of orchestras in three of the sub-periods. Perhaps this reflects more emphasis on middle parts in eighteenth-century concert repertory as compared with operas and church music. Otherwise venue does not seem to be much of a factor. Nor does orchestra size. Orchestras of different sizes use about the same proportions of violas, and no trends are apparent over time.

TABLE 9.5. *Classical orchestra balances: violas as a percentage of all strings*

	1754–59	1773–78	1791–96	1808–18
Country				
England	19	20	15	16
France	11	10	12	13
Germany	15	15	15	15
Italy	13	16	14	12
Venue				
Concert	16	14	16	16
Church	—	14	15	—
Kapelle	15	16	14	14
Theater	13	15	13	14
Size				
Small	14	16	14	13
Medium	15	14	15	14
Large	—	14	12	15
Huge	—	—	13	15

The proportion of wind instruments in orchestras (Table 9.6) again shows a strong effect by country: German orchestras are wind-heavy; Italian orchestras have relatively small wind sections. Again this corresponds to the ideal orchestras of German and Italian commentators. In the last sub-period (1808–18) the proportion of winds in different countries seems to become more similar: Italian, French, and English orchestras add winds, while the average proportion of winds in German orchestras declines slightly. Kapellen seem to have larger wind sections than orchestras in other venues, but, since almost all the Kapellen in the sample are German, this probably signifies an effect of geography rather than venue. Surprisingly, the proportion of winds does not seem to vary much by orchestra size. The balance that Koch complains about—small orchestras in which full pairs of winds overwhelm meager string sections—is not particularly apparent in Table 9.6, although in the final sub-period (1808–18) large orchestras seem to have proportionately fewer winds than small and medium-sized orchestras.

The percentages of instruments that played *basso* parts—cellos, double basses, bassoons—are shown in Table 9.7, averaged as before over country, venue, and orchestra size. Again regional differences are striking and persistent: French orchestras tend to use more *basso* instruments, Italian orchestras fewer. Venue and orchestra size do not appear to have much effect on the proportion of *basso* instruments. Over the

328 The Classical Orchestra

TABLE 9.6. *Classical orchestra balances: winds as a percentage of all instruments*

	1754–59	1773–78	1791–96	1808–18
Country				
England	30	33	32	36
France	29	27	31	33
Germany	34	32	39	36
Italy	21	26	24	27
Venue				
Concert	31	28	30	32
Church	—	29	25	—
Kapelle	35	37	38	41
Theater	25	27	34	34
Size				
Small	28	33	34	36
Medium	28	27	33	38
Large	—	31	33	29
Huge	—	—	34	28

TABLE 9.7. *Classical orchestra balances: basso as a percentage of all instruments*

	1754–59	1773–78	1791–96	1808–18
Country				
England	24	19	25	23
France	31	28	28	27
Germany	23	23	23	22
Italy	21	22	21	21
Venue				
Concert	27	24	25	23
Church	—	20	23	—
Kapelle	24	20	23	23
Theater	26	27	24	24
Size				
Small	24	20	24	23
Medium	25	26	23	23
Large	—	26	29	23
Huge	—	—	23	24

entire period the strength of the *basso* seems to decline slightly, and orchestras seem to get more similar to one another in this respect, so that by the final sub-period the range of averages is very narrow.

Ratios of cellos to basses are displayed in Table 9.8. Orchestras in which the numbers of cellos exceeds the number of basses have ratios higher than 1.0; orchestras with more basses than cellos have ratios below 1.0. Once again there are strong differences by country. French orchestras use more cellos than basses, Italian more basses than cellos.[57] English and German orchestras seem to begin with more French balances and shift over time toward Italian balances. In the very last sub-period French orchestras too shift toward the Italian pattern, so that by 1818 orchestras in different countries are much more similar to one another than they were in 1754. In the first sub-period it seems as though there are systematic differences by venue in the ratio of cellos to basses, but in the later sub-periods this effect seems to disappear. There seem to be no consistent relationships between orchestra size and the relative strength of the cello and bass sections.

Tables 9.4–9.8 suggest that national and regional practices explain most of the variability in the balances of the classical orchestra. Italian orchestras were characteristically heavy in violins, light on winds, light on cellos, heavy on basses. French orchestras had large numbers of *basso* instruments and many more cellos than basses.

TABLE 9.8. *Classical orchestra balances: ratio of cellos to double basses*

	1754–59	1773–78	1791–96	1808–18
Country				
England	1.8	1.5	1.6	0.9
France	2.5	2.3	2.2	1.4
Germany	1.6	1.1	1.0	1.4
Italy	0.7	0.8	0.9	0.6
Venue				
Concert	2.2	1.5	1.5	1.3
Church	—	1.5	1.1	—
Kapelle	1.5	1.1	1.1	1.7
Theater	0.9	1.3	1.5	1.0
Size				
Small	1.6	1.4	1.5	0.9
Medium	1.4	1.2	1.2	1.2
Large	—	1.2	2.0	1.4
Huge	—	—	1.5	1.2

[57] Many Italian orchestras had only two cellos, who functioned mainly as soloists.

German orchestras were distinguished by large numbers of wind instruments, English orchestras by large numbers of violas. These national differences persisted over the entire period of the classical orchestra; however, by the beginning of the nineteenth century they had become less pronounced. Venue and orchestra size do not seem to explain much of the variability in orchestral balances. Balances tended to be similar in Kapellen, concert, church, and theater orchestras, as well as smaller and larger orchestras over the entire period. This reinforces the impression that the classical orchestra was relatively stable over time and in a wide variety of contexts.

Tables 9.4–9.8 were constructed by averaging data from reports compiled for diverse purposes and based on differing premises. For a few orchestras, however, reports were compiled year after year according to the same principles. In these cases trends can be traced over time and compared with one another. Six orchestras were chosen for this comparison: the orchestras of the Opéra and of the Comédie-Italienne (Opéra Comique) in Paris, the orchestras of the Teatro Regio in Turin and the San Carlo theater in Naples, and the Dresden and Stuttgart Kapellen.[58] These analyses use the same categories as before; the results are displayed graphically in Figs. 9.1–9.5.

Figure 9.1 shows the number of violins as a percentage of all strings in the six orchestras from 1740 to 1815. Each orchestra appears as a line on the graph. The orchestra of the San Carlo Theater in Naples has a relatively high proportion of violins during most of the period, the orchestra of the Paris Opéra a relatively low percentage. The other orchestras fluctuate in between. In most of these orchestras the percentage of violins is highest in the 1780s and declines somewhat thereafter, confirming the impression from the averaged figures in Table 9.4. From the 1780s on, the lines for the different orchestras seem to converge: the spread in the 1740s between highest and lowest is 26 percent; by the 1790s it is only about 13 percent and by 1815 only around 10 percent. This supports the hypothesis that orchestras became more similar to one another toward the end of the eighteenth century.

The graph of violas as a proportion of orchestral strings (Fig. 9.2) shows all the orchestras fluctuating between 10 percent and 19 percent. No strong regional differences can be discerned, perhaps because there are no English orchestras in the sample. Nor does there seem to be any tendency for the proportion of violas to rise or fall over time. Even more than with the violins, however, the lines converge to the right of the graph, indicating that the percentage of violas in various orchestras becomes more similar toward the end of the period.

The trends in the proportion of wind instruments (Fig. 9.3) correspond to previous findings. Throughout the period the German orchestras have relatively more winds, the French and Italian orchestras relatively fewer. During the 1760s and 1770s the percentage of winds declines in several orchestras, not because wind instruments

[58] There are no extant reports for the orchestra of the Teatro Regio in Turin between 1791 and 1815. A set of regulations dated 1821 prescribing the composition of the orchestra was used as a proxy for 1811. The Comédie-Italienne merged with the Opéra Comique in 1762. See Ch. 6.

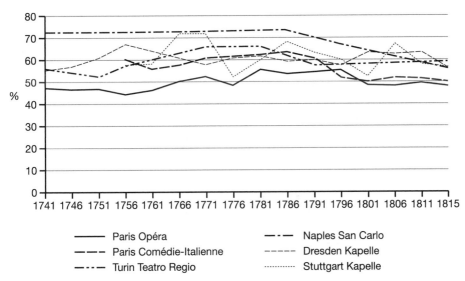

FIG. 9.1. Violins as a percentage of all strings in six orchestras, 1741–1815

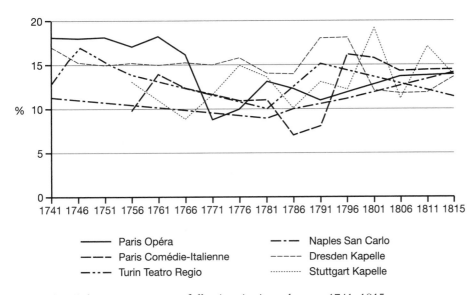

FIG. 9.2. Violas as a percentage of all strings in six orchestras, 1741–1815

are being eliminated but because string sections are being increased while maintaining wind pairs. From the 1780s on the percentage of winds tends to rise in all the orchestras, due to the addition of clarinets and trombones and also to wind doubling. By the end of the period the French and Italian orchestras have increased their proportion of winds significantly, so that the spread in 1815 between the most wind-heavy orchestra and the least is considerably less than it was in 1741.

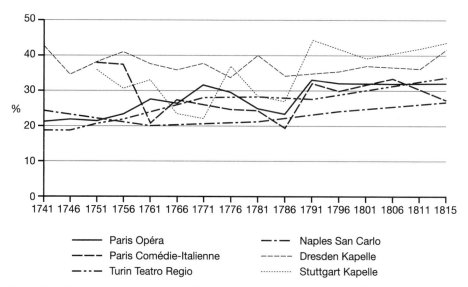

FIG. 9.3. Winds as a percentage of all instruments in six orchestras, 1741–1815

The strength of the *basso* as a percentage of these six orchestras is shown in Fig. 9.4. Again the regional differences seem clear: the two French orchestras have a consistently higher percentage of *basso* instruments than the German and Italian orchestras. Toward the end of the period the number of bass instruments increases in some orchestras (Stuttgart, Naples), while it declines slightly in others (Opéra, Comédie-

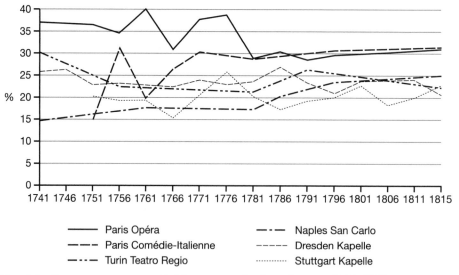

FIG. 9.4. *Basso* as a percentage of all instruments in six orchestras, 1741–1815

Italienne), so that at the end of the period the range of values is again narrower than at the beginning. Figure 9.5 shows the ratio of cellos to double basses in the same six orchestras, displayed on a logarithmic scale, so that values below 1.0 will not be unduly compressed. Because the addition or subtraction of one or two instruments makes a considerable difference in the ratio, the lines in Fig. 9.5 are more jagged than those in the previous graphs. The differences between regions, however, are just as clear as they were in Table 9.8: French orchestras always have more cellos than basses; Italian orchestras always have more basses than cellos; German orchestras fluctuate in between. Toward the end of the period the lines tend to converge. French orchestras added double basses until, by 1814, the ratio at the Opéra was 2 to 1 and at the Comédie-Italienne the number of basses actually matched the cellos. At the same time the orchestra of the San Carlo Theater was adding cellos so that by 1815 there were almost as many cellos as basses. Here is yet another example of orchestras becoming more like one another at the end of the classical period.

Tables 9.4–9.8 and Figs. 9.1–9.5 all point to the same conclusions. The balances and proportions of orchestras between 1740 and 1815 varied considerably but within a well-defined range. At the beginning of the period national differences were pronounced: French orchestras had a lower proportion of violins and a higher proportion of *basso* instruments than Italian, German, and English orchestras. German orchestras had a higher proportion of winds. Italian orchestras had more double basses than cellos; elsewhere cellos tended to predominate over basses. Over the 75 years from 1740 to 1815, these national differences tended to even themselves out: the proportion of violins rose in French orchestras; the proportion of winds rose

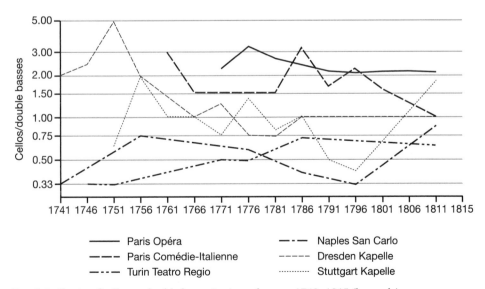

FIG. 9.5. Ratio of cellos to double basses in six orchestras, 1740–1815 (log scale)

in Italian; the proportion of double basses increased in Germany and France. By the end of the period European orchestras resembled one another considerably more than they had at the beginning.

THE ORCHESTRAL CONSENSUS

Increasing similarities between orchestras in different places and in different venues were promoted by the circulation of personnel and of repertory. This circulation was both local and international. Within a city or a region a small number of instrumentalists often played in a large number of venues. For example, a roster drawn up in 1783 of all the instrumentalists on the payrolls of various Viennese churches is filled with names from the orchestras of the Burg- and Kärntnertor theaters.[59] Similarly, in London the orchestras at pleasure gardens like Vauxhall and Ranelagh were staffed with players from the Covent Garden and Drury Lane theaters, and the orchestra of the Professional Concerts overlapped extensively with that of the opera (see Ch. 8). Sometimes an entire orchestra could be engaged to play in another venue, as when Mozart hired the orchestra of the Burgtheater in 1785 to play for his concert series at the Mehlgrube.[60] Court Kapellen played in several venues as part of their official duties. For example, the Mannheim Kapelle played in the Court chapel and in the Jesuitenkirche, in the opera house for both opera and spoken theater, for concerts in the Rittersaal at the palace, for court balls during Carnival, and in the outdoor pavilion at the Elector's summer residence in Schwetzingen.[61] Similarly, the Salzburg Kapelle performed for services at the cathedral, for graduation ceremonies at the Benedictine University, as well as for concerts and dinner music at the Archbishop's court.[62] Musicians from the Salzburg Kapelle also performed at private occasions like weddings and name-day celebrations for the nobles and merchants of the town.

When political boundaries permitted, orchestra musicians circulated more widely. Instrumentalists on the payroll of the cathedral at Bergamo, for example, played as supernumeraries in the opera orchestras of Turin, Milan, and Genoa.[63] In Emilia-Romagna opera seasons in neighboring towns were staggered, so that instrumentalists could travel from town to town, filling the first-chair positions in opera orchestras (see Ch. 12). In the late eighteenth and early nineteenth centuries a cadre of players from the London theaters staffed the orchestras at festival oratorio performances in

---

[59] Otto Biba, "Die Wiener Kirchenmusik."

[60] Zaslaw, *Mozart's Symphonies*, 393.

[61] Würtz, "Die Organisation der Mannheimer Hofkapelle," 46.

[62] Cliff Eisen, "Salzburg under Church Rule," in Neal Zaslaw (ed.), *The Classical Era* (Englewood Cliffs, NJ, 1989), 166–87.

[63] Paola Palermo, "La musica nella basilica di Santa Maria Maggiore a Bergamo all'epoca dell'infanzia di Locatelli," in Albert Dunning (ed.), *Intorno a Locatelli* (Lucca, 1995), 653–748 at 702, 709.

Birmingham, Manchester, and other English provincial towns, augmented by local professionals and amateurs (see Ch. 8). This circulation of musicians probably fostered similarities in proportions and balances between orchestras in different venues, and it also tended to discourage local differences in repertory and performance practices.

Orchestra musicians also circulated internationally with increasing freedom and frequency over the course of the eighteenth century. Italian string players poured into English, German, Spanish, and Russian orchestras, often arousing resentment on the part of natives who complained that the Italians got better positions and higher salaries. At the same time there were many German wind players in Italian orchestras, particularly in the north. Orchestras in Paris and London imported German wood-wind players and Bohemian hornists from the 1750s through the 1780s. International travel by wind players was made easier by an increasing standardization of orchestral pitch that took place in the second half of the eighteenth century.[64] In 1712 when Louis Rousselet, a French bassoonist, went to London, he found he had to order a special bassoon pitched higher than his old instrument, since the pitch in London was almost a quarter tone higher than it had been in Paris.[65] By the end of the eighteenth century, London and Paris orchestras (except for the Opéra) played at the same pitch—about A = 435—and wind players could use the same instruments in both countries.[66] Charles Burney saw this international circulation of personnel as a force for musical progress and good taste. "By travelling," he says in the final chapter of *The Present State of Music in Germany*, "musicians lose, among other local partialities, that veneration for a particular style, which . . . keeps them in such subjection."[67] Just as the international circulation of singers in the fifteenth and sixteenth centuries had contributed to the emergence of a pan-European choral style, so the circulation of instrumentalists in the eighteenth century helped foster an international orchestral consensus.

Even more vigorous than the circulation of performers was the circulation of orchestral repertory, both locally and internationally. Although eighteenth-century critics decreed that church, theater, and chamber each required a different musical style, in practice the same pieces were often pressed into service in all three contexts. This was particularly true with orchestral music, which did not have words that might mark it as inappropriate in its new venue. Movements from symphonies were often performed during mass, often during the offertory and communion, or as substitutes for mass movements.[68] Some of these were "church symphonies," composed specifically for such occasions. But in Italy and southern Germany secular symphonies,

---

[64] See Bruce Haynes, "Pitch Standards in the Baroque and Classical Periods" (Ph.D. diss., Université de Montréal, 1995); see also Ch. 11.

[65] Tula Giannini, "A Letter from Louis Rousselet, 18th-Century French Oboist at the Royal Opera in England," *American Musical Instrument Society Newsletter*, 16/2 (1987), 10–11.

[66] Haynes, "Pitch Standards," 349.   [67] Burney, *Present State of Music in Germany*, ii. 338.

[68] See Zaslaw, *Mozart's Symphonies*, 77–81.

concertos, and opera overtures were often used for the same purpose.[69] The spoken theater used a good deal of music originally composed for other venues. At Covent Garden and Drury Lane in the 1730s and 1740s the orchestra played concertos by Geminiani and Corelli and Handel's *Water Music* between the acts.[70] Somewhat later, symphonies by Stamitz and the Earl of Kelly served as act music.[71] At concerts operatic arias and scenes were repertory staples, along with overtures and *sinfonie*.

The circulation of repertory was facilitated by standardized scorings. If an orchestra could muster the four principal string parts plus oboes and horns, it could play the greater portion of the orchestral repertory. The same music could and did serve for an orchestra of 10, an orchestra of 40, or an orchestra of 80. This flexibility was abetted by the extensive double-handedness of eighteenth-century instrumentalists. If a piece called for flutes or clarinets, the oboists could usually handle the parts, or they could be transcribed for strings or keyboards. A hornist could double on trumpet, a violist on timpani; or the trumpet and drum parts could simply be omitted.

The circulation of repertory between orchestras and between venues was a two-edged sword. Reichardt pointed out in 1793

> how dangerous it is for a composer's reputation when works that have been written for a specific orchestra or concert society are performed in other places by less good musicians. Yet he can do nothing to prevent this; indeed, it is indispensible to the advancement of his reputation. All composers are therefore well advised to write music that is easy to play—particularly for the orchestral accompaniments [*begleitenden Instrumente*].[72]

Composers were taking Reichardt's advice long before he gave it: the difficulty of orchestral music in the eighteenth century was regulated by well-established conventions. Orchestral violin parts from the 1740s until the 1790s seldom exceed third position; most viola parts remain in first position.[73] The *basso* part, respecting the limitations of double basses and double bass players, seldom goes above the staff in bass clef, and almost never above *e'*. Passages above this note are usually written in tenor clef and intended for the cellos alone. These limitations apply to the orchestral string parts of Gluck, Hasse, Stamitz, Haydn, Mozart, and almost all their contemporaries.[74] Indeed, the fact that Reichart needed to give his advice at all may have been a sign that the system was beginning to break down. Orchestral violin parts that require

---

[69] Nicolai, *Beschreibung einer Reise*, i. 129. See Daniel Heartz, *Haydn, Mozart and the Viennese School, 1740–1780* (New York, 1995), 20.

[70] *The London Stage*, iii, p. clvii.   [71] Fiske, *English Theatre Music*, 260.

[72] Johann Friedrich Reichardt, "Winke und Regeln für Anführer der Musik in Concerten," *Berlinische musicalische Zeitung*, no. 21 (2 Nov. 1793), 162. The article is anonymous on the page but attributed to Reichardt in the index.

[73] Thus the highest note in many 18th-c. orchestral violin parts is *e'''*, which is played on the E-string in third position as an extension; in viola parts the highest note is usually *f''*. Parts marked "concertante" or "principale" go much higher.

[74] Since wind players were usually one on a part and often considered themselves virtuosos, conventions pertaining to the difficulty of their parts were less clear.

fifth position can be found in the later symphonies of Cannabich, in Haydn's London Symphonies, and in operas by Méhul and Spontini. Beethoven requires fifth position from his First Symphony (1800) on. No wonder John Marsh complained about the "elaborate symphonies of Haydn, Mozart, Beethoven &c," which were beyond the reach of the amateur orchestras that he organized and led in English provincial towns.[75] So long as composers scored for the standard "classical" orchestra and observed the conventions of difficulty in their string parts, large and small orchestras, standing orchestras and pick-up orchestras, professionals and dilettantes could all play the same pieces and hope to sound, if not the same, at least similar. When composers began to exceed these limits, the consensus began to break down.

THE END OF THE CLASSICAL ORCHESTRA

By the end of the 1790s the stability and uniformity that had marked the orchestra for 50 years were eroding. From about 1815 on orchestras again entered into a period of rapid change. New instruments were introduced, and the balances among instruments changed. Four-part scoring was replaced by organization into sections of instruments. A new kind of orchestra leader emerged: the conductor, who directed the orchestra with a baton rather than by playing an instrument. In addition the culture of the orchestra expanded tremendously during the first half of the nineteenth century: the number of orchestras increased, orchestras appeared in new venues and new roles. These developments will be sketched here only briefly.

Stringed instruments did not change much during the first half of the nineteenth century. Orchestra players continued to use instruments made on seventeenth-century patterns, with gut or overwound gut strings. Increasingly, however, the old instruments were rebuilt by luthiers to modernize them. The biggest change was in bows, where the Tourte bow, with its concave curve, weighted tip, and screw tensioner at the frog, replaced older models on violins, violas, and cellos. Woodwind instruments, on the other hand, were subjected to a frenzy of experimentation and improvement. Keywork was added to improve intonation, even out the timbre, eliminate awkward stretches, and make the instruments fully chromatic. The resulting instruments could play faster, louder, and more reliably in tune than eighteenth-century wind instruments. Instruments in extreme registers were added to the orchestra: piccolo flute, English horn, B-flat bass clarinet, contrabassoon. Changes among the brass instruments were even greater. Trombones, which in the eighteenth century had been used mainly in churches, were added to most orchestras. A succession of large instruments with cup mouthpieces—serpentone, bombardon, ophicleide, and cimbasso—were added to

---

[75] Charles Cudworth, "John Marsh on the Subscription Concert," 133. See above, Ch. 8.

orchestras in an attempt to give a bass voice to the brasses.[76] They were gradually replaced by tubas, beginning in the 1830s. Even more important was the addition of slides, then keys, then valves to trumpets and horns, which rendered them fully chromatic, enabling them to play melodies in their lower and middle registers and to play in various keys in rapid succession. During the first half of the nineteenth century valved and natural instruments played side by side in the same orchestras.[77] In the classical orchestra the only brass instruments had been horns and trumpets, and for the most part they had occupied very different niches: horns as a sustaining voice among the woodwinds, trumpets for festive fanfares with the drums. By the mid-nineteenth century an entire brass section had emerged, with instruments from the soprano to the bass, capable of playing as a brass choir or individually as melodic soloists.

Many orchestras grew larger during the first half of the nineteenth century.[78] The orchestra at the Berlin opera, for example, increased from 76 players in 1818 to 94 in 1831, the opera orchestra at La Scala in Milan from 45 in 1804 to 68 in 1825, the orchestra for the Gewandhaus concerts in Leipzig from about 27 in 1808 to 44 in 1839.[79] The orchestra of the Opéra in Paris, on the other hand, and the Kapellen at Dresden and Munich remained about the same size over the period. More striking are the huge orchestras assembled for festivals and other special occasions: 130 instrumentalists for a grand concert to honor Napoleon in Erfurt in 1811, 204 for the Lower Rhenish music festival in Cologne in 1835 (Mendelssohn conducting), 213 for the Handel Commemoration of 1834 in Westminster Abbey.[80] For the Handel festival at the Crystal Palace in 1857, the orchestra numbered almost 400.[81] In Paris Berlioz organized a succession of monster concerts: 450 singers and instrumentalists at the Opéra in 1840 for a program featuring music by Berlioz, Handel, Gluck, and Palestrina (!), and over 1,000 performers at the Palais de l'Industrie in 1844.[82] Orchestras at these monster concerts played for larger and socially more diverse audiences than classical orchestras ever had. In their size and their complexity they represented the wealth and the organizational capacities of an emerging industrial society.

---

[76] Renato Meucci, "The Cimbasso and Related Instruments in 19th-Century Italy," *GSJ* 49 (1996), 143–79.

[77] Daniel J. Koury, *Orchestral Performance Practices in the Nineteenth Century: Size, Proportions and Seating* (Ann Arbor, 1986), 94–95. Berlioz in the *Symphonie fantastique* (Paris, 1830) used natural trumpets, hand-stopped horns, and valved cornets; Halévy in *La Juive* (Paris, 1835) wrote parts for two valved horns plus two natural horns; Wagner in *Rienzi* (Dresden, 1842) called for the same combination, plus two natural trumpets, and two cornets with valves.

[78] Carse, *The Orchestra from Beethoven to Berlioz*, 46–59; Mahling, "Orchester und Orchestermusiker," *passim*; Koury, *Orchestral Performance Practices*, 117 ff.

[79] Berlin figures from Mahling, "Orchester und Orchestermusiker." La Scala from Pompeo Cambiasi, *La Scala, note storiche e statistiche di Pompeo Cambiasi* (Milan, 1889), 61, and Carse, *The Orchestra from Beethoven to Berlioz*, 55; Leipzig ibid. 51.

[80] Julian Herbage, *Messiah* (London, 1948), 60.

[81] Howard Smither, "Messiah and Progress in Victorian England," *EM* 13 (1985), 339–48; Michael Musgrave, *The Musical Life of the Crystal Palace* (Cambridge, 1995), 36.

[82] D. Kern Holoman, *Berlioz* (Cambridge, Mass., 1989), 271–73, 311.

The balances within the orchestra changed decisively in the first half of the nineteenth century. The proportion of strings to one another remained about the same—with the violins forming a slightly lower percentage of strings, a trend visible already in the 1790s (Fig. 9.1). The ratio of cellos to double basses still varied somewhat by region: many Italian orchestras still made do with only a pair of cellos against a much larger number of basses, while English, French, and German orchestras tended to use about equal numbers of cellos and basses.[83] The trend for wind instruments to form a higher percentage of the orchestra, evident in the last decades of the eighteenth century (Fig. 9.3), accelerated in the nineteenth century, both because of doubled woodwinds and because of added brass. By the 1840s brass instruments constituted 10 to 20 percent of many orchestras.

The *basso*, on the other hand—the combination of instruments on the bass line that had been central to the organization of the classical orchestra—disappeared rapidly at the beginning of the nineteenth century. Cellos, double basses, and bassoons were differentiated from one another and seated separately in the orchestra. The harpsichord, which had been the heart of the *basso* group, disappeared almost entirely from orchestras. Already in 1789 Rellstab commented that many German theater orchestras had abandoned the harpsichord: some of them had replaced it with the piano; others used no keyboard instrument at all.[84] Absent a keyboard, recitative was accompanied by the full orchestra, or another instrument had to realize the bass line. A cello method published by the Paris Conservatoire in 1804 instructs students on how to realize figured bass in order to accompany recitative on the cello.[85]

With the dissolution of the *basso* into its component parts and with the addition of woodwind and brass instruments, the "four principal parts" model of the classical orchestra was replaced by a new organization into sections of strings, woodwinds, and brass, each section containing a full range of instruments from treble to bass. This new sectional organization can be seen in paylists and seating charts from the first half of the nineteenth century.[86] In addition, the core of a percussion section began to appear in the early nineteenth century. Triangle, side drum, and bass drum were added to orchestras as needed, usually played by supernumeraries. Composers began to treat timpani independently from the trumpets (e.g. Haydn Symphony no. 103, Beethoven Symphony no. 5). While composers could score for choirs of strings, woodwinds, or brass in the nineteenth century, they could also pick and choose

[83] Carse, *The Orchestra from Beethoven to Berlioz*, 46 ff.

[84] Johann Carl Friedrich Rellstab, *Ueber die Bemerkungen eines Reisenden* (Berlin, 1789). Quoted in Thomas Drescher, "Johann Friedrich Reichardt als Leiter der Berliner Hofkapelle," *Basler Jahrbuch für historische Musikpraxis*, 17 (1993), 139–60 at 147.

[85] Pierre Marie Baillot, *Méthode de violoncelle et de basse d'accompagnement* (Paris, 1804). Edward Holmes mentions that in the 1820s cellists in London and in Vienna accompanied recitative with improvised chords and arpeggios even though there was a piano in the orchestra (Edward Holmes, *A Ramble among the Musicians of Germany* (London, 1828), 129). See also Valerie Walden, *One Hundred Years of Violoncello: A History of Technique and Performance Practice, 1740–1840* (Cambridge, 1998), 261 ff.

[86] Koury, *Orchestral Performance Practices*, 175 ff.

combinations of instruments from the various sections to create new timbres and tone colors. These procedures were formalized in a series of treatises on orchestration or instrumentation, culminating in the *Traité général d'instrumentation* (1837) by Georges Kastner and Berlioz's *Traité d'instrumentation* of 1843. By the second half of the nineteenth century "orchestration" was acknowledged as a distinct compositional activity.[87]

The baton conductor was another creation of the first half of the nineteenth century. The classical orchestra, insofar has it had a single leader, was directed by an instrumentalist, usually the first violinist.[88] Instrumentalist directors led by example, indicating the beat primarily by the way they played rather than by visible signs. To a great extent the musicians in the classical orchestra took responsibility for themselves: for keeping the beat, for playing in tune, with the correct dynamics, and with appropriate expression. A German commentator of 1779 says:

> Where an orchestra is arranged so that its members can all see and also hear one another, where it is staffed with virtuosos, where the composer has included performance indications in the parts, and where there are sufficient rehearsals, then no further direction is necessary: the piece plays itself, like a clock that has been wound up and set running.[89]

The exceptions to this system of leading by doing were in churches, where a timebeater marked the beat for the singers with vertical movements of his hand or a roll of paper, and the Opéra in Paris, where a *batteur de mesure* kept time with a baton. Both in church and at the Opéra timebeating was aimed primarily at vocalists—particularly chorus singers. Instrumentalists in the orchestra were expected to follow along, accompanying the singers as best they could. At the Opéra, however, the timebeater gradually assumed direction of the orchestra as well, concentrating authority in a single man, the *maître de musique*, who, as a contemporary commentator explained, "leads the orchestra without playing any instrument."[90] The *maître's* authority at the Opéra increased steadily during the last quarter of the eighteenth century. J.-B. Rey, *maître* from 1781 to 1810, was responsible not only for giving tempos but also for dynamics, phrasing, and the character of the music.[91]

The system at the Opéra, where the orchestra was led by a man who beat time rather than playing an instrument, spread to other theaters in France, then to Germany. It was particularly useful for choruses and large ensembles in operas. Already in 1778 Burney encountered a timebeating "maestro di capella" at the Théâtre de la Monnaie in Brussels.[92] According to a report from Berlin in 1788,

[87] Carse, *The History of Orchestration*; R. Larry Todd, "Orchestral Texture and the Art of Orchestration," in Joan Peyser (ed.), *The Orchestra: Origins and Transformations* (New York, 1986), 191–226. See also Ch. 13.

[88] For a discussion of orchestral leadership in the 18th c., see Ch. 11.

[89] Biedermann [anon.], *Wahrheiten die Musik betreffend, gerade herausgesagt von einem teutschen Biedermann* (Frankfurt, 1779), 43.

[90] Joseph de Meude-Monpas, *Dictionnaire de musique* (Paris, 1787), 90.

[91] David Charlton, "'A maître d'orchestre . . . conducts'."

[92] Burney, *Present State of Music in Germany*, i. 22–23.

J. F. Reichardt, the Kapellmeister at the Opera, had eliminated the harpsichord from the orchestra and beat time, though it is not known whether he used a baton.[93] At the Hamburg opera in 1799 the conductor, a Belgian, beat time with a small stick, "as seems to be the custom," explained the German commentator, "almost everywhere in France."[94] Similarly, at Kassel in 1810 Legaye directed the opera "in the French manner, with a baton."[95] By 1825 baton conductors could be found in theaters in London, Paris, Berlin, Stuttgart, Cologne, Vienna, Dresden, and Darmstadt. Baton conducting turned up on the concert stage as well as in the theater. Louis Spohr, a strong advocate of the new system, led an oratorio, a symphony, an overture, and other works at the Frankenhausen festival in 1810 by beating time with a roll of paper.[96] In the first concert of his works at the Gewandhaus in 1835, Mendelssohn led with a baton, "with a precision previously unheard of."[97] By the 1840s the public was beginning to think of the man who led an orchestra "without playing any instrument" not simply as a timebeater but as a performer and musical creator. Michael Costa at the Royal Italian Opera in London, according to the *Musical World* in 1847, is "applauded when he comes on, applauded when he goes off."[98] "Never," said the critic, "was such a fuss made about a conductor." Even more fuss was made of Costa's contemporary Louis Jullien, who organized his own orchestra, named it after himself, led it in the Promenade Concerts in London, and took it on a series of tours through England and the United States.[99] When Jullien stood in front of his orchestra and waved his jewel-encrusted baton, reported the Birmingham *Journal* in 1845, "it seems as if he alone were the performer."[100]

The changes that transformed the orchestra at the beginning of the nineteenth century—changes in size, organization, balance, and leadership—were connected to broader changes in the orchestra's social role. The orchestras of Lully, of Corelli, of Handel, of Stamitz, and even of Mozart had been creations and creatures of courts. They either formed part of princely households, or they were supported to a major extent by princely patronage. They accompanied the activities of court society: operas, dancing, public ceremonies, festive services in church, soirées, and academies. In the second half of the eighteenth century, beginning in England and then increasingly on the Continent, patronage began to shift toward a broader public, and orchestras began to function in more varied social contexts. This is not to say that the orchestra became the property of the "middle class." As William Weber has shown, patronage by royalty and aristocracy remained central to concert life during most of

[93] *Bemerkungen eines Reisenden über die zu Berlin von September 1787 bis Ende Januar 1788 gegebene öffentlichen Musiken, Kirchenmusik, Oper, Concerte und königliche Kammermusik betreffend* (Halle, 1788), 57. See Drescher, "Johann Friedrich Reichardt," 147–49.

[94] Friedrich Rochlitz, "Bruchstücke aus Briefen an einen jungen Tonsetzer," *AMZ* 2 (1799), col. 728.

[95] *AMZ* 12 (1810), col. 714. [96] Louis Spohr, *Lebenserinnerungen* (Tutzing, 1968), i. 137.

[97] Koury, *Orchestral Performance Practices*, 73.

[98] 3 Apr. 1847; quoted in Carse, *The Orchestra from Beethoven to Berlioz*, 339.

[99] Adam Carse, *The Life of Jullien* (Cambridge, 1951). [100] Quoted ibid. 113.

the nineteenth century.[101] In many European cities aristocracy and bourgeoisie shared and struggled over the patronage of orchestras and musical culture. During the first half of the nineteenth century, however, more and more people gained access to orchestras and orchestral music. Orchestras could be heard at concerts, in theaters, at festivals, in cafés, and in dance halls. In the rapidly growing cities of nineteenth-century Europe orchestras became ubiquitous. Access to orchestras was no longer regulated by social status or social connections but by price: whoever could afford a ticket could hear an orchestra. "M. Jullien," remarked a critic in 1855, "has taught the crowd that they can hear, for a shilling or half-a-crown . . . performances quite as good as those for which the Philharmonic directors charge one guinea."[102]

This shift from court to public milieux went along with the changes sketched above. Orchestras needed to be bigger because they played for larger audiences in larger halls. Rebuilt violins, doubled or tripled woodwinds, and the newly redesigned brass instruments helped orchestras project in large halls and outdoor venues. Flexible scorings and effects of orchestration enabled orchestras to convey moods and meanings in the absence of words and singers. The baton conductor provided the large audience with a single human figure who embodied the entire orchestra, and whose elaborate dance seemed to turn the sawing and puffing of a hundred instrumentalists into music.

The classical orchestra of the second half of the eighteenth century represented the emergence and consolidation of the orchestra as an institution. With the end of the classical orchestra in the early nineteenth century, the institution of the orchestra became central in an even broader way to European musical life.

---

[101] William Weber, *Music and the Middle Class: The Social Structure of Concert Life in London, Paris and Vienna* (London, 1975). In the United States aristocratic patronage was never a factor.

[102] *Musical World*, 14 July 1855; quoted in Carse, *The Orchestra from Beethoven to Berlioz*, 231–32.

Chapter Ten

Placement, Seating, and Acoustics

Queen Christina of Sweden, having abdicated her throne and announced her conversion to Catholicism, was welcomed to Rome in 1655. Her arrival was celebrated at the carnival of 1656 with a spectacular *Giostra delle caroselle* outside the Barberini palace, as shown in Plate XII. In the center Don Matteo Barberini and two other Roman noblemen pose as Amazonian Indians in feathered headdresses. Parade floats carry mythological and allegorical figures: Hercules and a monster, a winged Cupid, the sun, and the four seasons.[1] A contemporary account describes the music for this gala occasion:

In the great courtyard of the palace . . . were constructed two spacious grandstands capable of holding up to 3,000 persons. In between them a magnificent gateway was erected . . . On top of this gate was a loft [*coro*] for the singers [*musici*], who were placed behind screens at four large windows and who sang exquisite melodies, accompanied by a variety of instruments.[2]

On the top of the giant gate at left of the painting, the viewer can just make out a little band of singers and instrumentalists, one of whom plays a large lute, another a cornett, another a violin (Pl. XIIa). There may have been more instrumentalists at the other windows, but if so, the artist chose not to depict them.[3] The chronicler goes on

[1] The identification of the mythological characters is based on a published account by V. G. Priorato, *Historia della Sacra Reale Maestà di Christina Alessandra Regina di Svetia* (Rome, 1656), reprinted in Filippo Clementi, *Il carnevale romano—nelle cronache contemporanee* (Città di Castello, 1939), 525–33. This picture is discussed more fully in Spitzer, "The Birth of the Orchestra in Rome."

[2] Giovanni Incisa della Rocchetta, "Tre quadri Barberini acquistati dal Museo di Roma," *Bollettino dei musei comunali di Roma*, 6 (1959), 20–37 at 30. The chronicle mentions that several houses had to be demolished to make room for the gate.

[3] The two artists, Filippo Gagliardi and Filippo Lauri, raised the screen on the one window in order to display the musicians, who according to the chronicler were hidden from view.

to say that "from time to time this musical ensemble [*coro de' musici*] played harmonious symphonies."[4]

Plate XIII depicts a similarly lavish event almost a hundred years later, again in Rome: a festival to celebrate the marriage of the French Dauphin to Princesse Maria-Josepha of Saxony in 1747.[5] The painting, by Gian Paolo Panini, shows a performance in the Teatro Argentina of a *Componimento dramatico* by Niccolò Jommelli.[6] This time there is no need to search for the instrumentalists. An orchestra of over 70 members is installed on the theater stage, dressed in red and blue livery and surrounded by clouds. To the left and right of the four vocal soloists at the front are two harpsichordists, each with a continuo group of cellos and double basses. Behind them violins, violas, and some winds are arrayed in tiers. This is a much larger and more "orchestral" ensemble than the little band of 1656. It is based on violin-family instruments; it has several instruments to a part, 16-foot basses, and chordal continuo, all traits that came to characterize the orchestra in the eighteenth century.

The instrumental ensembles in these two pictures also differ in their placement and seating. "Placement" means where an orchestra is located with respect to its physical surroundings, the audience, and concomitant social activities. The 1656 ensemble is placed in an enclosed gallery, high above the participants in the pageant and behind the spectators in the grandstands. The ensemble is depicted as peripheral: at the edge of the picture and on the fringe of the event. The orchestra for Jommelli's *Componimento* of 1747 is central, both to the picture and to the event. It is placed on the theater stage, on a level with the occupants of the lower boxes. Orchestra and audience face one another directly: each instrumentalist can be seen by every member of the audience. Both visually and aurally the orchestra is at the center of the show.

"Seating" means how the members of an orchestra are oriented to one another and to the listeners. The musicians in the 1656 *Giostra* picture seem be packed at random into their balcony. Some are seated, some are standing; some face left, others right; strings, winds, and singers are mixed together in no apparent order. The onstage orchestra of 1747 presents a contrasting image of regimentation and symmetry. Singers and instrumentalists are separated.[7] The two continuo groups are arranged symmetrically facing the center. The rest of the instrumentalists stand in tiers on risers, all facing the same way, arranged symmetrically and grouped by instrument. The orchestra's seating seems to be calculated not only to facilitate musical coordination but also for maximum visual effect.

---

[4] Clementi, *Il carnevale romano*, 531.

[5] See Ferdinando Arisi, *Gian Paolo Panini* (Piacenza, 1961), 188–90; André Bourde, "Opera seria et scénographie: Autour de deux toiles italiennes du 18ème siècle," in *L'Opéra au 18ème siècle. Colloque, Aix-en-Provence 29 avril–1 mai 1977* (Aix-en-Provence, 1982), 229–53.

[6] Jommelli's music is lost, but a libretto preserves the text by F. Scarselli.

[7] Besides the four vocal soloists in the center, who represent Venus, Jupiter, Pallas Athena, and Mars, choirs of "Graces" and "Amoretti" are seated on either side above the string basses.

Finally, the orchestras in the two pictures are performing under very different acoustical conditions. The ensemble at the *Giostra* is playing outdoors: the listeners hear mainly direct sound plus a little sound reflected from the wall of the palace. The musicians compete with sounds of horses, marching feet, creaking machinery, and an unruly crowd trying to force its way into the square on the bottom right. The 1747 ensemble performs indoors in a theater, where the direct sound is enhanced by sound reflected from the ceiling and the plaster decorations on the walls. At the same time both direct and reflected sound are absorbed by the audience, the upholstery on the chairs, and the interiors of the boxes. Although knots of people are conversing, and servants can be seen making their way through the crowd with drinks, the environment was probably a good deal quieter than that of the *Giostra delle caroselle*.

Much of the evidence about the placement and seating of orchestras in the seventeenth and eighteenth centuries comes from drawings, engravings, diagrams, and paintings, like Pls. XII and XIII. Information about acoustics can be deduced from the same pictures, as well as from architectural drawings, contemporary reports, and measurements of surviving buildings. The interpretation of pictures as evidence of musical performance practices has been much criticized.[8] Often the proportions of an instrument or how it is held are implausible. For example, the cornett player in Pl. XIIa holds the instrument with his right hand above his left, an unusual, though not impossible, practice.[9] The artist may "telescope" events that took place in succession into a single picture: according to a contemporary report, the refreshments at the Teatro Argentina were not served during the performance of the serenata as the picture shows, but during an intermission.[10] Many pictures are fraught with connotative or symbolic meanings. Their underlying subject may not be music but social status, or etiquette, or the relations between men and women.[11] Finally, some pictures do not depict an actual occasion on which music is being played but rather are portraits in which musical instruments function as props. Nevertheless, pictures still provide valid and valuable evidence, particularly about general relationships, such as where orchestras were placed, whether they were large or small, what types of instruments they contained, how the musicians were seated in relation to one another and to the audience. Even if a picture misrepresents what actually took place at an event, it still represents musical practices possible at the time. Perhaps there were more instrumentalists on top of the gate in 1656; perhaps there were fewer on the stage of the Teatro Argentina in 1747. Nevertheless, the paintings still show how big

---

[8] See e.g. Emanuel Winternitz, "The Iconology of Music: Potentials and Pitfalls," in Barry Brook, Edward Downes, and Sherman Van Solkema (eds.), *Perspectives in Musicology* (New York, 1972), 80–119.

[9] Some 17th- and early 18th-c. wind instruments were designed so that they could be played with either hand uppermost. See Haynes, *The Eloquent Oboe*, 182–84.

[10] Arisi, *Panini*, 189. On telescoping in depictions of musical performances, see Hanning, "Iconography of a Salon Concert."

[11] Richard Leppert, "Men, Women, and Music at Home: The Influence of Cultural Values on Musical Life in Eighteenth-Century England," *Imago Musicae*, 2 (1985), 51–133.

TABLE 10.1. *Eighteenth-century orchestral configurations*

Placement	Venue	Seating	Function	Repertory	Acoustic
In a balcony	church large room	amorphous separate ensembles	church services dances banquets	sacred music symphonies sonatas dances	large room high reverb
In the pit	theater	single row facing rows semicircle	opera ballet spoken theater	opera symphonies ballet music	large room low reverb
On the floor	music room salon	around table around keyboard single row	concerts musical socializing	symphonies cantatas concertos	small room high reverb
On stage	outdoors theater large room	in tiers semicircle	concerts public celebrations	oratorio serenatas symphonies	outdoors low reverb

or how small the artists thought orchestras *should* be at events of this type in the 1650s and again in the 1740s. When pictures like these are corroborated by other contemporary images, and by documentary evidence like pay records, carpenters' bills, letters, and official accounts, then they can be taken as evidence of actual patterns of placement and seating.

Four placements turn up again and again in depictions of orchestras in the seventeenth and eighteenth centuries:[12]

1. In a balcony. Balconies can be choir lofts in churches, also galleries in large rooms or on the roofs of buildings.
2. In the pit. The characteristic placement of an orchestra in the theater is directly in front of the stage, on the ground level of the theater.
3. On the floor. For music in private, indoor spaces, instrumentalists are typically placed on the floor of the room in close proximity to the audience.
4. On stage. This is often the stage of a theater, but it can also be a temporary stage or a special structure like a bandstand.

These four placements were associated in turn with distinct venues, seating patterns, social functions, musical repertories, and acoustics to make four broad configurations, as shown in Table 10.1. In venues like churches and large rooms with high reverberation, orchestras tended to be placed in a balcony or in several balconies, and the players tended to be seated randomly with respect to one another and to the audience. This permitted the sound to reflect off the ceiling, reaching all corners of the room. Orchestras "in a balcony" were most often used for church services, dances, and banquets, and they typically played concerted sacred music, symphonies, sonatas, or dance music. In theaters, large rooms with less reverberation, orchestras were typically placed "in the pit," with the instrumentalists seated in a long row or in two facing rows. The configurations in Table 10.1 are general patterns and tendencies, and they admit of a great number of exceptions. The *Giostra* picture, for example, shows an instrumental ensemble in a balcony; however, it is not in a church or a hall but rather outdoors, and the occasion is a public celebration, which would seem to call for the placement of the orchestra on stage. The Teatro Argentina orchestra of 1747 fits the "on stage" configuration in many respects: seating in tiers, theater venue, public celebration, serenata repertory—but it performs in a theater rather than outdoors.

ORCHESTRAS IN BALCONIES

An orchestra in a balcony occupies an enclosed space above the listeners and other participants in the event. Balcony placement includes ensembles on top of buildings,

---

[12] This categorization was first proposed in Zaslaw, "The Origins of the Classical Orchestra."

on top of monuments, like the triumphal arch in the *Giostra* picture, and in choirlofts. Instrumentalists in balconies are often mixed in with singers. Often there are several balconies, containing independent choirs of instruments and singers or with the orchestra divided into two more more parts. An orchestra in a balcony tends to be peripheral to the event in which it participates. Often it cannot be seen by the listeners, because it is above eye level or because it is hidden behind grills or screens, as in Pl. XII. In the eighteenth century orchestras in balconies appeared most often in three contexts: in churches, at banquets, and for dances.

Most churches in the eighteenth century had two or more lofts for the musicians, a holdover from the multiple-ensemble, *cori spezzati* practices of the sixteenth and seventeenth centuries (see Ch. 2). Often two lofts faced one another across the chancel of a church. Each loft had its own organ, its own singers, and its own orchestra, as seen in Pl. IV.[13] Groups of singers and instrumentalists could also be placed in a series of lofts along the length of the nave, or at the back of the nave over the main door. This last placement had the disadvantage that it drew attention to the back of the church and away from the service. A visitor to Venice, who attended a mass at the church of S. Lorenzo in 1758, was surprised to see that the chairs were placed with their backs to the altar so that people could watch the orchestra and chorus.[14]

Dining at European courts in the seventeenth and eighteenth centuries was often accompanied by music, which added splendor to the occasion and also masked the noise of plates, glasses, conversations, and servants. To keep the musicians out of the traffic and also to maintain social distance between the musicians and the guests, the orchestra at a banquet was usually placed in a balcony. Figure 10.1 depicts a banquet given in Dresden by Friedrich August I of Saxony to celebrate his birthday in 1718. Fifteen or 20 singers and instrumentalists are squeezed together in a small balcony above the king. A bassoon, three singers, two violins, and a long-necked lute can be seen in the front row. The other instruments cannot be made out. Trumpet and drum ensembles occupy separate balconies on either side. The position of the orchestra in Fig. 10.1 seems to imply that it was central or at least very important to the banquet. In any event it must have been loud. Not only is the orchestra indoors, but the high balcony puts it very close to a rounded plaster ceiling, which reflects the sound toward the unseen spectators watching the Elector dine. When all the instruments including the trumpets played, the result must have had a considerable impact on the digestion of the Elector and his guests.[15]

---

[13] For more pictures of orchestras in multiple balconies, see Pl. I (Salzburg, 1682) and Fig. 7.3 (Königsberg, 1701).

[14] Grosley, *Observations*, 55. See Ch. 5. An engraving by J. E. Mansfeld in Richter's *Bildergalerie katholischer Misbräuche* (1784) shows a Viennese audience turning their backs on the altar to watch solo singers and an orchestra in a balcony. See Heartz, *Haydn, Mozart and the Viennese School*, 15–16.

[15] For another picture of an orchestra in a balcony at a banquet, see Fig. 7.6 (Hamburg, 1719).

FIG. 10.1. Banquet for the birthday of Friedrich August I of Saxony, Dresden, 1718

Orchestras for balls and social dancing were also placed in balconies, perhaps again to keep them out of the way. Figure 7.5, the imaginary dress ball, shows an orchestra of strings and winds crowded into two balconies, while some 15 couples dance stiffly below. Again, the placement of the orchestra near the ceiling probably helped reflect the sound to the audience. Plate XIV, a painting of a masked ball in Madrid *c.*1767, looks like more fun. The parterre of the theater has been turned into a ballroom, and a temporary balcony erected for the orchestra.[16] Masked dancers fill the room with a whirl of color and activity; spectators in masks observe from the theater boxes above. Here the artist has positioned the orchestra in the center of the picture rather than the periphery, perhaps to emphasize the noise and excitement of the scene.

The seating patterns of orchestras in balconies can usually be characterized as amorphous. Singers and instrumentalists seem to be squeezed together with no apparent regard to who is playing what instrument or which part. The other possible balcony seating is in tiers: the players sit or stand on risers with everyone facing the same way (Fig. 7.5). Dividing an orchestra among two or more balconies (Pl. I) created severe coordination problems, because of the amount of time it took for sound to travel from one orchestra to the other.[17] Churches continued to place instrumentalists in separate lofts, however, until the end of the eighteenth century. Orchestras for banquets were seldom divided, but a very large ballroom could have two dance orchestras. Perhaps they took turns, or perhaps they played simultaneously, since very likely neither orchestra by itself could be heard across the length of the ballroom.

ORCHESTRAS IN THE PIT

Orchestras in the seventeenth-century theater moved from place to place according to the demands of the particular production. Chappuzeau reports in 1674 that the "violins" at the Paris theaters could be placed backstage, in the wings, between the stage and the parterre, or in one of the rear loges.[18] Seventeenth-century English theaters sometimes had a "music room" built above the proscenium arch, hidden by shutters that could be opened to reveal the musicians.[19] Samuel Pepys, visiting the newly opened Drury Lane Theatre in 1663, complained that the instrumental ensemble had been placed *under* the stage, which ruined its sound: "the Musique being below, and most of it sounding under the very stage, there is no hearing of the bases at all, nor very well of the trebles . . ."[20]

As theater ensembles grew into orchestras, however, and as coordination became more important between the orchestra and the singers and actors on stage, theater orchestras moved to the space in front of the stage called the "orchestra" in Italy,

---

[16] Several 18th-c. theaters were designed with machinery under the floor that raised the parterre to the level of the stage, thus making the entire room into a single dance floor. See Michael Forsyth, *Buildings for Music* (Cambridge, 1985), 90.

[17] Galeazzi, *Elementi teorico-pratici*, i. 217.　　　[18] Chappuzeau, *Le Théâtre françois*, 146–47. See Ch. 2.

[19] Boswell, *The Restoration Court Stage*, 163, 169.

[20] Pepys, *Diary*, iv. 128. For additional discussion of the placement of the orchestra in 17th-c. theaters, see Patrizio Barbieri, "The Acoustics of Italian Opera Houses and Auditoriums (ca. 1450–1900)," *Recercare*, 10 (1998), 263–323 at 314 ff.

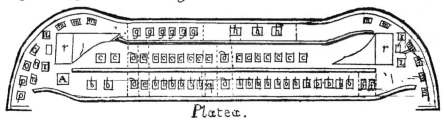

FIG. 10.2. Diagram of the orchestra at the Teatro Regio in Turin, *c.*1790

"orchestre" in France, and in the English theater the "pit."[21] This placement can be seen in Pl. XV, which depicts the opening of Turin's first permanent theater, in the ducal palace, with a performance of Pagliardi's *Lisimaco* (Carnival, 1681).[22] The orchestra has been placed directly in front of the stage, stretching from one side to the other, and a barrier has been erected between the orchestra and the audience. About 28 musicians can be seen, playing violins, archlutes, and violoni; the other instruments cannot be seen.

Placement in the pit had several advantages over the former locations in balconies, music rooms, or offstage. The orchestra was closer to the audience, so its sound was louder; singers and instrumentalists could see and hear one another clearly; and the sound of the orchestra reached the audience from the same direction as the actors' and singers' voices. On the other hand, the new placement had the disadvantage that the orchestra was in plain view. The audience was obliged to ignore it in order to maintain the theatrical illusion.

The classic eighteenth-century configuration of an orchestra in the pit can be seen in Fig. 10.2, a diagram of the orchestra in the Teatro Regio in Turin, published by Galeazzi in 1791. Two lines of violinists face one another across long music desks. The firsts (labeled "b") have their backs to the audience, so that their sound projects toward the singers rather than the listeners. The leader of the first violins ("A") sits on a raised chair so that all the musicians can see him. Violas (labeled "g") have been put in a third row at the lip of the stage, along with the bassoons ("h"). Oboes ("d") and clarinets ("e") are distributed among the rows of violins. To the left and right harpsichords form the core of two continuo groups: each harpsichordist has a solo cello on his right, a solo bassist on his left. Additional cellos and basses ("m") are gathered behind these groups. Hornists (who also played trumpet) are placed at the far edges of

[21] The "pit" was at floor level rather than below the parterre, like the orchestra pit in most modern opera houses.

[22] Mercedes Viale Ferrero, "Repliche a Torino di alcuni melodrammi veneziani e loro caratteristiche," in Maria Teresa Muraro (ed.), *Venezia e il melodramma nel Seicento* (Florence, 1978), 145–72 at 151–52.

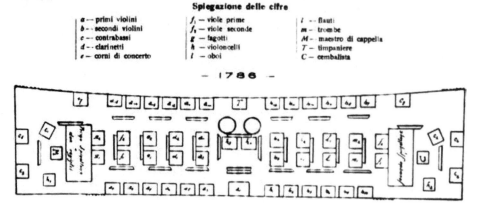

Piano della nuova pianta dell' orchestra per il Real Teatro San Carlo

La linea che guarda la platea deve essere diritta e di lunghezza pal: 52. La larghezza dell' orchestra in mezzo è di pal: 10 ¹/₂ e va gradatamente a pal: 12. Li sedili sono quelli in cui si trova scritto il nome dello strumento corrispondente a ciascheduno. Devono essere situati nel luogo ove sono e per la misura tutti devono essere simili cioè larghi pal: 1 ¹/₂ e lunghi pal: 1 ¹/₂ ad eccezione di quello del sedile *a*, che deve essere largo pal: ¹/₂ e lungo pal: 1 ³/₄. Li leggii sono quelli segnati in figura ═══ li quali, vedendosi in pianta devono essere larghi pal: 3 nel fondo e di sopra pal: 2 ³/₄ e di materiale veduto in pianta ³/₄ di pal: Il doppio segno di sotto significa il regolo che sostiene il libro della Musica. Ogni leggiino deve essere ad una sola faccia con una gamba sola e piede tondo lungo ¹/₂ palmo da imboccarsi nelle loro situazioni.

Spiegazione delle cifre

a — primi violini	*f₁* — viole prime	*l* — flauti
b — secondi violini	*f₂* — viole seconde	*m* — trombe
c — contrabassi	*g* — fagotti	*M* — maestro di cappella
d — clarinetti	*h* — violoncelli	*T* — timpaniere
e — corni di concerto	*I* — oboi	*C* — cembalista

— 1786 —

FIG. 10.3. Diagram of the San Carlo Theater orchestra, Naples, *c*.1786

the ensemble ("f" and "n"). Although it originated nearly a half-century later, Galeazzi's diagram closely resembles Olivero's painting of the Teatro Regio in 1740 (Pl. III). Because the orchestra was smaller in the earlier period, two rows sufficed for the violins. Violas and oboes were placed among the violins, and bassoons among the ripieno basses.

Essentially the same configuration—facing rows of violins, violas, and woodwinds, harpsichords, and continuo to the left and right, ripieno basses and brass at the margins—may be seen in Figs. 5.2 (Rome 1727) and 7.2 (Dresden 1719). When an orchestra had only one harpsichord, its place was on the left, with a single continuo group. In a few orchestras strings and winds were separated, strings in facing rows on one side, winds similarly arranged on the other—a configuration seen in the diagram of the Dresden orchestra that Rousseau published in his *Dictionnaire de musique* of 1768.[23] Galeazzi, comparing the two plans, remarks that the Dresden layout is better for maintaining ensemble but that the Turin plan is better for projecting a uniform orchestral sound to every corner of the theater.[24]

Seating plans of the late eighteenth century begin to orient themselves more around the orchestra itself rather than toward the stage. A "new plan" for the orchestra at the San Carlo Theater in Naples in 1786 (Fig. 10.3) retains the traditional lines

[23] Rousseau, *Dictionnaire de musique*, pl. G. Quantz (1752) and Scaramelli (1811) both propose seating plans for theater orchestras in which strings and winds are divided. See Quantz, *Versuch*, Eng. trans. 211–12; Scaramelli, *Saggio*, 14.

[24] Galeazzi, *Elementi teorico-pratici*, 223.

of violinists, but the rows have been moved farther apart, creating room for wind instruments between the lines of violins. Also, first and second violins are divided in a new way—firsts on the left, seconds on the right. Four violinists and two cellists ("a3, a4, b3, b4," "h3, h4") have been moved to the middle of the orchestra and turned to face the center. Now the principal strings form a tight semicircle around the violin-leader ("a") at the center of the ensemble. The winds, along with the violas, have also turned to face the center. Long music racks have been replaced by music stands, shared by players in pairs. A variation on this plan is seen in Pl. IX, Rowlandson's aquatint of the King's Theatre in London around 1808. The violinists at the front of the orchestra are still in facing rows, but toward the rear the strings are arranged in pairs, facing one another. The winds are in pairs also, but they face the center, where the violin-leader was presumably located (though he cannot be made out in the picture).[25] Where earlier seating plans encouraged instrumentalists to take individual responsibility for accompanying the singers, the new plans focused responsibility on a centrally placed leader.

In almost all eighteenth-century theaters the orchestra was placed at floor level, not below it. Most of the instrumentalists were seated, presumably to keep them from blocking the view of the stage. Only bass players stood, and occasionally a hornist or bassoonist; in most cases they were placed at the extreme left and right. The orchestra was separated from the audience by a barrier that kept audience members out of the orchestra's space and away from the stage. Like the proscenium, the orchestra's barrier marked the line between the real world of the audience and the imaginary world on stage. Because the stage apron extended well past the frontmost boxes, the orchestra's position in many theaters was toward the center of the room, as seen in Rowlandson's picture of the King's Theatre (Pl. IX) as well as the watercolor of the Opéra Comique in 1772 (Pl. VII). Presumably this enabled the direct sound of the orchestra to reach more of the audience.

ORCHESTRAS ON THE FLOOR

Pictures of eighteenth-century orchestras "on the floor" are usually set indoors: in a room of a house, a "chamber" in a palace, or a public assembly room. Most of them depict music-making in an atmosphere of sociability. Instrumentalists, singers, and audience are placed on the same level as one another, some sitting, some standing, and there is no barrier between orchestra and audience. Audience members sit among the performers or stand where they can see the music. Occasionally there is no audience at all—the musicians seem to be performing for their own pleasure or rehearsing

---

[25] A diagram of the orchestra of the Berlin opera in 1788 shows pairs of instrumentalists facing the concertmaster in the center (*Bemerkungen eines Reisenden*, 57). Many pictures from the early 19th c. present versions of this arrangement.

FIG. 10.4. Concerto performance, Zürich, 1777

privately (Fig 7.7). Pictures like Fig. 10.4, an engraving published in Zürich in 1777, give the impression that the audience and the performers belong to the same social circles. The hornist with the cap probably represents a professional musician, but the woman playing the harpsichord is almost certainly an amateur, and the flutists and

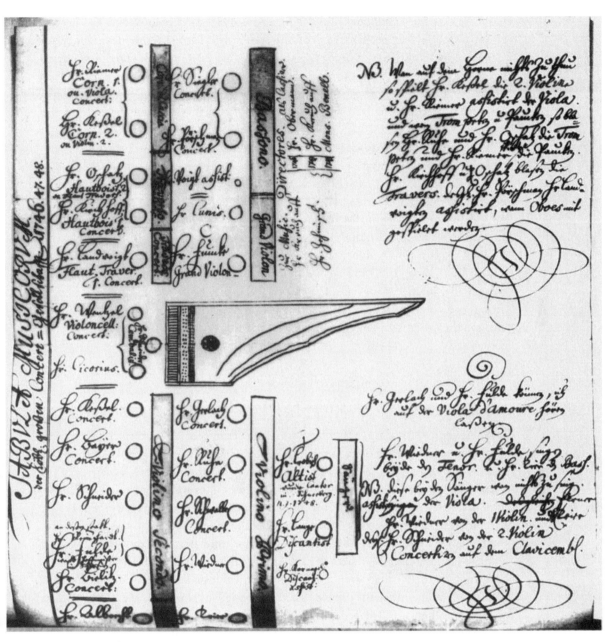

FIG. 10.5. Diagram of the Grosse Konzert, Leipzig, *c.*1746

violinists may very well be.[26] Two men and two seated ladies look over the harpsi-chordist's shoulder; perhaps one of the ladies will attempt the next concerto. Compared with the theater orchestras above, this little ensemble of eight instruments hardly looks like much of an orchestra. The caption insists, however, that they are playing a "keyboard concerto with instrumental accompaniment," and indeed one-on-a-part performances of concertos were common in Germany throughout the eighteenth century.[27]

The seating plans of on-the-floor orchestras tend to focus inward: the instrumentalists are arranged around a keyboard (Figs. 7.4, 7.7, 10.4) or in a semicircle (Pl. X), so they can see and hear each other well. Such self-contained seating plans were satisfactory when an orchestra performed for its own enjoyment or in an atmosphere of informality and social equality. In a more formal setting, however, it was inappropriate for the players to turn their backs to the audience, and the seating plan had to be adjusted. A plan for a public concert is shown in Fig. 10.5, a diagram of the Grosse Concert in Leipzig in 1746.[28] As in the theater, the instrumentalists are arranged in two parallel lines, but instead of facing one another, both lines face the audience. Strings and winds are separated. The harpsichord is placed at the center of the ensemble, and the other instruments are oriented not around the keyboard but toward the audience.

THE ORCHESTRA ON STAGE

In the seventeenth century the most common setting for an onstage orchestra was outdoors, usually for an occasion that involved civic display or a public celebration. Usually the stage or bandstand was specially built for the occasion. When Corelli's orchestra played outdoors, he assembled large ensembles and placed them in tiers on temporary stages. The tiered arrangement meant that most of the instruments had a hard, sound-reflecting surface immediately behind them. At the festival sponsored by the French ambassador in 1687, an orchestra of around 40 musicians was installed in a square bandstand in the Piazza di Spagna (Fig. 4.2). For the birthday of the Queen of Spain later that year an even larger orchestra was installed in a yet more elaborate bandstand: a magnificent convex structure topped by carytids (Fig. 4.1). Raised above the audience and placed in the center of the visual field, Corelli's orchestra did not just accompany the show: aurally and visually the orchestra *was* the show.

---

[26] For other pictures of amateur musicians in on-the-floor configurations, see Fig. 7.4 and Pl. X.

[27] Edge, "Manuscript Parts."

[28] This diagram was probably drawn by one of the members of the orchestra, who wrote in the names of all the performers and indicated instruments on which they doubled. For a discussion of this drawing see Claudius Böhm and Sven-W. Staps, *Das Leipziger Stadt- und Gewandhausorchester* (Leipzig, 1993), 10. On the Grosse Concert, see Ch. 12.

In the eighteenth century these temporary outdoor stages were sometimes turned into permanent bandstands, like the structure outside the castle walls in Milan where Sammartini's orchestra performed in the 1750s (Fig. 5.4), or the bandstand at Vauxhall Gardens in London, which contained a built-in organ (Fig 8.2). The shells that covered these outdoor bandstands protected the instruments from bad weather, projected the orchestra's sound toward the audience, and also served as a visual frame for the orchestra. Bandstands were also built indoors, particularly in large rooms, where the acoustics resembled those of the open air. Such bandstands—called "orchestras" in England—tended to be steeply raked, both to display the performers and also to provide plenty of reflecting surfaces to project the orchestra's sound toward the audience.

For opera and spoken theater, where the orchestra's primary role was to accompany singers and actors, the orchestra was rarely placed on stage. For scenes like triumphal processions and dances, in which the action called for onstage performance by instrumental ensembles, these ensembles were almost never composed of members of the regular theater orchestra but rather of supernumeraries hired for the occasion. For oratorios and serenatas on the other hand, the orchestra was very often placed on the stage rather than in the pit. As Panini's painting of the Teatro Argentina shows (Pl. XIII), the display of the orchestra on stage could contribute substantially to the effect of a *serenata*. In Fig. 5.2, the Christmas oratorio performed at Cardinal Ottoboni's palace in 1727, the orchestra is placed both on stage *and* in the pit. The onstage orchestra, on risers as usual, is framed by the elaborate scenery, and the orchestra in turn frames the singers, who sit at the center of the stage. For oratorios at Covent Garden and Drury Lane in the 1780s and 1790s the entire orchestra was placed on stage along with the chorus, though without scenery or costumes.[29] Oratorios at the Burgtheater in Vienna did use scenery. The poet Metastasio reported in 1744 that "the numerous orchestra and the many singers who serve in the chorus are placed on the stage, elevated on artfully constructed risers, and surrounded by scenery consisting of beautiful architecture."[30] The Tonkünstler Society concerts at the Burgtheater in the 1780s and 1790s placed the orchestra on the stage—not just for oratorios but also for symphonies and concertos.

The claim has been made that for ordinary concerts at the Burgtheater and other Viennese theaters, like the concerts that Mozart played in the Burgtheater in April 1784 and March 1785, the orchestra was not placed on stage but remained in its usual position in the pit. When an instrumental soloist played a concerto, he would have played from the stage, while the orchestra accompanied from the pit as it would a

---

[29] It is unclear whether this arrangement was already the pattern in Handel's day. Contemporary sources report that Handel and the vocal soloists were placed on stage "in a sort of a Gallery," but the placement of the orchestra is not known. See Donald Burrows, "Some Thoughts Concerning the Performance of Handel's Oratorios," *Händel-Jahrbuch* 35 (1989), 63–64; Donald Burrows, "Handel's Oratorio Performances," in id. (ed.), *The Cambridge Companion to Handel* (Cambridge, 1997), 266–70.

[30] Metastasio, *Tutte le opere*, iii. 981, quoted in B. A. Brown, *Gluck*, 117–18.

singer.[31] This argument, particularly as it pertains to Mozart and his piano concertos, is based on conjecture rather than evidence.[32] However, there is evidence of such a practice from other times and places. John Marsh in 1774 attended a concert of the Musicians Fund at the King's Theatre in London, which included concertos on the violin, cello, clarinet, oboe, and bassoon. The music, he says, "was all perform'd in the common orchestra [i.e. in front of the stage], except those that played solo concertos, who mounted the stage just above by themselves."[33] Considerably later, the Parisian violinist Pierre Baillot recommended in his *L'Art du violon* (1834) that the violin soloist should stand on stage to play a concerto while the orchestra accompanied from the pit.[34]

Concerts of vocal and instrumental music were often held in music rooms or assembly rooms, rather than theaters. Here the orchestra often played "on the floor," as seen above in Figs. 10.4 and 10.5, but it could also be placed on a bandstand. Plate XVI depicts a concert in the civic palace in Bologna in 1705.[35] The performers are raised above the audience on a bandstand and seated in tiers, singers in the upper row, instrumentalists in the lower row. Orchestra and audience face one another: the musicians are clearly the center of attention. The bandstand is draped with heavy cloth, perhaps to add to the impression of luxury and cover the scaffolding, perhaps to cut down on reverberation, since the concert is indoors. The same configuration—with orchestra and singers arrayed in tiers on a bandstand, raised above an attentive audience—can be seen in many later depictions of concerts, for example Guardi's painting of the concert of the Venetian *figlie di coro* in 1782 (Pl. V). When the Tottenham Street Concert Rooms in London were renovated in 1785 for the Concert of Ancient Music, the previous "on the floor" arrangement was replaced by a bandstand: "At the West end, where the band used to be, but without any fixed arrangement, there is now to be a regular series of enclosed fittings for the musicians, much in the manner of the oratorio disposition at Drury-lane, with the organ and harpsichord at the centre."[36] Similarly, when the concert room of the Lobkowitz Palace in Vienna was remodeled in 1804, a low stage was added, transforming an on-the-floor to an onstage placement.[37] In concert rooms the orchestra's platform was

[31] Otto Biba, "Concert Life in Beethoven's Vienna," in Robert Winter and Bruce Carr (eds.), *Beethoven, Performers, and Critics* (Detroit, 1980), 77–93 at 83; Daniel Heartz, "Nicholas Jadot and the Building of the Burgtheater," *MQ* 68 (1982), 1–31 at 23; Richard Maunder, "Performing Mozart and Beethoven Concertos," *EM* 17 (1989), 139–40; Neal Zaslaw, "Contexts for Mozart's Piano Concertos," in id. (ed.), *Mozart's Piano Concertos* (Ann Arbor, 1996), 1–16 at 14.

[32] Mary Sue Morrow, *Concert Life in Haydn's Vienna: Aspects of a Developing Musical and Social Institution* (Stuyvesant, NY, 1989), 183; Edge, "Mozart's Viennese Orchestras," 82; Heartz, *Haydn, Mozart and the Viennese School*, 64.

[33] Marsh, *Journals*, 119.

[34] Pierre Marie Baillot, *The Art of the Violin* (1834), ed. Louise Goldberg (Evanston, Ill., 1991), 463.

[35] Corrado Ricci, *I teatri di Bologna nei secoli XVII e XVIII* (Bologna, 1888), 270; Plessi, *Le insignia*, 200.

[36] *Public Advertiser*, 5 Feb. 1785. Quoted in McLamore, "Symphonic Conventions," 66.

[37] Tomislav Volek and Jaroslav Mrácek, "Beethoven's Rehearsals at the Lobkowitz's," *MT* 127 (1986), 75–80 at 77–78. This was the room in which Beethoven's Eroica Symphony was rehearsed.

MUZYK ZAAL
IN HET GEBOUW der MAATSCHAPPŸE FELIX MERITIS
BINNEN AMSTERDAM.

SALLE de CONCERT
DANS L'EDIFICE de la SOCIÉTÉ FELIX MERITIS
A AMSTERDAM

Fig. 10.6. Concert at the Felix Meritis Society, Amsterdam (1790s)

seldom as elaborate as an outdoor bandstand and not usually as steeply raked. In in Fig. 10.6, a concert of the Felix Meritis Society in Amsterdam in the 1790s, a low, convex platform fits into the ovoid curve of the wall behind.[38] The instrumentalists stand in pairs at music stands, facing the audience. C. L. Junker explains why this sort of stage is preferable to an on-the-floor placement:

These stages merit our hearty approval, not only because of their superior acoustics, but also because they afford greater freedom and independence to the orchestra musicians and

[38] On the Felix Meritis Society see Daniel F. Scheurleer, *Het muziekleven in Nederland* (The Hague, 1909), 305–7.

especially to the soloist, who is protected from noble amateurs, who can scrape and noodle a little bit and think this gives them license to stand behind the soloist, look at his music, and get in his way.[39]

Thus the sociability of on-the-floor placement was replaced in on stage placements by a desire for formality and distance.

In pictures of orchestras on stage—outdoors, on theater stages, and on bandstands—most of the musicians usually stand (Pl. XIII, Figs. 4.1 and 10.6). Standing, after all, was the position in which a person presented himself to his social betters in the eighteenth century. All the instrumentalists face the audience, and they are arranged in rows on risers, with each row a couple of feet higher than the last. The risers allowed each instrumentalist both to be heard clearly and also to be seen. The problem with this seating plan was that the audience could see the players, but the players could not see one another well enough to maintain good ensemble.[40] To solve this problem, Arnold recommends that the risers be curved into a kind of amphitheater as in Fig. 10.6, with the keyboard, the violin leader, and the vocal soloists in the center and the other instruments rising above them in concentric semi-circles.[41] The "new plan" for the orchestra at Haydn's first Salomon concert in 1791 seems to have been such an amphitheater arrangement.[42] Haydn used it again for the first public performance of *The Creation* at the Burgtheater in Vienna in 1799.[43] Amphitheater seating achieved the central focus and good ensemble of on-the-floor seating plans while maintaining the visual effect and social distance of onstage seating.

PLACEMENT AND THE ACOUSTICS OF THE ORCHESTRA

The last column in Table 10.1 extends the correlations among the placement, seating, function, venues, and repertory of orchestras in the seventeenth and eighteenth centuries to include the acoustics of orchestras, that is, the way sound was propagated and perceived in the spaces where orchestras performed. Each of the four placements for orchestras—in a balcony, in the pit, on the floor, on stage—can be associated with a characteristic acoustic environment.[44] The table shows that in large rooms with lots of reverberation (i.e. rooms in which sound is reflected efficiently and takes a long

---

[39] Carl Ludwig Junker, *Einige der vornehmsten Pflichten eines Kapellmeisters oder Musikdirektors* (Winterthur: 1782), 14–15.

[40] *Bemerkungen*, 13, 26.

[41] Ignaz Ferdinand Cajetan Arnold, *Der angehende Musikdirektor* (Erfurt, 1806), 308–9.

[42] See Landon, *Haydn*, iv. 52; Zaslaw, "Toward the Revival of the Classical Orchestra," 165–66, as corrected in id. *Mozart's Symphonies*, 464–65; Koury, *Orchestral Performance Practices*, 46.

[43] Heartz, *Haydn, Mozart and the Viennese School*, 64; A. Peter Brown, *Performing Haydn's* The Creation: *Reconstructing the Earliest Renditions* (Bloomington, Ind., 1986), 30.

[44] The categorization of acoustical environments in Table 10.1 is an extension of Bagenal's formulation that rooms for music have either the acoustics of the open air or the acoustics of a cave (Hope Bagenal, "Musical Taste and Concert Hall Design," *PRMA* 78 (1951–52), 11–29).

time to die away) orchestras tend to be placed in balconies. In large rooms with low reverberation they are placed in the pit. In small rooms with high reverberation they tend to be placed on the floor. Orchestras outdoors, where sound diffuses widely and there is little or no reverberation, are characteristically placed on a stage or bandstand.[45] These connections between placement and acoustics can be deduced from contemporary reports and from pictures of seventeenth- and eighteenth-century orchestras. At the same time there are exceptions. As previously mentioned, Pl. XII, the *Giostra* of 1656, depicts an instrumental ensemble in a balcony, but it is not playing in a large reverberant room but rather outdoors in an environment with little reverberation. Plate XVI (Bologna, 1705) depicts an orchestra on stage in a palace rather than outdoors. However, the majority of the depictions of orchestras discussed here and in previous chapters tend to support the connections suggested in Table 10.1.

To some extent these connections can be explained on the basis of acoustical principles. For example, in a large room like a theater with a high ceiling, the sound of the orchestra tends to dissipate upward; in addition much of the sound will be absorbed by the spectators and by the upholstered interiors of the boxes. Placing the orchestra in the pit helps to address these acoustical problems. Because the orchestra is located toward the center of the room, the audience receives the maximum amount of direct sound. Because the orchestra extends across the width of the stage, the singers and instrumentalists can hear one another clearly despite the deadness of the room. The balcony placement of orchestras in churches, banquet halls, and other large rooms reduces echo. The proximity of the orchestra to the walls and the ceiling means that its sound will be reflected almost immediately, and thus the delay between when direct and reflected sound reach the listeners is kept to a minimum. In a small room with high reverberation, on-the-floor placement puts the orchestra close to the audience, thereby increasing the amount of sound that is absorbed rather than reflected and ensuring that the listeners will hear more direct and less reflected sound. Thus on-the-floor placement helps compensate for the liveness of the room. In an outdoor acoustic, on the other hand, where there is little reverberation and where sound dissipates rapidly, placing the orchestra in tiers on a stage cuts down on the absorption of sound, while the bandstand reflects sound toward the audience. This increases the amount of orchestral sound that reaches the listeners in an acoustically dead environment. Social and musical factors need to be acknowledged as well as acoustics. Placement in the pit can be explained by the musical need for coordination between singers and their accompanists and by the social need to separate instrumentalists from audience members. Putting the orchestra on stage displays the size and discipline of

---

[45] "High" reverberation is used here to mean long reverberation time. "Live" and "reverberant" should also be understood as meaning having a long reverberation time. "Low" reverberation and "dead" designate spaces with short reverberation times.

the ensemble to a large audience and provides enough room for the orchestra to be divided into sections by instrument.

Since the orchestra was a new institution in the seventeenth and early eighteenth centuries, few of the spaces in which orchestras performed were designed with orchestras in mind. Theaters were designed for speaking and singing; churches were designed for ritual and ceremonial observances; palaces were designed for social inter-action and social display; gardens were designed for private, plazas for public social intercourse. Thus, except for a few concert rooms built in the late eighteenth century, almost all the venues in which orchestras played presented severe acoustical challenges. Placement does not seem to have been enough in many cases to overcome these challenges, and various adjustments were made to improve the way orchestras sounded in their assigned venues. When large orchestras played in churches, the interior was sometimes draped with cloth to cut down on reverberation (Pl. IV).[46] Draperies could also help cut down on reverberation in small rooms with an over-lively acoustic, particularly when the orchestra was placed on a stage rather than on the floor (Pl. XVI). The *Allgemeine musikalische Zeitung* complained that the oval shape of the Felix Meritis concert room in Amsterdam (Fig. 10.6) made the orchestra seem very loud and made it hard for the musicians to maintain an even tempo.[47] The only thing that seemed to improve this over-lively acoustic was a large audience, which absorbed some of the sound. Several commentators recommended that concert rooms be paneled with thin wood veneer, which they believed would cause the walls to resonate and thus improve the sound of the orchestra.[48] Actually, the wood probably absorbed sound rather than reflecting it, thus mitigating the live acoustic of such rooms.[49]

Theaters presented the opposite acoustical challenge: a large dead room in which much of the orchestra's sound was dissipated or absorbed. Eighteenth-century commentators tended to attribute the acoustical problems in the theater to the low placement of the orchestra in front of the stage and to way musicians and instruments were crowded into the pit.[50] Various sorts of acoustical enhancers were proposed to make orchestras sound louder and fuller in theaters.[51] Several writers advised that the "pit" should be constructed of wood laid over an empty cavity, like the sound box of a violin or a guitar.[52] The air space, they believed, would act as a resonator for the

---

[46] See Schnoebelen, "The Concerted Mass at San Petronio," 42; Snyder, *Dieterich Buxtehude*, 75; Barbieri, "Acoustics," 270–71.

[47] *AMZ* 16 (1814), col. 417.   [48] e.g. Unold, "Einige Bemerkungen," 784.

[49] See Leo Beranek, *Concert and Opera Halls: How They Sound* (Woodbury, NY, 1996), 432–35.

[50] Ancelet, *Observations sur la musique*, 10; Fröhlich, "Orchester," in *Allgemeine Encyklopedie der Wissenschaften und Künste*, ed. Johann Samuel Ersch and Johann Gottfried Gruber (Leipzig, 1818), 428–29.

[51] For a comprehensive review of the theory and practice of acoustical enhancement in theaters, see Barbieri, "Acoustics."

[52] Rousseau, *Dictionnaire de musique*, 302; Galeazzi, *Elementi teorico-pratici*, 219; Meude-Monpas, *Dictionnaire de musique*, 133.

orchestra.[53] This recommendation, derived from Vitruvius' descriptions of ancient Greek and Roman theaters, was actually implemented in several eighteenth-century theaters. At the San Carlo in Naples, an exceptionally large theater with notoriously dead acoustics, the pit was reconstructed in 1773 to create such a resonant cavity under the orchestra.[54] There was a similar cavity under the orchestra at the Teatro Regio in Turin, connected by air ducts to the stage, so that the singers could hear the resonating air. J. J. de Lalande, a French traveler to Italy in 1765, claimed that, as a result, the orchestra in Turin did not need to have as many players as in Paris, where there was no acoustical enhancement.[55] Ledoux's neoclassical theater in Besançon, finished in 1784, not only had a resonating chamber under the orchestra but also a semicircular shell above it, intended to reflect orchestral sound toward the audience. Acoustical enhancement was particularly necessary in Besançon, because the orchestra was placed in a true pit, below the level of the parterre and recessed beneath the stage.[56]

When orchestras were moved onto the stage for concert performances, a different set of acoustical issues arose. Instead of being near the center of the room, most of the instruments were now behind the proscenium arch. Acoustically they were in a different room from the audience, and much of their sound was lost above the stage or in the wings on either side. Listening to a performance of one of his symphonies at a concert of the Tonkünstler Society in Vienna, Paul Wranitzsky complained that he could see the large orchestra exerting itself, but he heard almost nothing.[57] Wranitzky, who was secretary of the Society, raised money to build a shell, similar to those used at outdoor concerts, which could be erected for the Tonkünstler concerts, then disassembled for opera and spoken theater.[58] Installed with considerable difficulty for a performance of Haydn's *Creation* in 1807, the shell proved to be a failure. Rather than improving the sound of the orchestra, it made the sound worse in the loges where important patrons sat, and it was soon abandoned. Other theaters addressed the problem by building steep risers for the orchestra or even a bandstand on stage in order to reflect more sound toward the audience. Like the acoustical shell, these remedies were based on the placement of orchestras outdoors.

These attempts at acoustical mitigation and enhancement were necessary because the placement and seating of orchestras was determined as much by social and

---

[53] Except for cellos and basses, which actually touch the floor, a wooden floor is more likely to absorb an instrument's sound than to amplify it. See Beranek, *Concert and Opera Halls*, 432–33.

[54] Prota-Giurleo, *La grande orchestra*, 24.

[55] Lalande, *Voyage d'un françois en Italie*, 116. See also George Saunders, *A Treatise on Theatres* (London, 1790), 35 and pl. I.

[56] Forsyth, *Buildings*, 112. The Teatro Argentina in Rome and the theaters at Breslau and Berlin also seem to have installed resonating chambers beneath their orchestras (Saunders, *Treatise on Theatres*, 17–18; Schreiber, *Orchester und Orchesterpraxis*, 210).

[57] Quoted in Morrow, *Concert Life*, 185, 501–2.

[58] Carl Ferdinand Pohl, *Denkschrift aus Anlass des hundertjährigen Bestehens des Tonkünstler-Societät* (Vienna, 1871), 36–37.

logistical considerations as by the physics of sound. Orchestras were moved onto the stage in theaters so that they could be displayed to the audience, even though the acoustics of the onstage orchestra were problematic. At a banquet or a dance there may have been acoustical reasons for putting the orchestra in a balcony, but it was just as important to keep the instrumentalists out of the way of the diners or dancers and to maintain the social separation between performers and audience. When an orchestra played outdoors, there were acoustical reasons to place it on a stage or a bandstand, but when *serenate* or concerti grossi were performed indoors in a lively room, the onstage placement was frequently retained, presumably for social and visual reasons, even though this often made the orchestra sound extremely loud.

ORCHESTRAS, ACOUSTICS, AND MUSICAL STYLE

People in the seventeenth and eighteenth centuries perceived a direct relation among acoustics, compositional style, and performance practice. J. G. Sulzer, for example, says that a composer writing church music needs to avoid "too much rapid movement in the lower parts, because in churches these instruments create a great deal of reverberation, and if the lower parts move quickly this will make the harmonies very confused."[59] For a banquet, on the other hand, says J. A. Scheibe, in a large room with lots of food and a big crowd, a composer needs to write music with lots of instruments and lots of activity in the middle parts, because otherwise the orchestra's sound will be dissipated or absorbed before anyone hears it.[60] Acoustics are also a consideration in the choice of repertory. "In a large room," says Quantz,

where there is lots of reverberation [*wo es stark schallet*] and where the accompanying orchestra is very numerous, fast pieces create more confusion than pleasure. For these occasions [a soloist] should choose concertos written in a majestic style with many unison passages and in which the harmonies change at the bar or the half bar.[61]

Arnold (1806) links acoustics to the selection of tempos. Outdoors or in a theater, he says, where there is little or no echo, an allegro can be taken very quickly. However, in a concert hall or a small room, the same piece needs to be taken at a slower tempo, because the liveness of the room makes rapid passages sound muddled.[62]

Modern commentators draw even more ambitious connections between acoustics and musical style. Thurston Dart, for example, categorizes music according to

---

[59] Johann Georg Sulzer, *Allgemeine Theorie der schönen Kunste* (Leipzig, 1771–74). iii. 23 (1786–87 edn., s.v. "Kirchenmusik"). This article was probably written by Johann Philipp Kirnberger, whom Sulzer acknowledges in the preface to this volume.

[60] Scheibe, *Critischer Musikus*, 620–21. See above, Ch. 7.   [61] Quantz, *Versuch*, 170.

[62] Arnold, *Der angehende Musikdirektor*, 274. Arnold remarks that singers who rehearse their arias in a small room are often alarmed at the faster tempos that the orchestra takes in the theater.

whether it was composed for a "resonant," a "room," or an "outdoor" acoustic.[63] Gabrieli's music for brass consort, he thinks, sounds different from Matthew Locke's brass music, because Gabrieli was composing for the "resonant" acoustic of St. Mark's, while Locke was writing for open-air performance. Other commentators, like acousticians Hope Bagenal and Leo Beranek and architect Michael Forsyth, historicize this line of reasoning, equating each style period of Western music with a distinctive acoustic.[64] Medieval and Renaissance music, according to Beranek, was composed for large churches with high reverberation; as a consequence medieval and Renaissance styles tend to favor simple textures and slow tempos. "Baroque" music, he claims, was written for small rooms with little reverberation and thus features the counterpoint of several individual lines. "Classical" music was conceived for small but resonant rooms, "romantic" music supposedly for large rooms with high reverberation.[65] This line of argument ultimately becomes a kind of acoustical determinism, in which changing architectural fashions generate a succession of musical styles.

Acoustical determinism is unconvincing for at least two reasons. First, it downplays the extent to which musical works migrated from one acoustical and social setting to another in the seventeenth and eighteenth centuries. Symphonies written for the theater were performed in private homes, in concert halls, and even in churches. Concertos written for church performance were heard in theaters and vice versa. Masses written for large cathedrals were performed in small chapels. Performance practices changed as these works changed venue; but the style of the work remained the same. Second, acoustical determinism implies that a historical period can be characterized by a single acoustical environment and a single musical style. Which was the typical "Baroque" acoustic: the Salzburg cathedral (Pl. I), the Civic Palace in Bologna (Pl. XVI), or the Marble Courtyard at Versailles (Fig. 3.3)? What is "Baroque" style: a Vivaldi concerto, a Lully ballet, or a Handel aria? Only by ignoring most of the music and many of the venues in a given historical period can acoustics and styles be arranged into a neat historical sequence.

Rather than generalizing about musical styles and acoustics of entire periods, it may be more productive to link specific works to specific acoustical environments. Jürgen Meyer, in an influential study published in 1978, analyzes the acoustics of four rooms where Haydn's symphonies were first performed.[66] The concert room at Eisenstadt, for which Haydn wrote many of his early symphonies, is a relatively large room with considerable reverberation, even when an audience is present. The music room at

---

[63] Thurston Dart, *The Interpretation of Music* (London, 1969), 57.

[64] Bagenal, "Musical Taste"; Beranek, *Concert and Opera Halls*, 1–12; Forsyth, *Buildings*, 1–17 and *passim*.

[65] Beranek, *Concert and Opera Halls*, 4–9.

[66] Jürgen Meyer, "Raumakustik und Orchesterklang in den Konzertsälen Joseph Haydns," *Acustica*, 41 (1978), 145–62. This analysis is amplified in id., *Akustik und musikalische Aufführungspraxis*, 2nd edn. (Frankfurt am Main, 1980), 213 ff.

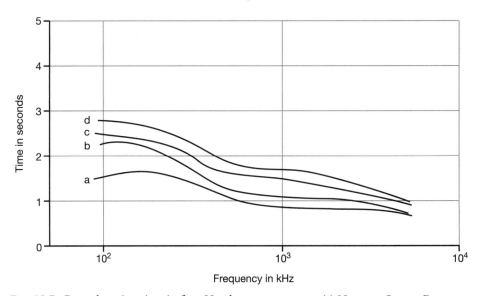

FIG. 10.7. Reverberation time in four Haydn concert rooms: (*a*) Hanover Square Rooms; (*b*) Concert room at Eszterháza; (*c*) King's Theatre concert room; (*d*) Concert room at Eisenstadt. Adapted from Jürgen Meyer, *Akustik und musikalische Aufführungspraxis* (1980)

Eszterháza is much smaller and drier, particularly when there is an audience.[67] Of the two music rooms in London, where Haydn's London symphonies were premiered, Hanover Square was medium sized and had a very short reverberation time; the concert room at the King's Theatre was somewhat larger and had more reverberation than either Hanover Square or Eszterháza.[68] Figure 10.7, based on Meyer's article, shows the reverberation times of the four rooms at various frequencies.[69]

Meyer asks whether stylistic differences between Haydn symphonies can be explained by differences in the acoustics of the rooms for which Haydn wrote them. He observes that the plateau dynamics found in many early Haydn symphonies are suited to the relatively high reverberation of the Eisenstadt room, while the quick dynamic shifts and nuances of the middle-period symphonies work better in the dry acoustic of Eszterháza. The Eszterháza symphonies also feature many soft passages and

[67] Meyer performed acoustical measurements in both the Eisenstadt and the Eszterháza rooms, which are still intact.

[68] The Hanover Square Rooms and the King's Theatre do not survive. Meyer's calculations are based on architectural reports and drawings. See also Forsyth, *Buildings*, 39.

[69] The horizontal axis in Fig. 10.7 represents the frequency of the sound, the vertical axis the time in seconds that it takes for the sound to die away. The graph thus shows that at every frequency the Eisenstadt room was more resonant than the King's Theatre concert room, which in turn was more resonant than Eszterháza and Hanover Square.

"chamber" effects, like the reduced scorings at the end of the "Farewell" Symphony (No. 45) or the *col legno* violins at the end of the second movement of Symphony No. 67. Meyer offers less insight into the style of the London symphonies. He does observe, however, that Symphonies 102–104, composed for the King's Theatre room, make prominent use of the orchestral grand pause, an effect that took advantage of the greater reverberation of that hall compared with Hanover Square. Haydn worked for many years in the Eisenstadt and the Eszterháza halls, whereas in London he was involved in only a limited number of concerts over the course of 34 months.[70] It stands to reason that the acoustics of Eisenstadt and Eszterháza would have made a greater impression on Haydn's orchestral style than the acoustics of the London halls.[71]

Meyer's findings about the relation between Haydn's symphonies and the acoustics of four concert rooms can be extended to make some more general observations about acoustics and orchestral styles. Many of the characteristic features of seventeenth- and eighteenth-century orchestral writing—string tremolo, rapid scale passages, sudden dynamic changes, crescendo, rhythmic repetition in the bass (*Trommelbass*), and orchestral unison—work best in an acoustic that has relatively little reverberation.[72] In a large, reverberant room string tremolo or *Trommelbass* become muddy and indistinct, crescendos are colored by unwanted overtones, dynamic effects are spoiled by the natural echo of the room. In a dry, non-reverberant environment, on the other hand, like a theater or outdoors, sudden dynamic changes and rapid scales come off cleanly, while crescendos, sustained chords, orchestral unisons, tutti chords, and echo effects help make the acoustic sound more reverberant than it really is. Composers and performers of the seventeenth and early eighteenth centuries not only compensated for the dry acoustic of theaters and outdoor venues, they took advantage of it to create a specifically orchestral style.

The original and typical environment of the seventeenth-century orchestra was outdoors. Most extant depictions of Lully's and of Corelli's orchestras show them performing in outdoor venues (Figs. 3.1–3.4, 4.1, 4.2). Additional outdoor performances are documented for both composers.[73] When Lully's orchestra played indoors, it often played in a large room full of people, like the Salle des Machines

---

[70] Besides the 24 subscription concerts at the Hanover Square Rooms in 1791–92 and 1793–94 and 11 at the concert room in the King's Theatre, Haydn was involved in benefit concerts at both venues (Landon, *Haydn*, iii. 255–57, 283–305).

[71] Zaslaw develops a parallel argument for Mozart. He demonstrates that for acoustical reasons Mozart tended to favor one flute plus two oboes in his symphonies and concertos for on-the-floor venues, but two flutes plus two oboes for theaters. Neal Zaslaw, "Mozart's Orchestral Flutes and Oboes," in Cliff Eisen (ed.), *Mozart Studies* (Oxford, 1991), 201–11.

[72] These effects are discussed with examples in Ch. 13.

[73] On Lully's outdoor performances, see Zaslaw, "Lully's Orchestra"; on Corelli, see Marx, "Die Musik am Hofe Pietro Kardinal Ottobonis."

at the Tuileries.[74] Corelli's orchestra played in churches, but typically in smaller, lavishly decorated churches like San Luigi dei Francesi and San Lorenzo in Damaso, which have less reverberation than larger Roman churches. Many other seventeenth- and early eighteenth-century pictures of orchestras are set outdoors (Figs. 5.4, 8.2) or in large and crowded rooms (Pls. V and XIV, Fig. 7.6). For most indoor venues an orchestra was unnecessary. When seventeenth-century instrumental ensembles played in churches, the reverberation could make a few instruments sound like many. Most seventeenth-century theatres were small enough that the direct sound of a few instruments accompanying opera could reach the audience without needing the help of reverberation. When an ensemble performed outdoors, on the other hand, the parts needed to be heavily doubled in order to amplify the sound for everyone to hear. From this perspective the birth of the orchestra can be seen, at least in part, as a response to the problem of outdoor performance and dry acoustics.

In the eighteenth century the orchestra came indoors. Beginning around 1730 something like a musical building boom took place, in which courts and cities competed with one another to erect new buildings designed specifically for music. First came a series of new opera houses, among them the San Carlo in Naples (1737), the Teatro Regio in Turin (1740), the Burgtheater in Vienna (1741), and new theaters in Mannheim (1742), Berlin (1748), Bologna (1763), Paris (1770), Versailles (1770), Milan (1778), Bordeaux (1780), and Marseilles (1787). Most of these theaters were considerably larger than seventeenth-century theaters, and they were more lavishly decorated. When they were filled with spectators, their acoustic resembled that of the outdoors, with rapid dissipation of sound and little reverberation. The small ensembles of seventeenth-century theaters could not make themselves heard in such spaces, and they were soon expanded into orchestras like those that played outdoors. Large orchestral ensembles had already been used in outdoor theaters, so the use of similar ensembles in opera houses was not a radical innovation. The tendency for orchestras to get larger during the first half of the eighteenth century was probably due, at least in part, to the acoustics of new, larger theaters.

Somewhat later in the eighteenth century a number of new halls were built specifically for concerts: The Holywell Room at Oxford (1748), St. Cecilia's Hall, Edinburgh (1762), the Hanover Square Rooms, London (1775), the Gewandhaus in Leipzig (1781), and the hall of the Felix Meritis Society in Amsterdam (1788). In addition rooms suitable for concerts were built in princely palaces, for example the music room at Sans Souci palace in Potsdam, the Rittersaal in Mannheim, the concert room at Eszterháza, and the concert room at the Lobkowitz palace in Vienna.

---

[74] Barbara Coeyman, "Theatres for Opera and Ballet during the Reigns of Louis XIV and Louis XV," *EM* 18 (1990), 22–37.

These new concert rooms tended to be small, with a capacity of something like 250 to 800 listeners; and most of them featured hard surfaces like plaster walls and windows. Because of their small size and relatively high reverberation, eighteenth-century music rooms delivered a great deal of sound to the listeners—more than other eighteenth-century venues and more than most modern concert halls.[75]

When orchestras were brought into concert rooms, as happened more and more often during the eighteenth century, the results were something new and stupendous. C. D. F. Schubart, who heard the famous Mannheim orchestra play in the Rittersaal, found the effect overwhelming: "its forte is like thunder, its crescendo a cataract . . ."[76] H. C. Koch availed himself of a similar metaphor to make the opposite point: "Putting too large an orchestra in a [small] room is yet more detrimental to any good effect of the music. The excess quantity of sound becomes burdensome and unpleasant to the ear, and the effect is similar to being blinded by too much light striking the eye."[77] For Schubart and Koch, bringing the orchestra into the concert hall was like bringing the forces of nature indoors. The volume and power of the orchestra in its new acoustical environment could create effects that competed with nature in grandeur and sublimity.

Only a few orchestras played in concert halls, however. In a theater or in a large hall with a large audience, much of the sound was diffused or absorbed. In these acoustic environments effects of grandeur and sublimity could only be achieved by enlarging the orchestra. The effects that could be created in Haydn's *Creation* with an orchestra of 20 in the concert room at Eisenstadt required an orchestra of 50 in the Festival Hall of the University in Vienna, an orchestra of over 100 at the Burgtheater, and an orchestra of almost 150 in the Théâtre des Arts in Paris. For this reason among others, theater orchestras tended to grow larger at the end of the eighteenth century, and the orchestras that played for concerts in theaters or in large halls grew very large indeed—over 100 musicians in many cases. These large orchestras, with doubled or tripled winds and added brass, could re-create the power and excitement of concert room performance for large audiences in large, acoustically challenged halls. Instead of musical styles being determined by acoustics, acoustics, orchestras, and musical styles accommodated themselves to one another in an ever-expanding spiral, leading to the orchestras, concert halls, and orchestral styles of the nineteenth century.

[75] Meyer, *Akustik und musikalische Aufführungspraxis*, 213–18. Meyer compares the energy level (i.e. loudness) of a selection of 18th-c. concert rooms to 18th-c. theaters and churches, and to modern concert halls. The concert rooms are by far the loudest and most live. See also Willem Kroesbergen and Jed Wentz, "Sonority in the 18th Century, *un poco più forte*?" *EM* 22 (1994), 483–95.

[76] Schubart, *Ideen zu einer Aesthetik der Tonkunst*, 130. Soft passages became equally effective by way of contrast: "a babbling brook, a spring breeze . . ."

[77] Koch, *Musikalisches Lexikon*, 238. The same point is made by Meude-Monpas, *Dictionnaire de musique*, article "Symphonie."

Chapter Eleven

Orchestral Performance Practices

Roger North, the English lawyer, parliamentarian, and musical amateur, in his manuscript notebooks written at the beginning of the eighteenth century, proposes a startling theory of instrumental ensemble:

[With] 2 violino's set to play the same lesson, if perfectly in tune with one another, it is better music when one goes a little before or behind the other, than when they play (as they zealously affect) to a touch together. For in that, nothing is gott by the doubling, but a litle loudness; but in the other way, by the frequent dissonances there is a pleasant seasoning obtained. And let anyone say why a consort of severall parts, performed by diverse hands, makes a better harmony than when the same accords are heard out of one and the same instrument, unless it be allowed that the various movements by reason of different manners of handling, intersperseth some dissonances which makes a seasoning to the consort.[1]

Violins playing two on a part, North says, sound better if their ensemble is a little less precise. He acknowledges that many of his contemporaries condemn this kind of improvised "seasoning," but he maintains that the practice is precisely what makes ensemble playing different from solo performance.

By the last quarter of the eighteenth century this sort of heterophonic ensemble playing could still be heard in England, but teachers and critics were even less willing to allow it. The music publisher Robert Bremner, writing in 1777, espouses an aesthetic very different from North's:

The concert, or orchestra player['s] . . . performance, with that of those who play the same part, must, like the unisons of an organ or harpsichord, coincide so as to pass for one entire sound, whether loud or soft. . . . All the parts being thus rendered pure, and the whole

---

[1] North, *Roger North on Music*, 172–73.

properly proportioned, then will that noble construction, *harmony*, strike the mind with pleasing astonishment.[2]

Where North thinks that two players on the same part should play a little differently, Bremner thinks they should play exactly the same; where North thinks that an ensemble should sound like many instruments, Bremner thinks that an ensemble should sound like a single organ or harpsichord; where North praises diversity, Bremner praises unity.

The differences between Bremner and North are not just a matter of personal taste. Between the beginning and the end of the eighteenth century ideas about ensemble performance changed greatly, not just in England but throughout Europe. In North's day there was no such thing as a "concert or orchestra player," at least not in England. An instrumentalist played the same way whether he played by himself, one on a part in consort, or several on a part in a large ensemble. By Bremner's time concert or orchestra players had become a distinct kind of musician, with their own performance practices. What Bremner called "concert or orchestra players," Italians called *suonatori d'orchestra* or *professori* (i.e. professionals). In Germany they were *Kapellisten* or *Ripienisten*, in France *symphonistes*.

Externally the orchestra changed relatively little between North's time and Bremner's: in numbers, types of instruments, venues, social functions, etc. The biggest changes were in performance practices. During the eighteenth century distinctly orchestral performance practices developed in at least five areas:

1. Bowing and articulation
2. Tuning and intonation
3. Control of improvised ornamentation
4. Rehearsal
5. Leadership

These orchestral performance practices were enforced and reinforced by new, specifically orchestral ways of thinking and talking—by what amounted to an ideology of the orchestra. This ideology was articulated in a series of books and articles published during the second half of the eighteenth century that explained and justified orchestral performance practices to musicians.

BOWING AND ARTICULATION

Soloists, says Georg Löhlein in his violin method of 1774, are never content with ordinary bowing patterns; they always want to play something special. For this

---

[2] Robert Bremner, "Some Thoughts on the Performance of Concert Music," published as an introduction to J. G. C. Schetky, *Six Quartettos for Two Violins, a Tenor and Violoncello, Op. VI* (London, 1777), transcribed and annotated in Neal Zaslaw, "The Compleat Orchestral Musician," *EM* 7 (1979), 46–57 at 50–52.

reason, he says, "they seldom make good orchestra players [*Ripienisten*]. They are like circus horses, trained to do all sorts of tricks; whereas everyday performance is like hauling a cart: the whole team must pull together at the wagon trace."[3] Brijon explains in his violin method (1763) how each orchestral violinist needs to bow the same as his fellows:

I need to make a special observation with regard to bowings in orchestral music [*symphonies*] where several people play together on each part; it is necessary for true expression and for precise execution, that all those who play on the same part observe the same bow stroke. Otherwise the unity and the ensemble will always be poor.[4]

Eighteenth-century composers seldom indicated bowings in their orchestral music; most of them wrote in rather few articulations of any sort. Therefore orchestra violinists needed some sort of rules or principles that would enable players on the same part to bow the same way.

There seem to have been three principles of orchestral articulation in the second half of the eighteenth century, though no commentator enumerated all of them. The first principle was that each note got its own bowstroke, unless marked with a slur in the music.[5] Following this principle, an orchestral violinist could procede through a piece by simply alternating downbows and upbows. Quantz says that in ripieno parts a "short, articulated, French-style bowstroke" works better than a long, drawn-out Italian stroke.[6] In orchestra music as in solo playing, slower tempos required a more sostenuto bowstroke, while quicker tempos were played more detached.[7] But in either case each note usually got a single stroke of the bow.

The second principle was that the bow should remain on the string, unless there was a rest or unless the music was marked staccato. Off-the-string techniques were for concertos, and even there they were not common.[8] In quick tempos, says Quantz, there is not enough time to lift the bow, even when staccato is marked, so a very short stroke should be used instead.[9] In an Adagio, according to Reichardt, the bow should remain on the string for continuity's sake.[10]

The third principle of orchestral articulation was the so-called "rule of the down-bow," which declared that the first beat of every measure should be played with a downbow—or, more generally, strong beats should be played downbow, weak beats

---

[3] Georg Simon Löhlein, *Anweisung zum Violinspielen* (Leipzig and Züllichau, 1774), 113.

[4] C. R. Brijon, *Réflexions sur la musique et la vraie manière de l'exécuter sur le violon* (Paris, 1763), 27.

[5] Johann Friedrich Reichardt, *Ueber die Pflichten des Ripien-Violinisten* (Berlin and Leipzig, 1776), 81: "All notes that are neither marked staccato nor slurred should be played with a single stroke of the bow, but not so separately as staccato notes."

[6] Quantz, *Versuch*, 199.   [7] Reichardt, *Ueber die Pflichten*, 25–27.

[8] See Robin Stowell, *Violin Technique and Performance Practice in the Late Eighteenth and Early Nineteenth Centuries* (Cambridge, 1985), 168 ff.

[9] Quantz, *Versuch*, 201. Quantz distinguishes between staccatos marked with dots and those marked with vertical strokes (*Strichelchen*). Only for strokes should the bow be lifted. For dots it remains on the string (pp. 193–94). This distinction may be unique to Quantz.

[10] Reichardt, *Ueber die Pflichten*, 25.

upbow. This "first and paramount rule" of articulation, as Leopold Mozart called it, was already prescribed by string instrument tutors in the early seventeenth century.[11] Georg Muffat, in his *Florilegium secundum* of 1698, calls it "the method of Monsieur Baptiste [Lully]" and says it creates the "uniformity" that French ensembles have but that German ensembles of his time sorely lack.[12] Solo players, says Brijon (1763), often begin a measure with an upbow, but "when several play on the same part" it is necessary to stick to the rule of the downbow, and when the pattern is disrupted to use two upbows in a row to return to form.[13]

By the late eighteenth century, however, not just soloists but orchestral violinists too seem to have become frustrated by "the wretched Rule of drawing the Bow down at the first Note of every Bar" (Geminiani).[14] Reichart argues that in orchestral music every phrase needs to begin with a downbow, but not every measure, "as many falsely believe." He gives several examples from orchestral music where the violinist should play two upbows or two downbows in a row or add slurs to his part. Reichardt also urges ripieno violinists to begin taking their bows off the string occasionally, for example at the end of a phrase or to shorten a note that resolves an appoggiatura.[15]

If ripieno violinists do not follow the rule of the downbow, then how can uniform bowing be maintained? Reichardt's answer is that composers should indicate articulation more explicitly in their orchestral music.[16] And indeed slurs and dots do become more frequent in late eighteenth-century orchestral parts. Another solution was for violinists to write bowings into their parts. Pisendel, the concertmaster at Dresden from 1730 to 1755, is said to have gone to the "unbelievable trouble" of writing each and every bowstroke in the parts.[17] This anecdote, transmitted by Reichardt, is undermined by the fact that orchestral parts preserved at Dresden do not have bowings written into them, although they sometimes contain dynamics.[18] Penciled-in bowings tend to be rare in eighteenth-century music altogether.[19] A third way for orchestral violinists to coordinate irregular bowings is through education and training. If all or most of the violinists in an orchestra have the same teacher or come from the same "school" of playing, then they will tend to bow a given passaqe the same way, particularly if they have played together for many years. Reichardt asserts, for example,

---

[11] Leopold Mozart, *Versuch einer gründlichen Violinschule* (Augsburg, 1756), 70. See also Boyden, *The History of Violin Playing*, 158 ff.

[12] Muffat, *Florilegium secundum*, ed. Rietsch, 21, 45.   [13] Brijon, *Réflexions*, 27–29.

[14] Francesco Geminiani, *The Art of Playing on the Violin* (London, 1751), 4. See Boyden, The History of Violin Playing, 401.

[15] Reichardt, *Ueber die Pflichten*, 11, 42.   [16] Ibid. 25–26.

[17] Johann Friedrich Reichardt, *Briefe eines aufmerksamen Reisenden die Musik betreffend*, (Leipzig, Frankfurt, 1774–76), i. 10.

[18] Personal communication from Ortrun Landmann. Dr. Landmann notes that performance indications are often written into the concertmaster's part only, suggesting that Pisendel communicated bowings and other performance indications to his musicians orally and by example.

[19] Clive Brown, "String Playing Practices in the Classical Orchestra," *Basler Jahrbuch für historische Musikpraxis*, 17 (1993), 41–64 at 46.

that the orchestra at Berlin plays with "unusual unanimity," because almost all the violinists were trained by Benda and Graun.[20] Galeazzi says that the orchestras of northern Italy bow together because "all the violins come from the same school."[21]

Uniform bowing often aroused admiring comments. The reviewer of a concert at the Paris Conservatoire in 1810 praises the fact that the students all play in the style of Viotti. This results, he says, "in such unity of performance in the symphonies that from a distance one would believe that there was only one violin on each part."[22] Similarly, Giovenale Sacchi boasts that the violinists in Milan are accustomed to play together with such unanimity that it is a delight not only to hear them, but also to watch them, because it seems as though a single hand pushes and pulls all the bows.[23] The correspondent of the *Allgemeine musikalische Zeitung*, describing the Mannheim orchestra in 1799, compares uniform bowing to military maneuvres: "I found an orchestra that marched in step like a well-trained bataillon. It was a joy to see how all the bows rose and fell together, and a joy to hear how each and every appoggiatura was executed to a man by this full orchestra of more than 50 persons."[24] The incredulous tone of these comments suggests that uniform bowing may still have been relatively rare in European orchestras. Löhlein (1774) says that it is "practically impossible" for orchestra violinists to maintain the same bowing patterns in triple meters.[25] As late as 1832 Spohr says that uniform bowing is "a most difficult undertaking" and that "even the best and most experienced orchestras leave much to be desired."[26] All the reports emphasize the visual impact of uniform bowing just as much as its aural benefits. This repeated emphasis on the visual and psychological effect of unanimity suggests that perhaps uniform bowing was not so much a musical imperative as a piece of showmanship, a visual metaphor for the skill, the discipline, and the unanimity of the orchestra.

TUNING AND INTONATION

"If one were to check the instruments in a large orchestra one by one," says Quantz, "it would turn out that not only is almost every instrument tuned poorly to itself, but usually no two or three instruments are in tune with one another."[27] Orchestral intonation provoked a steady chorus of complaint from eighteenth-century commentators, interspersed with a smattering of advice. In the debate over intonation, at least three issues can be discerned: (1) Tuning etiquette: when and where does the orchestra tune, and what behaviors are acceptable during the tuning period? (2) Tuning protocol: where does the orchestra get its pitch, and how are instruments

---

[20] Reichardt, *Briefe*, i. 9.
[21] Galeazzi, *Elementi teorico-pratici*, i. 211. See also Louis Spohr, *Violinschule* (Vienna, 1832), 248.
[22] A. M., "Sixième exercice du Conservatoire," *Tablettes de Polymnie*, 1ère Année (Apr. 1810), 4.
[23] Sacchi, *Della divisione del tempo*, 26. For a similar account of a Viennese orchestra in the 1780s, see Ch. 14.
[24] *AMZ* 1 (1799), col. 882. This comparison of orchestras with armies was common in the 18th c. See Ch. 14.
[25] Löhlein, *Anweisung*, 112.   [26] Spohr, *Violinschule*, 248.   [27] Quantz, *Versuch*, 239.

tuned to that pitch? (3) Pitch level: what is the absolute pitch level of an orchestra, and how does it compare with the level of other orchestras?

In the early years of the eighteenth century "preluding"—that is, tuning, warming up, and generally noodling around before the piece starts—was the normal way for instrumental music to begin. Fuhrmann (1706) explains that in church the organist should improvise, while the instrumentalists play along in the same key, adjusting their instruments until they are in tune with the organ.[28] Roger North, typically, appreciates the sound of this group improvisation, which he says "may be performed in severall manners by any number of instruments, with perpetuall variety of fancy in each, and no one much regard what another doth; and in all that disorder . . . the sound will be rich and amazing."[29] Muffat, on the other hand, advocates a more disciplined style. He advises aspiring Lullists to "abstain from all noise before the beginning of a piece, and all of these confused preludes that . . . cause more displeasure before the concert than any following pleasure can compensate for."[30]

By the second half of the eighteenth century opinion had turned decisively against preluding at the beginning of an orchestral performance. Quantz fears that preluding after tuning up will put the instruments out of tune again before the music begins.[31] Sartori, the Violinist-Director at the Darmstadt Hofkapelle, declares: "Since well-bred persons have a natural aversion to noise, it is to be expected that they will eschew preluding of their own accord . . . and that they will not turn the orchestra into a synagogue (*Juden Schule*), which is a miserable introduction for a musical performance."[32] For Sartori preluding contradicted propriety and court etiquette. In addition it ruined the effect of the *premier coup d'archet* at the beginning of the piece. An overture or a symphony movement, says Rochlitz, has a vastly better effect if it is preceded by "several minutes of complete silence, not by tuning, rustling, and fiddling around."[33] A couple of writers suggest that an orchestra should tune up in a separate room where it will not be heard by the audience.[34] The commentators also condemn tuning while the music is actually in progress. "Older players," says Veracini (*c.*1760), habitually begin without tuning, then tune up during vocal recitatives. It sounds, he says, like the buzzing of a wasp's nest [*un continuo Vespaio*], an incessant "zun, zun, zun" of violins and

---

[28] Fuhrmann, *Musikalischer-Trichter*, 74. See also John Butt, *Music Education and the Art of Performance in the German Baroque* (Cambridge, 1994), 105 ff.

[29] North, *Roger North on Music*, 143.   [30] Muffat, *Florilegium secundum*, 24, 48.

[31] Quantz, *Versuch*, 181.

[32] Quoted in Georg Sebastian Thomas, *Die grossherzogliche Hofkapelle, deren Personalbestand und Wirken unter Ludewig I*, 2nd edn. (Darmstadt, 1859), 32. Sartori's comment dates from around 1792. Armand Schmith uses the same metaphor of a synagogue [*Judenschule*] to criticize preluding in the orchestra (Amand Wilhelm Schmith, *Philosophische Fragmente über die praktische Musik* (Vienna, 1787), 88). This refers to the Jewish practice in which every member of the congregation chants the service at his own pace and in his own way.

[33] Rochlitz, "Bruchstücke," *AMZ* 2 (1799), col. 58. See also Schmith, *Philosophische Fragmente*, 89.

[34] See Schreiber, *Orchester und Orchesterpraxis*, 240. Dauscher claims that the orchestra at the Opéra in Paris tunes in a green room, and he urges German orchestras to follow this good example (Andreas Dauscher, *Kleines Handbuch der Musiklehre und vorzüglich der Querflöte* (Ulm, 1801), 136–37). Petri suggests that violinists should tune at home (*Anleitung,* 2nd edn., 176).

basses, who keep on tuning all the way to the final chorus without ever being in tune.[35]

Sartori at Darmstadt went beyond merely complaining about preluding. He outlined a detailed tuning protocol for his orchestra:

So as to miss no opportunity to uphold good order and to create good intonation, I will tune my violin to a tuning fork. I will then proceed from one player to the next, checking whether his A string agrees with mine. After this, the string players, all at the same time, should tune their remaining strings as quickly as possible, while the wind instruments play the various notes of the D major chord. As soon as I give a sign, tuning is over, and everyone should remain quietly in his place.[36]

By the end of the eighteenth century many orchestras were following a tuning protocol similar to the one described by Sartori. Some orchestras tuned to D rather than to A, though by the second half of the century this was considered old-fashioned.[37] Quantz (1752), Mozart (1756), and Reichardt (1776) all agree with Sartori that the concertmaster should tune his violin first, then tune each violinist individually in turn.[38] Marpurg in 1786 refers to this system as a novelty for German orchestras, though he says it has long been the practice at the "better concerts" in Paris and London.[39] Koch (1802), on the other hand, rejects individual tuning as "demeaning" both for concertmaster and ripienists: if a violinist can't tune his open strings by himself, how can he finger the notes in tune?[40]

Sartori's method of taking his A from a tuning fork was an innovation. Most orchestras tuned either to the keyboard (harpsichord or organ) or to one of the winds. Several authors say that a wind instrument should give the initial pitch to the orchestra, since wind pitch varies according to temperature and humidity. Bertezèn says this should be the trumpet; Vandenbroeck and Junker say the horn; Schmith says either oboe, horn, or flute.[41] Quantz, Veracini, Rochlitz, and Scaramelli, on the other hand, all agree that the orchestra should tune to the keyboard.[42] Koch in 1802 claims that many orchestras use a pitch pipe to tune the keyboard, so that the instrument will have the same pitch at every performance. However, a tuning fork works better, he says, because it is not affected by changes of temperature.[43]

[35]   Francesco Maria Veracini, *Il trionfo della prattica musicale* (n.d.), sec. 83.

[36]   Quoted in Thomas, *Die grossherzogliche Hofkapelle*, 32.

[37]   Mozart, *Versuch*, 255; Petri, *Anleitung,* 2nd edn., 179. See Boyden, *History of Violin Playing*, 247. Marpurg says that it was "formerly" the custom for the keyboard to give several pitches (E, A, D, G) and for the strings to tune according the one they preferred, a method he says gave very poor results (Friedrich Wilhelm Marpurg, *Legende einiger Musikheiligen* (Cologne, 1786), 197–98).

[38]   Authors who recommend tuning the violins individually include: Quantz, *Versuch*, 181; Mozart, *Versuch*, 255; Reichardt, *Ueber die Pflichten*, 89; Schmith, *Philosophische Fragmente*, 87; Scaramelli, *Saggio sopra i doveri*, 17.

[39]   Marpurg, *Legende*, 199.

[40]   Koch, *Musikalisches Lexikon*, cols. 145–46. See Ch. 14.

[41]   Salvatore Bertezèn, *Principj di musica teorico-prattica* (Rome, 1780), 333; Othon Vandenbroeck, *Methode nouvelle et raisonée pour apprendre à sonner du cor* (Paris, c.1789), 3; Junker, *Pflichten*, 10; Schmith, *Philosophische Fragmente*, 87.

[42]   Quantz, *Versuch*, 210; Veracini, *Trionfo*, sec. 81; Rochlitz, "Bruchstücke", 19; Scaramelli, *Saggio*, 17.

[43]   Koch, *Musikalisches Lexikon*, cols. 1441–42.

Tuning to a keyboard instrument raises the issue of temperament: string players like to tune their fifths pure (i.e. in the mathematical proportion of 3:2), whereas keyboard fifths are somewhat narrow both in mean-tone and in equal temperaments.[44] Quantz advises the orchestra violinist to tune his fifths a little narrow in order to match the keyboard, adding, however, that this is not a "rule" but his "opinion."[45] Tuning to a wind instrument creates a different problem. Wind instruments tend to go sharp as they play, while strings tend to go flat. To compensate for this, says Rousseau, the wind player who gives the initial pitch should overblow and force the sound, so that the strings will tune somewhat sharp.[46] With luck winds and strings will come into tune with one another as the concert proceeds.

Orchestras made up exclusively of stringed instruments, that is of bowed strings, plucked strings, and harpsichords, were able to tune at a range of pitch levels according to the circumstance of the moment. When wind instruments were added to the orchestra, however, pitch became more narrowly fixed. The pitch level of a wind instrument is determined at the time of manufacture, and it can be adjusted only marginally thereafter. It was critical, then, for the wind players in an orchestra to use instruments tuned at the same pitch level. One way to accomplish this was for the orchestra to buy its instruments from the same maker, because good makers took pains to produce instruments at consistent pitch levels. Makers in the same city or within a geographical region characteristically tuned their instruments to one another and to regionally accepted standards.[47] From one region to another, however, there could be considerable differences in the pitch levels of wind instruments and consequently large differences between the pitch levels of different orchestras.

Eighteenth-century musicians were well aware of these differences, particularly when they traveled. Ignazio Rion, for example, a virtuoso oboist from Venice, came to Rome in 1705, where he played in orchestras with Corelli and Handel. Rion's oboe was tuned to Venetian–northern Italian pitch, which at that time was about a whole step higher than Roman pitch.[48] To enable Rion to play with the Roman orchestra, Handel notated his oboe parts a whole step lower than he wanted them to sound.[49] Louis Rousselet, a French oboist who was working in London in 1712, wrote to a Parisian woodwind maker and ordered two bassoons, one right-handed and one left-handed. "It is necessary," he added, "that the bassoons and the oboes be the same pitch we play here, almost a quarter-tone higher than the pitch of the Opéra in Paris."[50] Singers too, as they traveled from one opera house to another, had to be aware of the different pitch levels of various orchestras. Tosi urged the aspiring cas-

---

[44] See Haynes, "Beyond Temperament." [45] Quantz, *Versuch*, 240–41.
[46] Rousseau, *Dictionnaire de musique*, 24. [47] Haynes, "Pitch Standards," 36–39. [48] Ibid. 90 ff.
[49] Haynes, *The Eloquent Oboe*, 311. The oboe parts for the cantata *Laudate pueri dominum* (HWV 237) are notated a whole tone below the string parts. Haynes points out that the oboe parts for some of Handel's English operas were also notated below their sounding pitch (ibid. 346–47).
[50] Giannini, "Letter from Louis Rousselet."

trato singer to practice at the higher pitch of Lombardy rather than the lower pitch of Rome, "not only to make him acquire and preserve high Notes, but also that he may not find it troublesome when he meets with Instruments that are tun'd high."[51] Regional variation in orchestral pitch levels persisted throughout most of the eighteenth century.

Even within regions there were disparities in pitch levels. In and around Paris during the first half of the eighteenth century there were two pitch standards: orchestras at Court tuned to the *ton de chambre*; the orchestra at the Opéra tuned to the *ton d'Opéra*, which was about a half step lower. The two standards could maintain themselves in such close proximity because players from Court were not supposed to play at the Opéra, and because both the Court and the Opéra owned sets of instruments, which they lent to the players.[52] There were two pitch levels in many German cities and courts as well. *Chorton* was the pitch that organs were tuned to; *Cammerton* was the pitch that most wind instruments were tuned to and to which most orchestras tuned in theater and chamber settings. Both *Chorton* and *Cammerton* varied considerably from place to place, but in general *Chorton* tended to be higher than *Cammerton* by a whole tone or even a minor third.[53] Here, unlike France, the two pitch levels did overlap: whenever an orchestra played in church, an accommodation had to be made between them. Usually this was done by transposing the organ part down or by transposing the winds up. The strings tuned either higher to match the organ or lower to match the winds.[54]

The pitch levels of various European musical centers in the mid-eighteenth century and, by inference, that of their orchestras are shown in Table 11.1. The table is based on the research of Bruce Haynes, who has examined and measured eighteenth-century woodwind instruments and organs and reviewed contemporary documents. The values for A represent average ranges of instruments manufactured or used in the cities or regions indicated. Just what pitch level a given orchestra tuned to cannot be known—presumably it varied over time anyway. Still, the table gives a fair idea of how various orchestras compared to one another during the period 1730–50. Many, but not all, of the pitch levels are below the modern pitch of A = 435–40. The highest tunings (leaving aside the German *Chorton*, which was an organ tuning) are those of northern Italy, the lowest those of Rome and Paris. The range of variation is about a minor third, from orchestras tuned so that their C sounded like a modern B♭ to

---

[51] Tosi, *Observations*, trans. Galliard (London, 1743), 26.

[52] Haynes, "Pitch Standards," 123–24.

[53] This is a simplification of a complicated but by now rather well understood subject. See Arthur Mendel, "On the Pitches in Use in Bach's Time," in *Studies in the History of Musical Pitch* (Amsterdam, 1968), 187–238, *passim*; id., "Pitch in Western Music since 1500: A Re-examination," *Acta musicologica*, 50 (1978), 1–93; Haynes, "Pitch Standards," 187–269.

[54] Mendel, "Pitch in Western Music," 13. J. S. Bach in Mühlhausen and Weimar wrote most of his scores at *Chorton* and transposed the wind parts up. In Leipzig he usually wrote at *Cammerton* and transposed the organ down.

TABLE 11.1. *Orchestral pitch levels, c.1730–50*

Name of standard	Where in use	Approximate level of *a'* in Hz.	Modern C becomes	Reference in Haynes, "Pitch Standards"
Corista di Lombardia	Milan, Bologna, Cremona	460–470	C♯	81 ff., 561 ff.
Corista di Veneto	Venice	430–440	C	85 ff., 561 ff.
Corista di mezzo	Naples, Florence	410–420	B	98 ff., 561 ff.
Corista di San Pietro	Rome	385–395	B♭	73 ff., 561 ff.
Ton d'Opéra	Paris	395–400	B♭	112 ff., 569
Ton de chambre	Paris, France	410–420	B	108 ff., 569 ff.
Chorton	Germany	450–495	C♯–D	187 ff., 578
Cammerton	[northern] Germany	410–420	B	222 ff., 579 ff.
Tief Cammerton	[northern] Germany	390–400	B♭	226 ff., 579 ff.
"Southern" Kammerton	Vienna	430–435	C	357 ff., 594
Opera pitch	London	400–410	B/B♭	342 ff., 587
New consort pitch	London	415–425	B	347 ff.
"Continental" pitch	London	430–440	C	349 ff.

Source: Based on Haynes, "Pitch Standards."

orchestras tuned so that their C would be a C-sharp today. It is easy to see why Sauveur, Quantz, Agricola, and others pleaded for the adoption of a single European pitch standard.[55]

A trend toward standardization seems in fact to have set in during the second half of the eighteenth century. Already in 1739 the Dutch organist Quirinus van Blankenburg claimed that, since wind instruments need to be in tune with one another "even when they come from different countries," the "whole world" has agreed to adopt "opera pitch."[56] In the event, it was not the French "opera pitch" but the Venetian pitch of A = 435–440 that European orchestras moved haltingly to adopt. Quantz in 1752 observed that pitch levels in Paris had risen until they were almost the same as Venetian pitch.[57] By the end of the eighteenth century all Parisian orchestras except the Opéra played in the neighborhood of A = 435, which in the 1790s became known as "ton d'orchestre."[58] Viennese orchestras too were playing at Venetian pitch by the 1760s, as were many other south German orchestras.[59] A flood of north Italian and south German musicians in the mid-eighteenth century brought the higher pitch to England, and by 1770, says Haynes, almost all English woodwinds were pitched around 435.[60] Standardization was fostered by the growth of an international musical circuit, in which singers and virtuoso instrumentalists traveled widely and performed with orchestras in many cities. The emigration of orchestra musicians (especially wind players) and the import and export of wind instruments also tended to foster the standardization of pitch. By the end of the century the standard of A = 435–440 was well on its way to European acceptance.[61]

IMPROVISED ORNAMENTATION

"If a soloist has a ripieno part to play," says Quantz, in his advice to orchestral musicians,

he must add nothing to a melody that might obscure it, especially if several people are playing on the same part. Otherwise he will produce great disorder in the melody. For it is not possible for one person always to divine the thoughts of another. For example, if one player were to make even a single appoggiatura that is not written, and the others were to play the note plain, an offensive dissonance, without preparation or resolution, would result, which would

---

[55] Joseph Sauveur, *Collected Writings on Musical Acoustics (Paris 1700–1713)*, ed. Rudolf Rasch (Utrecht, 1984), 159 ff.; Quantz, *Versuch*, 241–42; Johann Friedrich Agricola, *Anleitung zur Singkunst. Aus den Italiänisch des Herrn Peter Franz Tosi, mit Erläuterungen und Zusätzen* (Berlin, 1757), 45–46.

[56] Quirinus van Blankenburg, *Elementa Musica* (The Hague, 1739), 109. Translated in Haynes, "Pitch Standards," 196.

[57] Quantz, *Versuch*, 241.   [58] Haynes, "Pitch Standards," 139.   [59] Ibid. 364 ff.

[60] Ibid. 349.

[61] Many modern performers believe that pitch levels at the end of the 18th c. were considerably lower than modern pitch levels. Bruce Haynes convincingly refutes this "illusion" (ibid. 43 ff.).

greatly affront the ear, especially in a slow piece. . . . Ritornellos, in particular, must be played entirely without extempore additions. Such additions are permitted only to the performers of concertante parts.[62]

In the orchestral performance practice that Quantz describes, one or more violinists add appoggiaturas and other improvised ornamentation to the notes in their parts. Quantz condemns this practice unequivocally—and later he also warns violists, cellists, and bassists against improvising—but in condemning orchestral improvisation, he documents its existence. Indeed, later in the same passage he acknowledges that the practice is widespread: "Some musicians have the bad habit of introducing all sorts of fopperies, even in the ritornellos, and meanwhile they forget to read the notes correctly. Many end a piece, especially an aria, with a full chord where none is written. This they seem to have learned from tavern fiddlers."[63]

Other eighteenth-century writers, in Germany, France, Italy, and England, add their voices to the chorus condemning but at the same time documenting improvised ornamentation in orchestral performance.[64] For example John Potter in 1762:

If you suppose that the author is himself correct in the harmony of his parts, it is almost certain that the different gracings and additions of the players will destroy this harmony; one is flourishing his part one way and another, a quite different way; and as these things are done extempore, there is not the least probability that they can accord. Thus a beautiful author is frequently murder'd by introducing what he never thought of, or intended.[65]

Likewise Rousseau in his *Musical Dictionary* of 1768:

ORNAMENTS . . . Nothing shows better the good or bad taste of a musician than the choice and the employment that he makes of ornaments . . . So far as instruments are concerned, one may play as one likes during a solo, but a ripienist who embellishes [*symphoniste qui brode*] is never tolerated in a good orchestra.[66]

And Galeazzi in his *Elementi* of 1791:

If orchestra musicians were permitted to play diminutions and ornaments, if each could play whatever seemed best to him, they would jostle against one another in horrid dissonance, and the result would be an intolerable muddle. To avoid such things, it is necessary to play in the most straightforward manner possible and to abstain from even the slightest diminution.[67]

All these authors repeat the same argument in more or less the same form. They draw a contrast between orchestral playing, where ornamentation is forbidden, and solo style, where it is permitted. The spectre of unrestrained simultaneous ornamentation is invoked only to be indignantly condemned, and orchestra musicians are exhorted to play the notes on the page. The vividness of the portrait, however, and the vigor

---

[62] Quantz, *Versuch*, 246–47; Eng. ed., 272.   [63] Quantz, *Versuch*, 247.
[64] For more extensive quotations and citations see Spitzer and Zaslaw, "Improvised Ornamentation."
[65] John Potter, *Observations on the Present State of Music and Musicians* (London, 1762), 79–80.
[66] Rousseau, *Dictionnaire de musique*, 59–60.   [67] Galeazzi, *Elementi teorico-pratici*, i. 209.

of the condemnation suggest that each author has heard the phenomenon he complains about. Indeed Quantz and Potter both acknowledge that orchestra musicians frequently play this way.

Does this mean that eighteenth-century orchestras routinely "murdered" the music with improvised ornamentation? Such a conclusion is considerably justified. While many writers complain, others call for *more* improvisation in the orchestra, or at least for more of the right sort of ornamentation in the right place at the right time. Löhlein, for example, says in his violin tutor that composers seldom write in enough ornamentation to make their pieces successful in performance. Most ripienists, he says, "think they are doing their duty when they just saw away mechanically at the notes like woodcutters." An experienced and intelligent player, on the other hand, knows when and how to add ornaments that will "fulfill the composer's intent and enhance the melody with the decoration it needs."[68] The "Deutsche Biedermann" similarly criticizes ripienists who, where good taste calls for a trill or a turn, "grind out the poor old notes pitifully and ridiculously without any ornament whatsoever."[69] Rousseau in his dictionary entry on "Ensemble" contradicts what he said in his article on "Ornaments" (quoted above), declaring that ensemble depends "not only on the accuracy with which each player reads his part," but also on each player's ability, "to add to the ornaments marked on the page those others that are so obviously assumed by the composer that no one may omit them."[70] Even Quantz allows orchestral violinists to add a trill or a mordent to their part, so long as they rehearse it in advance and execute it unanimously.[71]

Much of the discussion and most of the criticism of improvised ornamentation was aimed at violinists, because the first violins were the most likely to play the melody that needed embellishing. The concertmaster, say the commentators, should take the lead in ornamentation as in other matters. "The other violinists," says Scheibe,

must apply no more and no fewer graces than he does. For if everyone were to add a caprice [*einen Schnörkel*] whenever he took it into his own head, who knows what nonsense would ensue. If not all the violinsts are competent enough to follow in every detail, then the concertmaster must leave off playing ornamentation altogether.[72]

"What I have seen more often," says Scheibe in another passage, "is a concertmaster who, when he is playing with a full orchestra and when the others have to follow him, plays nothing but ridiculous variations on . . . the melodies and other tasteless, convoluted figurations, so that no one can follow him at all."[73] The result, it seems, was a sort of heterophony where the first violin part was performed ornamented by the concertmaster and plain by the rest of the violinists.

---

[68] Löhlein, *Anweisung*, 45–46.   [69] Biedermann [anon.], *Wahrheiten die Musik betreffend*, 75–76.
[70] Rousseau, *Dictionnaire de musique*, 198. He may be referring here to a more modest kind of ornamentation than the "embellishment" he describes under the heading of "ornaments." See Spitzer and Zaslaw, "Improvised Ornamentation," 535 ff.
[71] Quantz, *Versuch*, 181.   [72] Scheibe, *Critischer Musikus*, 715.   [73] Ibid. 558–59.

Another situation in which orchestra musicians improvised ornaments in their parts were passages in which one instrument imitates what another has just played. If the first instrument ornaments his part, then the next should do likewise. Cellists, violists, even double basses, says Petri, should play the passage the way they have just heard it rather than the way they see it on the page.[74] In aria accompaniments the violins and also the winds were encouraged to imitate the singer's ornamentation. And when there was only one player on the part, the orchestra musician automatically acquired the rights of a soloist. This situation arose most often for wind players. Koch explains that when an oboist or a bassoonist sees "solo" written in his part, this means that he momentarily has the principal melody and that he should play accordingly.[75] Tromlitz, in the 1790s, tells flutists that, since the flute part is seldom played by more than one person, "it will not hurt anything very much if the flutist throws in a little embellishment [*ein Blümchen*] here and there—particularly in solo passages."[76] Descriptions of orchestral wind players ornamenting their parts persist well into the nineteenth century, particularly in Italy. The violinist Louis Spohr, performing in Rome in 1816, reports on the performance practices of the musicians in the orchestra that accompanied him:

The first horn, in a tutti section, instead of the simple cadence:

played the following

while at the same time the clarinets were playing something like this:

instead of:

---

[74] Petri, *Anleitung*, 2nd edn., 168. See also Quantz, *Versuch*, 213–14.

[75] Koch, *Musikalisches Lexikon*, col. 1412.

[76] Johann Georg Tromlitz, *Ausführlicher und gründlicher Unterricht die Flöte zu spielen* (Leipzig, 1791), 369. Tromlitz goes on to say that if there are two flutists on the part—something he considers a great error—then they must play the notes as written.

"Ornamentation," says Spohr, "has become so much second nature to them that they cannot stop."[77]

Although it is amusing to contemplate the sound of an eighteenth-century orchestra improvising simultaneously like a Dixieland band, it is important to remember that almost all the documentation of orchestral improvisation takes the form of condemnation. The earliest critiques turned up in France at the very beginning of the eighteenth century, perhaps as part of the effort to codify and preserve the performance practice of Lully's works.[78] In Germany and in England complaints about orchestral improvisation began to appear around mid-century, in Italy somewhat later. During the second half of the eighteenth century commentators and critics waged what amounted to a propaganda campaign to drive improvised ornamentation out of orchestral performance. The arguments were everywhere the same: improvised ornamentation destroys the unity of orchestral performance; improvised ornamentation is egotistical and self-indulgent; if everyone ornaments at the same time, the result will be chaos; if composers want ornaments, they should write them into the music. By the end of the eighteenth century the battle had been won, and the campaign tapered off, except in Italy, where orchestral ornamentation and its critique continued into the nineteenth century.

The suppression of improvised ornamentation may be seen as part of the imposition of new kinds of discipline on the orchestra. Other aspects of this new orchestral discipline were uniform bowing, dynamics, and intonation, and the suppression of preluding—all discussed above—as well as social behaviors like punctuality, sobriety, uniform dress, and neatness. A disciplined orchestra was no longer an aggregation of individuals making music in parallel; it was a single social unit, audibly and visibly acting as a group. Orchestral discipline functioned both as a means to an end, the successful performance of ensemble music, and as an end in itself, a demonstration of the power of social unity.

REHEARSAL

Almost every eighteenth-century author who presumed to give advice to ripienists says that an orchestra musician needs to be a good sightreader. Most orchestras did not permit players to take their parts home to practice, and musicians seem to have considered it inappropriate to practice orchestra music.[79] Therefore an orchestra

---

[77] Spohr, *Lebenserinnerungen*, 296–97.

[78] See e.g. Bourdelot and Bonnet, *Histoire de la musique*, i. 297–99.

[79] Heinrich Christoph Koch, "Über den Charakter der Solo- und Ripienstimmen," *Journal der Tonkunst*, 2tes Stück (1795), 143–55 at 155. In addition, parts could not be sent home because for instrumental music there was often no score available, and a lost part could not be replaced. See I. F. C. Arnold, *Der angehende Musikdirektor*, 229.

violinist, as Koch explains, "must perform his part either entirely *prima vista* or at best with one or two rehearsals, where he has no opportunity to practice difficult spots. Thus, playing ripieno parts requires great facility on the instrument and much practice in sightreading."[80] Sometimes eighteenth-century orchestras performed with no rehearsal at all. Junker reports that at Mannheim masses were often played without rehearsing them in advance.[81] Haydn in 1795 refused to participate in a performance of one of his symphonies in England because the organizers had not scheduled a rehearsal.[82]

Such examples, however, may not be as typical as they are sometimes made out to be. Many eighteenth-century orchestras rehearsed a good deal. Corelli, according to Geminiani's report, gathered his orchestra together for rehearsals, "which constantly preceded every public performance of his concertos."[83] La Pouplinière's private orchestra in Paris in the 1750s rehearsed each morning the symphonies on that evening's concert (see Ch. 6). The Darmstadt Kapelle held regular Wednesday rehearsals in the 1750s; by the end of the century the number of rehearsals had been increased to four or five per week.[84] Operas were extensively rehearsed: first with just singers and continuo players, then with singers and first-chair orchestra players, finally several rehearsals in the theater with full orchestra. The opera then typically ran for anywhere from 5 to 20 performances, which gave the ripienists plenty of opportunity to work out remaining rough spots. In many theaters full rehearsals were open to boxholders and to anyone else who could get past the doorman.[85] Ballets were usually rehearsed by a skeleton crew of two violins and cello with the dancers, then by the full orchestra at general rehearsals.[86] Instrumental music and music for concerts was rehearsed less than opera, but one rehearsal seems to have been considered the minimum for public performance, at least in Germany. Ditters says that at the Prince von Hildburghausen's household "a rehearsal was always held the evening before a concert, so that everything, especially new pieces, would go smoothly and accurately . . ."[87] Church music got the least rehearsal: except for oratorios, which, like operas, received several full rehearsals, church music was usually performed at sight.[88]

"The more often a piece is rehearsed," says J. A. Scheibe in his *Critischer Musikus* (1745), "the better it will go in performance, and the more certainly it will have its

---

[80] Koch, *Musikalisches Lexikon*, cols. 1263–64.   [81] Junker, *Pflichten*, 19.

[82] Joseph Haydn, *Gesammelte Briefe und Aufzeichnungen*, ed. Dénes Bartha (Kassel, 1965), 531.

[83] Burney, *General History of Music*, ed. Mercer, ii, 443. See Ch. 4, p. 132.

[84] Biermann, "Die Darmstadter Hofkapelle," 44; Thomas, *Die grossherzogliche Hofkapelle*, 35. The Landgraf at Darmstadt, who was a passionate music lover, attended evening rehearsals, where he frequently played first violin.

[85] Susan Burney attended rehearsals at the King's Theatre in London in 1779 and gives a vivid account in her diary. See Ch. 8, p. 282.

[86] B. A. Brown, *Gluck*, 90, 167. This rehearsal system was one of the reasons that the ballet was led by a different violinist than the concertmaster, who might be rehearsing with the singers at the same time. See Ch. 5.

[87] Ditters von Dittersdorf, *Lebensbeschreibung*, 59.   [88] Junker, *Pflichten*, 19.

desired effect."[89] He proceeds to outline what should happen at a rehearsal: (1) The director (in this case a keyboard leader) should assign players to the parts they will play in the performance. (2) The director should arrange the players physically in the performance space. (3) As the rehearsal proceeds, the parts should be checked for errors. (4) Singers should inquire about the pronunciation of unusual words; instrumentalists about dynamics. (5) The concertmaster must show the other violinists where to add unnotated ornamentation. (6) The director should acquaint the performers with the tempos of each movement. (7) The director should make suggestions about how the piece should go, and he should justify his suggestions with convincing reasons.

As the century goes on, authors seem to pay increasing attention to rehearsal. Music dictionaries and lexicons from the beginning of the century do not mention rehearsal at all.[90] One of the earliest entries for "rehearsal" is in Grassineau's *Musical Dictionary* of 1740, where it is defined as: "an essay or experiment of some composition made in private, previous to the representation or performance in publick, to habituate the actors or performers, and make them ready or perfect in their parts."[91] Rousseau in his *Dictionnaire de musique* (1768) adds that rehearsals are necessary to make sure that the music has been copied accurately and also to give composers a chance to hear and to revise their works.[92] Meude-Monpas in 1787 agrees that rehearsals are necessary to check the accuracy of the parts, and also to allow the composer to hear whether he calculated his effects correctly. And he adds another sort of reason: rehearsals are "very necessary . . . because they help the performers understand the spirit of the music."[93] The idea that rehearsal can be used to work out artistic interpretation turns up elsewhere in the late eighteenth century, for example in Petri (1787), who says that rehearsal is where the music director makes the players aware of "the hidden intentions of the composers."[94] For this very reason Arnold (1806) argues against sightreading: "so-called *prima-vista* concerts render pieces utterly without character, especially when the orchestra is inexperienced, because the performers have no idea what the effect of the piece should be. Rehearsal enables them to judge whether or not they have hit upon the composer's intent."[95]

By the early nineteenth century rehearsal had become institutionalized as a distinct and special realm, with its own rules and procedures. At rehearsals a piece could be stopped and started again; difficult passages could be played several times; different tempos could be tried out; the performers could talk about the music as well as playing it.[96]

---

[89] Scheibe, *Critischer Musikus*, 714.

[90] e.g. Sébastien de Brossard, *Dictionnaire de musique* (Paris, 1703), and Johann Gottfried Walther, *Musikalisches Lexikon* (Leipzig, 1732).

[91] James Grassineau, *A Musical Dictionary* (London, 1740), 196.

[92] Rousseau, *Dictionnaire de musique*, 411.   [93] Meude-Monpas, *Dictionnaire de musique*, 173.

[94] Petri, *Anleitung,* 2nd edn., 181.   [95] I. F. C. Arnold, *Der angehende Musikdirektor*, 58.

[96] See ibid. 213 ff.; also Rainer Nägele, " 'Hier ist kein Platz für ein Künstler': Das Stuttgarter Hoftheater, 1797–1816," in id. (ed.), *Musik und Musiker am Stuttgarter Hoftheater (1750–1918): Quellen und Studien* (Stuttgart, 2000), 110–28 at 122 ff.

As Koch puts it: "Rehearsals are really the private study of an orchestra, and whether they are managed better or worse determines how the whole orchestra plays, for better or for worse."[97]

LEADERSHIP

Orchestras had leaders from their earliest days. Lully and Corelli led the orchestras that they created; Handel, Bach, and Vivaldi led their orchestras, as did countless Kapellmeisters and *maestri di cappella*. The scope of leadership changed considerably over the course of the eighteenth century, however, as orchestras consolidated themselves and as orchestral performance practices developed. At the beginning of the period a musical leader, whatever his title, was responsible not just for the orchestra but for the entire musical establishment. Leading singers and instrumentalists in performance was only one aspect of his job. He was also a composer, an administrator, a vocal coach, sometimes a copyist, and often a teacher. By the end of the century the leader's duties had become more narrowly focused on the orchestra, and on leadership in performance. He made sure everyone was in tune, he set and maintained tempos, he oversaw dynamics and expression, and he interpreted the composer's intent to the performers. A number of men, most of them violinists, became famous not as composers or solo performers, but first and foremost as the leaders of their orchestras.

There were three principal ways of leading an orchestra in the eighteenth century and consequently three types of leader: (1) the timebeater; (2) the keyboard director; and (3) the violin leader. Of these the timebeater was the earliest. Beating time—with the hand, with a rolled-up scroll of music paper, or with a short, thick baton—had been the usual way of leading choral ensembles in the sixteenth and seventeenth centuries, and the practice persisted in church music throughout the eighteenth century.[98] Mozart (age 12) beat time when he led a performance of his mass, K. 139, for the Court in Vienna in 1768.[99] Burney attended a festival mass in Bologna in 1770, in which each movement had been written by a different composer and consequently "every author beat time to his own performance."[100] Often timebeating in church was audible as well as visible: at the beginning of the piece or when the chorus dragged, the director would strike the downbeats on his music desk. Complaints about noisy timebeating are an enduring refrain in descriptions of eighteenth-century performances of sacred music.[101]

---

[97] Koch, *Musikalisches Lexikon*, col. 1172.

[98] See Linda Faye Ferguson, "Col Basso and Generalbass in Mozart's Keyboard Concertos: Notation, Performance Theory, and Practice" (Ph.D. diss., Princeton University, 1983), 120 ff.

[99] Letter of 14 Dec. 1768. Mozart, *Briefe*, i. 286.

[100] Burney, *The Present State of Music in France and Italy*, 234.

[101] Fuhrmann, *Musikalischer-Trichter*, 75; Mattheson, *Der vollkommene Capellmeister*, 482; Scheibe, *Critischer Musikus*, 717; Petri, *Anleitung*, 2nd edn., 183. Leopold Mozart reports that at a performance in Salzburg of a

Another place where the orchestra was led by a timebeater was the Opéra in Paris. Lully evidently inaugurated the practice in the 1670s. The engraving of a performance of *Alceste*, not at the Opéra but at Versailles in 1674, shows a man, presumably Lully himself, standing at the stage apron, beating time with a short stick (Fig. 3.3). By the end of the seventeenth century the timebeater, under the name "batteur de mesure," had become a fixture at the Opéra. Charles Dufresny in 1699 describes him as "the sovereign of the orchestra," who governs by "raising and lowering his scepter in the form of a roll of paper that he holds in his hand."[102] The 1714 regulations for the Opéra distinguish between two official positions: the *batteur de mesure* and the *maître de musique*.[103] The *maître* is a vocal coach. The *batteur* beats time "both in performance and in rehearsals" and makes sure that the instrumentalists come to work on time and do not leave before the end of the performance. Around 1760 the positions of *batteur* and *maître* were merged, suggesting that musical control of the opera was being consolidated.[104] In the 1770s the *maître*, J.-B. Rey, set tempos, coordinated singers and instrumentalists, rehearsed singers and orchestra, and engaged in a considerable amount of what today would be called interpretation: dynamics, rubato, phrasing, etc.[105]

A timebeater also led performances at court concerts and at many provincial theaters. However, at the Italian theater and the Comédie Française the orchestras were led by the first violinist. The Concert Spirituel, which had a large chorus as well as an orchestra, seems to have wavered between the two methods of direction.[106] In 1760 Louis Aubert was listed both as first violin and as *batteur de mesure*.[107] The next year the *Almanach des spectacles* reported that M. Mondonville, the director, "beats the time himself" and that M. Aubert "only assists him."[108] In 1762 an experiment was tried whereby the orchestra was led by two violinists, one at the head of the firsts, one at the head of the seconds, and there was no *batteur* at all for instrumental music.[109] The system seems to have been abandoned as being too Italianate, and for the next few years the *Almanach* listed the timebeater as director, with a violinist as his assistant.[110] In 1774, however, the *batteur* disappeared again from the roster, and two violinists were listed as leaders, a system that obtained for the remainder of the century. Thus the Concert Spirituel, apparently over considerable opposition, moved away from baton direction toward a system of violin leadership.

---

mass by Michael Haydn three of the ripienists beat time on the shoulders of the wind players to help them keep time in fugal passages (letter of 1 Nov 1777, in Mozart, *Briefe*, ii. 96).

[102] Charles Dufresny, *Amusmens sérieux et comiques* (Amsterdam, 1699), 64. See Ch. 14, p. 512.

[103] Durey de Noinville, *Histoire du théâtre*, 136.

[104] *Almanach des spectacles* (1760), 3. Up until 1758 the *Almanach* lists the two positions separately. The *Almanach* published in 1759 (dated 1760) lists only a *maître de musique*, no *batteur*.

[105] Charlton, "'A maître d'orchestre . . . conducts,'" 348 ff.

[106] See Brenet, *Les Concerts en France*, 277–79.

[107] *Almanach des spectacles* (1760), 3.

[108] *Almanach des spectacles* (1761), 4.

[109] *Mercure de France* (Paris), 1762, i. 184.

[110] *Almanach des spectacles* (1763–71). See Ch. 6.

At the Opéra the *batteur* marked the beat, not with the traditional up and down movements of the choral timebeater but rather with a downbeat followed by "various movements of the hand to the right and to the left."[111] The bitter complaint of Grimm, Rousseau, and other critics was that for the downbeat the *batteur* struck his baton against a music stand or the stage apron, making a "noise as if he were splitting wood."[112] However, by the second half of the eighteenth century the audible beat seems to have been heard mainly in the choruses, particularly when the singers were stationed in the wings or at the back of the stage. During the rest of the opera direction was by visible signals.[113] The other complaint about timebeating—not just audible timebeating, but timebeating in general—was that it was mechanical and inflexible. "Orchestra musicians become cold and indifferent," says Grétry, "when they do not follow the singer directly. The stick that directs them humiliates them."[114] For an ensemble made up of individuals and artists, Grétry says, authoritarian leadership is less effective because it inhibits the performers' artistic skills and judgement.

To many people in the eighteenth century, leadership by example seemed far preferable to leadership by command. As Mattheson observed in 1739: "Things always work out better when I both play and sing along than when I merely stand there and beat time. Playing and singing in this way inspires and enlivens the performers."[115] Two instruments were the most suitable for leading an orchestra by example: keyboard (organ, harpsichord, fortepiano), and violin. Leading from the keyboard seemed natural because a keyboard player did not have to establish any new or special authority as a leader. The keyboardist often held an administrative post in the music establishment, as Kapellmeister, *maestro*, or director, so his authority to lead was reinforced by his official position. Also the keyboardist was often the composer of the music being performed, which again conferred a kind of natural authority. Finally, the keyboardist gained authority from his relationship with the singers: he coached and accompanied them whenever they sang.

It was the keyboardist's responsibility to set the tempo at the beginning of each piece and to make sure that the entire orchestra maintained that tempo. "The keyboardist," says C. P. E. Bach in 1753, "is and will always be the reference point for the beat." If the *basso* part has long notes, the keyboardist may subdivide them to maintain the audible beat; if the bass has repeated eighths or sixteenths, the keyboardist may want to play just the strong beats, both in order to ease the strain on his left hand and to make the pulse clearer. Bach recommends that the keyboardist should raise his hands off the keys between notes, both to get a more forceful sound and so

---

[111] Rousseau, *Dictionnaire de musique*, 52.   [112] Grimm, *Le Petit Prophète*, 10.

[113] Charlton, "A maître d'orchestre . . . conducts,' " 347–48.

[114] André Ernest Modeste Grétry, *Mémoires, ou essais sur la musique* (Paris, 1797), i. 40. Grétry acknowledges that baton direction is necessary at the Opéra for large choruses.

[115] Mattheson, *Der vollkommene Capellmeister*, 482.

that the rise and fall of his hands will mark the beat.[116] Other authors advise the keyboard leader to avail himself of stronger measures. Veracini tells him to start a piece by saying "ONE" in a loud voice and then "to begin marking the beat visibly with his body and audibly by stamping his feet until the entire orchestra has joined in at the desired tempo."[117] Schönfeld describes a Kapellmeister who "labors with his head, hands, and feet all at once to keep the tempo and the beat—indeed he is often obliged to leave off leading from the keyboard altogether and hack at the air with both hands."[118] Schönfeld compares such keyboardists to the "woodchopper" at the Opéra.

The keyboardists depicted above were forced to resort to extraordinary measures, it seems, because simply realizing the bass line at the keyboard did not always provide enough of an example to lead an entire orchestra. In full textures the harpsichord could not be heard; in thin textures it was too loud. And a harpsichord could not execute, much less lead, the dynamic nuances that were becoming increasingly important in orchestral performance. A fortepiano was capable of dynamics, but its attack was not loud or incisive enough for the orchestra to follow.[119] In the last analysis, it was hard for the keyboardist to lead by example because he did something fundamentally different from the other orchestra musicians: where they played melodies, he played a chordal accompaniment; where they played from written parts, he improvised. By 1806 I. F. C. Arnold had lost faith entirely in the ability of keyboardists to lead orchestras: "The keyboard director with his isolated instrument can gain little respect from the rest of the musicians. He will always be a stranger among them [*ein Fremdling unter ihnen*], and he has no responsibility for whether the performance succeeds or fails."[120]

As keyboard participation in orchestral music declined during the late eighteenth century, keyboard leadership declined correspondingly, until by the end of the century the harpsichordist or pianist, when he was found in the orchestra at all, was little more than a figurehead or a vestige. At Salomon's concerts in London in the 1790s Salomon, as concertmaster, led with his violin, while Haydn sat at the piano and "presided."

Given that something like half of the musicians in the orchestra were violinists, a violin leader was in a better position than a keyboardist or a timebeater to lead by example. As the author of a memorandum in the archives of the Opéra put it:

---

[116] Carl Philipp Emanuel Bach, *Versuch über die wahre Art das Clavier zu spielen* (Berlin, 1753–62), 5–6, 8, 252, 259.

[117] Veracini, *Trionfo*, sec. 74.

[118] J. von Schönfeld, *Jahrbuch der Tonkunst von Wien und Prag* (Vienna, 1796), 174.

[119] I. F. C. Arnold, *Der angehende Musikdirektor*, 137. See also Biedermann, *Wahrheiten*, 30, and Rochlitz, "Bruchstücke," 19.

[120] Arnold, *Der angehende Musikdirektor*, 139.

the baton of the *maître de musique* can indeed prevent them from rushing or dragging, but it will never be able to make them phrase uniformly, it will never be able to make them feel the different gradations of forte or piano, of dolce or crescendo. Only an able violinist leader can compel them to render delicate nuances with precision and uniformity.[121]

Violin leadership became increasingly prominent over the course of the eighteenth century.[122] The leader, as he was called in England—*primo violino* or *capo d'orchestra* in Italy, *Anführer* or *Konzertmeister* in Germany, *premier violon* in France—led by means of the strength and loudness with which he played the first violin part. He must have an instrument, says Reichardt,

that is louder than all the others; but this in itself is not enough to enable him to shout out his part over eighteen other violinists and all the other instruments too; he must also have a better arm than the others, that is, he must learn to exploit all the advantages of his instrument by means of clear and strong execution in order to make his tone as powerful and as penetrating as possible.[123]

Many sources emphasize that the concertmaster needs to play very loudly. "In order the keep the orchestra together," says a document in the Dresden archives, the concertmaster "must play twice as loud as the others."[124] According to Galeazzi, the first violin "must be a strong and incisive player [*un suonatore di forza e di brio*], so that he can be heard by everyone around him and also by the singer onstage."[125] Indeed the concertmaster must play so loudly, says Schmith, that his right arm becomes "heavy," and he is no longer suited for solo playing.[126]

Besides playing loudly the concertmaster also led by means of visual signs. He bowed vigorously to indicate the beat and to demonstrate articulations to the rest of the violinists.[127] Pisendel, according to Reichardt, marked the meter in the first few bars of a piece by moving the neck and scroll of his violin in a manner very similar to a timebeater: "If it was 4/4 time, he moved the violin first downwards, then up, then to the side, then up again; if it was 3/4, then he moved it down once, once to the side, then up."[128] The concertmaster, says Arnold, can also beat a single bar in the air with his bow before the piece starts, and then the orchestra will be able to enter "as though

---

[121] Paris, Archives nationales, AJ13/1: "Réflexions sur l'orchestre de l'Opéra" (*c.*1776–79?): "le bâton du Maître de Musique peut bien les empecher d'accelerer ou de retarder la mesure, mais il ne pourra jamais les faire phraser uniformement, jamais il ne pourra leur faire sentir les differentes gradations des forte ou piano, du dolce au crescendo. Un habile premier violon peut seul les forcer à rendre avec precision et uniformité [les] nuances delicates." We are grateful to William Weber for bringing this document to our attention.

[122] See Robin Stowell, " 'Good execution and other necessary skills': The Role of the Concertmaster in the Late 18th Century," *EM* 16 (1988), 21–33.

[123] Reichardt, *Briefe*, 39.

[124] Quoted in Landmann, "Die Entwicklung der Dresdener Hofkapelle," 188.

[125] Galeazzi, *Elementi teorico-pratici*, i. 224.

[126] Schmith, *Philosophische Fragmente*, 54. Schmith says that Dittersdorf is one of the few German violinists who manages to be both a good orchestra leader and a good soloist.

[127] Galeazzi, *Elementi teorico-pratici*, i. 224; Arnold, *Der angehende Musikdirektor*, 138.

[128] Reichardt, *Briefe*, 40.

it had been playing together all along."[129] Galeazzi even says that a concertmaster should shout cues to the players

to alert them to important features of the expression, which he needs to understand better than the others; and from time to time, when he senses the need, he should stamp his foot, which will put whole orchestra back on the right track, preserve equilibrium, prevent disorder, and restore unanimity when things go wrong.[130]

Often the violin leader was placed on a raised platform so that the entire orchestra (and also the singers) could see and hear him.[131]

Eighteenth-century sources give no directions for dividing leadership between keyboardist and violinist. Most commentators feel that instrumental music is best led from the concertmaster's position, vocal music from the keyboard.[132] In a poorly run orchestra this might lead to conflicts over leadership. But composers like J. S. Bach, Handel, Joseph Haydn, and Mozart could and did lead from either position according to circumstance. In the last quarter of the eighteenth century, however, as orchestral performance practices became acknowledged and codified, a debate arose over keyboard versus violin leadership. Biedermann (1779), Forkel (1783), Rochlitz (1799), and Koch (1802) each ask the question: who should lead the orchestra, the keyboard or the violin? Each of these authors weighs the issue, considers the several arguments, and comes down on the side of keyboard leadership.

By the time these keyboard-playing theorists asked the question, their cause was already lost, for by the end of the eighteenth century every major European orchestra was led by the first violinist—not only in the sense that the violin leader set tempos and managed rehearsals, but also in the sense that the concertmaster was acknowledged as the personification of the orchestra and as the individual responsible for how it played. Cannabich in Mannheim, Benda and Reichardt in Berlin, Pisendel and Babbi in Dresden, Giardini, Cramer, and Salomon in London, Pugnani in Turin, Rolla in Milan, La Houssaye and Saint-Georges in Paris—these successful violin leaders became famous not just as virtuosos but even more for the achievements of the orchestras they led.

A succession of treatises by and for concertmasters—Galeazzi (1791), Arnold (1806), and Scaramelli (1811)—confirmed the ascendancy of the violin leader and outlined his ever-expanding duties. He is responsible for selecting musicians to play in the orchestra, for leading rehearsals, for determining seating arrangements, for

---

[129] Arnold, *Der angehende Musikdirektor*, 359. [130] Galeazzi, *Elementi teorico-pratici*, i. 224.

[131] Biedermann, *Wahrheiten*, 44. See Fig. 10.2.

[132] Formulas for dividing responsibility between the keyboardist and the violinist do turn up in later sources. Busby in his *Complete Dictionary of Music* (*c*.1801) says that the leader "receives the time and style of the several movements from the conductor [at the keyboard] and communicates them to the rest of the band" (Thomas Busby, *Complete Dictionary of Music* (London, *c*.1801), s.v. "Leader"). The regulations of the theater orchestra at Rimini in 1806 say that the maestro at the keyboard directs the music at rehearsals, but "when the opera is put on, this duty falls to the first violinist" (quoted in Paolo Fabbri, "Un progetto dimezzato," in Conati and Pavarani (eds.), *Orchestre in Emilia-Romagna*, 495–508 at 503).

tuning, for setting and maintaining tempos, for giving cues to the singers, for filling in missed entrances, and for rescuing the performance in the event of disaster. The more responsibilities the concertmaster acquired, the more central his activities became to the orchestra's performance. "If an opera goes well," says Galeazzi, "it is the first violin who will receive the praise, and if it goes poorly, it is he who will be blamed."[133] "A mediocre orchestra with an excellent director," says Scaramelli, "plays much better than an excellent orchestra led by an incompetent first violinist."[134] No wonder Galeazzi and Scaramelli both complain that the *primo violino* doesn't make enough money![135]

THE IDEOLOGY OF ORCHESTRAL PERFORMANCE PRACTICE

Scaramelli's treatise stands at the end of a succession of books and articles that address themselves to orchestra musicians on the subject of orchestral performance. These treatises and commentaries document, promulgate, and promote specifically orchestral performance practices. The following are the most important:

J. J. Quantz: *On Playing the Flute* (Berlin, 1752)
J. F. Reichardt: *The Duties of the Ripieno Violinist* (1776)
R. Bremner: "Some Thoughts on the Performance of Concert Music" (1777)
C. L. Junker: "The Foremost Duties of a Capellmeister or Music Director" (1782)
F. Galeazzi: *Theoretical and Practical Elements of Music* (1791–96)
H. C. Koch, "The Character of Solo and Ripieno Parts" (1795)
I. F. C. Arnold: *The Aspiring Music Director* (1806)
G. Scaramelli: *Essay on the Duties of a First Violinist and Orchestra Director* (1811)

Taken together, these eight sources transmit what amounts to an ideology of orchestral performance practice. They are not just "how to" manuals that give performers tips on playing in orchestras. They also tell performers how to think in order to be orchestra musicians; they articulate the ideas that people need to have for the orchestra to maintain and reproduce itself as an institution. Their authors, from Quantz to Scaramelli, may thus be thought of as "ideologists" of the orchestra.

The ideology of the orchestra can be summarized in the form of seven principles, most of which are expressed in one form or another by all eight authors listed above.

1. *Playing in an orchestra requires special performance practices.* As Bremner puts it:

for ought I can learn, the difference between a solo and concert performance has not been treated of hitherto. Should gentlemen now see this difference in its true light, there is great

---

[133] Galeazzi, *Elementi teorico-pratici*, i. 226.   [134] Scaramelli, *Saggio*, 10.
[135] Galeazzi, *Elementi teorico-pratici*, i. 214; Scaramelli, *Saggio*, 49. Both men were themselves violin leaders, Galeazzi at the Teatro Argentina in Rome, Scaramelli at the Teatro Regio in Trieste.

reason to hope that they will not hereafter destroy their own entertainment by mingling these two styles of playing together; at least by carrying the first into the last.[136]

Bremner was not the first to insist on this difference; Quantz and Reichardt had already discussed it at length.

Most of the ideologists justify the dichotomy between solo and orchestral playing styles by pointing to the chaos that results when orchestra musicians play like soloists. In his essay on "The Character of Solo and Ripieno Parts," H. C. Koch proposes a more elaborate rationale, based on the theory of music as communication. Music, Koch claims, communicates human feelings. The soloist, when he performs, expresses his unique, individual feelings. The orchestra musician, on the other hand, is a member of a social group that is moved by a common feeling. People in a social group communicate their feelings through the power and unity of their expression. Therefore, Koch concludes, "a ripieno part must be played in exactly the same way by all the musicians who communally perform it."[137]

2. *An orchestral player is a special kind of musician.* All the ideologists draw a distinction between the concerto player and the orchestral player, between the soloist and the ripienist. Soloists and ripienists are different kinds of people, separated by aptitude, training, and employment. "When a young player," Galeazzi writes, "despite much study and long hours of practice, has still not earned a position of respect and has not distinguished himself above his fellows, he finds himself relegated to the status of a mere orchestral performer; as people say vulgarly, he's a member of the rank and file [*suona in truppa*]."[138] The ideologists agree that soloists usually make poor orchestra performers and that ripienists make poor soloists. "Concerto players," says Rochlitz,

are concerned in their performance with refinement, elegance, and tenderness—and rightly so, for these are central to their playing. But the ripienist, without neglecting such things entirely, has to make power and exactness his principal concerns. How is it possible for one and the same man to be a completely different person in one situation from what he is somewhere else?[139]

Only Arnold reexamines the assumption that soloists and ripienists are different classes of people. In order to be a musician at all, says Arnold, an orchestral violinist needs to develop his musical sensibilities. Arnold encourages a music director to give each of the members of his orchestra the opportunity to play concertos in public. Playing concertos gives everyone (even the timpanist) a sense of participation, and it imparts a "certain *delicatesse* in orchestral playing that will always stand a competent and experienced player in good stead."[140]

---

[136] Zaslaw, "The Compleat Orchestral Musician", 53.
[137] Koch, "Über den Charakter," 149, 154.
[138] Galeazzi, *Elementi teorico-pratici*, 208.
[139] Rochlitz, "Bruchstücke," col. 22.
[140] Arnold, *Der angehende Musikdirektor*, 75–77, 116, 122.

3. *What the orchestra player does is unique and valuable.* With the recognition of ripienists as a distinct class of people, the ideologists undertook what amounted to a public relations campaign to validate orchestral musicians in general and ripieno violinists in particular. Quantz observes that

as a result of the efforts of composers to come up with new ideas, modern ripieno parts are often far more challenging than such parts used to be. Many ripieno parts today are harder to play than a solo was in former times, and consequently today's ripienists must know far more than their predecessors, if they are to realize the intentions of composers.[141]

Rochlitz claims that "a truly good ripienist is more valuable and does better service than six . . . run-of-the mill soloists."[142] "Everyone underestimates the job of a ripienist." says Reichardt on the first page of his treatise. "In the following it will be shown how much is involved in being a really good ripienist, and people will learn to value him more."[143]

The Italian writers tend to give orchestra musicians less credit than the Germans do. Galeazzi observes dismissively:

Expression in an orchestra comes down to the mechanical exercise of accurately executing the pianos and the fortes as they are written on the page. A little practice and a little attention suffice to play a piece well in an orchestra. The case is entirely different for a soloist. His music requires the most profound mastery of all the techniques and the resources of the [violinist's] art. This requires genius, not mere talent.[144]

H. C. Koch responds to this point of view in the "Ripienist" article in his *Musikalisches Lexikon*:

Because soloists play one on a part and because their parts tend to be technically more difficult than ripieno parts, . . . a prejudice has established itself that ripienists lack genius and taste, that any poor devil is good enough to play a ripieno part. . . . To be a good ripienist requires just as much artistic education and artistic integrity as to be a good concerto player.[145]

If musicians are going to spend their entire adult lives playing at the back of the violin or viola section, they need to believe that what they are doing is worthwhile. "Many a good piece has been ruined," says Junker, "by the coarse and incorrect playing of sickly, depressed, downcast individuals."[146] "Treat the members of your orchestra," Rochlitz tells his young music director, "not as underlings, but as comrades in the quest of a praiseworthy goal."[147]

4. *Orchestral playing requires uniformity.* If orchestra musicians are to play several on a part, then each individual must play the same thing as his neighbor—not just the same notes, but the same bowing, the same articulation, the same dynamics, the same

---

[141] Quantz, *Versuch*, 175–76.   [142] Rochlitz, "Bruchstücke," col. 60.
[143] Reichardt, *Ueber die Pflichten*, 3.   [144] Galeazzi, *Elementi teorico-pratici*, i. 197.
[145] Koch, *Musikalisches Lexikon*, col. 1261–62.   [146] Junker, *Pflichten*, 44–45.
[147] Rochlitz, "Bruchstücke," col. 63.

ornamentation. Violinists must all bow uniformly (Quantz, Bremner, Galeazzi); dynamics must be executed uniformly by the entire orchestra (Quantz, Reichardt, Arnold); the orchestra must tune carefully to a uniform pitch (Quantz, Arnold, Scaramelli); the orchestra should maintain a uniform tempo from the beginning to the end of the piece (Quantz, Reichardt, Scaramelli). Reichardt even suggests that all the violinists in an orchestra should use the same type of mute.[148] Galeazzi waxes rhapsodic on the subject of uniformity:

> An orchestra player must always have his ear attuned to the unity of the ensemble: to slur if the others slur, to detach if the others detach, to press or relax the tempo as the others do (especially the concertmaster), to play loudly or softly as his fellows do, to watch the concertmaster, and finally to help out his neighbors if they are not as good as he is—for this too can be done without disturbing the most exact unity. . . . An entire orchestra, even as many as hundred strong, can play thus with perfect unity, as though they were a single player.[149]

5. *An orchestra is greater than the sum of its parts.* Although each orchestra musician does the same thing as his neighbors, their united performance transcends their individual performances. Bremner puts it succinctly: "The concert, or orchestra player . . . is only a member of that whole by which a united effect is to be produced; and if there be more than one to a part, he becomes no more than a part of a part."[150] In consequence, no performer should call attention to his particular part or to his individual abilities, for this will ruin the effect of the whole. Arnold expresses the same idea metaphorically: the individuals in an orchestra, despite their diverse technical levels and their different expressive capacities, must unite into a "single mechanical body."[151]

6. *An orchestra needs a leader.* All the ideologists agree that the orchestra should be led by a single person, and all but Junker and Koch say that the leader should be the concertmaster.[152] From Quantz to Scaramelli, the leader's duties are listed in ever-increasing scope and detail. In addition, the sources increasingly glorify the leader's position and skills. The directorship of an orchestra is a "luminous post," according to Galeazzi; for Scaramelli it is a "highly estimable calling."[153] Junker says that the Kapellmeister is like the "hero of a painting," prominently visible (and audible) in the foreground.[154]

For one man to lead, another must follow, so the ideologists also stress the idea of subordination. "It is the duty of each member of the orchestra," Quantz says, "to be guided by the concertmaster . . . and not to think it any disgrace to accede to a reasonable and necessary subordination without which there can be no good music."[155] Later authors grow even more insistent about notions of hierarchy, for example

---

[148] Reichardt, *Ueber die Pflichten*, 87. [149] Galeazzi, *Elementi teorico-pratici*, i. 210–11.

[150] Zaslaw, "The Compleat Orchestral Musician," 50.

[151] Arnold, *Der angehende Musikdirektor*, 63. For more metaphors of this sort, see Ch. 14.

[152] Junker does not raise the issue of who should direct the orchestra; Koch argues for keyboard leadership.

[153] Galeazzi, *Elementi teorico-pratici*, i. 214; Scaramelli, *Saggio*, 51. [154] Junker, *Pflichten*, 17.

[155] Quantz, *Versuch*, 247.

Galeazzi: "All the violinists of an orchestra must have complete, blind, and perfect subordination to the first violin, whoever he may be. Even in the case where he makes a mistake, they should all unite in following him, since he alone is responsible for the performance of the orchestra."[156] This ideology of hierarchy resonates in the titles of the treatises, with their talk of the duties (*Pflichten*) of ripienists and the obligations (*doveri*) of the director.

7. *All orchestras are the same.* Differences remained at the end of the eighteenth century between French orchestras and German orchestras, between opera orchestras and concert orchestras, and so on. Indeed, such differences remain today. The ideology of the orchestra as it evolved in the second half of the eighteenth century, however, held that orchestras everywhere were examples of a single institution. Consequently, the performance practices that obtained in one orchestra ought to be valid in all orchestras. A player trained in one orchestra ought to be able to play in any orchestra; an instrument used in one orchestra should be usable in any orchestra; a piece written for one orchestra should be playable in principle by all orchestras.

The internationalization of orchestral pitch levels was one manifestation of this principle. Other orchestral performance practices, like bowing, dynamics, and methods of leadership also tended to generalize themselves as performers moved from place to place. Orchestra leaders (both keyboardists and violinists) were especially influential in transmitting performance practices from one place to another. It is good, says Quantz, for a leader to have played in several different orchestras so that he will have broad experience with different performance practices.[157] Orchestral performance practices should also be internationalized by notation. Quantz, Reichardt, and Arnold all urge composers to indicate the performance practices they want on the page—to write in dynamics, articulation, and ornamentation—so that different orchestras will be able to play their music in the right style. If notation is standardized, says Arnold, and if orchestral performance practices are widely understood, then "a composer in Naples can send his score to Moscow or to London or to some other distant place and may be confident that, wherever the same rules and musical forms are recognized and implemented, his composition will sound the same and have the same effect."[158] By the end of the eighteenth century, not only did scores travel from Naples to London to Moscow, but singers, orchestra musicians, and orchestra leaders made the same trips. Isolated individual orchestras and distinct regional styles began to be replaced by an international network of orchestras, sharing the same repertory and the same performance practices.

---

[156] Galeazzi, *Elementi teorico-pratici*, i. 211.   [157] Quantz, *Versuch*, 178.
[158] Arnold, *Der angehende Musikdirektor*, 35.

Chapter Twelve

The Life and Times of an Eighteenth-Century Orchestra Musician

Who was an orchestra musician in the eighteenth century? What kind of life did he lead? Where did he live? What did he wear? How much money did he make? Who were his friends? What was his social standing? Answers to questions like these vary according to individual circumstances and also with place and time. The life of a violist in Salzburg in 1720 was very different from the life of a first violinist in Milan in 1750, different again from a London oboist in 1790. Yet there were similarities too. The life of the Salzburg violist was not all that different from that of instrumentalists in Bonn or Eszterháza or other German court Kapellen. In several ways the life of the London oboist resembled that of an orchestra musician in Paris or Venice during the same period.

The economic circumstances and the social milieux of eighteenth-century orchestra musicians fall into patterns according to how the musical life of the city, town, or court where they lived was organized. Three basic models can be distinguished:

1. *The Kapelle*. The orchestra forms part of the household of a king, a prince, or some other ruler. Orchestra musicians sign contracts for terms of at least a year and often serve the same patron for their entire lives.

2. *The free market*. Orchestras are formed by buying the labor of individual musicians and combining them into orchestras. Instrumentalists are hired for particular occasions or for single seasons.

3. *Civic music*. Musicians are civil servants and hold their positions as offices, usually for life. They form orchestras as needed and as numbers permit.

These three models should be seen as "ideal types."[1] Few cities, countries, or courts corresponded exactly to one model or another; several were mixtures of two or even of all three types. This chapter presents five case studies that exemplify the three models and show how they changed over the course of the eighteenth century.

THE ESTERHÁZY KAPELLE

A great deal is known about the musicians in Haydn's orchestras, from the time he arrived at Eisenstadt in 1761 to work for Prince Paul Anton, through his years at Eszterháza under Nicholas I, and into the early nineteenth century. The Esterházy establishment kept very good records—payrolls, musicians' contracts, petitions to the Prince, records of baptisms and wills, civil and criminal proceedings, etc.—and many of these records have been preserved.

The Esterházy orchestra exemplifies the principal features of Kapelle organization. The "Fürstlich Kammer- und Chormusik" was a department of the princely household (*Hofstaat*), just like the kitchen, the stable, the guards, the buildings and grounds crew, the personal servants, and other departments.[2] The Kapelle included not only orchestra musicians but also opera singers, plus singers and instrumentalists for the church at the Prince's hereditary residence in Eisenstadt. All the musicians were classified as "house officers," which meant that they were not servants. Like other members of the princely household, the orchestra musicians were lodged on the palace grounds. At Eszterháza, the Prince's magnificent palace on the Neusiedlersee, most of them lived in the "Musicians' House," a large building of 70 rooms, with furniture, linens, firewood, candles, and maids provided by the Prince. The musicians ate their main meal together with one another and other house officers at the "Officers' Table." If the musician had a wife and children, the family too was lodged on the Prince's estate, with full accommodations for them at Eisenstadt and limited ones at Eszterháza.[3] The Prince also clothed his orchestra. They received a new uniform every year—gray with silver or gold trim until 1776, then a red coat and pants with a green waistcoat.[4]

The Prince provided the musicians with musical instruments. No inventories of Esterházy instruments have survived, but princely ownership is documented by a stream of bills for instrument purchase and repair, as well as supplies like strings, bows, reeds, quills, mutes, and so on. Perhaps some of the musicians had instruments of their

---

[1] Max Weber, *From Max Weber: Essays in Sociology*, ed. Hans Gerth and C. Wright Mills (New York, 1958), 323–24.

[2] János Harich, "Das fürstlich Esterházy'sche Fideikommiss," *Haydn Yearbook*, 4 (1968), 5–35.

[3] Landon, *Haydn: Chronicle and Works*, ii. 29, 180.

[4] Harich, "Fideikommiss," 20; Landon, *Haydn: Chronicle and Works*, ii. 355. One year the musician received a "summer uniform," the next year a "winter uniform." A musician who kept his uniforms in good condition could request a cash payment instead of a new uniform.

DOCUMENT 12.1. *Contract of Carl Schiringer, 1767*

We take Carl Schiringer into our Service as a double bassist, and We graciously authorize his yearly provision or salary, namely:

In cash each month . . . . 20 f
For parade money, daily like the others . . . . — 17 Kreutzer
Lodging, candles, wood like the others
A suit of clothes yearly, or 2 suits every 2 years

In return his duties will be:

1. To appear diligently with the instrumental and choral music at the appointed hours, early or late, and to participate as long as We shall please, not only in Eisenstadt but also providing assiduous service in Vienna and in other places where he shall be called.

2. To render obedience to the Kapellmeister and to execute without back-talk whatever he [the Kapellmeister] may command in his Master's service.

3. He shall comport himself quietly and peacefully, as is appropriate for a respectable man in a Princely establishment, and he shall avoid any sort of disruption.

4. He shall not absent himself without Our permission from Eisenstadt, Vienna, or from any other place where the Court may be staying for a time, nor may he miss any performance of the instrumental or choral music, but report punctually to the Kapellmeister.

If the aforementioned conditions are acknowledged to be satisfactory, then on the same terms will Our Princely accord be granted.

Pressburg 1 March 1767. Nicolaus Prince Esterházy

Source: Translated from Harich, "Das Haydn-Orchester im Jahr 1780," 134.

own in addition to those the Prince provided. However, when hornists Franz Pauer and Joseph Oliva arrived at Eszterháza in 1769, the Prince bought their horns from them for 24 ducats, and henceforth he owned the instruments.[5]

The provisions and language of a typical Esterházy orchestra musician's contract reinforce the impression of paternalism. The initial contract, translated here, of Carl Schiringer, who played bassoon and double bass in the Esterházy Kapelle from 1767 to 1790, provides a typical example (Doc. 12.1).[6] Under its terms Schiringer is paid 20 florins a month (240 florins per year), plus an additional 17 Kreutzers per day when

---

[5] János Harich, "Das Haydn-Orchester im Jahr 1780," *Haydn Yearbook*, 8 (1971), 5–163 at 139.

[6] This contract calls Schiringer a "Violonist." In subsequent contracts he is listed alternately as a "Violonist" and as a "Fagotist." In 1788 he is listed as a flutist, probably an error. See Sonja Gerlach, "Haydns Orchestermusiker von 1761 bis 1774," *Haydn-Studien*, 4 (1976), 35–48 at 40; Harich, "Das Haydn-Orchester," 63–64.

the orchestra is "on parade," i.e. at Eszterháza rather than Eisenstadt.[7] He also receives his lodging, his uniform, and the same allotment of candles and firewood as the other musicians.[8] In return he is obliged to appear and play at whatever hour the Prince chooses, "whether early or late"; he is to show respect for the Kapellmeister (i.e. Haydn), follow orders without back-talk, and live an upright life. Finally, he is not to miss a performance of either instrumental or church music [*Cammer oder Chor Musique*] or leave the premises without permission. This means that he cannot play in any other orchestra besides the Prince's.

These restrictions on personal freedom are characteristic of Kapelle contracts at Eszterháza and elsewhere. And they were enforced. Violinist Antonio Rosetti, for example, was fined repeatedly in the late 1770s for leaving Eszterháza without permission, and in March 1780 his contract was terminated. The cellist Anton Kraft also went AWOL repeatedly during the 1780s, almost certainly to play concerts in Vienna. He was fined, but the Prince, who may have been disposed to give his star performers more leeway than the others, rescinded the penalty. Esterházy musicians also needed the Prince's permission to marry. The unfortunate Johann Hollerieder, fourth horn player, applied for permission in 1778 but was refused and allowed to stay in the orchestra only "on condition that he does not marry but remains single, especially since there are no more quarters available for married persons."[9]

In return for this loss of freedom, members of the Esterházy Kapelle received social benefits that extended in principle from cradle to grave. Besides room, board, candles, firewood, and clothing, instrumentalists had a medical plan: access to a hospital at Eisenstadt, endowed by the Prince and operated by the Barmherzige Brüder, and a hospital on the estate at Eszterháza, with three doctors and a surgeon.[10] When Carl Chorus, an oboist, was ill in 1774, the Prince sent him to take a cure at Baden.[11] Some Esterházy musicians played in the orchestra for only one or two contract periods, that is 2–4 years, then moved on, usually to another Kapelle. But a musician who settled in for the long haul could expect job security for life. If he got old and his playing got rusty, another job might be found for him on the estate, or he might be pensioned off at a portion of his salary.[12] When a musician died, his widow and minor children

---

[7] Soon after his appointment, Schiringer petitioned the Prince for a raise, but his request was denied (Landon, *Haydn: Chronicle and Works*, ii. 78–79). After 10 years of service, Schiringer's salary was raised to 343 Fl. 25 Kr. A Florin was the same as a Gulden, and there were 60 Kreutzer in either a Florin or a Gulden (Bernd Sprenger, *Das Geld der Deutschen* (Paderborn, 1991), 105). János Harich gives an idea of the purchasing power of Austrian currency in 1782. A pound of bread, he says, cost 1 Kreutzer, a pound of beef 4–5 Kreutzers. A suit of clothes cost anywhere from 7 to 45 Gulden, and a coat 14–26 Gulden (Harich, "Fideikommiss," 9–10). For prices of cows, pigs, cheese, rice, and cocoa, see Landon, *Haydn: Chronicle and Works*, ii. 33.

[8] In the 1760s the standard yearly allowance for the Eisenstadt musicians seems to have been 30 lbs. of candles and 6 Klaffter (fathom cords) of firewood (Landon, *Haydn: Chronicle and Works*, i. 317–22).

[9] Harich, "Das Haydn-Orchester," 60–61, 65. [10] Harich, "Fideikommiss," 7.

[11] Landon, *Haydn: Chronicle and Works*, ii. 70.

[12] Joseph Hofmann left the Kapelle after 12 years and became a bookkeeper in the Esterházy establishment; Joseph Purksteiner, after 16 years of service, was given a job as caretaker at Deutschkreuz Castle (Harich, "Das Haydn-Orchester," 60–61). Johann Hinterberger, a bassoonist, retired from the orchestra in 1780 after 17

received the pension. Sometimes the expected benefits failed to materialize, either because an individual musician was dismissed or because the entire Kapelle was dissolved, as it was in 1813, when Prince Nicholas, under the financial pressure of the Napoleonic wars, dismissed all but five members of the orchestra.[13] Offered only six weeks' severance pay and no pensions, the musicians sued. They produced documents the Prince had signed assuring them pensions in exchange for pledges of lifetime service. A settlement was reached with a year's severance pay for most of the musicians.

The musicians of the Esterházy orchestra were recruited from three principal sources. Some, like Nikolaus Kraft, Anton Tomasini, Alois Tomasini, and Antonio Polzelli, were children or relatives of Kapelle members; others, like Joseph, Johann, and Nikolaus Dietzl, came from local families of musicians who lived in the Prince's domains. Probably the largest number came to Eszterháza from other Kapellen. A roster drawn up in 1801 lists the previous employment of each musician. Out of 16 instrumentalists in the by then reduced Kapelle, eight had originally come from other aristocratic Kapellen, including the orchestras or wind bands of Prince Grassalkowitz, Prince-Archbishop Battyanyi, and Count Franz Esterházy.[14]

The salaries of musicians in the Esterházy orchestra, according to payroll records for 1780, ranged from a low of 250 Florins per year (the unfortunate Hollerieder) to 582 Florins (Luigi Tomasini, the concertmaster).[15] The majority of the musicians were paid between 300 and 450 Florins per year. Table 12.1 compares this with salary ranges for other occupations in Vienna and lower Austria at about the same time. The incomes of the Esterházy musicians seem comparable to those of lower-level government bureaucrats. With free room, board, clothing, and other in-kind emoluments, however, Esterházy orchestra musicians probably lived better than teachers and government functionaries at similar salary levels.

Whatever their standard of living, the social status and social aspirations of Esterházy instrumentalists seem to have been rather modest. The personnel list of 1801 notes the languages that Kapelle members speak. Most speak German plus a little Hungarian or Czech. Only Tomasini and his sons speak Italian; only Tomasini Sr. speaks French.[16] There is no sign in the personnel list or elsewhere that any of the musicians had received a liberal education or that any had ever attended a university.

---

years of service, because he was growing deaf. He drew a pension of 250 Gulden per year plus firewood until his death in 1801 (Harich, "Fideikommiss," 22).

[13] Roger Hellyer, "The Wind Ensembles of the Esterházy Princes, 1761–1813," *Haydn Yearbook*, 15 (1984), 5–92 at 16–19, 68 ff. The Prince retained four violinists and a bass player to play church services at Eisenstadt.

[14] Landon, *Haydn: Chronicle and Works*: v. 64–65. Of the rest three (Elssler, Alois Jr., and Anton Tomasini) were children of Esterházy Kapelle members, two (Ernst, Dietzel) came from families of local musicians, two (Düppe, Lendvay) had been playing in Viennese theater orchestras, one (Tomasini Sr.) had been recruited in Italy.

[15] Landon, *Haydn: Chronicle and Works*, ii. 429.

[16] Ibid. v. 65. Haydn is listed as speaking German, French, Italian, and English.

TABLE 12.1. *Wage levels in Vienna and Lower Austria, c.1780*

Occupation	Salary or wage	Income in kind?
Esterházy Kapelle	300–450 Florins / yr.	yes
Construction laborer (Vienna)	15 Kreutzers / day 75 Fl. / yr.	no
Porcelain factory: laborer (Vienna)	15 Kreutzers / day 75 Fl. / yr.	no
Porcelain factory: skilled worker (Vienna)	100–300 Fl. / yr.	no
Coachman	20 Fl. / yr.	yes
Maidservant	16–20 Fl. / yr.	yes
Tutor	50 Fl. / yr.	yes
Elementary school teacher	120–250 Fl. / yr.	no
Secondary school teacher	400 Fl. / yr.	no
Government servant (*Amtsdiener*)	300–500 Fl. / yr.	no
Government clerk (*Kanzlist*)	400–900 Fl. / yr.	no
Government official (*Hofsekretär*)	1,500–2,000 Fl. / yr.	no

Source: Figures compiled from Sandgruber, "Wirtschaftsentwicklung."

Their children did not get such an education either and did not tend to go into the professions. By and large the children of Esterházy orchestra musicians became musicians in their turn or employees on the Esterházy estate.

Nor were the manners of Esterházy orchestra musicians always exemplary. Records from 1771 describe a brawl between Marteau, a cellist, and Pohl, an oboist, in which Pohl lost an eye. A court deposition by the bassoonist Hinterberger, who witnessed the fight, tells the story in detail:

Witness arrived on the 23rd of June in the Eszterháza tavern with his wife, the Italian singer [Gertruda] Cellini, and the cellist Xavier Marteau to enjoy a glass of wine. . . . Meanwhile the oboist Pohl came over, picked up the dice, and invited Marteau to play. Marteau at first did not want to but then agreed, and they played, witness thinks, for a jug of wine, which Pohl won. They continued to play, and after Pohl had lost about a gulden, witness suggested to him that he should stop. Pohl, however, gestured to witness that this wasn't any of his business and began to curse, whereupon witness left. He had hardly reached the door when he heard a noise, and Cellini led him back, saying that Pohl and Marteau were fighting. When witness re-entered the room, some grenadiers . . . had separated the two. Marteau went upstairs with Cellini, while witness asked the landlady to apply compresses to Pohl; but when he examined [Pohl] more closely, he saw that the eye was very badly injured . . . [Witness] closed his testimony with the statement that Pohl was a gambler and used to curse and abuse people frequently.[17]

An investigation determined that Pohl's eye had been put out by a large ring that Marteau wore on his left hand but that Marteau had not meant to injure Pohl. Marteau had to pay Pohl's medical expenses, and both players remained in the orchestra. Mayhem at this level was not typical in the Esterházy orchestra, although accounts of other quarrels do turn up in the records.[18]

Haydn's orchestra at Eszterháza provides an example of the Kapelle model of orchestral organization in an almost pure, archetypal form. Orchestra musicians contracted not only their services but their entire persons to the Prince. They had no other jobs; they served no other master. In return, the Prince took responsibility for the welfare of each musician and (when the musician was permitted to marry) for the musician's entire family. The instrumentalists had no independent existence as an orchestra; along with singers and the church musicians, they formed part of the Prince's household. Their wages were paid by the year, and much of their salary was paid not in cash but in kind—clothing, lodging, food, and social services. Over the course of Haydn's service at Eszterháza somewhat more flexibility developed in the system. Contracts written in the 1780s tended to put fewer extra-musical demands on the players; and they tended to pay salaries more in cash and less in kind. The system remained thoroughly paternalistic, however, and in this as in many operational details it resembled most Kapellen, not only in Germany and Austria but in other countries as well.

THE LONDON MARKETPLACE

The life of an orchestra musician in London in the second half of the eighteenth century can be described by a model that is almost the opposite of the Kapelle model at Eszterháza. In this "free market" model the instrumentalist sells his labor, not his person. Music and music performance are commodities; patrons are consumers. A free market for the services of orchestra musicians was possible because of the great broadening of patronage that took place in eighteenth-century England, part of the process that J. H. Plumb calls "the commercialisation of leisure" (see Ch. 8). Compared with other European cities, London—then the largest city in Europe—had more patrons, more orchestras, and more instrumentalists. Instead of working for

---

[17] "Acta Musicalia of the Esterházy Archives (Nos. 175–200)," *Haydn Yearbook*, 17 (1992), 1–84 at 31, 39.

[18] In 1776 newly engaged bassoonist Joseph Purcksteiner complained in a petition to the Prince that horn player Franz Steinmetz had insulted him and boxed his ears (Landon, *Haydn: Chronicle and Works*, i. 32). In 1771 cellists Ignaz Küffl and Joseph Weigl engaged in a shouting match in front of the orchestra over the issue of which man would sit next to the cembalo player and accompany the opera recitatives ("Acta Musicalia," 22–23).

a single patron as in the Kapelle system, an orchestra musician in London sold his services to many patrons, and instead of being a member of a single musical establishment, he typically played in several orchestras in several venues.

The career of John Parke (1745–1829), an oboist, provides an example of how one of London's top orchestra musicians made his living.[19] As a 20-year-old virtuoso, Parke played in the orchestras at London's pleasure gardens: three nights a week at Ranelagh, another three nights at Marylebone. During Lent he played for oratorios at Drury Lane. In 1771 Parke took a job at Vauxhall Gardens, eliminating the commute between Marylebone and Ranelagh.[20] Also in 1771 he was engaged as first oboist for the theater year-round at Drury Lane, where he was paid considerably more than the other wind players. Parke soon became a member of the Prince of Wales' private orchestra and eventually of the King's Band of Musick, which performed only infrequently but which paid a salary of £200 per year. He was also a member of the Professional Concert and the Concert of Ancient Music, each of which gave weekly concerts during the winter season. In the summer Parke played at the provincial music festivals. Very likely his obligations as a member of at least six different orchestras sometimes overlapped, and presumably he solved these conflicts by sending a deputy.[21] All this work provided Parke with a good income, and he lived, as Sainsbury puts it in the *Dictionary of Musicians* (1825), "prudently though respectably" in a house that he owned in the fashionable district of Soho. His daughter became a singer, his son a successful architect. Sainsbury also notes that Parke was a close friend of David Garrick, the great actor who managed Drury Lane, and a friend as well of the Duke of Cumberland, brother of King George III, who frequently invited Parke to stay at Windsor Lodge and occasionally visited the oboist's home.[22]

Parke represented the elite of London's orchestra musicians, but the structure of his livelihood was typical. Campbell's *London Tradesman*, a career guide published in 1747, while complaining that music "effeminates the Mind," and "enervates the more Manly Faculties," acknowledged that an instrumentalist could make a decent living:

If a Parent cannot make his Son a Gentleman, and finds, that he has got an Itch of Music, it is much the best Way to allot him entirely to that Study. The present general Taste of Music in the Gentry may find him better Bread than what perhaps this Art deserves. The Gardens in the Summer Time employ a great Number of Hands; where they are allowed a Guinea a Week

---

[19] Parke's biography has been pieced together from John S. Sainsbury, *A Dictionary of Musicians from the Earliest Times* (London, 1824), 263–64, and Highfill et al., *A Biographical Dictionary*, xi. 199–200.

[20] In Rowlandson's painting of the Vauxhall orchestra (Fig. 8.2) John Parke is the musician to the left of the pillar in the front row.

[21] Ehrlich gives examples of the deputy system and its abuses in the 19th c. (Cyril Ehrlich, *The Music Profession in Britain since the Eighteenth Century: A Social History* (Oxford, 1985)).

[22] Sainsbury, *Dictionary of Musicians*, 263.

and upwards, according to their Merit. The Opera, the Play-Houses, Masquerades, Ridottoes and the several Music-Clubs, employ them in the Winter.[23]

The key was to hold down several jobs simultaneously in the London musical marketplace.[24] The schedules of the theaters and the pleasure gardens were coordinated by alternating nights or alternating seasons, and a good performer could play in at least two standing orchestras and sometimes more. On nights when he was not engaged in the theater or at a pleasure garden, the instrumentalist could play at concerts. The subscription concerts, like the Bach–Abel series or the Professional Concerts, maintained standing orchestras that shared personnel with the theater orchestras. "Benefit" concerts usually assembled a pickup orchestra for the event, although sometimes an entire theater orchestra was contracted as a unit.[25]

A few London orchestras were set up as private music establishments, like Continental Kapellen. Instrumentalists gained positions in these orchestras by appointment, usually on the basis of personal or political connections. Unlike Continental Kapellen, such appointments were not exclusive: the musician could hold as many other jobs as he liked. The Queen and the Prince of Wales intermittently maintained orchestras on this basis. A position in the King's Band of Musick was especially desirable, because the performance demands were minimal and the appointment was for life. In addition many orchestra musicians, whatever their primary instrument, held posts as organists at parish churches. Besides income from performing, a London instrumentalist earned money by teaching. His students might be young men who aspired to become professional musicians, but there was more money to be made giving lessons to the nobility, the gentry, and their children, who pursued music as an avocation and a social grace. Violinists and wind players often gave keyboard or singing lessons, because the demand for these skills was greater than for most orchestral instruments (except for the flute).

Besides performing and teaching, many orchestra musicians supplemented their incomes with non-musical or para-musical enterprises of various sorts. Giovanni Carbonnelli, for example, a violinist and Corelli pupil who immigrated to London in 1719 and led the orchestra at Drury Lane, became a successful wine merchant. Lewis August Lavenu, violinist at Covent Garden and the King's Theatre, started a music-publishing business in the 1790s, which survived until the 1840s under the proprietorship of his wife and son. Samuel Lyon, a violist and cellist at Drury Lane, ran a shop where he sold pianos and music that he published himself. James Oswald, who

---

[23] R. Campbell, *The London Tradesman* (London, 1747), 89, 93.

[24] See Rohr, *The Careers of British Musicians*, 120.

[25] "Benefit" concerts were organized by individual musicians for their own benefit. The musician rented the hall, hired the orchestra, printed announcements, sold tickets, paid for the candles, etc. Whatever was left of the receipts after the overhead was paid became his "benefit." Instrumentalists often played for free at benefit concerts, either out of friendship or in the expectation that the favor would be returned some day.

played cello intermittently at the Drury Lane Theatre, did a brisk business arranging and publishing Scotch tunes, which he sold from a shop in St. Martin's Lane. Oswald also produced an English version of Pergolesi's *Serva padrona* in 1758 at Marylebone Gardens and the next year at the Little Theatre in the Haymarket. When he died in 1768, Oswald left his heirs £2,000 in investments plus real estate and personal property.[26]

Not all instrumentalists made successful entrepreneurs. Thomas Vincent, oboist at Drury Lane and Covent Garden and a member of the King's Band, "had acquired a considerable sum of money in his profession, which he augmented by marriage."[27] Along with two partners he undertook the management of the opera at the King's Theatre in 1764, but in five years he had lost so much money that he had to assign his income from his Royal appointments to his creditors. English musicians seem to have had a strong penchant for free enterprise compared with their Continental cousins. Perhaps this was because it was easier to initiate a business in England than on the Continent, perhaps because English musicians moved in broader social circles and had more access to capital.

The apprenticeship system, regulated by statutes dating from the early sixteenth century, remained in force in eighteenth-century London, and a few instrumentalists were still articled to a master musician for seven years before becoming independent professionals.[28] Charles Burney, for example, was apprenticed at age 18 to Thomas Arne, composer and keyboardist at Drury Lane. Since Burney's father had little money, Arne waived the initial £100 fee. Burney played violin and viola in the Drury Lane orchestra, turning his wages of 5s. per night over to Arne. He also spent endless hours copying out Arne's compositions and bitterly resenting his "avaricious, selfish, sordid, and tyrannical" master.[29] Burney was rescued by a patron, Fulke Greville, who bought out the last three years of his apprenticeship for £300 and helped launch him on a career as a fashionable music teacher, critic, and author. John Parke had at least one apprentice: his brother William, who became an equally famous oboist and author of a set of *Musical Memoirs*.[30] As a means of recruiting and training orchestra musicians in London, however, the apprenticeship system had become obsolete. As another career manual, Collyer's *Parent's and Guardian's Directory*, recognized, "The youth in learning this science, is not to be put apprentice, but to attend different

---

[26] Highfill et al., *Biographical Dictionary*, iii. 54–55; ix. 167, 389–90; xi. 122–24.

[27] Burney, *A General History of Music*, ed. Mercer, 870. Vincent, who was apparently a favorite of the Prince of Wales, also held an appointment as "Barber to His Majesty" (Highfill et al., *Biographical Dictionary*, xv. 177).

[28] See Rohr, *The Careers of British Musicians*, 68–71.

[29] Charles Burney, *Memoirs of Dr. Charles Burney, 1726–1769*, ed. Slava Klima, Garry Bowers, and Kerry S. Grant (Lincoln, Nebr., 1988), 43–44, 50, 81.

[30] Highfill et al., *Biographical Dictionary*, xi. 201; William T. Parke, *Musical Memoirs* (London, 1830). Other examples of London instrumentalists who served full or partial apprenticeships include James Graves and John Hindmarsh (See Highfill et al., *Biographical Dictionary*). Musical apprenticeships were somewhat more common in provincial towns than in London.

masters at the practice."[31] The initial fees were too high, and the level of training was too low. Most of all there was too much demand in London for orchestra musicians. Why should a young musician spend seven long years as an apprentice when the pleasure gardens, the theaters, and the concert societies were begging for players? Nor did a young instrumentalist need to play for years without pay as a trainee, the standard practice in Continental Kapellen. If he was good enough to play, he was good enough to get paid, albeit at an entry-level wage.

The shortage of instrumentalists and the lack of training for English musicians were recognized in the eighteenth century, and several schemes were proposed to remedy the situation. Daniel Defoe, the novelist and pamphleteer, suggested in 1728 that an "Academy of Musick" be established at Christ's Hospital.[32] From the students at the charity school there, thirty boys would be selected with "good Ears and Propensity to Musick"—six for "Wind-Instruments, such as the Hautboy, Bassoon, and German-Flute," sixteen for "String-Instruments, or at least the most useful, *viz.* the Violin and Bass-Violin," and eight singers. In ten years, Defoe reasoned, "we shall find an Orchestre of forty Hands, and a Choir or Opera of twenty Voices." John Potter in his *Observations on the Present State of Music and Musicians* (1762) proposed a plan for a "Musical Academy," so that "vacancies . . . at churches, or in the bands at the playhouses or any other public places . . . will be sure to be filled by persons of genius and great abilities."[33] In 1774 Charles Burney and Felice Giardini suggested to the Governors of the Foundling Hospital that they should establish a "Public Music School in England After the Manner of an Italian Conservatorio" for both boys and girls.[34] They offered themselves as "superintending Masters" at salaries £200 apiece "for life." Although the need was obvious, no music school was established in England until the Royal Academy of Music in 1823.

The shortfall of orchestra musicians was made up to a great extent by immigration from abroad. The King's Band was closed to foreigners by the Settlement Act of 1701, but all other orchestras were open to immigrants, and the free market for musical labor in London meant that an immigrant did not have to have a job in hand when he arrived but could begin playing in one or two orchestras and put together a living as he went along. This musical immigration—of singers as well as instrumentalists—aroused considerable hostility on the part of English musicians and English audiences.

---

[31] Joseph Collyer, *The Parent's and Guardian's Directory and the Youth's Guide in the Choice of a Profession or Trade* (London, 1761), 198–99. Quoted in Ehrlich, *Music Profession*, 9.

[32] Brian Trowell, "Daniel Defoe's Plan for an Academy of Music at Christ's Hospital, with some Notes on his Attitude to Music," in Ian Bent (ed.), *Source Materials and the Interpretation of Music: A Memorial Volume to Thurston Dart* (London, 1981), 403–27.

[33] Potter, *Observations*, 100. Potter proposed that his Academy should act as a kind of musical censor—that the masters should have authority to review all music submitted for publication "and to make such alterations and corrections as they should think necessary, without which . . . no music should be suffered to be printed" (ibid. 101).

[34] Jamie Croy Kassler, "Burney's Sketch of a Plan for a Public Music School," *MQ* 58 (1972), 210–34.

TABLE 12.2. *Native vs. foreign instrumentalists in English orchestras, 1754–93*

Date and venue	Players in orchestra	Foreign born	Born in England	Undetermined	Source
1754: Founding Hospital (*Messiah*)	38	6 (16%)	30 (80%)	2 (4%)	Deutsch, *Handel*, 751
1760: Covent Garden	19	2 (11%)	14 (74%)	3 (15%)	*London Stage*, iv/2. 815
1778: Drury Lane	23	2 (9%)	20 (87%)	1 (4%)	*London Stage*, v/1. 194
1782: King's Theatre	34	14 (41%)	19 (56%)	1 (3%)	Price et al., *Italian Opera*, 286
1785: Professional Concert	31	17 (55%)	13 (42%)	1 (3%)	McVeigh, "Professional Concert," 40
1787: Concert of Ancient Music	40	2 (5%)	30 (75%)	8 (20%)	MS in US–Wc [ML 28 L8 A2]
1788: Professional Concert	31	12 (39%)	19 (61%)	—	McVeigh, "Professional Concert," 65
1790: Pantheon (opera)	39	15 (38%)	23 (60%)	1 (2%)	Milhous et al., *Italian Opera*, 424–25
1793: Professional Concert	36	7 (19%)	29 (81%)	—	McVeigh, "Professional Concert," 114–15

One of Defoe's primary arguments for establishing an Academy was that the free market for music had resulted in "over-loading the Town with . . . heaps of Foreign Musicians."[35] Potter claimed that his Musical Academy would injure no one "except a few Italian singers, and French dancers, who run away with what is strictly due to our own countrymen."[36]

The number of foreign instrumentalists in English orchestras does not seem to have been as high in actual fact, however, as it was in public perception.[37] Table 12.2 shows the percentages of foreign vs. native-born musicians in selected orchestras during the second half of the eighteenth century.[38] Only at the Professional Concert in 1785 did foreigners make up more than half of the orchestra. And that was not for long: by 1793 the Professional Concert too had transformed itself into an orchestra made up predominantly of native-born musicians. The opera orchestras at the King's Theatre and the Pantheon had substantial percentages of foreigners, but the orchestras at Covent Garden and Drury Lane were overwhelmingly native-born, as were the oratorio orchestras at the Foundling Hospital.[39] Compared with Continental Kapellen, the percentage of foreigners in English orchestras does not seem particularly high. In the Esterházy Kapelle in 1780 about 40 percent of the instrumentalists were foreign born.[40] It also depends on who is considered "foreign." If German Kapellen or Italian opera orchestras are tabulated so that only people born in that state or principality are considered "natives," then the percentage of "foreigners" at Eszterháza or Mannheim or the Venetian theaters rises above that of any of the London orchestras. The perception that English orchestras in the eighteenth century were being overrun by heaps of foreign musicians resulted more from English insularity and xenophobia than from actual immigration.

Because of short supply and high demand, wages for orchestra musicians in London tended to be relatively high during the second half of the eighteenth century. Table 12.3 shows wage scales for a few London orchestras whose pay records have been preserved. The entry-level wage seems to have been 5 to 8s. per night and the mean wage around 10s. sixpence (half a guinea). Top performers received over £1 per night.[41] Covent Garden paid its orchestra (and also its actors) considerably less than the other theaters. Remarks by contemporaries confirm the figures in Table 12.3. Burney says he made 5s. per night as a supernumerary at Drury Lane in 1744.

[35] Quoted in Trowell, "Daniel Defoe's Plan," 408.

[36] Potter, *Observations*, 104.

[37] See Simon McVeigh, "Italian Violinists in Eighteenth-Century London," in Reinhard Strohm (ed.), *The Eighteenth-Century Diaspora of Italian Music and Musicians* (Turnhout, 2001), 139–76 at 152.

[38] Table 12.2 was compiled by collating paylists of the orchestras with various biographical sources, especially Highfill et al., *Biographical Dictionary*.

[39] Earlier opera orchestras at the King's Theatre had higher percentages of foreigners: 56% in 1708, 45% for the Academy of Music in 1720. See Milhous and Hume, *Vice Chamberlain Coke's Theatrical Papers*, 78–79; Milhous and Hume, "New Light on Handel,"158.

[40] Landon, *Haydn: Chronicle and Works*, ii. 429.

[41] The salaries of violinist leaders have been excluded from Table 12.3. They were yet higher.

TABLE 12.3. *Wage scales (per service) in English orchestras, 1708–1818*

Date and venue	High wage[a]	Intermediate wage	Low wage	Source
1708: Haymarket Theatre	£1 5s.	10–15s.	8s.	Milhous and Hume, *Coke's Theatrical Papers*, 78–79
1754: Foundling Hospital	15s.	10s. 6d.	8s.	Deutsch, *Handel*, 751
1760: Covent Garden	6s. 8d.	5s.	3s. 4d.	*London Stage*, iv/2. 815
1778: Drury Lane	£1 3s.	10–16s.	8s.	*London Stage*, v/1. 194
1787: Concert of Ancient Music	1 G.	10–15s.	5s. 4d.	MS in US-Wc [ML 28 L8 A2]
1790: Pantheon opera	£1 3s.	15s.	10s. 6d.	Milhous et al., *Italian Opera*, 692–93
1818: Covent Garden	14s.	6s. 8d.	5s. 10d.	Rohr, *Careers*, 123

[a] Excluding violin leader.

Leopold Mozart comments in a letter of 1764 from London that "the ordinary players" in a London orchestra received "half a guinea" per night.[42] Charles Wesley's
account books show him paying half a guinea each to the string players at the small
subscription concerts he gave at his home in the 1780s.[43] George Smart received half
a guinea per night as a violist at the Salomon concerts in 1794.[44] Thus the standard
wage for a London orchestra musician seems to have been half a guinea (10*s*. 6*d*.), and
this wage seems to have remained stable for most of the century, until the inflation of
the Napoleonic wars.[45] During that same period an unskilled laborer in London
earned 1*s*. to 1*s*. 8*d*. per day, a skilled laborer around 2*s*. per day, and a highly skilled
worker (e.g. a typesetter) 3*s*. per day.[46] Compared with wages like these, orchestra
musicians were strikingly well paid.[47]

A London musician's wages, however, did not include any social benefits. Unlike
the paternalistic German Kapellen, English theaters and concert impresarios did not
feed, clothe, or house their musicians, and they felt no obligation to provide for the
players in sickness or old age. In a free-market system orchestra musicians were
obliged to look after their own social welfare. To this end the "Fund for the Support
of Decayed Musicians or their Families" (later the Royal Society of Musicians) was
founded in 1738.[48] Members paid an annual subscription of 10*s*. per year, later 20*s*. In
addition they raised money by giving benefit concerts. The "Grand Musical Festival"
at Westminster Abbey in commemoration of the centenary of Handel's birth was
such a benefit: it raised £6,000 for the Society.[49] Money raised by subscriptions and
benefits was invested at interest. A decrepit or destitute musician or his widow and
children applied to the Society for benefits, presenting a certificate signed by ten
other members stating that he was a "proper object" for relief. If the petition was
approved, he or his family drew benefits according to a fixed schedule.[50] The
Society's Board of Governors monitored cases to guard against welfare fraud—for

[42] Letter of 8 June 1764, in Mozart, *Briefe*, i. 153. For Wolfgang and Nannerl's benefit, however, most of
the performers played gratis.

[43] McLamore, "Symphonic Conventions," 188.

[44] George Smart, *Leaves from the Journals of Sir George Smart*, ed. H. Bertram Cox and C. L. E. Cox (London,
1907), 3.

[45] McVeigh gives "one guinea per night" as the standard rate at London concerts in the late 18th c. ("The
Professional Concert," 7). However, most of his examples are of ½ guinea wages.

[46] Rudé, *Hanoverian London*, 88.

[47] Adam Smith, the economist, was puzzled by the high wages paid to "players, opera-singers, opera-
dancers &c," compared with other professions that required a similar level of training. He attributed the anom-
aly to the public prejudice against musical occupations, which prevented many people from taking them up
(Adam Smith, *An Inquiry into the Nature and Causes of the Wealth of Nations* (1776), ed. R. H. Campbell and
A. S. Skinner (Oxford, 1976), 124).

[48] Pippa Drummond, "The Royal Society of Musicians in the Eighteenth Century," *M & L* 59 (1978),
268–89. Originally members of the Royal Society had to be practicing musicians, recommended by 10 other
members. By the middle of the 18th c., however, this requirement had been relaxed, and many people subscribed as a way of obtaining tickets to the Society's benefit concerts.

[49] Ibid. 279.

[50] Ibid. 271. Men without dependents received 10*s*. per week benefits; widows received 7*s*. per week.

example a musician who moonlighted or a widow who remarried. The records of the Society show that the system functioned vigorously and successfully during the entire second half of the eighteenth century. Musicians were supported in their old age, their children educated, their medical bills and their funerals paid, and their widows taken care of.

Free enterprise and welfare schemes notwithstanding, many London instrumentalists led lives that were marginal both financially and socially. A survey of life stories in Highfill's *Biographical Dictionary* turns up scores of musicians who went to prison for debt, who emigrated to America, or who were forced to turn to the Royal Society for relief.[51] To Friedrich August Wendeborn, a German clergyman who lived in London, it seemed as though the standard of living of English musicians, and particularly of immigrants, was falling at the end of the eighteenth century:

Those who are musicians by profession, and who earn part of their livelihood by teaching, have seen formerly, as it is said, better times than at present. I have heard of some receiving a guinea or half a guinea for a lesson, who now, perhaps must be content with five shillings. . . . Several of the principal German and Italian musicians in London, I have known to live in a most deranged state of their finances: they were involved in debt, and died wretchedly poor.[52]

Nevertheless London offered an orchestra musician possibilities for social status considerably above anything available to the member of a German Kapelle. Because their incomes were relatively high and because their work brought them into many different social settings, English orchestra musicians operated in a wider world than their German counterparts. Additionally, London social circles, while hardly egalitarian, were more mixed than anything on the Continent. William Parke in his *Memoirs* regales the reader with anecdote after anecdote in which London's orchestra musicians eat, drink, play music, hunt, and otherwise socialize with members of the gentry and the nobility. Such social mixing was a form of patronage less direct than ticket purchase or subscription: the patron supported the musician by providing access to students, employers, financial advisers, and subscribers.[53] At the same time an orchestra musician who had sufficient income to keep up appearances and sufficient education to keep up conversation could take advantage of this mixed society to effect a lasting improvement in his social status and the status of his family and heirs.

---

[51] Highfill et al., *Biographical Dictionary, passim*; Rohr, *The Careers of British Musicians*, 157 ff.
[52] Friedrich August Wendeborn, *A View of England towards the Close of the 18th Century* (Dublin, 1791), 174.
[53] See McVeigh, "Italian Violinists," 153, 160–61.

EMILIA-ROMAGNA: A REGIONAL MARKET FOR MUSICIANS

The Italian region of Emilia-Romagna provides an example of a free-market system in a less metropolitan setting. The market in this case operated not just within one city but connected several cities and towns in a regional network.[54]

Emilia-Romagna refers to an area of north central Italy, bounded on the north by the Po river, on the east by the Adriatic. It includes the cities of Piacenza, Parma, Reggio Emilia, Modena, Bologna, Ferrara, and Ravenna, as well as many smaller towns. In the eighteenth century the region was divided between the duchies of Parma and of Modena in the west and the Papal States in the east. Parma and Modena had court capellas that in many respects resembled the Esterházy Kapelle. The city of Bologna, which belonged to the Papal States, maintained an orchestra at the cathedral of San Petronio as well as a civic band, the Concerto Palatino.

In the other cities and towns of Emilia-Romagna orchestras were not standing institutions. The instrumentalists in town constituted a pool from which orchestras were assembled as needed—for an opera, for church services, for religious festivals, for academies and other concerts, for civic celebrations. Pay records from Ravenna churches during the 1790s demonstrate how the system worked.[55] For a festival at one church, a festive mass at another, and a funeral at a third, three distinct orchestras were assembled. However, the size and composition of the orchestras were almost identical—six or seven violins, one viola, one to two cellos, two or one basses, and two horns—and more or less the same instrumentalists played at all three functions. An impresario who wanted to put together an opera orchestra in Ravenna in the 1790s would presumably have used most of the same players. This kind of stable pick-up orchestra, assembled and reassembled year after year, at different venues for various events, is typical of the cities and towns of Emilia-Romagna in the eighteenth century; indeed it was typical of much of Italy. Corelli's orchestras in Rome already operated this way in the late seventeenth century (see Ch. 4).

Although there was no standing orchestra in most cities or towns, instrumentalists often organized themselves into a guild or syndicate of players. In Piacenza a "Università dei Filarmonici" was set up in 1781. Its members were 21 "professori di suono," playing violin, viola, cello, bass, oboe, horn, and organ, plus six "aggregati," who worked at other occupations but played instruments on the side. The "aggregati" included two barbers who played the violin, a glazier and another barber on bass, and a wigmaker and a gold-leaf worker, both of whom played horn. The Filarmonici claimed to include "all performers of music without exception" who

---

[54] We were able to choose this example because of an excellent collection of studies, *Orchestre in Emilia-Romagna nell'Ottocento e Novecento*, edited by Marcello Conati and Marcello Pavarani (Parma, 1982). "Emilia-Romagna" is a recent term; the region had no single name in the 18th c.

[55] Paolo Fabbri, "Le orchestre ravennati," in Conati and Pavarani (eds.), *Orchestre in Emilia-Romagna*, 419–40 at 420–22.

played in the churches or theaters of Piacenza.[56] The "university" maintained a fund for medical expenses, and it paid surviving widows and children based on the amount that the musician had paid into the fund during his lifetime.

In Imola, a small town southeast of Bologna, musicians created a similar organization, calling it initially a "corpo della musica," then, from 1803 on, the "Società dei Filarmonici." The organization monitored the employment and working conditions of instrumentalists in the town and took up cases of members who felt they had been unfairly passed over for employment.[57] In 1804 the Society prevailed upon the town council to instruct opera impresarios who came to Imola to hire players exclusively from the ranks of the "Filarmonici." The singers and instrumentalists of Ravenna, referring to themselves in 1768 as "the body of musicians, in effect the *cappella*, of this city" (*il corpo di musica o sia della capella di questa città*), drew up a table that prescribed pay rates for each of the various musical jobs in town. Wages ranged from 40 denari per service for the *maestro di cappella* to 25 denari for the first violinist to 20 denari for the cellist to 10 denari for the violist.[58] The "corpo di musica" also drafted a list of rules for its members: if they take a job, they must show up for work; if they want to send a substitute, the substitute must be approved by the maestro; they must play whatever music is set before them. It is not clear how long organizations like Piacenza's "Università," Imola's "Società dei Filarmonici," and Ravenna's "corpo di musica" survived or to what extent they succeeded in achieving their wage scales or enforcing their rules. In effect they were trying to take on the attributes and functions of a guild in a free-market environment.

In most of the cities and towns of Emilia-Romagna in the late eighteenth century the "corpus" of local instrumentalists provided enough players for day-to-day functions like church services. For the opera season, however, and for special gala events these instrumental forces were inadequate, and musicians had to be recruited from out of town. During most of the eighteenth century there was vigorous traffic of instrumentalists among the towns of Emilia-Romagna—in effect, a regional labor market. Instead of all the operas being given at the same time of year, opera seasons in neighboring towns were staggered, so that instrumentalists—as well as singers and dancers—could play the season in one town, then in the next town and the next. Piacenza, Parma, and Modena had their opera seasons at Carnival. Meanwhile Bologna, Ferrara, and Ravenna celebrated carnival with opera buffa, which used smaller orchestras, fewer singers, and modest sets. Smaller country towns did not attempt any theater whatever at Carnival time. They had their principal opera season either in the summer (Carpi, Lugo, Imola, Faenza) or in the fall (Mirandola,

---

[56] Dante Rabitti, "Orchestre e istituzioni musicali piacentine," in Conati and Pavarani (eds.), *Orchestre in Emilia-Romagna*, 37–60 at 38–40.

[57] Stefano Suzzi, "L'orchestra nella vita di una città di provincia: una prima ricognizione," in *Orchestre in Emilia-Romagna*, 393–418 at 397, 409.

[58] Fabbri, "Le orchestre ravennati," 419–20.

Correggio). Thus patrons who owned both palaces in town and country villas were provided with entertainment during both winter and summer.[59] Bologna had its big opera season in the fall; Reggio Emilia, Ferrara, and Ravenna held theirs in the spring (i.e. May and June).

This system of offset seasons resembled the scheduling of London's concerts, theaters, and pleasure gardens extended over an entire region. By the late eighteenth century impresarios were moving whole productions from one town to another. For example, the troupe that played for the June fair in Reggio often moved to Senigallia for the fair in July.[60] A certain number of instrumentalists went along with the singers and the sets; the rest were recruited in Senigallia. The system is documented by libretti from opera productions, which list first-chair instrumentalists and note their place of origin. At Reggio Emilia in the 1780s the first-chair men came from Modena, Parma, and Bologna, with the same players returning year after year.[61] Players in lower positions are not listed; they were presumably local residents. Rossini's father, a horn player, traveled around Emilia-Romagna along with a handful of instrumentalists from local towns (Lugo, Imola, Forlì) playing for the operas in one season after another.[62]

For special events instrumentalists were recruited from far and wide. For example, when the Teatro Comunale in Bologna opened in 1763 with Gluck's *Trionfo di Clelia*, the concertmaster was brought from Milan, along with six more violinists; two violinists were imported from Cremona; two horns were hired from Parma.[63] For the opening of the Teatro Comunale in Ferrara in 1798, Alessandro Rolla was brought from Parma as first violin, along with "altri professori esteri e ferraresi."[64] This rubric is typical. "Professori esteri" and "suonatori forestieri" appear in opera libretti and pay lists for gala events as well as for regular operas in almost every theater in Emilia-Romagna from the middle of the eighteenth century until well into the nineteenth.

As in London, these foreign orchestra musicians, usually in the first chairs, provoked a certain amount of resentment from local instrumentalists. Their participation was customary and necessary, and there never seems to have been a movement in any city to exclude them. But associations and societies of orchestra musicians tried to guarantee that locals got their fair share. Two local hornists in Imola, both of them

[59] We thank Emmanuele Senici for this insight.

[60] Adriano Cavicchi, "Musica e melodramma nei secoli XVI–XVIII," in Servio Romagnoli and Elvira Garbero (eds.), *Teatro a Reggio Emilia* (Florence, 1980), 97–134 at 130. Senigallia is not in Emilia-Romagna but in the neighboring Marches, on the Adriatic coast south of Ravenna.

[61] Paolo Fabbri and Roberto Verti, *Due secoli di teatro per musica a Reggio Emilia: repertorio cronologico delle opere e dei balli 1645–1857* (Reggio Emilia, 1986), 104 ff.

[62] Paolo Fabbri, "I Rossini, una famiglia in arte," *Bollettino del Centro Rossiniano di Studi*, 23 (1983), 125–50; Fabbri, "Le orchestre ravennati," 423; Alexis Azevedo, *G. Rossini: sa vie et ses œuvres* (Paris, 1864), 33.

[63] Ricci, *Teatri*, 614.

[64] Paolo Natali and Gianni Stefanati, "Le presenze orchestrali a Ferrara dalla fine del Settecento al Novecento," in Conati and Pavarani (eds.), *Orchestre in Emilia-Romagna*, 287–324 at 299. Rolla later played first violin at La Scala in Milan.

porters by trade, complained in a letter to the civic authorities in 1803 that they had been excluded from the opera orchestra in favor of a foreigner, Giuseppe Rossini (father of Gioacchino), and Antonio Giustiani, a beginner on the instrument.[65] Their complaint was apparently heeded, because the impresario's contract for the next year obliged him to use local musicians, and the charter of the theater in 1811 specified that "the professors of our community ought to have preference."[66] Similarly, a contract in Parma declared in 1807 that "professors of the local orchestra will be given preference over foreigners, except in cases where the former are not content with the contractual salary."[67] The "corpo di musica" in Ravenna took a different approach: their rules stipulated that when out-of-towners were brought in, the wages of local players should be doubled.[68]

Besides visiting professionals and local semi-professionals, like the barbers and the wigmaker in Piacenza, orchestras in Emilia-Romagna were filled out with dilettantes. At the Carnival opera in Carpi in 1778, for example, the singers were professionals from out of town, but the entire orchestra was composed of local amateurs.[69] Dilettantes seem to have played a particularly important role in Ravenna. They received instruction from the local "professori" in violin, cello, flute, keyboards, and winds. According to one report (perhaps apocryphal) a performance in Ravenna of a mass by the young Rossini in 1808 attracted so many amateurs that 11 flutes, seven clarinets, five oboes, and nine bassoonists showed up for the first rehearsal.[70]

The underlying problem, again, was a shortage of orchestra musicians. Even the large cities in Emilia-Romagna did not have enough resident instrumentalists to put together a really big orchestra, particularly not in the late eighteenth and early nineteenth century, as musical styles required larger string sections and a greater variety of winds.[71] Small cities and towns like Piacenza and Imola could not come close. A regional network of instrumentalists was a time-honored and viable solution to the problem.

Other regions of Italy may have had similar networks. John Rosselli proposes that the world of Italian opera in the eighteenth century was divided into a number of "regional circuits" or "zones."[72] For singers and composers these zones were rela-

---

[65] Fabbri, "I Rossini," 134–35.

[66] Suzzi, "L'orchestra nella vita," 398. Despite opposition from local musicians, Giuseppe Rossini turned up once again as first horn on the Imola payroll for 1804. The second horn was one of the porters who had complained in 1803.

[67] Gian Paolo Minardi, "L'orchestra a Parma: un prestigio europeo e il suo progressivo declino," in Conati and Pavarani (eds.), *Orchestre in Emilia-Romagna*, 75–144 at 79.

[68] Fabbri, "Le orchestre ravennati," 420.

[69] Mario Bizzoccoli, "Una volontà per una tradizione," in Conati and Pavarani (eds.), *Orchestre in Emilia-Romagna*, 275–84 at 275.

[70] Azevedo, *Rossini*, 49–50.

[71] The one exception may have been Parma, where the court under Marie Louise, Duchess of Parma (r. 1816–47) maintained a large court orchestra.

[72] John Rosselli, "Geografia politica del teatro d'opera nell'Emilia Romagna del tardo Settecento," in Susi Davoli (ed.), *Civiltà teatrale e Settecento emiliano* (Reggio Emilia, 1986), 335–41.

TABLE 12.4. *Wage scales (per service) for orchestras in Emilia-Romagna, 1752–1821*

City	Date	Venue	High wage[a]	Middle wage	Low wage	Source
Bologna	1763	Teatro Comunale		3 lire		Mioli, "Il Teatro Comunale," 327
	1778	Teatro Comunale	8.5 lire	2.5 lire	1 lira	Ricci, *Teatri*, 654–55
	c.1806	"Church"			0.1 lira	Radiciotti, *Aneddoti*, 16
	c.1806	"Theater"			0.6 lira	Ibid.
	1821	Teatro Comunale (*Spettacoli eroici*)	1.4 lire	0.5 lira	0.2 lira	Mioli, 332
	1821	Teatro Comunale (*Opera buffa / Accademia*)	0.7 lira	0.45 lira	0.4 lira	Ibid. 333
	1821	Teatro Comunale (spoken theater)	0.25 lira	0.25 lira	0.25 lira	Ibid.
Imola	1804	Teatro Comunale	45 denari	35 denari	20 denari	Fabbri, "I Rossini," 135–36
	1804	Balls (*Veglioni*)	75 denari	60 denari	30 denari	Ibid. 136
Piacenza	1752	Regio Ducal Teatro	8 lire	5 lire	4 lire	Rabitti, "Orchestre," 37–38
Ravenna	1768	"Funzioni ordinarie di città"	25 denari	20 denari	10 denari	Fabbri, 420
	1790	S. Giovanni Evangelista	60 denari	60 denari	45 denari	Ibid. 420–21
	1798	S. Romualdo	60 denari	50 denari	40 denari	Ibid. 422

[a] Excluding *maestro al cembalo* and violin director.

tively large: the northern Italian circuit, according to Rosselli, included Venice and the Veneto, Lombardy, and Emilia-Romagna. For instrumentalists, the zones were probably smaller. It was often difficult to cross political boundaries in eighteenth-century Italy, and orchestra musicians were easier to come by locally than singers. Of the "suonatori forestieri" in the Emilia-Romagna performances surveyed here, most came from other towns in Emilia-Romagna. In Milan, Brescia, Bergamo, and Verona, "foreign" instrumentalists tended to come from the cities and towns of Lombardy.[73] Venice and the Veneto may have constituted another zone for orchestra musicians, Lucca, Pisa, Livorno, Florence, and the rest of Tuscany yet another.[74] The fact that travel was so integral to the world of the Italian instrumentalist may help explain the large number of Italians in German, English, Spanish, even Russian orchestras in the eighteenth century. Perhaps travel around Emilia-Romagna or around Lombardy put Italian orchestra musicians in the frame of mind to set out for Dresden, London, Madrid, or St. Petersburg, where the shortage of qualified orchestral musicians was even more acute and the wages higher.

It is hard to get much of a feeling for the economic and social level of orchestra musicians in eighteenth-century Emilia-Romagna. Table 12.4 summarizes information on pay scales at theaters and churches in a few towns between the 1750s and the 1820s. The figures are difficult to interpret, because of the profusion of currencies in eighteenth- and early nineteenth-century Italy and because data are scarce on relative wages and costs of living. Rossini recalled that when he played keyboards in Bologna in 1806 or 1807, he earned 6 paoli for a night's work in the theaters, but only 1 paolo for a church service.[75] Six paoli in the currency of the Papal States equaled 60 baiocchi. Thus Rossini's recollection corresponds closely to the 50 baiocchi (½ lira) per service that the Teatro Comunale in Bologna paid its rank-and-file players according to a wage schedule published in 1821. Pay rates on the Bologna schedule range from a high of 1 lira 40 baiocchi per service (the first oboist) to a low of 20 baiocchi (the man who played cymbals and triangle).[76] These rates were for grand operas that included a ballet. For opera buffa and concerts (*accademie*) the rates were somewhat lower; for spoken theater they were lower still: 25 baiocchi for every member of the orchestra, no matter what his function. Records from Bologna 50 or 60 years earlier seem to indicate considerably higher rates of pay: 3 lire per night for the violinists who played Gluck's *Trionfo di Clelia* in 1763; 2½ lire per night for his *Armida* in 1778.[77] It

---

[73] On the exchange of musicians between towns in Lombardy, see Ch. 5.

[74] On traffic between Lucca and Pisa, see Alfredo Bonaccorsi, *Maestri di Lucca: i Guami e altri musicisti* (Florence, 1967), 48 ff.

[75] Giuseppe Radiciotti, *Aneddoti Rossiniani autentici* (Rome, 1929), 16.

[76] Piero Mioli, "Il Teatro Comunale: centottanta anni di presenza," in Conati and Pavarani (eds.), *Orchestre in Emilia-Romagna*, 325–42 at 332. According to the schedule the *maestro al cembalo* makes 1 lira 50 baiocchi per night, while the *primo violino direttore* makes 2 lire, indicating higher prestige and more responsibilities.

[77] The table reflects wage rates in 1763 and 1778 for local Bolognese musicians only. The account books for both operas document quite large payments to instrumentalists from out of town (Ricci, *I teatri di Bologna*,

looks as though wage rates had fallen disastrously at the beginning of the nineteenth century. The explanation, however, is that the value of the lira in the Papal States had increased as a result of the Napoleonic reforms of 1805, so that half a lira in 1820 was more or less equivalent to three lire in the 1770s.[78] The 5 lire per service that violinists earned in Piacenza in 1752 seems to reflect yet another value of the currency. When instrumentalists traveled to Imola, Piacenza, or Parma, they were paid in soldi and denari, whose exchange rate with lira-based currencies varied over time.

Table 12.4 implies that the shortage of orchestra musicians in Emilia-Romagna did not drive up wages or enhance the social possibilities for instrumentalists as it did in England. Leisure was not "commercialized" in Italy to nearly the extent it was in London. The number of musical patrons in a given town was small and rigidly limited by social class. There was only one "orchestra" per town, and it was a rotating rather than a standing orchestra, larger or smaller according to the needs of the particular event or season. Spoken theater did not compete with opera for instrumentalists; instead it shared the same theater and the same musicians (but paid them much less). There were no pleasure gardens; concerts were dominated in most towns by amateurs, with only a few professionals to lead the sections and to play unfashionable instruments. Nor could an orchestra musician do much to enhance his income by teaching. The only music school in the region was the Liceo di Bologna, founded in 1804, where members of the San Petronio orchestra and the Concerto Palatino served as teachers.[79] In many other towns of Emilia-Romagna the *primo violino direttore* and other first-chair players were contractually obliged to take students for free.[80] In turn their students played without pay in the theater for many years until a spot opened up on the payroll.[81] Evidently there was not enough demand for students to strike out on their own. The best they could do was to accompany their teacher from town to town, playing a succession of seasons and receiving a portion of his wages.[82] No wonder that Italian instrumentalists emigrated from Emilia-Romagna to France, Germany, and England.

614, 654). Probably these include travel and lodging expenses, but the *forastiere* may also have earned more per service than Bolognese instrumentalists.

[78] See Carlo M. Cipolla, *Le avventure della lira* (Milan, 1958), 78 ff.

[79] Nicola Gallino, "Lo 'scuolaro' Rossini e la musica strumentale al Liceo di Bologna: Nuovi documenti," *Bollettino del Centro Rossiniano di Studi*, 33 (1993), 5–54.

[80] Minardi, "L'orchestra a Parma," 79; Natali and Stefanati, "Le presenze orchestrali," 298.

[81] Minardi, "L'orchestra a Parma," 142; Mario Bizzoccoli, "L'importanza di una passione," in Conati and Pavarani (eds.), *Orchestre in Emilia-Romagna*, 285–90 at 286.

[82] Pay records often contain entries for a single payment to an out-of-town musician "e su allievo."

VIENNA IN TRANSITION

The world of the orchestra musician in Vienna during the second half of the eighteenth century was not a free market like London or even a regional market like Emilia-Romagna, but it did not correspond to the Kapelle model either. It was an example of a mixed system or a system in transition from Kapelle organization toward a free market.

During the seventeenth century the Hofkapelle—the music establishment of the Emperor—had been the principal employer of instrumentalists in Vienna. When Maria Theresia came to the throne in 1741, however, she embarked on a campaign of downsizing and fiscal restraint that shrank the number of instrumentalists in the Kapelle from 52 in 1740 to eight in 1765.[83] She split the opera orchestra off from the Kapelle, then privatized the two court theaters, the Burgtheater and the Kärntnertortheater, by leasing them to impresarios who operated them as businesses.[84] Each theater had a standing orchestra, which played for opera or Singspiel and also for the spoken theater. Churches also had orchestras, or at least a roster of instrumentalists who played on Sundays and feast days.[85] And increasingly in the second half of the century temporary orchestras were assembled for concerts, dances, and other one-time occasions.

These changes did not mean the end of the Kapelle system, however. As the Hofkapelle declined, the Kapellen of the Austrian upper aristocracy flourished. Some of these, like the Esterházy Kapelle, were based outside Vienna; others were headquartered in town, like the Liechtenstein and Lobkowitz Kapellen. Until the general collapse of the Kapelle system during the Napoleonic wars, aristocratic Kapellen remained a central feature of Viennese musical life.[86]

A typical Viennese instrumentalist in the second half of the eighteenth century, or at least a successful one, held a position in a Kapelle or in one of the theater orchestras, then took on additional jobs to supplement his income. For example, the composer Karl Ditters (later Ditters von Dittersdorf), as a talented young violinist in and around Vienna in the early 1750s, had a position in Prince Hildburghausen's Kapelle, where he was housed, clothed, and fed. He also performed at private concerts, he played concerti in churches, and he took students. In 1759 the Prince had to leave Vienna, and his Kapelle was dissolved. Through his patron's good offices Ditters obtained a position in the orchestra at the Burgtheater at the same salary. He

---

[83] Selfridge-Field, "The Viennese Court Orchestra," 125.

[84] Ludwig Ritter von Köchel, *Die kaiserliche Hof-Musikkapelle in Wien von 1543 nach 1867* (Vienna, 1869), 10–11. Although they were not part of the Imperial household, the theaters received large subsidies from the Empress, and she took an active hand in their administration (Brown, *Gluck and the French Theatre*, 64 ff.).

[85] Biba, "Die Wiener Kirchenmusik um 1783."

[86] Julia Moore gives a census and brief descriptions of 18th-c. Austrian Kapellen, and she discusses possible reasons for their decline ("Beethoven and Musical Economics," 563 ff.).

complained, however, that his new job cut down on his supplemental income ("Nebenverdienst"), and he negotiated with the theater director, Count Durazzo, to be excused from rehearsals four days a week in order to pursue his lucrative moonlighting career.[87]

A Viennese instrumentalist had many ways to increase his income. He could work as a substitute or supernumerary in a theater orchestra at the rate of one Gulden per service.[88] He could play at a benefit concert organized by a local or traveling virtuoso, again usually at one Gulden per service. He could play in a church orchestra, either on the regular payroll or as a supernumerary.[89] Dances required rather large orchestras. For example, at the Carnival balls organized at Court for the "junge Herrschaft" (i.e. the Imperial children and their attendants) in 1751, an orchestra was put together consisting of musicians from the Hofkapelle, the Burgtheater, and the Kärntnertortheater, plus several freelancers, including a young violinist named Joseph Haydn.[90] Viennese amateurs and dilettantes organized orchestras and gave concerts, either in private salons or as public concert series, like those in the Mehlgrube in 1781 and in the Augarten in the 1790s.[91] Amateur instrumentalists played most of the string parts, but professionals were usually hired as concertmasters, for the bass section, and for many of the wind parts.[92] All these constituted potentential sources of supplementary income for the freelancer.

A successful Viennese orchestra musician must have had a busy schedule. The Burgtheater orchestra on theater days ("Normatagen") rehearsed from 10 A.M. to 2 P.M., then played either for opera or spoken theater from 6:30 to 10 P.M.[93] Afterward there were often dances. On Fridays there were usually official concerts ("Academies") and occasionally benefit concerts at the theaters. On Sundays and holidays the instrumentalist had one or more services to play in church. Between rehearsals and performances, the musician taught as many students as he could manage and copied music or composed. All in all, there seems to have been enough work in Vienna that, even without a position in a Kapelle or a theater orchestra, a musician could make a living as a freelancer. This is how Haydn seems to have lived in the

---

[87] Ditters von Dittersdorf, *Lebensbeschreibung*, 108.

[88] Dexter Edge, review of Mary Sue Morrow, *Concert Life in Haydn's Vienna*, in *Haydn Yearbook* ,17 (1992), 108–66 at 126; Franz Hadamowsky, *Die Josefinische Theaterreform und das Spieljahr 1776/77 des Burgtheaters* (Vienna, 1978), 112.

[89] A roster of all music personnel in Viennese churches in the year 1782 shows that there was considerable overlap between the big churches like St. Stephans and St. Peters and the payrolls of the theaters and the Hofkapelle. See Biba, "Wiener Kirchenmusik," 20 ff.; also Edge, "Mozart's Viennese Orchestras," 68, 85. There was also overlap between the churches themselves, suggesting that either musicians ran from church to church on Sunday, or (more likely) that they often sent deputies.

[90] Dexter Edge, "New Sources for Haydn's Early Biography," paper read at the annual meeting of the American Musicological Society, Montreal, 7 Nov. 1993.

[91] Eduard Hanslick, *Geschichte des Concertwesens in Wien* (Vienna, 1869), 69–71; Otto Biba, "Grundzüge des Konzertwesens in Wien zu Mozarts Zeit," *Mozart-Jahrbuch* (1978–79), 132–43 at 137 ff.

[92] Morrow, *Concert Life in Haydn's Vienna*, 15; Biba, "Grundzüge," 138.

[93] Brown, *Gluck*, 96 ff.; Ditters von Dittersdorf, *Lebensbeschreibung*, 106–7.

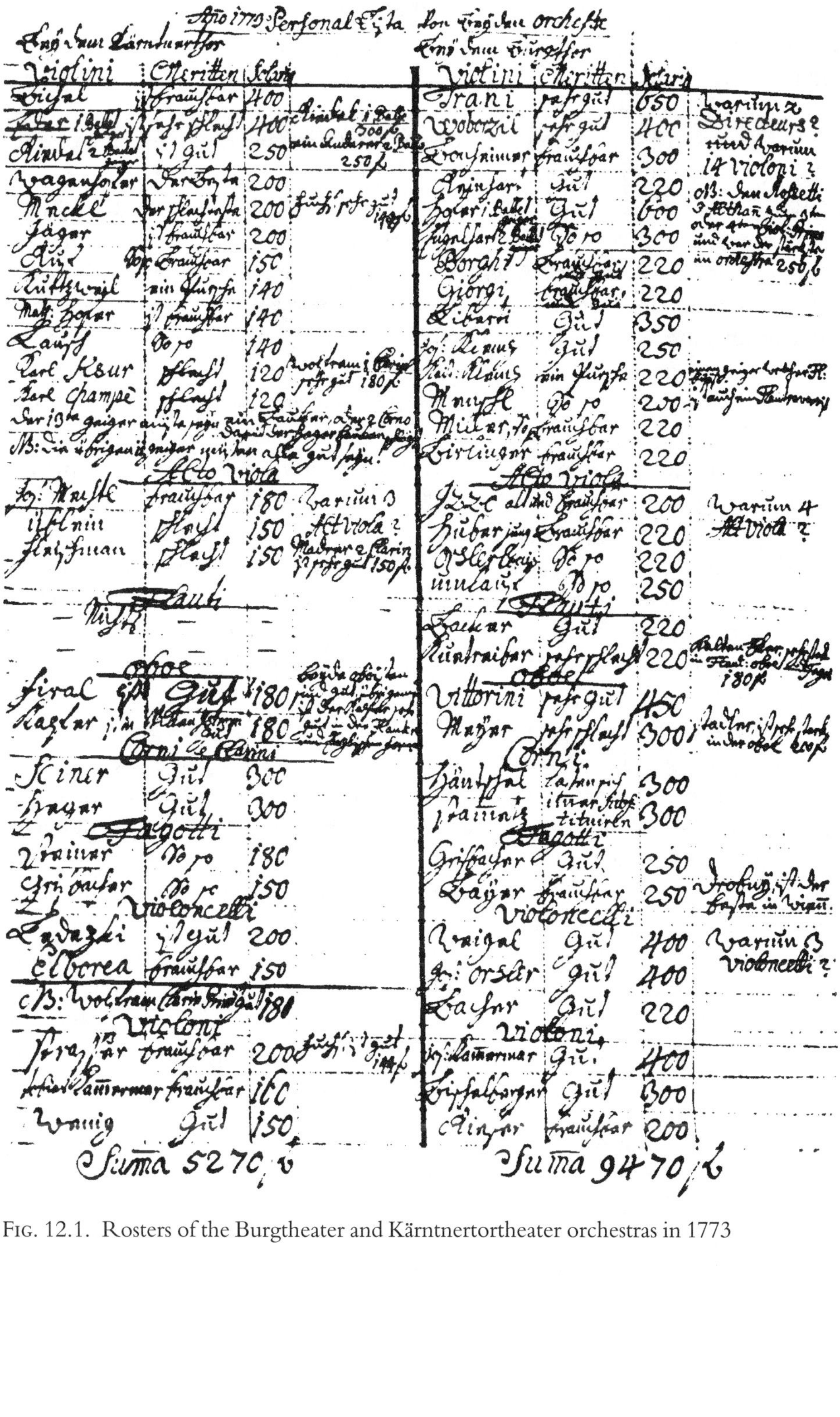

FIG. 12.1. Rosters of the Burgtheater and Kärntnertortheater orchestras in 1773

1750s and the Stadler brothers in the 1770s. Freelancing as the sole means of support, however, was probably only feasible in Vienna for a young musician with good chops and without a family.

Pay scales at the Burg- and the Kärntnertortheaters were comparable to the scales at aristocratic Kapellen. Figure 12.1 is a facsimile of orchestra rosters for both theaters in 1773; the Burgtheater is on the right, the Kärntnertor on the left. Salaries at the Kärntnertortheater range from 120 to 400 Gulden for the year; at the Burgtheater they range from 200 to 650 Gulden. The Burgtheater paid more because in this year its orchestra played six times a week, whereas the Kärntnertortheater orchestra had only four services per week.[94] The concertmasters who led the orchestras were paid considerably more than the others, first-chair men and both horns somewhat more. The second column is for "merit" (*Meritten*). Whoever compiled this list judges that Trani, the concertmaster at the Burgtheater, plays "sehr gut [very well]," but that Wenzel Pichl at the Kärntnertor is only "brauchbar [adequate]." Karl Champé, at the back of the the violin section in the Kärntnertor orchestra, is flatly "schlecht [poor]," which may explain why he earns only 120 Gulden. The salary range and the distribution of salaries in the Burgtheater in 1773 orchestra are quite similar to those of the Esterházy Kapelle in 1780. At the Burgtheater, however, there was no room and board, and the players had no uniforms but dressed in coats and waistcoats, which they had to buy for themselves. On the other hand, Burgtheater musicians gave management only six services per week plus rehearsals, not their entire lives. Their earnings at the theater represented only a portion of their total income. Given the Viennese wage levels shown in Table 12.1, it seems as though, starting with a foundation of 150 to 400 Gulden per year at a theater or in a Kapelle, an enterprising musician ought to have been able to lift himself to an economic status comparable to that of a secondary school teacher, a government servant ("Amtsdiener"), or even a government clerk ("Kanzlist").

Still, the circumstances of Viennese orchestra musicians were markedly inferior to those of London's instrumentalists of the same time. Julia Moore, who examined the estate inventories of Hofkapelle musicians, found that "the financial situations of most Hofkapelle members and the families who survived them were quite bad."[95] The largest estate was left by violinist Giacomo Conti, who was concertmaster at the Burgtheater in the 1790s. When he died in 1805 he left an estate with 483 Gulden in 1795 currency, that is, somewhat less than a year's earnings at the theater.[96]

---

[94] Gustav Zechmeister, *Die Wiener Theater nächst dem Kärntnerthor von 1747 bis 1776* (Vienna, 1971), 371.

[95] Moore, "Beethoven and Musical Economics," 466. She surveys estate inventories of members of the Hofkapelle who died between 1790 and 1830.

[96] Between 1795 and 1805 there was severe inflation in Austria, so that Conti's actual estate of 893 Gulden in 1805 Bankozettel was worth only 483 Gulden in 1795. See Moore, "Beethoven and Musical Economics," 119 ff. Besides the problems adjusting for inflation, Moore's figures have to be interpreted with caution because it was advantageous for family members to hide as much of an estate as possible from the assessors (Moore, "Beethoven and Musical Economics," 410).

Two-thirds of the instrumentalists in Moore's survey left 100 Gulden or less, mainly in goods rather than in cash. Many of them died in debt.[97] Their belongings tended to be mostly furniture and especially clothing, which constituted a large share of an eighteenth-century budget, particularly in the case of a musician who had to out-fit himself for public performance.[98] The estate inventories also record a striking number of watches and clocks. It seems as though musicians were already keeping calendars and rushing to get to the next rehearsal on time. It is equally striking that the estates did not tend to include musical instruments. Sixteen out of 24 instrumentalists surveyed by Moore did not own an instrument at the time of their death.[99] If they were members of Kapellen, they probably used instruments belonging to their patrons, many of whom, like Prince Esterházy, maintained a large inventory of instruments and kept them in good repair. Theaters also owned instruments, not just keyboards, but also cellos, basses, brass instruments, and perhaps others.[100] Some musicians might have had to sell their instruments after they became too old or too ill to perform, in order to support themselves and their families.

Orchestra musicians who moved from aristocratic Kapellen into the Viennese musical marketplace lost the social benefits that the Kapelle system provided. A the-ater orchestra might provide a steady income and perhaps even an instrument to play, but it did not provide medical attention, a pension, or survivors' benefits. Such social insurance was the purpose of the Tonkünstler Society, founded in 1771 as part of the project of transferring the costs of music out of the Imperial household.[101] Viennese singers and instrumentalists joined the Society by making an initial capital investment of 150 Florins (Gulden) and then contributing an additional premium of 12 Florins per year. Additional capital was raised at four big benefit concerts each year, two just before Christmas and two more at the end of Lent, for which composers, singers, and instrumentalists donated their services. Proceeds from the Society's investments went to retired members, their widows, and their orphaned children.[102]

The Stadler brothers, Anton and Johann, both active in Vienna from the 1770s until about 1800, can serve as examples of Viennese instrumentalists during the tran-sition from the Kapelle to the free-market system.[103] They came from modest social origins: their father was a shoemaker, their mother a midwife; and they grew up in

---

[97] Moore, "Beethoven and Musical Economics," 466–69.

[98] Roman Sandgruber, "Wirtschaftsentwicklung, Einkommensverteilung und Alltagsleben zur Zeit Haydns," in Gerda Mraz (ed.), *Joseph Haydn in seiner Zeit* (Eisenstadt, 1982), 72–90 at 85.

[99] A few of the musicians owned several instruments. Franz Oliva, who played at Eszterháza, then in the Schwarzenberg Kapelle, left 2 bassoons, 2 violins, 1 viola, and a clavichord (Moore, "Beethoven and Musical Economics," 493).

[100] Moore, "Beethoven and Musical Economics," 475; Hadamowsky, *Josefinische Theaterreform*, 112.

[101] Hanslick, *Geschichte*, 8–11.

[102] Pohl, *Denkschrift*, 6.

[103] Anton Stadler was the clarinetist for whom Mozart wrote his Clarinet Concerto, K. 622, and Clarinet Quintet, K. 581.

working-class neighborhoods of Vienna.[104] Anton married the daughter of a minor government official; around age 50 he left his wife and moved in with a seamstress with whom he lived for the rest of his life. Johann married the daughter of a tanner. One of Anton's sons became a musical instrument maker, the other a clarinetist like his father.[105] Neither brother ever owned property. They rented their lodgings, usually in the suburbs rather than the city, and they moved frequently. Often they shared lodgings, even after they had married and started families. Both brothers borrowed money repeatedly.[106] When Anton died in 1812, his estate inventory recorded little more than the clothes on his back and no musical instruments.

It is not known why, where, or how the Stadler brothers learned to play the clarinet, although it was common for pairs of brothers to play the same instrument. Their father, besides being a shoemaker, was a musician of some sort, but he does not appear on the pay lists of any theaters or Kapellen; most likely he played part-time, perhaps in taverns. The first record of a performance by the Stadler brothers was as joint soloists at a Tonkünstler Society concert in 1773; Anton was 20 years old, Johann only 17.[107] At this point they seem to have been freelancers. The Burgtheater orchestra, which did not include clarinets in the 1770s, hired them as supernumeraries during the 1779–80 and 1780–81 seasons. They had a few brief connections with Kapellen—with the wind band of Count von Palm in 1780, perhaps with Count Galitzin around the same time. In 1781 they applied unsuccessfully for jobs in the Wallerstein Kapelle.[108] Steady jobs finally came in 1781, when they were taken onto the payroll at the Burgtheater.[109] When in April 1782 Joseph II created a court wind octet or "Harmonie," the brothers were appointed as the clarinetists. This provided them with a second steady income in addition to the theater. In 1787 they were appointed—always as a pair—to the Hofkapelle.[110]

Like other Viennese orchestra musicians the Stadlers supplemented their earnings at the theater and the Hofkapelle with a large number of additional jobs. They participated in academies at the Burgtheater, sometimes as soloists.[111] They performed chamber music in aristocratic homes. Freemasons, the Stadler brothers played in performances at the Palmtree Lodge, where they were members, and also at the Crowned Hope, to which Mozart belonged.[112] It is unlikely that they were paid for

---

[104] K. M. Pisarowitz, " 'Müasst ma nix in übel aufnehma . . .': Beitragsversuch zu einer Gebrüder-Stadler-Biographie," *Mitteilungen der Internationalen Stiftung Mozarteum*, 19 (1971), 29–33.

[105] Pamela Poulin, "The Bassett Clarinet of Anton Stadler and its Music" (Ph.D. diss., Eastman School of Music, Rochester, NY, 1978), 77. Of Johann Stadler's children, one son became a clerk in a factory; a daughter may have worked at the court theater.

[106] Ibid. 78, 90.   [107] Ibid. 4.

[108] Pamela Poulin, "A Little Known Letter of Anton Stadler," *M & L* 69 (1988), 49–56.

[109] Edge, "Mozart's Viennese Orchestras," 71–74.

[110] Köchel, *Die kaiserliche Hof-Musikkapelle*, 91. Pisarowitz has the Stadler brothers entering the Hofkapelle in 1793, which is probably too late (Pisarowitz, "Müasst ma nix in übel aufnehma . . .," 30).

[111] Poulin, "The Bassett Clarinet," 33, 36.

[112] Ibid. 24–25; H. C. Robbins Landon, *Mozart and the Masons: New Light on the Lodge "Crowned Hope"* (London, 1982), 25–26.

these fraternal services, but at Masonic functions they made important contacts, including Johann Esterházy, who was a clarinet student of Anton's, and Michael Puchberg, from whom both brothers (like Mozart) borrowed money.[113] Anton Stadler accompanied Mozart to Prague in 1791 for the premiere of *La Clemenza di Tito*, in which he played the basset clarinet solo for "Parto, parto" in the first act. Then, with Mozart's newly-composed clarinet concerto in his luggage and a loan from Mozart, he undertook a concert tour that lasted four or five years and took him to Warsaw, Vilnius, Riga, St. Petersburg, Lübeck, Hamburg, and Hannover.[114]

On the one hand, the careers of the Stadler brothers serve as an example of the vicissitudes and marginality of the lives of Viennese orchestra musicians in the late eighteenth century—of the dangers of the transition from the Kapelle to the free-market system. The Stadlers were the outstanding clarinetists of their day; they played at the Burgtheater in what was probably the best orchestra in town; they were members of the Imperial Kapelle. Yet they lived in crowded conditions in rented lodgings in poor neighborhoods; they were constantly in debt; they died in poverty. On the other hand, the Stadlers' lives, Anton's in particular, also demonstrate some attractive possibilities of the new order. In the Masonic lodges they interacted with men from a comparatively broad social spectrum on a basis, if not of equality, at least of fraternity and good intentions.[115] Through their performances at private concerts, they came into contact with aristocratic music lovers like Countess Thun, whose name they gave as a reference when they applied for positions in the Wallerstein Kapelle.[116]

Another aristocratic acquaintance of the Stadlers was Count Georg Festetics, who in 1800 asked Anton to draft a proposal for a music conservatory that he intended to establish in an abandoned monastery on his Hungarian estate. The resulting "Music Plan" has been preserved at the National Library in Budapest. It shows that Anton, despite his humble origins, had acquired enough education somewhere to write literate, sometimes elegant German decorated with quotations in French (Rousseau) and Latin (Cicero, Servius).[117] He also demonstrates some familiarity with music theory (Fux, Riepel) and musical journalism (Reichardt, Mattheson). Music, Stadler insists, is not just a craft but part of general culture. "Whoever wants to achieve genuine mastery of music," he tells Count Festetics in the Music Plan, "must acquire a broad knowledge of the world, plus mathematics, poetry, rhetoric, and several languages."[118] This is an ambitious program for an orchestra musician, even today. Stadler's Music Plan expresses an Enlightenment sensibility that sounds fresh and

---

[113] Landon, *Mozart and the Masons*, 36; Poulin, "The Bassett Clarinet," 32, 71.

[114] Pamela Poulin, "Anton Stadler's Basset Clarinet: Recent Discoveries in Riga," *JAMIS* 22 (1996), 110–27.

[115] On social mixing among Viennese Masons, see Landon, *Mozart and the Masons*, 35–50.

[116] Poulin, "A Little Known Letter," 53.

[117] E. Hess, "Anton Stadlers 'Musick Plan,'" 48, 52. The ideal orchestras that Stadler proposed in his Music Plan are tabulated in Table 9.3.

[118] Ibid. 50.

remarkable coming from a shoemaker's son living a penurious existence in a work-ing-class suburb of Vienna.

CIVIC MUSIC IN LEIPZIG

Leipzig in the eighteenth century represents yet another model for the organization of orchestra musicians and their lives—the "civic music" model. Like Vienna, Leipzig was in transition during the course of the eighteenth century, in this case from the civic-music model to a free-market system.

Leipzig had no Kapelle because it had no court; the Saxon court was in Dresden, some 90 kilometers away. Leipzig was a "free city," a vigorous trading center and home to one of Germany's largest universities. Civic music in Leipzig was the respon-sibility of the city administration (*Rat*). On the city payroll were four *Stadtpfeifer* (city wind players) and three *Kunstgeiger* (art fiddlers), numbers that had not changed since the system was first established in the sixteenth century.[119] There were also journey-men and apprentices, but their names and their activities are not well documented. Despite the implications of their titles, the *Stadtpfeifer* and *Kunstgeiger* were all expect-ed to play both string and wind instruments. At an audition for one of the *Kunstgeiger* positions in 1745, J. S. Bach heard Carl Friedrich Pfaffe, a journeyman, perform on "every instrument that the *Stadtpfeifer* are required to play—namely violin, oboe, transverse flute, trumpet, horn, and various bass instruments."[120]

Stadtpfeifer enjoyed higher status than *Kunstgeiger*, because it was the *Stadtpfeifer* who played the "Abblasen," fanfares and other short numbers usually on brass instru-ments, from the Rathaus tower at 10 in the morning and 6 in the evening every day.[121] *Stadtpfeifer* and *Kunstgeiger* together played for services on Sundays and holidays at the Thomaskirche and the Nikolaikirche, the town's two principal churches in alternation. Because they had more duties, the *Stadtpfeifer* made more money than the *Kunstgeiger*, but neither made a great deal. In 1740 for example, a *Stadtpfeifer* earned 1 Thaler, 18 Groschen per week, while a *Kunstgeiger* made just 18 Groschen.[122] Besides their salaries, Leipzig civic musicians, like Kapelle musicians, received payments in kind. The city provided each musician with a house in the

---

[119] Arnold Schering, "Die Leipziger Ratsmusik von 1650 bis 1775," *Archiv für Musikwissenschaft*, 3 (1921), 17–53. On civic music in Germany, see Ch. 7.

[120] *Bach-Dokumente*, i. 147.

[121] Arnold Schering, *Musikgeschichte Leipzigs* (Leipzig, 1926–1941), ii. 271 ff.

[122] Ibid. iii. 156. The *Stadtpfeifer's* wage was similar to the wage of a carpenter, a stonemason, or a second-ary school teacher in Leipzig in the 1730s; the *Kunstgeiger's* wage approximated that of a day laborer. See Richard Petzoldt, "The Economic Conditions of the 18th-Century Musician," trans. Herbert Kaufman and Barbara Reisner, in Walter Salmen (ed.), *The Social Status of the Professional Musician from the Middle Ages to the 19th Century* (New York, 1983), 159–88 at 163, 170, 184. There were 24 Groschen in a Thaler. A pound of bread cost a little less than a Groschen, a pound of meat about 2 Groschen; a pair of men's stockings 1 Thaler 8 Groschen, a pair of boots 15 Thaler (Sprenger, *Das Geld*, 150).

Stadtpfeifergässlein.[123] The city also provided instruments for them to play, one set in the Rathaus tower, other sets in the churches.[124] *Stadtpfeifer* and *Kunstgeiger* did not need a pension system, because they held their jobs for life.[125] If they became too decrepit to play, a journeyman took their place for a nominal sum in expectation of the position when the incumbent died. Widows and minor children were provided for through the "Witwenbrief" (widows' letter) system, in which the deceased musician's family was entitled to remain in their house in the Stadpfeifergässlein for six months after his death, during which time they continued to draw his salary. In addition, the family was supposed to receive a portion of the income of the successor.[126] Thus the civic music system provided at least some of the social benefits of the Kapelle system.[127]

A civic musician's wages, however, did not come close to matching the salary of a Kapelle musician. At 100 Thalers per year, a *Stadtpfeifer's* wage was only about a third of the salary of the average member of the Esterházy Kapelle. The *Kunstgeiger's* wage was less than a sixth. To earn a decent living, *Stadtpfeifer* and *Kunstgeiger* supplemented their salaries with so-called *Accidentien*, jobs that they received as perquisites of their office. They played for weddings—both in the churches and at the celebrations that followed; they played for christenings; they played at banquets; they played at University ceremonies; they played in the theater during the spring fair.[128] All these jobs were monopolies, reserved by city ordinance for the *Stadtpfeifer*, *Kunstgeiger*, and their apprentices. The "major part" of a civic musician's living, the *Stadtpfeifer* and *Kunstgeiger* declared in a petition to the Town Council in 1758, consisted in these *Accidentien*.[129]

Salary plus benefits plus *Accidentien*, Hans-Joachim Schulze argues, added up to a reasonable income, a decent standard of living and respectable social status.[130] Analyzing estate inventories of Leipzig civic musicians, Schulze shows that they often owned the instruments they played, especially strings and woodwinds, which the City did not supply for the music the *Stadtpfeifer* played away from the Rathaus tower.

---

[123] Schering, *Musikgeschichte Leipzigs*, iii. 155. *Stadtpfeifer* had been provided with housing since the 16th c.; *Kunstgeiger* got housing only from 1725 on.

[124] Schering, "Die Leipziger Ratsmusik," 34; Terry, *Bach's Orchestra*, 20.

[125] Schering, "Die Leipziger Ratsmusik," 38.

[126] Schering says that some of these welfare provisions had fallen into desuetude by the mid-18th c. (*Musikgeschichte Leipzigs*, iii. 157).

[127] Many other German cities had systems similar to Leipzig's in the 17th and 18th cc. See Heinrich W. Schwab, "The Social Status of the Town Musician," trans. Herbert Kaufman and Barbara Reisner, in Salmen (ed.), *The Social Status of the Professional Musician*, 31–59.

[128] Schering, *Musikgeschichte Leipzigs*, iii. 149. When they played at a wedding the *Stadtpfeifer* earned 1 Thaler 6 Groschen apiece for the church service, another 1 Th. 6 Gr. for the banquet afterward, in all more than a week's wage (Petzoldt, "Economic Conditions," 181).

[129] Quoted in Schering, *Musikgeschichte Leipzigs*, iii. 156. Schering describes the life of a Leipzig civic musician as "an everlasting pursuit of supplementary income" (ibid. 158).

[130] Hans-Joachim Schulze, "Besitzstand und Vermögensverhältnisse von Leipziger Ratsmusikern zur Zeit Johann Sebastian Bachs," *Beiträge zur Bachforschung*, 4 (1985), 33–46 at 39–40.

Christian Rother (d. 1737) owned a lute, a violin, two cornetts, two oboes, two recorders, and an "old broken bass fiddle." Johann Caspar Gleditsch (d. 1747) owned three violins, three oboes, three horns, a cello, a bassoon, a trumpet, a lute, and a "useless" harpsichord or clavichord (*Clavier*). Johann Christian Oschatz (d. 1762) left two violins, a cello, an oboe, two flutes, and a trumpet. The three men also owned books and printed music. Rother apparently operated a pub ("Weinschenk") as yet another income supplement. He left 162 Thalers in liquid assets, offset, however, by 333 Thalers in debts. His widow complained that her husband had been "a man of means and considerable property" and that someone must have plundered the estate before the appraiser arrived. J. C. Gleditsch had little cash, but he owned a piece of property appraised at over 3,000 Thalers, the so-called Fisch-hof outside the city gates. These examples all suggest that Leipzig town musicians enjoyed a social status and a standard of living higher than members of the Esterházy Kapelle or Viennese instrumentalists of about the same period, but probably still not on the level of London orchestra musicians, certainly not the level of the top London players.

The civic-music system was adequate for *Abblasen*, for wedding music, and for old-style church music, but it was inadequate for newer eighteenth-century musical styles. In his "Necessary memorandum for well-appointed Church music," the *Entwurff* of 1730, J. S. Bach complained to the town council about the inadequacy of the instrumental forces available to him within the civic-music system.[131] Of 18 to 20 players in his ideal orchestra, the *Stadtpfeifer* and *Kunstgeiger* supply only eight.[132] He is compelled to fill out his orchestra, Bach says, with Thomasschule choirboys who play instruments and with student amateurs from the University. Bach's complaint is symptomatic of a general and chronic shortage of instrumentalists in eighteenth-century Leipzig. Johann Gotthelf Gerlach, organist at the Neukirche, complained about the same thing in a memo of his own to the Town Council in 1735.[133] The problem was that to protect the supplementary income on which their livelihoods depended, the *Stadtpfeifer* and the *Kunstgeiger* did their best to keep the supply of instrumentalists as low as possible. They remonstrated to the town council about the players Gerlach hired at the Neukirche; they objected to students and part-time musicians playing at weddings. But seven professionals plus occasional journey-men and apprentices could not come close to supplying the musical needs of one of the largest cities in Germany. The Neukirche continued to add non-civic musicians to its payroll. In the spring and fall during Leipzig's annual fair, bands of traveling

---

[131] *Bach-Dokumente*, i. 60–64. See above, Ch. 7, 248–49.

[132] Bach's eighth civic musican, in addition to the four *Stadtpfeifer* and three *Kunstgeiger*, was an apprentice. As he mentions the *Stadtpfeifer* and *Kunstgeiger*, Bach cannot resist complaining in passing about the low level of their playing: "As concerns their abilities and musical knowledge, discretion prevents me from speaking the entire truth" (*Bach-Dokumente*, i. 61).

[133] Schering, *Musikgeschichte Leipzigs*, iii. 70. Already in 1709, Kuhnau, Bach's predecessor at the Thomasschule, had written a memo to the Town Council complaining about the lack of instrumentalists in Leipzig. See above p. 248.

instrumentalists—particularly Bohemians, according to the *Stadtpfeifer* petitions—made their way to Leipzig where they played in the taverns and coffeehouses.[134] Wind bands from army regiments quartered nearby played concerts in town and (even worse) played at weddings in place of the *Stadtpfeifer*.

Bach thought he saw the solution to Leipzig's shortage of instrumentalists in the Kapelle system as he observed it in nearby Dresden. The Dresden Kapelle was large enough to play truly orchestral music; the King paid them well enough that they did not need *Accidentien* to make a living; they could concentrate on a single instrument instead of several. "One has only to go to Dresden," Bach wrote in the *Entwurff*, "to see how all the musicians there are salaried by his Royal Majesty. These musicians have no worries about feeding themselves . . . so they can excel on a single instrument. It is truly extraordinary and excellent to hear."[135]

The solution, however, lay in another direction. Bach mentions in the *Entwurff* that he has been forced to fill out his orchestra at the Thomas- and Nikolaikirchen not only with Thomasschule students but also with Leipzig University *studiosi*. Already in the 1720s and increasingly during the next few decades University students constituted a pool of instrumentalists from which players could be drawn to satisfy Leipzig's musical needs. In particular the generation of students that came to the University in the 1740s and 1750s constituted a cadre that transformed Leipzig from a civic music system to a freemarket system.

Student collegia in Leipzig were founded, disbanded, and refounded periodically, from the seventeenth century on, led by a succession of composer-directors that included Heinrich Schein, Johann Kuhnau, Georg Philipp Telemann, and Johann Friedrich Fasch. The collegia were voluntary associations of university students who had previous training as instrumentalists. At the time Bach wrote his *Entwurff* there were two functioning collegia: the one established by Telemann in 1704 and another founded by Görner in 1723. Bach directed the former from 1729 to 1737 and again from 1739 to perhaps 1744.[136] To a certain extent the collegia functioned as conservatories for students contemplating careers as cantors or organists.[137] For other students they provided recreation and a bit of supplemental income. The collegia played at formal and informal university events and at festivals for the King of Saxony's birthday and name-day.[138] More important were weekly meetings at taverns or coffeehouses. Bach's collegium met at Zimmermann's coffeehouse, indoors during most of the year, outdoors during summer weather. These meetings amounted to a concert series, with visiting soloists and with extra concerts during the Leipzig fairs.[139] Zimmermann, the proprietor, seems to have paid his student instrumentalists,

---

[134] Schering, *Musikgeschichte Leipzigs*, iii. 159–60.   [135] *Bach-Dokumente*, i. 63.

[136] Neumann, "Das 'Bachische Collegium Musicum,'" 10. See Ch. 7.

[137] Schering, *Musikgeschichte Leipzigs*, iii. 131–32.

[138] Neumann, "Das 'Bachische Collegium Musicum,'" 13 ff.

[139] Schering, *Musikgeschichte Leipzigs*, iii. 132.

but only poorly.[140] Since many of the students did not have instruments, Zimmerman acquired a number of instruments, which he lent out as needed.[141] "Loaner" instruments like this can be seen in Fig. 7.7, a portrait of the Jena collegium in the 1730s or 1740s. In addition Bach may have provided instruments from his own collection.[142] These coffeehouse meetings transformed themselves around the middle of the century into public orchestral concerts with paid admission: the Grosse Konzert, which operated from 1743 until around 1778; the Richter series (1756–93); and the Gewandhauskonzerte, which began in 1781 and continues today.[143]

The core of the orchestra for these concert series was formed by musicians who had come to Leipzig as university students. Their biographies can be pieced together from the *Lexikon* of Ernst Ludwig Gerber, who was himself was one of their number.[144] Most came from small towns in Saxony, and almost all of them came to study law. Some were the sons of Kantors; others came from professional families; only a couple were children of civic musicians. Several had attended a choir school like the Thomasschule; most had attended *Gymnasium*. They had learned to play, perhaps in choir school, perhaps from a father or an uncle, sometimes from a teacher. Violinist Johann Georg Häser (1729–1809), for example, was a carpenter's son who came to the university in 1752 to study law. He played to earn money for school, then around 1756 abandoned the law and committed himself entirely to music. He was first violinist and leader of the Grosse Konzert, then of the Gewandhauskonzert until 1800. In 1785 he was appointed Music Director of the University. Häser's children became musicians after him—three of his sons were musicians, his daughter a famous opera singer.[145] Thus Häser transformed not only himself but also his descendants into professional musicians operating on the free market.

Karl Gottlieb Goepfert (1733–93), another violinist, was the son of a Kantor.[146] He went to the Dresden Kreuzschule, where he sang in the choir, then came to Leipzig in 1753 to study law. He played simultaneously in the Grosse Konzert and the Richter concerts, where he was first violinist. In 1770 he became concertmaster in the Kapelle at Weimar, completing his transformation from law student to professional orchestra musician, now in a Kapelle rather than a free-market setting. Gerber himself (1746–1819) was trained at the choir school in Sondershausen and learned to play keyboards from his father, who was court organist and also Court Secretary (*Hofsecretär*). He also picked up the cello, more or less casually, in order to play in ensembles with his fellow students.[147] Following his father's wishes, he went to

---

[140] The accusation of poor pay comes from Mariane von Ziegler's report in 1730 (Schering, *Musikgeschichte Leipzigs*, iii. 133).

[141] Ibid. iii. 135.   [142] Terry, *Bach's Orchestra*, 20.

[143] For a diagram of the Grosse Konzert C. 1746, see Fig. 10.5.

[144] Ernst Ludwig Gerber, *Historisch-biographisches Lexikon der Tonkunstler (1790–92) und Neues historisch-biographisches Lexikon der Tonkunstler (1812–14)* (Graz, 1966–77).

[145] Schering, *Musikgeschichte Leipzigs*, iii. 405.   [146] Ibid. iii. 406.

[147] Gerber, *Historisch-biographisches Lexikon*, 293.

Leipzig in 1765 to study law, but he also played in the Richter concerts and in the theater orchestra, not for money but as a trainee (*Accessist*). The next year he was paid as a regular member of the orchestra. He did not own an instrument but borrowed a cello from the director of the concerts. Gerber, unlike Häser and Goepfert, did not become a professional musician but returned to Sondershausen and a career in the civil service. His involvement in music continued, however, in a series of iconographical and biographical projects, culminating in the *Historisch-biographisches Lexikon der Tonkünstler.*

Throughout the second half of the eighteenth century these students-turned-professionals staffed Leipzig concerts, operas, and theater music. At the Grosse Konzert in 1778 most of the players earned 12 or 15 Thalers for the season, while principals made 30 to 40 Thalers. The theater orchestra paid on a per-service basis. For example, when the Bustelli opera troupe came to town in 1773 for a run of 45 performances, it paid instrumentalists from the Grosse Konzert 16 Groschen a night.[148] The *Stadtpfeifer* and *Kunstgeiger* played in the same orchestra, but they were paid at a lower rate (12 Groschen), evidently because they did not play as well as the ex-students.

In this free-market environment instrumentalists did not receive the social benefits that the *Stadtpfeifer* and *Kunstgeiger* enjoyed. To address these needs, the ex-students in 1786 organized an "Orchesterinstitut," which aimed both to regulate wages and working conditions and to provide security to old and infirm musicians. Set up initially for the musicians who played in the theater, it was extended in 1789 to include the entire Gewandhaus orchestra. The original bylaws of the Institute included provisions for orchestra members to control auditions and hiring, and for members to show solidarity with a player who had been dismissed unjustly by "themselves no longer participating in the orchestra." The bylaws also established a "common fund" into which every member paid 2 Groschen per week and from which pensions could be drawn in case of sickness or in old age. The Institute did not put an end to conflicts with the theater and concert management, which continued to dismiss musicians arbitrarily, but the pension system seems to have worked as anticipated. The first pensioner was the oboist Hubrich, who retired in 1788 at the age of 74 with a pension of 2 Thalers, 6 groschen per week.[149]

CONCLUSIONS

The five case studies in this chapter present strikingly different pictures of orchestra musicians and their lives in the eighteenth century. Yet generalizations are not so hard to make. For instance, eighteenth-century orchestra musicians were all men. Women

---

[148] Schering, *Musikgeschichte Leipzigs*, iii. 428, 464.   [149] Ibid. iii. 592, 584 ff.

turn up as keyboardists and occasionally as violinists, but invariably as soloists rather than as members of the orchestra. Reading through hundreds of rosters, payrolls, and accounts of performances, one finds only a handful of instances of a female instrumentalist playing in an ensemble that could be called an orchestra. The harpist for the London rehearsals of Haydn's *Anima del filosofo* in 1795 was Anne-Marie Krumpholz (see Ch. 1). She was not a regular member of Salomon's orchestra, however, but was engaged especially for that opera, which in any case was never performed. Mme Krumpholz also seems to have played as a supernumerary in oratorios at Covent Garden.[150] Burney visiting Florence in 1770 says that at academies in private homes Signora Maddalena Morelli, a noble dilettante and student of Nardini, played ripieno parts on the violin—i.e. she was not a soloist but a member of the orchestra.[151] Mozart, describing the amateur concerts at the Augarten in 1782, notes that "there are women as well as men" in the orchestra.[152] John Marsh mentions a blind girl who played harpsichord with an amateur orchestra in the English town of Salisbury (see Ch. 8). Of course, women played in the orchestras at the Venetian *ospedali* (see Ch. 5). But these were all-woman orchestras, not orchestras in which women played alongside men. Besides the famous Venetian *ospedali* there were a few more all-female orchestras in the eighteenth century. Friedrich Nicolai in 1781 reported hearing a women's orchestra and choir at the Laurentian convent in Vienna, where the "pretty violinists" played out of tune, but the nun who played double bass got a bigger sound out of her instrument than many men.[153] At Piazzola sul Brenta north of Padua there was a conservatory called Il luogo delle vergini, where as many as 38 girls were taught instrumental and vocal music on the model of the Venetian *ospedale*.[154] The girls played concerts for visitors and also staffed the orchestra of a small theater on the premises.[155] Apart from these exceptional cases, women did not play—were not allowed to play—in orchestras in the eighteenth century.

Another generalization: orchestra musicians tended to be the sons or nephews of orchestra musicians, the brothers of orchestra musicians, and the fathers or uncles of still more orchestra musicians. Family provided the basic organizational structures of the profession. Instrumentalists were trained by family members; they were recruited into orchestras by other family members; they worked side by side with family members; they traveled with family members—to the fair in Senigallia, or to a new career in Vienna or London.

In all the cases presented above orchestra musicians were professionals. Even when an instrumentalist had several jobs, all the jobs revolved around music. A few artisan

---

[150] Highfill et al., *Biographical Dictionary*, ix. 78.

[151] Burney, *Present State of Music in France and Italy*, 259–60.

[152] Letter of 8 May 1782; Mozart, *Briefe*, iii. 208.　　[153] Nicolai, *Beschreibung einer Reise*, iv. 545–46.

[154] Robin Walton, "Piazzola sul Brenta," in *GroveO*, iii. 999–1000; C. M. Piccioli, *L'orologio del piacere* (1685).

[155] An engraving dated 1685 shows an orchestra of girls playing for a banquet. It is reproduced in Selfridge-Field, "Venice in an Era of Political Decline," 77.

instrumentalists were encountered in Emilia-Romagna, a few servant instrumentalists in the Austrian Kapellen, and a group of law student instrumentalists in Leipzig. By and large, however, orchestra musicians in eighteenth-century Europe constituted a distinct professional class. Amateurs played a significant role in orchestras in each of the environments discussed, but the distinction between amateurs and professionals seems to have been consistently maintained. Except for Leipzig, examples of amateurs crossing over to become professionals or professionals becoming amateurs were rare.

For most of the eighteenth century orchestra musicians operated in an expanding market; we might call it a seller's market. The audience for orchestral music was expanding, the number of orchestras was growing, orchestras themselves were getting bigger—adding new instruments and increasing the size of the string sections. As a consequence, orchestra musicians had at least an opportunity to make a decent living—if they had talent, if they didn't drink, if their families weren't too large. In the five cases presented, economic contexts and individual circumstances varied greatly, yet orchestra musicians always seemed to find their place on the economic scale somewhere at the level of master artisans and middle-range civil servants. They may or may not have had a middle-class lifestyle (whatever that was), but they had a reasonable chance at living free from hunger and want.

The three "ideal types" of orchestral organization presented in this chapter turn up widely in late eighteenth-century Europe. For the Kapelle model Eszterháza was presented as the example, but there were many others: large Kapellen in Mannheim, Dresden, Salzburg, Turin, and Madrid; small Kapellen in The Hague, Parma, Koblenz, and elsewhere. For the civic-music model, the example was Leipzig, but it could have been Hamburg, Bologna, or Danzig. Other examples of the free market besides London were Paris, Amsterdam, Venice, and Philadelphia. Over the course of the eighteenth century there was a general trend away from the first two models and toward a free market. The trend was traced in Vienna and Leipzig, but it can also be seen in Prague, Paris, Milan, Naples, Munich, and Berlin. This development had momentous consequences for orchestra musicians. On the one hand they gained freedom of movement, education, and possibilities for social advancement. On the other hand, what had been a position became a job, and a musician usually needed several jobs in several orchestras to make a living. To replace the security and the benefits of the Kapelle system or the civic system, orchestra musicians created new institutions—societies and mutual assistance funds in the eighteenth century, leading toward musicians' unions in the twentieth century.

Chapter Thirteen

The Birth of Orchestration

ORCHESTRAL EFFECTS

In an article on "Accompaniment" published in 1791, the French critic Jean-Baptiste Suard makes a pronouncement that contradicts a century or more of writing and thought about music. "The human singing voice," says Suard:

doubtless has a special charm that no instrument can equal; but the possibilities of the voice are limited in comparison to those of a large instrumental ensemble whose diverse timbres, wider range, and greater freedom and precision of execution lend infinite variety to the colors and shadings of the composer's palette. Indeed there are a multitude of effects [*une multitude d'effets*] that can be produced only by instrumental music.[1]

In this short passage Suard discards the assumption shared by eighteenth-century writers from Mattheson to Koch that the role of the orchestra is to "accompany" the singer or an instrumental soloist. He also challenges Rousseau's theory that musical expression derives exclusively from language and human speech. In Suard's formulation musical meanings are conveyed not just by words or by the imitation of words on an instrument, but also by "effects," that is by sounds and combinations of sounds that only instruments can make.

Suard's notion of an instrumental effect can be traced back at least to the middle of the eighteenth century. Diderot, in the article he wrote on instruments for the *Encyclopédie*, advises the composer that it is not enough to understand the character of each particular instrument: "He must also understand the effect that their sounds will have when combined with one another."[2] Chastellux in 1765 praises the "beautiful

---

[1] Jean Baptiste Antoine Suard, "Accompagnement, Accompagner," in *Encyclopédie méthodique: Musique*, ed. Nicolas Étienne Framery, Pierre-Louis Ginguené, and Jérôme Joseph de Momigny (Paris, 1791), i. 23.

[2] Denis Diderot, "Instrumens," in *Encyclopédie ou dictionnaire raisonné des sciences, des arts et des métiers*, ed. Denis Diderot and Jean Le Rond d'Alembert (Neufchâtel, 1765), viii. 803.

effects" that German composers know how to draw from a large number of different instruments.[3] Francoeur in his treatise on wind instruments (1772) speaks of "grands effets" in a tempest scene, "effets sombres" in a funeral march, and even the "bel effet" that a serpent can make in pathetic pieces.[4] Slightly later, English writers begin to speak of "effects," Italians of *effetti*, Germans of *Wirkungen*. The effects that these writers are talking about are created by instruments rather than by voices, and they communicate meanings to the listener by way of musical sounds rather than by words.[5] Moreover, these effects are specifically orchestral. They are created by large ensembles that include both strings and winds and in which players are multiplied on the string parts. Effects are distinct and distinctive; each effect has its own history, its characteristic contexts, and its meanings.

Orchestral effects may be divided for purposes of analysis into two categories: (1) effects of unity and grandeur, and (2) effects of variety and nuance. The first call attention to the size, power, and discipline of the orchestra; the second highlight the diversity of orchestral timbres and the various possibilities for combination and contrast among instruments. Take, for example, the opening bars of Mozart's Paris Symphony, K. 297, composed in 1778 (Ex. 13.1). The opening downbow for the entire string section, the repeated tutti chords in measures 1 and 2, the sixteenth-note scale by strings, flutes, and bassoons, the ringing silence in the fourth measure, the organ-like whole notes in the horns, oboes, and clarinets (m. 7)—all these can be considered effects of unity and grandeur. The subito piano in measure 4, on the other hand, the reduction of the texture to violins alone, the timbre of first and second violins in octaves (mm. 4–6), and the scoring of the dominant chord in measure 7, with the bass in the horns rather than the *basso* part—these are effects of variety and nuance. Each of the effects in this passage can be found in works by many other composers, not just Mozart's contemporaries but his predecessors and heirs as well. In general, effects of unity and grandeur were developed earlier than effects of variety and nuance, and they involved mainly strings. Effects of variety and nuance came later for the most part and tended to make more use of the winds. None of these orchestral effects involved plucked strings or keyboards. Although the continuo was a component of most eighteenth-century orchestras, composers tended to treat it as vocal accompaniment rather than as part of the orchestra.

Initially, orchestral effects appeared mainly in music for the theater and there only in certain contexts: in overtures, in "dramatic symphonies" depicting storms, battles, etc., in accompanied recitatives, and in a few stock arias (pastoral arias, military arias, etc.). As they became more familiar, orchestral effects tended to loosen their associations

[3] François-Jean de Chastellux, *Essai sur l'union de la poésie et de la musique* (The Hague, 1765), 49.

[4] Louis Joseph Francoeur, *Diapason général de tous les instrumens à vent avec des observations sur chacun d'eux . . .* (Paris, 1772), 7, 24, 71. A serpent was a bass cornett.

[5] See David Charlton, " 'Envoicing' the Orchestra: Enlightenment Metaphors in Theory and Practice," in id., *French Opera 1730–1830: Meaning and Media* (Aldershot, 2000), V, 1–31.

Ex. 13.1. W. A. Mozart, Symphony in D, K. 297 ("Paris")

with context, so that by Mozart's time they had come to signify the orchestra itself—its unity, grandeur, variety, and nuance. Similarly, effects tended to lose their association with particular instruments, and the two categories of effects tended to blend into one another. Thus in Ex. 13.1 flutes and bassoons participate in the sixteenth-note scale, a typical string effect, while the piano dynamic wind chord in measure 7 turns what was traditionally an effect of unity and grandeur into a coloristic nuance.

Mozart's deployment of orchestral effects in the Paris Symphony amounts to what today is called orchestration, that is, the division of a musical composition among the instruments of the orchestra for artistic effect.[6] In fact, the earliest treatises on orchestration date from the years just before the Paris Symphony. But these treatises, by Valentin Roeser and Louis Joseph Francoeur, limit themselves to wind instruments.[7] A theory of orchestration that considers the entire orchestra and treats instrumental combinations as an ongoing compositional process rather than as isolated special effects coalesced only slowly in the last decades of the eighteenth century. Most of the effects that Mozart uses in the opening measures of the Paris Symphony were already in widespread use by the 1760s. Yet people were slow to generalize about them, not only because musical theory characteristically lags behind musical practice, but perhaps also because people did not yet think of the orchestra as a musical subject. The emergence of a theory of orchestration at the end of the eighteenth century marked a final stage of the recognition of the orchestra as a distinct and distinctive institution.

EFFECTS OF UNITY AND GRANDEUR

The premier coup

Le premier coup d'archet, "the first bowstroke," means beginning a piece with a simultaneous downbow in all the string parts. It seems obvious today that beginning together is an effective way for an orchestra to start a piece, but such beginnings were rare in seventeenth-century ensemble music. Much more common were passages like the *sinfonia* to the second act of Landi's *Sant'Alessio* (Rome, c.1632), where the parts enter one by one in fugal imitation (Ex. 13.2). Beginning a piece this way is relatively easy. The first violin (along with the continuo) can decide when to start, set

[6] See Hugo Riemann, *Musiklexikon*, 8th edn. (Leipzig, 1916), 499. We do not differentiate between "instrumentation" and "orchestration," terms that have sometimes been used to make distinctions in English, French, German, and Italian. For an attempt to distinguish systematically between them, see Hans Bartenstein, *Hector Berlioz' Instrumentationskunst und ihre geschichtlichen Grundlagen*, 2nd edn. (Baden-Baden, 1974), 2.

[7] Valentin Roeser, *Essai d'instruction à l'usage de ceux qui composent pour la clarinette et le cor* (Paris, 1764); Francoeur, *Diapason général*. That the introduction of larger numbers and new types of wind instruments, and learning what constituted effective use of these resources, was seen as a key development—at least in France c.1750–1800, but also elsewhere—is confirmed by François-Joseph Gossec's self-aggrandizing account of c.1810, published posthumously as "Notice sur l'introduction des cors, des clarinettes et des trombones dans les orchestres français," *Revue musicale*, 3/5 (1829), 217–23.

Ex. 13.2. S. Landi, *Sant'Alessio*, Act II, Sinfonia

the tempo, and determine the style. The other instruments simply follow his lead. Such a beginning works equally well with one player on a part or with several. It does not require part doubling, but it can accommodate extra players if they are available. One-by-one entrances are the most common way for seventeenth-century Italian canzonas, sonatas, and *sinfonie* to begin.

Compare the *sinfonia* from *Sant' Alessio* with the overture to Lully's *Amadis*, composed in 1684 (Ex. 13.3(*a*)). Here the entire ensemble begins with a resounding downbow chord. The audience experiences the full power of the orchestra at the very beginning of the opera; the orchestra creates musical sound where a moment before there had been only ambient noise. Not until the second half of the overture (Ex. 13.3(*b*)) does Lully revert to the old style of individual entrances and fugal imitation, and, unlike *Sant' Alessio*, the entrances here are far from easy, because of the dotted rhythms and jagged shape of the melodic line. Lully seems to have borrowed the *premier coup d'archet* from the practices of Parisian string bands of the previous generation; indeed, this was the effect that cured the melancholy wife in Jean Denis's anecdote in Chapter 3. Corelli adopted the *premier coup* for his ensembles in Rome. His Concerto Grosso Op. 6 No. 8 ("Christmas" Concerto, 1714) begins not with one but with three *coups* (Ex. 13.4). The gesture emphasizes not just the size and power of Corelli's orchestra but also the skill and discipline of its members, who can start and stop together like a single man. Besides its acoustical effect Corelli's *premier coup* would also have made a visual impact: 30, 50, or even 80 musicians, dressed alike and displayed on risers, all executing the same movement in perfect synchronicity (see Fig. 4.1). Having

Ex. 13.3(*a*). J. B. Lully, *Amadis*, Ouverture:

Ex. 13.3(*b*). J. B. Lully, *Amadis*, Ouverture, second part

Ex. 13.4. A. Corelli, Concerto Grosso, Op. 6 No. 8

introduced the orchestra with *coups d'archet*, Corelli, like Lully, reverts after the double bar to the fugal entrances of individual instruments.

Explaining to German readers how to play Corelli-style concertos, George Muffat places great importance on the *premier coup*:

The very first note of the *concerto grosso*, which begins the piece or which begins again after a pause or a breath, has to be played forcefully and without hesitation by each and every musician, unless an indication of *piano* forbids this. For neglecting the first note or playing it timidly will weaken and confuse the entire harmony.[8]

---

[8] Muffat, *Sechs Concerti Grossi*, 9, 21.

By the second half of the century, however, the *premier coup* seems to have lost a good deal of its novelty. In a letter he wrote to his father in 1778 describing his Paris Symphony, Mozart mocks the pride that the French took in this gesture: "I have been careful not to neglect *le premier coup d'archet* and that should be enough for the oxen here who make such a fuss over it. The devil if I can see any difference! They all begin together, just as they do in other places. It is really a joke."[9] Hackneyed or not, the *premier coup* remained a mainstay of Mozart's orchestral style. Of the symphonies that he wrote after K. 297, only one (K. 550 in G minor) fails to begin with a *premier coup*.

The grand pause

In Ex. 13.4 above from Corelli's Christmas Concerto the *premier coup* at the beginning of the piece is followed by two beats of silence in all parts. This silence gives the sound of the orchestra time to die away; it also prepares for a repetition of the *coup* in measure 2 and again in measure 3. Silence itself has become an orchestral effect, calling attention by the absence of sound to the magnitude of the sound that has just been heard. Written-out silence in all parts is rare in seventeenth-century instrumental music. At any given moment at least one instrument is usually playing; when all the instruments stop, the piece is over.[10] Lully too keeps at least three parts going in instrumental passages, perhaps because silence is confusing for dancers, and much of his orchestral music was written for dancing.[11]

Eighteenth-century composers found new uses for the grand pause. In a D-major symphony composed around 1752, Johann Stamitz uses the gesture to mark a structural juncture (Ex. 13.5). After several measures of imitation between strings and winds, the full orchestra cadences in A major; then comes a grand pause in all parts (m. 32). When the instruments reenter the first violins alone introduce new thematic material, and they are playing in A minor rather than A major. Here the silence allows not only the sonority but also the tonality to die away, an insight that Haydn extended to create some astonishing modulations in his symphonies.[12] Thus an effect that was used at first mainly for acoustical reasons, to accommodate the reverberation of large ensembles in resonant spaces, proved useful for dramatic, structural, and harmonic purposes as well.

[9] Letter of 12 June 1778; Mozart, *Briefe*, ii. 379.

[10] Examples of silence in all parts do occur in music designed for large, resonant spaces, like St. Mark's in Venice or San Petronio in Bologna, for instance, the canzonas of Gabrieli, and the sonatas of Torelli.

[11] An exception occurs in *Les Amants magnifiques* (1670) in a dance for the "young princess," plus four dancers dressed as statues. After four measures of a chordal texture, the instruments stop and the statues engage in a silent pantomime. When the living character resumes her dance, the orchestra begins again. The grand pause in this passage serves in the first instance a representational function, then a musical one.

[12] Examples of Haydn's use of a grand pause to move to remote keys include his Symphony 45 ("Farewell"), first movement, m. 108; Symphony 100 ("Military"), first movement, m. 125; Symphony 102, first movement, m. 82.

Ex. 13.5. J. Stamitz, Symphony in D (Wolf D-5), 4th mvt.

Tutti chords

As an orchestral effect, the tutti chord, where the entire orchestra attacks and releases a chord together, is related both to silence and to the *premier coup d'archet*. A tutti chord is attacked with a *coup d'archet* by the entire orchestra, and it is often preceded and followed by silence (Ex. 13.4). Tutti chords often stand apart from any melodic

Ex. 13.6. N. Jommelli, *Artaserse*, Overture

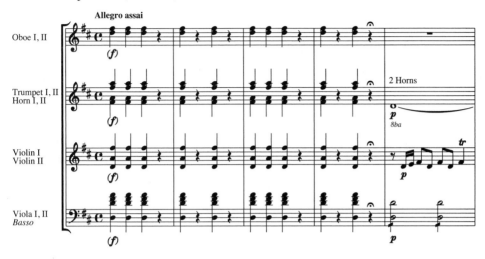

Ex. 13.7. D. Sarro, Sinfonia to *La Didone*

Ex. 13.8. A. Scarlatti, *Cambise*, Sinfonia, beginning

and contrapuntal context; typically they reiterate a static harmony or outline a simple progression. The use of tutti chords to introduce and define the orchestra at the beginning of a piece evolved in the first half of the eighteenth century into the familiar "curtain chords" of opera overtures and symphonies. Jommelli begins many of his overtures with this effect, for example in *Artaserse* (Rome, 1749) (Ex. 13.6). Here a single tutti chord is repeated 10 times in the same scoring, over the same D-major harmony, interspersed with orchestral silences and followed by a grand pause. Tutti chords can also serve to confirm endings. At the end of the overture to *La Didone* by Domenico Sarro (Naples, 1730), the tonic is reached with a weak cadence in the middle of measure 51 (Ex. 13.7). Sarro confirms it with a stronger cadence delivered by the full orchestra playing tutti chords (mm. 52–53). The orchestra ends the overture with three tutti chords on the tonic.

Tutti chords were put to other uses besides beginnings and endings. Alessandro Scarlatti, in his overture to *Cambise* (1719), overlaps tutti chords with a melody (Ex. 13.8). The violins launch the movement with a vigorous rhythmic figure, while the rest of the orchestra punctuates the melody with tutti chords that establish the tonic harmony and mark the beat. Having introduced tutti chords as quarter notes separated by rests, Scarlatti reduces their value in measure 2 to eighths. The diminution creates a clamor of trumpets, oboes, and strings that calls attention not only to the large number of the instruments in the orchestra but also to their diversity.

Orchestral unison

Example 13.9 shows the opening ritornello of J. S. Bach's harpsichord concerto in D minor (BWV 1052). The entire string orchestra in octaves plays an angular theme that stretches over seven measures, until the entrance of the harpsichord soloist finally introduces a contrapuntal texture. In sixteenth- and seventeenth-century ensemble music passages like this do not occur. Even in homophonic textures there are at least two voices, and contrapuntal voice leading prevails. An orchestral unison takes a single voice and amplifies it orchestrally—like pulling out the stops on an organ. Orchestral unison seems to have come into use around the beginning of the eighteenth century. Vivaldi uses the effect so often that it becomes almost a mannerism. In Ex. 13.10, a D-major violin concerto, he introduces the orchestra with a scalar, unison head motif terminating in a grand pause. When the violin solo begins (m. 5), the texture becomes contrapuntal, softer, and more differentiated. And finally, Vivaldi overlaps the two textures (mm. 12–13): the unison motif in the orchestra, a lyrical figure in the solo part.

Thanks to its bluntness and power, the orchestral unison often conveyed the suggestion of primitiveness or barbarism.[13] To depict Polyphemus, the ungainly Cyclops in *Acis and Galatea* (1732), Handel has the orchestra play in unison with the vocal part.[14] Osmin, the Turkish gardener *cum* harem guard in Mozart's *Abduction from the Seraglio*, is similarly accompanied by the strings in unison (Ex. 13.11). Osmin is one of several eighteenth-century middle Eastern heavies characterized by orchestral unison. The Kalender in Gluck's *Rencontre imprévu* (Vienna, 1764) and the chorus of dervishes in Beethoven's *Ruins of Athens* (1812) belong to the same family and are accompanied in the same manner. Turkish music, after all, was monophonic, and eighteenth-century Turkish instrumental groups played in unison from the beginning of a piece to the end.

[13] On extra-musical meanings of the orchestral unison, see Janet M. Levy, "Texture as a Sign in Classic and Early Romantic Music," *JAMS* 35 (1982), 482–531 at 507 ff.; Armin Raab, *Funktionen des Unisono — Dargestellt an den Streichquartetten und Messen von Joseph Haydn* (Frankfurt, 1990), 14 ff.; John A. Parkinson, "The Barbaric Unison," *MT* 114 (1973), 23–24.

[14] In the aria "Affanno tiranno," not shown here.

Ex. 13.9. J. S. Bach, Harpsichord concerto in D minor, BWV 1052

Ex. 13.10. A. Vivaldi, Violin concerto in D major, RV 226

As the effect of orchestral unison became more familiar, these extra-musical associations with rudeness and barbarism tended to fall away. The unison at the beginning
of Mozart's Paris Symphony (Ex. 13.1) does not refer to a Turk or a Cyclops but simply to the orchestra itself, the power of the 57 musicians who played at the Concert
Spirituel in 1778, beginning the symphony as one.[15] Mozart exploits the unison in

---

[15] A personnel list for the Concert Spirituel in 1778 is given in the *Almanach des spectacles de Paris* (1779), 3–6.

Ex. 13.11. W. A. Mozart, *Die Entführung aus dem Serail*, Act I, "Solche hergelauf'ne Laffen" ("These callow intruders")

more daring fashion at the beginning of the development section of the last movement of his G-minor symphony, K. 550 (Ex. 13.12). All the instruments (except the horns) race up a B♭ arpeggio together, leap back down to B♮, a half-step above where they started, then careen back and forth between widely separated pitches, until the winds enter with a legato passage in thirds that leads temporarily to D minor. Other orchestral effects—tutti chords, a tirade, a grand pause—are added to create an impression not just of size and power, but of the flexibilty and virtuosity of Mozart's orchestra.

Tirade

Georg Muffat, the German Lullist, calls the tirade "the liveliest of all figures."[16] He defines it as "several quick notes in a row, executed with great bow speed" and leading to a strong beat. Thus the tirade is an upward or, less often, a downward scale, played quickly, with alternating bowstrokes. Lully often added short tirades to orchestral passages, and occasionally longer ones, as in the "Entrée des songes funestes

Ex. 13.12. W. A. Mozart, Symphony in G minor, K. 550, 4th mvt.

[16] Muffat, *Florilegium secundum*, 50.

Ex. 13.13. J. B. Lully, *Atys*, Act III, Scene iv, "Entrée des songes funestes"

[dance of the bad dreams]" from *Atys* (Ex. 13.13), where both upward and downward tirades are written into the music, and in all parts, not just the *dessus*. These rapid scales, executed by all the players together, add brilliance and color to what would otherwise be a staid texture. They also show off the technique and alertness of Lully's violinists.[17] There is no need to play tirades with note-perfect execution; the bustle of many players headed quickly in the same direction is already a spectacular effect, particularly when it is preceded by silence and followed by a held note.

[17] Le Cerf claims that this was the passage that Lully used to audition players for the orchestra of the Paris Opéra (*Comparaison*, 209).

For many years after Lully the tirade functioned as a marker of the French style. Vivaldi in the first movement of a C-major ripieno concerto marked "alla francese" (Ex. 13.14) uses both tirades and dotted rhythms to allude to French music, although the steady italianate eighth notes in the bass give away the work's cisalpine origins.[18] Mozart refers appropriately to French tradition with the tirade in the opening measures of his Paris Symphony (Ex. 13.1). On the other hand, the tirade in Ex. 13.7 from Sarro's *Didone* (1730) is simply a rapid scale in the violins (descending in this case), without national implication—an easy way to add brilliance and to set off the tutti chords that follow. Jommelli in the overture to *Fetonte* (1768) makes much greater demands on his orchestra. He writes the violin tirade in thirds rather than unison, with the added timbres of flutes and oboes, then challenges the violas, cellos, and basses to match the effect (Ex. 13.15). This exchange of tirades served to show off the Stuttgart Kapelle, the "orchestra of virtuosos" for whom he wrote the opera (see Ch. 7).

Ex. 13.14. A. Vivaldi, Concerto in C major, RV 117

---

[18] Other examples of tirades in Vivaldi that seem to allude to the French style but are not labeled as such include violin concertos RV 582 and RV 583.

Ex. 13.15. N. Jommelli, *Fetonte*, Overture

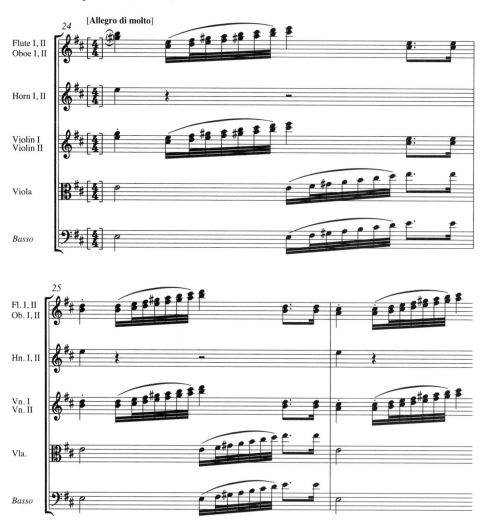

Tremolo

The tremolo—a quick and continuous repetition of a single pitch with alternating bowstrokes—is characteristic of instrumental as opposed to vocal music and of stringed as opposed to wind instruments. An early example of tremolo occurs in Monteverdi's *Combattimento di Tancredi e Clorinda* (1624, not shown) where it serves a doubly pictorial function: it depicts the agitated mental states of Tancred and Clorinda as they confront one another, and it depicts the actual clash of arms.[19]

[19] In the Preface to *Madrigali guerrieri ed amorosi* (1638) Monteverdi calls attention to the tremolo as a hallmark of his "agitated" (*concitato*) style. He says that playing the same note 16 times in a row initially aroused more laughter than praise (*Lettere, dediche e prefazioni*, ed. Domenico De' Paoli (Rome, 1973), 417–18).

Ex. 13.16. A. Vivaldi, *The Four Seasons*, RV 269, "Primavera"

Ex. 13.17. A. Scarlatti, *Cambise*, Sinfonia, mm. 18–21

Stewart Carter argues that most passages labeled "tremolo" in seventeenth-century instrumental music or marked with wavy lines call not for alternating bowstrokes but for a pulsating bow technique—what might today be called *ondeggiando* or bow vibrato.[20] Thus, in passages like the "Shivering Chorus" from Lully's *Isis* (1677) or the song of the "Cold Genius" from Purcell's *King Arthur* (1691) the orchestra would have

---

[20] Stewart Carter, "The String Tremolo in the 17th Century," *EM* 19 (1991), 43–59 at 56. See also Lionel Sawkins, "*Trembleurs* and Cold People: How Should they Shiver?" in Michael Burden (ed.), *Performing the Music of Henry Purcell* (Oxford, 1996), 243–64; Greta Moens-Haeren, *Das Vibrato in der Musik des Barock: Ein Handbuch zur Aufführungspraxis für Vokalisten und Instrumentalisten* (Graz, 1988), 253 ff.

played with long pulsating bowstrokes.[21] Alternating-bow tremolo, on the other hand, was usually indicated by written-out sixteenth or thirty-second notes, as in "Spring" from *The Four Seasons* (Ex. 13.16). For Vivaldi, as for Monteverdi, the tremolo is pictorial: it represents thunder (*tuoni*), while tirades in the violins depict lightning (*lampi*). Bach in the *St. Matthew Passion* (1727) sets the lines "and the earth did quake, and the rocks rent" with a tremolo in the bass part; he sets the parallel passage in the *St. John Passion* (1724) with a tremolo in the violins and violas.

Extra-musical references are absent, however, from the *Sinfonia* to Scarlatti's *Cambise* (Ex. 13.17). Here, as in many other Italian concertos and *sinfonie* of the early eighteenth century, the tremolo's function is not pictorial but rhythmic and textural. It enlivens and energizes what would otherwise be a simple succession of quarter-note chords, while the bustle of sixteenth notes calls attention to the multiplication of players on the parts. In the passage from *The Four Seasons* (Ex. 13.16) Vivaldi uses the tremolo structurally as well as pictorially: the tremolo defines the full orchestra, while the solo violin responds with contrasting triplets. Eighteenth-century opera composers often used the tremolo to keep the sound of the orchestra distinct from the sound of the singer. What in the seventeenth century was a pictorial gesture had become simply an orchestral effect. If it referred to anything, the tremolo referred to the orchestra itself.

Crescendo

The crescendo was the orchestral effect *par excellence* of the eighteenth century, or at least it was the effect that excited the most comment. J. F. Reichardt attributed its power to physiology:

The story goes that when Jommelli presented [the crescendo] for the first time in Rome, the listeners gradually rose from their seats during the crescendo and did not exhale until the diminuendo, at which point they noticed that they had been holding their breath. I myself have experienced this effect in Mannheim.[22]

Like the tremolo, the earliest instances of the crescendo are programmatic. Matthew Locke in his incidental music to Shakespeare's *Tempest* (1675) uses a crescendo to depict the storm that rages at the beginning of the first act (Ex. 13.18). Lacking any notation for crescendo, Locke simply says "louder by degrees." Other composers

---

[21] Sébastien de Brossard, in the entry on "tremolo" in his *Dictionnaire de musique* (1703), confirms that the "Shivering Chorus" requires a pulsating bow tremolo: "Tremolo . . . is used to tell those who play stringed instruments to play several notes on the same degree [of the scale] in a single bowstroke, in imitation of the Tremulant of an organ. It is also often marked in vocal parts, and we have an excellent example of both in the 'Shivering Chorus' from the opera *Isis* by Monsieur de Lully."

[22] Reichardt, *Briefe eines aufmerksamen Reisenden*, i. 11. The credibility of this account is diminished by the fact that Jommelli did not notate a diminuendo in any of his works. Crescendos in Jommelli are followed not by diminuendos but by forte passages or by subito pianos.

Ex. 13.18. M. Locke, *The Tempest*, Curtain Tune

Ex. 13.19. N. Jommelli, *Attilio Regolo*, Sinfonia

Ex. 13.20. J. Stamitz, Symphony in D (Wolf D-3), 1st mvt.

achieved the effect by indicating a succession of dynamic levels: piano, mezzoforte, forte, più forte.[23]

Jommelli too initially used the crescendo naturalistically, for example in his depiction of a storm in *Merope* (1741). Soon, however, he began to use the gesture without

---

[23] For surveys of the history of the crescendo see Rosamond Harding, *Origins of Musical Time and Expression* (Oxford, 1938), 85 ff.; Hell, *Die neapolitanische Opernsinfonie*, 354 ff.; Eugene K. Wolf, "On the Origins of the Mannheim Symphonic Style," in John Walter Hill (ed.), *Studies in Musicology in Honor of Otto E. Albrecht* (Kassel, 1980), 197–239.

Ex. 13.20. J. Stamitz, Symphony in D (Wolf D-3), 1st mvt. (*Cont.*)

programmatic implications, particularly in overtures. In the overture to *Attilio Regolo* (1753) he uses a crescendo to move from V of V to the dominant to the tonic at the end of the last movement (Ex. 13.19).[24] He enhances the crescendo with a tremolo in the violins, sustained notes in the horns, and oboe doublers from measure 47 on. All these effects combine to make the orchestra sound its most impressive as the overture comes to a close.

The crescendo became notorious in the works of Mannheim composers, who often used it at the beginning of symphonies, especially in conjunction with sequentially ascending melodies over a tonic pedal. Sometimes they used a crescendo several times in the course of a movement, as Stamitz does in a D-major symphony (*c.*1755, Ex. 13.20). He spreads his crescendo over a full eight measures (a long time for the audience to hold its breath), and he deploys it three times during the course of the movement: at the beginning in the tonic, in the dominant halfway through, and once

---

[24] The designation "rinforzando" in the brass in m. 48 is synonymous with "crescendo." Galuppi uses the term similarly in the overture to *Alessandro nell'Indie* (1750). See Reinhard Wiesend, "Zum Gebrauch des Crescendos in der italienischen Oper um 1750 (Baldassare Galuppi)," in *Mannheim und Italien: Zur Vorgeschichte der Mannheimer: Bericht über das Mannheimer Colloquium in März 1982*, ed. Roland Würtz (Mainz, 1984), 150–61 at 151–52.

again in the tonic at the very end of the piece. Thus, the crescendo becomes a sort of motif, marking the structural junctures of the movement and at the same time conveying the power and the virtuosity of the Elector's famous orchestra.

Trumpets and drums

Another way to increase the splendor and also the volume of the orchestra was to add trumpets and drums. During most of the seventeenth century trumpets and drums were were treated as a separate ensemble, often placed in a location separate from the orchestra—in a balcony, on a platform, or onstage. In operas they were used for battle scenes, like the four trumpets in Luigi Rossi's *Orfeo* (1640), "who sounded a call to battle along with drums, accompanying the assault of a French army on a fortified city."[25]

Lully too made use of a trumpet-and-drum ensemble for battle scenes, like the "Air des combattants" in the first act of *Amadis* (1684), which calls for trumpets in five parts plus timpani.[26] And he also combined the trumpets with his orchestra, for example in *Les Amants magnifiques* (1670), where trumpets and drums alternate with the five-part string ensemble (Ex. 13.21). Although Ex. 13.21 is labeled "Prélude . . . pour Mars," it is not a battle scene. The trumpets accompany the entrance of Apollo, portrayed by none other than Louis XIV himself. This annunciatory function of trumpets was transferred to opera overtures and *sinfonie*, where trumpets were added to the orchestra to strike a note of pomp and grandeur at the beginning of the entertainment. Alessandro Scarlatti's *Il prigioniero fortunato* (1698) opens with four trumpets playing virtuoso passagework, followed by the strings with an orchestral effect of their own, a tremolo (Ex. 13.22). Here the trumpets do not simply alternate with the strings but remain in the texture, marking the strong beats with blaring chords. The trumpets form part of the texture also in Scarlatti's *Cambise* above, doubling the strings and oboes in tutti chords and repeated notes (Ex. 13.8). Around the beginning of the eighteenth century, as horns were added to orchestras, they were used in similar ways, either doubling the trumpets, as in Ex. 13.6 (Jommelli, *Artaserse*) or replacing them with fanfares of their own, as in Handel's *Water Music* (1717; Ex. 13.23).

---

[25] Frederick Hammond, "Orpheus in a New Key," 118. See Ch. 1.

[26] For a discussion of Lully's scorings for trumpets and drums, the technical demands of the parts, and the capabilities of Lully's trumpeters, see Peter Downey, "Trumpet Style in 17th-Century France and the Music of *Les trompettes du Roy*," *Historic Brass Society Journal*, 7 (1995), 67–93.

Ex. 13.21. J. B. Lully, *Les Amants magnifiques*, "Prélude pour Mars"

Ex. 13.22. A. Scarlatti, *Il prigioniero fortunato*, Sinfonia

The wind organ

An even more characteristic use of horns for an effect of unity and grandeur appears at the beginning of a symphony by F. X. Richter (Ex. 13.24). Horns and oboes reinforce the opening harmony with a whole-note tonic chord played forte, then fade to piano as the violins play a descending staccato figure. Then the winds strike another chord, again forte (m. 3). The effect is something like an organ playing along with the string orchestra, and for this reason German scholars sometimes refer to this scoring as a "Bläserorgel" (wind organ).[27] Oboes and horns were the usual components of the wind organ, because these were the standard orchestral winds during most of the eighteenth century. Later in the eighteenth century flutes, clarinets, bassoons, and even trumpets were added to the oboes and horns of the wind organ. The wind organ is never used alone but always in combination with the strings, usually with the full orchestra.

The wind organ serves at least two purposes: (1) to increase volume, particularly when the strings are playing melodic motifs and figuration; (2) to sustain an ongoing

[27] See Hell, *Die neapolitanische Opernsinfonie*, 50.

Ex. 13.23. G. F. Handel, *Water Music*

Ex. 13.24. F. X. Richter, Symphony in F, Op. 4 No. 2

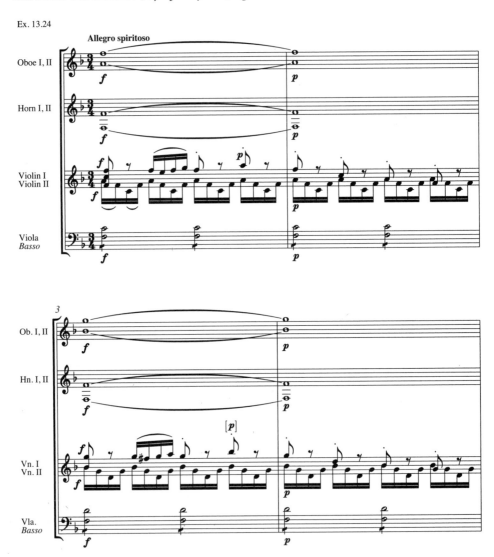

harmony or highlight harmonic changes. In Ex. 13.24 the wind organ provides a characteristic harmonic backdrop to the more agitated strings, outlining the very slow-moving I–II$^6_4$–V–I progression of the symphony's introductory flourish. In the overtures of Jommelli and the symphonies of Stamitz the wind organ often occurs in the context of a crescendo. In Exs. 13.19 and 13.20 the horns and oboes get louder, and additional instruments join in as the crescendo grows.

The earliest effects of unity and grandeur—the *premier coup d'archet*, the tirade, and the tremolo—made a string ensemble sound large and powerful. Later effects, like

Ex. 13.24. F. X. Richter, Symphony in F, Op. 4 No. 2 (*Cont.*)

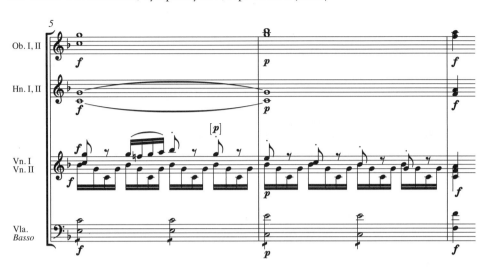

the crescendo and the wind organ, took advantage of the addition of winds to the orchestra. Several of the effects originally had symbolic meanings: the tremolo signified turmoil and agitation; trumpets and drums signified battles or parades. These meanings tended to disappear, however, as the effects became familiar. Tremolo became simply a way of adding energy to string parts; trumpets and drums served to increase volume and punctuate the tuttis. Thus effects of unity and grandeur came to refer to the orchestra itself. Tremolos, grand pauses, trumpets and drums, plus a crescendo or two combined simultaneously and in succession signified to the listeners: "This is orchestral music." In this sense the orchestra by the time of Corelli and Vivaldi had become self-referential.

EFFECTS OF VARIETY AND NUANCE

Effects of unity and grandeur treat the orchestra as a single entity, with all or most of the instruments playing together to make the orchestra sound large, powerful, and magnificent. Effects of variety and nuance take advantage of the diversity of the instruments in the orchestra and the combinations possible between them in order to create contrasts with effects of unity and grandeur and sometimes also to signify or depict sounds of the natural world.

Echo effects

Echo effects, the musical imitation of a natural phenomenon, were familiar already in sixteenth-century Italian madrigals.[28] They occasionally turn up in seventeenth-century

---

[28] See Werner Braun, "Echo," in *MGG²*, Sachteil 2, cols. 1623–37; also Harding, *Origins*, 85 ff.

instrumental music as well. Purcell obtains a naturalistic echo in Act II of *The Fairy Queen* (1692). He repeats a trumpet fanfare at three dynamic levels—"loud," "soft," and "softer"—each successive level repeating less of the initial phrase.[29] Where Purcell creates an echo effect by having the same instruments play louder, then softer, Alessandro Scarlatti (Ex. 13.25) calls for two groups of instruments, one loud and one soft. At the beginning of the aria "Quante frodi, quant'inganni" from *Il prigioniero fortunato* (1698), he instructs the first violins to play forte, the second violins to play piano; the seconds echo the firsts' melodic material throughout the aria. Each violin section gets a harpsichord of its own, with the second harpsichord marked "sempre piano," played perhaps with lute or buff stop. This represents a rare example of a keyboard instrument participating in an orchestral effect.

Ex. 13.25. A. Scarlatti, *Il prigioniero fortunato*, "Quante frodi, quanti inganni"

[29] Not shown. This echo piece for oboes and trumpets is itself the echo of the preceding song, in which Purcell obtains the same three-tier echo effect with voices. See Henry Purcell, *The Fairy Queen*, ed. J. S. Shedlock and Anthony Lewis (London, 1968), 43–45.

Corelli gets an echo effect in the seventh concerto of his Op. 6 (Ex. 13.26) by letting the concertino repeat material that the full orchestra has just played. Since the
concertino is smaller than the concerto grosso, the echo effect is automatic. Here the
echo seems less naturalistic than in the preceding example. For one thing, it is not
quite literal—the cello of the concertino moves up where the bass of the concerto
grosso had moved down. In addition, the echo effect is combined with tutti chords
and grand pauses—effects of unity and grandeur. Corelli's echo is artistic rather than
naturalistic.

Ex. 13.26. A. Corelli, Concerto Grosso, Op. 6 No. 7

Reduced scorings

Composers developed other scorings that created effects of variety and nuance but did not require a specially designated concertino. The simplest approach was to reduce the texture to violins alone. Even though many violins might be playing the part, their uniform timbre and the lack of harmony provided an effective contrast to the full orchestra. This effect was seen above in Mozart's Paris Symphony (Ex. 13.1), where after three bars of tutti chords and a tirade for the full orchestra, the violins answer alone with three measures of lively, contrasting material. Mozart sweetens the effect by scoring the violins in octaves rather than in unison. The same effect could be deployed on a smaller scale to create contrast within phrases. In the middle movement of the Sinfonia to F. B. Conti's *Pallade trionfante* (1722) tutti diminished 7th chords played by the full orchestra contrast with chromatic sigh figures played by violins (Ex. 13.27). Each loud–soft pair constitutes a phrase, which is then repeated over a chromatically falling bass-line.

Ex. 13.27. F. B. Conti, *Pallade trionfante*, Sinfonia, 2nd mvt.

Another way of reducing the scoring is to eliminate the *basso* from the texture and let the violas or even the second violins take the bass line. Following a cadence and a grand pause in C. P. E. Bach's string symphony in C, the *basso* part drops out and the violas take over the bass line (Ex. 13.28). Quantz (1752) calls this the "little bass" ("das Bassetchen," "la petite basse"), and he warns violinists and violists to be alert for the effect, because such a passage requires them to play their part more forcefully.[30] After four measures of reduced scoring, Bach brings the full orchestra in again, with the melody in the newly restored *basso*. If the *basso* included a keyboard (very likely in

---

[30] Quantz, *Versuch*, 205–6. Lully used the *petite basse* already in his operas, for example in the chaconne from *Phaëton* (Act III) and the passacaille from *Persée* (Act V, Scene viii).

Bach's and Quantz's north German milieu) then the *petite basse* effect would be made more striking by the absence of the harpsichord in the reduced texture.[31]

Instead of reducing the scoring, it is also possible to get variety in dynamics by having the entire orchestra play more softly, either gradually (decrescendo, diminuendo) or all at once (subito piano). Describing the "gran concerti di Roma" in 1711—presumably Corelli's orchestra—Scipione Maffei remarks not only on their skill at playing forte and piano in alternation, but also that they have "an artful way of letting the sound grow softer little by little and then all of a sudden resuming clamorously" with the full ensemble.[32] Corelli does not indicate a decrescendo in any of his published scores, so if his orchestra did engage in such an effect, it must have been an unwritten performance practice worked out at rehearsals. At the end of the Curtain Tune to Act I of Shakespeare's *Tempest* (Ex. 13.18), Matthew Locke writes in all parts "soft and slow by degrees" to depict the storm dying down as the curtain rises on Prospero's cave. Rameau in the Prologue to *Zaïs* (1748) uses the same effect to depict the calming of the waves. Like Locke, Rameau has no sign or word for decrescendo; he simply writes in successive measures: "fort," "moins fort," "doux." Diminuendo was much less common than crescendo in eighteenth-century orchestra music—perhaps because it is more difficult to execute, perhaps also because melodically descending, phrase-ending figures tend to get softer naturally, so, as an effect, decrescendo is not very distinctive.

Ex. 13.28. C. P. E. Bach, Sinfonia in C (Wq. 174/Helm 649), 1st mvt.

[31] For another example of the *petite basse*, see Ex. 13.10, m. 5.

[32] Scipione Maffei, "Nuova invenzione d'un gravecembalo . . ." in *Giornale dei letterati d'Italia* (Venice, 1711), v. 144. Quoted in Harding, *Origins*, 94.

Subito piano is indicated much more often in eighteenth-century scores than diminuendo, but in the majority of cases it is enhanced by alternation or reduction in forces. In many of the musical examples above a piano marking follows directly after a forte, and in almost every case a smaller and usually a contrasting group of instruments plays at the softer dynamic. An exception is the beginning of the F-major symphony above by Richter (Ex. 13.24). Here the forte and piano passages are identically scored: a melody in the first violins, an accompaniment figure in the rest of the strings, a wind organ in the horns and oboes. The piano effect depends entirely on the execution of the orchestra. Richter could count on the effect because the symphony was written for the Elector's orchestra at Mannheim, renowned for its execution of dynamics. The novelty effect lay in hearing and watching a large group of powerful instruments play loudly, then very softly.

The wind choir

Because the orchestra of the seventeenth and eighteenth centuries consisted first and foremost of bowed strings, string textures tended to be perceived as neutral. To achieve an effect with the strings, a composer needed something special: a *premier coup*, a tremolo, an orchestral unison, pizzicato, subito piano, etc. The winds were added to the orchestra gradually, beginning in the late seventeenth century, and for a long time they were considered supplementary or optional in most music. At first almost anything that wind instruments played could be an orchestral effect. Winds could be used as soloists, as pairs of instruments, or as a wind band with several parts.

Lully's winds were organized into four-part bands of different-sized instruments, parallel to the five-part texture of the strings but minus the *quinte* (see Ch. 3). He sometimes gives the wind band a number of its own to play, for example the "Concert champêtre de l'époux" for a four-part oboe ensemble in the *Ballet de l'amour malade*

Ex. 13.29(a). J. B. Lully, *Alceste*, Prologue

Ex. 13.29(b).J. B. Lully, *Alceste*, Prologue ("How sweet it is to combine glory and pleasure")

(1657), or the "Prélude pour l'Amour" for one transverse flute and three recorders in *Le Triomphe de l'Amour* (1681). In his later works Lully increasingly preferred a trio texture of two oboes and bassoon or two flutes and continuo, and he began to integrate strings and winds more closely. In the Prologue to *Alceste* (1674) he gets an especially bright tone color by doubling the oboes with the strings and instructing the oboes to play loudly, the violins softly (Ex. 13.29(*a*)). Later in the same passage he alternates a wind trio (two oboes and bassoon) with full five-part strings and chorus (Ex. 13.29(*b*)).

In the Sinfonia to *Il martirio di S. Giovanni Nepomuceno* by Nicolo Porpora (*c*.1730), the strings and winds alternate at closer quarters (Ex. 13.30). The strings play a four-measure figure, the oboes echo it in the dominant, then trumpets back in the tonic echo the oboes. Rather than oboe or trumpet bands, Porpora uses the instruments in pairs, and instead of separating strings and winds, he overlaps them. The strings provide tutti chords and even some unison reinforcement for the winds. In the already discussed Symphony in D major by Stamitz (Ex. 13.5) the alternation is further compressed: strings and winds trade a one-measure figure, the winds literally echoing the strings. Pairs of flutes, oboes, and bassoons are merged into a single choir of mixed wind timbres. In these eighteenth-century examples the wind choirs do not convey extra-musical associations. If they refer to anything, it is once again to the orchestra itself: to the variety of instruments available and the integration of winds and strings into a single ensemble. The repetition of melodic material is no longer heard as a naturalistic echo; now it simply highlights the variety of timbres in the orchestra and the skill of the performers in executing the same figure on their different instruments.

As the wind choir shed its extra-musical associations, composers began to use the alternation of strings and winds for purely structural purposes. In symphony first movements the beginning of the second group, the so-called second theme, is a familiar spot for the effect. Stamitz, in another D major symphony (Ex. 13.31), ends the first group with three tutti chords by the full orchestra. The violins alone enter with a repeated-note pedal, then a pair of oboes introduces a new, lyrical theme in the dominant. Here the wind choir is combined with several other orchestral effects,

Ex. 13.30. N. Porpora, *Il martirio di S. Giovanni Nepomuceno*, Sinfonia

Ex. 13.30. N. Porpora, *Il martirio di S. Giovanni Nepomuceno*, Sinfonia (*Cont.*)

Ex. 13.31. J. Stamitz, Symphony in D (Wolf D-2), 1st mvt.

both of grandeur and of nuance: tutti chords, a brief silence, reduction in forces, *petite basse* in the violins, concertante oboes, and a wind organ (at piano dynamic) in the horns. Another familiar place for the wind choir to make itself heard in a symphony is the trio of the minuet, where the new texture and new timbre reinforce the introduction of a new key.

Wind soloists

Distinct from the tradition of wind bands is the obbligato wind solo, where a single wind instrument plays an independent melodic part. Wind soloists appear most frequently in opera arias and in concertos, but occasionally also in single movements of symphonies. A striking feature in scores before about 1760 is that once a wind instrument takes a solo role, it seldom relinquishes it. In an aria with oboe obbligato, the oboe is introduced in the opening ritornello, it plays along with the singer or fills in at the ends of phrases, and in some cases it participates in the singer's cadenza at the end.[33] Often the obbligato is not one but two wind soloists, usually a pair of identical instruments, closely coordinated and treated as a single participant in the texture. Obbligato wind soloists often have strong extra-musical connotations. Flutes and oboes are associated with pastoral themes and also with love; trumpets are associated with war, horns with the hunt, and so on. In *Ariodante* (1735) Handel uses a pair of horns to represent Fame and her trumpet, which will "fly to spread the joyous news" of the king's daughter's wedding (Ex. 13.32). Horns, violins, and singer share similar melodic material: triads, neighbor-note motifs, and trills; the horns distinguish themselves, however, with consecutive trills (mm. 5–8), the violins with tirades (m. 12), the singer with passagework (mm. 23–26). The horns maintain their obbligato role throughout the first section of the aria.

In symphonies wind soloists turn up most typically in slow movements, where they assume the role of the absent singer. Here, as in arias, they usually maintain their obbligato role throughout the movement. In J. C. Bach's overture to *Lucio Silla* (1774, Ex. 13.33) the oboe takes a solo at the beginning, in the middle of the piece, then again at the end. The opening theme is echoed by a wind choir composed of flutes, clarinets, and bassoons—but no oboes, because here the oboe is the soloist. This solo oboe can be heard as amorous or as rustic, but no extra-musical association is really necessary. What the passage suggests more than anything is the variety and nuance possible in an orchestra that has enough instruments not just for an oboe solo but for a choir of contrasting winds as well.

Alternating concertante

By the middle of the eighteenth century the obbligato wind solo was a familiar orchestral effect, particularly in opera. However, the effect in Ex. 13.34, an aria from Jommelli's *Fetonte* (1753), was new. The strings play a one-measure phrase in unison, a pair of oboes answers with a contrasting one-measure phrase, followed by a pair of flutes with yet another phrase that accompanies the singer's first word. The entire sequence is repeated twice more before the aria really gets underway. Instead

---

[33] See Spitzer, "Improvised Ornamentation," 519.

Ex. 13.32. G. F. Handel, *Ariodante*, "Voli colla sua tromba" ("Let Fame fly with her trumpet")

Ex. 13.32. G. F. Handel, *Ariodante*, "Voli colla sua tromba" (*Cont.*)

Ex. 13.33. J. C. Bach, Sinfonia in B flat, Op. 18 No. 2 (Overture to *Lucio Silla*), 2nd mvt.

of monopolizing the solo for the entire aria, the wind soloists take turns, each pair relinquishing the solo role to the other or to the violins, then taking it back three measures later. Here the winds serve a dramatic function. They both introduce and

Ex. 13.34. N. Jommelli, *Fetonte*, Act I, "Penso, scelgo" ("I think, I decide, I regret my choice")

Ex. 13.35. C. Cannabich, Symphony in B flat (Wolf 72), 2nd mvt.

represent the singer, communicating his thoughts to the audience before he actually utters them.

Alternating wind concertante seems to have made its appearance first in opera, but it was soon adopted by symphony composers. Example 13.35 shows the second movement of a symphony in B flat by Christian Cannabich. Bassoons, clarinets, and horns all participate in the action, trading melodies, offering contrasting material, sometimes doubling the strings. The French critic Chastellux, writing in 1765,

Ex. 13.35. C. Cannabich, Symphony in B flat (Wolf 72), 2nd mvt. (*Cont.*)

recognized the novelty of this sort of wind writing and credited German composers with its invention:

The German symphonists . . . are less interested in finding good themes than in producing beautiful effects of harmony, which they create with the great number of different instruments that they use and by the way in which they employ them in succession [*les font travailler successivement*]. Their symphonies are like a kind of concerto, in which each instrument shines in turn.[34]

[34] Chastellux, *Essai*, 49.

Rapidly alternating and interwoven concertante, later sometimes referred to by German scholars as "open-work," became a hallmark of the Viennese Classical style, not just in symphonies but in operas and concertos as well.

From echo effects to alternating concertante, new effects of variety and nuance were invented and refined over the course of the seventeenth and eighteenth centuries. The earliest relied mainly on strings, but as more wind instruments became available and as players grew more skillful, composers discovered striking effects of timbral variety and nuance that could be created with winds. Where earlier composers had used one wind soloist, one texture, and one timbre per number, later composers called on several soloists to create a kaleidoscope of timbres and textures. In addition, wind instruments tended to lose their extramusical associations; now they were used for their timbres and their technical capabilities. "In the days before [instrumental] music was capable of declamation," says Grétry, "a flute meant love, a trumpet glory, a horn the hunt. But nowadays these diverse instruments must contribute together toward expression."[35]

CONTEXTS FOR ORCHESTRAL EFFECTS

In the seventeenth and eighteenth centuries orchestral effects were especially important in four musical contexts: in overtures, accompanied recitative, the "dramatic symphonies" of operas, and concert symphonies.

Overtures

The overture, often called French overture, was established as a genre by Lully, drawing on elements from earlier French string band music (see Ch. 3). It featured two sections, the first stately and homophonic, the second in a quicker tempo and beginning in an imitative texture, as seen in Lully's overture to *Amadis* (Ex. 13.3). The overture's first section offered many opportunities for effects of unity and grandeur. It inevitably began with a *premier coup d'archet* by the entire orchestra, and it made liberal use of tutti chords and tirades. The hallmark of the French overture, at least of its first section, was trochaic rhythm—dotted quarter followed by an eighth, dotted eighth followed by a sixteenth, etc. Dotted rhythms are easy to execute on violin-family instruments, with downbows on the long note and upbows on the short. The players can adjust to one another on the short notes, so that everyone arrives at the downbeat together. Dotted rhythms soon became appreciated for their own sake, as signs of large ensembles and the magnificence of the courts that sponsored them. Example 13.3 above features dotted rhythms in both the slow and the quick sections.

[35] Grétry, *Mémoires*, i. 237. Vol. i of Grétry's memoirs was originally published in 1789.

Ex. 13.36(a). G. F. Handel, *Samson*, Sinfonia: mm. 1–9;

The second section (Ex. 13.3(*b*)), as in most French overtures, is not a true fugue: the instruments enter one at a time, but the imitation does not continue; once all the instruments have entered, the texture becomes homophonic. For an ensemble composed entirely of violin-family instruments, and with several instruments on each of five parts, a strict fugue would not be a promising endeavor, and Lully was probably wise not to attempt it. Kusser, Handel, Telemann, and other composers who wrote French overtures at the beginning of the eighteenth century followed Lully in

Ex. 13.36(b). G. F. Handel, *Samson*, Sinfonia: mm. 60–66

making the B section a pseudo-fugue rather than a real one, and Purcell sometimes made the B section entirely homophonic.[36]

Although it successfully projected an air of unity and grandeur, the French overture, with its two strongly characterized sections, was not readily amenable to effects of variety and nuance, nor to some of the newer grand effects, like crescendo or tremolo. This inflexibility may have been one of the reasons that the overture passed out of fashion and was supplanted by the Italian sinfonia in the 1730s and 1740s. Example 13.36, the Sinfonia to Handel's *Samson* (1743), represents a highly original attempt to update the overture and combine it with the sinfonia. Although Handel

---

[36] An exception was J. S. Bach, whose first, third, and fourth suites begin with overtures featuring large and quite strict fugues. These so-called Orchestral Suites may well have been one-on-a-part music. See Ch. 7.

calls the piece "Sinfonia," he retains the structure of the overture: a stately opening section in dotted rhythms (Ex. 13.36(*a*)), followed by a pseudo-fugue in quick tempo (Ex 13.36(*b*)). He does not neglect the *premier coup*, tutti chords, or tirades (m. 8). But he also finds a place for echoes (mm. 2–3), for string–wind alternation (m. 1 and *passim*), and for solo horns (m. 1). The fanfare-like fugue theme is conceived with the horns in mind, making it possible for them to share the final entrance with the basses (mm. 65–66). Toward the end of the movement the repeated notes in the theme turn into another orchestral effect—a string tremolo (not shown). Handel's experiment in merging the French overture with the sinfonia had few heirs, but composers continued to use the gestures of the overture as introductions to symphonies. Mozart begins his Linz symphony (K. 425) with dotted rhythms in a stately tempo, his Paris symphony (K. 297) with a tirade (Ex. 13.1).

Accompanied recitative

In Italian opera one of the principal contexts for orchestral effects was accompanied recitative. "Decked out with all the brilliance of the orchestra," says Rousseau in his musical dictionary,

> these alternating passages of recitative and melody are the most touching, most ravishing, and most energetic part of modern music. The singer, moved and transported by an emotion too strong to be spoken in its entirety [*une passion qui ne lui permet pas de tout dire*], breaks off, stops and falls silent, during which time the orchestra speaks for him [*l'orchestre parle pour lui*] . . .[37]

The third act of C. H. Graun's *Montezuma* (1755) opens with such an accompanied recitative (Ex. 13.37). As the captured Aztec king ponders his unhappy fate, the orchestra gives voice to his emotions with an orchestral unison and in the second measure with dotted rhythms. When Montezuma begins to sing, the orchestral effects cease; the instruments hold a diminished 7th chord and let the king express himself in words. Later in the same recitative the orchestra continues to speak for the King with tutti chords, grand pauses, and tirades. The orchestra in this passage of accompanied recitative may "speak for" King Montezuma, but it does not speak the same dialect as he does. The singer speaks in the rhythms and inflections of natural speech, musically heightened. The orchestra speaks in an idiom that consists mainly of orchestral effects of unity and grandeur. Not until the aria that follows do singer and orchestra begin to speak the same language. The contrast here between vocal and orchestral idioms is characteristic of accompanied recitative. It reflects, indeed it increases, the distance between speech and emotion, between what the character onstage says and what he feels.

---

[37] Rousseau, *Dictionnaire de musique*, 404.

Ex. 13.37. C. H. Graun, *Montezuma*, Act III, Scene i, "Qual orribil destino" ("Oh Gods, what terrible fate afflicts me! This morning the rising sun saw me happy")

Dramatic symphonies

One of the enduring conventions of seventeenth- and eighteenth-century French opera was the *symphonie dramatique*, in which the orchestra conveys in sounds the scene, the situation, or the action that the audience sees on the stage. Dramatic symphonies confined themselves to a limited number of situations: battle scenes, sleep scenes, landscapes, storms, earthquakes, descents of gods to earth, and an occasional erupting volcano.[38] At the Paris Opéra with its large orchestra, dramatic symphonies became a kind of laboratory for orchestral effects, where composers experimented with ever grander and more nuanced musical scene painting.

The aesthetic of dramatic symphonies was influenced by the prevailing doctrine of art as imitation of nature. Music, says André Morellet in 1771, chooses as its objects the sounds, actions, and movements in the natural world that can be imitated by voices and instruments.

It depicts natural sounds by the musical sounds that are most analogous . . . the turbulant sea by rapid notes slurred together, like waves surging one after another; . . . the peaceful flow of a brook by a short diatonic phrase repeated over and over by the softest instruments, support-ed by a steady, simple bass line . . .[39]

Morellet goes on to discuss several more natural phenomena, each characterized by a different combination of orchestral effects.

Many dramatic symphonies rely primarily on effects of unity and grandeur. Battles, for example, are characterized by dotted rhythms, tutti chords, tremolos, and of course trumpets and drums. Scenes in which a ghost appears or an oracle speaks often begin with string tremolos, bass ostinatos, timpani, and sometimes a wind organ, cre-ating an anticipation of the supernatural. Perhaps the most successful of all the descriptive symphonies was the *tempête* or storm, with thunder, lightening, driving rain, and whistling wind. An enduring model for the genre was provided by Marin Marais in *Alcione* (1706). Marais's tempest features tirades, tremolos, rolling timpani, and a double bass (Ex. 13.38).[40] Storm scenes by later composers used all of these effects, plus crescendos, tutti chords, shrill piccolos, and organ-like chords in the winds.[41] The popularity of storms in dramatic symphonies encouraged composers

---

[38] Wood presents a typology of dramatic symphonies and a discussion of the most characteristic types with many examples: Caroline Wood, "Orchestra and Spectacle in the *Tragédie en musique* 1673–1715: Oracle, *Sommeil* and *Tempête*," *PRMA* 108 (1981–82), 25–45. See also Jérôme de La Gorce, "Tempêtes et tremble-ments de terre dans l'opéra français sous le règne de Louis XIV," in Hervé Lacombe (ed.), *Le Mouvement en musique à l'époque baroque* (Metz, 1996), 171–88; Sylvie Bouissou, "Mécanismes dramatiques de la tempête et de l'orage dans l'opéra français à l'âge baroque," in Jean Gribenski, Marie-Claire Mussat, and Herbert Schneider (eds.), *D'un opéra l'autre: Hommage à Jean Mongrédien* (Paris, 1996), 217–30.

[39] André Morellet, "De l'expression en musique," *Mercure de France*, Nov. 1771, 113–43, 117–18. A note at the end of Morellet's essay says that most of the text was written in 1756. See Charlton, " 'Envoicing' the Orchestra," 7.

[40] Marais's *tempête* is sometimes cited as the first appearance of the double bass at the Paris Opéra. The instrument had been used earlier, however, for infernal scenes in *Scylla* by Gatti (1701) and in *Tancrède* by Campra (1702). See Sylvette Milliot, "Réflexions et recherches sur le viole de gambe et la violoncelle en France," *RMFC* 4 (1964), 179–238 at 226; Maurice Barthélemy, "Theobaldo di Gatti et la tragédie en musique 'Scylla,' " *RMFC* 9 (1969), 56–66 at 62.

[41] Examples include Matho, *Arion* (1714), iii/3; Rameau, *Castor et Pollux* (1737), v/4; Leclair, *Scylla et Glaucus* (1746), Prologue; Gluck, *Iphigénie en Tauride* (1779), i/1.

Ex. 13.38. M. Marais, *Alcione*, Act III, Tempête

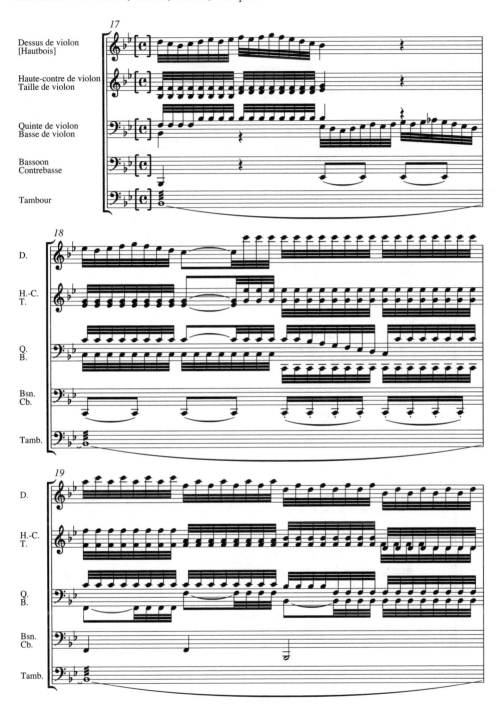

Ex. 13.38. M. Marais, *Alcione*, Act III, Tempête (*Cont.*)

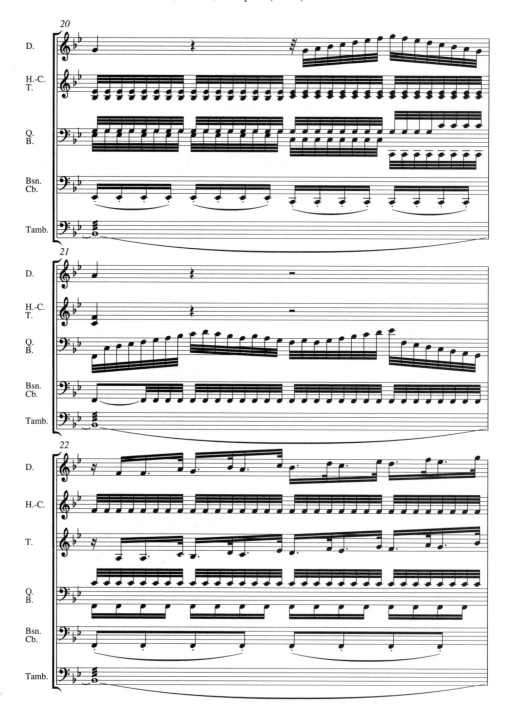

Ex. 13.38. M. Marais, *Alcione*, Act III, Tempête (*Cont.*)

like Vivaldi, Telemann, Holzbauer, and Haydn to include movements entitled
"storm" or "tempesta del mare" in concertos and concert symphonies as well.[42]

Effects of variety and nuance are less frequent in dramatic symphonies than effects
of unity or grandeur. One common setting for effects of nuance occurs when a character falls asleep onstage. Such scenes occur already in seventeenth-century Italian
operas, where they are set with sustained harmonies in the strings and ostinato

[42] Vivaldi, Concerto in E flat, RV 253; Telemann, "Der stürmende Aeolus," Ouverture in C; Holzbauer,
Symphony in E flat, Op. 4 No. 3; Haydn, Symphony No. 8 ("Le Soir").

Ex. 13.39(a). J. B. Lully, *Les Amants magnifiques*, Scene iv, Sommeil: mm. 1–8

Ex. 13.39(b). J. B. Lully, *Les Amants magnifiques*, Scene iv, Sommeil: mm. 18–25 ("Sleep, sleep fair eyes")

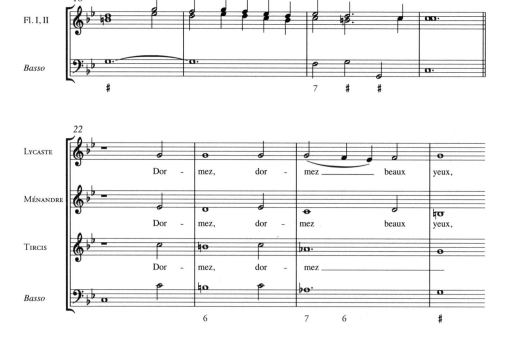

patterns in the bass.[43] In French opera they characteristically involve flutes, either alone or in alternation with the strings. An early example comes from from Lully's *Les Amants magnifiques* (1670). A pair of flutes, a pastoral signifier, accompanies a song by Caliste, a shepherdess. Then the two flutes plus continuo play as she falls asleep, and the chorus sings a lullaby (Ex. 13.39). The "Sommeil" in Atys (1676) is more elaborate. Flutes and strings alternate in the symphony, followed by ballets of pleasant and unpleasant dreams (Ex. 13.13), played by the string ensemble.

In the seventeenth century dramatic symphonies tended to depict a single natural object or a static scene and to use the same set of orchestral effects throughout, effects of unity and grandeur or effects of variety and nuance, but not both. As the vocabulary of orchestral effects grew during the first half of the eighteenth century, composers experimented with the depiction of changing states of nature, using gradations or combinations of effects. Rameau was particularly adventurous in this regard. An earthquake in *Les Indes galantes* (1735, ii/5) features tremolos and tirades at alternating dynamics of piano and forte (not shown). The overture to *Zaïs* (1748) depicts chaos by means of unaccompanied tympani followed by bizarre harmonies. In the Prologue proper an ambitious dramatic symphony (not shown) depicts a stream cascading down a mountain slope in sixteenth notes, then broadening and slowing as it reaches the plain, with a diminuendo and slower note values, finally becoming a river flowing among verdant fields, while piccolos imitate the songs of birds along the banks. To help the spectators draw the right inferences about which natural objects are being imitated, a narrator provides a "voice-over" description of the river's course.

Critics and spectators at the Opéra marveled at the faithfulness with which the orchestra imitated nature in dramatic symphonies. Yet the way that composers actually used orchestral effects in their symphonies belied the doctrine of imitation. The tremolo that imitated the sounds of battle in one symphony became the sound of thunder in another, the harbinger of the supernatural in yet another.[44] The piccolos that imitated the howling wind in the first act became twittering birds in the fourth. This is not to say that tremolos were not effective at evoking battles, thunder, or ghosts, or piccolos at suggesting birds or winds. Rather it implies that, just as a poet depicts the world with a finite number of words in ever-changing combinations, composers of the eighteenth century were creating a vocabulary of orchestral effects, capable if not of imitating, at least of evoking the whole world through a limited number of instrumental metaphors.[45]

---

[43] See Rosand, *Opera in 17th-Century Venice*, 338–42.

[44] See La Gorce, "Tempêtes et tremblements," 183.

[45] See Morellet, "De l'expression en musique," 120 ff.

Concert symphonies

Unlike dramatic symphonies, the *sinfonie* at the beginning of seventeenth- and eighteenth-century Italian operas did not usually depict anything. Instead they were an opportunity for the orchestra to make itself heard alone before the singers commanded the audience's attention; they were curtain-raisers, settling down the audience and the players. In fulfilling those functions, *sinfonie* made use of many orchestral effects, particularly effects of unity and grandeur. The excerpts above from *sinfonie* by Jommelli, Porpora, Scarlatti, and Conti featured *premiers coups*, tutti chords, trumpets and drums, crescendos, and other effects that make the orchestra sound large, unified, and impressive. In addition, opera *sinfonie* contained occasional effects of variety and nuance, particularly subito piano and string–wind alternation.

Symphonies composed specifically to be performed in concert relied even more than opera *sinfonie* on orchestral effects, because here the orchestra itself was the principal attraction. The first movement, according to J. A. P. Schulze in 1774, needs to have "grand and bold thoughts," "strongly marked rhythms," "unisons and powerful bass melodies," "concertante middle parts," "vivid shadings of forte and piano," and above all "the crescendo, which, when combined with a rising melodic line with intensifying expression, creates a tremendous effect."[46] Schulze praises the symphonies of the Belgian composer Pierre van Maldere as exemplifying all these orchestral effects but, he says, they can also be found in concert symphonies by Mannheim and Berlin composers and especially in the symphonies of Haydn.

The Symphony No. 6 ("Le Matin") was the first symphony that Haydn composed for the Esterházy court, and he seized the opportunity to show what he and his orchestra could do. Almost every orchestral effect available to a composer in 1761 can be heard in the introduction and exposition of the first movement of this up-to-date, forward-looking symphony (Ex. 13.40). The opening Adagio does not begin with a *premier coup* but rather pianissimo with first violins alone, an effect of nuance instead of grandeur. Haydn does allude, however, in measures 1 and 2 to the dotted rhythms of the French overture. Effects of unity and grandeur begin in measure 3 with the staggered entrance of the full orchestra and a rapid crescendo to a fortissimo, dominant chord.[47] The Allegro begins with a subito piano and with the melody not in the violins but a solo flute, a radical effect of variety and nuance for 1761. First and second violins play a *petite basse* accompaniment. In measure 11 the oboe takes over the solo (alternating concertante); in measure 14 the full orchestra enters with tremolo in

[46] In Sulzer, *Allgemeine Theorie der schönen Kunste*, iv. 479. For the articles on music in his dictionary of aesthetics, Sulzer enlisted the assistance of Johann Peter Kirnberger for the first part of the alphabet and Kirnberger's pupil Johann Abraham Peter Schulze toward the end of the alphabet. See the Introdution to Vol. iii of the second edition (1786–89).

[47] This opening adagio is sometimes said to depict the sun rising over the horizon, a sort of condensed dramatic symphony. See Landon, *Haydn: Chronicle and Works*, i. 555.

Ex. 13.40. J. Haydn, Symphony No. 6 ("Le Matin"), 1st mvt.

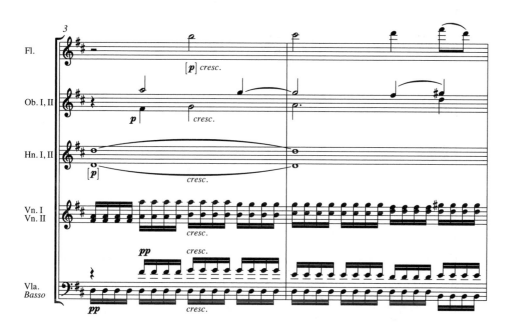

Ex. 13.40. J. Haydn, Symphony No. 6 ("Le Matin"), 1st mvt. (*Cont.*)

Ex. 13.40. J. Haydn, Symphony No. 6 ("Le Matin"), 1st mvt. (*Cont.*)

Ex. 13.40. J. Haydn, Symphony No. 6 ("Le Matin"), 1st mvt. (*Cont.*)

the violins and a wind organ in the horns. Effects of grandeur and effects of variety alternate: a grand pause in measure 20, subito piano in measure 21 for the second group, subito forte again in measure 27, with tirades in the violins and a wind organ in the horns, oboes, and flutes. Measure 35 initiates a quick, brilliant cycle of alternating concertante—second oboe, first oboe, flute, bassoon, both oboes—all over a forte–piano dynamic effect in the strings. Finally, the exposition ends with three

Ex. 13.40. J. Haydn, Symphony No. 6 ("Le Matin"), 1st mvt. (*Cont.*)

measures of orchestral unison. In less than 50 measures of music, Haydn has managed to make use of every orchestral effect discussed here except for the *premier coup*, and trumpets and drums, the last unavailable at Eszterháza in 1762.

Unlike a descriptive symphony, a concert symphony does not have to depict anything; unlike an accompanied recitative, it does not have to communicate any particular emotion. In their symphonies Haydn and other composers were free to alternate effects of grandeur and unity with effects of variety and nuance more freely

Ex. 13.40. J. Haydn, Symphony No. 6 ("Le Matin"), 1st mvt. (*Cont.*)

Ex. 13.40. J. Haydn, Symphony No. 6 ("Le Matin"), 1st mvt. (*Cont.*)

and more rapidly than in other musical genres. Concert symphonies were intended, as Schulze said, to "show off instrumental music in all its magnificence,"[48] and in this sense symphonies, insofar as they were about anything, were about the orchestra. By using the full range of orchestral effects to highlight the melodies, harmonies, rhythms, textures, and structures of the music, eighteenth-century symphony composers communicated the excellence of the orchestras for which they composed their symphonies and the excellence of orchestras in general.

THE THEORY OF ORCHESTRATION

The orchestral effects that composers invented and refined during the seventeenth and eighteenth centuries and the ways that they found to exploit these effects in their music amounted to what is now called orchestration. Yet neither the word "orchestration" nor its close relative, "instrumentation," was used in any European language until the nineteenth century. The German lexicographer H. C. Koch documents the arrival of the new usage. In his *Musikalisches Lexikon* of 1802 there is no entry for either word. Koch's comments about full vs. reduced scorings, the use of wind

---

[48] Sulzer, *Allgemeine Theorie*, iv. 478–79.

instruments, and other orchestral effects appear in an article on "Begleitung" (accompaniment).[49] But in a condensation of the lexicon, the *Kurzgefasstes Handwörterbuch der Musik* (1807), Koch adds an entry for "Instrumentirung," which he defines as "the manner in which a composer treats the instruments that he has chosen as accompaniment for the principal part, what effects he obtains from them, and how he works them more or less prominently into the texture."[50] Koch does not say what effects are possible or how the composer should obtain them; those matters still appear under the old rubric of "accompaniment." But instrumentation is named and conceptualized as a distinct phase of compositional activity.

Notwithstanding the lack of a word for orchestration, a small literature on instruments, their use in combination with one another, and the effects that they were capable of in large ensembles, began to emerge in the second half of the eighteenth century. Diderot addressed the topic briefly in an article he wrote around 1761 for the *Encyclopédie* under the heading "Instruments."[51] "The character of the instruments," he asserts, "is a vital part of a composer's study." A composer needs to be acquainted not only with each and every instrument but also with "the effects possible when the sounds of instruments are combined with one another." Once a composer understands how to use instruments, says Diderot, "there are no natural phenomena, no passions, no sentiments of the human heart that cannot be imitated by an instrument." In counterpoint to Diderot, his colleague d'Alembert complained about the excessive reliance on instrumental effects in French music: "Our French composers go wild, heaping instrument upon instrument: but the only effect they achieve thereby is noise."[52]

Jean-Laurent de Béthizy, in his *Exposition de la théorie et de la pratique de la musique* (1764) goes beyond aesthetic pronouncements to offer practical advice about the use of instruments in an orchestra. He devotes one paragraph apiece to the instruments that "are used in the majority of accompaniments: namely the flute, the oboe, the violin, [the viola], the bassoon, the cello, the bass viol, and the harpsichord."[53] The flute has a range from *d'* to *e'''* (even higher for good players). Its sound is "tender and sad," and it is useful to express sorrow. The oboe is gay and appropriate for rustic scenes. Its range extends from *c'* to *d'''*, and so forth. All the instruments of the orchestra are compressed into four pages. If the composer needs to know more, says Béthizy, he should consult performers.[54]

---

[49] Koch, *Musikalisches Lexikon*, cols. 232–37.

[50] Heinrich Christoph Koch, *Kurzgefasstes Handwörterbuch der Musik* (Leipzig, 1807), 192.

[51] Diderot, "Instrumens," 803. This article was written by Diderot rather than Rousseau, who wrote most of other articles in the *Encyclopédie* on musical topics. See Béatrice Didier, *La Musique des lumières* (Paris, 1985), 265, 269, 459.

[52] D'Alembert, *De la liberté de la musique*, 448.

[53] Jean-Laurent de Béthizy, *Exposition de la théorie et de la pratique de la musique*, 2nd edn. (Paris, 1764), 304. Béthizy in 1764 still lacks a word in French for viola. He calls it "the instrument which plays the *haute-contre*, *taille* and *quinte de violon* parts."

[54] Ibid. 307.

Diderot, D'Alembert, Béthizy, and even Koch do not seem to think of the orchestra as an ensemble, with an identity and a performance style of its own, but rather as "accompaniment" to a singer or to an instrumental soloist, the standard eighteenth-century conceptualization. Although they all acknowledge the orchestra as an institution, most eighteenth-century writers still conceive of the music that orchestras play as accompaniment to a principal part. This framework leaves little room for orchestral effects. Because the interest of music lies in the melody and expression of the principal part, effects are little more than a distraction. Only in dramatic symphonies, says d'Alembert, is the orchestra freed from its role as accompaniment. Since there is no principal part, the accompaniment is no longer a distraction, and orchestral effects have a legitimate role. Here, says d'Alembert, French music, particularly the dramatic symphonies of Rameau, is actually superior to Italian.[55]

The prevailing doctrine of the orchestra as accompaniment was challenged in a pair of articles both entitled "Accompaniment" in the *Encyclopédie méthodique: Musique* (1791).[56] The first, by Framery, discusses keyboard accompaniments for vocal numbers, then orchestral accompaniments, whose main precept is to support the voice and not to compete with it. Framery acknowledges, however, that in accompanied recitative the orchestra takes on a different role: it enters into dialogue with the voice; sometimes it becomes a rival to the voice; indeed the orchestra itself occasionally becomes the principal part. The orchestra's special role in accompanied recitative and also in dramatic symphonies can be highlighted by effects like unison, tremolo, *petite basse*, wind organ, and wind obbligato, each of which he describes in considerable detail. Framery still feels obliged, however, to warn his readers against the overuse of wind instruments, and he ends the article with a diatribe against trumpets and drums:

these instruments are useful only to accompany marches and depict battle scenes. The mania for effects has become so great, however, while the means for producing such effects remain so limited, that by now hardly an opera is staged without trumpets and drums. We hear them even in pastoral airs.[57]

Framery's ambivalence is typical of many commentators on orchestration in the late eighteenth and early nineteenth centuries: he acknowledges the importance of the orchestra and the effects it can create, but he complains about how these effects are actually used in contemporary music.

J. A. B. Suard, in his article "Accompaniment," sheds all ambivalence.[58] In a lengthy historical presentation he argues that "it was the destiny of instrumental composition to produce the most diverse effects and gradually to build up an infinite

---

[55] D'Alembert, *De la liberté de la musique*, 455.

[56] Nicolas Étienne Framery, "Accompagnement," in *Encyclopédie méthodique: Musique*, ed. Nicolas Étienne Framery, Pierre-Louis Ginguené, and Jérôme Joseph de Momigny (Paris, 1791–1818), i. 13–20; Suard, "Accompagnement, Accompagner."

[57] Framery, "Accompagnement," 20.

[58] Suard, "Accompagnement, Accompagner," i. 22–24. See the beginning of this chapter, and also Charlton, "'Envoicing' the Orchestra," 29–31.

multitude of novel combinations." In contemporary music, he says, the orchestra can no longer be considered an accompaniment to the singers; it is a "chorus" of independent voices, which expresses its own sentiments in a language of its own. The concept of "accompaniment" has misled people into thinking of the orchestra as subordinate to the voice and of orchestral effects as inferior to melody, whereas in reality the most striking, expressive, sublime moments in music almost always come from the orchestra ("les plus beaux effets de la musique peuvent donc se trouver dans ce qu'on appelle les accompagnements"). Concludes Suard: "those who believe that genius, charm, and expression are the exclusive property of vocal melody rather than of instruments, are listening to music without hearing it."[59]

The history of orchestration traditionally begins with three books published in the second half of the eighteenth century, all of them in French, on how to compose for wind instruments. They are the *Essai d'instruction à l'usage de ceux qui composent pour la clarinette et le cor* by Valentin Roeser (1764), Louis Joseph Francoeur's *Diapason général de tous les instruments à vent* (1772), and the *Traité général de tous les instruments à vent* by Othon Vandenbroeck (1793).[60] Because the winds, particularly horns and clarinets, were relatively new to the orchestra, composers were not as familiar with them as they were with strings. Composing for winds required mastery of the vocabulary of orchestral effects, because just about any intervention of the winds, beyond simply doubling the strings or the voice, amounted to an orchestral effect.

Francoeur's *Diapason général* (1772) can serve as an example of these treatises as a genre. Proceeding instrument by instrument, Francoeur advises composers about the range of each instrument, about which keys are best for that instrument, about which notes are good and which are bad, which intervals are easy and which difficult, which trills are possible, which impossible. Finally he discusses the appropriate use of that instrument—what its associations and connotations are, what kinds of passages are typical. He illustrates these uses with printed musical examples.

Francoeur's treatise evidently remained in use for the rest of the eighteenth century and beyond, for in 1813 Alexandre Choron issued a new edition under a new title: *Traité général des voix et des instruments d'orchestre*.[61] Although the chapters on wind instruments remained exactly as Francoeur had written them in 1772, the new title indicated a fundamental change: the treatise is now addressed not just to winds but to the entire orchestra. Choron adds chapters on stringed instruments, percussion, and even voice. For Choron the orchestra is a single musical unit: winds are just as much the norm as strings; now both strings and winds are capable of orchestral effects.

---

[59] Suard, "Accompagnement, Accompagner," 24.

[60] For a review of 18th- and early 19th-c. orchestration manuels, see Hans Bartenstein, "Die frühen Instrumentationslehren bis zu Berlioz," *Archiv für Musikwissenschaft*, 28 (1971), 97–118.

[61] Alexandre Choron, *Traité général des voix et des instruments d'orchestre* (Paris, 1813).

One of the main purposes of these French treatises was to explain the orchestrations of German composers like Stamitz and Haydn. Yet the only eighteenth-century German treatise on orchestration seems to have been the "Short description of musical instruments" that J. G. Albrechtsberger, Beethoven's composition teacher, appended to his *Gründliche Anweisung zur Composition* (1790).[62] He devotes a paragraph to each of the orchestral instruments, giving their ranges, scales, good and bad notes, and symbolic connotations. He also discusses outmoded instruments like the baryton and the viola d'amore. He pays the most attention to the winds, warning composers about their bad notes, bad keys, and difficult registers, and giving musical examples to make his points. He has nothing to say about combinations of instruments or orchestral effects.

No English treatises address themselves exclusively to orchestration until the middle of the nineteenth century. However, Augustus Kollmann, a German-trained composer living in England, takes up the subject in his *Essay on Practical Musical Composition* (1799). Chapter 11 is a brief treatise on orchestration, laid out instrument by instrument, a format that had evidently become conventional. He characterizes the tone quality of the various instruments: the serpent and the trombone are "harsh," the trumpet, oboe, and bassoon "milder," the clarinet, French horn, and flute "mildest." He also tries to characterize each instrument's typical idiom: "The trumpet is calculated more for short and pointed notes than the French Horn, and this latter instrument more for holding notes than the former."[63] He devotes a section to "the combination of different instruments," the first writer on orchestration to address this issue systematically.

Although Kollmann's treatment of orchestration is brief, he comes closer than any other eighteenth-century theorist to an adequate description of the practices of contemporary composers. He considers the orchestra to be an independent musical unit, not just an accompaniment to a singer or a soloist. He gives systematic consideration to combinations of instruments, to orchestral effects, and to the special requirements of writing for an ensemble composed of many different types of instruments and with several players on each part. Finally, he does not complain about the overuse of wind instruments, not even the brass. He praises the orchestrations of modern composers, especially Haydn, and recommends passages from "the scores of all great composers" for his readers to study.

Orchestration developed during the seventeenth and eighteenth centuries as a stockpile of "effects" that composers invented, learned from one another, experimented with, refined, and applied in more and more musical contexts. Eighteenth-century theorists considered these orchestral effects as exceptions to ordinary four-part string scoring, which they thought of as fundamentally an "accompaniment" to a singer or an

---

[62] Johann Georg Albrechtsberger, *Gründliche Anweisung zur Composition* (Leipzig, 1790), 416 ff.

[63] Augustus Frederic Christopher Kollmann, *An Essay on Practical Musical Composition* (London, 1799), 91.

instrumental soloist. Effects were for dramatic symphonies, for accompanied recitative, and other special situations. Orchestral effects outside these contexts were criticized as noisy, distracting, and inappropriate. Yet composers persistently ignored these warnings and made use of their growing stockpile of effects in an ever-widening range of musical and dramatic situations. By the last quarter of the eighteenth century effects had become pervasive in orchestral music.

Not until the 1790s, however, did theory begin to catch up with practice. Albrechtsberger in 1790 considered the wind instruments as equal partners with the strings in the orchestra. Suard in 1791 criticized the old conceptualization of the orchestra as accompaniment and tried to persuade people that orchestral effects were one of the glories of modern music. Kollmann (1799) recognized combinations of instruments and effects of variety and nuance as everyday aspects of compositional technique in orchestral music. And Koch in his *Kurzgefasstes Handwörterbuch* (1807) finally gave this technique a name: "instrumentation." The timing is suggestive. As Chapter 9 has shown, the period from 1790 to 1815 marked the end of a long period of uniformity and stability for the "classical orchestra," after which the orchestra entered a period of rapid change. Chapter 11 showed how an ideology of orchestral performance practice consolidated itself in just the same period, as represented in treatises by Galeazzi (1791), Arnold (1806), and Scaramelli (1811). The articulation of a theory of orchestration was another aspect of the same process of consolidation and growing consciousness of the orchestra as a social institution.

Chapter Fourteen

The Meaning of the Orchestra

When it was born in the late seventeenth century the orchestra was a novelty. Never before had people heard music so loud, so grand, and so forceful. The orchestra, moreover, represented a new kind of social organization: a large number of people doing the same thing at the same time in precisely the same way. Because the orchestra was new and different, people found it hard to characterize in words. Sebastiano Locatelli, an Italian traveler, struggled to describe the French string band that he heard in Lyons in 1664: "The music in this region is made by, how should I say it, an assembly [*radunanza*] of players on violins, violas, and basses, as many as 40 or 50 at a time. They play in a full chorus [*a coro pieno*]; they all bow together with great bow strokes, as though they were marching into battle."[1] The anonymous chronicler who heard Corelli's orchestra playing for an "Academy" at Queen Christina's palace in Rome in 1687 was similarly impressed:

When the signal was given, the royal festival began with a grand symphony comprising 150 instruments of all sorts, played by master musicians, and directed and led by the famous Arcangelo Corelli, the Bolognese. With their almost celestial harmony they brought joy to the spectators, who could not comprehend how the clamor of so many instruments [*lo strepito di tanti stromenti*] could strike their ears with such sweet unanimity.[2]

A hundred years later the orchestra was no longer a novelty, but the same sense of astonishment can still be heard in Johann Kaspar Riesbeck's report on Viennese orchestras in 1783:

Here one can assemble four or five large orchestras, all of them incomparably good. The number of true virtuosos is small, but as far as orchestral music is concerned, one can hardly hear anything more beautiful in the whole world. I have heard 30 and 40 instruments play

[1] Locatelli, *Viaggio di Francia*, 169. See Ch. 2, p. 67, ch. 9, p. 306.
[2] Liess, "Neue Zeugnisse von Corellis Wirken in Rom," 134. See Ch. 4, p. 118.

together with such a correct, pure, and precise tone that one seems to hear a single supernat-
urally powerful instrument [*ein einziges übernatürlich starkes Instrument*]. One bowstroke sounds
all the violins; one breath animates all the winds.[3]

These three descriptions share a single rhetorical device: each explains what an
orchestra is by using a metaphor. Locatelli compares the orchestra to an army, the
Roman chronicler to a choir of angels, Riesbeck to a giant musical instrument. By
making a metaphorical equation between the orchestra and something else, the
authors assimilate the new institution to ideas and experiences already familiar to their
readers. At the same time they create a sense of astonishment by juxtaposing the
orchestra with something from which it initially seems quite different.

A metaphor, Aristotle says, gives a thing a name that belongs to something else.[4]
The topic of interest, in this case the orchestra, is explained or enhanced with words
that would seem to apply more properly to other topics: armies, angels, musical
instruments. I. A. Richards, in his classic essay on metaphor, called the topic of interest the "tenor," the word belonging to another object the "vehicle."[5] George Lakoff
and Mark Turner use a more intuitive terminology, calling the topic of interest the
"target" and the words drawn from elsewhere the "source" or the "source domain"
of the metaphor.[6] In Riesbeck's metaphor the target is orchestras in general and
Viennese orchestras in particular; the source is musical instruments, their technology
and performance practice. Attributes from the domain of musical instruments—each
instrument has a distinctive tone, stringed instruments are played with bows, etc.—
are transferred to the orchestra in order to highlight qualities that Riesbeck finds
extraordinary and admirable about Viennese orchestras. The account of the Corelli
performance draws metaphors from two contrasting source domains: the confusion
and chaos of the human world versus the harmony and order of heaven. Locatelli in
his description of French string bands draws metaphors from three source domains:
civil society and sociability ("an assembly"), vocal music ("a full chorus"), and finally
the army ("marching into battle").

Metaphors offer a path to uncover historical meanings.[7] One way to understand
what the orchestra meant to people during the period in which it was born as an institution is to look at the metaphors that people of the time used to describe orchestras.

---

[3] Johann Kaspar Riesbeck, *Briefe eines reisenden Franzosen über Deutschland* (1783), ed. Wolfgang Gerlach
(Stuttgart, 1967), 138–40.

[4] Aristotle, *Poetics*, ch. 21; Penelope Murray and T. S. Dorsch (eds.), *Classical Literary Criticism* (Oxford,
2000), 85.

[5] I. A. Richards, *The Philosophy of Rhetoric* (Oxford, 1936), 96.

[6] George Lakoff and Mark Turner, *More than Cool Reason: A Field Guide to Poetic Metaphor* (Chicago, 1989),
57 ff.

[7] For discussions of musical metaphors and their change over time, see Mark Evan Bonds, *Wordless Rhetoric:
Musical Form and the Metaphor of the Oration* (Cambridge, Mass., 1991); Charlton, " 'Envoicing' the Orchestra."
For a more general discussion see Hans Blumenberg, "Paradigmen zu einer Metaphorologie," *Archiv für
Begriffsgeschichte*, 6 (1960), 7–142.

The metaphors in the passages above—the orchestra as a musical instrument, as a heavenly choir, as chaos, as civil society, as an army—occur over and over in seventeenth- and eighteenth-century sources. Writers at different times and in different places draw from the same source domains to communicate in words what they know and believe about orchestras. This suggests that there are configurations of meaning that these authors share with one another and with their readers. The metaphors they choose reveal what they mean by orchestra and what the orchestra means to them.

The metaphors in our survey were gathered from a large number of texts in English, French, German, and Italian in which writers use the word "orchestra" or one of its cognates, or in which they describe an instrumental ensemble that today would be called an orchestra. The texts have been extracted from novels, letters, plays, and poetry, as well as from writings about music. The earliest date from the beginning of the seventeenth century, the latest from 1850.[8] In order to identify areas of meaning and trace meanings over time, the texts were classified according to source domain and arranged chronologically. Three broad findings emerge:

1. Metaphors of the orchestra are drawn from a limited number of source domains. Besides musical instruments, chaos, heavenly choirs, civil society, and the army, writers describe the orchestra with metaphors of the human body (or organisms in general), nature, machines, and works of art. Other metaphors are rarely encountered.[9]

2. Metaphors of the orchestra change over time. Those that were once common become scarce, while scarce metaphors become common. This suggests that what the orchestra meant to people changed as the orchestra developed.

3. At the beginning of the period the orchestra is exclusively the target of metaphor, that is, in order to explain the orchestra, it is compared to something else. In the mid-eighteenth century and increasingly thereafter, however, the orchestra begins to serve also as a source for metaphor. This suggests that it had become familiar enough and its meanings well enough understood that it could serve as a source domain to explain and enhance other topics of interest.

---

[8] Many of the texts were located by computer searches through full-text databases and electronic dictionaries. The largest full-text databases are ARTFL, which contains over 2,000 texts from French letters and literature (http://www.humanities.uchicago.edu/ARTFL/ARTFL.html) and Chadwyck-Healy's Literature Online, a database of English and American literature (http://lion.chadwyck.com). For Italian there is LIZ (Letteratura Italiana Zanichelli [Bologna: Zanichelli, 1998]), a CD-ROM. In addition we consulted *The Oxford English Dictionary on Compact Disc*, 2nd edn. (New York: Oxford University Press, 1992).

[9] The only other metaphor for the orchestra that occurs with any frequency before 1800 is of the orchestra as a pack or herd of animals. This can be regarded as a satirical inversion of the "orchestra as civil society" metaphor.

EARLY METAPHORS OF THE ORCHESTRA

The earliest metaphors of the orchestra date from the seventeenth century, when "pre-orchestral" instrumental ensembles began to arise at European courts. The most common metaphor in the seventeenth century seems to have been that of a hodge-podge of instruments and sounds. A typical example comes from Giovanni Battista Doni's *Tratatto della musica scenica*, written around 1630:

> But when instruments are used alone as a plain symphony [*mera sinfonia*] to spell the actors and tickle the ears of the spectators, I do not know whether it might not be more suitable, instead of a hodgepodge, like a Spanish stew [*oglia podrida alla spagnuola*], to group them into separate ensembles: sometimes of viols and violins, sometimes of lutes, theorbos, and lyras, sometimes of harps and harpsichords, sometimes of flutes or other wind instruments.[10]

Having no word for orchestra, Doni calls it a "plain symphony," that is, instruments playing together without voices. He condemns this newfangled ensemble of diverse instruments as an undesirable and unpleasant musical stew, and argues instead for traditional consorts of similar instruments playing one on a part.

Michel de Pure, in his *Idée des spectacles* (1668), likewise has no word for orchestra, so he chooses a similar metaphor in French to describe what was either an ensemble for one of the *ballets de cour* at the French court or perhaps one of Mazarin's Italian operas:

> I don't even need to mention other instuments, for they should be rejected and excluded from royal and public entertainments. I witnessed a shivaree [*un charivary*], for I don't know what else to call that huge company assembled a few years ago. Not only did the large number of performers create impossible problems, but sour notes and poor intonation were almost inevitable. And in the end this conflation [*amas*], which seemed curious and novel at the time, turned out to be nothing but foolishness, and gave rise only to mockery and scorn.[11]

Doni and de Pure both choose metaphors with negative connotations, because both disapprove of orchestras—at least they condemn the combination of instruments of different types and the multiplication of instruments on parts. In the eighteenth century, however, when such ensembles became much more common, the negative connotations tended to disappear. L.-S. Mercier, in a novel published in 1776, finds the cacophony of an orchestra tuning up downright pleasant: "The chaotic but agreeable sound of the instruments tuning in the adjoining room, the tumult, and the continuous symphony, announced to the world that this house, or rather this palace, was the home of a tax farmer."[12] As orchestras became more familiar, and perhaps also as

---

[10] Giovanni Battista Doni, *Tratatto della musica scenica*, in *Lyra Barberina amphichordos: accedunt eiusdem opera I–II*, ed. A. F. Gori and G. B. Passari (Florence, 1763), 110.

[11] Michel de Pure, *L'Idée des spectacles* (Paris, 1668), 272.

[12] Louis-Sébastien Mercier, *Jezennemours: Roman-dramatique* (Amsterdam, 1776), 3. Mercier may be be thinking here of La Pouplinière. See Ch. 6.

improvisation was eliminated from orchestral performance practice, confusion became less common and less threatening, and metaphors of hodgepodge, confusion, and stews grew rare in descriptions of the orchestra.

In the description above of Queen Christina's academy, the confusing clamor of massed instruments is contrasted with the celestial harmony of Corelli's orchestra. The metaphor of heavenly choirs was familiar in descriptions of sixteenth- and seventeenth-century vocal music, and it was available for instrumental ensembles too. It still took something akin to divine intervention, however, to make a large group of instruments play with heavenly concord. A 1701 description of Corelli's orchestra claims that the composer has "left the heavenly choir to come to earth, bringing with him from that bright world a unity of sound never heard before on earth, so that one would believe that a hundred instruments were a single one."[13] A description of Lully's orchestra for *Alcidiane* (1658) employs the same metaphor, although the source domain is a pagan rather than a Christian heaven:

> A grand concert, to all intents,
> Made up of eighty instruments
> (Indeed, they say, of eighty-four)
> Opens the show with an overture.
> Thirty-six violins all play,
> An Apollo each in his own way,
> A heavenly melange.[14]

"Melange" in the last line recalls the metaphor of hodgpodge and confusion, softened and sweetened now by its heavenly associations.

By the late eighteenth century metaphors of the heavenly orchestra had become scarce. Vocal choirs, whose primary venue was churches, retained their heavenly connections, but the associations of orchestras, which played in theaters and at pleasure gardens, were earthly. Mme de Staël in 1810 criticizes German churches for relying too much on orchestral music: "Church music is not so beautiful in Germany as in Italy, because the instruments always dominate. When you have been to Rome and heard the *Miserere* sung by voices a cappella, all instrumental music, even that of the Dresden Kapelle, seems earth-bound by comparison."[15] Most likely, the metaphors of chaos versus concord faded because of changes in the orchestra. As the orchestra became more familiar and more widely used in secular contexts, it became less appropriate to map characteristics of heaven onto it, and that metaphor gave way to others.

---

[13] G. B. Zappi and G. M. Crescimbeni, *Il Ferragosto* (1701); quoted in Rinaldi, *Arcangelo Corelli*, 256.

[14] Jean Loret, *La Muze historique*, ed. Ch.-L. Livet (Paris, 1877), 444 (letter of 16 Feb. 1658): "Un grand Concert, des plus charmans, / Compozé d'octante Instrumens, / (Encor, dit-on octante-et-quatre) / Fait l'ouverture du Théatre; / Sçavoir trente-et-six Violons, / Qui sont, presque, autant d'Apollons, / Formans un mêlange céleste. . . ."

[15] Germaine de Staël, *De l'Allemagne* (1810) (Paris, 1991), 85. Mme de Staël refers to the famous *Miserere* by Allegri as performed by the papal choir in Rome.

THE ORCHESTRA AS CIVIL POLITY

Writers of the late seventeenth century began to draw metaphors from a new source to characterize the orchestra: politics, government, and civil society. As the activities of individuals are combined and regulated in society, so an orchestra combines instruments and performers to make music. And in the orchestra, as in politics, harmony is achieved by the imposition of external authority. Charles Dufresny in 1699 describes the *batteur de mesure* at the Paris Opéra in terms of royal absolutism: "Everyone depends on the sovereign of the orchestra, a prince whose power is so absolute that by raising and lowering his scepter, the roll of paper that he holds in his hand, he regulates every movement of this fickle populace."[16] Dufresny adapts a cluster of elements from the source domain of society and governance. The timebeater is a ruler, the rolled-up score in his right hand is a scepter, and the instrumentalists are the "populace," capricious and difficult to govern. The ruler of France in 1699 was Louis XIV, who sponsored the Opéra and its orchestra. The "absolute" power of the *batteur de mesure* was a reflection of the absolute power of the Sun King. The metaphor of the orchestra as civil polity not only served to characterize the new institution, it also reinforced the ideology of absolutism.

Johann Beer, in his *Musicalische Discurse*, written in the 1690s, asks whether an orchestra can exist at all without a director.[17] Some people claim, he says, that instrumentalists are all equally good performers, and that one cannot be singled out and set above his fellows; others claim that a musical artist is a free spirit and by nature cannot be subjected to another's will. Christian humility, however, and civil order both teach us, he says, that

musical subjugation resembles neither civic duty nor slavery. People obey not of their own free will but out of deference to authority. . . . [Musicians] must give this obedience to their leader [*der Majestro*] during the time that he is leading, even though they are an aristocracy in other respects.[18]

Beer undertakes this convoluted metaphorical argument because orchestras and orchestral behaviors were new to Germany in 1719. People are not sure what to call an orchestra, and they do not know how such a large group of instrumentalists should be organized or how its members should relate to one another. Perhaps because Beer himself was both court musician and court counselor to the Duke of Saxe-Weissenfels, he decides that the orchestra corresponds best to an autocratic form of government and that therefore it needs a single leader or director. When Dufresny or Beer compare the orchestra to an absolute monarchy, they do more than describe an

---

[16] Dufresny, *Amusmens sérieux et comiques*, 64.

[17] Johann Beer, *Musicalische Discurse* (Nuremberg, 1719), 3. Beer died in 1700, but his treatise was not published until 1719.

[18] Ibid. 5–6.

emerging institution. By choosing an absolutist model of civil society as the source for their metaphor, they assert the validity of that particular style of authority and that particular form of government.

Other eighteenth-century writers had other political agendas. A letter from John Vanbrugh to the Earl of Manchester concerning arrangements for Italian opera in London in 1708 invokes the same metaphor of the orchestra as civil polity, but here the sovereign is a violin leader rather than a timebeater: "if yr Ldship brought a perfect good Violin to Lead & Govern the Orcastre, 'twou'd be of great Service. Nicolini that belong'd to the Duke of Bedford & is now at Rome, is thought by the Skilfull here, to be as good as any in Europe for that particular Service."[19] Vanbrugh's "Orcastre" may have referred primarily to a place in the theater rather than the instrumental ensemble that occupied that place. But the language of government applied in either case. If engaged, Nicolini would govern both the orchestra pit and the musicians in it. This time, however, government is not "absolute power" or "obedience" but "service," reflecting the political differences between the Continent and England, a "constitutional" monarchy since 1688.

The author of a bit of anonymous verse published in France during the Querelle des bouffons puts a different spin on the same metaphor to criticize the timebeater at the Opéra:

> He confines himself solely to flogging the time,
> As though the poor singers and orchestra supine,
> Were led by a chieftain with menacing threats,
> And could not proceed unless beaten to death.[20]

The writer implies that Italian orchestras, which did not use a timebeater, sound better than the orchestra of the Opéra, and that professional musicians do not need an absolute monarch to make them play. Perhaps he implies more. If the metaphor is reversed, if the orchestra is taken as the source and government the target, then this anonymous bit of doggerel suggests that the French nation may not need a timebeater either. Perhaps absolute monarchy is not the only or the best kind of government for France.[21]

Friedrich Rochlitz, in his "Letters to a Young Musician" (1799), rejects the authoritarian model of social organization explicitly: "Never treat the members of your orchestra as subordinates but rather as helpmates in pursuit of a noble goal [*Gehülfen zur Erreichung eines löblichen Zwecks*]. Try to raise them up, as a rational

---

[19] Letter from John Vanbrugh to the Earl of Manchester, 27 July 1708; quoted in Milhous and Hume, *Vice Chamberlain Coke's Theatrical Papers*, 113.

[20] *Réforme de l'Opéra*, quoted in *La Querelle des bouffons*, ed. Launay, i. 395: "Il se borne à l'emploi d'assomer la mesure, / Comme si nos Acteurs, ou l'Orchestre peu sure, / Gouvernés par un chef qui semble menacer, / Sans les coups de bâton ne pouvoient avancer."

[21] The Querelle des bouffons had strong political overtones. See Ch. 6.

teacher does his pupils, rather than humiliating them and beating them down."[22] Here the metaphor of top-down government is replaced by metaphors of cooperation and education. Rochlitz seems to be influenced by the vocabulary and values of the Enlightenment and the French Revolution, ongoing at that very moment. For him the unity of a good orchestra does not result from the exercise of absolute authority; rather it is the product of voluntary cooperation for the common good.

Gottfried Weber in 1807 debates with himself between the ideals of the Revolution and those of the ancien régime:

During a performance the director (*Direktor*) . . . can be seen, like the regent of a state, as the representative of the general will. But when decisions have to be made in the course of a performance, it is impossible for this regent to consult first with the privy council and the lords of the realm, and therefore no other constitution is possible for this state but monarchy or despotism—at least during performance.[23]

Weber comes down on the side of reaction, but only for reasons of expediency. His vocabulary comes from Rousseau, and his political sympathies seem to be liberal. Leadership in the new model is based not on birth or office but on law. Castil-Blaze articulates the new ideology in 1820:

The ability of the conductor [*chef d'orchestre*] influences an orchestra's performance a great deal. Each individual musician may be capable of playing his part perfectly, but when many musicians play together, they must unite into a single will and even the most proficient must submit to the common law.[24]

Castil-Blaze was writing during the Restoration, but the ideals of the Revolution and the Napoleonic era resonate in his prose. In both the orchestra and French political life authority must be derived from voluntary association, social unity, and the rule of law.

In this sequence of "orchestra as society" metaphors from the end of the seventeenth to the early nineteenth century, the relationship between source and target remains the same. The orchestra is described using words from the source domain of social relations and government. However, the source domain has changed. Between 1699 and 1820 people's ideas about the nature of civil authority shifted from a model of subordination to top-down, divine-right authority toward a model of voluntary association regulated by laws. As the source domain changed, the meaning of the orchestra changed too. Where Dufresny and Beer saw the orchestra as yet another example of the legitimacy of royal absolutism, Rochlitz and Castil-Blaze see it as the promise of a new social order.

---

[22] Rochlitz, "Bruchstücke aus Briefen an einen jungen Tonsetzer," col. 62.
[23] Gottfried Weber, "Praktische Bemerkungen," *AMZ* 9 (1807), col. 805.
[24] Castil-Blaze [François-Henri-Joseph Blaze], *De l'Opéra en France* (1820), 2nd edn. (Paris, 1826), i. 431.

THE ORCHESTRA AND THE ARMY

By far the favorite metaphor for the orchestra in the eighteenth century was the army. J. A. Birnbaum's essay on J. S. Bach in 1738 provides a typical example. Defending Bach against the criticism that his music is too intricate and too hard to play, he says:

If an entire army can be trained so that at a given sign one sees many thousand men carry out a maneuver as though they were a single man, then the same precision ought to be even more possible in a musical ensemble, which consists of many fewer persons. . . . Whoever has had the fortune to see the famous orchestra of the great Saxon court play a concert will no longer be able to doubt the truth of this statement.[25]

Birnbaum constructs his metaphor systematically and explicitly. He emphasizes traits that orchestras and armies have in common: they consist of many individuals; these individuals do the same thing at the same time; their actions are prescribed in advance; they are commanded by signals from a leader. If an army can achieve unity in its maneuvers, then an orchestra, the metaphorical equivalent of an army, ought to be able to play with steady tempos and good ensemble.

Other eighteenth-century authors select different features from the military domain to project onto orchestras. F. M. Veracini equates violins with the muskets of the soldiers; the *premier coup d'archet* represents the opening salvo in an battle: "The composer is advised never to begin a musical engagement, whether in the church, in the theater, or elsewhere, without first having given a general sign to all his harmonic soldiers [*soldati Armonici*], so that they will all be ready to open fire [*dar fuoco*] at exactly the same moment."[26]

Battles between rival ensembles, armed with violins, oboes, and basses, became a stock element of plays and picaresque novels as well as satirical drawings and engravings. Charles Molloy, in an English comedy of the early eighteenth century, introduces two bands of serenaders from opposite wings of the stage. The leader of one declares: "Let us draw up our Fidlers against theirs and fight it out. It signifies nothing if two or three Dozen of 'em are kill'd for you know they are but Vermin. For the honor of England, no Quarter to Cat-gut scrapers."[27] The father of the young lady who is the object of the serenade appears onstage with a non-metaphorical blunderbuss and disperses both bands.

Other writers emphasize the coordinated movements of soldiers on the march or on parade and compare this to the uniform bowing of orchestral string sections. Francesco Galeazzi in 1791 praises the orchestras of Lombardy for their military pre-

[25] Johann Abraham Birnbaum, *Verteidigung J. S. Bachs*; text in *Bach-Dokumente,* ed. Neumann and Schulze, ii. 304. Although Birnbaum refers here to "many" performers, other parts of his essay indicate that he is probably thinking of one-on-a-part performance of Bach's music.

[26] Francesco Maria Veracini, *Il trionfo della prattica musicale* (n.d.), cap. 80.

[27] Charles Molloy, *The Coquet: or, the English Chevalier* (London, 1718), Act IV.

cision: "Nothing is more beautiful than to experience the perfect unity that is to be found here and to see with what uniformity all the bows move. It is exactly like watching military maneuvers by well-trained and disciplined troops. Such orchestras fully reward both the eye and the ear."[28] To describe the relations between King Frederick the Great of Prussia and his Kapelle, Charles Burney has recourse to the military metaphor, particularly apt here, since the King was both a famous general and an outstanding flutist:

> In the opera house, as in the field, his majesty is such a rigid disciplinarian that if a mistake is made in a single movement or evolution, he immediately marks, and rebukes the offender; and if any of his Italian troops dare to deviate from strict discipline, by adding, altering, or diminishing a single passage in the parts they have to perform, an order is sent *de par le Roi*, for them to adhere strictly to the notes written by the composer, at their peril.[29]

Here the metaphor has become especially rich, filled with points of similarity between armies and orchestras: musicians are troops, a musical passage is an "evolution" (the technical term for a single military maneuver), improvised ornamentation is a breach of discipline, and the orchestra leader is a general—in this case both figuratively and literally.[30]

This metaphorical equation of the orchestra leader with an army commander became commonplace in eighteenth-century writing about music. Mozart, describing the Mannheim orchestra in a letter to his father in 1778, assigns the general's role to Christian Cannabich, the concertmaster:

> If only music [in Salzburg] were as well organized as it is in Mannheim. The discipline [*Subordination*] that rules this orchestra!—the authority that Cannabich wields. Here everything is taken seriously. Cannabich, who is the best director I have ever seen, commands the love and the fear of his subordinates. Moreover he is respected by the entire town, and so are his soldiers. But they behave quite differently [from Salzburg musicians]. They have good manners, they are well dressed, they don't go to the taverns and get drunk.[31]

Mozart assumes, and he imagines his father will too, that orchestras are like armies, that instrumentalists are like soldiers, that orchestras and armies should follow their leaders, and so on. But he extends the metaphor one additional step. Like soldiers, orchestra musicians should behave themselves off duty as well as on, something that both seem to have trouble doing—particularly when they walk into a bar.

The argument over the leadership of the orchestra, which broke out toward the end of the eighteenth century—whether the orchestra should be led by a keyboard-

---

[28] Galeazzi, *Elementi teorico-pratici*, i. 208.

[29] Burney, *Present State of Music in Germany*, ii. 234–35. On Frederick the Great as a flutist, see Ch. 7.

[30] At the end of the passage Burney cannot resist adding a political observation to his military metaphor: "his majesty allowing no more liberty in [music] than he does in civil matters of government: not contented with being sole monarch of the lives, fortunes, and business of his subjects, he even prescribes rules to their most innocent pleasures." Ibid. 235.

[31] Letter of 9 July 1778; Mozart, *Briefe*, ii. 395.

continuo player or by the first violinist—became a metaphorical discussion of military organization.[32] "The Capellmeister should be the director," said J. N. Forkel in 1783, "and he should lead from the keyboard. The first violinist is like his aide-de-camp [*sein Adjutant*] . . . but he can never be the leader, except in cases where the director entrusts him with a limited expedition, for example in a symphony or some other instrumental work."[33] Forkel goes on to explain how small "sallies," undertaken by "irregulars," can be led by "subalterns," like the French horn player who might take charge during a wind solo. Amand Schmith, an advocate of violin leadership, uses the same simile in 1787 to make the opposite point:

A musical director, like an experienced general, must survey the field, so to speak, at a single glance. . . . No instrument is better suited to direct than the violin. . . . As tonal commander-in-chief [*Befehlshaberinn der Ton*], it leads the band, and the other voices must bend themselves as subalterns to its will in order to create a harmonic whole.[34]

Military discipline and the command structure of the army can be mapped onto the orchestra, but the coordinates of that map can still be manipulated by the writer to suit his purpose.

Armies provided a rich source for eighteenth-century metaphors of the orchestra because of major changes that had taken place in European military institutions. Mercenary forces raised for particular expeditions and campaigns were replaced during the seventeenth century by standing professional armies in the employ of central governments.[35] Infantry tactics based on rows of soldiers with muskets necessitated greater emphasis on coordination and discipline. Drill—both weapons drill and marching drill—became an important component of military training, displayed to the public at military exercises and parades.[36] A well-trained and well-commanded army became an object of admiration, even of aesthetic pleasure. The discipline of the Prussian infantry, wrote an Austrian officer who faced them at the battle of Mollwitz in 1741,

was something admirable. Despite the relentless fire that our troops directed at them, they assembled themselves in the most beautiful order. . . . The whole line seemed to be moved by a single force. They advanced step by step with astonishing uniformity. . . . Before our very eyes they carried out movements with such rapidity and exactness that it was a joy to watch them.[37]

[32] On the debate over leadership, see above, Ch. 11.

[33] Johann Nicolaus Forkel, "Genauere Bestimmung einiger musicalischen Begriffe," *Magazin der Musik*, 1 (8 Nov. 1783), 1039–82 at 1064–65.

[34] Amand Wilhelm Schmith, *Philosophische Fragmente über die praktische Musik* (Vienna, 1787), 53.

[35] Johannes Kunisch, "Das 'Puppenwerk' der stehenden Heere," *Zeitschrift für Historische Forschung*, 17 (1990), 49–83 at 49.

[36] Richard Preston, Alex Roland, and Sydney Wise, *Men In Arms* (Fort Worth, 1991), 123; William McNeill, *Keeping Together in Time: Dance and Drill in Human History* (Cambridge, Mass., 1995), 127 ff.; John Keegan, "Keeping in Time," review of William H. McNeill: *Keeping Together in Time*, in *Times Literary Supplement*, no. 4867 (12 July 1996), 3–4.

[37] Quoted in Carl Hans Hermann, *Deutsche Militärgeschichte: Eine Einführung* (Frankfurt am Main, 1968), 112.

Perhaps the aesthetic aspects of the writer's experience were magnified in retrospect as his wounds healed. In any case his language, closely resembling contemporary descriptions of orchestras, emphasizes how easy it was to move metaphorically from one domain to the other.

Around the beginning of the nineteenth century army metaphors seem to take on a more critical tone. The chronicler of the local theater in Reggio Emilia invokes the military metaphor to complain about orchestral absenteeism:

One might want to invest an orchestra with the dignity of military nomenclature: the concertmaster would be the colonel, the leader of the seconds a major; the first cello and bass would be lieutenant colonels, and all the various first-chair winds would be captains. But what would happen if . . . the colonel were killed, the major were wounded, and the two lieutenant colonels and five of the captains went AWOL? I know that under military discipline the authority of the leader passes to the subordinate who takes his place; but the outcome of the battle will not be the same.[38]

The orchestra, the commentator implies, should not pretend to be an army unless the musicians are steadfast in their duties. On the other hand, H. C. Koch, in his *Musikalisches Lexikon* (1802), suggests that military-style discipline may not be appropriate for an orchestra at all: "The custom that has been introduced in some places of having each string player tune his instrument individually under the eye of the leader, like new recruits at weapons drill under the command of a corporal, is thoroughly demeaning for artists."[39] Armies and orchestras, he implies, despite their similarities and notwithstanding literary tradition, may not be metaphorical equivalents after all.

The new tone heard in "orchestra as army" metaphors in the early nineteenth century can be attributed to changes in both the source and target domains—that is, in both orchestras and armies. In the colonial wars of the late eighteenth century the old tactics of the line proved unsuccessful, and new companies of "rangers" were organized, in which soldiers operated more as individuals and less as a unit.[40] Not just the structure but also the meaning of the army changed at the end of the eighteenth century. During the French Revolution and Napoleonic wars European armies became national rather than royal armies, symbolizing patriotism and national identity, rather than the glory of the ruler.[41] Orchestras too were, in many cases, no longer expressions of princely authority. Theater orchestras, civic orchestras, philharmonic societies, and conservatory orchestras, although they often received royal subventions, were sponsored and patronized by a broad spectrum of the monied classes. Neither

---

[38] [C. Ritorni], *Annali del teatro della città di Reggio. Anno 1831* (Bologna, 1831), 17; quoted in Paolo Fabbri, "L'orchestra . . . sarà bene che sia . . . stabile," in Conati and Pavarani (eds.), *Orchestre in Emilia-Romagna nell'Ottocento e Novecento*, 199–216 at 204.

[39] Koch, *Musikalisches Lexikon*, col. 1445, s.v. "Stimmung."

[40] Preston, Roland, and Wise, *Men in Arms*, 122.

[41] Ibid. 163–64; Henning Eichberg, "Geometrie als barocke Verhaltensnorm—Fortifikation und Exerzitien," *Zeitschrift für historische Forschung*, 4 (1977), 17–50 at 40–41.

the army nor the orchestra meant the same thing in the nineteenth century as they had in the eighteenth.

MECHANISM VS. ORGANISM

Another metaphor that flourished during the eighteenth century was that of the orchestra as a machine. "The music of an orchestra," said J. N. Forkel in 1783,

> can be considered just like the mechanism of a clock. It stops at the end of each movement, like a clock whose mainspring has unwound or whose weight has reached bottom. To continue operating, each needs to be set in motion again. Setting the tempo for the orchestra at the beginning of a movement is like winding up the musical clock [*das Aufziehen des musicalischen Uhrwerks*].[42]

Burney used the same metaphor to describe the 250-member orchestra at the Handel festival at Westminster Abbey in 1784: "When all the wheels of that huge machine, the Orchestra, were in motion, the effect resembled clock-work in every thing, but want of feeling and expression."[43] From the source domain of machines Forkel and Burney draw attributes like large size, motion, complexity, and diversity of the parts. Like a machine, when an orchestra is functioning properly, all components work together toward a single product or result.

Continuing his description of the Handel festival orchestra Burney switches to a seemingly contradictory metaphor: "The pulsations in every limb, and the ramifications of veins and arteries of an animal, could not be more reciprocal, isochronous, and under the regulation of the heart, than the members of this body of Musicians under that of the Conductor and Leader."[44] Here the orchestra is not a machine but an animal, with flesh and blood and a beating heart, namely the conductor who beats time. What seems to be a contradiction between organism and mechanism is actually typical of the late eighteenth century, when the body was often described as a machine.[45] Indeed Burney's language—"reciprocal," "isochronous," "regulation"— implies a considerably mechanical approach to mammalian physiology.

Metaphors of machinery and of organism were combined by several other writers, for example, I. F. C. Arnold in 1806: "The performance of a musical work must address two sets of issues: mechanism and feeling. . . . A large number of individuals entrust their very different capabilities and sensibilities to the leadership of a single

---

[42] Forkel, "Genauere Bestimmung," 1063–64.

[43] Charles Burney, *An Account of the Musical Performances in Westminster Abbey and the Pantheon . . . in Commemoration of Handel* (London, 1785), 15. On the orchestra for the Handel festival, see Table 8.4.

[44] Ibid. 15.

[45] Carsten Zelle, "Maschinen-Metaphern in der Ästhetik des 18. Jahrhunderts," *Zeitschrift für Germanistik*, NF 3 (1997), 510–20 at 512; Blumenberg, "Paradigmen", 69–71. For an insightful discussion of organic metaphors as well as of musical metaphors more generally, see Charlton, " 'Envoicing' the Orchestra."

man, whose job it is to . . . unite them in one single mechanical body."[46] François Arnaud, discussing Gluck's approach to instrumentation, draws a contrast between this newer organic metaphor and the older metaphor of the orchestra as society:

Why haven't *Iphigénie* and *Orphée* trained you to listen more attentively to the orchestra? This neglect is excusable in other operas, where, with only a few exceptions, the instruments accompany the voice as a valet accompanies his master, and not as a person's arms, hands, eyes, and facial and body movements accompany a discourse of sentiment and passion.[47]

Most composers, says Arnaud, treat the orchestra in the old framework of hierarchical social relations; Gluck points the way to the future by treating it like a living organism.

Both mechanical and organic metaphors were applied in the eighteenth century to many other things besides orchestras. The Encyclopedists and other writers of the French Enlightenment used the metaphor of clockwork or machinery to describe the natural world, the human body, and even human emotions.[48] On the other hand, Neoplatonists like Shaftesbury and romantics like Herder and Goethe saw the universe as infused with a life force or a soul and interpreted the world in terms of organic development and growth.[49] Around the beginning of the nineteenth century there was a tendency in literary criticism and political theory for organic metaphors to replace mechanical.[50] Clockwork passed out of fashion as a model for the world, for the state, and for human activities; and the life cycle became the paradigm of choice. Similarly, in the language of music theory, according to Mark Evan Bonds, the metaphor of organism replaced the metaphor of rhetoric and discourse.[51]

For the orchestra, on the other hand, both mechanical and organic metaphors remained popular during the first half of the nineteenth century. However, their connotations turned from positive to negative. The orchestra of the Paris Opéra, writes G. L. P. Sievers in 1817, is a "lifeless machine. Its performance is as regular as clockwork, and it generates no more interest than a clock. The skeleton is intact, but the flesh is gone."[52] Here both mechanical and organic metaphors have been given a negative spin; the machine is lifeless, nothing remains of the organism but a skeleton. Balzac's portrait of the Opéra orchestra in 1839 is even more sinister:

[46] Arnold, *Der angehende Musikdirektor*, 63.

[47] François Arnaud, "La Soirée perdue à l'Opéra" (1776), in *Querelle des Gluckistes et des Piccinnistes*, ed. François Lesure (Geneva, 1984), i. 54.

[48] See Zelle, "Maschinen-Metaphern."

[49] M. H. Abrams, *The Mirror and the Lamp: Romantic Theory and the Critical Tradition* (New York, 1958), 184 ff.

[50] See ibid. 156 ff.; Ahlrich Meyer, "Mechanische und organische Metaphorik politischer Philosophie," *Archiv für Begriffsgeschichte*, 13 (1969), 128–99.

[51] Bonds, *Wordless Rhetoric*.

[52] G. L. P. Sievers, "Ueber den jetzigen Zustand der Musik in Frankreich, besonders in Paris (Beschluss)," *AMZ* 19 (1817), cols. 297–304 at 299.

For me the orchestra has never been anything but a haphazard and bizarre assemblage of carved wood and twisted tubes . . . a visible monster, born over these last two centuries out of the miscegenation of man with wood. . . . This hydra with a hundred bows sullies my pleasure by forcing me to witness its labors. Yet this crew of galley slaves is indispensible to the majestic course of that noble ship we call an opera.[53]

In Balzac's nightmarish vision clockwork has become a contraption, and the organism has become a monster.

Again it seems as though the change in the metaphor resulted from changes in both target and source. Machines in the eighteenth century were still considered to a great extent curiosities and toys; by Balzac's time they had become instruments of oppression in factories and mills. Orchestras too were turning into factories of a sort, in which instrumentalists sold their labor for an insecure and inadequate wage. Organisms, on the other hand, did not generally acquire negative associations in the nineteenth century; indeed philosophers and poets proposed organic theories and metaphors as antidotes to the cold power of machines.[54] But as orchestras grew larger, and with the advent of baton conductors, the metaphorical equation of the entire orchestra with a single living creature became problematic. Organic attributes tended to be transferred to the conductor, who came to embody the human aspects of the orchestra, while the instrumentalists became, as Berlioz put it, "machines endowed with intelligence but subject to the action of an immense keyboard played by the conductor under the direction of the composer."[55]

ART AND NATURE

Machine and organism metaphors were joined in the late eighteenth century by another contradictory yet complementary pair: the orchestra as a work of art and the orchestra as a natural phenomenon. The nature metaphor can be heard in C. D. F. Schubart's description, written around 1780, of the Mannheim orchestra: "No other orchestra in the world can match the execution of the Mannheim orchestra. Its forte is like thunder, its crescendo a cataract, its diminuendo a clear brook babbling in the distance, its piano a spring breeze."[56] In this purple passage Schubart projects four different natural phenomena onto the orchestra—thunder, a waterfall, a brook, and a breeze—one for each of the dynamic effects for which the Mannheim orchestra was

---

[53] Letter of 29 May 1837, to Maurice Schlesinger (Honoré de Balzac, *Correspondance*, ed. Roger Pierrot (Paris, 1960–69), iii. 292).

[54] Meyer, "Mechanische und organische Metaphorik."

[55] Hector Berlioz, *Traité d'instrumentation et d'orchestration* (Paris, 1843), 293: "machines devenues intelligentes, mais soumises à l'action d'un immense clavier touché par le chef d'orchestre, sous la direction du compositeur."

[56] Schubart, *Ideen zu einer Aesthetik der Tonkunst*, 130: "Sein Forte ist ein Donner, sein Crescendo ein Catarakt, sein Diminuendo — ein in die Ferne hin plätschernder Krystallfluss, sein Piano ein Frühlingshauch."

famous. Caroline von Greiner's description of the first performance in Vienna of Haydn's London Symphonies mixes many of the same nature metaphors in verse:

> Hark how the music rushes along,
> The current of tones
> In harmonious tumult,
> Coursing in flood!
> Astonished, our senses
> Scarce make out the tune,
> As it's tossed in the billows,
> Nor capture its meaning sublime.[57]

Here the emphasis is on orchestral effects of unity and grandeur, which are compared to powerful forces of nature, like rivers and floods. Natural forces and music are both characterized in the poem as sublime.

The sublime in the eighteenth century designated a rhetorical, literary, or artistic mode suitable for conveying grand objects or ideas, a style that aroused overwhelming emotions in the listener or viewer.[58] Nature was the source and the primary locus of the sublime. "As nothing is more grand and admirable than nature," declares Thomas Stackhouse in 1731, "that which imitates it perfectly, and presents us with lively and resemblant images, will always appear truly great and sublime."[59] Joseph Priestley's catalog of sublime objects begins with natural phenomena:

Objects of the first rank in point of magnitude, and which chiefly constitute the sublime of description, are large rivers, high mountains, and extensive plains; the ocean, the clouds, the heavens, and infinite space; also storms, thunder, lightning, volcanos, and earthquakes, in nature; and palaces, temples, pyramids, cities &c. in the works of men.[60]

Several of the sublime objects on Priestley's list—rivers, the heavens, storms, and thunder—turn up during the same period as metaphors of the orchestra.

Besides trumpets and drums and other effects of unity and grandeur, orchestral effects of variety and nuance also invited comparison with nature. Birds were a favorite theme, as in the following bit of a poem by the English poet George Dyer:

---

[57] Her poem was published in the *Wiener Theater Almanach für das Jahr 1795*. It is quoted in full in Landon, *Haydn: Chronicle and Works*, iii. 227–28: "Wie rauscht die laute Musik, wie wälzt / im harmonischen Gange / Der Strom der Töne sich reissend dahin! / Kaum folgt das erstaunte Gehör dem kühn / verschlungnen Gesange, / Und fasset seinen erhabenen Sinn!"

[58] Samuel H. Monk, *The Sublime: A Study of Critical Theories in XVIII-Century England* (New York, 1935). Also Elaine Sisman, *Mozart: The "Jupiter" Symphony* (Cambridge, 1993); Nicholas Waldvogel, "The Eighteenth-Century Esthetics of the Sublime and the Valuation of the Symphony" (Ph.D. diss., Yale University, 1992).

[59] Thomas Stackhouse, *Reflections on the Nature and Property of Languages* (1731), excerpt in Andrew Ashfield and Peter de Bolla (eds.), *The Sublime: A Reader in British Eighteenth-Century Aesthetic Theory* (Cambridge, 1996), 50.

[60] Joseph Priestley, *A Course of Lectures on Oratory and Criticism* (1777), excerpt in Ashfield and de Bolla, *The Sublime*, 119. Priestley is best known as the "discoverer" of oxygen.

> So great a stir the warblers made,
> In their orchestras over head
> There seem'd a concert of the groves.[61]

What is interesting and significant about Dyer's metaphor is that the orchestra is not the target. Instead the orchestra is the source for the metaphor, and nature has become the target. The simultaneous songs of many species of birds are equated with the variety of sounds in an orchestra. Heine in *Neue Gedichte* (1844) uses the same metaphor in a more complex way:

> All the trees are ringing,
> All the nests are singing.
> Who is the Kapellmeister
> In this green forest-orchestra?[62]

None of the birds, he concludes at the end of the stanza, is directing the orchestra; rather it is his own enamoured heart that beats time. Longfellow in *Hyperion* (1839) imagines he hears a bass line for the orchestral birds. It is provided by "those green-coated musicians, the frogs. . . . They too, belong to the orchestra of Nature."[63] In a poem entitled "To the Moon" (1825), Bernard Barton expands nature's orchestra to include both animate and inanimate performers:

> For the softest of sounds shed their harmony round,
> More musical far in a calm so profound;
> The murmur of brooks, and the nightingale's song,
> And the sigh of the breeze, sweeping gently along:
> These alone form thy orchestra.[64]

The use of the orchestra as a source of nature metaphors, rare in the eighteenth century, is common in the nineteenth. As the public became familiar with orchestras, how they worked and how they sounded, the orchestra became available as a source domain for metaphors. Things about orchestras—they are made up of many different kinds of instruments, they are led by a Kapellmeister, the players wear frock coats, etc.—could be used to illustrate and explicate the natural world.

Alongside the nature metaphor, the orchestra began to be characterized in the second half of the eighteenth century in terms of artifice and art. The simplest version of this metaphor is almost tautological: the orchestra is compared to a keyboard instrument. Robert Bremner buttresses his argument against orchestral improvisation with this simile:

---

[61] George Dyer, *Poetics, or A Series of Poems and Disquisitions on Poetry* (London, 1812), Ode XIV.

[62] Heinrich Heine, *Historisch-kritische Ausgabe der Werke* (Hamburg, 1973–), ii. 15: "Es erklingen alle Bäume / Und es singen alle Nester, / Wer ist der Kapellenmeister / In dem grünen Wald-Orchester?"

[63] Henry Wadsworth Longfellow, *Hyperion, A Romance* (1839) (Cambridge, Mass., 1845), 89.

[64] Bernard Barton, *Poems by Bernard Barton*, 4th edn. (London, 1825).

The concert, or orchestra player . . . if there be more than one to a part . . . becomes no more than a part of a part; therefore his performance, with that of those who play the same part, must, like the unisons of an organ or harpsichord, coincide so as to pass for one entire sound, whether loud or soft.[65]

Bremner's metaphor alludes to both musical art and mechanical artifice: an orchestra should emulate the couplers of an organ or harpsichord and blend the various instruments into a single sound.

Eighteenth-century writers also describe the orchestra in terms of the visual arts, most often painting. From contemporary art criticism, they adopted the term *chiaroscuro* (light and shade) to characterize orchestral dynamics, which came into vogue in the second half of the eighteenth century. "As Discords in Music are like Shades in Painting," says Charles Avison in his *Essay on Musical Expression* (1753), "so is the Piano like the fainter Parts of Figures in a Picture."[66] Burney extends the metaphor in the entry he wrote under the heading "orchestra" in Rees's *Cyclopedia*: "The orchestra is a composer's palette, and each solo instrument a colour and a pencil. The tone of these, whether alone, or in the aggregate, should have their peculiar and general effect, occasionally, and contribute to the colouring of the piece."[67] Here Burney transfers several elements from the source domain of painting to the orchestra as a target: the composer is the painter, the orchestra is his palette, an instrument is like a color, a piece of music like a painting. Burney's metaphor, like the keyboard metaphor, makes orchestras seem somewhat passive. The orchestra is merely a source of shades and colors; it is the composer who gives the music its artistic form and content.

If orchestras could be described in terms of painting, then, paintings could also be described in terms of the orchestra. L.-S. Mercier in 1773 explains the difference between Italian and Netherlandish paintings as follows:

these large-scale Italian paintings . . . do not have the polish of the Flemish school, because they require broad strokes rather than an exact and detailed manner. A symphony requires an orchestra! When all the instruments enter at the same moment, we apprehend the combination of all the sounds, and we become aware of the fundamental bass.[68]

By the nineteenth century the orchestra was providing a source domain for literature, as well as painting. Flaubert, in a letter written in 1850, uses the metaphor to criticize modern writers, himself included: "What we all lack is not style, nor do we

---

[65] Bremner, "Some Thoughts on the Performance of Concert Music," in Zaslaw, "The Compleat Orchestral Musician," 50. See Ch. 11, 370.

[66] Charles Avison, *An Essay on Musical Expression*, 2nd edn. (London, 1753), 143.

[67] Abraham Rees, *The Cyclopaedia, or, Universal Dictionary of Arts, Sciences, and Literature* (London, 1819–20), s.v. "Orchestra." Burney wrote his encyclopedia articles on music between 1801 and 1805. See Roger Lonsdale, *Dr. Charles Burney: A Literary Biography* (Oxford, 1986), 424 ff.

[68] Louis-Sébastien Mercier, *Du théâtre ou nouvel essai sur l'art dramatique* (Amsterdam, 1773), 294.

lack the suppleness of bow and fingers that passes for talent. We have a well-staffed orchestra, a rich palette, varied resources. . . . No, what we lack is the guiding principle, the soul of things, the very idea of the subject."[69] Flaubert's easy move from the literature-as-orchestra metaphor to a literature-as-painting metaphor suggests that he sees all the arts overlapping in a metaphorical equivalency of sensibility and technique.

The typical metaphors for the orchestra at the end of the eighteenth and the beginning of the nineteenth centuries—machines, organisms, nature and art—resemble one another in a telling way. Earlier metaphors—the shivaree, the army, civil polity—considered orchestras as aggregations of human beings, initially and potentially chaotic, but formed into cohesive groups by the exercise of authority. The later metaphors do not consider orchestras as people at all. As the orchestra developed and matured as an institution, it was perceived less as an aggregation of individuals, more as a single impersonal entity, sometimes superhuman, sometimes subhuman, but characteristically non- or even inhuman. By the mid-nineteenth century the orchestra had become a thing.

A WEB OF METAPHORS

Civil polity, the army, clockwork, the human body, nature, paintings. . . . What, if anything, do the characteristic source domains for seventeenth- and eighteenth-century metaphors of the orchestra have in common? They tend to involve complex entities, composed of discrete and often disparate elements or members that work together toward a common goal. Moreover these entities are unified by a single will or creative intelligence. In the body the unifying force is the brain, in the army the commander, in a painting the artist, in a clock the mechanic, in nature God. Based on their perceived similarities, these domains all served in the seventeenth and eighteenth centuries as reciprocal sources and targets for one another.[70] People described the army as a machine, nature in terms of civil polity, the state and society in military terms, and so on. All these large-scale, complex, unified, purposeful entities, it seems, meant similar things to people, and people understood and interpreted them in terms of one another. Together they formed a larger metaphor system, a web of metaphors. We could even call it a "meta-metaphor"—an interconnected set of natural, social, and cultural domains that over a long period were considered as metaphorical equivalents. The orchestra joined this metaphor system around the end of the seventeenth century, at first as the target of metaphors from the other domains, then, as it became better established and understood, as both a target and a source. The metaphorical

---

[69] Gustave Flaubert, *Correspondance* (Paris, 1973), i. 627.
[70] Blumenberg, "Paradigmen"; Eichberg, "Geometrie."

equivalence of all these domains suggests that to people of the seventeenth and eighteenth centuries civil polity, the body, art, nature, and the orchestra all meant the same thing in an important sense.

The web of metaphors was fostered and held together by centralized monarchy and political absolutism, a system in which political power was concentrated in a single hereditary monarch, whose authority was unbounded by legal, political, or moral constraints.[71] As absolute monarchies developed during the seventeenth and eighteenth centuries, they justified and legitimized themselves with this web of metaphors. "The State," says Hobbes, combining organic and mechanical metaphors, "is but an artificial man . . . in which the sovereignty is an artificial soul, . . . the magistrates . . . artificial joints, . . . counsellors . . . are the memory, etc."[72] As the project of absolutism progressed, the state itself became a metaphor—for the body, for the world of nature, for the orchestra. The absolutist state also fostered the metaphor system in concrete ways: kings raised standing armies, they commissioned clocks, automatons, and other mechanical contrivances, they assembled and maintained orchestras. All these things signified, advertised, and magnified the state and its ruler.

Although all the domains implicated in this metaphor system can be related to the absolutist state, it is hard to propose specific mechanisms connecting one domain to another. William McNeill speculates that the connections between armies, bodies, and music were a matter of social psychology.[73] The military reforms introduced by Prince Maurice of Nassau at the beginning of the seventeenth century, he claims, turned armies from chaotic aggregations of individual fighters into tight-knit units responsive to a single command. Frequent military drill and marching in step to the beat of a drum disciplined soldiers' bodies and inculcated a spirit of solidarity in their minds. The officers who drilled the troops were the same men who danced intricate and highly disciplined minuets, gavottes, and bourrées at court to the sound of the orchestra. McNeill claims that they applied the same principles and the same values to dance as they did to drill. His account has been criticized by both military historians and historians of the dance, because parade drill, with its mechanical precision, fancy dress, and pomp, did not emerge until the second half of the eighteenth century, long after the codification of courtly dance.[74] In addition, the domain of dance is conspicuously absent from the web of metaphors discussed in this chapter. On the other hand, as demonstrated by passages cited above, people frequently drew parallels between orchestras and armies, between the coordinated tempos and uniform

---

[71] A. D. Lindsay, "Absolutism," in *Encyclopaedia of the Social Sciences*, ed. Edwin Seligman (New York, 1951), 380.

[72] Thomas Hobbes, *Leviathan* (1651), ed. Michael Oakeshott (New York, 1962), 19.

[73] McNeill, *Keeping Together in Time*, 127 ff.

[74] Keegan, "Keeping in Time." See also Kate Van Orden, "Descartes on Musical Training and the Body," in Linda Phyllis Austern (ed.) *Music, Sensation, and Sensuality* (New York and London: Routledge, 2002), 17–38 at 26 ff.

bowing of orchestras and the movements of troops on parade. Perhaps the connection lay in patronage rather than participation. The kings and princes who paid for both armies and orchestras expected that the same principles should obtain in each domain.

Henning Eichberg, in an article on "Geometry as a norm of behavior in the Baroque era," connects the domains of the meta-metaphor in a more abstract way.[75] He notes the importance of "geometrical" patterns of organization in several different areas of seventeenth- and eighteenth-century life: in mathematics, in military fortifications, in military drill, in fencing, in horsemanship, in dance, in gardening. He does not mention music, but it could surely be added to the list. Eichberg attributes these correspondences to a "conceptual model" of spatial analysis and a "behavioral norm," which actualized this analysis in various human activities. The actions of a soldier with a gun, a rider on a horse, or a dancer were analyzed in the same fashion as Kepler analyzed the motion of a planet or Newton a falling apple. These analyses became behavioral norms, enforced by codes of taste and deportment. Applying Eichberg's scheme to the metaphors under consideration here, the connections among armies, clocks, and orchestras would seem to have originated in mental representations rather than in human activities. Over time, however, human activities can alter mental representations. Eichberg claims that the social and political changes of the late eighteenth century led to a breakdown of the geometrical model and its replacement by a model based on process or evolution, in which time and movement were more important than pattern and space. The new model, says Eichberg, led to new styles of warfare (mobile tactics), horsemanship (English riding), dance (couples dances like the waltz), and so on. The organization of the orchestra into sections and the techniques of orchestration that emerged at the end of the eighteenth century could be seen as similarly based on process rather than pattern, although most other changes in the orchestra were in the direction of tighter coordination and discipline, not decentralization.

Rather than looking for connections between representations, sociologists Paul DiMaggio and Walter Powell look at similarities between institutions.[76] They observe that in a given society different institutions tend to have similar organizational structures. This phenomenon they call "institutional isomorphism," and they propose three mechanisms to account for it: (1) coercive isomorphism, in which a ruler or a governmental entity imposes the same structures on two or more institutions; (2) mimetic isomorphism, in which a new institution models itself on an older, successful institution; (3) normative isomorphism, where people move from one institution to another, carrying habits and behavioral norms with them and recreating the old structures in their new surroundings. All three mechanisms help explain the metaphorical connections between orchestras and other institutions in

---

[75] Eichberg, "Geometrie," 40 ff.   [76] DiMaggio and Powell, "The Iron Cage Revisited."

the seventeenth and eighteenth centuries. Rulers demonstrably imposed the same structures on orchestras as on other institutions. In France, Germany, and England the earliest orchestras were part of the ruler's household, and they were organized according to the same rules as the army, the stable, and the kitchen staff. Corelli's orchestra in Rome mimicked the organization of church choirs; amateur orchestras were modeled in England on gentlemen's clubs, in Italy on learned societies. Normative isomorphism was seen in the movement of personnel between orchestras and town waits, orchestras and regimental bands, orchestras and companies of actors and dancers, and also between orchestras in different countries. DiMaggio and Powell's theory of institutional isomorphism can explain metaphorical correspondences between orchestras and armies or between orchestras and choirs (even heavenly choirs), but it is hard to see how it can account for the metaphor of the orchestra as an organism or the orchestra as a machine. Those seem to call for an explanation that involves ideology as well as organizational structures.

Several commentators have interpreted the orchestra of the seventeenth and eighteenth centuries in the context of industrialism and the rise of the middle class. For Jacques Attali in *Noise: The Political Economy of Music*, the orchestra is a metaphor for the rational organization of production and the alienation of labor:

> The emergence of large orchestras and the limitations on their growth would have offered the system, if anyone had cared to listen, a premonitory indication of its evolution. . . . The constitution of the orchestra and its organization are symbols of power in an industrial economy. The musicians, who are anonymous, hierarchically ranked, and usually salaried workers, are the image of programmed labor in our society. Each of them produces only a part of the whole, which has no value in itself.[77]

In the eighteenth century, however, mechanization and the factory system were rare in most of Europe, and where they appeared, they were often sponsored by the state and protected by monopoly. Thus, Attali is obliged to consider the orchestra as a "premonitory indication," a metaphorical harbinger of a future social and economic order. The problem with Attali's notion of metaphorical prophecy is that orchestras of the seventeenth and eighteenth centuries were not so anonymous, hierarchical, rational, or industrial as he imagines. They were organized very much like other preindustrial institutions on the basis of corporate privilege and personal relationships. Leadership, hierarchy, orchestral discipline, and the free market for orchestral labor established themselves only gradually. Moreover, seventeenth- and eighteenth-century orchestras were content in their metaphorical present. People of the seventeenth and eighteenth centuries integrated the orchestra easily and comfortably into the web of metaphors surrounding absolutism. Rather than look for the meaning of the early orchestra 200 years after its birth, it is more reasonable to understand it as its

---

[77] Jacques Attali, *Noise*, trans. Brian Massumi (Minneapolis, 1985), 65–66.

contemporaries did: as a large-scale, unified organization with centralized leadership that signified the wealth, power, and legitimacy of the ruler and the state.

To say that the orchestra meant absolutism is not to say that all seventeenth- and eighteenth-century orchestras were created and maintained by absolute monarchs. Lully's orchestra was the creation and reflection of such a regime, as were many German Kapellen and a few Italian orchestras, for example in Naples, Turin, and Milan. Corelli's orchestra, on the other hand, had a variety of patrons, some more absolute, some less. The orchestras in most Italian theaters were sponsored by an aristocratic consortium rather than by a single ruler. In England the Stuart kings drew the nascent orchestra into their project of absolutism, but after 1688 almost all English orchestras depended on the patronage of the public, in theaters, concert series, pleasure gardens, and festivals. In Paris and Vienna too concert orchestras and theater orchestras eclipsed the royal musical establishment in importance during the course of the eighteenth century.

In 1805 the English poet George Huddesford, in a satirical attack on Napoleon, still evoked the metaphorical association between the orchestra and absolutism, but now the connotations of the metaphor were negative:

> Great Master! to your potent lay
> Each heart in unison replies
> When You, like Orpheus, sound your A,
> All our brute cat-guts symphonize![78]

Napoleon is the concertmaster, the French public is the orchestra, tuning their hearts and minds to his A-string. Frenchmen follow Bonaparte's lead mechanically and instinctually, as orchestra musicians follow the first violin. Napoleon's message of liberty, equality, and fraternity, the poet implies, is actually a siren song of slavery.

The image of Napoleon as Orpheus recalls the musical representations of Orpheus in Chapter 1. But whereas Lully's "charming lyre" in the *Ballet des muses* of 1666 sang the praises of Louis XIV, Huddesford's Orpheus is himself the autocrat. It is also striking that the orchestra is the source rather than the target of this Orpheus metaphor. Lully's Petits Violons represented his "lyre" literally to his audience of courtiers. For them the meaning of the "orchestra" was limited and specific. Huddesford's readers understand concertmasters, tuning-up protocols, and orchestral discipline well enough that he can use the orchestra to make a broader point about European politics.

Changes in metaphor reflect changes in meaning. The orchestra meant something different to people in 1805 from what it had meant in 1666. In part this was because the orchestra itself changed. The eighteenth-century campaigns for uniform bowing and against improvised improvisation made orchestras less chaotic and more like

---

[78] George Huddesford, *Les Champignons du Diable, or Imperial Mushrooms: A Mock-heroic Poem in Five Cantos* (London, 1805), 62.

armies than those of earlier times. The consolidation of leadership in the person of the concertmaster made orchestras seem more monarchical and autocratic. The development of the practice and theory of orchestration drew orchestral music closer to works of art. The meaning of the orchestra also changed as values changed. Under the ancien régime where social hierarchy and deference were highly valued, the orchestra was understood in terms of order and discipline. As individual initiative and responsibility became preferred social values, the orchestra became an example of participation and social solidarity.

By the second decade of the nineteenth century the orchestra was no longer a novelty. In almost every European city and in North and South America as well there were orchestras in theaters, in pleasure gardens, dance halls, cafés, and spas. There were concert societies and concert series; there were festivals with giant orchestras and choirs. At the same time there were more organizations of other kinds, in which a large number of people did the same thing at the same time, just as they did in orchestras. Workers in textile mills or clerks in offices carried out the same tasks side by side with their fellows, though not so closely coordinated in time as orchestra musicians. So did agricultural laborers on plantations or work crews building roads and (slightly later) railroads. Orchestras and other organizations of many people working side by side toward a common goal became part of the everyday experience of a large proportion of European city-dwellers.

With these social and political transformations the entire web of metaphors—armies, bodies, civil polity, clockwork, etc.—was realigned. The new web of metaphors emphasized history, evolution, and process. The orchestra retained its metaphorical associations with nature, with machines, and with art; it lost its connections with heaven, with the human body, with the army. Most important, the system was no longer predicated on absolutism. Politically the new web of metaphors revolved around the nation rather than the ruler. To the extent that the orchestra was still connected with monarchy, its connotations tended to be negative, as in Huddesford's poem about Napoleon as Orpheus. Associated with civil society or the nation, the orchestra's connotations were positive. Finally, the orchestra functioned in the new system both as target and as source for metaphor. Because people knew what an orchestra was, how it worked, and what it meant, the orchestra could serve both as an explanation for other phenomena and as a model for them.

For the orchestra to serve in the nineteenth century as a source of metaphor is yet another marker of the birth of the orchestra as an institution. The birth of the orchestra, it should be clear by now, was not an event but a process—a long process that began in the early seventeenth century and completed itself, more or less, in the early decades of the nineteenth century, as the orchestra became recognizable as the ancestor and the model of modern orchestras. Besides the instruments and performers in the pit or on the stage, the process involved repertories, performance practices, administrative structures, systems for training players, techniques of scoring and orchestration, the acoustics of theaters and concert halls, and many other things. Finally, the birth of the orchestra was a matter of people's beliefs—what people thought orchestras were and what orchestras meant.

Orchestras, it is similarly clear, did not mean just one thing. They meant many things to many people, and their meanings changed over time. As has been shown in this chapter, however, the meanings of the orchestra fit into broader systems of meanings, and the changes over time were systematic insofar as they changed in concert with other changes in other social institutions. For historians too, or for anyone who contemplates the birth of the orchestra from the perspective of the twenty-first century, the orchestra can and should mean many things. It can mean court culture and absolutism, but it can also mean the rise of the middle class. It can mean musical innovation and invention, or it can mean the conservation of cultural heritage. Any historical interpretation, however well founded on historical fact, is in the last analysis just another metaphor.

APPENDICES

APPENDIX A

Sample orchestras, 1754–1759

Date	Place	Bowed strings	Woodwinds	Brass and drums	Keyboard and plucked	Total excl. kbd.	Source
1754	Berlin Kapelle	12 violins 3 violas 4 cellos 1 viola da gamba 2 double basses	5 flutes 3 oboes 4 bassoons	2 horns	1 harpsichord 1 theorbo	37	Marpurg, *Beyträge*, 76
1754	London: Foundling Hospital (*Messiah*)	14 violins 6 violas 3 cellos 2 double basses	4 oboes and flutes 4 bassoons	2 horns 2 trumpets 1 drum	1 organ/ harpsichord	38	Deutsch, *Handel*, 751
1755	Munich Kapelle	20 violins 5 violas 2 cellos 4 double basses	2 oboes 4 bassoons	2 horns 4 trumpets	[2 harpsichords]	43	Mahling, "Orchester" (1971)
1755	Turin: Teatro Regio	21 violins 5 violas 2 cellos [4] bassi di rip. 2 double basses	3 oboes [2 bassoons]	4 horns [and trumpets]	2 harpsichords	43	Bouquet, *Teatro*, 172
1755	Paris: Concert Spirituel	17 violins 2 violas 6 cellos 2 double basses	5 oboes and flutes 4 bassoons	2 horns 1 trumpet 1 timpani	1 organ	40	*Almanach* (1756), 4
1755	Vienna: Jungen Herrschafts-Ballen	12 violins and violas 2 cellos 1 double bass	1 flute 1 oboe 1 bassoon	2 horns		20	Edge, "New Sources"

Year	Ensemble	Strings	Woodwinds	Brass & Timpani	Keyboard / Other	Number	Source
		7 violas 12 cellos and basses	4 bassoons			22	Daub, "Music," 186
1756	London: King's Band	10 violins 2 violas 2 cellos 1 double bass	2 oboes 2 bassoons	2 trumpets 1 timpani			
1756	Dresden Kapelle	19 violins 4 violas 3 cellos 1 viola da gamba 2 double basses	3 flutes 5 oboes 6 bassoons	3 horns [2 trumpets] [1 timpani]	[2 harpsichords] 1 pantaleon	50	Mahling, "Orchester"
1756	Bologna: San Petronio Cathedral	8 violins and violas 1 cello 1 double bass			1 organ	10	Gambassi, *Cappella musicale,* 189
1756	Paris: Comédie-Italienne	6 violins 1 viola 3 cellos	2 oboes and flutes 2 bassoons	2 horns		16	Charlton, "Orchestra," 94
1756	Madrid: Royal Chapel	12 violins 4 violas 3 cellos 3 double basses	4 oboes and flutes 2 bassoons	2 horns 2 trumpets	2 organs	32	Bordas, "Musical Instruments," 183
1756	Vienna: Grosse Hof-Ballen	15 violins and violas 2 cellos 1 double bass	2 oboes 1 bassoon	2 horns		23	Edge, "New Sources"
1756	Vienna: Burgtheater	12 violins 2 violas 2 cellos 2 double basses	1 flute 2 oboes 1 bassoon	2 horns	[1 harpsichord]	24	Haas, *Gluck,* 22
1757	Ludwigslust: Mecklenburg-Schwerin Kapelle	6 violins 2 violas 2 cellos 1 double bass	2 flutes 2 oboes 1 bassoon	2 horns [2 trumpets] [1 timpani]	[1 harpsichord]	21	Marpurg, *Beyträge,* 339

Date	Place	Bowed strings	Woodwinds	Brass and drums	Keyboard and plucked	Total excl. kbd.	Source
1757	Salzburg Kapelle	10 violins 2 violas 2 cellos 2 double basses	3 oboes and flutes 4 bassoons	2 horns 1 trombone	2 organs	26	Ibid. 183 ff.
1757	Schwarzburg–Rudolstadt Kapelle	7 violins 3 violas 3 cellos 2 double basses	2 oboes 1 bassoon	2 horns 3 trumpets 1 timpani	[1 harpsichord]	24	Ibid. 77
1757	Paris: Comédie-Française	5 violins 2 cellos	2 oboes and flutes 1 bassoon			10	*Almanach* (1758), 42
1758	Rome: Teatro Argentina	16 violins 4 violas 2 cellos 4 double basses	2 oboes	4 horns [and trumpets]	2 harpsichords	32	Rostirolla, "La professione," 168
1758	Paris: Opéra Comique	7 violins 1 viola 2 cellos 1 double bass	2 oboes 2 bassoons	2 horns		17	*Almanach* (1759), 91
1758	Stuttgart Kapelle	14 violins 3 violas 4 cellos 3 double basses	2 flutes 3 oboes	4 horns [2 trumpets] [1 timpani]	2 organs	36	Mahling, "Orchester"
1759	Cremona: Teatro Nazari	10 violins and violas 1 cello 2 double basses	2 oboes	2 horns	1 harpsichord	17	Santoro, *Il teatro*, 239
1759	Naples: San Carlo Theater	28 violins 4 violas 3 cellos 4 double basses	4 oboes [2 bassoons]	4 trumpets [and horns]	2 harpsichords	49	Prota-Giurleo, *La grande orchestra*, 16

Sample orchestras, 1773–1778

Date	Place	Bowed strings	Woodwinds	Brass and drums	Keyboard and plucked	Total excl. kbd.	Source
1773	Turin: Teatro Regio	28 violins 5 violas 2 cellos 8 double basses	6 oboes [flutes, and clarinets] 4 bassoons	4 horns 2 trumpets 1 timpani	2 harpsichords	60	Bouquet, *Teatro*, 171
1773	Cremona: Teatro Nazari	8 violins 2 violas 1 cello 3 double basses	1 oboe	2 horns	1 harpsichord	17	Santoro, *Teatro*, 267
1773	Paris: Opéra	20 violins 3 violas 8 cellos 7 double basses	7 oboes [flutes] 2 clarinets 8 bassoons	2 horns 1 trumpet 1 timpani 1 drum	1 harpsichord	60	*Almanach* (1774)
1773	Paris: Comédie-Française	11 violins 2 violas 3 cellos 1 double bass	2 oboes 2 bassoons	2 horns		23	Ibid.
1773	Mannheim Kapelle	21 violins 7 violas 4 cellos 3 double basses	3 flutes 3 oboes 4 clarinets 4 bassoons	6 horns [2 trumpets] [1 timpani]	2 harpsichords	58	Wolf, "On the Composition," 118
1773	Vienna: Burgtheater	12 violins 3 violas 3 cellos 3 double basses	1 flute 2 oboes 2 bassoons	2 horns	[1 harpsichord]	28	Zechmeister, *Die Wiener Theater*, 356

Date	Place	Bowed strings	Woodwinds	Brass and drums	Keyboard and plucked	Total excl. kbd.	Source
1773	Stuttgart Kapelle	17 violins 6 violas 3 cellos 4 double basses	2 flutes 3 oboes 2 bassoons	3 horns		40	Mahling, "Orchester"
1774	Bath: Orchard St. Theatre	[5] violins [2] violas 1 cello	1 oboe 1 bassoon	1 horn 1 trumpet		12	James, "Concert Life," 1050
1774	Paris: Comédie-Italienne	11 violins 2 violas 3 cellos 2 double basses	2 oboes [flutes] 2 bassoons	2 horns		24	Charlton, "Orchestra," 97
1774	Paris: Concert Spirituel	26 violins 4 violas 10 cellos 4 double basses	2 flutes 3 oboes 2 clarinets 4 bassoons	2 horns 2 trumpets 1 timpani		60	*Almanach* (1775)
1774	Vienna: Kärntnertor Theater	13 violins 2 violas 3 cellos 4 basses	2 oboes 2 bassoons	2 horns	[1 harpsichord]	26	Edge, "Mozart's Viennese Orchestras," 68
1775	Kassel Kapelle	8 violins 2 violas 1 cello 1 double bass	2 flutes 1 oboe 1 bassoon	2 horns [2 trumpets] [1 timpani]		21	Mahling, "Orchester"
1775	Dresden Kapelle	19 violins 5 violas 3 cellos 3 double basses	3 flutes 4 oboes 5 bassoons	2 horns [2 trumpets] [1 timpani]	[1 harpsichord]	47	Ibid.
1775	Rome: Accademia del Disegno di San Luca	18 violins 2 violas 2 cellos 2 double basses	2 oboes	4 trumpets 4 horns		34	Piperno, "Musica," 560

Year	Ensemble	Strings	Woodwinds	Brass/Timpani	Keyboard	Total	Source
	of Ancient Music	5 violas 4 cellos 2 double basses	4 bassoons	2 trumpets 1 trombone 1 timpani			
1776	Salisbury: Concerts	7 violins 2 violas 1 cello 1 double bass	1 flute 1 oboe	2 horns		15	Marsh, *Journals*, 93
1776	Bologna: San Petronio	12 violins and violas 1 cello 1 violone 1 double bass	3 oboes	2 trumpets 1 trombone	1 organ	21	Gambassi, *Cappella musicale*, 201
1776	Esterházy Kapelle	7 violins 2 violas 1 cello 1 double bass	2 oboes 2 clarinets 2 bassoons	2 horns 1 timpani		20	Landon, *Haydn*, ii. 225
1776	Salzburg Kapelle	10 violins 1 viola 3 double basses	2 oboes 2 bassoons	3 horns [2 trumpets] [1 timpani]	[1 organ]	24	Hintermaier, "Die Salzburger Hofkapelle"
1776	Munich Kapelle	26 violins 5 violas 5 cellos 4 double basses	4 flutes 4 oboes 1 clarinet 3 bassoons	7 horns [2 trumpets] [1 timpani]	2 harpsichords	62	Mahling, "Orchester"
1776	Stuttgart Kapelle	14 violins 4 violas 5 cellos 4 double basses	4 flutes 3 oboes 2 bassoons	4 horns [2 trumpets] [1 timpani]	1 organ	43	Ibid.
1777	Paris: Comédie-Française	12 violins 2 violas 3 cellos 1 double bass	2 oboes 2 bassoons	2 horns		24	*Almanach* (1778)

Date	Place	Bowed strings	Woodwinds	Brass and drums	Keyboard and plucked	Total excl. kbd.	Source
1777	Mannheim: High Mass	20 violins 4 violas 4 cellos 4 double basses	2 flutes 2 oboes 2 clarinets 4 bassoons	2 horns 2 trumpets 1 timpani	1 organ	47	Mozart, *Briefe*, ii. 101
1777	Baden Kapelle	9 violins 2 violas 1 double bass	3 oboes [flutes] 2 bassoons	2 horns	1 harpsichord	19	Mahling, "Orchester"
1777	Würzburg Kapelle	6 violins and violas 1 cello 1 double bass	1 flute 2 oboes 2 clarinets 1 bassoon	2 horns [2 trumpets] [1 timpani]	1 organ	19	Ibid.
1777	Vienna: Burgtheater	12 violins 4 violas 3 cellos 3 double basses	2 oboes 2 bassoons	2 horns	[1 harpsichord]	28	Edge, "Mozart's Viennese Orchestras," 71
1778	London: Drury Lane	9 violins 3 violas 4 cellos and basses	2 oboes 2 bassoons	2 horns	1 harpsichord	22	*London Stage*, v. 194
1778	Milan: La Scala	30 violins 8 violas 12 cellos and basses	2 flutes 6 oboes 2 bassoons	4 horns 4 trumpets	2 harpsichords	68	Barblan, "La musica strumentale," 654
1778	Bologna: Teatro Comunale	25 violins 8 violas 2 cellos 7 double basses	2 flutes 2 oboes 1 English horn 2 bassoons	4 horns 4 trumpets 4 trombones 1 timpani	2 harpsichords	62	Ricci, *Teatri*, 654
1778	Berlin: Italian opera	13 violins 4 violas 5 cellos 3 double basses	2 flutes 2 oboes 2 bassoons	2 horns	2 harpsichords	33	*Gothaer Theaterkalendar* (1778), 229

	Salzburg, Count Czernin's dilettante orchestra	14 violins 2 violas 5 cellos 3 double basses	2 oboes				
1778	Leipzig: Gewandhaus Concert	16 violins 3 violas 2 cellos 2 double basses	1 flute 2 oboes 2 bassoons	2 horns	1 harpsichord 1 lute	31	Schering, *Musikgeschichte Leipzigs*, iii. 427
1778	Leipzig: special concerts	8 violins 2 violas 1 cello 2 double basses	2 flutes 2 oboes 3 bassoons	2 horns		22	Ibid. 428

APPENDIX C

Sample orchestras, 1791–1796

Date	Place	Bowed strings	Woodwinds	Brass and drums	Keyboard and plucked	Total excl. kbd.	Source
1791	London: Opera at the Pantheon	17 violins 4 violas 4 cellos 3 double basses	2 flutes 2 oboes 2 clarinets 2 bassoons	2 horns 2 trumpets 1 timpani	1 harpsichord	41	Milhous et al., *Italian Opera*, 424
1791	Berlin: Königl. Ital. Oper	22 violins 4 violas 6 cellos 4 double basses	5 flutes 4 oboes 2 clarinets 5 bassoons	6 horns	2 harpsichords 1 harp	59	Mahling, "Orchester"
1791	Stuttgart Kapelle	15 violins 3 violas 2 cellos 4 double basses	4 flutes 6 oboes 2 bassoons	4 horns 2 trumpets 1 timpani		43	Ibid.
1791	Paris: Concert Spirituel	18 violins 4 violas 10 cellos 4 double basses	7 flutes, oboes, clarinets 3 bassoons	5 horns and trumpets 1 trombone 1 timpani		53	*Almanach* (1791)
1791	Karlsruhe Kapelle	10 violins 2 violas 2 cellos 3 double basses	2 flutes 2 oboes 4 bassoons	6 horns [2 trumpets] 1 timpani	[harpsichord]	34	Mahling, "Orchester"
1791	London: Drury Lane	7 violins and violas 3 cellos 1 double bass	2 oboes 2 bassoons	2 horns/trumpets	[1 harpsichord] 1 harp	18	*London Stage*, v. 1383

Year	Location	Strings	Woodwinds	Brass/Percussion	Keyboard/Other	No.	Source
	Giovanni Evangelista	1 viola 2 cellos 1 double bass					
1791	Venice: San Marco	12 violins 6 violas 4 cellos 5 double basses	4 oboes [flutes]	4 horns [trumpets]	[2 organs]	35	Caffi, *Storia*, 69
1791	Berlin: Königl. National-Theater	6 violins 2 violas 1 cello 1 double bass	2 flutes 2 oboes 2 clarinets 2 bassoons	2 horns		20	Mahling, "Orchester"
1791	Bonn Kapelle	16 violins 4 violas 3 cellos 3 double basses	2 flutes 2 oboes 2 clarinets 2 bassoons	2 horns [2 trumpets] 1 timpani		39	*Musikalische Korrespondenz* (1791), 220
1791	Berlin Kapelle	27 violins 6 violas 9 cellos 5 double basses	4 flutes 5 oboes 3 clarinets 5 bassoons	5 horns 4 trombones 2 trumpets 1 timpani 1 serpent	2 harpsichords 1 harp	78	*Musikal. Monatsschrift* (July 1792), 19
1791	Venice: Ball for Duke of Tuscany	8 violins 2 violas 2 double basses	1 flute 2 oboes 2 bassoons	2 horns		19	Arnold, "Russians," 128
1791	Vienna: Tonkünstler Akademie	37 violins 8 violas 8 cellos 6 double basses	2 flutes 7 oboes 2 clarinets 4 bassoons	4 horns 2 trumpets 1 timpani		81	Edge, "Mozart's," 80
1791	Rudolstadt Kapelle	10 violins 3 violas 3 cellos 2 double basses	2 oboes 2 clarinets 1 bassoon	3 horns 2 trumpets 1 timpani		29	*Musikal. Korr.* (1791), 126

Date	Place	Bowed strings	Woodwinds	Brass and drums	Keyboard and plucked	Total excl. kbd.	Source
1791	Paris: Théâtre de Monsieur	16 violins 3 violas 4 cellos 3 double basses	2 flutes 3 oboes 2 clarinets 2 bassoons	4 horns 1 trumpet 1 trombone		43	*Almanach* (1791), 157
1791	Darmstadt Kapelle	11 violins 2 violas 4 cellos and basses	3 oboes and flutes 2 bassoons	2 horns		24	Mahling, "Orchester"
1792	Manchester Musical Festival	[17 violins] [4 violas] 5 cellos [2 double basses]	1 flute 3 oboes 3 bassoons	2 horns 1 trumpet 1 timpani	1 organ 1 harp	40	Pritchard, "Some Festival," 17
1792	London: Professional Concert	12 violins 4 violas 3 cellos 3 double bassees	2 flutes 2 oboes 2 clarinets 2 bassoons	2 horns 2 trumpets 1 trombone 1 timpani	1 pianoforte	36	McVeigh, "Professional Concert," 103
1792	Marseilles: Théâtre National	9 violins 2 violas 5 double basses	3 flutes and oboes 2 bassoons	2 horns 1 trumpet and trombone		24	*Almanach* (1793), 351
1792	Marseilles: Grand Théâtre	16 violins 2 violas 4 cellos 2 double basses	2 flutes 2 oboes	2 horns 1 trumpet 2 trombones 1 timpani		34	Ibid. 348
1792	Paris: Opéra	24 violins 5 violas 10 cellos 5 double basses	2 flutes 4 oboes 2 clarinets 5 bassoons	4 horns 4 trumpets and trombones 2 serpents 1 timpani		68	Ibid. 62
1792	Paris: Théâtre de l'Ambigu Comique	8 violins 2 violas 3 cellos	1 flute 2 clarinets 2 bassoons	2 horns		21	Ibid. 291

Year	Place	Strings	Woodwinds	Brass	Other	No.	Source
	Vienna: Tonkünstler Akademie	12 violins 4 violas 3 cellos 3 double basses	2 oboes 2 clarinets 2 bassoons				
1792	Lisbon: Convent of Odivellas	8 violins and violas 2 cellos 2 double basses	2 flutes 2 oboes 2 bassoons	2 horns 2 trumpets 1 timpani	1 organ	23	Scherpereel, *L'Orchestre*, 245
1793	The Hague (Tafelmusik at Court)	12 violins 4 violas 2 cellos 2 double basses	2 flutes 2 clarinets 3 bassoons	2 horns		29	Smet, *La Musique*, 132
1793	Rouen: Théâtre de Rouen	10 violins and violas 2 cellos 2 double basses	2 oboes 1 clarinet 2 bassoons	2 horns		21	*Amanach* (1794), 61
1793	Paris: Théâtre du Vaudeville	9 violins 2 violas 3 cellos 1 double bass	3 clarinets and oboes 2 bassoons	2 horns 1 drum		23	Ibid. 30
1793	Bordeaux: Grand Théâtre National	13 violins 2 violas 5 cellos 2 double basses	2 oboes and flutes 2 bassoons	2 horns 1 trumpet 1 timpani		30	*Almanach* (1793), 336
1793	Trieste: Teatro S. Pietro	10 violins 2 violas 1 cello 2 double basses	2 oboes	2 horns	1 harpsichord	19	Curiel, *Teatro*, 481
1793	Bologna: San Petronio	11 violins 2 violas 1 cello 1 violone 1 double bass	2 oboes	2 trumpets 1 trombone		21	Gambassi, *Cappella musicale*, 210
1793	London: Covent Garden (Oratorios)	13 violins and violas 2 cellos 3 double basses	2 oboes 1 clarinet 2 bassoons	2 horns 2 trumpets 1 trombone	2 organs	28	*London Stage*, v. 1577

Date	Place	Bowed strings	Woodwinds	Brass and drums	Keyboard and plucked	Total excl. kbd.	Source
1793	London: Salomon's Concert	16 violins 4 violas 5 cellos 4 double basses	2 flutes 2 oboes 2 bassoons	2 horns 1 trombone 2 trumpets 1 timpani	[1 harpsichord]	41	McVeigh, "Professional Concert," 121
1793	Toulouse: Théâtre de Toulouse	10 violins 2 violas 4 cellos 2 double basses	2 flutes 2 oboes 2 bassoons	2 horns		26	*Almanach* (1794), 57
1793	Munich Kapelle	34 violins 6 violas 7 cellos 5 double basses	8 flutes 5 oboes 2 clarinets 6 bassoons	10 horns [2 trumpets] [1 timpani]		86	Mahling, "Orchester"
1795	Rome: Accademia del Disegno di San Luca	20 violins 2 violas 3 cellos 4 double basses	2 oboes 2 clarinets 2 bassoons	2 trumpets 2 horns 2 drums	1 harpsichord	41	Piperno, "Musica," 560
1795	Cremona: Teatro della Nob. Assoc.	5 violins and violas 1 cello 1 double bass	1 oboe	2 horns	[1 harpsichord]	10	Santoro, *Teatro*, 309
1796	Vienna: Burgtheater	12 violins 4 violas 3 cellos 4 double basses	2 flutes 2 oboes 2 clarinets 2 bassoons	2 horns 2 trumpets 1 timpani		36	Schönfeld, *Jahrbuch*, 92
1796	Vienna: Theater auf der Wieden	6 violins 2 violas 1 cello 2 double basses	2 flutes 2 clarinets 2 oboes 2 bassoons	2 horns 2 trumpets 1 timpani		24	Ibid. 96

Year	Location	Strings	Woodwinds	Brass/Timpani	No.	Source
1796	Prague: Theater auf dem Kapuzinerplatze	4 violins / 2 violas / 1 cello / 1 double bass	2 flutes / 2 oboes / 2 clarinets / 2 bassoons	2 horns / 2 trumpets / 1 timpani	21	…
1796	Naples: Teatro San Carlo	25 violins / 4 violas / 2 cellos / 6 double basses	2 oboes / 2 clarinets / 4 bassoons	4 horns [and trumpets]	49	Prota-Giurleo, *Grande orchestra*, 53
1796	Prague: Deutscher Nazionaltheater	8 violins / 2 violas / 1 cello / 2 double basses	2 flutes / 2 oboes / 2 clarinets / [2 bassoons]	2 horns / 2 trumpets / 1 timpani	26	Schönfeld, 152
1796	Paris: Comédie-Italienne	19 violins / 6 violas / 9 cellos / 4 double basses	3 flutes / 3 oboes / 2 clarinets / 3 bassoons	4 horns [and trumpets] / 1 trombone	54	Charlton, "Orchestra," 103
1796	Dresden Kapelle	20 violins / 6 violas / 4 cellos / 4 double basses	3 flutes / 4 oboes / 2 clarinets / 3 bassoons	4 horns / [2 trumpets] / [1 timpani]	53	Mahling, "Orchester"

APPENDIX D

Sample orchestras, 1808–1818

Date	Place	Bowed strings	Woodwinds	Brass	Keyboard and plucked	Total excl. kbd.	Source
1808	Leipzig: Gewandhaus	8 violins 2 violas 2 cellos 2 double basses	2 flutes 2 oboes 2 clarinets 2 bassoons	2 horns 2 trumpets 1 timpani		27	Koury, *Orchestral*, 149
1808	Vienna: Italian Theater (Burgtheater)	12 violins 4 violas 3 cellos 3 double basses	2 flutes 2 oboes 2 clarinets 2 bassoons	2 horns 2 trumpets 1 timpani		35	Morrow, *Concert Life*, 175
1808	Vienna: Adelige Liebhaberkonzerte (Beethoven 4th Symphony)	25 violins 7 violas 6 cellos 4 double basses	2 flutes 2 oboes 2 clarinets 2 bassoons	2 horns 2 trumpets 1 timpani		55	Biba, "Concert Life," 88
1810	Frankenhausen: Festival performance of Haydn's *Creation*	42 violins 12 violas 11 cellos 9 double basses	4 flutes 4 oboes 4 clarinets 4 bassoons	4 horns 3 trumpets 3 trombones 2 timpani 1 Basshorn	2 organs 1 harpsichord	103	*AMZ* 12 (1810), 747
1810	Bologna: San Petronio	9 violins 1 viola 1 cello 2 double basses	2 oboes	1 horn 1 trumpet 1 trombone	1 organ	18	Gambassi, *Cappella musicale*, 221
1810	Frankfurt am Main: Opera	14 violins 3 violas 2 cellos 2 double basses	2 flutes 2 oboes 2 clarinets 2 bassoons	3 horns 3 trombones 2 trumpets 1 timpani		38	*AMZ* 12 (1810), 644

Year	Ensemble	Strings	Woodwinds	Brass/Percussion	Keyboard	No.	Source
1810	Paris: "Grand Concert"	24 violins 8 violas 12 cellos 6 double basses	2 flutes 4 oboes 2 clarinets 4 bassoons 1 contrabassoon	4 trumpets 3 trombones 1 percussion	1 pianoforte		
1810	Dresden: Charity concert	42 violins 8 violas 8 cellos 8 double basses	6 flutes 4 oboes 4 clarinets 8 bassoons	6 horns 4 trombones 4 trumpets 1 timpani		103	Mahling, "Orchester"
1810	Edinburgh: Canongate Theatre	4 violins 1 viola 1 cello 1 double bass	1 flute 1 oboe 1 bassoon	2 horns		12	Johnson, *Music*, 47
1810	Rome: Accademia del Disegno di San Luca	18 violins 2 violas 3 cellos 4 double basses	2 oboes 2 clarinets 2 bassoons	2 trumpets 2 horns 2 timpani	1 harpsichord	39	Piperno, "Musica," 560
1811	Schwarzburg-Rudolstadt Kapelle	10 violins 2 violas 2 cellos 1 double bass	1 flute 2 oboes 2 clarinets 2 bassoons	2 horns 2 trumpets 1 timpani		27	Mahling, "Orchester"
1811	Meiningen Kapelle	6 violins 2 violas 2 cellos 2 double basses	2 flutes 2 oboes 2 bassoons	2 horns 2 trumpets 1 timpani		23	Ibid.
1811	Berlin Kapelle	25 violins 5 violas 11 cellos 5 double basses	4 flutes 4 oboes 4 clarinets 4 bassoons	7 horns 2 trumpets 3 trombones 1 timpani		75	*AMZ* 13 (1811), 607
1811	Erfurt: Grosse Musikal. Akademie	52 violins 17 violas 17 cellos 12 double basses	6 flutes 4 oboes 4 clarinets 6 bassoons 1 contrabassoon	4 horns 3 trumpets 3 trombones 1 timpani	1 pianoforte 1 organ	130	Ibid. 643

Date	Place	Bowed strings	Woodwinds	Brass	Keyboard and plucked	Total excl. kbd.	Source
1812	Kassel Kapelle	17 violins 4 violas 6 cellos 3 double basses	2 flutes 4 oboes 2 clarinets 3 bassoons	4 horns 2 trumpets 1 timpani		48	*AMZ* 14 (1812), 158
1812	Mecklenburg Kapelle	8 violins 2 violas 2 cellos 1 double bass	2 flutes 2 oboes 2 clarinets 2 bassoons	2 horns [2 trumpets] 1 timpani		26	Ibid. 500
1812	Vienna: Tafelmusik for Emperor	8 violins 2 violas 2 cellos 2 double basses	2 flutes 2 clarinets 2 bassoons 2 oboes	2 horns 2 trombones 1 timpani		27	J. Moore, "Beethoven," 421
1812	Leipzig: Gewandhaus	14 violins 4 violas 3 cellos 3 double basses	2 flutes 2 oboes 2 clarinets 2 bassoons	2 horns 2 trumpets 3 trombones 1 timpani		40	*AMZ* 15 (1813), 454
1813	Paris: Odéon	14 violins 2 violas 4 cellos 6 double basses	2 flutes 2 oboes 3 clarinets 5 bassoons	5 horns [and trumpets]		43	*Annuaire* (1814), 141
1813	Paris: Théâtre des Variétés	12 violins 2 violas 3 cellos 2 double basses	1 flute 2 clarinets 1 bassoon	2 horns [and trumpets] 1 trombone		26	Ibid. 178
1813	Paris: Opéra Comique	14 violins 4 violas 5 cellos 5 double basses	3 flutes 3 oboes 3 clarinets 3 bassoons	4 horns 1 trumpet 1 timpani	1 harp	47	Ibid. 116

Year	Location	Strings	Woodwinds	Brass/Percussion	Keyboard	No.	Source
1813	Paris: Opéra	22 violins / 6 violas / 12 cellos / 6 double basses	2 flutes / 4 oboes / 3 clarinets / 4 bassoons	3 horns / 2 trumpets / 3 trombones	2 harps	73	Ibid. 71
1813	Paris: Théâtre de l'Ambigu Comique	8 violins / 2 violas / 2 cellos / 2 double basses	2 flutes / 2 oboes / 2 clarinets / 1 bassoon	2 horns [and trumpets] / 1 drum		22	Ibid. 201
1814	Milan: La Scala	25 violins / 6 violas / 3 cellos / 8 double basses	2 flutes / 2 oboes / 2 clarinets / [2 bassoons]	4 horns / 2 trumpets / 1 trombone / 1 timpani / 1 percussion		59	*AMZ* 16 (1814), 252
1814	Weimar Kapelle	8 violins / 2 violas / 2 cellos / 2 double basses	2 flutes / 2 oboes / 2 clarinets / 2 bassoons	2 horns / 2 trumpets / 1 timpani		27	Ibid. 296
1818	Naples: San Carlo	24 violins / 6 violas / 6 cellos / 7 double basses	2 flutes / 2 oboes / 2 clarinets / 2 bassoons	4 horns / 2 trumpets / 1 timpani / 1 bass drum	1 pianoforte	59	*AMZ* 20 (1810), 495 (diagram)
1818	London: Covent Garden	12 violins / 2 violas / 2 cellos / 2 double basses	1 flute / 2 oboes / 1 clarinet / 2 bassoons	2 horns / 2 trumpets / 1 trombone		29	Carse, *Orchestra* (1948), 489
1818	London: King's Theatre	19 violins / 4 violas / 4 cellos / 5 double basses	2 flutes / 2 oboes / 2 clarinets / 2 bassoons	2 horns / 2 trumpets / 1 trombone / 1 timpani	[1 piano]	46	Ibid. 488

Bibliography

A. M., "Sixième exercice du conservatoire," *Tablettes de Polymnie*, 1ère Année (Apr. 1810), 3–4.

ABRAMS, M. H., *The Mirror and the Lamp: Romantic Theory and the Critical Tradition* (New York: Norton, 1958).

ACADÉMIE FRANÇOISE, *Dictionnaire de l'Académie françoise, revu, corrigé et augmenté par l'Académie elle-même* (Paris: J. J. Smits, 1798).

—— *Nouveau Dictionnaire de l'Académie françoise*, 2nd edn. (Paris: Coignard, 1718).

"Acta Musicalia of the Esterházy Archives (Nos. 175–200)," *Haydn Yearbook*, 17 (1992), 1–84.

Actes du colloque international de musicologie sur le grand motet français 1663–1792, ed. Jean Mongédien and Yves Ferraton (Paris: Presses de l'Université de Paris-Sorbonne, 1986).

ADELUNG, JOHANN CHRISTOPH, *Versuch eines vollständigen grammatisch-critischen Wörterbuches der hochdeutschen Mundart* (Leipzig: Breitkopf, 1777).

ADEMOLLO, ALESSANDRO, *I teatri di Roma nel secolo decimosettimo* (Rome: Pasqualucci, 1888).

AGRICOLA, JOHANN FRIEDRICH, *Anleitung zur Singkunst. Aus den Italiänisch des Herrn Peter Franz Tosi, mit Erläuterungen und Zusätzen* (Berlin: George Ludewig Winter, 1757).

ALBRECHTSBERGER, JOHANN GEORG, *Gründliche Anweisung zur Composition* (Leipzig: Breitkopf, 1790).

ALEMBERT, JEAN LE ROND D', *De la liberté de la musique* (Amsterdam: Chatelain, 1759); repr. in *La Querelle des bouffons*, ed. Launay, 2199–2282.

ALLSOP, PETER, *Arcangelo Corelli—New Orpheus of our Times* (Oxford: Oxford University Press, 1999).

—— *The Italian Trio Sonata* (Oxford: Clarendon Press, 1992).

—— "Problems of Ascription in the Roman *Sinfonia* of the Late Seventeenth Century: Colista and Lonati," *Music Review*, 50 (1989), 34–44.

Almanach des spectacles de Paris . . . [title varies] (Paris, 1752–91).

ANCELET, *Observations sur la musique, les musiciens et les instruments* (Amsterdam: Aux depens de la Compagnie, 1757; repr. 1984).

ANGELO, HENRY, *Reminiscences, with Memoirs of his Late Father and Friends*, 2 vols. (London: Coburn, 1828–30).

Annuaire dramatique (Paris: Cavanagh, 1805–18).

Anthologie du motet latin polyphonique en France (1609–1661), ed. Denise Launay (Paris: Heugel, 1963).

ANTHONY, JAMES R., *French Baroque Music from Beaujoyeulx to Rameau*, 2nd edn. (Portland, Ore.: Amadeus Press, 1997).

—— "More Faces than Proteus: Lully's *Ballet des muses*," *EM* 15 (1987), 336–44.

ANTONINI, ANNIBALE, *Dictionnaire italien, latin, et françois*, new edn., 2 vols. (Lyon: Frères Duplain, 1760).

ARBINAU, LÉON, "Fragments des mémoires inédits de Dubois, Gentilhomme servant du Roi," *Bibliothèque de l'École des Chartes—Revue d'Érudition*, 9 (II/4) (1847–48), 1–45.

Arisi, Ferdinando, *Gian Paolo Panini* (Piacenza: Cassa di Risparmio, 1961).

Arnaud, François, "La Soirée perdue à l'Opéra" (1776), in *Querelle des Gluckistes et des Piccinnistes*, ed. Lesure, i. 46–61.

Arnold, Denis, "Con ogni sorti d'istromenti: Some Practical Suggestions," *Brass Quarterly*, 2 (1958), 99–109.

—— *Giovanni Gabrieli* (London: Oxford University Press, 1974).

—— " 'L'Incoronazione di Poppea' and its Orchestral Requirements," *MT* 104 (1963), 176–8.

—— "Instruments and Instrumental Teaching in the Early Italian Conservatoires," *GSJ* 18 (1965), 72–81.

—— "Orchestras in Eighteenth-Century Venice," *GSJ* 19 (1966), 3–19.

—— "Orphans and Ladies: The Venetian Conservatoires (1680–1790)," *PRMA* 89 (1963), 31–47.

—— and Arnold, Elsie, *The Oratorio in Venice* (London: Royal Musical Association, 1986).

—— —— "Russians in Venice: The Visit of the *Conti del Nord* in 1782," in Malcolm Brown and Roland John Wiley (eds.), *Slavonic and Western Music: Essays for Gerald Abraham* (Ann Arbor: UMI Research Press, 1985), 123–30.

Arnold, Ignaz Ferdinand Cajetan, *Der angehende Musikdirektor* (Erfurt: Henningsschen Buchhandlung, 1806).

Arte e musica a l'ospedaletto: schede d'archivio sull'attività musicale degli ospedali dei Derelitti e dei Mendicanti di Venezia (Sec. XVI–XVIII) (Venice: Stamperia di Venezia Editrice, 1978).

Arteaga, Esteban de, *Le rivoluzioni del teatro musicale italiano della sua origine fino al presente* (Venice: Stamperia di C. Palese, 1785; repr. 1969).

Ashbee, Andrew, *Records of English Court Music*, 9 vols. (Aldershot: Scolar Press, 1986–96).

Ashfield, Andrew, and Bolla, Peter de (eds.), *The Sublime: A Reader in British Eighteenth-Century Aesthetic Theory* (Cambridge: Cambridge University Press, 1996).

Attali, Jacques, *Noise*, trans. Brian Massumi (Minneapolis: University of Minnesota Press, 1985; first publ. 1977).

Auld, Louis E., *The Lyric Art of Pierre Perrin, Founder of French Opera*, 3 vols. (Henryville, Pa.: Institute of Medieval Music, 1986).

Aulnoy, Marie-Catherine, *Les Contes des fées par Madame d**** (1698) (London [i.e. Paris]: [n.p.], 1782).

Avison, Charles, *An Essay on Musical Expression*, 2nd edn. (London: Davis, 1753; repr. 1967).

—— *Six Concertos in Seven Parts, Op. 3* (London: J. Johnson, 1751).

Azevedo, Alexis, *G. Rossini: sa vie et ses œuvres* (Paris: Heugel, 1864).

Bach, Carl Philipp Emanuel, *Versuch über die wahre Art das Clavier zu spielen* (Berlin, 1753–62; repr. 1969; Eng. trans. William J. Mitchell, 1949).

Bach, Johann Sebastian, *Ratswahlkantaten I*, ed. Christiane Fröde (Neue Ausgabe sämtlicher Werke Johann Sebastian Bachs, I/32.1; Kassel: Bärenreiter, 1992).

Bach-Dokumente, i: *Schriftstücke von der Hand Johann Sebastian Bachs*; ii: *Fremdschriftliche und gedruckte Dokumente zur Lebenszeit Johann Sebastian Bachs, 1685–1750*; iii: *Dokumente zum Nachwirken Johann Sebastian Bachs, 1750–1800*, ed. Werner Neumann and Hans-Joachim Schulze (Kassel: Bärenreiter, 1963–72).

Bachaumont, Louis Petit de, *Mémoires secrets pour servir à l'histoire de la république des lettres en France . . .* (London: John Adamson, 1780–89).

BAETJER, KATHERINE, and LINKS, J. G., *Canaletto* (New York: Metropolitan Museum of Art, 1989).

BAGDON, ROBERT J., "Musical Life in Charleston, South Carolina, from 1732 to 1776, as Recorded in Colonial Sources" (Ph.D. diss., University of Miami, 1978).

BAGENAL, HOPE, "Musical Taste and Concert Hall Design," *PRMA* 78 (1951–2), 11–29.

BAILLOT, PIERRE MARIE, *The Art of the Violin* (1834), ed. Louise Goldberg (Evanston, Ill.: Northwestern University Press, 1991).

—— *Méthode de violoncelle et de basse d'accompagnement* (Paris: Imprimerie du Conservatoire, 1804; repr. 1974).

BALDAUF-BERDES, JANE, *Women Musicians of Venice: Musical Foundations, 1525–1855* (Oxford: Clarendon Press, 1993).

BALZAC, HONORÉ DE, *Correspondance*, ed. Roger Pierrot, 5 vols. (Paris: Garnier, 1960–69).

BARBIERI, PATRIZIO, "The Acoustics of Italian Opera Houses and Auditoriums (ca. 1450–1900)," *Recercare*, 10 (1998), 263–323.

—— "Cembalaro, organaro, chitarraro e fabbricatore di corde armoniche nella 'Polyanthea technica' di Pinaroli (1718–32). Con notizie sui liutai e cembalari operanti a Roma," *Recercare*, 1 (1989), 123–209.

—— "Conflitti di intonazione tra cembalo, liuto e archi nel 'concerto' italiano del Seicento," in *Studi corelliani IV*, ed. Pierluigi Petrobelli and Gloria Staffieri (Florence: Olschki, 1990), 123–53.

BARBLAN, GUGLIELMO, "La musica strumentale e cameristica a Milano nel '700," in *Storia di Milano* (Milan: Fondazione Treccani degli Alfieri per la storia di Milano, 1962), 619–60.

BARDET, BERNARD, "Dumanoir (les)," in *Dictionnaire de la musique en France*, ed. Benoit, 251–52.

—— "Violons, Petits," ibid. 724.

—— "Violons, Vingt-quatre," ibid. 724–28.

BARNES, CLIFFORD R., "Instruments and Instrumental Music at the 'Théâtres de la foire' (1697–1762)," *RMFC* 5 (1965), 142–68.

BARONCINI, RODOLFO, "Organici e 'orchestre' in Italia e Francia nel XVII secolo: differenze e omologie," *Studi musicali*, 25 (1996), 373–408.

BARTENSTEIN, HANS, "Die frühen Instrumentationslehren bis zu Berlioz," *Archiv für Musikwissenschaft*, 28 (1971), 97–118.

—— *Hector Berlioz' Instrumentationskunst und ihre geschichtlichen Grundlagen*, 2nd edn. (Baden-Baden: Koerner, 1974; first publ. 1939).

BARTHA, DÉNES, and SOMFAI, LÁSZLÓ, *Haydn als Opernkapellmeister: Die Haydn-Dokumente der Esterházy-Opernsammlung* (Budapest: Ungarischen Akademie der Wissenschaften, 1960).

BARTHÉLEMY, MAURICE, "Theobaldo di Gatti et la tragédie en musique 'Scylla,'" *RMFC* 9 (1969), 56–66.

BARTON, BERNARD, *Poems*, 4th edn. (London: Baldwin, Cradock & Joy, 1825).

BASHFORD, CHRISTINA, "Perrin and Cambert's *Ariane, ou Le Mariage de Bacchus* Re-Examined," *M & L* 72 (1991), 1–26.

BAUER, WILHELM A., and Deutsch, Otto Erich (eds.), *Mozart: Briefe und Aufzeichnungen*, 7 vols. (Kassel: Bärenreiter, 1962–75).

BAUMAN, THOMAS, "Musicians in the Marketplace: The Venetian Guild of Instrumentalists in the Later 18th Century," *EM* 19 (1991), 345–55.

BEAUJOYEULX, BALTASAR DE, *Le Balet Comique de la Royne* (Paris: Le Roy, Ballard, & Pattison, 1582; repr. 1982).

BECKER, ALEXANDER, SCHILLING-WANG, BRITTA, and KUSAN-WINDWEH, KARA, "Orpheus als Opernthema," in *MGG²*, Sachteil 7, cols. 1103–8.

BEEKS, GRAYDON, "Handel and Music for the Earl of Carnarvon," in Peter Williams (ed.), *Bach, Handel, Scarlatti: Tercentenary Essays* (Cambridge: Cambridge University Press, 1985), 1–20.

BEER, JOHANN, *Musicalische Discurse* (Nuremberg: Monath, 1719; repr. 1982).

BEKKER, PAUL, *The Story of the Orchestra* (New York: Norton, 1936).

Bemerkungen eines Reisenden über die zu Berlin von September 1787 bis Ende Januar 1788 gegebene öffentlichen Musiken, Kirchenmusik, Oper, Concerte und königliche Kammermusik betreffend (Halle: [n.p.], 1788).

BENOIT, MARCELLE, *Musiques de cour: Chapelle, chambre, écurie, 1661–1733* (Paris: Picard, 1971).

—— *Versailles et les musiciens du roi, 1661–1733: Étude institutionelle et sociale* (Paris: Picard, 1971).

BENSTOCK, SEYMOUR, "Venice: Four Centuries of Instrument Making," *Journal of the Violin Society of America*, 8 (1984), 41–56.

BERANEK, LEO, *Concert and Opera Halls: How They Sound* (Woodbury, NY: Acoustical Society of America, 1996).

BERETHS, GUSTAV, *Die Musikpflege am kurtrierischen Hofe zu Koblenz-Ehrenbreitstein* (Mainz: Schott, 1964).

BERLIOZ, HECTOR, *Traité d'instrumentation et d'orchestration* (Paris: Lemoine, 1843).

BERNARDI, GIAN GIUSEPPE, *La musica nella Reale Accademia Virgiliana di Mantova* (Mantua: Mondovi, 1923).

BERNARDINI, ALFREDO, "Carlo Palanca e la costruzione di strumenti di fiato a Torino nel Settecento," *Il flauto dolce*, 13 (1985), 22–26.

—— "The Oboe in the Venetian Republic, 1692–1797," *EM* 16 (1988), 373–87.

—— "Woodwind Makers in Venice, 1790–1900," *JAMIS* 15 (1989), 52–73.

BERTEZÈN, SALVATORE, *Principj di musica teorico-prattica* (Rome: Salomoni, 1780).

BESSELER, HEINRICH, *Sechs Brandenburgische Konzerte: Kritischer Bericht* (Neue Ausgabe sämtlicher Werke Johann Sebastian Bachs, VII/2; Kassel: Bärenreiter, 1956).

BÉTHIZY, JEAN-LAURENT DE, *Exposition de la théorie et de la pratique de la musique*, 2nd edn. (Paris: Dechamps, 1764; repr. 1972).

BIANCONI, LORENZO, and WALKER THOMAS, "Production, Consumption, and Political Function of Seventeenth-Century Italian Opera," *Early Music History*, 4 (1984), 209–96.

BIBA, OTTO, "Concert Life in Beethoven's Vienna," in Robert Winter and Bruce Carr (eds.), *Beethoven, Performers, and Critics* (Detroit: Wayne State University Press, 1980), 77–93.

—— "Grundzüge des Konzertwesens in Wien zu Mozarts Zeit," *Mozart-Jahrbuch* (1978–9), 132–43.

—— "Die Wiener Kirchenmusik um 1783," *Beiträge zur Musikgeschichte des 18. Jahrhunderts. Jahrbuch für österreichische Kulturgeschichte*, 1/2 (1971), 7–79.

BIEDERMANN [anon.], *Wahrheiten die Musik betreffend, gerade herausgesagt von einem teutschen Biedermann* (Frankfurt: Eichenbergsche Erben, 1779).

BIERMANN, JOANNA COBB, "Die Darmstadter Hofkapelle unter Christoph Graupner, 1709–1760," in Oswald Bill (ed.), *Christoph Graupner, Hofkapellmeister in Darmstadt 1709–1760* (Mainz: Schott, 1987), 27–72.

BILL, OSWALD, "Dokumente zum Leben und Wirken Christoph Graupners in Darmstadt," in id. (ed.), *Christoph Graupner, Hofkapellmeister in Darmstadt (1709–1760)* (Mainz: Schott, 1987), 82–181.

BIZZOCCOLI, MARIO, "L'importanza di una passione," in Conati and Pavarani (eds.), *Orchestre in Emilia-Romagna nell'Ottocento e Novecento*, 285–90.

—— "Una volontà per una tradizione," in Conati and Pavarani (eds.), *Orchestre in Emilia-Romagna nell'Ottocento e Novecento*, 275–84.

BJURSTRÖM, PER, *Feast and Theatre in Queen Christina's Rome* (Stockholm: Nationalmusei, 1966).

BLANKENBURG, QUIRINUS VAN, *Elementa Musica* (The Hague: Berkoske, 1739).

BLUMENBERG, HANS, "Paradigmen zu einer Metaphorologie," *Archiv für Begriffsgeschichte*, 6 (1960), 7–142.

BLUMENTHAL, ARTHUR R., *Theater Art of the Medici* (Hanover, NH: University Press of New England, 1980).

BÖHM, CLAUDIUS, and STAPS, SVEN-W., *Das Leipziger Stadt- und Gewandhausorchester* (Leipzig: Verlag Kunst und Touristik, 1993).

BONACCORSI, ALFREDO, *Maestri di Lucca: i Guami e altri musicisti* (Florence: Olschki, 1967).

BONDS, MARK EVAN, *Wordless Rhetoric: Musical Form and the Metaphor of the Oration* (Cambridge, Mass.: Harvard University Press, 1991).

BONONCINI, GIOVANNI, *Il Trionfo di Camilla, Regina de' Volsci*, ed. Howard Mayer Brown (New York: Garland, 1978).

BONTA, STEPHEN, "The Church Sonatas of Giovanni Legrenzi" (Ph.D. diss., Harvard University, 1964).

—— "From Violone to Violoncello: A Question of Strings," *JAMIS* 3 (1977), 64–99.

—— "Terminology for the Bass Violin in Seventeenth-Century Italy," *JAMIS* 4 (1978), 5–42.

—— "The Uses of the *Sonata da Chiesa*," *JAMS* 22 (1969), 54–84.

BORDAS, CRISTINA, "Musical Instruments: Tradition and Innovation," in Malcolm Boyd and Juan José Carreras (eds.), *Music in Spain during the Eighteenth Century* (Cambridge: Cambridge University Press, 1998), 175–91.

BORGIR, THARALD, *The Performance of the Basso Continuo in Italian Baroque Music* (Ann Arbor: UMI Research Press, 1987).

BOSSA, RENATO, "Corelli e il Cardinal Benedetto Pamphilj," in *Nuovissimi studi corelliani: Atti del Terzo Congresso Internazionale*, ed. Sergio Durante and Pierluigi Petrobelli (Florence: Olschki, 1982), 211–23.

BOSWELL, ELEANORE, *The Restoration Court Stage (1660–1702)* (Cambridge, Mass.: Harvard University Press, 1932).

BOUISSOU, SYLVIE, "Mécanismes dramatiques de la tempête et de l'orage dans l'opéra français à l'âge baroque," in Jean Gribenski, Marie-Claire Mussat, and Herbert Schneider (eds.), *D'un opéra l'autre: Hommage à Jean Mongrédien* (Paris: Presses de l'Université de Paris-Sorbonne, 1996), 217–30.

BOUQUET, MARIE-THÉRÈSE, *Musique et musiciens à Turin de 1648 à 1775* (Turin: Accademia delle Scienze, 1968).

—— *Il Teatro di Corte dalle origini al 1788* (Storia del Teatro Regio di Torino, 1; Turin: Cassa di Risparmio di Torino, 1976).

BOURDE, ANDRÉ, "Opera seria et scenographie: Autour de deux toiles italiennes du 18ème siècle," in *L'Opéra au 18ème siècle. Colloque, Aix-en-Provence 29 avril–1 mai 1977* (Aix-en-Provence: Université de Provence, 1982), 229–53.

BOURDELOT, PIERRE, and BONNET, JACQUES, *Histoire de la musique et de ses effets* (1715) (Amsterdam: Le Cene, 1725; repr. 1966).

BOWERS, JANE, "Mozart and the Flute," *EM* 20 (1992), 31–42.

BOWLES, EDMUND A., *Musical Ensembles in Festival Books, 1500–1800: An Iconographical and Documentary Survey* (Ann Arbor: UMI Research Press, 1989).

BOYCE, WILLIAM, *Three Birthday Odes for Prince George*, ed. Robert J. Bruce (Music for London Entertainment 1660–1800, Ser. F, vol. 4; New York: Garland, 1987).

BOYDELL, BRIAN, "The Dublin Musical Scene 1749–50 and its Background," *PRMA* 105 (1978–9), 77–89.

——"Music at the Rotunda Gardens in Dublin, 1771–91," *Irish Musical Studies*, 1 (1990), 99–116.

——"Music in Eighteenth-Century Dublin," in id. (ed.), *Four Centuries of Music in Ireland* (London: British Broadcasting Corporation, 1979).

BOYDEN, DAVID D., *The History of Violin Playing from its Origins to 1761* (London: Oxford University Press, 1965).

BOYSSE, ERNEST, *Le Théâtre des Jésuites* (Paris: Vaton, 1880).

BRAUER, JAMES LEONARD, "Instruments in Sacred Vocal Music at Braunschweig-Wolfenbüttel: A Study of Changing Tastes in the Seventeenth Century" (Ph.D. diss., City University of New York, 1983).

BRAUN, WERNER, "Echo," in *MGG²*, Sachteil 2, cols. 1623–37.

——"The 'Hautboist': An Outline of Evolving Careers and Functions," trans. Herbert Kaufman and Barbara Reisner, in Salmen (ed.), *The Social Status of the Professional Musician from the Middle Ages to the 19th Century*, 123–58.

BRENET, MICHEL [Marie Bobillier], *Les Concerts en France sous l'ancien régime* (Paris: Fischbacher, 1900; repr. 1970).

BRIJON, C. R., *Réflexions sur la musique et la vraie manière de l'exécuter sur le violon* (Paris, 1763; repr. 1972).

BROCKPÄHLER, RENATE, *Handbuch zur Geschichte der Barockoper in Deutschland* (Emsdetten: Lechte, 1964).

BROOK, BARRY S., *La Symphonie française dans la seconde moitié du XVIIIᵉ siècle* (Paris: Institut de Musicologie de l'Université de Paris, 1962).

BROSSARD, SÉBASTIAN DE, *Dictionnaire de musique* (Paris: Ballard, 1703; repr. 1964).

BROSSARD, YOLANDE DE, "La Vie musicale en France d'après Loret et ses continuateurs, 1650–1688," *RMFC* 10 (1970), 115–73.

BROSSES, CHARLES DE, *Lettres familières*, ed. Giuseppina Cafasso (Naples: Centre Jean Bérard, 1991).

BROWN, A. PETER, *Performing Haydn's* The Creation*: Reconstructing the Earliest Renditions* (Bloomington: Indiana University Press, 1986).

BROWN, BRUCE ALAN, *Gluck and the French Theatre in Vienna* (Oxford: Clarendon Press, 1991).

BROWN, CLIVE, "String Playing Practices in the Classical Orchestra," *Basler Jahrbuch für historische Musikpraxis*, 17 (1993), 41–64.

BROWN, HOWARD MAYER, "A Cook's Tour of Ferrara in 1529," *Rivista italiana di musicologia*, 10 (1975), 216–41.

—— *Sixteenth-Century Instrumentation: The Music for the Florentine Intermedii* (n.p.: American Institute of Musicology, 1973).

BROYLES, MICHAEL, "Ensemble Music Moves out of the Private House: Haydn to Beethoven," in Peyser (ed.), *The Orchestra: Origins and Transformations*, 97–122.

BRUFORD, WALTER, *Germany in the Eighteenth Century: The Social Background of a Literary Revival* (Cambridge: Cambridge University Press, 1935).

BRUNORO, GIOIA SOFIA SERAFINA, "The Life and Works of Giovanni Lorenzo Lulier" (Ph.D. diss., Victoria University of Wellington, 1994).

BRYANT, DAVID, "Liturgy, Ceremonial and Sacred Music in Venice at the Time of the Counter-Reformation" (Ph.D. diss., King's College, University of London, 1981).

—— "La musica nelle instituzioni religiose e profane di Venezia," in *Storia della cultura veneta*, iv/1, ed. Girolamo Arnaldi and Manlio Pastore Stocchi (Vicenza: Neri Pozza, 1983), 433–47.

BUCH, DAVID, *Dance Music from the* Ballets de Cour, *1575–1651: Historical Commentary, Source Study, and Transcriptions from the Philidor Manuscripts* (Stuyvesant, NY: Pendragon, 1995).

BUELOW, GEORGE J., "Dresden in the Age of Absolutism," in id. (ed.), *The Late Baroque Era*, (Music and Society; Englewood Cliffs, NJ: Prentice Hall, 1993), 216–29.

—— "Protestant North Germany," in Curtis Price (ed.), *The Early Baroque Era* (Music & Society; Englewood Cliffs, NJ: Prentice Hall, 1993), 185–205.

BUKOFZER, MANFRED, *Music in the Baroque Era from Monteverdi to Bach* (New York: Norton, 1947).

Bullarii Romani continuatio, Summorum Pontificum Benedicti XIV . . . Pii VIII, 14 vols. (Prati: Typographia Aldina, 1840–).

BURCHELL, JENNY, *Polite or Commercial Concerts? Concert Management and Orchestral Repertoire in Edinburgh, Bath, Oxford, Manchester, and Newcastle, 1730–1799* (New York and London: Garland Publishing, 1996).

BURKE, PETER, *The Fabrication of Louis XIV* (New Haven: Yale University Press, 1992).

—— "The Invention of Leisure in Early Modern Europe," *Past and Present*, 146 (1995), 136–50.

BURNEY, CHARLES, *An Account of the Musical Performances in Westminster Abbey and the Pantheon . . . in Commemoration of Handel* (London: Payne, 1785; repr. 1979).

—— *A General History of Music* (1776, 1786–9), ed. Frank Mercer (New York: Harcourt Brace, 1935).

—— *Memoirs of Dr. Charles Burney, 1726–1769*, ed. Slava Klima, Garry Bowers, and Kerry S. Grant (Lincoln: University of Nebraska Press, 1988).

—— *Memoirs of the Life and Writings of the Abate Metastasio, in which are Incorporated Translations of his Principal Letters*, 3 vols. (London: Robinson, 1796).

—— *The Present State of Music in France and Italy* (London: Becket, 1773; repr. 1969).

—— *The Present State of Music in Germany, the Netherlands and United Provinces*, 2 vols. (London: Becket, 1775; repr. 1969).

BURROWS, DONALD, *Handel* (New York: Oxford University Press, 1994).

—— "Handel's Oratorio Performances," in id. (ed.), *The Cambridge Companion to Handel* (Cambridge: Cambridge University Press, 1997), 262–81.

—— "Some Thoughts Concerning the Performance of Handel's Oratorios," *Händel-Jahrbuch*, 35 (1989), 63–68.

Burrows, Donald, and Hume, Robert D., "George I, the Haymarket Opera Company and Handel's Water Music," *EM* 19 (1991), 323–41.

Busby, Thomas, *Complete Dictionary of Music* (London: Phillips, *c*.1801).

Busch-Salmen, Gabriele, "'. . . Auch unter dem Tache die feinsten Wohnungen': Neue Dokumente zu Socialstatus und Wohnsituation der Mannheimer Hofmusiker," in Ludwig Finscher (ed.), *Die Mannheimer Hofkapelle im Zeitalter Carl Theodors* (Mannheim: Palatium, 1992), 21–35.

Butt, John, *Music Education and the Art of Performance in the German Baroque* (Cambridge: Cambridge University Press, 1994).

Buxtehude, Dietrich, *Sacred Works for Four Voices and Instruments—Part 2*, ed. Kerala Snyder (Dietrich Buxtehude, Collected Works; New York: Broude Trust, 1987).

Caccini, Francesca, *La liberazione di Ruggiero dall'isola d'Alcina* (Northampton, Mass.: Smith College, 1945).

Caffi, Francesco, *Storia della musica sacra nella già cappella ducale di San Marco in Venezia*, 2 vols. (Venice: Antonelli, 1855).

Cambiasi, Pompeo, *La Scala, note storiche e statistiche di Pompeo Cambiasi* (Milan: Ricordi, 1889).

Cametti, Alberto, "I musici di Campidoglio ossia il 'concerto di cornetti e trombone del senato e inclito popolo romano' (1524–1818)," *Archivio della R. Società Romana di Storia Patria*, 48 (1925), 95–135.

Campardon, Émile, *Les Comédiens du Roi de la troupe française* (Paris: Champion, 1879).

—— *Les Comédiens du Roi de la troupe italienne* (Paris: Berger-Levrault, 1880).

—— *Les Spectacles de la foire* (Paris: Berger-Laurault, 1877; repr. 1970).

Campbell, R., *The London Tradesman* (London: T. Garner, 1747; repr. 1969).

Campion, Thomas, *Lord Hay's Masque* (1607) (facs.; Menston: Scolar Press, 1973).

Campra, André, *Le Carnaval de Venise*, ed. James R. Anthony (French Opera in the 17th and 18th Centuries, 17; New York: Pendragon Press, 1989).

Careri, Enrico, "Giuseppe Valentini (1681–1753)," *Note d'archivio per la storia musicale*, NS 5 (1987), 69–125.

Carse, Adam, *The History of Orchestration* (London: Kegan Paul, Trench, Trubner & Co., 1925; repr. 1964).

—— *The Life of Jullien* (Cambridge: Heffer, 1951).

—— *The Orchestra from Beethoven to Berlioz* (Cambridge: Heffer, 1948).

—— *The Orchestra in the XVIIIth Century* (Cambridge: Heffer, 1940).

Carter, Stewart, "The String Tremolo in the 17th Century," *EM* 19 (1991), 43–59.

Carter, Tim, "A Florentine Wedding of 1608," *Acta musicologica*, 55 (1983), 89–107.

Carver, Anthony F., *Cori Spezzati*, 2 vols. (Cambridge: Cambridge University Press, 1988).

Casimiri, Raffaele, "Oratorii del Masini, Bernabei, Melani, Di Pio, Pasquini, e Stradella in Roma nell'Anno Santo 1675," *Note d'archivio*, 13 (1936), 116–29.

Castil-Blaze [François-Henri-Joseph Blaze], *De l'Opéra en France* (1820), 2nd edn., 2 vols. (Paris: chez l'auteur, 1826).

Cavicchi, Adriano, "Corelli e il violinismo bolognese," in *Studi corelliani*, ed. Cavicchi, Mischiati, and Petrobelli, 33–47.

—— "Musica e melodramma nei secoli XVI–XVIII," in Servio Romagnoli and Elvira Garbero (eds.), *Teatro a Reggio Emilia* (Florence: Sansoni, 1980), 97–134.

—— "Prassi esecutiva (IV Tavola Rotonda)," in *Studi corelliani*, ed. Cavicchi, Mischiati, and Petrobelli, 111–25.

CESARI, GAETANO, "Giorgio Giulini musicista," in *Memorie storiche intorno alle chiese, ai monasteri ed ai benefici ecclesiastici . . . nello Stato di Milano. Opera Inedita di Giorgio Giulini* (Milan: Comune di Milano, 1916).

CESSAC, CATHERINE, *Marc-Antoine Charpentier* (1988), trans. E. Thomas Glasow (Portland, Ore.: Amadeus Press, 1995).

CHABANON, MICHEL-PAUL-GUY DE, *Tableau de quelques circonstances de ma vie* (Paris: Forget, 1795).

CHAFE, ERIC THOMAS, *The Church Music of Heinrich Biber* (Ann Arbor: UMI Research Press, 1987).

CHAPPUZEAU, SAMUEL, *Le Théâtre françois* (1674), ed. Georges Monval (Paris: Jules Bonnassies, 1875).

CHARLTON, DAVID, " 'Envoicing' the Orchestra: Enlightenment Metaphors in Theory and Practice," in id., *French Opera 1730–1830: Meaning and Media*, V (Aldershot: Ashgate, 2000).

—— " 'A maître d'orchestre . . . conducts': New and Old Evidence on French Practice," *EM* 21 (1993), 341–53.

—— "Orchestra and Chorus at the Comédie-Italienne (Opéra Comique), 1755–99," in Malcolm Brown and Roland John Wiley (eds.), *Slavonic and Western Music: Essays for Gerald Abraham* (Ann Arbor: UMI Research Press, 1985), 87–108.

—— "Rehearsal—(iii) France," in *GroveO*, 1269–70.

CHASTELLUX, FRANÇOIS-JEAN DE, *Essai sur l'union de la poésie et de la musique* (The Hague: Merlin, 1765; repr. 1970).

CHEILAN-CAMBOLIN, JEANNE, "La Première Décentralisation des opéras de Lully en province: La création de l'Opéra de Marseille au XVIIe siècle," in *J.-B. Lully, Actes du Colloque/Kongressbericht, 1987*, ed. Jérôme de La Gorce and Herbert Schneider (Heidelberg: Laaber, 1990), 529–38.

CHORON, ALEXANDRE, *Traité général des voix et des instruments d'orchestre* (Paris: Des Lauriers, 1813).

CHRYSANDER, FRIEDRICH, "Zwei Claviere bei Händel," *AMZ* 12/13 (1877), cols. 177–80, 193–98.

CIPOLLA, CARLO M., *Le avventure della lira* (Milan: Edizioni di Comunità, 1958).

CLEMENTI, FILIPPO, *Il carnevale romano—nelle cronache contemporanee* (Città di Castello, 1939).

COELHO, VICTOR, "Public Works and Private Contexts: Lorenzo Allegri and the Florentine Intermedi of 1608," in *Luths et luthistes en Occident—Actes du colloque organisé par la Cité de la Musique, 13–15 mai 1998* (Paris: Cité de la Musique, 1999), 121–32.

COEYMAN, BARBARA, "Theatres for Opera and Ballet during the Reigns of Louis XIV and Louis XV," *EM* 18 (1990), 22–37.

COLLINS, MICHAEL, "L'orchestra nelle opere teatrali di Vivaldi," in Antonio Fana and Giovanni Morelli (eds.), *Nuovi studi vivaldiani* (Florence: Olschki, 1988), 285–312.

COLONNA, GIOVANNI PAOLO, *Messa a nove voci concertato con stromenti*, ed. Anne Schnoebelen (Recent Researches in Music of the Baroque Era, 17; Madison: A-R Editions, 1974).

CONATI, MARCELLO, and PAVARANI, MARCELLO (eds.). *Orchestre in Emilia-Romagna nell'Ottocento e Novecento* (Parma: Orchestra Sinfonica dell'Emilia-Romagna "Arturo Toscanini," 1982).

CONGREVE, WILLIAM, *Letters and Documents*, ed. John C. Hodges (New York: Harcourt Brace, 1964).

CORELLI, ARCANGELO, *Sonate da chiesa: Opus I und III*, ed. Max Lütolf (Historisch-kritische Gesamtausgabe, 1; Laaber: Laaber Verlag, 1987).

—— *Werke ohne Opuszahl*, ed. Hans Oesch and Hans Joachim Marx (Historisch-kritische Gesamtausgabe, 5; Cologne: Arno Volk Verlag, 1976).

CORRETTE, MICHEL, *L'Art de se perfectionner dans le violon* (Paris, n.d.; repr. 1972).

COUPERIN, FRANÇOIS, *Musique de Chambre I* (Œuvres complètes de François Couperin, 7; Paris: L'Oiseau-Lyre, 1933).

COWDERY, WILLIAM, "The Early Vocal Works of Johann Sebastian Bach: Studies in Style, Scoring, and Chronology" (Ph.D. diss., Cornell University, 1989).

CROWTHER, VICTOR, "A Case-Study in the Power of the Purse: The Management of the Ducal *Cappella* in Modena in the Reign of Francesco II d'Este," *PRMA* 115 (1990), 297–319.

—— *The Oratorio in Bologna (1650–1730)* (Oxford: Oxford University Press, 1999).

CUCUEL, GEORGES, *La Pouplinière et la musique de chambre au XVIIIᵉ siècle* (Paris: Fischbacher, 1913; repr. 1971).

CUDWORTH, CHARLES, "John Marsh on the Subscription Concert," *GSJ* 19 (1966), 132–34.

—— "The Vauxhall 'Lists,'" *GSJ* 20 (1967), 24–42.

CURIEL, CARLO, *Il Teatro di S. Pietro di Trieste* (Trieste: Archetipografia di Milano, 1937).

CYR, MARY, "*Basses* and *Basse continue* in the Orchestra of the Paris Opéra 1700–1764," *EM* 10 (1982), 155–70.

CZOK, KARL, *Am Hofe Augusts des Starken* (Stuttgart: Deutsche Verlags-Anstalt, 1989).

D'ACCONE, FRANK, *The History of a Baroque Opera: Alessandro Scarlatti's* Gli Equivoci nel Sembiante (New York: Pendragon, 1985).

DAINVILLE, FRANÇOIS DE, *L'Éducation des Jésuites (XVIᵉ–XVIIIᵉ siècles)* (Paris: Minuit, 1978).

DANIELS, DAVID W., "Alessandro Stradella's Oratorio 'San Giovanni Battista': A Modern Edition and Commentary" (Ph.D. diss., University of Iowa, 1963).

DART, THURSTON, *The Interpretation of Music* (London: Hutchinson, 1969).

DAUB, PEGGY ELLEN, "Music at the Court of George II (r. 1727–1760)" (Ph.D. diss., Cornell University, 1985).

DAUSCHER, ANDREAS, *Kleines Handbuch der Musiklehre und vorzüglich der Querflöte* (Ulm: Stettin, 1801).

DAVERIO, JOHN, "In Search of the Sonata da camera before Corelli," *Acta musicologica*, 57 (1985), 195–214.

DAVIS, SHELLEY, "The Orchestra under Clemens Wenzeslaus: Music at a Late-Eighteenth-Century Court," *JAMIS* 1 (1975), 86–112.

DEAN, WINTON, "A French Traveller's View of Handel's Operas," *M & L* 55 (1974), 172–8.

—— *Handel's Dramatic Oratorios and Masques* (London: Oxford University Press, 1959).

—— and Knapp, John Merrill, *Handel's Operas, 1704–1726* (Oxford: Clarendon Press, 1987).

DELLA LIBERA, LUCA, "La musica nella basilica di Santa Maria Maggiore a Roma, 1676–1712: nuovi documenti su Corelli e sugli organici vocali e strumentali," *Recercare*, 7 (1995), 87–157.

DELUMEAU, JEAN, *Rome au XVIᵉ siècle* (Paris: Hachette, 1975).

DENIS, JEAN, *Traité de l'accord de l'espinette* (1650), ed. Alan Curtis (New York: Da Capo, 1969). Eng. trans. as *Treatise on Harpsichord Tuning*, trans. and ed. Vincent J. Panetta, Jr. (Cambridge and New York: Cambridge University Press, 1987).

DEUTSCH, OTTO ERICH, *Handel: A Documentary Biography* (New York: Norton, 1955).

—— (ed.), *Mozart und seine Welt in zeitgenössischen Bildern* (Kassel: Bärenreiter, 1961).

Dictionnaire de la musique en France aux XVIIe et XVIIIe siécles, ed. Marcelle Benoit (Paris: Fayard, 1992).

DIDEROT, DENIS, "Instrumens," in *Encyclopédie ou dictionnaire raisonné des sciences, des arts et des métiers,* ed. Denis Diderot and Jean Le Rond D'Alembert (Neufchâtel: Samuel Faulche, 1765), viii. 803.

DIDIER, BÉATRICE, *La Musique des lumières* (Paris: Presses Universitaires de France, 1985).

DIES, ALBERT CHRISTOPH, *Biographische Nachrichten von Joseph Haydn* (1810), ed. Horst Seeger (Kassel: Bärenreiter, 1964).

DIMAGGIO, PAUL J., and POWELL, WALTER W., "The Iron Cage Revisited: Institutional Isomorphism and Collective Rationality in Organizational Fields," *American Sociological Review,* 48 (1983), 147–60.

Discours au vray du ballet dansé par le Roy le dimanche 29. jour de Janvier, 1617 (Paris: Ballard, 1617).

DITTERS VON DITTERSDORF, KARL, *Lebensbeschreibung—Seinem Sohne in die Feder diktiert* (1800), ed. Norbert Miller (Munich: Kösel-Verlag, 1967).

DIXON, GRAHAM, "The Origins of the Roman 'Colossal Baroque,'" *PRMA* 106 (1979–80), 115–28.

DOANE, JOSEPH, *A Musical Directory for the Year 1794* (London: Westley, 1794).

DONI, GIOVANNI BATTISTA, *Tratatto della musica scenica,* in *Lyra Barberina amphichordos: accedunt eiusdem opera,* ed. A. F. Gori and G. B. Passari, 2 vols. (Florence: Stamperia imperiale, 1763).

DOUSSOT, JOËLLE, "Dijon," in *Dictionnaire de la musique en France au XVIIe et XVIIIe siècles,* ed. Benoit, 240.

DOWNEY, PETER, "Performing Mr. Purcell's 'Exotick' Trumpet Notes," in Michael Burden (ed.), *Performing the Music of Henry Purcell* (Oxford: Clarendon Press, 1996), 49–60.

—— "Trumpet Style in 17th-Century France and the Music of *Les trompettes du Roy,*" *Historic Brass Society Journal,* 7 (1995), 67–93.

DRATWICKI, ALEXANDRE, "La Réorganisation de l'orchestre de l'Opéra de Paris en 1799: de nouvelles perspectives pour le répertoire de l'institution," *Revue de musicologie,* 88 (2002), 297–325.

DRESCHER, THOMAS, "Johann Friedrich Reichardt als Leiter der Berliner Hofkapelle," *Basler Jahrbuch für historische Musikpraxis,* 17 (1993), 139–60.

DREYFUS, LAURENCE, *Bach's Continuo Group: Players and Practices in his Vocal Works* (Cambridge, Mass.: Harvard University Press, 1987).

DRUMMOND, PIPPA, "The Royal Society of Musicians in the Eighteenth Century," *M & L* 59 (1978), 268–89.

DUFOURCQ, NORBERT, "En parcourant la 'Gazette' 1645–1654," *RMFC* 23 (1995), 176–202.

—— *La Musique à la cour de Louis XIV et de Louis XV d'après les Mémoires de Sourches et Luynes, 1681–1758* (Paris: Picard, 1970).

DUFRESNY, CHARLES, *Amusmens sérieux et comiques* (Amsterdam: Desbordes, 1699; repr. 1976).

DUHAMEL, JEAN-MARIE, *La Musique dans la ville de Lully à Rameau* (Lille: Presses Universitaires de Lille, 1994).

DUNNING, ALBERT (ed.), *Intorno a Locatelli: studi in occasione del tricentenario della nascita di Pietro Antonio Locatelli (1695–1764)* (Lucca: Libraria Musicale Italiana, 1995).

DUREY DE NOINVILLE, JACQUES-BERNARD, *Histoire du théâtre de l'Académie Royale de Musique en France* (Paris, 1757; 2nd edn., repr. 1972).

DYER, GEORGE, *Poetics, or A Series of Poems and Disquisitions on Poetry* (London: Johnson, 1812).

EBERSOLD, GÜNTHER, *Rokoko, Reform und Revolution: Ein politisches Lebensbild des Kurfürsten Karl Theodor* (Frankfurt am Main: Verlag Peter Lang, 1985).

EDGE, DEXTER, "Manuscript Parts as Evidence of Orchestral Size in the Eighteenth-Century Viennese Concerto," in Neal Zaslaw (ed.), *Mozart's Piano Concertos: Text, Context, Interpretation* (Ann Arbor: University of Michigan Press, 1996), 427–60.

—— "Mozart's Viennese Orchestras," *EM* 20 (1992), 64–88.

—— "New Sources for Haydn's Early Biography," paper read at the annual meeting of the American Musicological Society, Montreal, 7 November 1993.

—— Review of Mary Sue Morrow, *Concert Life in Haydn's Vienna*, in *Haydn Yearbook*, 17 (1992), 108–66.

L'effimero barocco: strutture della festa nella Roma del '600, ed. Maurizio Fagiolo Dell'Arco and Silvia Carandini (Rome: Bulzoni, 1977–78).

EHRLICH, CYRIL, *The Music Profession in Britain since the Eighteenth Century: A Social History* (Oxford: Clarendon Press, 1985).

EICHBERG, HENNING, "Geometrie als barocke Verhaltensnorm — Fortifikation und Exerzitien," *Zeitschrift für historische Forschung*, 4 (1977), 17–50.

EISEN, CLIFF, "Salzburg under Church Rule," in Neal Zaslaw (ed.), *The Classical Era* (Englewood Cliffs, NJ: Prentice Hall, 1989), 166–87.

EISENSTADT, SCHMUEL N., "Social Institutions," in *International Encyclopedia of the Social Sciences*, ed. David L. Sills (New York: Macmillan, 1968), 409–29.

ELKIN, ROBERT, *The Old Concert Rooms of London* (London: Edward Arnold Ltd., 1955).

Encyclopaedia Britannica, 11th edn. (Cambridge: University Press, 1911).

ENRICO, EUGENE, *The Orchestra at San Petronio in the Baroque Era* (Washington, DC: Smithsonian Institution Press, 1976).

EPPELSHEIM, JÜRGEN, *Das Orchester in den Werken Jean-Baptiste Lullys* (Tutzing: Schneider, 1961).

ERLEBACH, PHILIPP HEINRICH, *Harmonische Freude musikalischer Freunde — Erster und anderer Teil* (1693), ed. Otto Kinkeldey (Denkmäler Deutscher Tonkunst, 1. Folge, 46–47; Leipzig: Breitkopf & Härtel, 1914).

État de la France, ou, l'on voit tous les princes, ducs & pairs, maréchaux de France . . . (Paris: Guillaume De Luyne, 1649–1749) (title varies).

FABBRI, PAOLO, "L'orchestra . . . sarà bene che sia . . . stabile," in Conati and Pavarani (eds.), *Orchestre in Emilia-Romagna nell'Ottocento e Novecento*, 199–216.

—— "Le orchestre ravennati," ibid. 419–40.

—— "Un progetto dimezzato," ibid. 495–508.

—— "I Rossini, una famiglia in arte," *Bollettino del Centro Rossiniano di Studi*, 23 (1983), 125–50.

—— and Verti, Roberto, *Due secoli di teatro per musica a Reggio Emilia: repertorio cronologico delle opere e dei balli 1645–1857* (Reggio Emilia: Teatro Municipale Valli, 1986).

FAUCHIER-MAGNAN, ADRIEN, *Les Petites Cours d'Allemagne au XVIIIème siècle* (Paris: Flammarion, 1947).

FAWCETT, TREVOR, *Music in Eighteenth-Century Norwich and Norfolk* (Norwich: Centre of East Anglian Studies, 1979).

FÉLIBIEN, ANDRÉ, *Les Plaisirs de l'isle enchantée, ou, Les festes et divertissements du Roy à Versailles diviséz en trois journées et commencéz le 7me. jour de may de l'année 1664* (Paris: Imprimerie royale, 1673).

FENNER, THEODORE, *Opera in London: Views of the Press, 1785–1830* (Carbondale: Southern Illinois University Press, 1994).

FERGUSON, LINDA FAYE, "Col Basso and Generalbass in Mozart's Keyboard Concertos: Notation, Performance Theory, and Practice" (Ph.D. diss., Princeton University, 1983).

FÉTIS, FRANÇOIS-JOSEPH, "Notice d'une collection manuscrite d'ancienne musique française, recueillie par Michel Danican Philidor, en 1690," *Revue musicale*, 1/2 (1829), 9–13.

FISKE, ROGER, *English Theatre Music in the Eighteenth Century*, 2nd edn. (Oxford: Oxford University Press, 1986).

FITZPATRICK, HORACE, *The Horn and Horn-Playing and the Austro-Bohemian Tradition from 1680 to 1830* (London: Oxford University Press, 1970).

FLAUBERT, GUSTAVE, *Correspondance* (Paris: Gallimard, 1973).

FORKEL, JOHANN NIKOLAUS, "Genauere Bestimmung einiger musicalischen Begriffe," *Magazin der Musik*, 1 (8 Nov. 1783), 1039–72.

—— *Ueber Johann Sebastian Bachs Leben, Kunst und Kunstwerke* (Leipzig: Hoffmeister & Kühnel, 1802; repr. 1950, 1999).

FORSYTH, MICHAEL, *Buildings for Music* (Cambridge: Cambridge University Press, 1985).

FOURNEL, VICTOR, *Les Contemporains de Molière* (Paris: Didot Frères, 1866).

FRAMERY, NICOLAS ÉTIENNE, "Accompagnement," in *Encyclopédie méthodique: Musique*, ed. Nicolas Étienne Framery, Pierre-Louis Ginguené, and Jérôme Joseph de Momigny (Paris: Panckoucke, 1791–1818; repr. 1971), i. 13–20.

FRANCOEUR, LOUIS JOSEPH, *Diapason général de tous les instrumens à vent avec des observations sur chacun d'eux . . .* (Paris: Des Lauriers, 1772).

FRANÇOIS-SAPPEY, BRIGITTE, "Le Personnel de la musique royale de l'avènement de Louis XVI à la chute de la monarchie (1774–1792)," *RMFC* 26 (1988–90), 133–72.

FRANZ, EKHART G., and WOLF, JÜRGEN RAINER, "Hessen-Darmstadt und seine Fürsten im Zeitalter des Barock und Rokoko (1678–1780)," in *Darmstadt in der Zeit des Barock und Rokoko*, ed. Eva Huber (exh. cat.) (Darmstadt: Magistrat der Stadt Darmstadt, 1980), 13–19.

FRÖHLICH, "Orchester," in *Allgemeine Encyklopedie der Wissenschaften und Künste*, ed. Johann Samuel Ersch and Johann Gottfried Gruber (Leipzig: Gleditsch, 1818), 428–31.

FUCHS, MAX, *Lexique des troupes de comédiens au XVIIIᵉ siècle* (Paris: Droz, 1944).

FUHRMANN, MARTIN HEINRICH, *Musikalischer-Trichter* (Frankfurt an der Spree: Verlegung des autoris, 1706).

FULLER, DAVID, "Les Arrangements pour clavier des oeuvres de Lully," in *Jean-Baptiste Lully—Actes du colloque / Kongressbericht, Saint-Germain-en-Laye–Heidelberg 1987*, ed. Jérôme de La Gorce and Herbert Schneider (Laaber: Laaber-Verlag, 1990), 471–82.

FÜRSTENAU, MORITZ, *Zur Geschichte der Musik und des Theaters am Hofe zu Dresden* (Dresden: Rudolf Kuntze, 1861; repr. 1971).

FUX, JOHANN JOSEPH, *Orfeo ed Euridice*, ed. Howard Mayer Brown (facs.; New York: Garland, 1978).

GABRIELI, GIOVANNI, *Mottetta (Sacra Symphoniae, 1615)*, ed. Denis Arnold (Opera omnia, 5; Rome: American Institute of Musicology, 1969).

GALEAZZI, FRANCESCO, *Elementi teorico-pratici di musica*, 2 vols. (Rome: Pilucchi Cracas, 1791–96).

GALLINO, NICOLA, "Lo 'scuolaro' Rossini e la musica strumentale al Liceo di Bologna: nuovi documenti," *Bollettino del Centro Rossiniano di Studi*, 33 (1993), 5–54.

GAMBASSI, OSVALDO, *La cappella musicale di S. Petronio* (Florence: Olschki, 1987).

GASPARI, GAETANO, *Catalogo della biblioteca musicale G. B. Martini di Bologna* (Bologna: Forni, 1961).

GECK, MARTIN, "Gattungstraditionen und Altersschichten in den Brandenburgischen Konzerten," *Die Musikforschung*, 23 (1970), 139–52.

GEMINIANI, FRANCESCO, *The Art of Playing on the Violin* (London, 1751; repr. 1952, ed. David Boyden).

GERBER, ERNST LUDWIG, *Historisch-biographisches Lexikon der Tonkunstler (1790–92) und Neues historisch-biographisches Lexikon der Tonkunstler (1812–14)* (Graz: Olms, 1966–77).

GERKENS, GERHARD, *Das fürstliche Lustschloss Salzdahlum und sein Erbauer Herzog Anton Ulrich von Braunschweig-Wolfenbüttel* (Selbstverlag des braunschweigischen Geschichtsvereins, 1974).

GERLACH, SONJA, "Haydns Orchestermusiker von 1761 bis 1774," *Haydn-Studien*, 4 (1976), 35–48.

—— "Haydns Orchesterpartituren: Fragen der Realisierung des Textes," *Haydn-Studien*, 5 (1984), 169–83.

GIANNINI, TULA, "A Letter from Louis Rousselet, 18th-Century French Oboist at the Royal Opera in England," *American Musical Instrument Society Newsletter*, 16/2 (1987), 10–11.

GIANTURCO, CAROLYN, *Alessandro Stradella, 1639–1682: His Life and Music* (Oxford: Clarendon Press, 1994).

GIBSON, ELIZABETH, "The Royal Academy of Music (1719–28) and its Directors," in Stanley Sadie and Anthony Hicks (eds.), *Handel Tercentenary Collection* (Ann Arbor: UMI Research Press, 1985), 138–64.

GLOVER, JANE, *Cavalli* (New York: St. Martin's Press, 1978).

GOODKIND, HERBERT K., *Violin Iconography of Antonio Stradivari, 1644–1737* (Larchmont, NY: [n.p.], 1972).

GOSSEC, FRANÇOIS-JOSEPH, "Notice sur l'introduction des cors, des clarinettes et des trombones dans les orchestres français," *Revue musicale*, 3/5 (1829), 217–23.

GRASSINEAU, JAMES, *A Musical Dictionary* (London: Wilcox, 1740; repr. 1966).

GRÉTRY, ANDRÉ ERNEST MODESTE, *Mémoires, ou essais sur la musique*, 3 vols. (Paris: Imprimerie de la République, 1797 [L'an V]; repr. 1971).

GRIFFIN, THOMAS EDWARD, "The Late Baroque Serenata in Rome and Naples: A Documentary Study with Emphasis on Alessandro Scarlatti" (Ph.D. diss., University of California, Los Angeles, 1983).

GRIMM, FRIEDRICH MELCHIOR VON, Baron, *Correspondance littéraire, philosophique et critique par Grimm, Diderot, Raynal, Meister, etc.*, ed. Maurice Tourneux (Paris: Garnier, 1879).

—— *Lettre de M. Grimm sur Omphale* (1752); repr. in *La Querelle des bouffons*, ed. Launay, 3–54.

—— *Le Petit Prophète de Boehmischbroda* (1753), repr. in *La Querelle des bouffons*, ed. Launay, 133–92.

GROSLEY, PIERRE JEAN, *Observations sur l'Italie et sur les italiens, données en 1764*, 2nd edn. (London: [n.p.], 1774).

GUION, DAVID, "The Instrumentation of Operas Published in France in the 18th Century," *Journal of Musicological Research*, 4 (1982), 115–43.

HADAMOWSKY, FRANZ, *Die Josefinische Theaterreform und das Spieljahr 1776/77 des Burgtheaters* (Quellen zur Theatergeschichte; Vienna: Verband der Wissenschaftlichen Gesellschaften Österreichs, 1978).

HÄFNER, KLAUS, "Johann Caspar Ferdinand Fischer und die Rastatter Hofkapelle: Ein Kapitel südwestdeutscher Musikgeschichte im Zeitalter des Barock," in *J. C. F. Fischer in seiner Zeit—Tagungsbericht Rastatt 1988*, ed. Ludwig Finscher (Frankfurt am Main: Peter Lang, 1994), 137–79.

HALFPENNY, ERIC, "The 'Entertainment' of Charles II," *M & L*, 38 (1957), 32–44.

HAMMOND, FREDERICK, *Girolamo Frescobaldi* (Cambridge, Mass.: Harvard University Press, 1983).

—— "Girolamo Frescobaldi and a Decade of Music in Casa Barberini: 1634–1643," *Analecta musicologica*, 19 (1979), 94–124.

—— *Music and Spectacle in Baroque Rome* (New Haven: Yale University Press, 1994).

—— "Orpheus in a New Key: The Barberini and the Rossi–Buti *l'Orfeo*," *Studi musicali*, 25 (1996), 103–25.

HANDEL, GEORGE FREDERICK, *Poro*, ed. Friedrich Chrysander (Georg Friedrich Händel Werke, 79; Leipzig: Breitkopf & Härtel, 1880).

—— *Sosarme*, ed. Friedrich Chrysander (Georg Friedrich Händel Werke, 81; Leipzig: Breitkopf & Härtel, 1880).

HANNING, BARBARA RUSSANO, "The Iconography of a Salon Concert: A Reappraisal," in Georgia Cowart (ed.), *French Musical Thought, 1600–1800* (Ann Arbor: UMI Research Press, 1989), 129–48.

HANSELL, KATHLEEN KUZMICK, "Il ballo teatrale e l'opera italiana," in *Storia dell'opera italiana*, v, ed. Lorenzo Bianconi and Giorgio Pestelli (Turin: Edizioni di Torino, 1987), 175–302.

HANSLICK, EDUARD, *Geschichte des Concertwesens in Wien* (Vienna: Braunmüller, 1869).

HARDING, ROSAMOND, *Origins of Musical Time and Expression* (Oxford: Oxford University Press, 1938).

HARICH, JÁNOS, "Das fürstlich Esterházy'sche Fideikommiss," *Haydn Yearbook*, 4 (1968), 5–35.

—— "Das Haydn-Orchester im Jahr 1780," *Haydn Yearbook*, 8 (1971), 5–163.

HARRIS-WARRICK, REBECCA, "Ballroom Dancing at the Court of Louis XIV," *EM* 14 (1986), 41–63.

—— "A Few Thoughts on Lully's *Hautbois*," *EM* 18 (1990), 97–106.

—— "From Score into Sound: Questions of Scoring in Lully's Ballets," *EM* 31 (1993), 355–62.

—— "Magnificence in Motion: Stage Musicians in Lully's Ballets and Operas," *Cambridge Opera Journal*, 6 (1994), 189–203.

—— "Paris (3) 1725–89," in *GroveO*, 860–64.

HAWKINS, JOHN, *An Account of the Institution and Progress of the Academy of Ancient Music* (London: [n.p.], 1770).

—— *General History of the Science and Practice of Music* (1776) (London: Novello, 1875).

HAYBURN, ROBERT F., *Papal Legislation on Sacred Music, 95 A.D. to 1977 A.D.* (Collegeville, Minn.: The Liturgical Press, 1979).

HAYDN, JOSEPH, *L'anima del filosofo*, ed. Helmut Wirth (Joseph Haydn: Werke, XXV/13; Munich: Henle, 1974).

—— *Gesammelte Briefe und Aufzeichnungen*, ed. Dénes Bartha (Kassel: Bärenreiter, 1965).

HAYES, JOHN, *Rowlandson: Watercolours and Drawings* (London: Phaidon, 1972).

HAYNES, BRUCE, "Beyond Temperament: Non-keyboard Intonation in the 17th and 18th Centuries," *EM* 19 (1991), 357–81.

——*The Eloquent Oboe: A History of the Hautboy, 1640–1760* (Oxford: Oxford University Press, 2001).

—— "Lully and the Rise of the Oboe as Seen in Works of Art," *EM* 16 (1988), 324–38.

—— "Pitch Standards in the Baroque and Classical Periods" (Ph.D. diss., Université de Montréal, 1995).

HEARTZ, DANIEL, *Haydn, Mozart and the Viennese School, 1740–1780* (New York: Norton, 1995).

—— "Nicholas Jadot and the Building of the Burgtheater," *MQ* 68 (1982), 1–31.

HEINE, HEINRICH, *Historisch-kritische Ausgabe der Werke*, 23 vols. (Hamburg: Hoffmann and Campe, 1973–).

HELL, HELMUT, *Die neapolitanische Opernsinfonie in der ersten Hälfte des 18. Jahrhunderts* (Tutzing: Schneider, 1971).

HELLYER, ROGER, "The Wind Ensembles of the Esterházy Princes, 1761–1813," *Haydn Yearbook*, 15 (1984), 5–92.

HELM, EUGENE, *Music at the Court of Frederick the Great* (Norman: University of Oklahoma Press, 1960).

HENNEBELLE, DAVID, "Nobles, musique et musiciens à Paris à la fin de l'Ancien Régime: Les transformations d'un patronage séculaire (1760–1780)," *Revue de musicologie*, 87 (2001), 395–417.

HERBAGE, JULIAN, *Messiah* (London: Parrish, 1948).

HERMANN, CARL HANS, *Deutsche Militärgeschichte: Eine Einführung* (Frankfurt am Main: Bernard & Graefe, 1968).

HERSCHEL, SIR WILLIAM, *The Scientific Papers of Sir William Herschel* (London: The Royal Society, 1912).

HESS, CHRISTEL, "Mannheimer Alltagsleben im 18. Jahrhundert: Impressionen jenseits höfischer Kultur," in Karin von Welck and Liselotte Homering (eds.), *176 Tage: W. A. Mozart in Mannheim* (Mannheim: Reiss-Museum der Stadt Mannheim, 1991), 100–10.

HESS, ERNST, "Anton Stadlers 'Musick Plan,'" *Mozart-Jahrbuch* (1962–3), 37–52.

HEYER, JOHN HAJDU (ed.), *Jean-Baptiste Lully and the Music of the French Baroque: Essays in Honor of James Anthony* (Cambridge: Cambridge University Press, 1989).

HIGHFILL, PHILIP H., Jr., et al., *A Biographical Dictionary of Actors, Actresses, Musicians, Dancers, Managers & Other Stage Personnel in London, 1660–1800*, 16 vols. (Carbondale: Southern Illinois University Press, 1973–93).

HILL, JOHN WALTER, "Veracini in Italy," *M & L* 56 (1975), 257–76.

HILL, W. HENRY, HILL, ARTHUR F., and HILL, ALFRED E., *Antonio Stradivari, his Life and Work (1644–1737)*, 2nd edn. (London: Macmillan, 1909).

HINTERMAIER, ERNST, "The Missa Salisburgensis," *MT* 116 (1975), 965–6.

—— "'Missa Salisburgensis': Neue Erkenntnisse über Entstehung, Autor und Zweckbestimmung," *Musicologica Austriaca*, 1 (1977), 154–96.

—— "Die salzburger Hofkapelle von 1700 bis 1806, Organisation und Personal" (Diss., Universität Salzburg, 1972).

HOBBES, THOMAS, *Leviathan* (1651), ed. Michael Oakeshott (New York: Collier, 1962).

HOFERICHTER, CARL HORST, "Der Hofstaat Ernst Ludwigs," in Eva Huber (ed.), *Darmstadt in der Zeit des Barock und Rokoko* (Darmstadt: Magistrat der Stadt Darmstadt, 1980), 69–79.

HOLBACH, BARON D', *Lettre à une dame d'un certain âge, sur l'état présent de l'Opéra* (1752); repr. in *La Querelle des bouffons*, ed. Launay, 121–31.

HOLMAN, PETER, "The British Isles: Private and Public Music," in Julie Ann Sadie (ed.), *Companion to Baroque Music* (New York: Schirmer, 1990), 261–69.

—— *Four and Twenty Fiddlers: The Violin at the English Court, 1540–1690* (Oxford: Clarendon Press, 1993).

—— "Music for the State I: Before the Civil War," in *Music in Britain—The Seventeenth Century*, ed. Ian Spink (The Blackwell History of Music in Britain, 3; Oxford: Blackwell, 1992), 282–305.

—— "Purcell's Orchestra," *MT* 137 (1996), 17–23.

—— "Thomas Baltzar (?1631–1663), the 'Incomparable *Lubicer* of the Violin,'" *Chelys*, 13 (1984), 3–38.

HOLMES, EDWARD, *A Ramble among the Musicians of Germany* (London: Hunt and Clark, 1828).

HOLMES, WILLIAM, *Opera Observed: Views of a Florentine Impresario in the Early Eighteenth Century* (Chicago: University of Chicago Press, 1993).

HOLOMAN, D. KERN, *Berlioz* (Cambridge, Mass.: Harvard University Press, 1989).

HUCKE, HELMUT, "Verfassung und Entwicklung der alten neapolitanischen Konservatorien," in Lothar Hoffmann-Erbrecht and Helmut Hucke (eds.), *Festschrift Helmuth Osthoff zum 65. Geburtstag* (Tutzing: Schneider, 1961), 139–54.

HUDDESFORD, GEORGE, *Les Champignons du Diable, or Imperial Mushrooms: A Mock-heroic Poem in Five Cantos* (London: J. Ginger, 1805).

HUME, ROBERT D., "Handel and Opera Management in London in the 1730s," *M & L* 67 (1986), 347–62.

INCISA DELLA ROCCHETTA, GIOVANNI, "Tre quadri Barberini acquistati dal Museo di Roma," *Bollettino dei musei comunali di Roma*, 6 (1959), 20–37.

JAMES, KENNETH EDWARD, "Concert Life in Eighteenth-Century Bath" (Ph.D. diss., Royal Holloway College, University of London, 1987).

JANDER, OWEN, "Alessandro Stradella and his Minor Dramatic Works" (Ph.D. diss., Harvard University, 1962).

—— "Concerto Grosso Instrumentation in Rome in the 1660's and 1670's," *JAMS* 21 (1968), 168–80.

JENKINS, NEWELL, and CHURGIN, BATHIA, *Thematic Catalogue of the Works of Giovanni Battista Sammartini* (Cambridge, Mass.: Harvard University Press, 1976).

JOHNSON, DAVID, *Music and Society in Lowland Scotland in the Eighteenth Century* (London: Oxford University Press, 1972).

JOHNSON, JOYCE L., *Roman Oratorio, 1770–1800: The Repertory at Santa Maria in Vallicella* (Ann Arbor: UMI Research Press, 1987).

Journal de musique (Paris, 1770–77).

JUNKER, CARL LUDWIG, *Einige der vornehmsten Pflichten eines Kapellmeisters oder Musikdirektors* (Winterthur: Steiner, 1782); repr. in *Magazin der Musik*, 1 (1786), 741–77.

JURGENS, MADELEINE (ed.), *Documents du minutier central concernant l'histoire de la musique, 1600–1650*, i (Paris: S.E.V.P.E.N., 1967).

KAHL, WILLI, *Selbstbiographien deutscher Musiker des XVIII. Jahrhunderts* (Cologne: Staufen Verlag, 1948).

KAISER, HERMANN, *Barocktheater in Darmstadt* (Darmstadt: Eduard Roether Verlag, 1951).

KAPP, REINHARD, "Chronologisches Verzeichnis (in progress) der auf Orpheus bezogenen oder zu beziehenden Opern, Kantaten, Instrumentalmusiken, literarischen Texte,

Theaterstücke und Filme," in Sigrun Anselm and Caroline Neubaur (eds.), *Talismane: Klaus Heinrich zum 70. Geburtstag* (Basel: Stroemfeld, 1998), 425–57.

KARSTÄDT, GEORG, *Thematisch-systematisches Verzeichnis der musikalischen Werke von Dietrich Buxtehude: Buxtehude-Werke-Verzeichnis (BuxWV)*, 2nd edn. (Wiesbaden: Breitkopf & Härtel, 1985).

KASSLER, JAMIE CROY, "Burney's Sketch of a Plan for a Public Music School," *MQ* 58 (1972), 210–34.

KEEGAN, JOHN, "Keeping in Time," review of William H. McNeill, *Keeping Together in Time*, in *Times Literary Supplement*, no. 4867 (12 July 1996), 3–4.

KELLY, THOMAS FORREST, "'Orfeo da Camera': Estimating Performing Forces in Early Opera," *Historical Performance*, 1 (1988), 3–9.

KIRKENDALE, URSULA, "The Ruspoli Documents on Handel," *JAMS* 20 (1967), 222–73.

KLEEFELD, WILHELM, "Das Orchester der Hamburger Oper 1678–1738," *Sammelbände der Internationalen Musik-Gesellschaft*, 1 (1899–1900), 219–89.

KOCH, HEINRICH CHRISTOPH, *Kurzgefasstes Handwörterbuch der Musik* (Leipzig: J. F. Hartknoch, 1807).

—— *Musikalisches Lexikon* (Frankfurt am Main: Hermann, 1802).

—— "Über den Charakter der Solo- und Ripienstimmen," *Journal der Tonkunst*, 2tes Stück (1795), 143–55.

KÖCHEL, LUDWIG RITTER VON, *Die kaiserliche Hof-Musikkapelle in Wien von 1543 nach 1867* (Vienna: Beck'sche Universitäts-Buchhandlung, 1869; repr. 1976).

KOHLHASE, THOMAS, "Anmerkungen zur Generalbasspraxis der Dresdener Hofkirchemusik der 1720er bis 1740er Jahre," in id. (ed.), *Zelenka Studien I* (Kassel: Bärenreiter, 1993), 233–40.

KOLLMANN, AUGUSTUS FREDERIC CHRISTOPHER, *An Essay on Practical Musical Composition* (London: printed for the author, 1799; repr. 1973).

KÖNIG, ERNST, "Die Hofkapelle des Fürsten Leopold zu Anhalt-Köthen," *Bach-Jahrbuch*, 46 (1959), 160–67.

KOURY, DANIEL J., *Orchestral Performance Practices in the Nineteenth Century: Size, Proportions and Seating* (Ann Arbor: UMI Research Press, 1986).

KREBS, CARL, *Dittersdorfiana* (Berlin: Gebrüder Paetel, 1900; repr. 1972).

KROESBERGEN, WILLEM, and WENTZ, JED, "Sonority in the 18th Century, *un poco più forte?*" *EM* 22 (1994), 483–95.

KRÜGER, LISELOTTE, *Die hamburgische Musikorganisation im 17. Jahrhundert* (Strasburg: Heitz & Co, 1933).

KRUTTGE, EGIL, *Geschichte der Burgsteinfurter Hofkapelle, 1750–1817* (Cologne: Arno Volk Verlag, 1973).

KÜBLER, SUSANNE, "Die musikalische Ohnmacht des *Orfeo* von Antonio Sartorio," in Antonio Baldassarre, Susanne Kübler, and Patrick Müller (eds.), *Musik denken: Ernst Lichtenhan zur Emeritierung* (Berne: Peter Lang, 2000), 35–46.

KUNISCH, JOHANNES, "Das 'Puppenwerk' der stehenden Heere," *Zeitschrift für historische Forschung*, 17 (1990), 49–83.

KUSSER, JOHANN SIGISMUND, *Suiten für Orchester*, ed. Rainer Bayreuther (Musikalische Denkmäler, 11; Mainz: Schott, 1994). Modern edition of *Composition de musique suivant la Methode Françoise* (Stuttgart, 1682).

LAFONTAINE, HENRY CART DE, *The King's Musick* (London: Novello, 1909).

LA GORCE, JÉRÔME DE, "L'Académie royale de Musique en 1704, d'après de documents inédits conservés dans les archives notariales," *Revue de musicologie*, 65 (1979), 160–91.

—— "L'Orchestre de l'Opéra et son évolution de Campra à Rameau," *Revue de musicologie*, 76 (1990), 23–43.

—— "Some Notes on Lully's Orchestra," in Heyer (ed.), *Jean-Baptiste Lully and the Music of the French Baroque*, 99–112.

—— "Tempêtes et tremblements de terre dans l'opéra français sous le règne de Louis XIV," in Hervé Lacombe (ed.), *Le Mouvement en musique à l'époque baroque* (Metz: Éditions Serpenoise, 1996), 171–88.

LAGRAVE, HENRI, *Le Théâtre et le public à Paris de 1715 à 1750* (Paris: Klincksieck, 1972).

—— MAZOUER, CHARLES, and REGALDO, MARC, *La Vie théâtrale à Bordeaux* (Paris: CNRS, 1985).

LAKOFF, GEORGE, and TURNER, MARK, *More than Cool Reason: A Field Guide to Poetic Metaphor* (Chicago: University of Chicago Press, 1989).

LALANDE, JOSEPH JÉRÔME DE, *Voyage d'un françois en Italie, fait dans les années 1765 et 1766* (Paris: Desaint, 1769).

LA LAURENCIE, LIONEL DE, *L'École française de violon de Lully à Viotti* (Paris: Delagrave, 1922–24; repr. 1971).

LANDMANN, ORTRUN, "Die Dresdener Hofkapelle zur Zeit Johann Sebastian Bachs," *Concerto*, 51 (1990), 7–16.

—— "Die Entwicklung der Dresdener Hofkapelle zum 'klassischen' Orchester: Ein Beitrag zur Definition dieses Phänomens," *Basler Jahrbuch für historische Musikpraxis*, 17 (1993), 175–90.

LANDON, H. C. ROBBINS, *Haydn: Chronicle and Works*, i: *Haydn: the Early Years 1732–1765*; ii: *Haydn at Esterháza 1766–1790*; iii: *Haydn in England 1791–1795*; iv: *Haydn: The Years of "The Creation" 1796–1800*; v: *Haydn: The Late Years 1801–1809* (Bloomington: Indiana University Press, 1976–80).

—— *Mozart and the Masons: New Light on the Lodge "Crowned Hope"* (London: Thames & Hudson, 1982).

LASOCKI, DAVID, "The French Hautboy in England, 1673–1730," *EM* 16 (1988), 339–57.

—— "Professional Recorder Playing in England, 1500–1740," *EM* 10 (1982), 23–29; 182–91.

—— "The Recorder in the Elizabethan, Jacobean and Caroline Theater," *American Recorder*, 25 (1984), 3–10.

LA VIA, STEFANO, "Il Cardinale Ottoboni e la musica: nuovi documenti (1700–1740), nuove letture e ipotesi," in Dunning (ed.), *Intorno a Locatelli*, 319–526.

—— "Il violoncello a Roma al tempo del Cardinale Ottoboni: ricerche e documenti" (diss. Università di Roma, 1983).

LAVIN, IRVING, "On the Unity of the Arts and the Early Baroque Opera House," in Barbara Wisch and Susan Munshower (eds.), *Art and Pageantry in the Renaissance and Baroque* (State College: Pennsylvania State University Press, 1990), 518–79.

LAWSON, COLIN, "Single Reeds before 1750," in id. (ed.), *The Cambridge Companion to the Clarinet* (Cambridge: Cambridge University Press, 1996), 1–15.

LE CERF DE LA VIÉVILLE, JEAN-LAURENT, *Comparaison de la musique italienne et de la musique françoise*, 2nd edn. (Brussels: Foppens, 1705; repr. 1972).

LEFKOWITZ, MURRAY, "The Longleat Papers of Bulstrode Whitelocke: New Light on Shirley's *Triumph of Peace*," *JAMS* 18 (1965), 42–58.

—— *Trois Masques à la cour de Charles Ier d'Angleterre* (Paris: CNRS, 1970).

LEMAÎTRE, EDMOND, "Les Sources des *Plaisirs de l'Isle enchantée*," *Revue de musicologie*, 77 (1991), 187–200.

LEPPERT, RICHARD, "Men, Women, and Music at Home: The Influence of Cultural Values on Musical Life in Eighteenth-Century England," *Imago Musicae*, 2 (1985), 51–133.

LESURE, FRANÇOIS, *Dictionnaire musical des villes de province* (Paris: Klincksieck, 1999).

—— "Les Orchestres populaires à Paris vers la fin du XVIe siècle," *Revue de musicologie*, 36 (1954), 39–54.

—— "Le Recueil de ballets de Michel Henry," in Jean Jacquot (ed.), *Les Fêtes de la Renaissance* (Paris: CNRS, 1956), 205–11.

—— "Die 'Terpsichore' von Michael Praetorius und die französische Instrumentalmusik unter Heinrich IV," *Die Musikforschung*, 5 (1952), 7–17.

Lettre sur le mechanisme de l'opera italien (Naples [i.e. Paris]: Duchesne, 1756). Formerly attributed to Josse de Villeneuve.

LEVY, JANET M., "Texture as a Sign in Classic and Early Romantic Music," *JAMS* 35 (1982), 482–531.

LIBBY, DENNIS, "Introduction," in *Giovanni Battista Pergolesi: Salustia* (Giovanni Battista Pergolesi Complete Works Edition; forthcoming).

—— "Italy: Two Opera Centres," in Neal Zaslaw (ed.), *The Classical Era* (Englewood Cliffs, NJ: Prentice Hall, 1989), 15–60.

LIESS, ANDREAS, "Materialien zur römischen Musikgeschichte des Seicento: Musikerlisten des Oratorio San Marcello 1664–1725," *Acta musicologica*, 29 (1957), 137–71.

—— "Neue Zeugnisse von Corellis Wirken in Rom," *Archiv für Musikwissenschaft*, 14 (1957), 130–37.

LINDLEY, MARK, *Lutes, Viols, and Temperaments* (Cambridge: Cambridge University Press, 1984).

LINDSAY, A. D., "Absolutism," in *Encyclopaedia of the Social Sciences*, ed. Edwin Seligman (New York: Macmillan, 1951), 380–81.

LIONNET, JEAN, "La Musique à Saint-Louis des Français de Rome au XVIIème siècle," *Note d'archivio per la storia musicale*, NS, Supplement III–IV (1985–86).

LOCATELLI, SEBASTIANO, *Viaggio di Francia: costume e qualità di quei paesi (1664–1665)*, ed. Luigi Monga (Moncalieri: Centro Interuniversitario di Ricerche sul "Viaggio" in Italia, 1990).

LOCKE, MATTHEW, *The Rare Theatrical*, ed. Peter Holman (Music for London Entertainment 1660–1800: Series A, vol. 4; London: Stainer & Bell, 1989).

—— and GIBBONS, CHRISTOPHER, *Cupid and Death*, ed. Edward J. Dent (London: Stainer & Bell, 1951).

LÖHLEIN, GEORG SIMON, *Anweisung zum Violinspielen* (Leipzig and Züllichau: Waisenhaus- und Frommannische Buchhandlung, 1774; 3rd edn., 1797).

The London Stage, 1660–1800, ed. William Van Lennep, Emmet L. Avery, Arthur H. Scouten, and George W. Stone, Jr., 5 vols. (Carbondale: Southern Illinois University Press, 1960–68).

LONGFELLOW, HENRY WADSWORTH, *Hyperion, A Romance* (1839) (Cambridge, Mass.: J. Owen, 1845).

LONSDALE, ROGER, *Dr. Charles Burney: A Literary Biography* (Oxford: Clarendon Press, 1986).

LORET, JEAN, *La Muze historique*, ed. Ch.-L. Livet (Paris: Daffis, 1877).

LOVE, HAROLD, "The Fiddlers on the Restoration Stage," *EM* 6 (1978), 391–99.

Lowe, Robert W., *Marc-Antoine Charpentier et l'opéra de collège* (Paris: Maisonneuve & Larose, 1966).

Lowenstein, Uta, "Voraussetzungen und Grundlagen von Tafelzeremoniell und Zeremonietafel," in Jörg Jochen and Thomas Rahn Berns (eds.), *Zeremoniell als höfische Ästhetik in Spätmittelalter und früher Neuzeit* (Tübingen: Max Niemeyer Verlag, 1995), 266–79.

Lubbock, Constance A., *The Herschel Chronicle* (Cambridge: Cambridge University Press, 1933).

Lully, Jean-Baptiste, *Ballet des Saisons, Les Amours déguisés, Ballet royal de Flore*, ed. Rebecca Harris-Warrick (Oeuvres Complètes, 1/vi; Hildesheim: Olms, 2001).

—— *Oeuvres complètes de J. B. Lully*, ed. Henry Prunières (Paris: Éditions de la Revue musicale, 1930–39).

McCredie, Andrew, "Instrumentarium and Instrumentation in the North German Baroque Opera" (Diss., Universität Hamburg, 1964).

McGowan, Margaret M., *L'Art du ballet de cour en France, 1581–1683* (Paris: CNRS, 1963).

McGuinness, Rosamond, and Johnstone, H. Diack, "Concert Life in England I," in *The Eighteenth Century*, ed. H. Diack Johnstone and Roger Fiske (The Blackwell History of Music in Britain, 4; Oxford: Blackwell, 1990), 31–95.

Machard, Roberte, "Les Musiciens en France au temps de Jean-Philippe Rameau d'après les actes du Secrétariat de la Maison du Roi," *RMFC* 11 (1971), 5–177.

McLamore, Laura Alyson, "Symphonic Conventions in London's Concert Rooms, circa 1755–1790" (Ph.D. diss., University of California, Los Angeles, 1991).

McNeill, William, *Keeping Together in Time: Dance and Drill in Human History* (Cambridge, Mass.: Harvard University Press, 1995).

McVeigh, Simon, "Italian Violinists in Eighteenth-Century London," in Reinhard Strohm (ed.), *The Eighteenth-Century Diaspora of Italian Music and Musicians* (Turnhout: Brepols, 2001), 139–76.

—— "The Professional Concert and Rival Subscription Series in London, 1783–1793," *RMA Research Chronicle*, 22 (1989), 1–135.

—— *The Violinist in London's Concert Life, 1750–1784* (New York: Garland, 1989).

Maertens, Willi, *Georg Philipp Telemanns sogenannte hamburgische Kapitainsmusiken (1723–1765)* (Wilhelmshaven: Florian Noetzel Verlag, 1988).

Magazin der Musik, ed. Carl Friedrich Cramer (Hamburg, 1783–6; repr. 1971).

Mahling, Christoph-Hellmut, "Con o Senza Fagotto? Bemerkungen zur Besetzung der 'Bassi' (1740 bis ca. 1780)," in id. (ed.), *Florilegium Musicologicum: Hellmut Federhofer zum 75. Geburtstag* (Tutzing: Schneider, 1988), 197–207.

—— "Orchester und Orchestermusiker in Deutschland von 1700 bis 1850" (Diss., Universität Saarbrücken, 1971).

—— "The Origin and Social Status of the Court Orchestral Musician in the 18th and Early 19th Century in Germany," trans. Herbert Kaufman and Barbara Reisner, in Salmen (ed.), *The Social Status of the Professional Musician from the Middle Ages to the 19th Century*, 219–64.

—— and Rösing, Helmut, "Orchester," in *MGG²*, Sachteil 7, cols. 812–54.

Mainwaring, John, *Georg Friedrich Händel: Biographie*, trans. Johann Mattheson, ed. Hedwig Mueller von Asow and E. H. Mueller von Asow (Lindau: Frisch und Perneder, 1949).

MANGSEN, SANDRA, "The Trio Sonata in Pre-Corellian Prints: When Does 3 = 4?," *Performance Practice Review*, 3 (1990), 138–64.

MARAL, ALEXANDRE, *La Chapelle royale de Versailles sous Louis XIV: Cérémonial, liturgie et musique* (Mémoires et documents de l'École des Chartes, LXVII; Sprimont, Belgium: Pierre Mardaga, 2002).

MARCELLO, BENEDETTO, *Il teatro alla moda* (*c*.1720) (Udine: Pizzicato Edizioni Musicali, 1992).

MARMONTEL, JEAN-FRANÇOIS, *Mémoires* (1804), ed. Jean-Pierre Guicciardi and Gilles Thierriat (Paris: Mercure de France, 1999).

MARPURG, FRIEDRICH WILHELM (ed.), *Historisch-kritische Beyträge zur Aufnahme der Musik* (Berlin: Verlag Joh. Jacob Schutzens, 1754–78; repr. 1970).

—— *Legende einiger Musikheiligen* (Cologne: Peter Hammer, 1786).

MARSH, JOHN, *The John Marsh Journals: The Life and Times of a Gentleman Composer (1752–1828)*, ed. Brian Robins (Stuyvesant, NY: Pendragon, 1998).

MARX, HANS JOACHIM, "Die 'Giustificazioni della Casa Pamphilj' als musikgeschichtliche Quelle," *Studi musicali*, 12 (1983), 121–87.

—— "The Instrumentation of Handel's Early Italian Works," *EM* 16 (1988), 496–505.

—— "Die Musik am Hofe Pietro Kardinal Ottobonis unter Arcangelo Corelli," *Analecta musicologica*, 5 (1968), 104–77.

—— "Ein neuaufgefundenes Autograph Arcangelo Corellis," *Acta musicologica*, 41 (1969), 116–18.

—— "Römische Weihnachtsoratorien aus der ersten Hälfte des 18. Jahrhunderts," *Archiv für Musikwissenschaft*, 49 (1992), 163–99.

—— *Die Überlieferung der Werke Arcangelo Corellis: Catalogue raisonné* (Cologne: A. Volk, 1980).

—— "Unveröffentlichte Kompositionen Arcangelo Corellis," in *Studi corelliani: Atti del Primo Congresso Internazionale*, ed. Adriano Cavicchi, Oscar Mischiati, and Pierluigi Petrobelli (Florence: Olschki, 1972), 53–69.

Masses by Giovanni Rovetta, Ortensio Polidori, Giovanni Battista Chinelli, Orazio Tarditi, ed. Anne Schnoebelen (Seventeenth-Century Italian Sacred Music, 5; New York: Garland, 1996).

MASSIP, CATHERINE, *La Vie des musiciens de Paris au temps de Mazarin (1643–1661): Essai d'étude sociale* (Paris: Picard, 1976).

MATES, JULIAN, *The American Musical Stage before 1800* (New Brunswick, NJ: Rutgers University Press, 1963).

MATTHESON, JOHANN, *Grundlage einer Ehren-Pforte* (Hamburg: in Verlegung des Verfassers, 1740; repr. 1910, 1969).

—— *Der musicalische Patriot* (Hamburg, 1728).

—— *Das neu-eröffnete Orchester* (Hamburg: der Autor und Benjamin Schillers Witwe, 1713; repr. 1997).

—— *Der vollkommene Capellmeister* (Hamburg: Christian Herold, 1739; repr. 1954); Eng. trans. E. C. Harriss, 1981.

MAUNDER, RICHARD, "Performing Mozart and Beethoven Concertos," *EM* 17 (1989), 139–40.

MÉLÈSE, PIERRE, *Le Théâtre et le public à Paris sous Louis XIV, 1659–1715* (Paris: Droz, 1934; repr. 1976).

MENDEL, ARTHUR, "On the Pitches in Use in Bach's Time," in *Studies in the History of Musical Pitch* (Amsterdam: Knuf, 1968), 187–238.

——— "Pitch in Western Music Since 1500: A Re-examination," *Acta musicologica*, 50 (1978), 1–93.

MERCIER, LOUIS-SÉBASTIEN, *Du théâtre ou nouvel essai sur l'art dramatique* (Amsterdam: Van Harrevelt, 1773).

———*Jezennemours: Roman-dramatique* (Amsterdam: [n.p.], 1776).

Mercure de France (title varies) (Paris, 1620–1820).

MERSENNE, MARIN, *Harmonie universelle* (Paris: Sébastien Cramoisy, 1636; repr. 1963).

MESSISBUGO, CRISTOFORO DA, *Banchetti, composizione di vivande e apparecchio generale* (1549), ed. Fernando Bandini (Venice: Neri Pozza, 1960).

MEUCCI, RENATO, "The Cimbasso and Related Instruments in 19th-Century Italy," *GSJ* 49 (1996), 143–79.

——— "La costruzione di strumenti musicali a Roma tra XVII e XIX secolo, con notizie inedite sulla famiglia Biglioni," in *La musica a Roma attraverso le fonti d'archivio—Atti del convegno internazionale, Roma 4–7 giugno, 1992*, ed. Bianca Maria Antolini, Arnaldo Morelli, and Vera Vita Spagnuolo (Lucca: Libreria Musicale Italiana Editrice, 1994), 581–93.

——— "Horn," in *NG II*, xi. 709–25.

——— "On the Early History of the Trumpet in Italy," *Basler Jahrbuch für historische Musikpraxis*, 15 (1991), 9–34.

MEUDE-MONPAS, JOSEPH DE, *Dictionnaire de musique* (Paris: Knapen, 1787; repr. 1981).

MEYER, AHLRICH, "Mechanische und organische Metaphorik politischer Philosophie," *Archiv für Begriffsgeschichte*, 13 (1969), 128–99.

MEYER, JÜRGEN, *Akustik und musikalische Aufführungspraxis*, 2nd edn. (Frankfurt am Main: Verlag Das Musikinstrument, 1980).

——— "Raumakustik und Orchesterklang in den Konzertsälen Joseph Haydns," *Acustica*, 41 (1978), 145–62.

MILHOUS, JUDITH, and HUME, ROBERT D., "New Light on Handel and the Royal Academy of Music in 1720," *Theatre Journal*, 35 (1983), 149–67.

——— *Vice Chamberlain Coke's Theatrical Papers, 1706–1715* (Carbondale: Southern Illinois University Press, 1982).

———DIDERIKSEN, GABRIELLA, and HUME, ROBERT D., *Italian Opera in Late Eighteenth-Century London*, ii: *The Pantheon Opera and its Aftermath, 1789–1795* (Oxford: Oxford University Press, 2001).

MILLIOT, SYLVETTE, "Réflexions et recherches sur le viole de gambe et la violoncelle en France," *RMFC* 4 (1964), 179–238.

——— "Vie de l'orchestre de l'Opéra de Paris à travers les documents du temps," in *L'Opéra au XVIIIᵉ siècle: Actes du Colloque organisé à Aix-en-Provence par le Centre Aixois d'Études et de Recherches sur le XVIIIe siècle, les 29, 30 avril et 1ᵉʳ mai 1977*, ed. André Bourde (Aix-en-Provence: Université de Provence, 1982), 263–85.

MINARDI, GIAN PAOLO, "L'orchestra a Parma: un prestigio europeo e il suo progressivo declino," in Conati and Pavarani (eds.), *Orchestre in Emilia-Romagna nell'Ottocento e Novecento*, 75–144.

MIOLI, PIERO, "Il Teatro Comunale: centottanta anni di presenza," in Conati and Pavarani (eds.), *Orchestre in Emilia-Romagna nell'Ottocento e Novecento*, 325–42.

MISCHIATI, OSCAR, "Una statistica della musica a Roma nel 1694," *Note d'archivio per la storia musicale*, NS 1 (1983), 209–27.

MOENS-HAENEN, GRETA, *Das Vibrato in der Musik des Barock: Ein Handbuch zur Aufführungspraxis für Vokalisten und Instrumentalisten* (Graz: Akademische Druck und Verlagsanstalt, 1988).

MOFFA, ROSY, *Storia della regia cappella di Torino dal 1775 al 1870* (Turin: Centro Studi Piemontesi, 1990).

MOINE, MARIE-CHRISTINE, *Les Fêtes à la cour du roi soleil (1653–1715)* (Paris: Lanore, 1984).

MÖLLER, DIRK, "Zur Generalbassbesetzung in den Opern Georg Friedrich Händels," *Göttinger Händel-Beiträge*, 2 (1986), 141–54.

MOLLOY, CHARLES, *The Coquet: or, the English Chevalier* (London: E. Curll, 1718).

MONGRÉDIEN, GEORGES, and ROBERT, JEAN, *Les Comédiens français du XVIIe siècle, suivi d'un inventaire des troupes, 1590–1710* (Paris: CNRS, 1981).

MONK, SAMUEL H., *The Sublime: A Study of Critical Theories in XVIII-Century England* (New York: Modern Language Association, 1935).

MONTAGNIER, JEAN-PAUL C., "The Problems of 'Reduced Scores' and Performing Forces at the Chapelle Royale of Versailles during the Tenure of Henry Madin (1738–1748)," *Journal of Musicological Research*, 18 (1998), 63–93.

MONTÉCLAIR, MICHEL PIGNOLET DE, *Principes de musique* (Paris: veuve Boivin, 1736; repr. 1972).

MONTEVERDI, CLAUDIO, *Lettere, dediche e prefazione*, ed. Domenico De' Paoli (Rome: De Santis, 1973).

——— *L'Orfeo–Favola in musica*, ed. Wolfgang Osthoff (facs. of 1609 Venice edn.; Kassel: Bärenreiter, 1998).

MOORE, JAMES HAROLD, *Vespers at St. Mark's: Music of Alessandro Grandi, Giovanni Rovetta and Francesco Cavalli* (Ann Arbor: UMI Research Press, 1981).

MOORE, JULIA, "Beethoven and Musical Economics" (Ph.D. diss., University of Illinois, Urbana-Champaign, 1987).

MORELLET, ANDRÉ, "De l'expression en musique," *Mercure de France*, Nov. 1771, 113–43.

MORLEY-PEGGE, R., *The French Horn*, 2nd edn. (London: Benn, 1973).

MORROW, MARY SUE, *Concert Life in Haydn's Vienna: Aspects of a Developing Musical and Social Institution* (Stuyvesant, NY: Pendragon Press, 1989).

MOZART, LEOPOLD, *Versuch einer gründlichen Violinschule* (Augsburg: Verlag des Verfassers, 1756; 3rd edn. 1787, repr. 1956; trans E. Knocker, 1948).

——— (attrib.), "Nachricht von dem gegenwärtigen Zustande der Musik Sr. Hochfürstlichen Gnaden des Erzbischoffs zu Salzburg im Jahr 1757," in *Historisch-kritische Beyträge zur Aufnahme der Musik*, iii, ed. Friedrich Wilhelm Marpurg (Berlin: J. J. Schützens Witwe, 1757; repr. 1970), 183–98.

MOZART, WOLFGANG AMADEUS, *Briefe und Aufzeichnungen*, ed. Wilhelm A. Bauer and Otto Erich Deutsch (Kassel: Bärenreiter, 1962–75).

MUFFAT, GEORG, *Armonico tributo: 1682 . . . concerti grossi, zweiter Teil*, ed. Erich Schenk (Denkmäler der Tonkunst in Österreich, 89; Vienna: Österreichischer Bundesverlag, 1953).

——— *Florilegium primum* (1695), ed. Heinrich Rietsch (Denkmäler der Tonkunst in Österreich, 2; Vienna: Artaria, 1894; repr. 1959).

——— *Florilegium secundum* (1698), ed. Heinrich Rietsch (Denkmäler der Tonkunst in Österreich, 4; Vienna: Artaria, 1895; repr. 1959).

—— *Sechs Concerti Grossi I: Auserlesene mit Ernst und Lust gemengte Instrumentalmusik—nebst einem Anhange: Auswahl aus Armonico tributo* (1701), ed. Erwin Luntz (Denkmäler der Tonkunst in Österreich, 23; Vienna: Artaria, 1904; repr. 1959).

MÜNSTER, ROBERT, "Die Sinfonien Toeschis" (Diss., Ludwig-Maximilians-Universität, Munich, 1956).

MURATA, MARGARET, *Operas for the Papal Court, 1631–1668* (Ann Arbor: UMI Research Press, 1981).

MURRAY, PENELOPE, and DORSCH, T. S. (eds.), *Classical Literary Criticism* (Oxford: Penguin Books, 2000).

MUSGRAVE, MICHAEL, *The Musical Life of the Crystal Palace* (Cambridge: Cambridge University Press, 1995).

Musikalische Korrespondenz der Teutschen Filharmonischen Gesellschaft, ed. Heinrich Philipp Carl Bossler (Speier, 1790–2).

MUTEAU, CHARLES, *Les Écoles et collèges en province depuis les temps les plus reculés jusqu'en 1789* (Dijon: Barantière, 1882).

NÄGELE, RAINER, "'Hier ist kein Platz für ein Künstler': Das Stuttgarter Hoftheater, 1797–1816," in id. (ed.), *Musik und Musiker am Stuttgarter Hoftheater (1750–1918): Quellen und Studien* (Stuttgart: Württembergische Landesbibliothek, 2000), 110–28.

Narrazione delle solenne reali feste fatte in Napoli di sua Maestà il Re delle due Sicilie Carlo Infante di Spagna per la nascita del suo primogenito Filippo, reale principe delle Due Sicilie (Naples: [n.p.], 1749).

NATALI, PAOLO, and STEFANATI, GIANNI, "Le presenze orchestrali a Ferrara dalla fine del Settecento al Novecento," in Conati and Paravani (eds.), *Orchestre in Emilia-Romagna nell'Ottocento e Novecento*, 297–324.

A Neapolitan Festa a Ballo and Selected Instrumental Ensemble Pieces, ed. Roland Jackson (Recent Researches in the Music of the Baroque Era, 25; Madison: A-R Editions, 1978).

NETTEL, REGINALD, *The Orchestra in England: A Social History* (London: Jonathan Cape, 1946).

NETTL, PAUL, *Forgotten Musicians* (New York: Philosophical Library, 1951).

—— "Die Wiener Tanzkomposition in der zweiten Hälfte des siebzehnten Jahrhunderts," *Studien zur Musikwissenschaft*, 8 (1921), 45–175.

NEUMANN, WERNER, "Das 'Bachische Collegium Musicum,'" *Bach-Jahrbuch*, 47 (1960), 5–27.

NICOLAI, FRIEDRICH, *Beschreibung einer Reise durch Deutschland und die Schweiz, im Jahre 1781* (Berlin: 1783–96; repr. in Gesammelte Werke, 15–20, 1994).

NICOLL, ALLARDYCE, *The Garrick Stage: Theatres and Audience in the Eighteenth Century*, ed. Sybil Rosenfeld (Manchester: Manchester University Press, 1980).

NOACK, ELISABETH, *Musikgeschichte Darmstadts vom Mittelalter bis zur Goethezeit* (Mainz: Schott, 1967).

NORTH, ROGER, *Roger North on Music*, ed. John Wilson (London: Novello, 1959).

NUSSDORFER, LAURIE, *Civic Politics in the Rome of Urban VIII* (Princeton: Princeton University Press, 1992).

ODELL, GEORGE, *Annals of the New York Stage*, ii: *1798–1821* (New York: Columbia University Press, 1927).

O'DETTE, PAUL, "Plucked Instruments," in Jeffery T. Kite-Powell (ed.), *A Performer's Guide to Renaissance Music* (New York: Schirmer, 1994), 139–53.

O'REGAN, NOEL, "The Performance of Roman Sacred Polychoral Music in the Late

Sixteenth and Early Seventeenth Centuries: Evidence from Archival Sources," *Performance Practice Review*, 8 (1995), 107–46.

ORGEL, STEPHEN, and STRONG, ROY C., *The Theatre of the Stuart Court* (Berkeley: University of California Press, 1973).

OWENS, SAMANTHA KIM, "The Württemberg Hofkapelle, c.1680–1721" (Ph.D. diss., Victoria University of Wellington, 1995).

PADOAN, MAURIZIO, *La musica in S. Maria Maggiore a Bergamo nel periodo di Giovanni Cavaccio (1598–1626)* (Como: AMIS, 1983).

—— "La musica liturgica tra funzionalità statutoria e prassi," in A. Colzani, A. Luppi and Maurizio Padoan (eds.), *La musica sacra in Lombardia nella prima metà del Seicento* (Como: AMIS, 1987), 369–94.

PALERMO, PAOLA, "La musica nella basilica di Santa Maria Maggiore a Bergamo all'epoca dell'infanzia di Locatelli," in Dunning (ed.), *Intorno a Locatelli*, 653–748.

PARKE, WILLIAM T., *Musical Memoirs* (London: Colburn and Bentley, 1830; repr. 1970).

PARKINSON, JOHN A., "The Barbaric Unison," *MT* 114 (1973), 23–24.

PAVANELLO, AGNESE, "Locatelli e il Cardinale Camillo Cybo," in Dunning (ed.), *Intorno a Locatelli*, 749–92.

PELKER, BÄRBEL, "Musikalische Akademien am Hof Carl Theodors in Mannheim," in Ludwig Finscher (ed.), *Die Mannheimer Hofkapelle im Zeitalter Carl Theodors* (Mannheim: Palatium Verlag, 1992), 49–58.

PEPYS, SAMUEL, *The Diary of Samuel Pepys*, ed. Robert Latham and William Matthews (Berkeley: University of California Press, 1970–74).

—— *Private Correspondence and Miscellaneous Papers of Samuel Pepys, 1679–1703*, ed. J. R. Tanner (London: G. Bell and Sons, 1926).

PERI, JACOPO, *Le musiche sopra l'Euridice* (Florence: Giunti, 1600; repr. 1973).

PERRAULT, CHARLES, *Les Hommes illustres qui ont paru en France pendant ce siècle avec leurs portraits au naturel* (Paris: Antoine Dezallier, 1696–1700).

PERUFFO, MIMMO, "Italian Violin Strings in the Eighteenth and Nineteenth Centuries: Typologies, Manufacturing Techniques and Principles of Stringing," *Recercare*, 9 (1997), 155–201.

PETRI, JOHANN SAMUEL, *Anleitung zur praktischen Musik*, 1st edn. (Lauban: J. C. Wirthgen, 1767).

—— *Anleitung zur praktischen Musik*, 2nd edn. (Leipzig: Breitkopf, 1782; repr. 1969).

PETZOLDT, RICHARD, "The Economic Conditions of the 18th-Century Musician," trans. Herbert Kaufman and Barbara Reisner, in Salmen (ed.), *The Social Status of the Professional Musician from the Middle Ages to the 19th Century*, 159–88.

PEYRONNET, PIERRE, "Le Théâtre d'éducation des Jésuites," *Dix-huitième siècle*, 8 (1976), 107–21.

PEYSER, JOAN (ed.), *The Orchestra: Origins and Transformations* (New York: Scribner's, 1986).

PFEIFFER, RÜDIGER, "Der französische, inbesondere Lullysche Orchesterstil und sein Walten in der deutschen Musikkultur des ausgehenden 17. Jahrhunderts," in *Der Einfluss der französischen Musik auf die Komponisten der ersten Hälfte des 18. Jahrhunderts: Blankenburg/Harz, Juni 1981*, ed. Eitelfriedrich Thom (Michaelstein: Forschungsstätte, 1982), 15–20.

Pièces pour le violon, à 4 parties, de differents autheurs, 1665, ed. Martine Roche (Paris: Heugel, 1971).

PIÉJUS, ANNE, *Le Théâtre des demoiselles: Tragédie et musique à Saint-Cyr à la fin du grand siècle* (Paris: Société française de musicologie, 2000).

PIERRE, CONSTANT, *Histoire du Concert Spirituel 1725–1790* (Paris: Heugel, 1975). "Programmes du Concert spirituel" compiled by Antoine Bloch-Michele.

PINCHERLE, MARC, *Corelli: His Life, his Work*, trans. Herbert Russell (New York: Norton, 1956; first publ. 1954).

PIPERNO, FRANCO, "'Anfione in Campidoglio': presenza corelliana alle feste per i concorsi dell'Accademia del Disegno di San Luca," in *Nuovissimi studi corelliani: Atti del Terzo Congresso Internazionale*, ed. Sergio Durante and Pierluigi Petrobelli (Florence: Olschki, 1982), 151–208.

—— "'Concerto' e 'concertato' nella musica strumentale italiana del secolo decimo settimo," *Recercare*, 3 (1991), 169–202.

—— "Corelli e il 'concerto' seicentesco: lettura e interpretazione dell'opera VI," in *Studi corelliani IV: Atti del Quarto Congresso Internazionale*, ed. Pierluigi Petrobelli and Gloria Staffieri (Florence: Olschki, 1990), 359–80.

—— "Musica e musicisti per l'Accademia del Disegno di San Luca (1716–1860)," in Bianca Maria Antolini, Arnaldo Morelli and Vera Vita Spagnuolo (eds.), *La musica in Roma attraverso le fonti d'archivio* (Lucca: Libreria Musicale Italiana, 1994), 553–63.

—— "Le orchestre di Arcangelo Corelli. Pratiche musicali romane. Lettura dei documenti," in Giovanni Morelli (ed.), *L'invenzione del gusto: Corelli e Vivaldi* (Milan: Ricordi, 1982), 42–48.

PIRROTTA, NINO, "Orpheus, Singer of *Strambotti*," in id. and Elena Povoledo, *Music and Theatre from Poliziano to Monteverdi*, trans. Karen Eales (Cambridge: Cambridge University Press, 1982), 3–36.

PISAROWITZ, K. M., "'Müasst ma nix in übel aufnehma . . .': Beitragsversuch zu einer Gebrüder-Stadler-Biographie," *Mitteilungen der Internationalen Stiftung Mozarteum*, 19 (1971), 29–33.

PLANYAVSKY, ALFRED, *The Baroque Double Bass Violone*, trans. James Berket (Lanham, Md.: Scarecrow Press, 1998).

PLATEN, EMIL, "Collegium musicum," in *MGG²*, Sachteil 2, cols. 943–51.

PLESSI, GIUSEPPE, *Le insignia degli anziani del comune dal 1530 al 1796: Catalogo-inventario* (Rome: Ministero dell'interno, 1954).

PLUMB, JOHN H., *The Commercialisation of Leisure in Eighteenth-Century England* (Reading: University of Reading, 1973).

POHL, CARL FERDINAND, *Denkschrift aus Anlass des hundertjährigen Bestehens des Tonkünstler-Societät* (Vienna: Selbstverlage des Vereins, 1871).

POTTER, JOHN, *Observations on the Present State of Music and Musicians* (London: Henderson, 1762).

POULIN, PAMELA, "Anton Stadler's Basset Clarinet: Recent Discoveries in Riga," *JAMIS* 22 (1996), 110–27.

—— "The Bassett Clarinet of Anton Stadler and its Music" (Ph.D. diss., Eastman School of Music, Rochester, NY, 1978).

—— "A Little Known Letter of Anton Stadler," *M & L* 69 (1988), 49–56.

POWELL, ARDAL, *The Flute* (New Haven: Yale University Press, 2001).

POWELL, JOHN S., *Music and Theatre in France, 1600–1680* (Oxford: Oxford University Press, 2000).

PRAETORIUS, MICHAEL, *Syntagma Musicum*, ii (Wolfenbüttel: E. Holwein, 1619; repr. 1959).

—— *Terpsichore* (1612), ed. Günther Oberst (Gesamtausgabe der musikalischen Werke von Michael Praetorius, 15; Wolfenbüttel: G. Kallmeyer, 1929).

PRESTON, RICHARD, ROLAND, ALEX, and WISE, SYDNEY, *Men in Arms* (Fort Worth, Tex.: Holt, Rinehart & Winston, 1991).

PRICE, CURTIS, "Restoration Stage Fiddlers and their Music," *EM* 7 (1979), 315–22.

—— MILHOUS, JUDITH, and HUME, ROBERT D., *Italian Opera in Late Eighteenth-Century London*, i: *The King's Theatre, Haymarket, 1778–1791* (Oxford: Clarendon Press, 1995).

PRITCHARD, BRIAN W., "The Provincial Festivals of the Ashley Family," *GSJ* 22 (1969), 58–77.

—— "Some Festival Programmes of the Eighteenth and Nineteenth Centuries— 3. Liverpool and Manchester," *RMA Research Chronicle*, 7 (1969), 1–25.

—— and REID, DOUGLAS J., "Some Festival Programmes of the Eighteenth and Nineteenth Centuries—4. Birmingham, Derby, Newcastle Upon Tyne and York," *RMA Research Chronicle*, 8 (1970), 1–22.

PROTA-GIURLEO, ULISSE, *La grande orchestra del R. Teatro San Carlo nel Settecento* (Naples: L'autore, 1927).

PRUNIÈRES, HENRY, *Le Ballet de cour en France avant Benserade et Lully* (Paris: Laurens, 1914; repr. 1970).

—— "Notes sur les origines de l'ouverture française," *Sammelbände der Internationalen Musik-Gesellschaft*, 12 (1910–11), 565–85.

—— "Notice historique: Les premiers ballets de Lully," in *Œuvres complètes de J.-B. Lully*, i, pp. xiii–xxiii (Paris: Éditions de la Revue musicale, 1931; repr. 1966).

—— "Les Petits Violons de Lully," *L'Écho musical*, 5/4 (30 Apr. 1920), 125–31.

PURCELL, HENRY, *The Fairy Queen*, ed. J. S. Shedlock and Anthony Lewis (The Works of Henry Purcell, 12; London: Novello, 1968).

PURE, MICHEL DE, *L'Idée des spectacles* (Paris: Brunet, 1668; repr. 1972).

QUANTZ, JOHANN JOACHIM, *Versuch einer Anweisung die Flöte traversiere zu spielen* (Berlin: Voss, 1752; repr. 1988; Engl. trans: Edward R. Reilly, 1966).

La Querelle des bouffons: Textes des pamphlets avec introduction, commentaires et index (1752–4), ed. Denise Launay, 3 vols. (Geneva: Minkoff, 1973).

Querelle des Guckistes et des Piccinnistes, ed. François Lesure (Geneva: Minkoff, 1984).

QUOY-BODIN, JEAN-LUC, "L'Orchestre de la Société Olympique en 1786," *Revue de musicologie*, 70 (1984), 95–107.

RAAB, ARMIN, *Funktionen des Unisono—Dargestellt an den Streichquartetten und Messen von Joseph Haydn* (Frankfurt: Haag & Herchen, 1990).

RABITTI, DANTE, "Orchestre e istituzioni musicali piacentine," in Conati and Pavarani (eds.), *Orchestre in Emilia-Romagna nell'Ottocento e Novecento*, 37–60.

RADICIOTTI, GIUSEPPE, *Aneddoti Rossiniani autentici* (Rome: Formiggini, 1929).

RAGUENET, FRANÇOIS, *A Comparison between the French and Italian Musick and Opera's* (London: W. Lewis, 1709; repr. 1968).

—— *Parallele des Italiens et des François en ce qui regarde la Musique et les Opéra* (Paris: Moreau, 1702; repr. 1976).

RAYNOR, HENRY, *The Orchestra* (New York: Charles Scribner's Sons, 1978).

REES, ABRAHAM, *The Cyclopaedia, or, Universal Dictionary of Arts, Sciences, and Literature* (London: Longman, Hurst, Rees, Orme, & Brown, 1819–20).

REGAZZI, ROBERTO, "The Situation of Violin Making in Bologna in the Eighteenth Century," paper read at the Fourth Tiverton Violin Conference. East Devon College, 23–24 Sept. 1989.

REGNARD, JEAN-FRANÇOIS, *Œuvres* (Paris: E. A. Lequin, 1820).

REICHARDT, JOHANN FRIEDRICH, *Briefe eines aufmerksamen Reisenden die Musik betreffend* (Leipzig and Frankfurt (vol. i); Frankfurt and Breslau (vol. ii), 1774–76; repr. 1977).

——*Ueber die Pflichten des Ripien-Violinisten* (Berlin and Leipzig: George Jacob Decker, 1776).

——"Winke und Regeln für Anführer der Musik in Concerten," *Berlinische musicalische Zeitung*, no. 21 (2 Nov. 1793), 161–2.

REID, DOUGLAS J., assisted by Brian W. Pritchard, "Some Festival Programmes of the Eighteenth and Nineteenth Centuries—1. Salisbury and Winchester," *RMA Research Chronicle*, 5 (1965), 51–60.

——"Some Festival Programmes of the Eighteenth and Nineteenth Centuries—2. Cambridge and Oxford," *RMA Research Chronicle*, 6 (1966), 3–22.

RICCI, CORRADO, *I teatri di Bologna nei secoli XVII e XVIII* (Bologna: Successori Monti, 1888; repr. 1965).

RICE, ALBERT, *The Baroque Clarinet* (Oxford: Clarendon Press, 1992).

——"A History of the Clarinet to 1820" (Ph.D. diss., Claremont Graduate School, 1987).

RICHARDS, I. A., *The Philosophy of Rhetoric* (Oxford: Oxford University Press, 1936).

RICHELET, PIERRE, *Dictionnaire françois* (Geneva: Widerhold, 1679; repr. 1994).

RIELY, JOHN, *Rowlandson Drawings from the Paul Mellon Collection* (exh. cat., New Haven: Yale Center for British Art, 1978).

RIEMANN, HUGO, *Musiklexikon*, 8th edn. (Leipzig: Max Hesse Verlag, 1916).

RIESBECK, JOHANN KASPAR, *Briefe eines reisenden Franzosen über Deutschland* (1783), ed. Wolfgang Gerlach (Stuttgart: Steingrüben Verlag, 1967).

RIFKIN, JOSHUA, "More (and Less) on Bach's Orchestra," *Performance Practice Review*, 4 (1991), 5–13.

RILEY, MAURICE, *The History of the Viola* (Ann Arbor: Braun-Brumfield, 1980).

RINALDI, MARIO, *Arcangelo Corelli* (Milan: Curci, 1953).

RINUCCINI, CAMILLO, *Descrizione delle feste fatte nelle reali nozze de' serenissimi principi di Toscana d. Cosimo de' Medici e Maria Maddalena Arciduchessa d'Austria* (Florence: Giunti, 1608).

ROBINSON, MICHAEL F., "The Governors' Minutes of the Conservatory S. Maria di Loreto, Naples," *RMA Research Chronicle*, 10 (1972), 1–97.

——"A Late 18th-Century Account Book of the San Carlo Theatre, Naples," *EM* 18 (1990), 73–81.

——*Naples and Neapolitan Opera* (Oxford: Clarendon Press, 1972).

ROCHE, JEROME, *North Italian Church Music in the Age of Monteverdi* (Oxford: Clarendon Press, 1984).

——"North Italian Liturgical Music in the Early 17th Century: Its Evolution around 1600 and its Development until the Death of Monteverdi" (Ph.D. diss., Cambridge University, 1967).

ROCHLITZ, FRIEDRICH, "Bruchstücke aus Briefen an einen jungen Tonsetzer," *AMZ* 2 (2, 9, 23 Oct.; 27 Nov.; 4 Dec. 1799), cols. 1–5, 17–20, 57–63, 161–70, 177–83.

ROESER, VALENTIN, *Essai d'instruction à l'usage de ceux qui composent pour la clarinette et le cor* (Paris: Mercier, 1764; repr. 1972).

ROGERS, PATRICK J., *Continuo Realization in Handel's Vocal Music* (Ann Arbor: UMI Research Press, 1989).

ROHR, DEBORAH, *The Careers of British Musicians, 1750–1850: A Profession of Artisans* (Cambridge: Cambridge University Press, 2001).

ROLLIN, MONIQUE, "Les Oeuvres de Lully transcrites pour le luth," in *Jean-Baptiste Lully: Actes du colloque / Kongressbericht, Saint-Germain-en-Laye–Heidelberg 1987*, ed. Jérôme de La Gorce and Herbert Schneider (Laaber: Laaber-Verlag, 1990), 483–94.

ROSAND, ELLEN, *Opera in 17th-Century Venice* (Berkeley: University of California Press, 1991).

ROSETTI, ANTON, *Ausgewählte Sinfonien*, ed. Oskar Kaul (Denkmäler der Tonkunst in Bayern, 22; Leipzig: Breitkopf & Härtel, 1912).

RÖSING, HELMUT, "Zum Begriff 'Orchester' in europäischer und aussereuropäischer Musik," *Acta musicologica*, 47 (1975), 134–43.

ROSOW, LOIS, "How Eighteenth-Century Parisians Heard Lully's Operas: The Case of *Armide*'s Fourth Act," in Heyer (ed.), *Jean-Baptiste Lully and the Music of the French Baroque*, 213–37.

—— "Lully's *Armide* at the Paris Opéra: A Performance History: 1686–1766" (Ph.D. diss., Brandeis University, 1981).

ROSSELLI, JOHN, "Geografia politica del teatro d'opera nell'Emilia Romagna del tardo Settecento," in Susi Davoli (ed.), *Civiltà teatrale e Settecento emiliano* (Reggio Emilia, 1986), 335–44.

ROSTIROLLA, GIANCARLO, "L'organizzazione musicale nell'ospedale veneziano della Pietà al tempo di Vivaldi," *Nuova rivista musicale italiana*, 13 (1979), 168–95.

—— "La professione di strumentista a Roma nel Sei e Settecento," *Studi musicali*, 23 (1994), 87–174.

ROUSSEAU, JEAN-JACQUES, *A Complete Dictionary of Music*, 2nd edn., trans. William Waring (London: J. Murray, 1779; repr. 1975).

—— *Dictionnaire de musique* (Paris: Duchesne, 1768; repr. 1969).

—— (attrib.), *Lettre à M. Grimm au sujet des Remarques ajoutées à sa Lettre sur Omphale* (1752), repr. in *La Querelle des bouffons*, ed. Launay, 87–117.

—— *Lettre d'un symphoniste de l'Académie Royale de Musique à ses camarades de l'orchestre* (1753), repr. in *La Querelle des bouffons*, ed. Launay, 648–64.

—— *Lettre sur la musique françoise* (1753), repr. in *La Querelle des bouffons*, de Launay, 669–764.

RUDÉ, GEORGE, *Hanoverian London: 1714–1808* (Berkeley: University of California Press, 1971).

RUHNKE, MARTIN, *Beiträge zu einer Geschichte der deutschen Hofmusikkollegien im 16. Jahrhundert* (Berlin: Verlag Merseburger, 1963).

SABOL, ANDREW J., "New Documents on Shirley's Masque 'The Triumph of Peace,'" *M & L* 47 (1966), 10–28.

SACCHI, GIOVENALE, *Della divisione del tempo nella musica nel ballo e nel poesia* (Milan: Giuseppe Mazzucchelli, 1770).

SACHS, CURT, "Die Ansbacher Hofkapelle unter Markgraf Johann Friedrich (1672–1686)," *Sammelbände der Internationalen Musik-Gesellschaft*, 9 (1909–10), 105–37.

—— *Musik und Oper am Kurbrandenburgischen Hof* (Berlin: J. Bard, 1910; repr. 1977).

SADIE, STANLEY, "Concert Life in Eighteenth-Century England," *PRMA* 85 (1958–9), 17–30.

SADLER, GRAHAM, "Rameau's Singers and Players at the Paris Opéra: A Little-Known Inventory of 1738," *EM* 11 (1983), 453–65.

—— "The Role of the Keyboard Continuo in French Opera 1673–1776," *EM* 8 (1980), 148–57.

SAINSBURY, JOHN S., *A Dictionary of Musicians from the Earliest Times* (London: Sainsbury, 1824; repr. 1966).

SAINT DIDIER, ALEXANDRE-TOUSSAINT LIMOJON, SIEUR DE *The City and Republick of Venice, in three parts, Originally written in French by Monsieur de S. Desdier* (London: Brome, 1699).

SAINT-ÉVREMOND, CHARLES, *Sur les opéra*, in *Œuvres meslées*, xi (Paris: Claude Barbin, 1684; repr. 1987), 77–119.

SALMEN, WALTER (ed.), *The Social Status of the Professional Musician from the Middle Ages to the 19th Century* (New York: Pendragon Press, 1983).

SANDFORD, FRANCIS, *The History of the Coronation of the Most High, Most Mighty, and Excellent Monarch, James II* (London: Thomas Newcomb, 1687).

SANDGRUBER, ROMAN, "Wirtschaftsentwicklung, Einkommensverteilung und Alltagsleben zur Zeit Haydns," in Gerda Mraz (ed.), *Joseph Haydn in seiner Zeit* (Eisenstadt: Amt der Burgenländischen Landesregierung, 1982), 72–90.

SANTORO, ELIA, *Il teatro di Cremona* (Cremona: Edizioni Pizzorni, 1969–72).

SARDELLI, FEDERICO MARIA, *La musica per flauto di Antonio Vivaldi* (Florence: Olschki, 2001).

SARRI, DOMENICO, *Arsace* (New York: Garland, 1978).

SARTORIO, ANTONIO, *L'Orfeo*, ed. Ellen Rosand (Drammaturgia Musicale Veneta, 6; Milan: Ricordi, 1983).

SAULE, BÉATRIX, *Versailles triomphant: Une journée de Louis XIV* (Paris: Flammarion, 1996).

SAUNDERS, GEORGE, *A Treatise on Theatres* (London: Printed for the author, 1790; repr. 1968).

SAUNDERS, HARRIS SHERIDAN, "The Repertoire of a Venetian Opera House (1678–1714): The Teatro Grimani di San Giovanni Grisostomo" (Ph.D. diss., Harvard University, 1985).

SAUVEUR, JOSEPH, *Collected Writings on Musical Acoustics (Paris 1700–1713)*, ed. Rudolf Rasch (Utrecht: Diapason Press, 1984).

SAWKINS, LIONEL, "*Trembleurs* and Cold People: How Should they Shiver?," in Michael Burden (ed.), *Performing the Music of Henry Purcell* (Oxford: Clarendon Press, 1996), 243–64.

SCARAMELLI, GIUSEPPE, *Saggio sopra i doveri di un primo violino direttore d'orchestra* (Trieste: G. Weis, 1811).

SCHÄFFER, GOTTFRIED, *Das fürstbischöfliche und königliche Theater zu Passau (1783–1883)* (Passau: Verlag des Vereins für ostbairische Heimatforschung, 1973).

SCHEIBE, JOHANN ADOLF, *Critischer Musikus. Neue, vermehrte und verbesserte Auflage* (Leipzig: Bernhard Christoph Breitkopf, 1745; repr. 1970).

SCHERING, ARNOLD, "Die Leipziger Ratsmusik von 1650 bis 1775," *Archiv für Musikwissenschaft*, 3 (1921), 17–53.

—— *Musikgeschichte Leipzigs*, ii: *Von 1650 bis 1723*; iii: *Das Zeitalter Johann Sebastian Bachs und Johann Adam Hillers (von 1723 bis 1800)* (Leipzig: Kistner & Siegel, 1926–41; repr. 1974).

SCHERPEREEL, JOSEPH, *L'Orchestre et les instrumentistes de la Real Camara a Lisbonne de 1764 à 1834* (Lisbon: Fundacao Calouste Gulbenkian, 1985).

SCHEURLEER, DANIEL F., *Het muziekleven in Nederland* (The Hague: Nijhoff, 1909).

SCHIEDERMAIR, LUDWIG, "Die Oper an den badischen Höfen des 17. u. 18. Jahrhunderts," *Sammelbände der Internationalen Musik-Gesellschaft*, 13 (1912–13), 191–207, 369–449, 510–50.

Schmidt, Carl B., "Antonio Cesti's *Il pomo d'oro*: A Reexamination of a Famous Hapsburg Court Spectacle," *JAMS* 29 (1976), 381–412.

—— "The Geographical Spread of Lully's Operas during the Late Seventeenth and Early Eighteenth Centuries: New Evidence from the *Livrets*," in Heyer (ed.), *Jean-Baptiste Lully and the Music of the French Baroque*, 183–211.

—— *The Livrets of Jean-Baptiste Lully's* Tragédies Lyriques*: A Catalogue Raisonné* (New York: Performer's Editions, 1995).

—— "Pomo d'oro, Il," in *GroveO*, iii. 1051–54.

Schmidt, Günther, "Die Musik am Hofe der Markgrafen von Brandenburg-Ansbach" (Diss. Ludwigs-Maximilians-Universität, Munich, 1953).

Schmierer, Johann Abraham, *Zodiaci musici, in XII Partitas balleticas . . . Pars I.* (1698), ed. Ernst von Werra (Denkmäler deutscher Tonkunst, 10; Leipzig: Breitkopf & Härtel, 1902).

Schmith, Amand Wilhelm, *Philosophische Fragmente über die praktische Musik* (Vienna: K. K. Taubstummeninstitutsbuchdruck, 1787).

Schneider, Herbert, "The Amsterdam Editions of Lully's Orchestral Suites," in Heyer (ed.), *Jean-Baptiste Lully and the Music of the French Baroque*, 113–30.

—— *Die Rezeption der Opern Lullys im Frankreich des Ancien Régime* (Tutzing: Schneider, 1982).

Schnoebelen, Anne, "The Concerted Mass at San Petronio in Bologna: c. 1660–1730" (Ph.D. diss., University of Illinois, 1968).

—— "Performance Practices at San Petronio in the Baroque," *Acta musicologica*, 41 (1969), 37–55.

—— "The Role of the Violin in the Resurgence of the Mass in the 17th Century," *EM* 18 (1990), 537–42.

Scholes, Percy A., *The Puritans and Music in England and New England* (London: Oxford University Press, 1934).

Schönfeld, J. von, *Jahrbuch der Tonkunst von Wien und Prag* (Vienna: Selbstverlag, 1796; repr. 1976).

Schreiber, Ottmar, *Orchester und Orchesterpraxis in Deutschland zwischen 1780 und 1850* (Berlin: Junker & Dünnhaupt Verlag, 1938).

Schubart, Christian Friedrich Daniel, *Ideen zu einer Aesthetik der Tonkunst*, ed. Ludwig Schubart (Vienna: Degen, 1806; repr. 1969).

Schulze, Hans-Joachim, "Besitzstand und Vermögensverhältnisse von Leipziger Ratsmusikern zur Zeit Johann Sebastian Bachs," *Beiträge zur Bachforschung*, 4 (1985), 33–46.

—— "Johann Sebastian Bach's Orchestra: Some Unanswered Questions," *EM* 17 (1989), 3–15.

Schwab, Heinrich W. ,"The Social Status of the Town Musician," trans. Herbert Kaufman and Barbara Reisner, in Salmen (ed.), *The Social Status of the Professional Musician from the Middle Ages to the 19th Century*, 31–59.

Scudéry, Madeleine de, *Artamène; ou, Le Grand Cyrus* (Paris: Courbé, 1656; repr. 1972).

Segerman, Ephraim, "Strings through the Ages," *The Strad*, 99 (Jan., Mar., Apr. 1988), 52–55, 195–200, 295–98.

Sehnal, Jiri, "Die Musikkapelle des Olmützer Bischofs Karl Liechtenstein-Castelcorn in Kremsier," *Kirchenmusikalisches Jahrbuch*, 51 (1967), 79–123.

Seiffert, Max, "Matthias Weckmann und das Collegium Musicum in Hamburg," *Sammelbände der Internationalen Musik-Gesellschaft*, 2 (1900–1), 76–132.

SELFRIDGE-FIELD, ELEANOR, "Bassano and the Orchestra of St. Mark's," *EM* 4 (1976), 153–58.

—— "Italian Oratorio and the Baroque Orchestra," *EM* 16 (1988), 506–13.

—— *Pallade Veneta: Writings on Music in Venetian Society, 1650–1750* (Venice: Edizioni Fondazione Levi, 1985).

—— *Venetian Instrumental Music* (Oxford: Blackwell, 1975).

—— "Venice in an Era of Political Decline," in George J. Buelow (ed.), *The Late Baroque Era* (Englewood Cliffs, NJ: Prentice Hall, 1993), 66–93.

—— "The Viennese Court Orchestra in the Time of Caldara," in Brian W. Pritchard (ed.), *Antonio Caldara: Essays on his Life and Times* (Aldershot: Scolar Press, 1987), 115–51.

—— "Vivaldi's Esoteric Instruments," *EM* 6 (1978), 332–38.

SÉNECÉ, ANTOINE BAUDERON DE, "Lettre de Clément Marot à M. de ★★★ touchant ce qui s'est passé à l'arrivée de Jean Baptiste de Lulli aux Champs Elysées" (1688), in *Œuvres choisies de Sénecé* (Paris: P. Jannet, 1855), 291–334.

Seventeenth-Century Instrumental Dance Music in Uppsala Univ. Library Instr. mus. hs. 409, ed. Jaroslav Mrácek (Monumenta Musicae Svecicae, 8; Stockholm: Reimers, 1976).

SHACKLETON, NICHOLAS, "Clarinet," in *The New Grove Dictionary of Musical Instruments*, ed. Stanley Sadie (London: Macmillan, 1984), i. 389–403.

SHARP, SAMUEL, *Letters from Italy, Describing the Customs and Manners of that Country, in the Years 1765 and 1766*, 3rd edn. (London: Henry and Cave, 1767).

SIEGELE, ULRICH, "Bachs Endzweck einer regulierten und Entwurf einer wohlbestallten Kirchenmusik," in Thomas Kohlhase and Volker Scherliess (eds.) *Festschrift Georg von Dadelsen zum 60. Geburtstag* (Stuttgart: Hänssler, 1978), 313–51.

SIEVERS, G. L. P., "Ueber den jetzigen Zustand der Musik in Frankreich, besonders in Paris (Beschluss)," *AMZ* 19 (1817), cols. 297–304.

SIMI BONINI, ELEONORA, *Il fondo musicale dell'Arciconfraternita di S. Girolamo della Carità* (Rome: Ministero per i Beni Culturali e Ambientali, 1992).

SIMPSON, ADRIENNE, "The Orchestral Recorder," in John Mansfield Thomson (ed.), *The Cambridge Companion to the Recorder* (Cambridge: Cambridge University Press, 1995), 91–106.

SINGH, DULEEP, "Portraits in Norfolk Houses," *Volumes of the Walpole Society*, 46 (1978), 71–90. First published in 1927.

SISMAN, ELAINE, *Mozart: The "Jupiter" Symphony* (Cambridge: Cambridge University Press, 1993).

SITTARD, JOSEF, *Geschichte des Musik und Concertwesens in Hamburg vom 14. Jahrhundert bis auf die Gegenwart* (Altona: Reher, 1898; repr. 1971).

—— *Zur Geschichte der Musik und des Theaters am württembergischen Hofe* (Stuttgart: W. Kohlhammer, 1891; repr. 1970).

SLATFORD, RODNEY, and SHIPTON, ALYN, "Double Bass," in *NG II*, vii. 519–25.

SMART, GEORGE, *Leaves from the Journals of Sir George Smart*, ed. H. Bertram Cox and C. L. E. Cox (London: Longman, Green & Co., 1907).

SMEND, FRIEDRICH, *Bach in Köthen*, trans. John Page, ed. and revised with annotations by Stephen Daw (St. Louis, Mo.: Concordia House, 1985).

SMET, MONIQUE DE, *La Musique à la cour de Guillaume V, prince d'Orange* (Utrecht: Oosthoek, 1973).

SMITH, ADAM, *An Inquiry into the Nature and Causes of the Wealth of Nations* (1776), ed. R. H. Campbell and A. S. Skinner (Oxford: Clarendon Press, 1976).

SMITH, J. SUTCLIFFE, *The Story of Music in Birmingham* (Birmingham: Cornish Brothers, 1945).

SMITHER, HOWARD, *A History of the Oratorio*, i: *The Oratorio in the Baroque Era: Italy, Vienna, Paris* (Chapel Hill: University of North Carolina Press, 1977).

—— "Messiah and Progress in Victorian England," *EM* 13 (1985), 339–48.

—— "Oratorio and Sacred Opera, 1700–1825: Terminology and Genre Distinction," *PRMA* 106 (1980), 88–104

SNYDER, KERALA J., *Dieterich Buxtehude: Organist in Lübeck* (New York: Schirmer Books, 1987).

SOLERTI, ANGELO, *Gli albori del melodramma* (Milan: Sandron, 1904–5; repr. 1969).

—— *Musica, ballo e drammatica alla Corte Medicea dal 1600 al 1637* (Florence: R. Bemporad, 1905; repr. 1968).

SOLUM, JOHN, *The Early Flute* (Oxford: Clarendon Press, 1992).

SONNECK, OSCAR, "A Contemporary Account of Music in Charleston, S.C., of the Year 1783," in William Lichtenwanger (ed.), *Oscar Sonneck and American Music* (Urbana: University of Illinois Press, 1983), 94–99.

—— *Early Concert-Life in America* (Leipzig: Breitkopf & Härtel, 1907; repr. 1978).

—— *Early Opera in America* (New York: Schirmer, 1915).

SOREL, CHARLES, *Histoire comique de Francion (Livres I a VII)*, ed. Yves Giraud (Paris: Garnier-Flammarion, 1979).

SPIELMANN, MARKUS, "Der Zink im Instrumentarium des süddeutsch-österreichischen Raumes 1650 bis 1750," in *Johann Joseph Fux und die barocke Bläsertradition — Kongressbericht Graz, 1985*, ed. Bernhard Habla (Tutzing: Schnieder, 1987), 121–55.

SPITTA, PHILIPP, *Johann Sebastian Bach* (Leipzig: Breitkopf & Härtel, 1921; repr. 1979).

SPITZER, JOHN, "The Birth of the Orchestra in Rome: An Iconographic Study," *EM* 19 (1991), 9–28.

—— "Improvized Ornamentation in a Handel Aria with Obbligato Wind Accompaniment," *EM* 16 (1988), 514–22.

—— "Metaphors of the Orchestra: The Orchestra as a Metaphor," *MQ* 80 (1996), 234–64.

—— and ZASLAW, NEAL, "Improvised Ornamentation in Eighteenth-Century Orchestras," *JAMS* 39 (1986), 524–77.

—— —— "Orchestra," in *GroveO*, iii. 719–35.

—— —— "Orchestra," in *NG II*, xviii. 530–84.

SPOHR, LOUIS, *Lebenserinnerungen* (Tutzing: Schnieder, 1968). First published as *Selbstbiographie* (Kassel, 1860–61; Eng. trans. 1865).

—— *Violinschule* (Vienna: Haslinger, 1832; Eng. trans. 1833).

SPRENGER, BERND, *Das Geld der Deutschen* (Paderborn: Ferdinand Schöningh, 1991).

STAEHELIN, MARTIN, "Orchester," in *Handwörterbuch der musikalischen Terminologie*, ed. H. H. Eggebrecht (Wiesbaden: Steiner, 1972–).

STAËL, GERMAINE DE, *De l'Allemagne* (1810) (Paris: Garnier Flammarion, 1991).

STAFFIERI, GLORIA, "Arcangelo Corelli compositore di 'sinfonie': nuovi documenti," in *Studi corelliani IV: Atti del Quarto Congresso Internazionale*, ed. Pierluigi Petrobelli and Gloria Staffieri (Florence: Olschki, 1990), 335–57.

STAMPFL, INKA, *Georg Muffat: Orchesterkompositionen* (Passau: Verlag Passavia, 1984).

STAUFFER, GEORGE, "The Modern Orchestra: A Creation of the Late 18th Century," in Peyser (ed.), *The Orchestra: Origins and Transformations*, 37–68.

STEIN, LOUISE, *Songs of Mortals, Dialogues of the Gods* (Oxford: Clarendon Press, 1993).

STERNFELD, FREDERICK W., "Orpheus," in *GroveO*, ii. 776–7.

—— "Orpheus, Ovid and Opera," *PRMA* 113 (1988), 172–202.

STOCKIGT, JANICE, "Zelenka and the Dresden Court Orchestra 1735: A Study," *Studies in Music*, 21 (1987), 69–85.

STORZ, GERHARD, *Karl Eugen, Der Fürst und das "alte gute Recht"* (Stuttgart: Klett-Cotta, 1981).

STOWELL, ROBIN, "'Good execution and other necessary skills': The Role of the Concertmaster in the Late 18th Century," *EM* 16 (1988), 21–33.

—— *Violin Technique and Performance Practice in the Late Eighteenth and Early Nineteenth Centuries* (Cambridge: Cambridge University Press, 1985).

STRAHLE, GRAHAM, *An Early Music Dictionary: Musical Terms from British Sources, 1500–1740* (Cambridge: Cambridge University Press, 1995).

STROHM, REINHARD, "Italian Operisti North of the Alps, c.1700–c.1750," in id. (ed.), *The Eighteenth-Century Diaspora of Italian Music and Musicians* (Turnhour: Brepols, 2001), 1–59.

—— *Italienische Opernarien des frühen Settecento (1720–1730) = Analecta musicologica*, 16/1–2 (Cologne: Arno Volk Verlag, 1976).

Studi corelliani: 1° Congresso Internazionale di Studi Corelliani (Fusignano, 1968), ed. Adriano Cavicchi, Oscar Mischiati, and Pierluigi Petrobelli (Florence: Olschki, 1972).

SUARD, JEAN BAPTISTE ANTOINE, "Accompagnement, Accompagner," in *Encyclopédie méthodique: Musique* ed. Nicolas Étienne Framery, Pierre-Louis Ginguené and Jérôme Joseph de Momigny (Paris: Panckoucke, 1791–1818; repr. 1971), i. 20–24.

SULZER, JOHANN GEORG, *Allgemeine Theorie der schönen Kunste* (Leipzig: Weidmann Reich, 1771–4; rev. edns. 1778–9, 1786–7, 1792; repr. 1967).

SUZZI, STEFANO, "L'orchestra nella vita di una città di provincia: una prima ricognizione," in Conati and Pavarani (eds.), *Orchestre in Emilia-Romagna nell'Ottocento e Novecento*, 393–418.

TALBOT, MICHAEL, "Musical Academies in Eighteenth-Century Venice," *Note d'archivio per la storia musicale*, NS 1 (1983), 21–65.

—— "A Rival of Corelli: The Violinist-Composer Giuseppe Valentini," in *Nuovissimi studi corelliani: Atti del Terzo Congresso Internazionale*, ed. Sergio Durante and Pierluigi Petrobelli (Florence: Olschki, 1982), 347–65.

—— "The Serenata in Eighteenth-Century Venice," *RMA Research Chronicle*, 18 (1982), 1–40.

TALLEMANT DES RÉAUX, GÉDÉON, *Les Historiettes de Tallemant des Réaux* (Paris: Garnier, 1938).

TAMPIERI, DOMENICO, "Le orchestre communali tra produzione contemporanea e responsabilità aziendale nella Romagna dell'Ottocento: una prima ricognizione," in Conati and Pavarani (eds.), *Orchestre in Emilia Romagna nell'Ottocento e Novecento*, 445–94.

TARR, EDWARD H., "Ein Katalog erhaltener Zinken," *Basler Jahrbuch für historische Musikpraxis*, 5 (1981), 11–262.

—— "The Trumpet before 1800," in Trevor Herbert and John Wallace (eds.), *The Cambridge Companion to Brass Instruments* (Cambridge: Cambridge University Press, 1997), 84–102.

—— and WALKER, THOMAS, "'Bellici carmi, festivo fragor': Die Verwendung der Trompete in der italienischen Oper des 17. Jahrhunderts," *Hamburger Jahrbuch für Musikwissenschaft*, 3 (1978), 143–203.

TARTINI, GIUSEPPE, *Traité des agréments de la musique* (1771), ed. Erwin Jacobi (New York: Moeck, 1961).

TAYLOR, CAROLE, "From Losses to Lawsuit: Patronage of the Italian Opera in London by Lord Middlesex, 1739–45," *M & L* 68 (1987), 1–25.

TEMPERLEY, NICHOLAS, "Music in Church," in *The Eighteenth Century*, ed. H. Diack Johnstone and Roger Fiske (The Blackwell History of Music in Britain, 4; Oxford: Blackwell, 1990), 357–96.

TERRY, CHARLES SANFORD, *Bach: A Biography* (London: Oxford University Press, 1928).

—— *Bach's Orchestra* (London: Oxford University Press, 1932).

TESSIER, ANDRÉ, "Un Document sur les répétitions du *Triomphe de l'Amour*," in *Actes du Congrès d'Histoire de l'art, Paris 26 Sept.–5 Oct., 1921*, iii (Paris: Presses Universitaires de France, 1924; repr. 1979), 874–94.

THIBLOT, R., "Le Séjour de Mozart à Dijon en 1766," *Mémoires de l'Académie des sciences, arts et belles-lettres de Dijon* (1937), 139–43.

THOINAN, ERNEST, *Maugars: célèbre joueur de viole . . . suivie de sa Response faite à un curieux sur la sentiment de la musique en Italie . . . 1639* (London: A. Claudin, 1865; repr. 1965).

THOMAS, GEORG SEBASTIAN, *Die grossherzogliche Hofkapelle, deren Personalbestand und Wirken unter Ludewig I*, 2nd edn. (Darmstadt: Jonghaus, 1859).

TILMOUTH, MICHAEL, "A Calendar of References to Music in Newspapers Published in London and the Provinces, 1660–1719," *RMA Research Chronicle*, 1 (1961), 1–107.

—— "Some Early London Concerts and Music Clubs, 1670–1720," *PRMA* 84 (1957–58), 13–26.

TODD, R. LARRY, "Orchestral Texture and the Art of Orchestration," in Peyser (ed.), *The Orchestra: Origins and Transformations*, 191–226.

TOSI, PIETRO FRANCESCO, *Observations on the Florid Song*, trans. J. E. Galliard (London: Wilcox, 1743; repr. 1978; 1st Italian edn.: Bologna, 1723).

TROIANO, MASSIMO, *Dialoghi di Massimo Troiano* (Venice: Zaltieri, 1569); modern edn.: *Die münchner Fürstenhochzeit von 1568*, ed. Horst Leuchtmann (Munich: Katzbichler, 1980).

—— *Discorsi delli trionfi, giostre, apparati, et delle cose piu notabile . . .* (Munich: Montano, 1568).

TROMLITZ, JOHANN GEORG, *Ausführlicher und gründlicher Unterricht die Flöte zu spielen* (Leipzig, 1791; repr. 1973; Eng. trans. 1991).

TROWELL, BRIAN, "Daniel Defoe's Plan for an Academy of Music at Christ's Hospital, with some Notes on his Attitude to Music," in Ian Bent (ed.), *Source Materials and the Interpretation of Music: A Memorial Volume to Thurston Dart* (London: Stainer & Bell, 1981), 403–27.

TURRENTINE, HERBERT C., "The Prince de Conti: A Royal Patron of Music," *MQ* 54 (1968), 309–15.

'T Uitnement Kabinet–Vol Paduanen, Allmanden, Sarbanden, Couranten, Balletten, Intraden, Airs &c . . . Amsterdam 1646, 1649, ed. Rudi Rasch (Amsterdam: Groen, 1973–).

UNOLD, GEORG VON, "Einige Bemerkungen über die Stellung der Orchester und Einrichtung der Musiksäle," *AMZ* 4 (Aug. 1802), cols. 782–4.

VALLAS, LÉON, *Un Siècle de musique et de théâtre à Lyon, 1688–1789* (Lyons: Masson, 1932).

VAN ORDEN, KATE, "Descartes on Musical Training and the Body," in Linda Phyllis Austern (ed.) *Music, Sensation, and Sensuality* (New York and London: Routledge, 2002), 17–38.

—— *Music, Discipline, and Arms in Early Modern France* (Chicago: University of Chicago Press, forthcoming).

VANDENBROECK, OTHON, *Methode nouvelle et raisonée pour apprendre à sonner du cor* (Paris: Nadermann, c.1789).

—— *Traité général de tous les instruments à vent à l'usage des compositeurs* (Paris: Boyer, 1793).

Vann, James Allen, *The Making of a State: Württemberg, 1593–1793* (Ithaca, NY: Cornell University Press, 1984).

Veracini, Francesco Maria, *Il trionfo della prattica musicale*, n.d. MS at Florence Conservatory Library; transcribed by Bernhard Paumgartner; translated by Helen Margaret Smith (Ph.D. diss., Indiana University, 1963).

Viadana, Lodovico Grossi da, *Salmi a quattro chori*, ed. Gerhard Wielakker (Recent Researches in the Music of the Baroque Era, 86; Madison: A-R Editions, 1998).

Viale Ferrero, Mercedes, "Repliche a Torino di alcuni melodrammi veneziani e loro caratteristiche," in Maria Teresa Muraro (ed.), *Venezia e il melodramma nel Seicento* (Florence: Olschki, 1978), 145–72.

Viano, Richard J., "Salons," in *Dictionnaire de la musique en France*, ed. Benoit (Paris: Fayard, 1992), 631–33.

Vierhaus, Rudolf, *Germany in the Age of Absolutism*, trans. Jonathan B. Knudsen (Cambridge: Cambridge University Press, 1988).

Vingt suites d'orchestre du XVIIᵉ siècle français, ed. Jules Écorcheville, 2 vols. (Paris: Marcel Fortin, 1906).

Voiture, Vincent, *Lettres*, in *Œuvres de Monsieur de Voiture* (Paris: Courbé, 1654). Available in full text at http://gallica.bnf.fr.

Volek, Tomislav, and Mrácek, Jaroslav, "Beethoven's Rehearsals at the Lobkowitz's," *MT* 127 (1986), 75–80.

Walden, Valerie, *One Hundred Years of Violoncello: A History of Technique and Performance Practice, 1740–1840* (Cambridge: Cambridge University Press, 1998).

Waldvogel, Nicholas, "The Eighteenth-Century Esthetics of the Sublime and the Valuation of the Symphony" (Ph.D. diss., Yale University, 1992).

Walker, Daniel P., *Musique des intermèdes de "La Pellegrina"* (Paris: CNRS, 1963).

Walkling, Andrew W., "Masque and Politics at the Restoration Court: John Crowne's Calisto," *EM* 24 (1996), 27–62.

Walls, Peter, "The Violin Family," in Howard Mayer Brown and Stanley Sadie (eds.), *Performance Practice: Music after 1600* (New York: Norton, 1989), 44–67.

Walsh, T. J., *Opera in Dublin, 1705–1797: The Social Scene* (Dublin: Figgis, 1973).

Walter, Friedrich, *Geschichte des Theaters und der Musik am kurpfälzischen Hofe* (Leipzig: Breitkopf & Härtel, 1898; repr. 1968).

Walter, Michael, "Italienische Musik als Representationskunst der Dresdener Fürstenhochzeit von 1719," in Barbara Marx (ed.), *Elbflorenz—Italienische Präsenz in Dresden 16.–19. Jahrhundert* (Amsterdam and Dresden: Verlag der Kunst, 2000), 177–202.

Walter, Rudolf, *Johann Caspar Ferdinand Fischer, Hofkapellmeister der Markgrafen von Baden* (Frankfurt: Verlag Peter Lang, 1990).

Walther, Johann Gottfried, *Musicalisches Lexikon* (Leipzig: Wolfgang Deer, 1732; repr. 1953).

Walton, Robin, "Piazzola sul Brenta," in *GroveO*, iii. 999–1000.

Weaver, Robert, "The Orchestra in Early Italian Opera," *JAMS* 17 (1967), 83–89.

—— "Sixteenth-Century Instrumentation," *MQ* 47 (1961), 363–78.

—— and Weaver, Norma Wright, *A Chronology of Music in the Florentine Theater, 1751–1800* (Warren, Mich.: Harmonie Park Press, 1993).

Weber, Gottfried, "Besetzung," in *Allgemeine Encyclopedie der Wissenschaften und Künste*, ed. Johann Samuel Ersch and Johann Gottfried Gruber (Leipzig: Gleditsch, 1822), 284–85.

—— "Praktische Bemerkungen," *AMZ* 9 (16 Sept. and 23 Sept. 1807), cols. 805–11, 821–24.

WEBER, MAX, *From Max Weber: Essays in Sociology*, ed. Hans Gerth and C. Wright Mills (New York: Oxford University Press, 1958).

WEBER, WILLIAM, *Music and the Middle Class: The Social Structure of Concert Life in London, Paris and Vienna* (London: Croom Helm, 1975).

—— *The Rise of Musical Classics in Eighteenth-Century England* (Oxford: Clarendon Press, 1992).

WEBSTER, JAMES, "On the Absence of Keyboard Continuo in Haydn's Symphonies," *EM* 18 (1990), 599–608.

WEISS, SUSAN F., "Medieval and Renaissance Wedding Banquets and Other Feasts," in Martha Carlin and Joel Rosenthal (eds.), *Food and Eating in Medieval Europe* (London: Hambledon Press, 1999), 159–74.

WELLESZ, EGON, "Zwei Studien zur Geschichte der Oper im XVII. Jahrhundert," *Sammelbände der Internationalen Musik-Gesellschaft*, 15 (1913–14), 124–33.

WENDEBORN, FRIEDRICH AUGUST, *A View of England towards the Close of the 18th Century* (Dublin: William Sleater, 1791).

WESTRUP, JACK, and ZASLAW, NEAL, "Orchestra," in *NG*, xiii. 679–91.

WIESEND, REINHARD, "Zum Gebrauch des Crescendos in der italienischen Oper um 1750 (Baldassare Galuppi)," in *Mannheim und Italien: Zur Vorgeschichte der Mannheimer. Bericht über das Mannheimer Colloquium in März 1982*, ed. Roland Würtz (Mainz: Schott, 1984), 150–61.

WILSON, PETER H., *War, State and Society in Württemberg, 1677–1793* (Cambridge: Cambridge University Press, 1995).

WINTERNITZ, EMANUEL, "The Iconology of Music: Potentials and Pitfalls," in Barry Brook, Edward Downes, and Sherman Van Solkema (eds.), *Perspectives in Musicology* (New York: Norton, 1972), 80–119.

WOLF, EUGENE K., "The Mannheim Court," in Neal Zaslaw (ed.), *The Classical Era* (Englewood Cliffs, NJ: Prentice Hall, 1989), 213–39.

—— "On the Composition of the Mannheim Orchestra ca. 1740–1778," *Basler Jahrbuch für historische Musikpraxis*, 17 (1993), 113–38.

—— "On the Origins of the Mannheim Symphonic Style," in John Walter Hill (ed.), *Studies in Musicology in Honor of Otto E. Albrecht* (Kassel: Bärenreiter, 1980), 197–239.

—— *The Symphonies of Johann Stamitz: A Study in the Formation of the Classical Style* (Utrecht: Bohn, Scheltema & Holkema, 1981).

WOLFF, CHRISTOPH, *Bach: Essays on his Life and Music* (Cambridge, Mass.: Harvard University Press, 1991).

—— "Bach's Leipzig Chamber Music," *EM* 13 (1985), 165–75.

WOOD, ANTHONY À, *The Life and Times of Anthony Wood, Antiquary, of Oxford, 1632–1695, Described by Himself*, ed. Andrew Clark (Oxford: Oxford Historical Society, 1891).

WOOD, CAROLINE, *Music and Drama in the* Tragédie en Musique, *1673–1715: Jean-Baptiste Lully and his Successors* (New York: Garland, 1996).

—— "Orchestra and Spectacle in the *Tragédie en musique* 1673–1715: Oracle, *Sommeil* and *Tempête*," *PRMA* 108 (1981–82), 25–45.

WOODFIELD, IAN, *The Celebrated Quarrel between Thomas Linley (senior) and William Herschel: An Episode in the Musical Life of 18th-Century Bath* (Bath: University of Bath, 1977).

WROTH, WARWICK, *The London Pleasure Gardens of the Eighteenth Century* (London: Macmillan, 1896; repr. 1979).

WÜRTZ, ROLAND, "Die Organisation der Mannheimer Hofkapelle," in Ludwig Finscher (ed.), *Die Mannheimer Hofkapelle im Zeitalter Carl Theodors* (Mannheim: Palatium Verlag, 1992), 37–48.

YORKE-LONG, ALAN, *Music at Court: Four Eighteenth-Century Studies* (London: Weidenfeld & Nicolson, 1954).

ZASLAW, NEAL, "The Compleat Orchestral Musician," *EM* 7 (1979), 46–57.

—— "Contexts for Mozart's Piano Concertos," in id. (ed.), *Mozart's Piano Concertos: Text, Context, Interpretation* (Ann Arbor: University of Michigan Press, 1996), 1–16.

—— "The First Opera in Paris: A Study in the Politics of Art," in Heyer (ed.), *Jean-Baptiste Lully and the Music of the French Baroque*, 7–23.

—— "Lully's Orchestra," in *J.-B. Lully, Actes du Colloque/Kongressbericht, 1987*, ed. Jérôme de La Gorce and Herbert Schneider (Heidelberg: Laaber, 1990), 539–79.

—— "Mozart's European Orchestras," *Musicology Australia*, 17 (1994), 13–18.

—— "Mozart's Instruments," *EM* 20 (1992), 5–6.

—— "Mozart's Orchestral Flutes and Oboes," in Cliff Eisen (ed.), *Mozart Studies* (Oxford: Oxford University Press, 1991), 201–11.

—— *Mozart's Symphonies: Context, Performance Practice, Reception* (Oxford: Clarendon Press, 1989).

—— "Observations: At the Paris Opéra in 1747," *EM* 11 (1983), 515–16.

—— "The Origins of the Classical Orchestra," *Basler Jahrbuch für historische Musikpraxis*, 17 (1993), 9–40.

—— "Three Notes on the Early History of the Orchestra," *Historical Performance*, 1 (1988), 63–9.

—— "Toward the Revival of the Classical Orchestra," *PRMA* 103 (1976–77), 158–87.

—— "When is an Orchestra not an Orchestra?," *EM* 16 (1988), 483–95.

ZECHMEISTER, GUSTAV, *Die Wiener Theater nächst dem Kärntnerthor von 1747 bis 1776* (Vienna: Hermann Böhlaus Nachfolger, 1971).

ZELLE, CARSTEN, "Maschinen-Metaphern in der Ästhetik des 18. Jahrhunderts," *Zeitschrift für Germanistik*, NF 3 (1997), 510–20.

Index

Boldface numbers refer to plates, figures, documents, tables, and musical illustrations.